From the Wadsworth Series in Mass Communication and W9-ALK-361

General Mass Communication

Anokwa/Lin/Salwen, *International Communication: Issues and Controversies*

Biagi, *Media/Impact: An Introduction to Mass Media,* Seventh Edition

Bucy, *Living in the Information Age: A New Media Reader,* Second Edition

Craft/Leigh/Godfrey, *Electronic Media*

Day, *Ethics in Media Communications: Cases and Controversies,* Fourth Edition

Dennis/Merrill, *Media Debates: Great Issues for the Digital Age,* Third Edition

Fellow, *American Media History*

Gillmor/Barron/Simon, *Mass Communication Law: Cases and Comment,* Sixth Edition

Gillmor/Barron/Simon/Terry, *Fundamentals of Mass Communication Law*

Hilmes, *Connections: A Broadcast History Reader*

Hilmes, *Only Connect: A Cultural History of Broadcasting in the United States*

Jamieson/Campbell, *The Interplay of Influence: News, Advertising, Politics, and the Mass Media,* Fifth Edition

Kamalipour, *Global Communication*

Lester, *Visual Communication: Images with Messages,* Third Edition

Overbeck, *Major Principles of Media Law,* 2005 Edition

Straubhaar/LaRose, *Media Now: Understanding Media, Culture, and Technology,* Fourth Edition

Zelezny, *Cases in Communications Law,* Fourth Edition

Zelezny, *Communications Law: Liberties, Restraints, and the Modern Media,* Fourth Edition

Journalism

Bowles/Borden, *Creative Editing,* Fourth Edition

Chance/McKeen, *Literary Journalism: A Reader*

Craig, *Online Journalism*

Fischer, *Sports Journalism at Its Best: Pulitzer Prize-Winning Articles, Cartoons, and Photographs*

Fisher, *The Craft of Corporate Journalism*

Gaines, *Investigative Reporting for Print and Broadcast,* Second Edition

Hilliard, *Writing for Television, Radio, and New Media,* Eighth Edition

Kessler/McDonald, *When Words Collide: A Media Writer's Guide to Grammar and Style,* Sixth Edition

Laakaniemi, *Newswriting in Transition*

Miller, *Power Journalism: Computer-Assisted Reporting*

Poulter/Tidwell, *News Scene: Interactive Writing Exercises*

Rich, *Writing and Reporting News: A Coaching Method,* Media Enhanced Fourth Edition

Rich, *Writing and Reporting News: A Coaching Method, Student Exercise Workbook,* Media Enhanced Fourth Edition

Stephens, *Broadcast News,* Fourth Edition

Wilber/Miller, *Modern Media Writing*

Photojournalism and Photography

Parrish, *Photojournalism: An Introduction*

Public Relations and Advertising

Diggs-Brown/Glou, *The PR Styleguide: Formats for Public Relations Practice*

Hendrix, *Public Relations Cases,* Sixth Edition

Jewler/Drewniany, *Creative Strategy in Advertising,* Eighth Edition

Newsom/Haynes, *Public Relations Writing: Form and Style,* Seventh Edition

Newsom/Turk/Kruckeberg, *This Is PR: The Realities of Public Relations,* Eighth Edition

Sivulka, *Soap, Sex, and Cigarettes: A Cultural History of American Advertising*

Woods, *Advertising and Marketing to the New Majority: A Case Study Approach*

Research and Theory

Baran/Davis, *Mass Communication Theory: Foundations, Ferment, and Future,* Third Edition

Baxter/Babbie, *The Basics of Communication Research*

Littlejohn, *Theories of Human Communication,* Seventh Edition

Merrigan/Huston, *Communication Research Methods*

Rubin/Rubin/Piele, *Communication Research: Strategies and Sources,* Sixth Edition

Sparks, *Media Effects Research: A Basic Overview*

Wimmer/Dominick, *Mass Media Research: An Introduction,* Seventh Edition

THOMSON
WADSWORTH

Publisher: *Holly J. Allen*

Assistant Editor: *Shona Burke*

Editorial Assistant: *Laryssa Polika*

Senior Technology Project Manager: *Jeanette Wiseman*

Senior Marketing Manager: *Kimberly Russell*

Marketing Assistant: *Andrew Keay*

Advertising Project Manager: *Shemika Britt*

Project Manager, Editorial Production: *Jane Brundage*

Interior Design Director: *Carolyn Deacy*

Print/Media Buyer: *Doreen Suruki*

Permissions Editor: *Sarah Harkrader*

Production Service: *Sara Dovre Wudali, Buuji Inc.*

Text Designer: *Roy Neuhaus*

Copy Editor: *Adrienne Armstrong*

Proofreader: *Virginia Aretz, Buuji, Inc.*

Indexer: *Marji Toensing, Buuji, Inc.*

Cover Designer: *Brittney Singletary*

Printer: *Webcom, Limited*

Compositor: *Buuji, Inc.*

Printed in Canada

2 3 4 5 6 7 08 07 06 05

For more information about our products, contact us at:
Thomson Learning Academic Resource Center
1-800-423-0563

For permission to use material from this text or product, submit a request online at
http://www.thomsonrights.com.

Any additional questions about permissions can be submitted by email to
thomsonrights@thomson.com.

Library of Congress Control Number:

ISBN 0-534-61296-2

Thomson Wadsworth
10 Davis Drive
Belmont, CA 94002-3098
USA

Asia
Thomson Learning
5 Shenton Way #01-01
UIC Building
Singapore 068808

Australia/New Zealand
Thomson Learning
102 Dodds Street
Southbank, Victoria 3006
Australia

Canada
Nelson
1120 Birchmount Road
Toronto, Ontario M1K 5G4
Canada

Europe/Middle East/Africa
Thomson Learning
High Holborn House
50/51 Bedford Row
London WC1R 4LR
United Kingdom

Latin America
Thomson Learning
Seneca, 53
Colonia Polanco
11560 Mexico D.F.
Mexico

Spain/Portugal
Paraninfo
Calle Magallanes, 25
28015 Madrid, Spain

THOMSON
WADSWORTH

Publisher: *Holly J. Allen*

Assistant Editor: *Shona Burke*

Editorial Assistant: *Laryssa Polika*

Senior Technology Project Manager: *Jeanette Wiseman*

Senior Marketing Manager: *Kimberly Russell*

Marketing Assistant: *Andrew Keay*

Advertising Project Manager: *Shemika Britt*

Project Manager, Editorial Production: *Jane Brundage*

Interior Design Director: *Carolyn Deacy*

Print/Media Buyer: *Doreen Suruki*

Permissions Editor: *Sarah Harkrader*

Production Service: *Sara Dovre Wudali, Buuji Inc.*

Text Designer: *Roy Neuhaus*

Copy Editor: *Adrienne Armstrong*

Proofreader: *Virginia Aretz, Buuji, Inc.*

Indexer: *Marji Toensing, Buuji, Inc.*

Cover Designer: *Brittney Singletary*

Printer: *Webcom, Limited*

Compositor: *Buuji, Inc.*

Printed in Canada

2 3 4 5 6 7 08 07 06 05

For more information about our products, contact us at:
Thomson Learning Academic Resource Center
1-800-423-0563

For permission to use material from this text or product, submit a request online at
http://www.thomsonrights.com.

Any additional questions about permissions can be submitted by email to
thomsonrights@thomson.com.

Library of Congress Control Number:

ISBN 0-534-61296-2

Thomson Wadsworth
10 Davis Drive
Belmont, CA 94002-3098
USA

Asia
Thomson Learning
5 Shenton Way #01-01
UIC Building
Singapore 068808

Australia/New Zealand
Thomson Learning
102 Dodds Street
Southbank, Victoria 3006
Australia

Canada
Nelson
1120 Birchmount Road
Toronto, Ontario M1K 5G4
Canada

Europe/Middle East/Africa
Thomson Learning
High Holborn House
50/51 Bedford Row
London WC1R 4LR
United Kingdom

Latin America
Thomson Learning
Seneca, 53
Colonia Polanco
11560 Mexico D.F.
Mexico

Spain/Portugal
Paraninfo
Calle Magallanes, 25
28015 Madrid, Spain

Dedicated to former co-author Bob J. Carrell, and all public relations writers who care about communicating clearly and effectively.

Contents

CHAPTER TWO
Ethical and Legal Responsibilities of the PR Writer   15

CHAPTER THREE
Persuasion   38

CHAPTER FOUR
Research for the Public Relations Writer 61

PART 2

Writing Principles   81

PART 3

Writing for Select Publics   131

CHAPTER   SEVEN
Email, Memos, Letters, Reports and Proposals   132

CHAPTER TWELVE
Message Design Concepts   228

CHAPTER FOURTEEN
Writing for Web Sites   277

P A R T 5

CHAPTER NINETEEN
Magazines and Annual Reports   371

CHAPTER TWENTY
Crisis Communication and the Planning Process 394

APPENDIX A
Readability Formulas 421

APPENDIX **B**
Copyfitting 426

Preface

The seventh edition introduces a new co-author, Jim Haynes. Longtime friend and professional associate of Doug Newsom, Haynes brings a wealth of professional experience to the task as well as his considerable talents as a teacher. You'll find evidence of his assistance to this book in expressions of thanks included in the Preface of the sixth edition. You'll notice that this edition is dedicated to former co-author, the late Dr. Bob J. Carrell.

Many changes were made with the sixth edition, but the public relations field changes so quickly that we decided to fine-tune some chapters while retaining the same basic structure that was revised for the sixth edition. For example, we changed the focus of Chapter 15 to working with media, including contacting media with ideas as well as stories themselves. This new content seems to work well with the media kits that remain in that chapter but includes more on electronic versions. Planning for communication during crises and ongoing public relations programs is the focus of the last chapter. In Chapter 20 we have redirected all of the content to strategic public relations writing. Content about keeping centered on mission statements that previously was in the campaign writing chapter seems to fit well here since that's an essential element in all crisis communication.

The basic sections remain the same, with Part One providing background for public relations writing tasks by explaining the special qualities of these efforts and by examining legal and ethical obligations of what is essentially persuasive writing. Research is essential not only for the writing task itself but also to determine the impact of your writing efforts. Part Two covers style and techniques.

Part Three has the basic writing assignments that students must master early such as crafting messages for letters, emails and Web sites. The section includes more organizational writing for both internal and external audiences: reports and proposals, backgrounders and position papers. Writing for the mass media is covered in Part Four. That section includes news releases for Web sites, print and broadcast media as well as the types of advertising that often are the responsibility of public relations, rather than marketing.

More complex writing appears in Part Five, where you'll find media kits and messages for the news media, including announcements of upcoming events. This section also includes speeches and other presentations, newsletters, brochures, magazines and annual reports. The last chapter involves strategic planning and messages for campaigns and crises.

As always, the focus of the text remains the same: to make competent writers of students who can meet the many demands of the workplace and discover the rewards of being able to turn a phrase that tells a story for any audience in any medium.

We appreciate the reviewers who suggested some of these changes and gave us guidance: Coy Callison, Texas Tech University; Bill Haldin, California State University, Sacramento; John L. Naccarato, University of Nevada, Las Vegas; James L. Terhune, University of Florida; and Diane F. Witmer, California State University, Fullerton. Thanks is due also to Holly Allen, publisher; Jane Brundage, project manager; Kimberly Russell, marketing manager; Adrienne Armstrong, copy editor; and Sara Dovre Wudali from Buuji, Inc.

PART 1

PR Writing: Role and Responsibility

Finding facts, communicating effectively in all media, knowing the law and being ethical—all are essential for the PR writer.

Public Relations and the Writer

Public relations writing—that's all about putting a "spin" on things. Right? Wrong! It is about tailoring messages for particular media and publics. Clients and employers may not understand this, but it is imperative that you do, as a writer. Writing for public relations takes many forms, as you will realize as you go through these chapters. The more you know about different media, the more facile you are with all writing assignments, the better off you will be in the kaleidoscopic job market.

The changing job market is bringing together various demands on the writer that used to be more distinctly categorized along separate job lines. Some public relations people will tell you that they don't write advertising copy. Too bad for them. They may get into a job where that skill is needed. Many public relations people are still learning about Web sites, and some are just relinquishing the task to a graphics designer. The results are dreadful if the designer is not a word person too. The demands on today's writers are for more versatility, greater under-standing of the requirements of different media and increased competence in using visuals and sounds to help convey a message.

At the same time the demand for versatility is growing, there is more emphasis on accountability—evidence that the messages work. Employers want proof of results from com-munication efforts. There is no open checkbook for communication. Yet there is no need to despair. The writer who is genuinely good at the task of researching information, learning its meaning and communicating that effectively is and always will be needed.

You must understand what makes public relations writing different, though, from liter-ary writing, news writing or selling although you may be involved in all three.

Public relations writers do prepare messages for any medium that can convey informa-tion. Furthermore, much of the time these messages—words, images and often sound—are conveyed electronically. Potentially these messages can be received anywhere in the world.

The difference for public relations writing lies in the power and responsibility of the public relations person who is in the position of brokering goodwill between an institution and its publics. There are two aspects to this responsibility. Strategically, public relations involves the ways an organization's operations and policies affect people—the face-to-face interaction of employees with customers or clients and the organization's participation in the affairs of the community. Tactically speaking, though, good policies and good performance are worth little if people don't understand the policies and don't know about the performance. The heart of public relations practice remains in communication, particularly writing.

Good public relations requires communication skills, expertise in dealing with news media and a knowledge of mass communication, the dynamics of public opinion and the principles of persuasion. Further, the communicator must know when and what to communicate. This involves analysis, judgment, counseling and planning—in addition to and prior to communicating. In this chapter we'll try to clarify the nature of this complex task and the writer's role in it, beginning with a definition of the discipline, public relations.

Defining Public Relations

Even people who practice public relations don't all agree on just what public relations is. Each practitioner probably has a slightly different definition, depending on his or her particular public relations experience. That experience is affected by the social, political and economic environment. Thus the practice of public relations in many countries is different and the demands on the writers vary. Nevertheless, certain definitions express the meaning of public relations to the satisfaction of most professionals. One accepted definition was adopted in 1978 in Mexico City during the First World Assembly of Public Relations Associations and the First World Forum of Public Relations:

> Public relations practice is the art and science of analyzing trends, predicting their consequences, counseling organization leaders, and implementing planned programs of action which will serve both the organization's and the public interest.

It's a broad definition but a useful one. By examining it more closely, we can get a better understanding of what public relations is and where the writer fits in.

Analyzing, Predicting and Counseling

The central part of this definition of public relations outlines the main roles of the professional public relations person: "analyzing trends, predicting their consequences, counseling organization leaders." These roles fall into the management context, in which personnel help to frame, implement, adjust and communicate the policies that govern how an institution interacts with its publics. It is through public relations that a company acts with responsibility and responsiveness—in policy and information—to the best interests of the institution and its publics.[1]

Doing this job well requires a broad educational background, expertise in many areas and, most of all, good judgment. Unlike the corporate attorney or accountant, the public relations practitioner cannot refer to a body of laws or procedures that prescribe behavior under given circumstances. Instead, the public relations person must know human behavior and combine that knowledge with specific information about people within the institution and people out-side whom the institution deals with. For example, the PR director for a bank must consider the views of bank officers and bank employees as well as those of customers, the community, legislators and government regulatory agencies. The public relations person for the local school district must be aware of the feelings of students, parents, voters and the regional accrediting agency. Any institution has many publics, and the public relations director must be able to advise management about the possible impact on those publics of various plans, policies and actions.

In addition to analyzing publics and counseling management on the effects of policy, the PR person must be alert for signs of change. The right policy today will not necessarily be the right policy tomorrow. People's attitudes and opinions evolve, and the composition of the public changes. The capable PR person notes trends in public opinion and predicts the consequences of such trends for the institution.

Usually, the public relations director also serves as spokesperson for the organization and overseer of the entire public relations program. The PR person at the top of the department spends little time on basic public relations techniques such as writing. The basics are handled by entry-level people, the staff writers.

Frank Wylie, a former president of the Public Relations Society of America, describes the division of public relations labor in this way: Senior-level public relations people are likely to spend 10 percent of their time with techniques, 40 percent with administration and 50 percent with analysis and judgment; at entry level it's 50 percent techniques, 5 percent judgment and 45 percent "running like hell."[2]

Advertising, Publicity and PR

Much of the "running like hell" is done to carry out those "planned programs of action" mentioned in the definition of public relations. These programs, the most visible part of public relations practice, usually reach the public in the form of advertising or publicity.

However, as the lines between publicity and advertising are increasingly blurred, there's room for confusion about these two terms. Strictly speaking, *advertising* is time or space in a medium, purchased to display a message that has been prepared or approved by the buyer. Both content and placement—time and place, as well as duration—are controlled by the buyer. *Publicity* is information provided to a public without charge. The supplier controls content but relinquishes further control. When information goes to a news medium, the decision whether to use the publicity and the determination of its final form are controlled by the medium. Only when the medium itself is controlled by the source of the information is there full control of the message. Examples of controlled media would be employee communications of all types from magazines, newsletters and annual reports to video presentations and Web pages.

Confusion begins when advertising is not purchased, but is donated by a news medium to nonprofit organizations. Is this advertising or publicity? Technically, it's advertising because it looks like commercial advertising and is used in the time or space reserved for advertising. Further confusion arises over promotional letters and brochures. Are these direct sales (and consequently advertising), or are they promotions?

Adding to the problem is the fact that image, identity or institutional advertising is usu-ally written by someone in a public relations department. On the other hand, ads for products or services, marketing-type advertising, often are handled exclusively by advertising agencies and their copywriters. Catalogs, which require more promotional kinds of writing, fall somewhere between publicity and advertising.

In any case, both publicity and advertising demand strong writing and conceptual skills. Most business executives are able to identify what they expect out of both, even when the lines begin to blur. However, many still equate publicity with public relations. Again there's an important difference. A publicist merely disseminates information. A public relations person, as we discussed, is involved in the analysis, counseling and planning that precede the dissemination of information. Or as PR authority the late Edward L. Bernays says, "Publicity is a one-way street; public relations is a two-way street."[3] PR incorporates publicity, press agentry and public information, with the emphasis depending on the type of institution.[4]

The Two-Way Street

The last part of the Mexico City definition of PR speaks of serving "both the organization's and the public interest." Publicists who simply transmit their organization's views to the media are not likely to serve the public interest. As Bernays said,

> Public relations is not a one-way street in which leadership manipulates the public and public opinion. It is a two-way street in which leadership and the public find integration with each other and in which objectives and goals are predicated on a coincidence of public and private interests.[5]

This means that the task of PR people is not simply to communicate management's view to the public. The task also involves communicating the views of the public to management. The objectives of an institution and its public relations program must be designed with the needs and desires of the public clearly in mind.

Going one way, the PR person analyzes public opinion and the needs of the community, and opens channels of communication that allow such information to flow into the institution. Using this information, the PR person advises management on the policies that are likely to be of mutual benefit to the institution and the public—or at least acceptable, if not beneficial, to the public.

Then—going the other way down the PR street—the PR person opens channels of communication that reach out from the institution to the public. These channels are used to interpret the institution's policies and actions to its various audiences. Communication in this direction is largely the responsibility of the PR writer.

Publics, Channels and the Role of the Writer

It is a simple thing to say that the task of public relations writers is to communicate with the public. But in practice there is nothing simple about it. It's not as though there were one single "public" to write for. Rarely is a public relations message important to everybody in the "public."

News that a theme park is creating a new thrill ride is important information to youngsters who enjoy such entertainment, but what they want to know about it is quite different from what businesses and residents near the theme park want to know. Concerns of businesses and residents are about increased traffic to the area and more noise. What that group is concerned with is different from what the city's safety engineers and the theme park's insurance people want to know. These groups' needs are all different from what the local and state tourism departments want to know. The tourism departments' needs for information are different from those of investors in the theme park, and even those interests are not the same. If the theme park belongs to a publicly held company, its stock is traded on the open market so securities analysts are another public. Publicly held companies are also responsible to the Securities and Exchange Commission. If the theme park is your client or your employer, you have to prepare information to reach all of these publics, and the information for each has a different focus. This focus is not a "spin." It is a responsible communication to satisfy the information needs and interests of particular publics.

A *public* is any group of people tied together by some common factor. And as public relations writers soon discover, there are many, many such groups. As some public relations people say, and as we've acknowledged through usage in this book, the *public* in public relations should really be *publics*.

The Public in Public Relations

In his book *The Mass Media*, the late Stanford professor Bill Rivers describes the endless variety of publics in this way:

> There are as many publics as there are groups with varying levels of income, education, taste, and civic awareness; as many as there are groups with different political allegiances, different religions and so on. What concerns and convinces one public may seem trivial to another. Furthermore, the definition of each public is never static; it changes as the issues change. When California is voting for a governor, a Los Angeles college student becomes one member of a large and diverse public that includes a San Francisco stevedore and excludes a college professor at the University of Maine. But, when higher education in the United States is the issue, the college student is one member of a public that includes the professor but excludes the stevedore—except that the stevedore's working partner may have a daughter who attends the University of Idaho . . . and so on in bewildering variety.[6]

Obviously, each of us belongs to many different publics. If you're a student, you're naturally a member of a public important to the university or college you attend. If you're about to graduate, you belong to a public important to prospective employers in the community. If you've just married, you're part of a public important to real estate agencies eager to sell you a house. If you belong to the local chapter of the Sierra Club, you're part of a public important to politicians and energy companies.

Just as each individual belongs to many publics, each institution must communicate with many publics—from customers and suppliers to employees and stockholders. A public relations writer for a university must write for faculty, students, administrators, alumni, financial benefactors, community leaders, legislators and sports fans. The public relations writer for a political candidate tailors messages to fund-raisers, voters, reporters and precinct workers.

The global proliferation of electronic technology also means that messages may be received by "unintended audiences," or nimbus publics.[7] An awareness of these publics, knowledge of them and sensitivity to their potential reactions are critical because misunderstandings, some of crisis proportions, can result. As an example, a casual comment in a speech by a high-level business or political figure might characterize the citizens of a nation in such a way as to cause outrage when it is seen by them on television or reported in their other news media. Such a communications misstep can jeopardize trade negotiations or business deals.

The variety of publics is so vast that PR people often find it useful to divide the publics they deal with into two broad classes: internal and external. *Internal publics* are groups within the organization (such as employees or the board of directors). *External publics* are groups outside the organization (such as the media, your company's customers or the state legislature). The distinction between the two is not always clear-cut; stockholders, for example, though essentially an external public, can have close ties to the institution. One definition of internal publics is "all those who share the institution's identity." Broad categories of publics appear in Tables 1.1 and 1.2.

T A B L E   1 . 1 a   *Discovering and Prioritizing Publics*   Publics for any organization fall into these categories, developed by Jerry Hendrix.

Major Publics			
Media Publics	National trade, industry and association publications	Other uniformed personnel	Organization employees
Mass media		Union representatives	Organization officers
Local	National organizational house and membership publications	Other nonmanagement personnel	Organization members
Print publications			Prospective organization members
Newspapers	National ethnic publications	**Member Publics**	
Magazines		Organization employees	Related or other allied organizations
TV stations	Publications of national special groups	Headquarters management	
Radio stations			**Community Publics**
National	National specialized broadcast programs and networks	Headquarters nonmanagement (staff)	Community media
Print publications		Other headquarters personnel	Mass
Broadcast networks			Specialized
Wire services	**Employee Publics**	Organization officers	Community leaders
Specialized media	Management	Elected officers	Public officials
Local	Upper-level administrators	Appointed officers	Educators
Trade, industry and association publications	Mid-level administrators	Legislative groups	Religious leaders
	Lower-level administrators	Boards, committees	Professionals
Organizational house and membership publications		Organization members	Executives
	Nonmanagement (staff)	Regular members	Bankers
Ethnic publications	Specialists	Members in special categories—sustaining, emeritus, student members	Union leaders
Publications of special groups	Clerical personnel		Ethnic leaders
	Secretarial personnel		Neighborhood leaders
Specialized broadcast programs and stations	Uniformed personnel		Community organizations
	Equipment operators	Honorary members or groups	Civic
National	Drivers		Service
General business publications	Security personnel	Prospective organization members	Social
			Business
		State or local chapters	Cultural

(*continued*)

1 . 1 a   *(continued)*

Major Publics			
Religious	City	Minorities	Public officials
Youth	Mayor or city manager	Other	Professional leaders
Political	City council	Activist consumer groups	Ethnic leaders
Special interest	Other city officials, commissions, departments	Consumer publications	Neighborhood leaders
Other		Consumer media, mass and specialized	Organizations composing this public
Government Publics	**Investor Publics**	Consumer leaders and organizations	Civic
Federal	Shareowners and potential shareowners	**International Publics**	Political
Legislative branch	Securities analysts and investment counselors	Host country media	Service
Representatives, staff, committee personnel	Financial press	Mass	Business
Senators, staff, committee personnel	Major wire services: Dow Jones & Co., Reuters Economic Service, AP, UPI	Specialized	Cultural
Executive branch		Host country leaders	Religious
President	Major business magazines: *Business Week, Fortune* and the like— mass circulation and specialized	Public officials	Youth
White House staff, advisers, committees		Educators	Other
Cabinet officers, departments, agencies, commissions	Major newspapers: *The New York Times, The Wall Street Journal*	Social leaders	Customers
State		Cultural leaders	New customers
Legislative branch	Statistical services: Standard and Poor's Corp., Moody's Investor Service and the like	Religious leaders	Old customers
Representatives, delegates, staff, committee personnel		Political leaders	Potential customers
Senators, staff, committee personnel	Private wire services: PR Newswire, Business Wire	Professionals	Employees
Executive branch	Securities and Exchange Commission (SEC) for publicly owned companies	Executives	Management
Governor		Host country organizations	Nonmanagement
Governor's staff, advisers, committees	**Consumer Publics**	Business	Media
Cabinet officers, departments, agencies, commissions	Company employees	Service	Mass
County	Customers	Social	Specialized
County executive	Professionals	Cultural	Investors
Other county officials, commissions, departments	Middle class	Religious	Shareowners and potential shareowners
	Working class	Political	Financial analysts
		Special interests	Financial press
		Other	Suppliers
		Special Publics	Competitors
		Media consumed by this public	Government regulators
		Mass	
		Specialized	
		Leaders of this public	

Source: From Jerry A. Hendrix, *Public Relations Cases*, 5th ed., 2001. Reprinted with permission of Wadsworth Publishing, a division of Thomson Learning.

T A B L E   1 . 1 b   *Discovering and Prioritizing Publics*   Prioritizing publics may be done in a number of ways. One informal method is called the PVI: *P*, the Potential to influence a public, plus *V*, the Vulnerability of the organization to that public (which may change over time and in different situations), equals *I*, the Impact of that public on the organization. Here is a tabular form for "computing" a PVI index.

Audience or Public	*P* Potential for Organization to Influence (Scale 1–10)	+	*V* Vulnerability of Organization to Be Affected (Scale 1–10)	=	*I* Importance of Audience to Organization
_____	_____		_____		_____
_____	_____		_____		_____
_____	_____		_____		_____

Source: Jim Haynes, *Instructor's Guide for This Is PR,* 3d ed., by Doug Newsom and Alan Scott (Belmont, Calif.: Wadsworth, 1985), p. 6.3.

Priority Publics

On any one project it is impossible to direct attention equally to all publics. Therefore, PR people must select the publics that are most important for the communication effort. They may include the group that a new policy will affect the most or the groups whose opinions are especially important. In any event, the groups considered most important for a communication effort are called the *target publics* or *priority publics*.

But demographic information alone does not tell writers all they need to know about a public. Statistics such as age, sex and income are not useful in predicting whether a person would be likely to subscribe to the magazine *Dog World,* for example. Dog lovers come in all ages, both sexes and most income levels—groups that might seem totally unrelated if defined by demographics alone.

In fact, what public relations people call *psychographics* is frequently more important to the PR writer than demographics. Psychographics classifies people by what they think, how they behave and what they think about—their special interests, such as dogs. Psychographic information is not merely helpful to the PR writer; it is often necessary. Consider the public relations director responsible for a university's alumni association magazine, who admitted with some dismay that she didn't know how to appeal both to an 80-year-old graduate of the engineering school and a 22-year-old sociologist. She did a research study that revealed a psychographic pattern binding all the alumni to the institution. This information suggested the sorts of articles that would interest alumni. The public relations director was then able to make informed decisions—and she now felt a great deal more confident in her choices.

Channels

To reach different publics, the PR writer must choose channels of communication carefully. To get the message across, the channel must be one that the target audience will receive and believe. For example, the amusement park that wants middle-school students to try its new

T A B L E   1 . 2   *Internal and External PR*

	Internal	External	
		Direct	**Indirect**
Publics	Management (top and middle) Staff and employees (union and employee organizations—nonunion) Stockholders Directors	(marketing communications) Customers Sales representatives Traders and distributors Suppliers Competitors	(institutional communications) Potential customers Potential investors (stockholders) Financial community Special community of institution Government (local, state, federal) Community (environmental)
Media	Personal (person to person/person to group) Audiovisual (specialized media: films, slides, videotape, closed-circuit TV, computer networks—i.e., on intranet) Publications (specialized media: books, magazines, newspapers, newsletters) Direct mail Exhibits (including posters and bulletin board materials internally displayed as well as personalized items such as pins and awards) Critics (individuals and institutions) Email Fax (or facsimile) CD-ROMs Web pages	Personal (person to person/person to group) Audiovisual (Web pages with art and sound, films, slides, videotape, mass media, specialized media available to external audiences such as externally distributed CD-ROMs, videos, etc.) Publications (mass and specialized, including controlled and uncontrolled publicity as well as institutional and commercial advertising) Direct mail (personalized, institutional and sales promotion) Exhibits (mass and specialized externally displayed and product packaging, graphics, including point-of-sale promotions) CD-ROMs Broadcast fax Listserve (email) Internet site (on World Wide Web)	

ride would be foolish to run an ad in *Harper's* magazine. Few middle-school students even know that *Harper's* exists. They would not receive a message placed in that medium. But they do listen to radio and watch TV, so programs in those media are the channels that the amusement park would probably use, as well as maintaining an Internet presence.

The channel must also be appropriate for the message. Radio is not a good channel for conveying messages on complex subjects such as a university's endowment. These subjects are better suited to a magazine, a channel that readers can spend time with. Radio, though poorly suited for discussing endowments, works just fine for telling students the dates for fall registration. Channels may be individuals or media and may be mass media or specialized media. Each medium has characteristics that make it suitable for sending a particular message to a particular audience at a particular time.

People may be channels—for example, in person-to-person meetings or person-to-group interactions such as speeches or meetings. When communication media are mentioned, you are likely to think of publications and audiovisuals. Publications may be books, magazines, newspapers, newsletters or reports. Audiovisuals may be films, videotapes, slides, Web pages, CD-ROMs or television—mass or closed circuit. But people, publications and audiovisuals aren't the only channels of communication. Another channel is direct mail or email of personalized letters or institutional or promotional pieces. Exhibits are another channel. They encompass everything from trade-show displays to campaign buttons.

Specialized Media   Media designed for a particular audience are called specialized, to distinguish them from media for general audiences. Specialized media include the internal publications that institutions produce to communicate with employees, staff, management and others close to the institution, such as directors and stockholders. Also included in specialized media are an organization's intranet, computerized message boards and audiovisuals intended for internal use only: videotapes, closed-circuit television, CD-ROMs, films and slides. Among these specialized media are electronic information networks of personal computer users. Most specialized media are controlled by the institution using them. Email is a good example. Although not usually heavily monitored, there often is a "postmaster" to clean up the network storage system periodically.

Mass Media   The mass media include magazines, books, newspapers, radio, television and the Internet. Because neither the circulation nor the audience of such media is controlled by the institution, mass media are mostly for communication with external publics. Public relations writers using mass media to reach large audiences must remember, however, that such media are seen by internal publics as well. For example, a leading metropolitan daily newspaper's female employees objected to a promotional campaign that displayed women as sex objects. French police did not like billboards portraying them as "helpful" rather than as crime fighters facing danger.

The Role of the Writer

Public relations writers must be knowledgeable not only about publics and channels, but about all aspects of their institution as well. The PR writer for a social services agency must understand welfare eligibility rules and federal funding guidelines. A writer for the highway department must know about everything from road-building materials to traffic laws. PR writers must know enough about the financial aspects of a business to prepare the right message for securities analysts and to develop an annual report that stockholders can comprehend and auditors will approve.

In addition to possessing a broad knowledge of their company's business, public relations writers must be able to research specific subjects to determine what is and what isn't important. They must be able to borrow ideas from other fields—psychology, social psychology, sociology and political science, for example—to help put their research in perspective. PR writers must be alert to changing patterns of thought and behavior in society and must fully comprehend the issues of the day.

Finally, and most important, the public relations writer must be an expert in communication. If you want to be a public relations writer, you must know how to write effectively in many different styles and for all media. You must understand the principles of good writing and be familiar with the vast body of scientific research on communication, persuasion and public opinion. Your goal is to be an efficient, effective communicator.

You must accept that your writing is management-oriented, strategic communication and therefore likely to be persuasive in nature. Because of the scope of your communication, you must command a knowledge of publics and their cultures—their corporate or work environment culture, their personal or lifestyle culture and their indigenous or ethnic culture. Beyond that, you must know the international communication networks and media systems and how they operate. No matter what message you communicate, what audiences you communicate with and what media you use to reach those audiences, you have to know which words will work and why. You are critical to the PR function.

Preparing you for these varied writing tasks is what this book is all about.

Conclusions

- A kaleidoscopic job market demands increasing flexibility and a greater command of technical skills from writers.
- More accountability for results is demanded by today's employers and clients—they want proof that the messages worked.
- Messages—a combination of words, images and often sound—are frequently communicated electronically and may be received anywhere in the world, whether or not that is the intent of the sender.
- A public relations writer is responsible for helping an organization establish good relationships with its publics.
- There are two aspects to this responsibility: *strategy* of determining what and when to communicate to whom and *tactics* of handling that communication through the appropriate channels so that receivers understand the policies and performance of the institution.
- The lines between advertising and publicity are blurred and frequently not clear to clients or employers.
- Advertising is time or space bought to carry a buyer's message, but public service announcements, although appearing in the same time or space as commercial copy, are carried at the discretion of the medium.
- Publicity is information supplied to the public without charge but also without control unless the employer or client owns the medium. Information supplied as publicity can appear in any form, and whether it appears at all is at the discretion of the medium.
- Public relations communication is a two-way street, a conduit for incoming as well as outgoing messages.
- Publics are people tied together by some common factor(s).
- Factors binding people together as audiences may be uncovered through demographics (statistics such as age, sex and geography) and psychographics (interests and attitudes).

- Priority publics or target audiences are public relations publics selected for special attention and specific messages.
- Channels of communication may be specialized media or mass media.
- A public relations writer's role is to know about the institution for which that writer is working, the audiences or publics of that institution and the channels of communication through which to reach them.
- Public relations writers must be effective, efficient writers in all media.

Exercises

1. Collect materials from your admissions office about your school. Analyze them for message statements about the school. Are different appeals addressed to first-year students, transfers, graduate students, older-than-average students? What are these appeals?
2. Examine the different types of materials from your school's public relations office. List all of the publics these suggest.
3. Look at ads for your school (commercials too, if you have them). Compare these message statements with the admission materials and the publicity about the school. What message statements are consistent? Are any of them inconsistent? For example, does admission material suggest it's easy to get into the school while publicity talks about the high standards for admission?

 Use InfoTrac® College Edition to access information on topics in this chapter from hundreds of periodicals and scholarly journals.

Notes

1. Doug Newsom, Judy VanSlyke Turk and Dean Kruckeberg, *This Is PR: The Realities of Public Relations,* 8th ed. (Belmont, Calif.: Wadsworth, 2004), p. 2.
2. Frank Wylie, "The New Professionals." Speech to the First National Student Conference, Public Relations Student Society of America, Dayton, Ohio, October 24, 1976. Published by Chrysler Corporation, p. 5.
3. Edward L. Bernays, *Public Relations* (Norman, Okla.: University of Oklahoma Press, 1952), p. 5.
4. James E. Grunig and Todd Hunt, *Managing Public Relations* (New York: Holt, Rinehart & Winston, 1984), pp. 22–24.
5. Bernays, *Public Relations,* p. 83.
6. William L. Rivers, *The Mass Media* (New York: Harper & Row, 1975), p. 22.
7. David Sturgis et al., "Crisis Communications Management: The Public Opinion Node and Its Relationship to the Environmental Nimbus," *SAM Management Journal* 56(3) (Summer 1991): 22–27.

Selected Bibliography

Arnold S. De Beer and John C. Merrill, eds., *Global Journalism: A Survey of International Communication,* 4th ed. (Boston: Allyn and Bacon, 2004).

Hugh M. Culbertson and Ni Chen, eds., *International Public Relations: A Comparative Analysis* (Mahwah, N.J.: Lawrence Erlbaum Associates, 1996).

Hugh M. Culbertson, Dennis W. Jeffers, Donna Besser Stone and Martin Terrell, *Social, Political and Economic Contexts in Public Relations, Theory and Cases* (Hillsdale, N.J.: Lawrence Erlbaum Associates, 1993).

Scott Cutlip, Allen H. Center and Glen M. Broom, *Effective Public Relations,* 8th ed. (Englewood Cliffs, N.J.: Prentice Hall, 1999).

Thomas L. Harris, *The Marketer's Guide to Public Relations: How Today's Top Companies Are Using PR to Gain a Competitive Edge* (New York: John Wiley & Sons, 1993).

Thomas L. Harris and Philip Kotler, *Value-Added Public Relations: The Secret Weapon of Integrated Marketing* (New York: McGraw-Hill, 1999).

Jim Haynes, *Instructor's Guide for This Is PR,* 3d ed., by Doug Newsom and Alan Scott (Belmont, Calif.: Wadsworth, 1985).

Jerry A. Hendrix, *Public Relations Cases,* 5th ed. (Belmont, Calif.: Wadsworth, 1998).

Doug Newsom, Judy VanSlyke Turk and Dean Kruckeberg, *This Is PR: The Realities of Public Relations,* 8th ed. (Belmont, Calif.: Wadsworth, 2004).

Dennis L. Wilcox, Phillip H. Ault, Warren K. Agee and Glen T. Cameron, *Public Relations: Strategies and Tactics,* 7th ed. (New York: HarperCollins, 1999).

Dennis L. Wilcox and Patrick Jackson, *Public Relations: Writing and Media Techniques,* 3d ed. (White Plains, N.Y.: Longman, 2000).

Ethical and Legal Responsibilities of the PR Writer

Jobs in public relations generally are not high in status. Some individuals and organizations are clear exceptions to that indictment. Why are they exceptions rather than the rule? Many reasons are possible, but we'll focus on just four. First, they have a highly developed sense of personal and professional ethics that drives them to meet the spirit of the law as well as its explicit provisions. Second, they believe that their highest professional obligation is to advocate policies and techniques that are socially responsible. Third, they uphold the idea that looking after the best interests of priority publics is in the best interests of their organizations. Fourth, the organizations for which they work are managed by people who are proactive in outlook and behavior.

Public relations professionals and their organizations that don't meet those standards often cause problems for themselves as well as others. They sometimes are cited by critics as the reason public relations practice is seen in a negative light. Critics can find plenty of things to cite in support of their view.

The new century began with the Firestone/Bridgestone v. Ford controversy over which of the companies was responsible for crashes that killed or injured hundreds of people—most, but not all, in the USA. The problem was with Firestone's 15-inch ATX tires and the unusual way these were made at the company's Decatur, Illinois, plant. Firestone said it wasn't the tires; it was low inflation, too-high load limits and the design of the Ford Explorer on which the tires were standard equipment. At one point there was some question about whether the Firestone brand would even survive, and the parent company, Bridgestone, based in Japan, subsequently emphasized its name, rather than Firestone. Bridgestone/Firestone and Ford fought the issue in the media first and then sued each other. Ford's CEO, William Clay Ford Jr., was in an especially awkward position because he is a Bridgestone as well as a Ford. Ford called in Explorers and replaced the tires. Bridgestone/Firestone began a recall of 6.5 million tires in August 2000—one of the largest recalls in USA history.

But that was just the beginning of critical legal and ethical issues of the 21st century. The overpowering one was the collapse of energy giant Enron, which caused the demise of one of the oldest accounting firms in the nation, Arthur Andersen, and left Enron employees penniless with no jobs and their pension funds invested in the company's now worthless stock. The Board and top management had taken out their money earlier. Right on the heels of the Enron story of lying to its investors and government regulators was the fall of WorldCom, essentially for the same reason. This was during 2001 and 2002.

Then, on the first of February in 2003, the space shuttle burned up on re-entry and was spread over east Texas and parts of Louisiana. The aging spacecraft had some damage at liftoff that went undetected until re-entry. NASA's credibility was damaged, despite a remarkable openness during and after the disaster.

Crises can always damage credibility if not handled well, but in each of these cases, ethical issues and judgment calls created the crisis and the resulting litigation. Poor judgment got a photojournalist who was covering the war in Iraq fired from his newspaper and created a stir of discussions about ethics. He merged two images of the same scene to make a better picture.[1] This is not the first time digital imaging has created some ethical issues.

Dustin Hoffman has consistently refused to allow his likeness to be used in commercial messages except in movies in which he stars. But *Los Angeles* magazine, using digital technology, showed Hoffman dressed in an evening gown and high heels in the magazine's spring fashion promotion, "Grand Illusions." He sued and was awarded $1.5 million in damages.[2] A simple question asking permission for this use would have been much less expensive and would have avoided some bad publicity.

Even if such practices don't result in legal actions, what image of public relations is apparent when a campaign worker plants false information about an opponent? Or what about the so-called spin doctors, who distribute information more as propaganda than as news? Video news releases are now staples of PR practice, but they are often seen as palming off "fake news" on an unsuspecting public.[3]

Former *Playboy* bunny Terri Welles decided to use the words "Playboy" and "Playmate" when she set up her Web site to provide hard-core porn. The two words were used as meta tags, electronic flags used by some search engines to locate information. *Playboy* brought suit, stating that these tags lead customers away and cause economic loss.[4] In London, the Hoover Company's promotion offering free-flight package holidays caused a furor when vacationers found the airfare was free but hotel rates were premium.[5]

Sensitivity to publics is sometimes a problem. For instance, a photograph of a dead, bloodied body atop an automobile appeared in *The Straits Times,* Singapore. The victim, a 70-year-old male Malaysian walking along a road in Negeri Sembilan, was hit by a car and died instantly.[6] The picture brought a lengthy series of letters of protest.

You might pass off each of these events as nothing more than good business. Even so, if you set aside legal issues, the question remains: Do these practices reflect good business ethics? Perhaps the question should be: What *are* good business ethics?

John Wanamaker, a famous retailer at the turn of the 20th century, had his personal credo etched into a marble column in his Philadelphia store: "Let those who follow me continue to build with the plumb of honor, the level of truth and the square of integrity, education, courtesy and mutuality." That credo is as valid today as when Wanamaker penned it. It applies just as much to the professional practice of public relations as to the conduct of any organization that interacts with the public.

Embedded in that quote are two guidelines especially relevant to public relations. One is the idea of being genuinely *sensitive* to the feelings and needs of others. The other is the will to practice the *Golden Rule,* which says you should treat other people as you want to be treated by them. Although these two guidelines are at the center of responsible professional practice, they are too simple to fully describe the complex set of influences affecting how you approach and complete any writing task.

Public relations writers often initiate or implement practices that draw criticism, much of it justified. Although some public relations writing practices are legally prescribed, others are set by *moral principles.* Ethics are founded on moral principles that are themselves grounded in effects. Moral principles consist of a set of beliefs and values that reflect a group's sense of what is *right* or *wrong*—regardless of how these terms are defined in formal rules, regulations or laws.

This is the case whether you agree with the idea that a moral judgment must fulfill *formal conditions* or you think a moral judgment must also meet some *material condition.* The difference is that formal conditions call for moral guidelines or rules that are regarded as universal and prescriptive. But material conditions represent considerations that deal with the welfare of society as a whole and emphasize basic human good or purpose. For example, agreements in the Geneva Conventions are prescriptive, but they do not address restrictions on the freedoms of individuals within a society such as apartheid or immigration quotas.

If you ask for a public's view of your ethics, don't be surprised if your organization is seen as unethical. The public view of an organization's ethics is likely to be based less on a definition of morality than on the consequences of what the organization says and does, which will be seen as either moral or not moral by each and all of its publics. This sense of rightness, even if it later proves to be in error, is the stuff of which *public opinion* is formed.

Clearly, public opinion is important. Much of what you will do as a professional will be directed toward influencing, if possible, the opinion of publics. In the USA, our treasured First Amendment is, in a real sense, the product of public opinion. That's a sobering thought because it implies that the First Amendment can be abridged or voided if public opinion no longer supports it. So if you write, say or do something that violates society's sense of "rightness," you may be undercutting your constitutional right to free speech. That's a heavy responsibility. As a writer, how can you meet it?

Core Values and Personal/Professional Behavior

Our core values are based on our personalized belief system—what we believe to be right or wrong. We are influenced in these by our family, friends, education and a faith we endorse, if we do. This core of values we take into the world, where it is often tried and tested, but probably no more so than in the workplace.

The reason is that organizations, like individuals, develop around a core set of values, often set forward in a mission statement or even a formal statement of values. These values are operationalized in the corporate culture that is often set by the organizational leadership. In looking for a place to work, you need to find an organization that fits within your own value system. In all probability, the organization that hires you will be looking also for a "good fit" between the corporate culture and a potential employee.

Even when there is a "good fit," initially, situations change and so may your level of comfort in working there. One way to understand ethical responsibility is to look carefully at the interplay of different levels of influence on your personal and professional behavior.

Dynamics

Pressures in the workplace come from the economic, political and social system in which the organization exists. As we live and work in a more global society, these pressures have increased significantly. It's an understatement to say there is little consistency in cultures. You are more likely to hear the term "cultural conflicts."

Governments are a big part of that. Governments change and with them the philosophy of governance as well as the laws themselves and the rules of regulators. Public relations is a recognized discipline, but it is practiced in many different ways around the world because it too must be responsive to the environment in which it functions in representing businesses and nonprofit organizations. Additionally, the organization itself for which you as a public relations person work is responsive to standards and practices set by its own industry. If you work for a PR firm or agency, you may have clients from a number of different industries. The relationship between you and an organization changes with time. Provisions of communication law are always in flux because a new court decision may put a different spin on a law, rule or regulation. And society's expectations and judgments about what is right or wrong are notoriously capricious. An example of changed expectations is the effect of what's happening in cyberspace to the old protocol of a clear division between advertising and editorial content. Web site editorial independence is seldom carefully defined, and search engines finding information on a topic cannot sort out the independent news from the sponsored information.[7] Compounding the problem are the many organizations that have placed their Web sites in the hands of management information systems specialists instead of public relations people. Because building and maintaining relationships are not necessarily high on their list of priorities, the result can be damaging to the corporate image.[8]

Trying to follow your own moral compass in the swirl of this social, legal and economic storm is not easy. You can easily get "off course," confused in your ability to know with certainty your ethical and legal responsibilities as a writer.

Things simply change. What is wrong today may be right tomorrow, or vice versa. It is your responsibility to be sensitive to these changes; otherwise, you and your organization may get into lots of trouble stemming from the volatility of today's values.

Values

The concept of *values* is another way of talking about ethics. The study of ethics falls into two broad categories: *comparative ethics* and *normative ethics*. Normative ethics are studied by theologians and philosophers. Comparative ethics—sometimes called *descriptive ethics*—are studied by social scientists, who look at the ways different cultures practice ethical behavior. Values form the foundation of our institutions and organizations, as well as of our informal and formal rules of behavior.

We're taught from an early age that some values are eternal verities. But if we see them violated repeatedly without sanctions, we begin to wonder whether they really are verities or eternal. A deceptive public relations practice, for example, may go unpunished or even unnoticed, and its users may gain significant advantages to the detriment of others. Which are the values we are expected to exhibit as responsible public relations writers?

Remember that ethics, being value-based, are different in different cultures, something to be sensitive to when communications go to other countries and to be aware of in countries of diverse cultures, such as the USA. When the *limits* of what your primary public will tolerate turn out to be narrower than those of your organization or yourself, your ethical behavior will be open to public debate, which may result in censure or withdrawal of support. In such cases, your first concern should be with examining your own personal and professional standards.

Influence of Personal Standards

Your personal and professional ethical standards come from your core values. If you find that your own standards are in conflict with those of your colleagues (especially your supervisor) in an organization, it can be personally and professionally upsetting.

Suppose that your task is to write, say or do something that, although legal, can't readily be reconciled with your own standards. What is your responsibility? To resolve this problem, you must explore your options realistically. Four basic strategies are apparent: (1) try to educate those in your organization to your standards; (2) refuse the task; (3) ask that you be given another task; or (4) take the assignment.

Educating

You can try to convert those around you to your point of view. The character of an organization tends to reflect its top leadership. The leadership hires managers, who then hire people whom they perceive as fitting into and contributing to the goals of the organization. To say that you must be a clone of the top leadership is absurd, but it is equally absurd to believe that you would be in the job if those doing the hiring had not assumed that you "fit the mold" to some extent.

That assumption will be in your favor as you attempt to educate others in the organization to your point of view, because you are presumed to be much like them. If you use this identification tactic, you'll probably find that some colleagues are open-minded but others aren't. If your organization encourages dialogue, however, your chances of getting a fair hearing are greater. But even with a fair hearing, you may not convert them to your view of the world; besides, you may be wrong. A lot depends on how carefully and thoughtfully you have drawn the personal and professional circles of influence around yourself.

How pliable is your position? What is the absolute limit beyond which you will not compromise? What justification can you offer to support your position? Is the basis of your justification appropriate to the situation? You must ask and carefully answer these questions and many like them before you attempt to implement a strategy of conversion.

Suppose you ask and answer such questions to your own satisfaction and mount a campaign to change the organization's course of action. Can you win? Yes. Even if you aren't successful at converting your colleagues, you still may win in two important ways.

First, your colleagues will respect a well-articulated, well-reasoned argument, even if they disagree with it. That's because the subject of contention is a matter of judgment. Neither you nor they can be absolutely certain of the truth of the matter, but each of you may recognize and appreciate sincere efforts to divine it.

Second, you also win because, when you articulate a different or unpopular standard, you accept the highest responsibility of being a professional public relations person. You are expected to counsel your organization against doing something you believe is wrong. Any lesser standard of behavior is not worthy of being called professional.

If you don't convert the others to your point of view, you can then adopt a strategy of refusal.

Refusing

A position of refusal is often greeted with arguments that "It's OK because everybody does it." If those arguments don't succeed, they are often replaced by anger—even retribution—that may get you fired. Your willingness to risk being fired is the severest test of your conviction. If your belief is strong enough, getting fired may be a personal and professional favor to you. That's because it tells you clearly that the organization does not respect you or your professional judgment and abilities. You need to know this so you can find one that does. Also, you will not be subject to criticism when the action of the organization draws fire.

No one and no organization can make you do something you believe is wrong, even if it is not illegal. If you cave in because you need the money, you like your position, you're really counting on an attractive retirement program or the like, your convictions are mostly for show. That's your fault. Don't blame the organization, society or some generalized "other" for the bottom-line decisions you make.

If you don't have the courage of your convictions, you may tend to assume that others don't either. This may be true of some, but not of all. And such an assumption is likely to make you less sensitive to the feelings, needs and values of others. As a result, you may write, say or do things that are harmful to pertinent audiences, without even recognizing it. Thus you may feed on and perpetuate stereotypes, confuse form with substance and promote behaviors detrimental to the best interests of your target publics. If left uncorrected, this behavior can end in alienation and loss of support for your organization, thereby setting the stage for program or organization failure.

To paraphrase the Golden Rule, the way you are treated as a writer is a reflection of how you, as a writer, treat your target publics.

Requesting Reassignment

If you like what you are doing and your prospects for the future look good, you may seek an alternative to refusing the task. One approach is to ask that you be assigned to something else of equal or greater importance. The problem is that there may be no one else to take the assignment. Assuming that someone else is available, this strategy will produce three important results. First, by stating your case clearly, calmly and logically, you will find out just how persuasive you really are. Second, whatever the response to your request, you also discover how you are valued by your supervisor and organization. Third, you'll get a clearer picture of the people you work with and for—what their values are and how they relate to the organization and industry with which they are identified.

"Now, when we explain this to Mom and Dad,
let's make sure we give it the right spin."

Reprinted by permission of Bunny Hoest.

Taking the Assignment

Taking the assignment, even if you are sincerely opposed to it, labels you as a team player who puts the values and needs of the organization above personal values. You are seen as fitting into the culture of the organization. You won't rock the boat. You will safeguard the values of the organization because you are loyal and trustworthy. You may even get a raise, a promotion or both.

The problem with all this is that you may be expected to write, say or do things that, although not strictly illegal, may violate a primary public's sense of right and wrong. If you push beyond what your target public will tolerate, you are likely to find yourself on trial in the court of public opinion. The judgments can be harsh. Even if you later clean up your act, you may never win an appeal or get a pardon. That will depend to some extent on the values and standards of practice exhibited by your organization and industry.

Influence of Organization and Industry Standards

Will having high personal and professional standards mean that you'll always be swimming upstream in your organization? That depends on the organization you work for and the industry sector it is part of. Some organizations and industry sectors are seen as monoliths whose only purpose is to make more money or gain additional power and influence. Such perspectives often are based not on facts but on perceptions that masquerade as facts. Some organizations and industry sectors seem more gifted than others at keeping facts and "facts" in close harmony.

Perceptions

Johnson & Johnson is remarkably successful at marketing a wide range of medical products and supplies. This long-term success can be traced in part to its standards of practice, as explained simply in its corporate credo. (See Figure 2.1.)

The credo places top priority on the welfare of its customers. Most organizations say no less, but J&J is perceived as really meaning it. That's because J&J tries to respond quickly and responsibly to any threat to the welfare of its priority publics.

This was demonstrated dramatically when the company immediately removed all Tylenol (made by a subsidiary company) from retailer shelves after a psychopath laced some capsules with cyanide, resulting in the random deaths of several people.

The economic loss to the organization was enormous. But the decision in 1982 to remove Tylenol from the public was both quick and decisive because management believes the J&J credo means what it says. More importantly, the public perceived the decision as the "right" thing to do. It was not mandated by law; it was simply the most responsible thing to do. Performance that is perceived positively earns lots of favorable support. That support has carried J&J through subsequent crises as well.[9]

On the other hand, Exxon's response in 1989 to the aftermath of the Valdez oil spill provoked extensive criticism from many quarters. Whether Exxon did everything it could do as quickly as possible will likely be debated for years. But Exxon was perceived as not responding quickly and responsibly. In fact, you expect to see comments about Exxon on every anniversary of the spill. Remember that perceptions become "facts" in the court of public opinion. Once those judgments are made, they may be very hard to overturn. And even when they can be overturned, the process is usually slow.

Organizational Culture and Values

When you start a new job, you'll go through a period of training in the culture and values of the organization. This may include attending a formal training program whose announced purpose is to acquaint you with the principal processes, techniques and policies that are to guide your behavior as an employee. These also reflect, but often not as obviously, the values and culture of the organization. But much of your training comes from simply watching and interacting with your new associates. That's how you learn the rules governing how you should behave in an organization. These rules of conduct may become so much a part of you that you hardly notice them. You may even respond automatically to new cues.

Automatic Responses

When you do things automatically, you're less likely to question your behavior or that of the organization. And if you don't question what you do, and how and why you do things, you aren't much more than an automaton. The only real difference is that you draw a salary. Automatons are machines whose greatest expense comes in the form of an initial capital investment, supplemented by routine maintenance to keep them productive. When they wear out or become outdated, they are simply replaced.

Our Credo

We believe our first responsibility is to the doctors, nurses and patients,
to mothers and fathers and all others who use our products and services.
In meeting their needs everything we do must be of high quality.
We must constantly strive to reduce our costs
in order to maintain reasonable prices.
Customers' orders must be serviced promptly and accurately.
Our suppliers and distributors must have an opportunity
to make a fair profit.

We are responsible to our employees,
the men and women who work with us throughout the world.
Everyone must be considered as an individual.
We must respect their dignity and recognize their merit.
They must have a sense of security in their jobs.
Compensation must be fair and adequate,
and working conditions clean, orderly and safe.
Employees must feel free to make suggestions and complaints.
There must be equal opportunity for employment, development
and advancement for those qualified.
We must provide competent management,
and their actions must be just and ethical.

We are responsible to the communities in which we live and work
and to the world community as well.
We must be good citizens—support good works and charities
and bear our fair share of taxes.
We must encourage civic improvements and better health and education.
We must maintain in good order
the property we are privileged to use,
protecting the environment and natural resources.

Our final responsibility is to our stockholders.
Business must make a sound profit.
We must experiment with new ideas.
Research must be carried on, innovative programs developed
and mistakes paid for.
New equipment must be purchased, new facilities provided
and new products launched.
Reserves must be created to provide for adverse times.
When we operate according to these principles,
the stockholders should realize a fair return.

Johnson & Johnson

FIGURE 2.1

Johnson & Johnson Credo   *"Our Credo" is Johnson & Johnson's attempt to state clearly its standards of practice with reference to its primary publics.*

Source: Reprinted with permission of Johnson & Johnson.

A responsible public relations writer should be a thinking, constructively critical and contributing member of the organization. In fact, the highest contribution you can make is not your technical skill but your sensitivity to the needs of your organization's relevant publics. If you become so immersed in the culture and standards of the organization that you lose touch with the values of those publics, you can do little more than a machine can do.

Problems may arise when the messages you shape undergo significant changes in the process of obtaining necessary approvals. The challenge for you is to see that these changes don't affect the sense of what must be communicated. This problem is aggravated by "editors" who excise segments or change things just to prove they can. You are supposed to be good enough with words and language that you can retain the sense of the message without compromising its integrity and without challenging the ego of those who have authority to approve what you write.

Because you are part of your organization, you are expected to know as much about what you write as anyone in the organization. You can't rely on your wordsmithing skills alone. You must know your organization and its industry thoroughly. You won't get much support or respect if you repeatedly make simple mistakes, such as using jargon incorrectly. You are supposed to know, and you shouldn't have to be told over and over. That's part of an organization's culture and values. But the practice of professional public relations also has its own culture and values, thus representing another area of influence on your behavior.

The complexity of this overlay of influences makes ethical decisions anything but clear cut.

Influence of Public Relations Standards of Practice

Every professional field has its own code of ethics and standards of practice. One of the most widely acknowledged codes in public relations is one adopted in 2000 to replace the 1988 code. (The Public Relations Society of America adopted its first code in 1950.) The code has lots to say about standards of practice, but a few key points are especially pertinent to your role as a writer.

Accuracy

Credibility with primary publics is probably the most important asset a writer or an organization can have. Without credibility, it is very difficult to succeed at what you want to do. Factual inaccuracies usually are pretty easy for primary publics to detect. The more difficult such inaccuracies are to discover, the more damaging they may appear in the eyes of your audience. Publics may conclude that you have deliberately distorted or misrepresented the facts for some ulterior motive.

They may label you and your organization as dishonest—and you are if you misrepresent the facts. But you and your organization can also make "honest" mistakes. These may seep into your writing as a result of rushed, sloppy editing, failure to verify details and the like. But if you simply rationalize them as "honest" mistakes, you're really not being very responsible. You are paid to do things correctly, and this includes preventing "honest" mistakes from getting by.

To illustrate, the annual report of a major oil company contained an out-of-place decimal that dramatically reduced estimates of its oil reserves from those it had claimed in previous reports. The financial community immediately became alarmed because it feared the company had been puffing up earlier estimates of its reserves. Frantic phone calls and a dramatic drop in share prices ensued. The company quickly issued a corrected estimate, so the damage, though costly, was temporary—all because the writers, editors and proofreaders made an "honest" mistake. You can also bet that market analysts and brokers looked at the next year's annual report with an extra dose of skepticism. "Honest" mistakes are sometimes no less damaging than dishonest ones.

Honesty, Truth and Fairness

The concept of honesty goes beyond the idea of accuracy and raises questions of truth and fairness. You can deal with documentable facts as a writer and still be dishonest, untruthful and unfair. So factual accuracy is not enough. The selection of facts and the way you weave them into the fabric of a message are what establish you as honest, truthful, fair and credible.

Must you use all the facts, even the bad? No. But to ignore the negatives is not fair. Even if members of your primary audience are not highly sophisticated, they are not dumb. If you fail to acknowledge damaging information, you simply invite disbelief. Not only will you not be believed, you may be perceived as unfair. Honesty and forthrightness served American Airlines well when one of its jets ran into a mountain in Colombia. The airline's chief pilot said, "Human error on the part of our people may have contributed to the accident." Years ago, the legal department might have been in an uproar because of concern over protecting the company from liability. Now most organizations see that a greater loss may come from a failure to speak out. A loss of credibility translates to a loss of customers.[10]

False or Misleading Information

Misleading information can lead audiences to make bad decisions. When they discover they have been misled, they withdraw their support. Although you and your organization may enjoy some advantage because of a deception, the advantage is usually temporary. And the consequences of misleading people can be enormous as well as long term. In fact, disaffected audiences may seek retribution through legal action, boycotts or other means.

The excesses of false and misleading information that came from Enron and WorldCom provoked the Sarbanes-Oxley Act of 2002, designed to make publicly held companies more accountable. As a result, the Securities and Exchange Commission and the New York Stock Exchange issued new orders. Although the public relations implications fall largely on the investor relations (IR) specialists, other corporate communications people must also be watchful.

New disclosure regulations require more explicit information about earnings and empha-size the SEC's fair disclosure regulation made in 2000. These regulations require that invest-ing decisions be made more accessible to the public and that anytime material information is intentionally disclosed it must be made available simultaneously to all publics. If uninten-tionally, the information must be made public as soon as possible. Disclosure also has to be made through a combination of means to reach as broad an audience as possible. Many IR officers now post news releases immediately on the corporate Web site as well as sending them on the Dow Jones wire, the AP wire and PR newswire.

Public relations practitioners also were affected by the Campaign Reform Act of 2002 which created new disclosure requirements and requires prompt compliance with earlier reg-ulations so that there's more public information available about politically active groups and individuals.[11]

Truth has a way of emerging in spite of extraordinary efforts to keep it hidden. In the vast majority of cases, false information is destined to fail. Writers who knowingly write and dis-tribute false information, for whatever reason, violate one of the trusts explicit in the Public Relations Society of America (PRSA) code and risk losing the respect and acceptance of their primary publics. False information corrupts not only a writer but also the channels of com-munication used to distribute it. Hence, false information supplied to a newspaper and relayed to readers damages the newspaper, as well as the primary source, in the eyes of the readers. The result is that the newspaper may be reluctant to accept subsequent information from you. Moreover, not only will you find it more difficult to get information into that newspaper, but so will all other public relations people. The assumption will simply be that all public relations professionals are alike: You can't trust any of them.

Influence of Laws and Regulations

Everything you write has the potential to spark litigation. You must know your freedoms under the First Amendment (if you are in the USA) and the laws governing commercial speech as well to bulletproof your writing as much as possible. If your material is going into other countries, check on your rights and restraints there too. You can't fully immunize it from legal action, but you can minimize the potential for losses. And you don't have to be an attorney to do this. Just follow some simple guidelines.

Negative Laws

The first guideline is to realize that laws are generally negative. They define what is not legal. They generally don't define what is. You may suppose that something is legal because it has not been defined as illegal. But although that may be true at the time, you may be in for a surprise later.

A further guideline is to remember that case law is built on a series of court decisions, each citing previous decisions. Even when a substantial line of cases evolves from a seminal decision—often one that turns on some question of constitutionality—each new case has the potential to produce a different interpretation of what is illegal, thereby setting a precedent. One thing you should guard against is doing something that will turn you or your organization into a legal precedent.

A case in point was a U.S. Supreme Court decision in 1989 declaring that the copyright of creative work is the property of the freelancer or vendor unless its ownership passes to someone else in a legal contract at the time the work is authorized. Organizations and PR agencies have sometimes acted as if they owned such creative work, even when no contract existed. The only way they can own it now is to contract for it ahead of time or to obtain permission to use it, which may involve paying fees for each additional usage. That now includes making the print version available on a Web site.

Simply because you or an organization has always done things in a certain way does not mean that those procedures will be acceptable tomorrow. It is your responsibility to keep up with court decisions and new laws affecting communication in general and your organization and industry specifically. Copyright laws continue to change regarding materials available through cyberspace.

That brings us to another guideline. Read and study each new issue of *Media Law Reporter.* This publication specializes in timely reports and summaries of laws and court decisions affecting every aspect of mass communication, including public relations. If you have any doubts about a new law or court decision, consult an attorney who specializes in communication law. Don't depend on other attorneys, because they may know no more about communication law than you do.

Contracts

You'll find that your organization probably uses many outside vendors—writers, producers, photographers, printers and the like. Because they are working for you, you are responsible for their actions in the process of preparing and presenting their material. You must know the nature of agreements with each of these suppliers. Otherwise you are liable to make a grievous error that may cost your organization lots of money and perhaps you your job. One of the most important contract areas is work done "for hire." Unless a vendor signs away ownership of his or her creative work to your organization in a legal contract, you may not use it for any additional or subsequent purpose unless you get legal permission and, sometimes, pay additional fees. This applies to all kinds of creative work.

Additionally, any time a photographer—whether staff or freelance—supplies you with pictures, each one that includes people (especially professional models) must be accompanied by a photo release form duly signed, thus "releasing" his or her likeness for use in the specified situation. If you're using a freelance photographer, determine who owns the rights to the negatives before shooting begins. Ownership of the negatives may fall under the "for hire" provision too. But unless a contract says otherwise, the photographer retains the negatives and controls subsequent uses of them.

One contractual arrangement now simplified is for the organizational use of music—either for meetings or to entertain phone callers put on hold. The American Society of Composers, Authors and Publishers now has an umbrella contract covering the playing of copyrighted music in public. Some organizations play their own promotional jingles, which for copyright reasons they usually have written especially for that purpose unless they use music "in the public domain," music on which the copyright has expired. There are some risks here because special arrangements of such music and performances of it may still carry a copyright, especially now with changes in the USA and the European Union (EU).

In addition to explicit contracts governing outside vendor relationships, there is an implied contract between you and your employer that you will maintain confidentiality. Some firms actually write this into a separate employee contract, although most of the time it's understood that you will keep to yourself what you learn about a client or an organization. That you will protect confidential information is an implied contract. You won't share information with anyone outside the organization and will use a "need to know" basis inside. Such discretion is especially important when you're dealing with financial matters that may constitute "insider information" and thus be of concern to the Securities and Exchange Commission. The fact is that if you tip someone who uses that information for personal gain in the stock market, you are as guilty for "tipping" as they are for "insider trading."

Commercial Free Speech

In the USA, no First Amendment rights for organizations are constitutionally guaranteed. However, over the years, a commercial free speech doctrine has evolved. Advertising is clearly covered. The doctrine is less clear about public relations communication, as Nike discovered in defending itself from a lawsuit filed by activist Marc Kasky. Nike had been accused of using sweatshop labor in contracting factories abroad to make its shoes and not monitoring working conditions there. Nike wrote letters to educators and opinion leaders defending its operations and also wrote op-ed commentaries for newspapers as well as sending news releases to the papers.

The USA's Supreme Court has always supported First Amendment privileges for *political* free speech, even when it is inaccurate. But, Kasky sued Nike for false *advertising*. So, the question really is the definition of Nike's action: commercial speech, as Kasky claimed, or noncommercial, as Nike claimed. Commercial speech is held to high standards of truth so consumers will not be deceived. Earlier cases, like the 1983 Texas Gulf Sulphur case where a news release was held to be "false and misleading," suggest that news releases are also under the umbrella of truth.

The problem is that commercial free speech is determined by case law, to which the Nike case contributes. In the past, decisions have moved back and forth across the spectrum of just how free are organizational and institutional voices.

Beyond case law, organizations and institutions also have to deal with possible contempt of court in trying to defend themselves in lawsuits. Litigation journalism (or litigation PR as some prefer to call it) has relaxed some earlier threats. But all it takes is for the opposing side to make the case to the judge handling the case that anything being said about the case is likely to prejudice the jury. When that occurs, you can't write a position paper about the case that you make public or write commentaries or interpretations of the case for public consumption without inviting a contempt of court charge. Furthermore, you can't go on talk shows, issue news releases, buy advertising space or time or take other actions to convey the position of your organization on the case. This can be very frustrating because it effectively gags an organization until the case has been decided.[12]

Libel Laws and Privacy Issues

When you defame someone in writing, it's libel and to do so in speech that is not written is slander. Defamation is an attack on someone's character, good name or reputation.

If people believe they have been libeled by what you have written, they can bring legal actions for actual and punitive damages. Your best defense against libel is to be accurate and truthful to a fault—so much so that you can document anything you say. Public figures (elected officials and people in the public eye) who bring libel actions must prove you libeled them "with malice." You should realize, however, that current case law makes it difficult to determine exactly who is a public figure.

You need to be very careful when dealing with both public and private figures. Stick with provable facts. You can't play fast and loose with words and avoid libel actions. Look at the list of "red flag" words in Table 2.1. Any time you use them, you are inviting a court appearance. Figure 2.2 walks you through the steps of a self-check for possible trouble with claims of libel.

Privacy laws are most often of concern when you want to use a person's likeness and name in publicity, advertising or other promotional materials. People in pictures of crowds at public gatherings represent fair use, but you can't single out people in the crowd and use them for promotional purposes without their consent. If they happen to be celebrities, you'll also need a legal contract to back up the usage. Otherwise, you may be guilty of invasion of privacy.

Defending yourself in these cases is not easy. In the case of libel, the documentable *truth* must be admissible in court, and that's up to the judge. *Privilege,* another defense, is a fair and true report of a public, official or judicial hearing, but who determines whether the report is "fair"? The *fair comment* defense, which used to protect people such as reviewers and columnists who often exaggerated statements about public figures for humor, has suffered some severe blows in the courts. Some claim that now such protection doesn't exist. The privacy issue is often ignored within organizations when they assume that because people work there it's all right to use their names and pictures without permission. This is not true, and the problems multiply if the representation is in something designed to make money for the organization, such as an ad or a brochure. There are also problems if the employee no longer works for the organization. The protection is a release form giving you *permission.*

Copyrights and Other Rights

A 2003 Supreme Court decision upheld a 1998 congressional action that extended by 20 years all existing copyrights. The premise of a copyright is that creators of creative works should own what they create. Consequently, it provides a means of protecting a person's or organization's creative property against unlawful appropriation and use by others. By copyrighting what you write, you serve notice that the work is yours. Always use the copyright symbol (©) with the word *Copyright* adjacent to it. Copyrighting does not automatically invoke legal action in instances of suspected infringement. It only makes it possible for you to seek legal redress. The initiative lies with you, not the law. Copyright protects the specific expression of an idea, but ideas, as such, are not protected.

T A B L E   2 . 1   *"Red Flag" Words*   Words can be semantic land mines. It is best not to step on them. These "red flag" words and expressions are typical of ones that may lead to a legal action if they are not carefully handled in news releases or other messages from an organization.

adulteration of products	co-respondent	gambling house	kept woman	short in accounts
	corruption	gangster	Ku Klux Klan	shyster
adultery	coward	gay (in context of		skunk
altered records	crook	"homosexual")	liar	slacker
ambulance chaser		gouged money		smooth and tricky
atheist	deadbeat	grafter	mental disease	sneak
attempted suicide	deadhead	groveling office	moral delinquency	sold his influence
	defaulter	seeker		sold out to a rival
bad moral character	disorderly house		Nazi	
bankrupt	divorced	humbug		spy
bigamist	double-crosser	hypocrite	paramour	stool pigeon
blackguard	drug addict		peeping Tom	stuffed the ballot
blacklisted	drunkard	illegitimate	perjurer	box
blackmail		illicit relations	plagiarist	suicide
blockhead	ex-convict	incompetent	pockets public funds	swindle
booze-hound		infidelity	price cutter	
bribery	false weights used	informer	profiteering	unethical
brothel	fascist	intemperate		unmarried mother
buys votes	fawning sycophant	intimate	rascal	unprofessional
	fool	intolerance	rogue	unsound mind
cheats	fraud		scam	unworthy of credit
collusion		Jekyll-Hyde	scandalmonger	
communist (or red)		personality	scoundrel	vice den
confidence man			seducer	villain
			sharp dealing	

Any words or expressions imputing: a loathsome disease; a crime, or words falsely charging arrest, or indictment for or confession or conviction of a crime; anti-Semitism or other imputation of religious, racial or ethnic intolerance; connivance or association with criminals; financial embarrassment (or any implication of insolvency or want of credit); lying; involvement in a racket or complicity in a swindle; membership in an organization that may be in ill repute at a given period of time; poverty or squalor; unwillingness or refusal to pay or evading payment of a debt.

Source: Bruce W. Sanford, *Synopsis of the Law of Libel and the Right of Privacy,* rev. ed., Scripps-Howard and World Almanac, 1981. Used by permission.

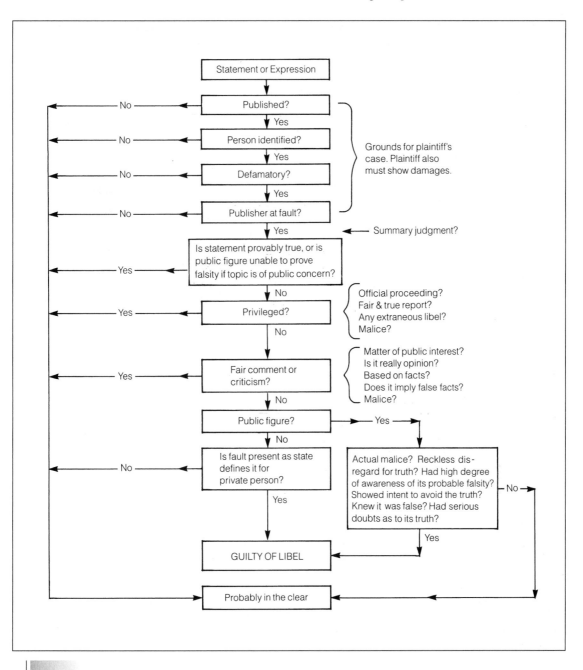

F I G U R E   2 . 2

A Guide to Libel   *Is it libel? Libel is the culpable (careless or knowing) publication of false information damaging to a person's reputation.*

Source: Albert Skaggs and Cleve Mathews, "Is This Libelous? Simple Chart Helps Student Get Answer," *Journalism Educator* (Autumn 1982), pp. 16–18. Revised chart (1992) reprinted with permission of Cleve Mathews.

The extension of copyrights means that the works of individuals on which the copyright would have ended in 50 years after the creator's death, now are still in effect for 70 years. If a creative property, such as songs and compositions, movies or cartoon characters, is owned by a corporation, the previous 75-year copyright protection is now 95 years. There is a Digital Millennium Copyright Act of 1988 that outlaws electronic copyright infringement, at least in the USA. When the European Union was created, it brought the diverse copyright laws of its member nations under one umbrella. The result was a 70-year rule that began in 1995. File for copyright protection with the Library of Congress (http://www.loc.gov/copyright/).

You should also be aware that many publications routinely copyright their contents. However, unless the individual messages in these publications were written by staff personnel, their creators retain ownership of what they have created.

Violations of copyright often take the form of plagiarism. Public relations writers have to be acutely aware of not usurping others' creations while doing research. If you are going to quote the source, put your notes in quotation marks, and register all of the information you will need for attribution. Furthermore, if you want to use more than 100 words from one source, less if it is a song, poem or relatively small work, you must get legal permission.

Much to the dismay of fans of historian Doris Kearns Goodwin, in 2002, she admitted to copying passages from other sources and using them in her own writing. She was asked to take a leave of absence from PBS's *The News Hour,* resigned from the Pulitzer Prize Committee and had speaking engagements canceled. She wasn't the only high-profile public figure to admit to incorporating others' work into her own. If you do it as a public relations person, not only will you be fired when it is discovered, you will have to find your own attorney and pay all of the expenses. Furthermore, it is highly unlikely that you will be able to find PR employment again.

When you use somebody's trademark, service mark, trade character or the like, make sure that you show the ownership. For example, the ™ symbol must appear immediately after the mark, usually accompanied by a line of small type that says something like "[product name] is a registered trademark of [company name]."

Government Regulators

Most of the things you write will fall under the purview of four major government agencies. One is the U.S. Postal Service. That agency is concerned with classes of mail, fraud, lotteries and the like. The range of regulations is staggering. And you'll find the interpretation of some of them varies significantly, depending on whom you ask. So, if you're not sure about something, ask the postmaster at the site where you expect to do a mailing. That's the only way you can really be sure.

The Securities and Exchange Commission is especially concerned with information dealing with or relating to the stock market and the financial community in general. Particular concerns that may affect you as a writer involve executives and their compensation, annual reports and news releases dealing with the financial condition or direction of your organization and potential opportunities for insider trading.

The Federal Trade Commission has a wide range of interests. In relation to writers, however, the FTC is most concerned with maintaining fair competition. Hence, seemingly deceptive advertising or other promotional materials draw FTC attention and action.

The Food and Drug Administration watches over information from food and health industries and is very protective of the consumer. In fact, it considers information drug companies circulate about their products to be promotional, and it closely monitors educational or scientific activities.

Other regulatory groups can affect what you write too. In fact, the Bureau of Alcohol, Tobacco and Firearms threatened to close Leeward Winery in California because the winery quoted in a newsletter to customers information from a CBS *60 Minutes* show that suggested red wine may help reduce the risk of heart disease. Another winery got into trouble for using similar information in an ad. A liquor store was also stopped from using an in-store wine sales campaign that had heart signs reading "Wines to your health" and "Be heart smart."[13]

Your responsibility is to know the applicable rules and regulations affecting your organization and industry. If you don't know the answer, ask someone who does. But you'd be wise to go to the original source, rather than risk acting on someone's well-intentioned but possibly wrong advice.

Influence of Primary Publics

Although the four major areas of influence already mentioned are vital to your success as a writer, none is more important than the influence of primary publics. Every organization, public or private, must be keenly aware of the influence of its primary publics. Indeed, the organization can exist only with their permission.

Permission does not always mean approval of all that the organization is doing. However, the critical limits of an organization's ethical and legal behavior are determined by its primary or closest publics—those who share organizational identity, such as employees and (often) former employees, and those with whom it has an ongoing relationship, such as suppliers, distributors and customers.

Shared Values

The stronger a public's identity with the organization, the stronger its reaction will be to what the organization is saying and doing. Primary publics perceive themselves as having shared values with the organization. Any violation of these values is often reacted to very strongly and personally. For example, a customer sued for violation of privacy because a company hired a contractor to process survey data, and the contractor used prisoners. The customer discovered this when she got a 12-page letter from an inmate who used detailed information from the survey and who mentioned the magazine that had conducted the original survey. In his letter the prisoner created a sexual fantasy based on a product the customer said she had used.[14]

Adversarial Groups

Another group whose reactions are anticipated in the planning process and closely monitored thereafter is composed of those who are likely to have an adversarial relationship with the organization, such as regulators, competitors, special-interest groups and activists concerned about certain aspects of society (the environment, endangered species, animal rights and so on). These groups typically perceive themselves as having a different, not shared, set of values.

That's not always the reality, but it is almost always the perception. For this reason, adversarial groups exhibit little tolerance for "mistakes" or "poor policy decisions."

Although the closest publics may respond quickly and personally to something they don't like or something they see as a violation of shared values, they are much more forgiving than adversarial publics. These two groups set the boundaries within which an organization must operate to be successful. Understanding their ethical standards and values is therefore crucial to planning.

Conclusions

- You have to be genuinely sensitive to the feelings and needs of others, and you must treat others as you want to be treated.
- Public relations writers often initiate or implement practices that draw criticism of public relations.
- Some public relations writing practices are legally prescribed; others are set by moral principles.
- Moral principles consist of a set of beliefs and values that reflect a group's sense of what is *right* or *wrong,* regardless of how these terms are defined in formal rules, regulations or laws.
- *Formal conditions* call for moral guidelines or rules that are regarded as universal and prescriptive. *Material conditions* represent considerations that deal with the welfare of society as a whole and emphasize basic human good or purpose.
- The public view of an organization's ethics is likely to be based less on a definition of morality than on the consequences of what the organization says and does, which will be seen as either moral or not moral by each and all of its publics. This sense of rightness is what creates public opinion.
- If you write, say or do something that violates society's sense of "rightness," you may be undercutting your constitutional right to free speech.
- One way to understand your responsibilities is to look carefully at the interplay of several levels of influence on your personal and professional behavior.
- Society's expectations and judgments about what is right or wrong are notoriously capricious, so it's your responsibility to be sensitive to changes and even to anticipate them.
- The study of ethics falls into two broad categories: comparative ethics and normative ethics. Normative ethics are studied by theologians and philosophers. Comparative ethics—sometimes called descriptive ethics—are studied by social scientists, who look at the ways different cultures practice ethical behavior.
- Remember that ethics are culture-bound. This can create controversies in ethnically diverse societies like the USA and provoke problems in other countries where values are different.
- Because your own ethical standards are at the core of your behavior, you have to decide what to do when your standards conflict with those of the organization. You have four strategy options: (1) educate the organization and persuade them to accept your standards; (2) refuse the task; (3) ask that you be given another task; or (4) take the assignment.
- Publics work with perceptions of facts, and these perceptions become the "facts" on which opinions are based.

- When you go to work for an organization, you may be given formal training in the corporate culture or value system, or you may pick it up informally by watching and interacting with new associates.
- Your real worth to an organization consists of your ability to be in tune with relevant publics. When you know these publics well, you can construct messages that are valued and accepted by them.
- Professional associations of public relations practitioners have standards with which you must comply in order to be accepted.
- Credibility with publics is essential for the success of an organization, and this quality depends on accuracy, honesty, truth and fairness.
- False and misleading information destroys credibility, and truth has a way of emerging. Besides, in some cases, giving out false information is against the law.
- This is a litigious society, and you need to bulletproof your writing as much as possible.
- Most laws are negative, defining things you cannot do. In addition to the laws themselves, there is a body of case law consisting of judicial decisions interpreting these laws. Because case law is in flux, you have to keep up with the changes.
- Watch for changes in the laws, especially those governing materials available in cyberspace.
- Contracts can keep you out of a lot of legal difficulty, but you must know what you need to specify in contracts and what is bound by contract.
- Commenting on a situation that is under litigation can earn you a contempt of court charge.
- Libel laws and privacy considerations can cause you legal problems if you don't understand them thoroughly, even when you are dealing with public figures.
- Copyrights protect your creative works but not your ideas. You need to be sure that you observe the copyrights of others. The trademarks and such of an organization are protected by law, but legal protections are sometimes difficult to enforce. You need to get permission when using materials protected by such registry. Plagiary is a violation of copyright.
- Federal government regulators that figure most prominently in public relations writing are the U.S. Postal Service, the Securities and Exchange Commission, the Federal Trade Commission and the Food and Drug Administration.
- When in doubt, consult a good attorney who is a specialist in communication law.

Exercises

Situation: You are the vice president for corporate communication at Enodyne, a conglomerate. You are in a corporate board meeting, having just finished presenting the communication plan and budget for next year, when an emergency phone call from Ben McConkle—the public relations director of a subsidiary, Fielding Works, which manufactures industrial solvents and other chemicals—advises you that a Fielding transport on its way to a toxic waste dump had an accident near North Platte, Nebraska, about three hours ago. The truck turned over three times and several containers of toxic chemicals ruptured, posing high danger to officers on the scene and to people within a 5-mile radius, depending on the speed and direction of the wind. No one was injured seriously, but the driver and his companion suffered minor abrasions and bruises. The driver is Burl B. Benton, 33, an employee of 10 years with a spotless record. The companion is Helene A. Haven, 30, a female nonemployee. McConkle wants quick guidance on how to handle inquiries, especially those related to these facts: (1) tests showed that Benton and Haven had been drinking; (2) neither was legally drunk; (3) tests showed that Haven had traces of cocaine in her system; and (4) McConkle has not yet notified Mrs. Benton and her two children of the accident. McConkle needs your advice now, not later, because the news media will pick up these facts very soon.

1. What guidance will you offer McConkle? Is your guidance fully responsible to Enodyne, to the driver and his family, to the driver's companion and her family, to the people in the area of the accident and to others? How so? Why so?
2. Write a one-page summary of the ethical problems involved in this situation, and explain how they might affect you as a writer.
3. Write a one-page summary of the potential legal problems in this situation, and explain how they might affect you as a writer.

Use InfoTrac College Edition to access information on topics in this chapter from hundreds of periodicals and scholarly journals.

Notes

1. Various news reports, print and broadcast, on Monday, March 31, 2003, as well as listserve messages from the VisCom Division members of AEJMC commented on the poor judgment of Brian Walski, who was fired from his newspaper, the *Los Angeles Times,* when editors noticed that some members of a crowd were duplicated in his photo from Iraq. His in-camera composition was not very tight, so he corrected by merging two shots of the same scene.
2. "'Dressed-Up' Hoffman Wins Suit," *The Sunday Times,* London, U.K., January 24, 1999, p. 9.
3. David Lieberman, "Fake News," *TV Guide,* February 22–28, 1996, pp. 10–16.
4. Janet Kornblum, "*Playboy* Files Trademark Suits Against Web Sites," *USA Today,* February 12, 1999, p. 8A.
5. John Harlow and Christopher Lloyd, "Hoover Holiday Deal Stirs the Dust," *The Sunday Times,* London, U.K., December 20, 1992, p. P7.
6. "Hit by a Car," *The Straits Times,* Singapore, February 13, 1999, p. 20.
7. Bart Ziegler, "Old-Fashioned Ethic of Separating Ads Is Lost in Cyberspace," *The Wall Street Journal,* July 25, 1996, p. B1.
8. John Pavlik and David Dozier, research quoted in "Study Details Bumps to Watch Out for on Info Superhiway," *pr reporter,* August 5, 1996, p. 2.
9. See Lawrence G. Foster, "Tylenol 20 Years Later," *The Strategist* 8 (4) (New York: Public Relations Society of America, Fall 2002), pp. 16–20.
10. Terry Maxon, "Weighing the Financial Fallout of Speaking Out," *The Dallas Morning News,* January 14, 1996, p. H1.
11. Go to U.S. government Web sites for information about laws and to the sites of the regulatory institutions for their decisions and new regulations. Also note the section in this chapter on government regulators.
12. For more information look on the Internet for the Nike case, and see the law chapter of *This Is PR,* 8th edition, Doug Newsom, Judy VanSlyke Turk and Dean Kruckeberg (Belmont, Calif.: Wadsworth, 2004) as well as *Advertising and Public Relations Law* by

Roy L. Moore, Ronald L. Farrar and Erik Collins (Mahwah, N.J.: Lawrence Erlbaum, 1998).

13. Carrie Dolan, "Wineries and Government Clash over Ads That Toast Health Benefits of Drinking," *The Wall Street Journal,* October 19, 1992, pp. B1, B4.

14. James P. Miller, "Privacy Issue Raised in Direct-Mail Case," *The Wall Street Journal,* May 6, 1996, p. B8.

Selected Bibliography

Books

Joseph L. Badaracco, Jr., *Defining Moments: When Managers Must Choose Between Right and Right* (Boston, Mass.: Harvard Business School Press, 1997).

Clifford G. Christians, Kim B. Rotzoll and Mark Fackler, *Media Ethics: Cases and Moral Reasoning,* 4th ed. (New York: Longman, 1994).

Barnaby Conrad and Monte Schulz, eds., *Snoopy's Guide to the Writing Life* (Cincinnati, Ohio: Writer's Digest Books, 2002).

Charles Conrad, *Ethical Nexus* (Norwood, N.J.: Ablex, 1993).

Louis A. Day, *Ethics in Mass Communication: Cases and Controversies,* 2d ed. (Belmont, Calif.: Wadsworth, 1997).

John P. Ferre and Shirley C. Willihnqanz, eds., *Public Relations & Ethics, A Bibliography* (New York: Macmillan, 1991).

Conrad C. Fink, *Media Ethics* (Needham, Mass.: Allyn & Bacon, 1995).

Donald L. Gillmor, Jerome A. Barron, Todd F. Simon and Herbert A. Terry, *Mass Communications Law,* 8th ed. (Belmont, Calif.: Wadsworth, 1999).

Philip Meyer, *Ethical Journalism* (New York: Longman, 1987).

Kent R. Middleton and Bill F. Chamberlin, *The Law of Public Communication,* 6th ed. (New York: Longman, 2004).

Roy L. Moore, *Mass Communication Law and Ethics: A Casebook* (Mahwah, N.J.: Lawrence Erlbaum Associates, 1999).

Ron Smith and H. Eugene Goodwin, *Groping for Ethics in Journalism,* 6th ed. (Ames, Iowa: Iowa State University Press, 1999).

Lynne Masel Walters, Lee Wilkins and Tim Walters, eds., *Bad Tidings: Communication and Catastrophe* (Mahwah, N.J.: Lawrence Erlbaum Associates, 1993).

Lee Wilkins and Philip D. Patterson, *Media Ethics: Issues and Cases* (New York: McGraw-Hill, 2001).

Journals

Jay Black and Ralph Barney, eds., *Journal of Mass Media Ethics* (Hillsdale, N.J.: Lawrence Erlbaum Associates, semiannual).

Sheila Garrett, ed., *Communications and the Law* (Littleton, Colo.: Fred B. Rothman & Co., quarterly).

Government publications are useful, especially those from regulatory groups such as the U.S. Postal Service, Federal Trade Commission, Food and Drug Administration, Securities and Exchange Commission and Environmental Protection Agency.

CHAPTER THREE

Persuasion

Wwhen you identify yourself as a public relations writer, some people may regard you with skepticism because they think of what you do as manipulation. Be prepared for that, but there's no need to apologize for it. Persuasion is implicit, if not explicit, every time a person tries to communicate with another. It is just that public relations is widely known for trying to persuade publics to a particular point of view.

Persuasion is explicitly part of the public relations fabric. If it is done ethically and legally, it logically is no more objectionable than most other human activities. Persuasive efforts now may seem more focused than in the past. That's because more and more companies are taking an *integrated* approach to planning and implementation. Integration simply means that a single communication strategy undergirds all messages from an organization. It is intended to give them unity and consistency.

The literature labels this approach variously as *integrated marketing communications, marketing communication* or simply *integrated communication*. We prefer integrated communication because it seems to encompass a range of activities not often central to the selling emphasis of marketing. The term used is not important, but it is important that you recognize that public relations efforts by many companies now seem to have a sharper focus than in the past. That tends to sensitize people to the persuasive role of public relations.

This integrated approach affects every public relations writer in at least two ways. First, writers will be expected to adapt any message to any medium. That certainly is not a new development, but an integrated communication philosophy will make it far more common than in the recent past. Second, writers who can think about persuasion at the strategic level will be at a premium. It is clear that a writer who knows how will always have a job. But the writer who knows why will always be the boss. That piece of wisdom is the focus for this chapter. Although persuasion has always been important in public relations, now it is critical that you understand the why, as well as the how, of persuasion. To begin, consider the following scenario.

A nuclear engineer especially good at explaining technical matters once gave a talk to a civic club in a small town. He used dozens of slides, charts and graphs to describe the operation of nuclear power plants and to explain how safe they were.

At the end of his talk, an elderly lady thanked the engineer for his presentation. "I don't understand anything you said," she told him, "but I agree with you a hundred percent." The point: People rely on information and logic in forming their opinions, but only up to a degree.

It is true that people are rational. But that only means they can think. People are also emotional. Were people driven only by logic, there would never be a need to persuade. The fact is, however, that people in economically advanced societies such as ours base most of their decisions and behaviors on emotion rather than logic. Most of us don't have to spend every waking hour just getting enough food, clothing and shelter to sustain life. As these things are easier to attain, we spend more and more time on improving their quality. That's where emotion comes in. And it is the context in which persuasion is most often used.

As we pursue our enlightened self-interest, we are often motivated more by emotions than by logic. Nevertheless, we place great value on information. It is the stuff of which good public relations is made. But a lot of public relations writing also attempts to persuade people to adopt a particular point of view.

To be a persuasive writer, you need to have some idea of the arguments—both factual and emotional—that will work best with your target publics. Common sense can give you some clues, but you'll do a much better job if you know something about the science of persuasion. Common sense is no substitute for what decades of research have revealed about how and why people form their opinions. As public relations pioneer Edward L. Bernays put it, "Like Columbus, you can sail west and reach new land by accident. But if you have charts, you can do better; you can arrive at a destination decided upon in advance."[1]

When engineers design bridges or buildings, Bernays pointed out, they apply a knowledge of physics, chemistry and other sciences. Doctors treat patients using a knowledge of biochemistry and medical research. In the same way, public relations people should apply the relevant findings of social sciences such as psychology, sociology and communication when they embark on efforts to persuade.

Persuasive writing focuses attention on these message areas: *recipients* of the message, intended and unintended; message *construction* with the emphasis on what consequences are intended—increased knowledge, attitude or behavior change; *source* for the message—who the source is and the credibility of that source with the intended recipients and the credibility of the organization identified with the source. Decisions have to be made at every level.

Primary, though, are the recipients: Who are they? What do they know or think they know? What do they believe about the issue/the organizations involved? You can't construct a message until you know that. The message construction then has to have a purpose: What do you want to happen as a result of communicating that message? What effect is it likely to have on each of the intended recipients? What about unintended recipients such as competitors, activists or other critics? Then there's the choice of a source: Who is the most credible, overall, with particular publics? In a crisis, there is another consideration of source because there will be many message sources from all parties involved. You know from personal experience that coverage of an apartment fire means you're likely to see and hear statements from fire officials, police, hospitals, owners of the apartment complex, residents as well as their friends and relatives.

The intent of maintaining credibility is to be sure there is consistency in the message statements. Many questions come up time and again in persuasive writing. Should you give both sides of the story or only your side? If you give both, which side should you give first? Should you draw an explicit conclusion, or is it better to let the audience figure it out for itself? Which should you give first, the good news or the bad news? How effective are fear techniques? Should you make a point once or repeat it several times to make sure it sinks in? These are the sorts of questions that social scientists can *help* you answer.

Of course, research findings can only help you answer these questions. Research results can be valuable guides in planning persuasive communication, but they are not laws of nature. In many cases, the findings collected so far are not conclusive. At times, you have to rely on personal experience and knowledge of your audience.

Nevertheless, social science has found out a lot about the nature of persuasion, and it would be foolish not to put that knowledge to use. Research data is better than off-the-top-of-the-head speculation about the how and why of opinion formation.

Opinion Formation and Change

The first thing you need to know as a persuasive writer is that you are not going to gain many converts to your point of view, at least not immediately. The reason is simple. The few minutes a person gives to reading your message are not likely to change attitudes built up over a lifetime. If you're going to make headway at all, you need to know something about what attitudes and opinions are and how they are formed.

Opinion, Attitude and Belief

Some authorities see little or no need to distinguish among opinions, attitudes and beliefs, at least in theory. On the practical level of trying to understand how and why people behave as they do, however, it may be useful to you to make such a distinction.

In this context, opinions are temporal, fleeting and unstable. They can change on a whim. Attitudes are a little more stable and are less likely to change immediately. Beliefs, however, are very stable, and they are very resistant to change. To illustrate the different levels involved, suppose we get in a time machine and travel back to 1950. At that time, products made in Japan were generally believed to be of poor quality. Opinions in the USA of products with the "Made in Japan" label were not charitable. With the introduction of import cars, a variety of electronic gear and camera systems of high quality, however, attitudes began to change. Now we believe that many brands of products made in Japan in these categories set the standards of quality against which all others are judged.

How did this change come about? As we began to experience products of higher quality from Japan, our opinions shifted to the extent that favorable attitudes began to be common, and these eventually came together in support of a belief that the label "Made in Japan" deserved respect.

When we accumulate information and experiences, we form opinions. Some of these opinions tend to cluster as especially relevant to a specific attitude. Attitude clusters then tend to gather in support of a specific belief. As used here, belief is the same thing as *engaged attitude* in Table 3.1 because the emphasis is on the effects. The point is that opinions can change with the wind. Beliefs can change too, but they are slow to do so. Attitudes fall somewhere between these extremes. In many respects, opinions, attitudes and beliefs are closely linked, so it makes sense for us to discuss them as one, using the term *attitude* to signify all three.

Models of Attitude Formation and Message Recipients

To begin with, an individual's personal background or historical setting plays an important role in his or her behavior. Where was the person born? Where did he or she grow up? What were the social and economic conditions of the day? These and similar factors help to shape personality. Historical factors also shape the issues that persuasive writers deal with—not only those of their audience, but their own as well.

All of these considerations are part of the social environment in which communication and persuasion take place. Individuals belong to groups with social norms that affect their opinions. A person's life experiences also play a large part in attitude formation. And naturally, the characteristics of the issue at hand are important.

One other major element of the social environment influences attitudes: available information. Here is the one door open to the persuasive writer. The writer has no power to change

T A B L E   3 . 1   *Communication Effectiveness Model*

		In order to be effective, a message must be:					
Field	**Discipline**	**Received**	**Attended to**	**Understood**	**Believed**	**Remembered**	**Acted on**
Marketing	Demographics	1	3	9	13		
	Psychographics	2	4		14		
Psychology	Persuasion				15		21
	Information processing		5			18	22
Communication	Linguistics			10			
	Writing		6	11		19	
	Design		7	12		20	
Social Sciences	Sociology				16		
	Anthropology				17		
	Economics		8				23

Just to get a message from here to there, from sender to receiver, requires a reasonable command of the social sciences, communication, psychology, marketing—and subdivisions of each. To be successful, a message must be *received* by the intended individual or audience. It must be the audience's *attention*. It must be *understood*. It must be *believed*. It must be *remembered*. And ultimately, in some fashion, it must be *acted upon*. Failure to accomplish any of these tasks means the entire message fails. It fails because it does not accomplish the purpose for which it was created.

Source: David Therkelsen, Christina L. Fiebich, "Message to Desired Action," *Journal of Communication Management*, Vol. 5, No. 4, May 2001. Used by permission.

a person's personal history or the norms of social groups, although persuasive messages may be woven into those fabrics of experience. You can't expect to change someone's life situation or provide a significant new experience with your message. As a writer, however, you can hope to add to the information on which attitudes may be based.

If you look at the situation objectively, it does not appear to be encouraging. Why spend all the effort and resources necessary to shape and send persuasive messages if there isn't much hope for change? The fact is that providing information is your only chance of making an impact. Even if the impact is minimal, you have to try. That's why you need to understand the nature of persuasion.

The Nature of Persuasion

As a writer, you can look at persuasion in three basic ways. One is as a learning process, whereby you impart information and members of your audience seek information because they want to know something. Another way of looking at persuasion is as a power process, whereby you attempt to "force" information on someone. The third broad view is that persuasion is simply an emotional process. No single perspective of persuasion is likely to be adequate, because the formation of attitudes is a complex process. But we can outline some aspects of the process that, when taken together, offer some useful insights.

Aspects of Persuasion

One of the best outlines of this process appears in Otto Lerbinger's *Designs for Persuasive Communication.* Lerbinger describes five "designs" of persuasion: (1) stimulus-response, (2) cognitive, (3) motivational, (4) social and (5) personality.[2]

Stimulus-Response   The concept of stimulus-response is the simplest approach to persuasion and, perhaps, the least useful. It is based on the idea of association. If two things are seen together many times, people tend to think of one when they see the other. Clearly, stimulus-response behavior does not involve any intricate thought on the part of the audience. It is useful only when a low level of response is acceptable. It seems to work as well with animals as it does with people, or perhaps even better. The classic illustration of this approach is Pavlov's experiments with dogs, in which a tuning fork was struck each time meat powder was fed to the dogs. Soon, whenever the tuning fork was struck, the dogs began to drool in anticipation of food. Similarly, a cat owner (a nonscientist) discovered that she could call her cats from any hiding place by starting up the electric can opener. The cats associated the sound of the can opener with food and thus with dinner.

Obviously, this design is not a very good way to persuade someone regarding a complex issue. If, however, you simply want to establish an "association" between an idea and your organization in the public mind, stimulus-response may provide an adequate model to follow. For example, Avis has been successful in associating its name with the idea of trying harder. But this design seems not to be as effective with internal audiences. The reason appears to be that they usually have much more cognitive information about the organization, so they tend to regard such low-level messages as fluff.

Cognitive   The concept behind the cognitive design is that people can think and reason about what they read, see or hear. And they will come to the right conclusion if they are given the right information in an understandable way. The "right conclusion" is not necessarily the one you advocate, but it is the one that is "right" by the standards of individual members of the audience.

The cognitive approach can be effective in many situations. If a person has no personal stake in an issue, for example, or has no preconceived notions about it, the simple presentation of information may be effective. Also, if you have a complex story to tell, a cognitive approach may be your best choice. People like to think of themselves as fair and reasonable, and if you provide reasonable arguments, they are likely to agree with you—other things being equal.

Of course, other things seldom are equal. You can't expect to dump your message (whether stimulus-response or cognitive) into people's heads without considering what is already in them. To persuade someone to take a certain position, you have to know what will motivate the person to take that position. This idea is the basis of the motivational design of persuasion.

Motivational   Generally, the motivational design is based on the idea that a person will change an attitude to fulfill a need. In essence, your message to the audience will offer some kind of emotional reward for accepting your message and responding to it as you suggest.

What are some needs that motivate people? A convenient outline of human needs was devised by the psychologist Abraham Maslow, who grouped human needs into a hierarchy ranging from the most basic to the least tangible. At the bottom of the hierarchy are physical needs such as food, water, air and sleep. One step up is the general need for safety, or the need to be free from fear of harm. Then come social needs: the need to belong to groups, the need to associate with others, the need for love. Next come personal needs, such as the desire for self-respect, the desire to feel important, the need for status. At the top of the scale are the self-actualizing needs: to fulfill potential, to be creative and to have a rewarding life.

Whether these needs are being fulfilled—and in what measure—may play a major role in an individual's response to your attempts at persuasion. Persuasion that ignores these needs in order to concentrate on reason and logic is not likely to get very far. It is also important for you, as a writer, to identify the relevant needs of the members of your audience. If your target audience is mostly at the social needs level and you're appealing to them at the ego level, your chances of success are diminished. Attempts at persuasion that do not meet individuals' needs will fail.

Social   Closely related to the motivational design is the social design of persuasion. This design takes into account an individual's background, social class and group norms. Often, group membership is the most important element in determining attitudes. On issues in which attitudes are closely tied to social conditions, persuasion must be designed to address the social factors that influence the individual.

Essential to this design is the idea that we learn from society which values are best and worst and which patterns of behavior are most acceptable. The key point here is that if you are trying to persuade across major regional, ethnic or national boundaries, the same message is unlikely to be appropriate in every case. You'll have to prepare separate messages, based on different social influences.

Continuous monitoring of program effectiveness is recommended for all of these designs, but it is especially important with the social design because norms change. They are dynamic. It is necessary, then, that you continue to take the pulse of your public. The norm today may not be the norm tomorrow. You'll need to know when, why and how the norm changes so that you can adjust your messages to the new conditions.

Personality   Finally, you can't ignore the fact that each individual is unique. Personality characteristics can determine which arguments will work best with a given person or public. Of course, a persuasive message is frequently directed at a large group containing a number of different personality types, so the personality design cannot be used effectively in many instances. Even if your message is directed at a large group—that is, it is designed for the masses—you should always remember that it will be received separately by individuals. As a writer, you need to remain aware of how personality characteristics affect persuasibility.[3]

Rokeach's Value Hierarchy

Values are a major contribution to the way recipients of messages respond to them. A hierarchy of values developed by Milton Rokeach complements, rather than competes with, the Maslow hierarchy.[4] Rokeach says that values are more important than attitudes and beliefs as primary influencers of our behavior. His values system, however, is based on attitudes and beliefs that cluster together to form values that are even more resistant to change than needs in the Maslow construct.

Rokeach thinks of values as specific clusters of attitudes and beliefs that act as long-term goals. He further asserts that values fall into two categories: *terminal* and *instrumental.* Terminal values represent ultimate life goals, but instrumental values are the tools we use to achieve terminal goals. Rokeach divides his values system into five levels.

Primitive values exist on two levels. At the first level are those core beliefs that are seldom challenged such as expectations that the sun will rise in the east. Writers are wise not to challenge messages that contradict basic beliefs because these disturb people, who will dismiss them. At another level of primitive beliefs are values that are somewhat idiosyncratic and personal and for which there is no consensus. We may feel undervalued by our employer or our family, for instance, but we seldom articulate these beliefs. Instead we hold them internally, but seldom do we change them very much. Such values are difficult to change and the most effective messages are those that reinforce these values rather than contradict them.

Authority values depend upon our interaction with parents, friends, colleagues or others. An example may be the parental advice not to lie because then you don't have to remember the fiction you created. Although beliefs on which these values are founded can change, the values may not change much. The writer may challenge the beliefs with persuasive messages but don't directly challenge authority values.

Derived values are ones we develop from our vicarious interaction with trusted sources such as books we read, Internet sites we have bookmarked, television shows we like to watch or radio shows we listen to regularly. These derived values are better targets for persuasive messages because they are more easily influenced.

Inconsequential values are those based on individual preferences and tastes. These are more easily changed because they express a personal preference, such as preferring to live in a warm, dry climate, but they are not so substantive as to be self-defining.

Taken together these values, beliefs and attitudes define our self-concept—the way we see ourselves. If something arises that challenges our self-concept, we move quickly to re-establish our sense of well-being. Shifts in beliefs or attitudes ordinarily result in short-term changes in behavior, but the values on which they are based seem to control our lifelong set of behaviors.

Steps in the Persuasion Process

Once you have considered all the different designs for the art of persuasion, how do you actually go about persuading someone?

To answer that, we must first identify the steps in the persuasion process. Social psychologist William McGuire lists six such steps: presenting, attending, comprehending, yielding, retaining the new position and acting.[5]

Presenting   You can't persuade anyone of anything unless he or she is in the right place at the right time to perceive a message. A person who does not own a television set probably will not see your public service announcement on TV. If he or she has a set but it is tuned to another channel, the result will be the same. In both cases, it will not matter how beautifully you have written the announcement. The same is true of the story in the newspaper about the benefit concert to help the hospital. If a person does not subscribe to the paper or does not buy one at the newsstand, your message is not going to penetrate and persuade that individual at all.

Attending   The nonviewer's next-door neighbor probably has a TV set, and he might see your announcement. But he might not pay the least attention to it. He might be looking straight at the screen but thinking about who's going to win the upcoming football game. If so, he's not getting your message either. He must *attend* to the message—that is, pay attention —if you're to have any hope of persuading him.

Comprehending   Suppose this guy's wife is paying attention. She is watching the screen and listening intently to the sounds. But she's Belgian and does not speak a word of English. She likes to watch football games even though she can't understand the announcers. But she can't understand the public service announcements either, so there isn't much chance that you'll persuade her. The point is, you have to use message symbols that your audience can comprehend. If you don't, your message, even if delivered and technically defined as sent, will fail to communicate.

Yielding   In the house next door is another woman who sees the same message. She understands English, so she comprehends what your announcement says about the concert and its benefit to the hospital. And she happens to work at the hospital. But her reaction is somewhat neutral because she isn't very fond of the musical group. "They just try to make up for a lack of talent by playing and yelling louder," she says to herself. She got your message, but she did not yield to it. Although communication occurred, persuasion did not.

Retaining the New Position   Let's assume that the first woman's husband isn't daydreaming about football scores after all, but sees the commercial and is impressed. "That looks like a great idea," he says. "I think we should go to the concert because it will not only be fun, it will help the hospital." But the concert does not happen for another month. By that time, he may have forgotten about the concert and the benefit to the hospital. Your attempt at persuasion has been successful in getting the viewer to accept it. But because the viewer didn't retain his new attitude, for all practical purposes this attempt at persuasion has failed.

This element, of course, represents one of the main arguments for sustained public relations programming. It is not enough to get the message through. The message has to be retained by the audience long enough for the desired action to occur. Frequent repetition of the message is necessary to reinforce the adopted position until a person can act on it.

Acting   Now let's assume that the viewer didn't forget your message. Perhaps he saw the same announcement again and once more expressed a desire to go to the benefit concert. He may even have gone downtown with the intention of buying tickets, discovering when he got there, to his surprise, that his favorite pop singer was scheduled for a concert on the next weekend. So rather than buying the benefit concert tickets, he opted for the pop concert. Your announcement, then, did persuade him to a new attitude, but the persuasion was not strong enough to get him to act on it.

To be successful, persuasion must accomplish all six of these steps. You must get your message to the audience. More important, you must get someone to pay attention to it. And the message must be understandable; people are more likely to read things that are easy to understand. In any event, they aren't likely to come over to your side if they don't understand what your side is. But understanding isn't enough. Your arguments must be convincing. The audience must be willing to give in, or yield. Then they must remember that they gave in, and then they must act.

You'll need to consider all these steps when designing persuasive messages. Techniques that work well for some steps might be useless for others. Some persuasive writing gets people to pay attention, but it might not be memorable. Messages designed only to produce yielding might not get the audience to act. For example, one research study tried to decide which persuasive methods were best for getting new mothers to go to the maternity ward for examinations. As it turned out, the best method depended on how the results were measured. One method got the most mothers to say they would come back a month later, but another method produced the most mothers who actually did go back a month later.[6] Obviously, one method was good at inducing yielding, but the other was better for retention and action.

Typology of Steps in Persuasion

In David Therkelsen's typology of the steps in the persuasion process, each step relates to the content areas of social science, communication, psychology and marketing and to such root functional areas as segmentation and writing. This typology in Table 3.1 shows demographics, for instance, as relevant primarily to the first four steps in the persuasion process.[7] But writing relates mostly to the attention, comprehension and memorability steps.

You may find this typology to be a handy guide that helps you draw on information from a variety of courses, as well as from your personal experience, when you're confronted with writing a persuasive message.

Compare these steps in persuasion to a model with which you are probably also familiar: steps in the adoption process, adoption of a product, practice or idea. The first step is awareness, followed by interest, then some evaluation of the new information. If it is a product or a practice, this is followed by a trial and if that works to the benefit of the experimenter, adoption follows. This early model used for encouraging innovation in agriculture attracted more attention in public relations as the diffusion model.[8] This model indicates some elements that affect steps along the way as well as the personality of individuals taking those steps.

Persuasion and Logic

Although strategies and the steps in the persuasion process are easy to grasp, another element is often ignored. This element often makes people uncomfortable because, in its purest form, it demands rigorous thought. We're talking about *logic,* specifically *applied logic.* To understand the idea, consider this scene. A grandfather standing on the porch of his country home remarks to an adult grandson, as they peer into a cloudless sky, that a storm is coming. The grandson says that it is amazing how old people can predict weather. "How do you do it, Gramps?" he asks, adding, "Is your arthritis acting up or is it the woollies again?" To which the grandfather replies, "Nope. The cable TV just went out."

Although fiction, the scene symbolizes what applied logic is all about. Look again at how the characters interact. If you analyze them closely, you'll see that several major principles are illustrated.

Expectations

The elder character may be a little flighty, especially in the eyes of the grandson. The young man *expects* his gramps to behave in certain ways. His expectations seemed to influence his view of his grandfather's behavior. Like this young man, audiences have expectations. If these expectations are met, your message clears one major hurdle toward effective persuasion. If these expectations aren't met, or if messages tend to contradict expectations and experience, the opportunity to persuade may be nil or, at least, quite limited.

This means that you must know the expectations of your audience. You have expectations too, so don't let them blind you to what an audience wants. These expectations are formed from applied logic—that is, thinking about experiences and observations of life around us.

Experience

Perhaps the cable TV system failed often at the grandfather's house and he'd noticed that this failure was sometimes followed by a storm. Therefore, he concluded that the failure of the cable TV system was the result of a distant storm that would soon come his way. Never mind that it is not fully logical for him to conclude this cause-effect relationship. His experience tells him that it is a fact of life. Applied logic tells him that it is the way the world works.

You'll find that the quirkiness of the applied logic of your public may keep you from a real understanding of that audience. That means that you must work hard to grasp what goes on in its collective head. One key to this understanding is to recognize how perceptions influence reality for publics.

Perceptions

Perceptions are tricky. Both grandfather and grandson looked out on a cloudless sky. One saw nothing but an aging grandparent; the other saw a storm coming. Perceptions are like that. They are individual, not collective, visions of the world around us. What we perceive may have little or no basis in reality, because our perceptions are our realities. Therefore, when the cable TV system goes down, it is perfectly clear, from the grandfather's perspective, that a storm is approaching. Because he had not had the same experience or concluded that there was cause and effect involved, the grandson could not perceive what his grandparent perceived.

One reason we can't fully perceive what others perceive is that we think in abstractions. We use verbal language as a tool inside our heads to give meaning and value to the reality around us. Because words merely represent reality, our understanding of reality is limited by our command of language. As a writer, you can only be as successful as your ability to select words that represent basically the same thing to your audience as they do to you. If you don't, you'll see a sky that has no hint of a storm. Therefore, you may fail to see the connections between things that your public sees.

Connections

The principle of connectivity is simple, although vexing at times. The concept of connection is self-descriptive—that is, it refers to the way people see relationships between ideas, events, issues, processes and so on. Obviously, connectivity relates closely to perception. In fact, you can think of it as the next step after perception. It is the idea of "What does this mean?" or "How is this related to that?" or "What does this mean to me?" When the cable TV system went out, it meant to the grandfather that a storm was coming. That the system went out meant nothing to the grandson because he had not made a connection between the two events.

If strict rules of logic are applied, there may be no connection between the two events. Our experience is not that of the old man, so we can understand the grandson's skepticism. But if the grandfather is in your target public, you must make every effort to understand how he may have made that connection. Otherwise, you're not likely to frame a message that is meaningful to him. Meaningfulness suggests that you must also look at the values of your audience.

Values

Our personal values are always important to us. And they become even more important, and more rigid, as we age. The grandfather's observation that a storm was on the way may seem trivial to us. That may be because we tend to forget that he lives in the country where weather is an important part of his daily existence. Developments that reinforce our values are welcome. Those that contradict them, or call them into question, are often ignored as not worthy of consideration.

Values are at the core of our behavior. They are rooted in our basic beliefs, such as our convictions about what is right or wrong, important or unimportant, valuable or not valuable and so on. Value systems, once formed, remain pretty much unchanged throughout our lives; they are much like the leopard that can't change its spots. It is our value system that influences the way we apply logic to what we experience and perceive and the kinds of connections we make between our perceptions of reality.

Applied logic—the way we see relationships between developments, things or issues—often provides the motive behind our own efforts to persuade others to our points of view.

Persuasion and Communication

Persuasion is a special type of communication. To understand the persuasion process fully, then, we must understand something about communication. Like persuasion, the communication process can be divided into a number of elements.[9]

As with persuasion, the communication process has many models. None of them is adequate in every situation. Some are clearly more relevant than others in certain situations. However, the principal paradigm of the communication process, as formulated by Harold Lasswell, is this: Who says what, through what channel, to whom, with what effect?[10] By using this paradigm, we can say that communication involves a source, a message, a medium (channel), a public and an effect. Changes in the characteristics of any of these elements can cause differences in the communication's persuasiveness.

Source

At first glance, it does not seem likely that you can change the "who"—the source of the message. You're stuck with who you are or who employs you. But then again, it is sometimes possible to change some of your characteristics (or some characteristics of your company).

At the very least, you can design your messages to take advantage of any helpful qualities that your organization has.

What qualities of the source of the message influence the effectiveness of persuasion? One of the most important is credibility. Usually, the more credible a source, the more persuasive it is.[11] This means that your organization must constantly strive to remain believable if your message is to be effective. And the best way to remain credible is to tell the truth—even when it hurts. Thus, even if you are trying to persuade, you must remember to be honest and accurate. What you write must correspond to your company's actions. If the organization is not acting the part of a good member of the community, it does not really matter much what you say, because your message won't be believed. As Lerbinger puts it, "The communicator realizes that what he says must correspond to the realities of a given situation. The management he represents cannot be doing one thing while he is saying something else."[12]

Credibility can be viewed as having two major elements: *expertise* and *objectivity*. The audience is more likely to believe you if its members think you know what you're talking about. But to believe you completely, they must also think you are telling the truth. If you have a vested interest in an issue, your objectivity will be suspect. McGuire says, "For maximum believability, the source must be perceived as not only knowing the truth but being objective enough to be motivated to tell it as he sees it."[13] Recent research also shows that people tend to rate expertise higher in writers who use big words and longer, more involved sentences, compared to those who use common words and simpler syntax, especially when dealing with complex issues. The same study also indicates that people who already have a fairly clear understanding of an issue are more critical of what they read and who writes it.[14] Also, several research studies have confirmed that disinterestedness makes a source more persuasive to audiences. In fact, a source is most persuasive of all when arguing *against* his or her own best interests.

Credibility isn't the only source characteristic that can aid persuasion. Your audience is likely to be persuaded too by sources it likes. Of course, the audience's feelings about the

source aren't always clear. Is an audience persuaded by a source because it likes the source, or does it like the source because it agrees with the message? In any event, being liked helps make persuasion more successful. So does *being similar* to the audience members in some way, especially when the similarity is ideological and not merely physical or social. Your persuasion, then, is more likely to be effective if you can establish some *ideological similarities* between yourself and your audience.

A third source characteristic that leads to effective persuasion is perceived power. Put simply, this means that your boss is more likely to persuade you than your neighbor is. Your boss has power over you; your neighbor does not.

Because many different source qualities affect persuasive success, it isn't always possible to predict what will happen when one of these qualities is changed. For example, if you work hard to appear to be an expert, your audience may very well perceive your expertise but may not agree with you as much as they would otherwise. By becoming more of an expert, you have become less similar to your nonexpert audience.

The increase in agreement produced by greater expertise can be more than offset by the loss of agreement caused by the decrease in similarity. In many cases, then, some intermediate level of expertise is probably best. Audiences tend to believe people who know more than they do, but not too much more.

Although these points are all supported by contemporary research findings, it is worth noting that the value of a reputation for personal truthfulness and expert experience was treated long ago by Aristotle under the general term *ethos.*[15]

Most of the time, you can choose your sources for expertise and credibility. However, in a crisis, that may not be the case. Others involved in the situation will be speaking out, and still others may be sought for their views. The proactive public relations practitioner gets those others involved in the situation to help tell the story and goes forward with the first news of the crisis, incident or situation in order to frame the issue in the minds of those hearing the news either through mass or specialized media or interpersonal communication.

Message

From the standpoint of the persuasive writer, the message element in the process is often the most important. At least, the message is the one element of communication over which the writer has complete control. In writing the message, you have to decide what things to say and how and when to say them. In doing this, you will be faced with many difficult decisions. Here is what communication research says about some of the questions surrounding those decisions.

Should you give one side or both sides?

In general, studies show that it is better to give both sides of the story. One-sided arguments are frequently dismissed, especially if a public is highly sophisticated or tends to oppose your point of view at the beginning. If the public does not like you, or if the public does not already agree with you on the issue at hand, it's usually best to give both sides. It's also better to give both sides if the public is likely to hear the other side of the story.

Is there any time when stressing your side of the story *only* is a good idea? Possibly, if circumstances include *all three* of the following conditions: The public is poorly educated, the public is friendly to you, and the public probably will not hear any arguments from the other side. Only rarely, however, are all of these requirements met. Generally that means you must introduce and refute other points of view.

A related question is occasionally faced by public relations writers: Should an issue be raised at all? Sometimes people (especially corporate executives) prefer to "let sleeping dogs lie" and not bring up a potentially controversial subject until somebody else does it first. This is usually a mistake. If there is any chance at all that someone will bring up an issue in the future, you should strike first with your side of the story. In fact, most research indicates that the first communicator has a significant advantage in winning over public opinion because of the inoculation effect. That is, you can try to "inoculate" an audience against the opponent's views, just as a person can be inoculated against a disease by an injection of a weakened form of the same disease. Thus it is generally more effective to raise the issues yourself, before your opponent does, but don't expect "inoculation" to work miracles. In fact, many scholars question its value.

Nonetheless, a smart public relations writer will supply a weakened form of the opposition arguments and then refute them before the opposition can present its case. The public will resist persuasion by the opposition at a later date. This strategy, studies show, works better than providing the public with large amounts of propaganda designed merely to promote the persuader's point of view while ignoring the existence of conflicting opinions.

Which side should you give first?

If, as in most cases, you use both sides of the story, whose side should you give first? Unfortunately, the evidence on this question is not conclusive. Giving the opposition arguments first is apparently better when dealing with controversial issues, but not when dealing with noncontroversial ones.

Which should come first, the good news or the bad news?

In general, give the good news first. This approach will probably get you the widest overall agreement with your message.

Should you make conclusions explicit or let the target public draw its own conclusions?

In essence, this question asks whether it's better to tell people what to think or to offer the facts and let them figure it out. It's true that a person drawing his or her own conclusions is likely to hold the new opinion more strongly. The problem is that the conclusion might not be the one you are after. Generally, then, it is safer to make the conclusion explicit, especially when the issue under consideration is complex.

There are exceptions to this general guideline, however. A highly intelligent public can probably be trusted to form an obvious conclusion, based on the weight of evidence presented to it. In fact, such a public may consider an explicit conclusion in such situations insulting. Sometimes an initially hostile public reacts negatively to explicit conclusions. And when the issues are very personal and members of the target public have a high ego involvement with your conclusions, it's definitely wiser not to make the conclusions explicit.

Do fear techniques work?

Research on this question seems to indicate that fear appeals do enhance persuasion, but only up to a point. Mild fear appeals seem to be more effective than strong fear appeals. Even then, you need to offer a resolution to the fear.

McGuire offers an explanation for this. Fear may be effective in passing the yielding step of persuasion. But high fear levels may work against other steps in the process, such as comprehension or remembering. If you scare people too much, they won't get the substance of your message, they will put it out of their minds and forget it or they will modify it to a less threatening form. Thus as with expertise, some medium level of fear is probably the best approach. Keep in mind, though, McGuire's observation that the more complex the message, the less fear arousal is desirable.[16]

Is it better to use emotional or factual arguments?

Evidence on this question is simply not conclusive. Sometimes emotional appeals are the most persuasive, and sometimes factual ones are. It all depends on the issue involved and the composition of the public. There are no good general guidelines to follow.

It is probably safe to say, however, that the best persuasive writing employs both factual and emotional arguments. Because information by itself seldom changes attitudes, some writers tend to rely on emotional presentations. But information is also important to persuasion, if only to provide people with a rational basis for justifying attitudes that are primarily based on emotion. Information can strengthen or weaken attitudes. It can blunt the criticism of a public opposed to your position. It can strengthen the opinions of those already on your side. Furthermore, providing information to supporters of your view gives them a way to verbalize their feelings—and to defend them. This reduces the chances that subsequent persuasion from the opposition will undo what your message has accomplished.

Medium

Although it may be a bit of an exaggeration, Marshall McLuhan's contention that "the medium is the message" certainly responds to the question of how the channel, or medium, can influence a persuasive outcome.

It should be obvious that the medium is important in both the presentation and attention steps of persuasion. As a writer, you must use a medium that will get your message to the target public, and the medium has to be one that the audience will pay attention to. But research studies indicate that the medium is also important for other steps of persuasion.

One finding is that spoken communication is usually more likely than written communication to bring about yielding.[17] This does not mean that you should spend all your time writing speeches while ignoring print media. But it is useful to keep in mind that speech has more power to change minds than writing. The pen might be mightier than the sword, but the tongue can outdo both.

This is not an endorsement of "fiery oration," either. In fact, studies have been unable to show much difference between the persuasive effects of intense, enthusiastic speeches and more subdued ones. In both cases, however, the spoken word wins over the written word in persuasive power.

On the other hand, studies also show that the written word achieves better comprehension. But complete understanding is not always needed for successful persuasion. The spoken word diminishes understanding a little, but it increases yielding a lot.

These findings seem to recommend television and radio as media for carrying your message. But though the evidence shows that oral persuasion is more effective than written persuasion, it also shows that face-to-face encounters are more persuasive than messages in the mass media, especially in attempts to influence voting behavior.[18] This evidence suggests that spending a lot of money on media time and space may not be worth the price. But if mass media messages aren't effective, then the nation's businesses are wasting billions of dollars annually to promote their products, services and ideas via mass media. And there are reasons to believe that the media can play a role in persuasion, though perhaps an indirect one such as reinforcement. Some of the debate on this issue may simply reflect the fact that the effects of the media are too difficult to isolate and to measure.

Studies show that the mass media can successfully convey information to people (though not in all cases, and not always to the extent that the communicator would like). And though information alone is usually not enough to get people to change their attitudes, it does play a part. Even if most people are not persuaded much by the media, opinion leaders—those who influence others in face-to-face contacts—do pay attention to the media and base their opinions at least in part on media messages.

The idea that opinion leaders transmit media messages to others is usually described as the "two-step flow" of mass communication. More recent research has cast some doubt on some of the details of this idea. For example, many people do receive input from the media, but they turn to opinion leaders for interpretations of facts more than for the facts themselves. Furthermore, the opinion leaders may receive information from sources other than the mass media.[19] Nevertheless, opinion leaders do provide a possible avenue for mass media to influence public opinion.

Another important influence of the media has been described as "agenda setting." Research seems to show that issues considered important by the population often are also issues that the media devote much time and space to. Thus it has been suggested that even if the media don't tell people what to think, they do tell them what to think about. Of course, it is possible that the situation is the other way around—that people decide what's important first, and then the media begin to run stories on those subjects. Much recent work has established, though, that media coverage often comes first. So if your intention is to raise an issue to public consciousness, you must first get the attention of the media.

Given that the mass media can be used as channels for your messages, which media are best to use? That's a difficult question to answer. Because the media's measurable effects on attitudes are small, it isn't easy to tell if one medium is more effective than another. Looking at credibility alone, the evidence suggests that people are more likely to believe television than newspapers and newspapers than radio. But, although television is generally given the highest believability ratings, members of higher socioeconomic groups usually rate newspapers and magazines higher for accuracy and truthfulness.[20]

Looking at the question from the standpoint of complexity of message, highly complex messages are generally more understandable and believable in print media. Messages charged with emotion appear to work best in broadcast media.

Public

The greatest lesson of social science research on the question of persuasion is a lesson that all good writers should already know: Know your public. Techniques that will work wonders persuading a football team may flop with a group of engineers. Most of the guidelines for preparing a message or choosing a channel depend on the characteristics of the public.

The public is made up of individuals. And all individuals, as receivers of your message, possess a common characteristic: They tend to forget things. This fact usually works to your disadvantage, because you must repeat messages often to combat forgetfulness. But attitudes built up over a long period of time are hard to forget. If your organization has a long history of exploiting employees or making a poor product, and if the company is perceived this way by your audience, you will have a difficult job writing credible messages. Before you can ever hope to be believed and accepted, your company will have to clean up its act. And you will have to tell the "good news" often over a long period of time before the new truth about the company will replace the old perceptions.

On the other hand, if your organization is generally perceived as a good place that is sensitive to employee needs, you'll be able to weather a damage suit filed by an employee with only moderate and temporary dents in your "white knight" armor.

The point is that the "retention" step in the persuasion process is a particularly difficult one.

The human tendency to forget can sometimes be helpful, especially to communicators with low credibility. If you are not a very credible source (because the target public believes you are biased), your message may not induce any immediate change. But months later, perhaps, the public may show some agreement with your point of view. It is possible that they will remember your message but forget where it came from. Thus the message, no longer associated with the low-credibility source, may now be believed, which is what you wanted in the first place. It just takes a while for it to happen.

This is sometimes called the *sleeper effect,* and whether it actually exists is a matter of some debate. Nevertheless, it's useful to know that even a low-credibility source can be effective in persuasion under some circumstances.

Forgetfulness probably carries no such benefits for high-credibility sources who want the target public to remember everything. High-credibility sources often repeat their messages over and over to make sure the point is retained. Research on this issue indicates that repetition (as with a commercial announcement presented many times) may indeed achieve greater effects, but mostly because it increases the likelihood that more people will hear the message.

On this point, however, it is wise to remember that people tend to forget information at about the same rate as they learn it. Hence, if you stop the flow of messages about your organization, you can expect awareness of your company to drop, though it apparently never goes back to zero. This point, viewed from the stance of economy, supports the idea of sustained programming, because it is more efficient to sustain awareness than to build it in the first place.

Effect

When you sit down to write a message about your company to its public, you have some objective in mind. You want the audience to think about an issue in a certain way, or you want the audience to do something. In other words, there is a motive, or intent, not only behind the message you want to convey but behind the way you will formulate and deliver it. Thus the overall "effect" question is: Did the audience do what you wanted it to do?

You begin the process of writing with an intended effect in mind. It has to be "intended" because you don't know what the actual effect will be ahead of time. You can only guess—and hope. Nevertheless, you must ask yourself how your intended effect influences your success in persuasion.

The most obvious intention of any persuasive speaker or writer is to persuade. If the audience knows it is being persuaded, its resistance may increase. If, however, people merely overhear a message, without knowing that the message is intended for their ears, they might be more susceptible to the argument.

This fact suggests that it might be helpful to disguise your persuasive intent. Some evidence supports this view, but some does not. At times the opposite effect can be seen. Although there is little doubt that disguising the intent to persuade enhances yielding, such a disguise may hinder presentation, attention and comprehension. The benefits of making sure your audience gets the message may outweigh the disadvantages of letting your intent be clearly seen.[21]

A companion issue regarding intent is the matter of how extreme your appeal should be. Should you try to persuade people to change their minds just a little or a lot? This question has been the focus of many research studies. It seems, generally, that increasing the level of intended change helps to increase persuasion, but only up to a point. If you ask for too much attitude change, effectiveness decreases.[22]

An Alternative Theory

Because of conceptual problems with certain methods by which some of the foregoing ideas have been tested, you will be wise as a writer to use them simply as guidelines, not gospels. Some research findings are contradictory or, at least, inconclusive. James E. Grunig has introduced yet another perspective that may help us to better understand the effects of persuasion.

Put simply, Grunig proposes a situational theory asserting that "how a person perceives a situation explains whether he will communicate about the situation, how he will communicate, and whether he will have an attitude relevant to the situation."[23] This perspective involves six key concepts: problem recognition, constraint recognition, referent criterion, involvement, information seeking and information processing.

Problem Recognition   A person must perceive that something is missing or indefinite in a situation in order to stop and think about it. The importance of this to the public relations writer is that recognition of a problem or issue increases the chances that a person will respond to a situation or express a need for more information about it. This idea is closely related to the *attending* and *comprehending* functions cited earlier.

Constraint Recognition   If the receiver of a public relations message thinks his or her options to respond to the situation are limited by group, institutional, legal, economic or other external constraints, there is less need for information about the situation. These constraints may be perceived as so compelling that people simply ignore the information because they feel impotent to use it or, perhaps, to do anything about it. Therefore, even if your message is loaded with relevant material, it may have little impact because the receiver is resigned to a limited response or no response at all. This idea is related to the retaining and acting functions discussed earlier.

Referent Criterion   A person brings to a situation some prior information that is relevant to the situation. If the situation is common, the prior information tends to lessen the person's need for additional information. This suggests that the person probably won't be very open to new information from a public relations writer. On the other hand, if the situation is new, related prior experience tends to serve initially as a guide to seeking information about behavior pertinent to the situation. This referent concept suggests that a public relations writer should be prepared to provide extensive information in new situations. This concept is related to Lerbinger's *designs of persuasion,* especially cognitive, motivational and social.

Involvement   The more salient or important the issue is perceived to be, the more likely a person will be to respond to it. Involvement seems to suggest not only if a person will respond but also *how.* Remember to attempt in every message to make its importance clear to the public.

Information Seeking   Deliberate acts by a person to get more information about the situation are characterized as information-seeking behavior. A need is perceived and behavior is directed at fulfilling the need. The concept of information seeking tends to suggest behavior that has risen to a higher level of involvement. Individuals with these higher levels of involvement are much more eager to receive and accept your persuasive messages. As a public relations writer, you won't have to work as hard to communicate with these individuals, but they will probably demand a lot more salient material.

Information Processing   Information processing implies a much lower level of involvement because some—maybe a lot of—information is encountered and processed incidentally, if not accidentally, about the situation. A large proportion of information acquisition is unplanned. It arises in the context of other behavior. For example, if there's nothing else to do, a person may switch on the television set and watch whatever appears on it, including your public service announcement on your community's blood drive. To reach this segment of your public, you will have to work especially hard to make your persuasive messages relevant. That's why we emphasize repeatedly in this book how important it is to know your audience. If you don't know your audience intimately, you probably will not be successful as a persuasive writer.

Conclusions

Because the results of research in persuasive communication are inconclusive or contradictory in some cases, the following conclusions should be interpreted as general guidelines, not rules, that may apply in many situations.

- Behavior is both rational and emotional. Effective persuasion uses appeals based on one or both characteristics.
- Attitude formation is a complex process. It involves our personal experience and history, social environment, personality characteristics, predispositions and communication.
- Persuasion can be viewed as a learning process, a power process or an emotional process.
- The communication-design aspects of persuasion include stimulus-response, cognitive, motivational, social and personality.
- The six steps in the process of persuasion are presenting, attending, comprehending, yielding, retaining and acting.
- As it involves the communication process, persuasion has five major considerations: source, message, medium, public and effect.
- It is generally better to give both sides of an issue rather than just your side, especially if your public is sophisticated.
- If there is a chance that the opposition will raise an issue, it is generally better for you to raise it first and try to "inoculate" your public against opposing views.
- When dealing with controversy, give your opponent's views first; then follow with your own.
- In general, tell the good news first and then the bad.
- It is safer to draw clear conclusions in your messages than to let the public draw its own.
- Mild fear appeals seem to work better than strong ones, but a resolution to the fear should also be offered.
- Use both factual and emotional appeals.
- The spoken word is more persuasive than the printed word.
- Opinion leaders base their views on the mass media, then use face-to-face contact to persuade others.
- If you want to raise an issue for public debate, you have to get the attention of the media, because they set the agenda.
- You must know your public very well to be able to shape effective persuasive messages to it.
- Attitudes built up over long periods of time are resistant to change. Even if you appear to be unsuccessful at promoting change in the short term, change might occur much later.
- A persuasive writer must know clearly what he or she wants to happen before writing the message. This intended effect may be quite different from the actual effect.
- If you ask for major attitude change, you will get more results than if you ask only for a little, up to a point. However, asking for too much change diminishes your effectiveness.

Exercises

1. Your parents bought you a computer when you went to college, but now you feel you really need a laptop. There are many times you need access to your computer. You feel that you lose time when you are in between classes and there's not a computer lab convenient for you to work in. You've been thinking about this for quite a while, and now you've decided to write your parent(s) to explain why you need a laptop. Although the style of your letter can be fairly informal, it needs to be persuasive enough for you to get the money to buy the model you've chosen as well as some additional software you need. You have all of the information, including the prices; now you must apply persuasive writing. Before starting this assignment, you might want to take another look at the chapter on letter writing. Remember: message, sources (quote experts?) and the medium (paper or email?).

2. You have been working as an intern this semester for a small public relations firm that has given you a great deal of responsibility. However, two of their clients are in the retail business, and you know that November and December are going to be extremely busy for you in working with them. You are concerned that if you devote the time the clients need, your grades will suffer and you may lose a scholarship. You want to write your employer a letter that will persuade your boss to give you a week off before exams. You know that others who have asked for favors have been told they are "not professional," and one was even fired. How can you write your letter so you won't suffer such consequences? This needs to be fairly formal.

3. Write a persuasive piece on any topic you know a great deal about but something that is fairly controversial. This will be an opinion piece for the student newspaper. Analyze how you constructed your argument and explain the rationale for your choices based on some of the theories in this chapter.

 Use InfoTrac College Edition to access information on topics in this chapter from hundreds of periodicals and scholarly journals.

Notes

1. Edward L. Bernays, *Public Relations* (Norman, Okla.: University of Oklahoma Press, 1952), p. 130.
2. Otto Lerbinger, *Designs for Persuasive Communication* (Englewood Cliffs, N.J.: Prentice Hall, 1972).
3. See, for example, Irving L. Janis, "Personality as a Factor in Susceptibility to Persuasion," in *The Science of Human Communication,* ed. Wilbur Schramm (New York: Basic Books, 1963), pp. 54–64.
4. Milton Rokeach, *The Nature of Human Values* (New York: Free Press, 1973).
5. William J. McGuire, "Persuasion, Resistance, and Attitude Change," in *Handbook of Communication,* eds. Ithiel de Sola Pool et al. (Chicago: Rand McNally, 1973), p. 221.

6. Stanley Lehmann, "Personality and Compliance: A Study of Anxiety and Self-Esteem in Opinion and Behavior Change," *Journal of Personality and Social Psychology* 15 (1970): 76–86. Cited in McGuire, "Persuasion," p. 233.

7. David J. Therkelsen and Christina L. Fiebich, "Message to Desired Action: A Communication Effectiveness Model," *Journal of Communication Management* 5 (4) (2001): 374–390.

8. Everett M. Rogers, *Diffusion of Innovations* (New York: Free Press of Glencoe, 1962). Also see Everett M. Rogers and Rodolfo N. Salcedo, "Mass Media and Interpersonal Communication," in *Handbook of Communication,* eds. Ithiel de Sola Pool and Wilbur Schramm with Frederick W. Frey, Nathan Maccoby and Edwin B. Parker (Chicago: Rand McNally, 1973), pp. 290–310.

9. McGuire calls the relationship between the steps in the persuasion process and those in the communication process the "matrix of persuasive communication."

10. Wilbur Schramm, "The Challenge of Communication Research," in *Introduction to Mass Communication Research,* eds. Ralph O. Nafziger and David M. White (Baton Rouge, La.: Louisiana State University Press, 1963), p. 29.

11. This is not always true, however. See B. Sternthal, L. Phillips and R. Dholakia, "The Persuasive Effect of Source Credibility: A Situational Analysis," *Public Opinion Quarterly* 42 (Fall 1978): 285–314.

12. Lerbinger, *Designs,* p. 25.

13. McGuire, "Persuasion," p. 231.

14. Duangkamol Chartprasert, "How Bureaucratic Writing Style Affects Source Credibility," *Journalism Quarterly* 70 (Spring 1993): 150–159.

15. Aristotle, *Rhetoric,* trans. W. Rhys Roberts (New York: Modern Library, 1954).

16. McGuire, "Persuasion," p. 234.

17. William J. McGuire, "Nature of Attitudes and Attitude Change," in *Handbook of Social Psychology,* eds. Gardener Lindzey and Elliot Aronson (Reading, Mass.: Addison-Wesley, 1969), p. 225.

18. Ibid., pp. 228–229.

19. Everett M. Rogers, "Mass Media and Interpersonal Communication," in *Handbook of Communication,* eds. Ithiel de Sola Pool et al. (Chicago: Rand McNally, 1973), pp. 292–298.

20. McGuire, "Nature," pp. 230–231.

21. McGuire, "Persuasion," p. 231.

22. Elliot Aronson, Judith Turner and J. M. Carlsmith, "Communicator Credibility and Communication Discrepancy as Determinants of Opinion Change," *Journal of Abnormal and Social Psychology* 67 (1963): 31–36.

23. James E. Grunig, "Communication Behaviors and Attitudes of Environmental Publics: Two Studies," *Journalism Monographs* 81 (March 1983): 9–14.

Selected Bibliography

Books

T. William Boxx and Gary M. Quinlivan, eds., *The Cultural Context of Economics and Politics* (Lanham, Md.: University Press of America, 1994).

Robert B. Cialdini, *Influence: Science and Practice,* 3d ed. (Glenview, Ill.: Scott, Foresman, 1992).

Theodore L. Glasser and Charles T. Salmon, *Public Opinion and the Communication of Consent* (New York: Guilford Press, 1994).

James Haggerty, *In the Court of Public Opinion: Winning Your Case with PR* (New York: John Wiley & Sons, 2003).

J. David Kannamer, *Public Opinion, the Press and Public Policy* (Westport, Conn.: Praeger, 1994).

Charles U. Larson, *Persuasion: Reception and Responsibility,* 8th ed. (Belmont, Calif.: Wadsworth, 1998).

Richard M. Perloff, *The Dynamics of Persuasion* (Hillsdale, N.J.: Lawrence Erlbaum Associates, 1993).

Vincent Price, *Public Opinion* (Newbury Park, Calif.: Sage Publications, 1992).

Everett M. Rogers, *Diffusion of Innovation* (New York: Free Press, 1995).

Annette Simmons, *The Story Factor: Inspiration, Influence and Persuasion Through the Art of Storytelling* (Cambridge, Mass.: Perseus Publishing, 2002).

Journals

The International Journal of Public Opinion Research, Oxford Journals Online, Oxford University Press for the World Association of Public Opinion Research and assisted by Stanford University Library HighWire Press.

Public Perspective, A Roper Center Review of Public Opinion and Polling, The University of Connecticut, Roper Center for Public Opinion Research, Storrs, CT 06269-1164, USA. Back issues only because the publication ceased in 2003.

Research for the Public Relations Writer

It is much easier and quicker today, but a lot riskier, to find facts by using computers. You simply tell a search engine what you're looking for and it will scour the World Wide Web for the information. The problem is that the search engine can't recognize the difference between biased and unbiased information. Only you can make that distinction.

You must develop basic strategies that help you select and use information. One approach is to rely on information from reputable sources, including the Web sites of organizations such as the U.S. Bureau of the Census and other government agencies, *The New York Times* and *The Wall Street Journal.* Even then, the information may be less than dependable. For example, reports on the number of deaths that occurred as a result of the September 11, 2001, terrorist attacks vary tremendously. Data compiled by the U.S. Department of State indicate that 2,829 died at the World Trade Center, 189 at the Pentagon and 44 in the airliner that crashed in western Pennsylvania—a total of 3,062.[1] But the Web site for the United States Senate Republican Policy Committee reported 5,350 deaths in the attack on the World Trade Center, 189 at the Pentagon and 44 near Pittsburgh, for a total of 5,583.[2] The Coalition for Global Solidarity and Social Development reports that the attacks "resulted in the deaths of more than 6,000 human beings."[3] The point is that when searching for facts, be prepared for ambiguity that sometimes may be hard to reconcile.

Information from newsgroups and independent electronic newsletters may or may not be biased. That doesn't mean you can't use it. It does mean, however, that before you use it you must seek other sources to confirm it.

Getting information from the Web is problematic, at best, because there are no traffic cops on the information superhighway. You may find that you still must visit a traditional library now and then, or do some original research on questions that can't be answered by existing information.

T A B L E   4 . 1   *Prewriting Checklist*

1. Gather the facts of the matter and get them right.
2. Gather authoritative opinions and interpretations of the matter.
3. Evaluate facts and opinions for their pertinence. Discard those not directly related to the matter.
4. Synthesize the remaining facts and opinions into a cohesive body of information.
5. Organize the information for writing.
6. Develop a writing outline that moves logically from one point to the next.
7. Write. Edit. Rewrite.

Keep in mind that action data, according to the newsletter *pr reporter,* is what is needed by public relations writers, including data that

1. *Answers questions essential to planning projects, programs and campaigns.* The most desirable research methods focus on the latent readiness of audiences to behave in certain ways and on how audiences get information and how they use it to arrive at decisions.
2. *Tests, if possible, and deflates assumptions.* Conventional wisdom—often what leads senior management to decisions—may be wrong.
3. *Produces baseline data that permits accurate evaluation.* Good baselines help us to know how far we've moved, if at all, whether a process is working and whether behavioral change goals are met.[4]

Research, then, is the key element in professional success—research at the beginning and at the ending of any endeavor. Research is as important to the beginner as it is to a senior counselor, although the focus of research may change as you move up the career ladder. Because most entry-level jobs in public relations are directly related to the writing process, it is important that you learn as much as you can about research and how to use it as a writer. For this reason, you should review and remember the prewriting checklist in Table 4.1.

Research in Public Relations

Careful planning is central to the process and practice of professional public relations. Plans are generally successful in direct proportion to the quality of the information on which they are built. That's why research is so important to the overall success of a public relations plan. Planning usually begins with what is known as a *situational analysis.* This is where answers are sought for all sorts of questions.

What are the significant trends? What is the overall economic situation? What are the political considerations for the action we are contemplating? How is our organization perceived by target publics? How are our competitors viewed by target publics? How much support can we expect from affected publics? These and other questions unique to the situation must be raised and answered.

You may not be directly involved in public relations planning, especially early in your career, but you still need to know a good bit about research because you'll use a lot of information unearthed through research. This information generally falls into six broad categories:

1. Policy and purpose
2. Background material
3. Public
4. Message
5. Media
6. Program evaluation

All six are important in every PR situation, but rarely are they all equally important. Your sensitivity to the problem at hand will help you determine which category or combination of categories is especially important in a particular case.

Categories of Research for the PR Writer

Policy   The "company line" is a euphemism that hardly does justice to the full concept behind the term *policy.* Policy is a considered statement of purpose, position or direction that is expected to guide the behavior of those it covers.

Every company or organization in both the public and private sectors has a set of policies. Anyone working for or with the company or organization is expected to know the provisions of applicable policies.

Policy is of two general types: internal and external. *Internal policy* is that of your employer. It is a set of guidelines that directs and controls the collective behavior of the organization and the job behavior of each employee. Such policies may range from a policy governing employee benefits to a policy of public candor in the face of a community crisis.

External policy comes from a source outside the organization's immediate control but bears on the organization's behavior toward its constituencies. For example, if you are writing the annual report for a publicly held company, you must know and observe certain Securities and Exchange Commission policies and requirements.

It is critical that you know applicable policies in order to avoid problems. This not only may save your job, it may even get you promoted.

Some policies you may need to know are available to you only in oral form. Oral policy can be especially frustrating, for three main reasons. First, oral policy is easily distorted. What you believe today to be a clear understanding of the policy may be completely obsolete a year from now. Second, management may be unsure of itself and thus reluctant to put a decision in writing. Third, management may have a hidden agenda. To understand this point, suppose you are about to write a series of releases for the local media about your country club's gala next month, some proceeds of which will go to the United Negro College Fund. Club policy does not bar blacks from membership, but there are no black members in the club. And you are told, when you ask the club manager, that no blacks are invited to or expected to attend the gala. Written policy may say one thing, but unwritten policy may say something else.

If you find yourself relying more on oral than written policy, urge management to put the oral policy in writing. If management resists this suggestion unreasonably, start looking for another job.

Background Material   Successful public relations writing is based on a solid, fully developed body of facts. The kinds of facts necessary will vary, depending on the situation.

For example, suppose you are retained to write a brochure in support of a bond election to double the community's hospital bed space. What facts do you need to know before you begin to write?

For starters, here are a few: What has been the community's rate of growth over the last 20 years? How much is the community expected to grow in the next 20? What accounts for this rate of growth? What is the ratio of community patients to patients from outside the community? Why? Has this ratio changed in the last few years? Is the ratio expected to change in the future? Why? Is the interest rate on the bonds favorable? How do local financial leaders view the bonding program? Why?

The questions you might ask about this project may number into the hundreds. The number is not the issue. The point is that public relations planning, decision making and writing depend on the careful accumulation of facts and ideas.

As you begin the task of assembling background materials, you should assume the traditional role of the news reporter by asking who, what, where, when, how and why—especially why. As you ask these questions, you'll begin to build an elaborate, sophisticated, project-specific system of information that will help you handle assignments ranging in diversity from staging a small symposium to handling a crisis at a chemical plant.

If your search for the proper background material leads you into legal or government documents and you find that an office or agency is uncooperative, you may want to request the needed information, if it qualifies, under the Freedom of Information Act. For guidance and materials on how to make an FOIA request, contact the Freedom of Information Clearinghouse at (202) 588-1000 or write to 1600 20th St. NW, Washington, DC 20009.

One of the key points to remember about background materials is that, even if the public relations situation is new to you, it is not new. Others have faced the same situation or a similar one. Learn from their experiences.

Public   As noted earlier, professionals in public relations are fond of talking about publics, audiences or constituencies. These terms are used synonymously. It is rare in public relations that you will deal with a single public. Even when it appears that way, closer examination usually turns up two or more subsegments, each with its unique characteristics, concerns and needs.

Thus the question is: How can you identify the public or subsegments? This requires research, perhaps at different levels of sophistication. To illustrate this point, consider the following situation.

You are director of public relations for a new bank with a national charter in a metropolitan area. The bank's management is aware that deregulation allows savings and loans and investment companies, such as Merrill Lynch, to provide many financial services previously available only at banks.

Your management decides to "sell" the bank to certain types of potential customers—specifically, those whose annual incomes are $100,000 or more. This rules out many potential depositors from your target audience. And it focuses attention on specific segments of the community, such as physicians, dentists, attorneys, retailers, owners of manufacturing or service companies, architects, designers and engineers.

In this situation you will first try to divide the priority public into segments by using demographic information—income, sex, education, occupation, marital status, home ownership and the like, as discussed earlier. Once the demographic profile is complete, the picture of this public comes into sharper focus. But does it tell you all you need to know? Perhaps. Perhaps not.

What you may need now is psychographic information—information about lifestyle, attitudes and behavior. Information of this type may give you important clues indicating that your public relations program should communicate differently with, say, physicians and dentists than with retailers and manufacturers. For example, physicians and dentists may be more concerned with long-range financial planning, whereas retailers and manufacturers may be more concerned with managing cash flow. If so, messages going to these two groups must be different.

Research helps you to understand to the fullest extent the needs of your public and its components so that you can shape messages that speak to their distinct needs. (See Figure 4.2.)

Message   What you say and how you say it may have a great deal to do with your success. Recall our discussion about publics. If you are lucky enough to have a single public with which to communicate, your job will be easier. But when you have several publics, your job can be complex.

Whether it is one public or several, you are generally well advised to begin by reducing your message to a single simple idea. Remember, though, that a single simple idea is not necessarily an insignificant or simpleminded idea. Reducing what you want to say to this level is necessary to help keep you on the right track as you shape your message.

Because different methods can be used to construct a message for maximum impact, you should select an approach based primarily on your purpose for the message. Is the purpose to change or to reinforce behavior? If it is to change, you must remember to make a reward obvious to the receiver of your message. If it is to reinforce, your message must avoid information that contradicts current behavior.

Should you use a conclusion-drawing technique? In this method you select and present information that will lead your audience to draw the conclusion you want it to draw. Communication-research literature suggests that this is a good method of communicating with sophisticated audiences. However, this technique can be fatal if used with unsophisticated audiences.

There are many techniques of message presentation in addition to the ones discussed. You should review the communication-research literature and develop a personal understanding of these methods. What are they? How do they work? Under what conditions do they appear to work best? A good way to begin is to review Chapter 3.

Media   As you work your way through a public relations problem, you will have to make choices about which channels of communication to use and how to use them. Before you can make these decisions, however, you need to know the characteristics of the various media available to you. What are their technical qualities and requirements? What can they or can't they do? What are their emotional qualities? How do people react to them? How and why do people use them as they do? Should you use general media, specialized media or a combination of the two types? These are serious questions, the answers to which are not easy and may involve large amounts of time and money. But you need to know, not guess.

Once you have chosen the media, you'll need to assess whether they are effective and efficient in implementing this particular public relations program. This suggests that you'll need to monitor progress and evaluate success. Four questions are important here. Did you reach

online User Free Subscription Form

ONLINE USER—PREMIERE ISSUE

A New, How-to Magazine For...
Corporate Management and Staff Who Use Electronic Information Resources • Media • Finance • Law & Government
Don't miss this chance to read the one magazine written and edited for you!

**QUALIFY FOR YOUR FREE ONE-YEAR SUBSCRIPTION
BY SENDING IN THE FORM BELOW TODAY!**

Please list your COMPANY NAME and STREET ADDRESS below. This address is required to qualify your subscription.

❏ Mr. ❏ Mrs. ❏ Ms.

First Name _____ Last Name _____
Title _____
Company _____
Division _____
Street Address _____
City _____ State _____ ZIP _____
Telephone _____ Fax Number _____
Internet/Email Address _____ URL _____

❏ Yes! I would like to receive a complimentary one-year subscription to *ONLINE USER.* I understand that I will begin receiving *ONLINE USER* with the December issue and will receive each issue after that.

❏ No, thank you.   **Signature**_____
                       SIGNATURE REQUIRED

                     Date _____

**PLEASE COMPLETE THE FORM BELOW. REMEMBER TO SIGN AND DATE IT.
ALL QUESTIONS MUST BE ANSWERED, INCOMPLETE FORMS CANNOT BE PROCESSED.**

1. I am in a corporate office in the following department:
- ❏ Advertising
- ❏ Finance
- ❏ Human Resources
- ❏ LAN Management
- ❏ M&A
- ❏ Marketing
- ❏ Public Relations
- ❏ Shareholder Relations
- ❏ Other_____
- ❏ Corporate Planning
- ❏ Goverment Relations
- ❏ International
- ❏ Legal
- ❏ Market Research
- ❏ MIS
- ❏ R&D
- ❏ Sales

2. If none of the above apply, I am a professional in the following field:
- ❏ Finance
- ❏ Legislative/Govt. Research
- ❏ Media
- ❏ Public Sector Planning
- ❏ R&D
- ❏ Other_____
- ❏ Legal
- ❏ Private Investigation
- ❏ Real Estate
- ❏ Library

More ➔

FIGURE 4.1

Researching Your Audience—Mailed Questionnaire   *Note the simplicity of the responses required and yet the enormous value of the guidance that will accrue to an editor planning the content of the publication, and to the people charged with promoting it. This is one of "twin" mailed questionnaires for a magazine directed to people who use electronic information resources. The other questionnaire was an*

3. How many people work in your current location?
□ 1-5   □ 6-25   □ 26-100
□ 101-500   □ Over 500

4. Who makes the decisions about which electronic information resources are available in your department?
□ I do
□ Upper management
□ MIS Dept.
□ Corporate library/info center

5. Do you have a local area network at your office? □ Yes □ No

6. If so, which of the following information tasks do you use your LAN for? (check all that apply)
□ Internal email
□ External email
□ Internet connections
□ External news service
□ Database searching for research

7. Which electronic information services do you use? Please check all that apply. Please put a number 1 by your most heavily used service, and numbers 2, 3, etc., by the next most heavily used services.
□ America Online
□ CompuServe
□ Delphi
□ Dow Jones
□ GEnie
□ Individual, Inc. (HeadsUp, First!)
□ LEXIS-NEXIS
□ M.A.I.D. (Profound)
□ Network MCI
□ Prodigy
□ SandPoint (Hoover)
□ WESTLAW
□ Other _____

□ AT&T Interchange
□ DataTimes (EyeQ)
□ DIALOG
□ Dun & Bradstreet
□ InfoSeek
□ Internet
□ Investext
□ Lotus Notes Newsstand
□ Microsoft Network
□ NewsNet
□ Questel•Orbit
□ STN

8. For what purpose do you use electronic databases?
□ News updates
□ Simple lookups of names or facts
□ Quick searches for info on companies or industries
□ Comprehensive retrieval on broad topics
□ Statistics
□ Legal
□ Personal

9. Do you go online monthly? □ Yes □ No
Weekly? □ Yes □ No
Daily? □ Yes □ No

10. How much time do you spend online in a typical week?
□ 1-15 minutes   □ 16-30 minutes
□ 31-60 minutes   □ 1-2 hours
□ Over 2 hours

11. Do you have access to the World Wide Web? □ Yes □ No

12. Do you use CD-ROMs to research business/professional information?
□ Often   □ Sometimes
□ Rarely   □ Never

13. Does your company have a library or information center?
□ Yes □ No
Have you used it in the past month?
□ Yes □ No

14. Do you sometimes act as a "librarian" by helping others obtain electronic information?
□ Yes □ No

15. Do you go online for leisure and recreational purposes from home or after work hours?
□ Yes □ No

(Please fold, tape, and mail. DO NOT STAPLE! Thank you!)

NO POSTAGE
NECESSARY
IF MAILED
IN THE
UNITED STATES

BUSINESS REPLY MAIL
FIRST-CLASS MAIL   PERMIT NO. 29   WILTON, CT
POSTAGE WILL BE PAID BY ADDRESSEE

ONLINE INC
SUBSCRIPTION DEPARTMENT
462 DANBURY ROAD
WILTON CT 06897-9819

4.1 *(continued)*

identical "twin" except for spacing. The one shown here has space for an address label. Why send two? There's a good chance there's more than one computer user at that address. The motivator for completing the questionnaire and returning it postage free is the possibility (note, not promise) of getting a free subscription.
Source: Reprinted by permission of Online Inc.

your priority public? Was your message really heard and accepted? Was your message acted upon? Was the use of the media cost-effective?

Evaluation   Public relations programs have to prove their worth. This means that one of your tasks as a writer is to evaluate the cost-effectiveness of the program. You will need to know what worked well, what did not and why. Most of the techniques discussed earlier are used in this phase too. It is simply a matter of employing questionnaires, interviews and secondary sources to evaluate what has been accomplished. Of course, such common pieces of physical evidence as how many people attended an event, how many people were exposed to your message and how many people responded to a special coupon offer are critical in basic program evaluation.

Research for Storage and Retrieval

Public relations professionals would have more serious communication problems than they do if intensive spadework in policy, background material, public, message and media had to be fresh with each new program. However, professionals routinely accumulate pertinent research information, initiate research for later use and plan for future research needs.

A large proportion of public relations research is borrowed from the social sciences, especially from behavioral areas. Useful research studies are accumulated and indexed for future use. Research about publics and about media is continually reviewed and stored. Much of the information about publics comes from comprehensive studies done by the commercial media about their audiences. Other studies come from product and service institutions concerned about their own publics. Research on internal policies is mined from organizational sources, whereas external policies are gleaned from various municipal, state and federal organizations, professional or associational groups and the like.

A particular public relations situation may require some original fact-finding. In conducting original research or in hiring a research company to do it, the public relations practitioner must know clearly what is needed. Otherwise, the resulting information may be imposing but inadequate.

Organizing   Because public relations information comes from such a wide variety of sources, organizing it can be a problem. One common organizational pattern follows the lines of our earlier discussion. Information is categorized according to policy (pertinent internal and external guides), background material (substantive facts bearing on the situation), public (facts about the people you want to reach), message (facts about successes of message types in similar situations) and media (the most effective ways of delivering your message).

Presenting   The organization of the research should reflect the ways in which it will later be presented and used. In presenting this information, it is important to explain the implications of the findings when these are not obvious and to suggest what bearing the research has on the situation. The information should also indicate what other research is needed to make the picture clearer.

Updating   Organization of the research should allow for easy updating, especially when ongoing research, such as periodic opinion measurement (as in an election campaign), is critical. Today most organizational information is stored in computers, and the PR professional must know enough about the method of storage to use the system effectively. What works best for information-systems people may not always be what works best for the public relations person trying to use the information.

Reusing   Adding to or reusing research information is difficult if the information is not readily accessible. The retrieval process, therefore, is critical. PR professionals must work with information-systems people to tell them how the information will be used—what will be needed, under what conditions, when and in what form. For PR research needs, the system must be designed so that data is well organized, is presented in a meaningful way and can easily be updated.

Sources for PR Writers and Researchers

Writers and researchers of all types—not just public relations professionals—depend on research from two basic sources: paper and people. Of course, "paper" doesn't always mean books. It can mean CD-ROMs, magnetic tape or disks, film, videotape, audiotape, Internet sites or some other form of storage. The important point to remember is that sources are either secondary (paper or other form of stored information) or primary (people).

Secondary Sources for Research

Every public relations writer should have at least a working library in the office that contains a dictionary, a thesaurus, appropriate reference volumes and bibliographies, and pertinent professional and technical journals and documents. Completing this working library is a file system where information can be placed for easy and immediate access. This office library will be your first line of attack when you need secondary information. For some writers, all of this will be in one place—their computer. Computer software can include many language references and fact-storage packages. Computer access to databases is also available. Much information can be accessed electronically with a good search engine.

If you need help, call a reference librarian. You will save time if you can succinctly describe the information you want. Some reference librarians will answer simple questions on the phone.

Library   Most metropolitan areas have public libraries containing adequate resources for basic research. They also usually have cooperative agreements with other libraries to get information on loan. College and university libraries contain scholarly material you may need. Some university libraries are repositories for government documents. These documents represent a large body of research in many different areas. Some churches have substantial holdings of religious works, and many cities have law libraries. Some libraries have special collections that are open to qualified researchers.

Reference Works   The primary tools of both the reference librarian and the researcher in the library are collections of information and reference works. These are "maps" that enable you to find the treasures of information you seek. Standard reference works include encyclopedias, biographical dictionaries, dictionaries of quotations, concordances of the Bible and other famous works, atlases and gazetteers, chronologies or other books of dates, handbooks and sourcebooks such as dictionaries of all languages and areas of specialization.

Bibliographies   One reference source that is especially important is the bibliography. In compiling and categorizing bibliographies, authors provide you with paths through mazes of footnotes. Bibliographies usually identify reliable sources of information that you will want to tap. Many libraries offer electronic access to stored bibliographies so that you can call up on a screen all the most likely sources. Hard (printed) copies are also available from material listed in these databases.

Periodicals/Databases   One resource accessible in electronic systems is *The New York Times Index.* Using this database, you can track, call up and read any story that has appeared in *The New York Times* within a specific number of years. Because *The New York Times* makes an effort to be a newspaper of record, it is possible to do a great deal of research through this index alone. LexisNexis, CompuServe, Dow Jones News/Retrieval Service and others are electronic databases that can be tapped through the Internet by public relations writers for research purposes. Many newspapers in addition to *The New York Times,* such as *The Washington Post, The Daily Oklahoman* and the *Fort Worth Star-Telegram,* provide database services that may be helpful. For commercial publications, the most useful index is the *Readers' Guide to Periodical Literature.* ADTRACK is a database consisting of all ads of a quarter page or more in 148 USA magazines. You can also find indexes and databases that focus on highly specialized fields, such as law (LEXIS) or medicine (Mediline).

Some scholarly organizations, such as the International Communication Association (ICA), offer CD-ROMs for reference articles.

An extensive database on public opinion is available from the Roper Center for Public Opinion Research. Opinions were gathered from 1,606 respondents on 560 variables, including measures of scientific and environmental knowledge, personal involvement in environmental activities, and concern for issues such as air pollution, pesticides, nuclear energy and global warming. The data is available on a disk formatted for analyses using the Statistical Package for the Social Sciences (SPSS), a statistical analysis program. Another source is PRFORUM, a network of more than 200 subscribers from nine countries. PRFORUM is an interactive exchange network through which professionals can seek information from or offer it to colleagues in many places around the world. Indexes and databases also exist for most scholarly publications and even for a few newsletters issued by national institutions or organizations. (The database for most communication materials, for example, is ERIC—the Educational Resources Information Center.)

Other good references for events and issues of the day are *Facts on File* and encyclopedia yearbooks.

Public Records   Government records at all levels—local, state and federal—are available to you unless they contain classified information. Some government agencies offer significant research assistance. For example, the Library of Congress (LOC) is helpful in locating information and will often offer advice to put you on the right trail.

Government Records   Most government offices are storehouses of information, and many government offices distribute their own materials. The federal government has its materials published by the U.S. Government Printing Office (GPO). A central store in Washington, D.C., contains information on every imaginable subject, as do GPO regional offices in cities with federal centers. Ask to be put on the GPO's mailing list. One essential source of information for PR people is the *Statistical Abstracts of the United States,* published annually by the U.S. Bureau of the Census, even though it is said to underestimate minorities. Much data is available on the www.census.gov Web site.

Public Access to Information   The Freedom of Information Act has opened many files of both public and private institutions to examination. This means that normally you now have access to all documents—titles to property, budgets of state institutions, court proceedings and the like—that have been filed in a public place. A wealth of information exists in these documents.

Primary Sources for Research

When you must research primary sources, generally you have two ways of gathering information from people. One is the interview, and the other is the questionnaire. Whether you're asking questions face-to-face or through a questionnaire, you must prepare yourself ahead of time so the answers you receive will give you the information you want. Let's look at each of these methods.

Interviewing   After you have done some fundamental research, you are ready to begin asking questions of people who might be knowledgeable in your subject. In any interview you may want to begin by asking yes/no questions, but always use these as the basis for asking open-ended questions in the body of the interview. Find authorities through your research, develop questions for them and then follow up any leads they may give you.

Although some people seem to have a natural talent for getting information from others, every public relations person should develop and practice interviewing skills. Like people who play musical instruments by ear, natural interviewers—and all others—become even better with practice.

Go to an interview prepared with questions on paper. Keep information in mind that you have gained from your research. Then, if the opportunity arises, you can follow a different line of questioning. Take notes and use a tape recorder, and try not to rely solely on one or the other. It is unquestionably ethical to advise your interviewee that you want to record the conversation and to seek consent. No federal law requires prior consent in a face-to-face interview, but if the interview is recorded via interstate telephone without prior consent, it is illegal. A few states require prior consent to record intrastate telephone conversations. Be sure to check out legal provisions in the state where you work.

Listen to what the person is telling you, and try to remember the information by putting it into the context suggested by your prior research. Encourage full responses by asking relevant questions and by participating in the conversation. Avoid being judgmental. You are asking, not telling. Table 4.2 provides an interviewing checklist.

TABLE 4.2   *Checklist for Interviewing*

1. Research your subject before the interview.
2. Know something about the person you are interviewing.
3. Prepare a list of questions in advance.
4. Inform the interviewee in advance of the kinds of questions you will be asking.
5. Whenever possible use a tape recorder *and* take notes. Never put complete trust in a machine or in your memory.
6. Ask for explanations if you don't understand something.
7. Ask specific questions. Vague questions elicit vague answers.
8. Ask one question at a time. Don't throw several questions into the same sentence and expect the interviewee to answer—or even to remember—them all.

Some of the important information you get from the interview will come from keen observation of the behavior of the person you are interviewing. Watch for nonverbal communication cues, and note both physical characteristics and environmental factors that could be telling. In particular, note gestures that indicate personality characteristics and remember emotional emphases. The latter are particularly evident in the way something is said: the inflection of the voice, the expression on the face. Be cautious, however, about reading more into these details than is there. Be aware of your own bias and involvement with the subject, so you don't misinterpret what you experience. To safeguard against misinterpretation, some researchers prefer to videotape interviews so that they can capture this information and isolate it later.

Keep in mind that there are several characteristics of a good interview. First, you need to present yourself as a warm, responsive person to the interviewee. If you cultivate that impression consistently, people you interview will respond warmly to you. That goes a long way toward convincing respondents that their interaction with you will be both pleasant and personally satisfying. Second, you need to create a permissive atmosphere in which the person being interviewed does not feel inhibited by your questions but that invites candid responses. If respondents see your interview as important, they'll tend to be more cooperative. Third, you must be sure not to apply pressure of any kind, real or implied, on the person you are interviewing. If you maintain a detached, but permissive posture in the interview, respondents are more likely to "open up" with more candor than you may have expected.

To achieve these purposes, it is recommended that you follow these steps:

1. Introduce yourself by name and explain your affiliation (show documentation if it is needed or is asked for).
2. Explain clearly what it is that you are doing.
3. Explain to the interviewee how he or she was chosen to be interviewed.
4. Adapt your behavior to the personality of the person being interviewed.
5. Build rapport.

Focus Group Interview   A focus group interview, or FGI, is with a group, not an individual. Its original intent was to be a useful preresearch tool. It was intended to help researchers identify and use terms in their questions to respondents that had common meanings to people in a target public.

The procedure is to select 8–12 people from a target public, bring them to a central location and talk with them for about two hours on some topic. While the atmosphere should appear to be casual, the moderator always works from a prepared list of questions designed to get participants to begin talking and interacting with each other. Their conversations usually are recorded, sometimes with video. A transcript of the dialogue can be analyzed to identify words or phrases that people use consistently to mean certain things. These words and phases are then used to form questions to be asked of a sample of respondents.

Suppose your client is a materials testing laboratory that does nondestructive and destructive testing for a wide variety of clients. Tests might range from stress tests on alloys to air quality. Many lab personnel become expert witnesses, especially in product liability cases. Your client wants feedback from quality control engineers representing a broad range of manufacturing in which testing is both routine and regular. Further suppose that you know nothing about how a materials testing laboratory operates. How can you shape appropriate questions to a sample of quality control engineers? Don't try until you've done an FGI. You should then have enough insights to put together a group of unambiguous questions that get the information you need.

Questionnaires   The second means of getting information from people is the questionnaire. The questionnaire is a research workhorse. Drafting a questionnaire is difficult, however. Several simple questions are sometimes necessary to get a single piece of information.

It can be difficult to ask a question so that the respondent knows exactly what you mean by it. For example, a national survey once asked a question about "consumer movement leaders." Another researcher, attempting to replicate part of the study, used the same expression with different audiences and was asked by one respondent for a definition of "consumer leader." Did the researcher want to know about movement activists, government appointees or civil servants involved in consumer information, or corporate employees charged with responding to consumers? The question was invalid because it was being interpreted in different ways. One technique that helps to safeguard against this is to pretest the questions with focus groups before actually using the questionnaire.

All questions should be phrased in such a way that they are bias-free. Consider this question: Do you still drink too much? Even a negative response signifies that the respondent drank too much at some previous time, though in fact the respondent may have never indulged in liquor at all. Questions asked in this fashion are not only ineffective but also unethical.

To develop a questionnaire, begin by simply listing all the information you want to know. Then begin to draft questions that will get at the information. Next, consider your respondents. Who will be responding to these questions and under what circumstances? Some people get impatient with long telephone questionnaires, especially if the questions are on a topic that is personally uninteresting. A questionnaire that can be returned by mail gives the respondent the choice of answering on his or her own schedule. However, because you cannot control who responds to mail questionnaires, problems may arise regarding the representativeness of the sample.

The age and educational level of respondents may also be factors in how questions should be phrased. Familiarity with the subject is another possible factor. The less familiar respondents are with the topic, the simpler the questions and the longer the response times need to

be. It is also important to arrange questions in logical sequence so that answers develop naturally in the respondent's mind.

In writing the questions, it is also important to consider how the questionnaire will be administered and scored. If a questionnaire is to be used in a busy shopping mall, for example, or in a phone call, the respondent may not want to take time to answer long or involved questions. Open-ended questions are difficult to evaluate and score. How you ask a question affects the response, and that determines whether the information you get from the questionnaire will be valid and useful.

Some open-ended questions and some interview responses are later subjected to content analysis. This just means that words are counted to see how often they appear, and in what context. At least two national research agencies use in-depth interviewing and content analysis extensively. The system involves transcribing oral interviews and entering these in the computer, as would other open-ended responses. The computer can rank the words by their frequency of usage, and a social science software program can be used to analyze each word in relation to others. Subtle themes often emerge from such analyses, making it possible for researchers to determine accurately what people *mean* by what they say.

Caveats   Much of the information you get from secondary and primary sources will be in simple statistical form that relies on your understanding of concepts like sum, mean (average), median and mode. If you are not adept with these terms now, get a mathematics book and study it until you are. Otherwise, you run the risk of misinterpreting factual information, drawing poor conclusions and eventually misleading your public.

Research information that infers cause-effect relationships usually entails more sophisticated statistics and research methodologies. There are several good books you can consult for help in these areas. One is Frederick Williams and Peter Monge's *Reasoning with Statistics,* a paperback designed for people who lack a statistical background but who need to know how to interpret and use information that is available only in statistical form.

Whether you are using secondary or primary data, be skeptical about their meaning, especially if the compilers claim that it is based on a random sample. The term *random* has a very strict scientific meaning when applied to survey research. It means that every person in your public should have an equal and known statistical probability of being included in the sample. The key point to remember here is that only when the sample is truly random can the findings be generalized to the total public being researched.

You should look for certain research protocols in every piece of research data you use. These are listed in the form of questions in Table 4.3. If answers to these questions are missing from the research report or if they are so vague you can't get a clear view of how the information was gathered, be wary of the data and of any conclusions based on it. It is possible, of course, that the information is reliable, but you should still use it with caution.

Verifying

When you start putting information together from all your sources, you will want to cross-check your sources. Check primary sources against each other. If you find areas of conflict, look for more primary sources so that the weight of information will clearly support your conclusions.

In addition, check primary sources against secondary sources. People have fallible memories. In attempting to check out information, you'll often find conflicts among secondary sources. Historians, for example, sometimes spend years tracking down an elusive date for an event. Most PR researchers don't do that type of research, nor do they have the time for it, but

---

T A B L E   4 . 3   *Checklist of Research Protocols*

1. What is the name of the person(s) or organization that did the research? What was the date on which it was done? For whom and why was it done?

2. If a sample was used, what steps were taken to ensure randomness?

3. What steps were taken to validate the questions before they were asked of respondents?

4. What steps were taken to ensure the reliability of the research methods?

5. Is a copy of the questionnaire (or measuring instrument) included in the research report?

6. How will this material help you or your organization to make a decision?

it pays to be careful, especially now that so much information is highly specialized and technical. If authorities disagree, you need to know it and to find out why. Check and keep checking until a pattern emerges.

Communication Audits

A special kind of research is the communication audit. This is an audit of how well information flows from one place to another in an organization and, sometimes, to special external publics such as selected financial analysts and media representatives. A great deal of emphasis also is placed on the credibility of sources. When an organization takes stock of its communication functions, it must rely on a wide range of research approaches, including individual interviews, content analyses, focus group interviews and questionnaires.

A lot of information can be gleaned from simply reading, analyzing and systematically evaluating newsletters, employee magazines, emails, memos, letters, announcements, Web sites and other sources. An audit also produces a lot of empirical evidence. For example, it may involve FGIs with representatives of employee groups at various organizational levels. Several questionnaires may be used and may be sent through the mail, distributed in person at meetings, or posted on intranet or Internet sites using specialized survey software. Some of this software allows survey participants to complete the online questionnaire in a choice of numerous languages.

The reason for using a variety of research devices is one of the maxims of research: People sometimes are guilty of telling you what they think you want to hear rather than what they really think. This can be a significant problem when employees believe their responses may be monitored, even if that is not possible. Personal in-depth interviews also are necessary, especially when you're looking for blockages in information flow.

A well-executed communication audit can yield a wealth of information that can help you as a public relations writer and also help all levels of management. Its results usually cause an extensive review of communication policies.

Non Sequitur © 1999 Wiley Miller. Dist. by Universal Press Syndicate. Reprinted with permission. All rights reserved.

Skepticism—A Requisite for All Research

Research involves digging, thinking, verifying and analyzing. It is the act of deciding between the probable and the improbable, the true and the false, the likely and the doubtful, the acceptable and the unacceptable and the right and the wrong. These are vital decisions in any PR situation. They call for sustained reasoning, a dedication to knowing the truth and a determination to be satisfied with nothing less.

Questions to Ask

Every writer should be from the "Show Me" state, because skepticism is the hallmark of all successful writers, including those in public relations. Skepticism should not be confused with cynicism. The former is a mindset that says, "I will believe but you have to prove it to me." The cynic often rejects proof without considering it.

This skeptical approach is especially important for you to adopt as a public relations writer, as it is for other writers in mass communication, even when presenting your side of the story, because you are legally accountable for false information. You simply can't afford to take the word of any one person as "the truth." You should always insist on documentation and then cross-check the documentation just to be safe.

Probe with questions such as these: Who says this is true? What documentation is available? Where is the evidence? Is there outside authority to substantiate this? What is the experience within the industry? Can I test this myself? What does other research suggest might be the case? What is my instinctive reaction to the credibility of each source? Just remember that the only dumb question is the one not asked.

Answers Prompt Questions

When you begin researching secondary and primary sources, you'll discover that answers to your questions suggest more questions. These questions become an agenda for future research. The point is that, if you expect to make it in PR, you'll need to dedicate yourself to being a good researcher who is always pursuing new questions.

A good model is to use FGIs to frame questions for a survey, prepare the questionnaire and test it, launch the survey and tabulate the results, then use post-survey FGIs to gain insight into why questions were answered the way they were.

Fact Sheets—Basic PR Tools

A good bit of research is internal—finding facts about your organization and its activities. Standard fact sheets present the fundamental facts about the organization. These should be readily available, either on a single sheet or in folder form. You also need a historical fact sheet covering landmarks in the organization's development. Special-event fact sheets not only tell others what's going on, they'll help you preserve your sanity.

A special event is one of the most common activities PR people get involved with. Such events are held for various purposes, such as to raise money or just to draw media attention (the so-called media event). Whatever the purpose of the special event, the first thing to do when you're faced with one is to prepare a fact sheet.

The fact sheet should contain a description of all activities, plus the day, date, time and duration of each activity and the name of the person responsible for each. Give each person's title (in relation to the event) too. Once you have drafted the timetable, add all the background: where and when the event will be held; charges (if any); sponsors; and your name, plus all the places and phone numbers where you can be reached. Your fact sheet will then be essentially complete.

On a separate page, you might want to add a brief history of the event, giving dates and milestones, as another basic element in your media kit. (Chapter 15 discusses media kits.) To update a fact sheet on a pro-am (professional-amateur) benefit, you might add a single sheet describing past benefits, naming participants and stating who won, what their scores were, how many dollars were raised, who benefited, who the sponsors were and where previous benefits were held (if different from the current location).

Conclusions

- Computer accessible data is easier to use but can be less reliable, depending on its origin.
- Public relations planning generally succeeds in direct proportion to the quality of the information on which it is built.
- Research is vital to the public relations writer.
- The focus of research for the public relations writer is on applicable internal and external policy, relevant background material, appropriate publics, methods of message presentation, the most effective media for delivering the message and evaluation of program success.
- Research information must be stored in such a way that it can be easily accessed, updated and used.
- The most common sources of secondary information include Internet sites, libraries, reference works, bibliographies, periodicals, databases and government records.
- A principal use for focus group interviews is to help identify words and phrases used commonly by a target public regarding a topic.
- An FGI can give insights into a situation but results from it can't be generalized to a target public.
- Primary information is developed mostly through interviews and questionnaires. To get information by these means, you must prepare yourself carefully to ask good questions of the right people under the right circumstances.
- Gathering information is not enough. The data you collect has to be cross-checked and verified before you can base decisions on the data. Be skeptical.
- It is in the nature of research that answers to questions prompt still more questions.
- You can secure a place in public relations by becoming a skilled researcher.
- Communication audits are used to evaluate how well information flows within an organization. A great deal of emphasis is on credibility.
- Communication audits use a full range of research techniques to get answers to questions.

- Employees sometimes tell researchers what they think they want to hear rather than what they really think.
- Although it is not yet common in public relations research, virtual reality offers exciting prospects for the future.
- A good bit of your fact-finding is internal. Much of an organization's basic internal information is produced in fact sheets.
- Fact sheets for organizations are of two types: functional and historical. The functional ones may be organizational or devoted to special events.
- Fact sheets should always be included in media kits but are also used with other publics such as investors, donors, volunteers and supporters.

Exercises

1. Locate 10 Web sites for reliable reference material.
2. Compile a bibliography of at least 10 publications whose primary emphasis is on public relations.
3. Develop a bibliography of at least 10 reference sources on manufacturing in your state.
4. Analyze the bias in the following questions. Rewrite them as necessary to eliminate bias.

   a. What did you like about the product you just tried?
   b. How good a job do you believe the President is doing?
   c. Do you believe that jogging does serious damage to the bone structures of the foot and joint?

5. Do research for and draft a questionnaire that probes the attitudes of the target audience toward physical fitness. The target audience is young men and women, ages 21–35, upwardly mobile in their professions, most with college degrees or some college, living in metropolitan areas. They lead very active social lives, but their careers are generally stressful.

Use InfoTrac College Edition to access information on topics in this chapter from hundreds of periodicals and scholarly journals.

Notes

1. U.S. Department of State, "September 11 One Year Later, A Selected Chronology of Key Events, September 11, 2001–Present," Compiled by the Office of International Information Programs, September 11, 2001, http://usinfo.state.gov/journals/itgic/0902/ijge/gjchron.htm (February 10, 2003: Washington, D.C.).
2. "Prelude to September 11, 2001, A Decade of Terrorist Attacks," United States Senate Republican Policy Committee, October 2, 2001, http://www.senate.gov/~rpc/releases/1999/fr100201.htm (March 12, 2003: Washington, D.C.).
3. Kai Frithjof Brand-Jacobsen, "September 11," The Coalition for Global Solidarity and Social Development, December 19, 2001, http://www.globalsolidarity.org/articles/kaj_sept11.html (March 12, 2003: New York, N.Y.).

4. "PR Needs Its Own Research Modes, Not Borrowed Ones," *pr reporter* (January 4, 1993): 1–2.

Selected Bibliography

Earl Babbie, *The Practice of Social Research,* 10th ed. (Belmont, Calif.: Wadsworth, 2004).

Leslie A. Baxter, *The Basics of Communication Research* (Belmont, Calif.: Wadsworth, 2004).

Glen M. Broom and David M. Dozier, *Using Research in Public Relations: Applications to Program Management,* 2d ed. (Englewood Cliffs, N.J.: Prentice Hall, 1990).

Sheldon R. Gawiser and G. Evans Witt, *A Journalist's Guide to Public Opinion Polls* (Westport, Conn.: Praeger, 1994).

Jerry A. Hendrix, Public Relations Cases, 6th ed. (Belmont, Calif.: Wadsworth, 2004).

John E. Hocking, et al., *Communication Research,* 3d ed. (Boston, Mass.: Allyn & Bacon, 2002).

Kenneth F. Kister, *Best Encyclopedias: A Guide to the Best Specialized Encyclopedias,* 2d ed. (Phoenix: Oryx Press, 1994).

Mary McGuire, Linda Stilborne, Melinda McAdams and Laurel Hyatt, *The Internet Handbook for Writers, Researchers, and Journalists,* 2002–2003 ed. (New York: Guilford Press, 2002).

Rebecca B. Rubin, Alan M. Rubin and Linda Piele, *Communication Research: Strategies and Sources,* 5th ed. (Belmont, Calif.: Wadsworth, 2000).

Michael B. Salwen and Don W. Stacks, eds., *An Integrated Approach to Communication Theory and Research* (Mahwah, N.J.: Lawrence Erlbaum Associates, 1996).

Don Stacks, *Primer of Public Relations Research* (New York: Guilford Press, 2002).

Thomas D. Stewart, *Principles of Research in Communication* (Boston, Mass.: Allyn & Bacon, 2002).

Frederick Williams and Peter Monge, *Reasoning with Statistics,* 5th ed. (New York: Harcourt College Publishers, 2002).

Roger D. Wimmer and Joseph D. Dominick, *Mass Media Research: An Introduction,* 7th ed. (Belmont, Calif.: Wadsworth, 2003).

PART 2

Writing Principles

Remember that all readers, listeners and viewers of PR writing are volunteers! Make their experience rewarding.

CHAPTER FIVE

Writing to Clarify and Simplify the Complex: Style and Content

Public relations writers seldom prepare materials that are required reading, listening or viewing. Occasionally, as a PR writer, you may prepare a handbook or manual or training video that eventually is required consumption for some audience. That's rare. Most publics you do research and write for are volunteers. You have a great deal of competition too, at all levels. You have to compete for attention with all kinds of compelling messages. When you are trying to get messages into the media, over which you and your organization have no control, you have to compete with materials prepared by skillful staff writers and freelance sources from all over the world. That means you have to be a very good writer, offering excellent information in an extraordinarily interesting way.

Most important, you need to remember that good writing is writing that succeeds in communicating. Bad writing is writing that fails to communicate.

Writer and teacher of writing at Yale, William Zinsser, says that every successful piece of nonfiction should leave the reader with one provocative thought not previously held. Not two thoughts or five, just one.[1] But all the advice in all the books about writing is worthless if you don't learn the most important point first: *Write so people will understand what you mean.* That is the one provocative thought you should take with you from this chapter. To do that you must consider both style and content.

You won't be very successful in communicating if you simply enter words into a computer without giving them much thought beforehand, or if you are more concerned with displaying your vocabulary than with communicating with your readers. You have to think about who your readers or listeners are. What do they know? What do they think they know? You can't get by with just telling them what you want to in the words you choose. Furthermore, much of what you write is expected to have a specific effect. PR writing is results-oriented, and it is a craft that must be learned and practiced.

How do you produce prose that succeeds in communicating? There is no magic formula, but you start with the basics—message, public, medium. Then be sure the message, however complex, is simplified.

Message, Public, Medium

An important part of good writing is being properly prepared before you start. You must do the necessary research on the subject matter so you will understand the material, know what is important and have in mind just what you want to communicate and what results you want. You must also know who will receive your communication and how best to reach them. In short, you must know your message, your public and your medium.

Message

Most writing, whether for public relations purposes or otherwise, has one goal: to convey a message. The goal of any writer is to transfer thoughts to other people's minds, whatever the medium. Step one, then, is deciding just what you want to say. If you don't understand what you're trying to say, neither will others.

This means you must know exactly what you are trying to say. Don't express your message in hazy, abstract terms. Make sure you understand the message before you begin to write. If you can't write a short, simple sentence that summarizes the point you want to make, you probably need to do a little more thinking. Remember: What do you want to happen as a result of your communication effort?

Public

It is not enough, however, for you to understand your message. You must phrase it so the public will also understand. You must know who your readers or listeners are (see the discussion of priority publics in Chapter 1), and you must know something of their characteristics, values and beliefs so you can reach them (see the discussion of demographics and psychographics in Chapter 4). Otherwise, you won't be able to communicate effectively. In short, you must tailor your message to the public.

Medium

An important part of tailoring your message consists of choosing the right medium to reach that public. In addition, different media are appropriate for different types of messages. Choosing the right medium is an important aspect of successful communication. (See Chapter 1.)

The choice of medium in turn affects the way you should frame the message. Articles written for magazines are done in an entirely different style than public service announcements for radio. You must use the style appropriate for the medium, being aware of the medium's technological advantages and limitations.

These three rules—know your message, know your public and know your medium—will take you a long way toward successful writing. Both the substance and the style of what you write depend on them.

These rules, however, apply only to the planning stages of writing. Even if you know your message, your public and your medium, your writing may fail. The execution is just as important as the preparation. So add three other rules for successful execution: Write clearly, make what you write interesting and simplify the complex to make information easily accessible.

Style

Clarity, of course, is the number one aim of writing style. If your public doesn't understand what you've written, your efforts will have been wasted. But even if your writing is clear, a dull style can put your readers to sleep, and your message still won't get across.

Readability/Listenability

Given a strong enough motivation, a person will "plow through any complexity of words, signs or hieroglyphs," says readability expert Robert Gunning.[2] That's true. Someone intensely interested in a subject will read through the worst writing trying to glean the slightest bit of new information. Usually, though, interest is not that high. People bombarded from all sides with innumerable public relations messages from different communicators are likely to ignore any messages that demand too much time or effort.

Although the desire to understand may be strong, the ability to understand may be inadequate. In the USA 20 percent of the population read at or below the fifth-grade level and another 27 percent have reading challenges. These challenges may stem from medical problems, such as dyslexia, from a lack of educational opportunities or from having English as a second language.[3]

What qualities make writing "easy to read"? This question has been the subject of a vast amount of research, finally focusing on two key qualities: sentence length and word length.

Sentence Length   The first principle of readable writing is to keep most sentences short. For the meaning to be clear, the reader must be able to grasp at once the relationship among the words in a sentence. Long, tangled sentences tend to obscure those relationships.

Of course, not every sentence should be short. An endless stream of short sentences makes for dull reading. And it is possible for long sentences to be clear—if they are properly constructed.

The key to readability, then, is average sentence length. An occasional long sentence is no problem. But a never-ending series of long sentences leaves readers dizzy. According to Gunning, modern prose read by the public has an average sentence length of about 16 words.[4] If your sentences are much longer than that on the average, your prose probably isn't as readable as it should be.

There are two major reasons why sentences are too long. One is that writers tend to connect independent clauses with coordinating conjunctions or add details that could be left for later sentences. The other is that too many unnecessary words are present. The cures are easy: Use more periods and fewer words.

Some long sentences, for example, can simply be cut in two with a period at the right spot. Avoid connectives like *however.* Use a period and start a new sentence. Look at this example:

> The Registrar's office said graduating seniors would be given priority in signing up for classes that have limited enrollments; however, all seniors needing to take advantage of this opportunity must come to registration with a letter from their adviser that documents the number of hours needed to graduate.

A period after *enrollments* forces a reworking of the next part to:

> When registering, those seniors must bring an adviser's letter listing the number of hours and courses needed for graduation.

A sentence of 48 words becomes two, each 19 words long. See if you can make them the more desirable 16 words each.

Excessive words in much writing result from temptations to overwrite—overusing modifiers, especially words that intensify and may be redundant. Some modifiers are so trite they are meaningless, such as *spectacular* or *amazing.* Some are redundant, like *dog puppies* or *young children.* The fewer words, the stronger the statement.

> The Provost said he never in his 10 years at the university ever had witnessed such a debacle, and he was surprised and shocked by the students' outrageous and destructive behavior at the game, although he realized it was not all students, just a disruptive few.

It is better to say, "The Provost said the students' outrageous and destructive behavior at the game shocked him."

The original sentence would have been worse if the attribution had not been clear. Much writing is made murky by needless attribution. Introductions and personal commentary also inflate, and commentary is not welcomed in news releases. These writing flaws are quite common in what is euphemistically called "business writing."

An example is: "Structural integrity has been found to be difficult to measure." All you need is: "Structural integrity is difficult to measure." If the statement is something that needs documenting, cite a source, don't write around it.

Weak information also causes protracted introductions. Another cause may simply be a lack of focus. People are in a hurry and if you want on their agenda, you have to earn the right with a clean, clear appeal.

> It is important for students to listen to the news media in the winter and know that the University will be officially closed on severe weather days.

Try this: "University closings on bad weather days will be announced on radio and television."

The personal commentary problem is so common in letters that one of the authors forbids students from using *I* to begin any sentence in a cover letter, memo or media advisory. The reason? People are likely to intuitively respond with "Who cares?" Of course few are rude enough to express it, but the reaction is there. It disengages the reader, whereas a *you* involves the reader.

Keeping sentences short is just the starting place in writing clearly, though. Short sentences won't make reading easy if the words within those sentences don't make sense. You can't write clear sentences if you don't use clear words.

Word Length   A student with an exceptional vocabulary once turned in what he thought was an especially well-written paper. The professor's comment scribbled across the top of the paper was simply: "Avoid sesquipedalianism." Because the student's vocabulary wasn't *that* large, he scurried to a dictionary to look up *sesquipedalianism.* He found it to mean the excessive use of long words.

The professor could easily have written, "Don't use so many long words," and the student would have understood immediately. The point for public relations writers is twofold. First, if you use long words, some readers won't understand them. Second, even if the long words you use have well-known meanings, they slow the reader down.

There is no need to say *precipitation* when you mean *rain.* There is nothing wrong with saying *use* instead of *employ* or *utilize. Fair* is just as good a word as *equitable.*

Some writers can't resist filling their prose with important-sounding phrases like "integrated conceptual analysis" or similar verbose nonsense. At least twice in every sentence they use words ending in *-ment, -any, -ial, -ization, -action* and *-ability.* Avoid such words when you can. They make reading more difficult and diminish the forcefulness of your statement. As public relations writer Alden S. Wood asks, who would have responded to these words?

> Retain your earth! Abstain from engagement in interpersonal ballistic relationships unless these relationships are initiated by the power incumbents. If, however, it becomes apparent that overt hostile interaction is to commence, let this commencement have its genesis in this geopolitical region.

The average sentence length in this paragraph is less than 14 words. But the words are so foggy that the meaning is completely lost. Fortunately, Captain John Parker didn't talk like that. Instead he uttered the famous command, "Stand your ground. Don't fire unless fired upon. But if they mean to have a war, let it begin here."

Why do long words make reading more difficult? One reason is that long words tend to be abstract. Readers comprehend more quickly if words are concrete—that is, if they evoke visual images and avoid ambiguity. If an oil company says it's spending money on "petroleum exploration facilities," for example, the average reader won't have a very clear notion of what the company is buying. They will, however, if the company says "drilling rigs."

Long words are often unfamiliar to readers. Common words, which readers recognize immediately, are usually short. Why say *remuneration* when *pay* will do?

Readability Formulas   Short sentences and short words are the prime ingredients of clear writing. These ideas have been incorporated into various formulas to gauge the readability of a piece of writing. (See Appendix A.) Such formulas—notably those devised by Gunning and Flesch—can be very useful to writers who want to check the clarity of their prose. Readability is much easier to check now that most word processing software comes with readability formulas. Everything from the technical writing of industry to the often-obscure prose of accounting is now being measured for clarity by using readability formulas. This shift toward plain language almost demands that writers measure their writing for level of comprehension. Keep in mind, though, that a high readability score doesn't guarantee good writing. Readability formulas are actually nothing more than measures of structural simplicity, and as Gunning points out, "nonsense written simply is still nonsense."[5]

Besides, clarity may be the first goal of writing, but it's not the only one. Clear writing can be stilted and unnatural. Writing can be so simple that it's just plain boring. Clarity is worthless if the writing isn't also interesting, because writing that isn't interesting usually isn't read.

What makes writing interesting? Primarily, the subject matter. Some subjects are interesting to some people but not to others (which is why you should know your public).

Here, though, we're concerned with style. The basic goals of style are, in addition to clarity, the logical development of ideas and a smooth transition from one idea to the next. Of course, style must also help maintain the reader's interest. Writing must be lively, with generous use of active verbs and vivid phrases. Interesting writing sounds natural, is not monotonous and, in general, is "pleasing to the ear." Interesting writing uses personal words such as *you* and *people* to enhance human interest. Thus besides the fundamental goal of clarity, good writers strive for naturalness, variety, euphony and human interest.

Naturalness

Reading is easiest if the style is conversational. Readability experts agree that one of the basic rules of readable writing is "write like you talk." Of course, you can't write exactly like you talk. There is a difference between written and spoken language. Spoken sentences are not carefully structured, and they often contain much repetition. In speaking, meaning can be shaded by intonation, inflection, facial expressions and gestures. You can't duplicate such features of the spoken language in your writing. But you can write prose that sounds natural, as though someone could have spoken it.

The following sentence, for example, is clear, but it sounds like a written, not a spoken, sentence:

> Smith was not disturbed that Johnson had submitted his resignation. He said that the position held by Johnson was not of high significance.

The same thing could have been written in a more natural, conversational manner:

> Johnson's resignation didn't bother Smith. He said Johnson's job wasn't important, anyway.

A good test of naturalness is to read aloud what you've written. If you stumble over phrases and your tongue gets twisted, the sentence is not easy enough to read. Try again. If you still have trouble writing sentences that sound natural, try this approach. Write what you want to say as you would say it in conversation. Then go back and rewrite the sentence with proper syntax, making sure the pronouns are in the right place and the meaning is clear. Part of making writing conversational is using active, not passive, verbs.

Notice the improvement that results when we substitute the active voice for the passive in the following sentences:

Passive: Everything possible was done by company engineers to restore service.
Active: Company engineers did everything they could to restore service.
Passive: It was requested by the company president that the exhibit be kept open by the museum officials.
Active: The company president asked museum officials to keep the exhibit open.

Another device that helps writing sound natural is the contraction. Use contractions freely. Everybody uses contractions in speech, and no matter what your grammar-school teacher told you, there is absolutely nothing wrong with using them in writing. You suffer no loss of meaning when you use *don't, won't* or *can't* instead of *do not, will not* or *cannot.* Avoiding contractions does nothing but slow the reader down, and readers don't like to be slowed down.

Variety

Monotony can poison an otherwise good style. You haven't gained anything by stringing clear and natural-sounding sentences together if their structure and vocabulary are so similar that readers get bored. You enrich meaning and help comprehension when you search for different words. Refreshingly new words help the pace too. The style must push readers along and keep them going. Readers shouldn't feel they have to force themselves through sentence after sentence.

Variety means following the rules wisely. For example, we already mentioned that not all sentences need to be short. True, a series of long sentences makes it hard for a reader to follow the flow. And it's easy to get lost in a maze of adverbial and prepositional phrases. But an occasional long sentence, if constructed properly, can improve the flow of the narrative. A compound sentence can take the reader from one idea to the next. An occasional inversion of subject and verb reduces monotony and can emphasize the action in the sentence. You need to be cautious with this technique, however, to avoid altering meaning.

Many writers, although aware of the need for judicious variety in sentence structure, still go too far in trying to achieve variety in word choice. This leads to the use of three or four words to describe the same thing. For example,

> When my books arrived, I took the hardbound texts from the package and placed the treasured volumes on my bookcase next to my other bound publications.

Usage experts call this pitfall "elegant variation." "There are few literary faults so widely prevalent," says one expert.[6] No doubt the problem stems from the widespread belief that you should never use the same word twice in one sentence. But no such prohibition exists in any rule book, and a single repetition is seldom as terrible as some writers think. Of course, repeating the same word several times can get boring. But you don't have to thumb through a thesaurus to find a synonym. And often a pronoun works well enough: "I took the books out of the box and put them on the shelf with my others."

In other cases, there's no need to repeat the word at all: "Jones, Smith and Brown all won races; it was Jones' first win, Smith's third victory, and Brown's fourth triumph." But the vocabulary lesson is unnecessary. It's just as clear to say, "It was Jones' first win, Smith's third and Brown's fourth."

If there's no way to get around repetition, go ahead and use the same word again. It won't hurt you. And the reader won't have to figure out whether you used different words because of some real difference or because you were trying to avoid repetition at all costs or, worse, trying to show off your vocabulary.

As for the thesaurus, don't throw it away. But use it only when you are looking for a specific word, the exactly right word, which you know but just can't think of at the moment. It is rarely wise to pick a word you've never heard of or used before. Always check a dictionary to make sure the word you choose is appropriate.

Euphony

The main reason so many writers worry about sentence uniformity and word repetition is that they want to achieve euphony in their writing. Indeed, writing that is rhythmic and makes proper use of figures of speech is usually more enjoyable to read than straightforward stilted prose.

The only way to achieve euphony is to read good writing and develop an ear for it. If you discover a good style that is used successfully by someone else, don't worry about copying it. Just don't get carried away. As one observer puts it, a "concatenation of mellifluous phrases may indicate more polish than insight."[7] First make sure your thoughts are clear and your message is pleasing to the mind. Then worry about pleasing the ear.

Human Interest

If you are writing about people, your writing will naturally contain elements of human interest. But if your subject is something mechanical, impersonal or abstract, your task will be more difficult. How can you achieve human interest when writing about inanimate objects? The trick is to remember that you're writing *to* people even when you're not writing *about* them. When appropriate, address the reader as *you.* Use the pronoun *we* to refer to people in general when discussing common knowledge, as in, "We know today that the world is round." Rhetorical questions and direct quotations help give writing a personal sound. If you don't find any and you never use *we* or *you,* your prose isn't likely to be very interesting.

Trite Expressions

"The performance *highlights* . . . ," "The series *features* . . ." and similar noun-into-verb conversions are trite. News releases burdened with such creaking turns of phrase as "colorful scenery," "dramatic new move" and "spearheading the effort" deserve their usual fate—a quick trip to the trash. Clichés make your copy seem old because the words are so familiar. Public relations writing demands freshness and vitality. But don't try to freshen a cliché. And don't try to be coy by putting it in quotes—as though you really know better but are speaking colloquially—as that just calls attention to its triteness. Simply avoid using expressions you constantly hear or read.

Eliminating Bias

A writer's word choice can be unintentionally disparaging. A careless construction can offend people with disabilities, members of ethnic groups, people in certain age groups—especially the very young and the very old—or women. Using gender-neutral language should become routine for you. Avoid expressions like business*men,* which excludes businesswomen. Use *people in business* or be specific: *merchants, retailers* and so on. Avoid using the masculine pronoun in a generic sense. Either use a noun or use the nongeneric plural pronoun (they, them, their). Gender-neutral language is much more common now as state constitutions have adopted changes as have most businesses.

You need to watch titles too. Don't make assumptions about gender in addressing a letter. Be sure your professor has an earned doctorate before using Dr., but if she or he has a Ph.D., use it. Some students inappropriately use Dr. for all male instructors and Mrs. for all female instructors. More than one student has been castigated by a female professor for using a social title in an instructional setting. Some male instructors without a doctorate are embarrassed when students use Dr. to address them.

Don't mention ethnicity or disabilities unless they are important to content. Be careful not to use stereotypes in language or art. Active seniors are offended by rocking-chair representations of their age group, and children resent being portrayed as miniature, but imbecile, adults.

Edit your copy mercilessly. You can do this better if you put it away for a day and go back to it. Get others to read it and offer critiques. The checklist in Table 5.1 provides a guide for assessing drafts of writing.

Content: Simplifying the Complex

The need for clear and simple writing has never been greater. With email messages flashing through cyberspace and faxes going around the world, your prose will be translated and interpreted in the idiom of another culture, another experience.

If you always remember to use simple language, you'll be able to write clearly about even the most complex ideas. That is important because the world has become exceedingly complex.

In his first paper on the theory of relativity, written in 1905, Albert Einstein penned one of the simplest sentences you'll ever find in a scientific paper. In explaining a point about time and simultaneity, Einstein wrote (in English translation):

> If, for instance, I say, "That train arrives here at 7 o'clock," I mean something like this: "The pointing of the small hand of my watch to 7 and the arrival of the train are simultaneous events."[8]

You can't get much simpler than that.

Einstein treasured simplicity in writing, and though his scientific papers did get technical in places, his public writings were always clear and readable. Einstein could write simply on subjects like relativity because he understood them so completely himself. He could write clearly, without too many technical terms, because he knew his subject well enough to express the ideas in plain language and retain absolute accuracy.

Public relations writers are not likely to be as knowledgeable about any subject as Einstein was about physics. Yet they are still called on to translate complex subjects into understandable language. There is nothing simple about nuclear power, pollution chemistry or petroleum economics. Medicine, urban affairs and social services can be as complex as advanced calculus. Yet such issues are becoming more and more important to the average citizen. Public relations people must be able to explain the implications of government and corporate actions in these areas, as well as to interpret the latest research findings. It's advisable to have authorities check the final drafts to be sure your translations are accurate. It takes special writing skills to simplify the complex without explaining it inaccurately.

Some authorities think it's impossible to explain complex things like scientific research to the general public. Even Rudolf Flesch, the ultimate advocate of simplifying the complex, advises writers not to try to give complete scientific explanations. You can describe the mean-

T A B L E   5 . 1   *Writing Checklist*

1. Is the message clear? Have you said exactly what you want to say?

2. Have you identified important publics? Does your writing speak to those publics?

3. Is the style of writing appropriate for the intended medium?

4. Are your sentences instantly clear? Are they free from confusing constructions?

5. Are sentences, on average, fairly short? Have you avoided stringing long sentences together?

6. Is your writing concise and free from needless words?

7. Have you used common, concrete words that evoke visual images?

8. Is your language natural? Can your writing be easily read aloud?

9. Is the sentence structure varied?

10. Are most sentences in the active voice?

11. Have you made sufficient use of personal words and sentences?

12. Have you substituted creative language for trite expressions?

13. Is your writing free from bias?

14. Is this your best effort?

ing of a discovery, he says, and indicate its importance. But a complete scientific explanation? Flesch wouldn't even try that with his own readability formula:

> Here I would have to get into statistical regression formulas and multiple correlation and whatnot, and nobody who hasn't had a course in statistics would know what I am talking about. . . . There is only one bit of advice I can offer in this business of giving laymen an exact scientific explanation: don't try.[9]

Not everybody agrees with this attitude. William Zinsser says, "a complex subject can be made as accessible to the layman as a simple subject. It's just a question of putting one sentence after another."[10]

In practice, explaining subtle scientific principles to nonscientists isn't often of much use—not because lay readers can't understand, but because most aren't really interested. If a reader is interested in a subject, however, a good writer can explain it. You can even explain statistics to people who haven't had statistics courses, if they are interested enough to follow what might be a fairly lengthy explanation.

Today, in many cases, people aren't merely interested in scientific explanations. They demand them. If your company is building a chemical plant near a town, you'd better be able to explain to the people who live there what that plant will do and how its safety systems will work. You won't get by with saying, "Don't worry—it's safe."

Conflicting scientific advice also gets into the public agenda, leaving people confused about what to believe or to do. With people increasingly concerned about health issues, in 1998 the Harvard School of Public Health and the International Food Information Council Foundation convened an advisory group of experts. Later this was broadened to include nutrition researchers, food scientists, journal editors, university media relations officers, broadcast and print reporters, consumer groups and food industry executives. The result was a set of guidelines to provide a context in which people can evaluate information.[11]

Another solution is to use the same system both internally and externally to develop a document called a position paper. (See Chapter 8.) Such documents should be developed with input from legal, marketing, customer service, operations, public relations and public affairs and consideration of opposing points of view from activist groups and competitors. Position papers then provide a launching pad for all public statements on an issue about a product, service or project.

And if the public doesn't ask technical questions directly, newspaper reporters and electronic journalists will. Today, the mass media deal with more technical subjects in greater detail than ever before. When reporters working on such stories don't understand something themselves, they often go to PR people for explanations. PR writers, frequently trained only in journalism or English and not in the technical fields they must try to interpret, often find themselves at a loss. When an activist group accuses your company of cheating on taxes, how do you explain the complexities of accelerated depreciation and the investment tax credit? How does the public relations person for a factory suspected of polluting the air explain the difference between primary ambient air standards and secondary emission limits? How does the spokesperson for a nuclear plant explain the meaning of "10 picocuries of radioactivity"?

It isn't easy, but these things can be explained. You can simplify the complex, and you can simplify it accurately—but only if, like Einstein, you know your subject.

Know Your Subject

There is an old saying among newspaper editors that a good reporter can cover any story. If the reporter doesn't know much about the subject, he or she can simply call an expert, ask a few questions and then explain it all to readers in words they'll understand. Or so the theory goes.

This adage may have been true once, but it isn't anymore. And it's no truer for PR writers than for reporters. Nevertheless, pamphlets on complex subjects are often written this way. An engineer produces a technical description of some process or machine in words specific to the profession. The copy is given to the PR person, who edits and rewrites to simplify the language but keep the facts as the engineer wrote them. In theory the PR person need know nothing about the subject; the engineer provides the facts. The PR writer just needs to know how to write clearly.

The problem is that you can't simplify complex writing unless you know what it means. You must understand it thoroughly yourself before you can explain it to somebody else. You must know more about the subject than you'll ever put into print. If you don't, you won't be able to tell when a simplified statement can stand alone or should be qualified. And you won't know the difference between a correct statement and a false one.

Consider this example from a writer trying to describe the dangers of cigarettes in simple terms:

> Opening another front in its war on smoking, the federal government plans to publicize a new peril—carbon monoxide—to prod the cigarette industry to reduce its use of that substance in cigarettes just as it has reduced tar and nicotine.

This sentence is simple enough, but also sheer nonsense. Carbon monoxide is not a substance that exists inside tobacco, waiting to be unleashed. It is a gas created when carbon (in the tobacco) combines with oxygen (from the air) as tobacco burns. The writer simply didn't

PORTERFIELD   **BY JOE MARTIN**

Source: Porterfield. Reprinted with permission of Neatly Chiseled Features.

know much about the subject. The sentence is also nonsense because carbon monoxide is not a "new peril." It's neither new in the sense of being a new phenomenon associated with burning cigarettes nor is it new in the sense of being recently identified as a health hazard by scientific evidence. "Hyping" a story, often with carelessly chosen adjectives, damages credibility.

The same is true of the reporter who attempted to describe nuclear fast breeder reactors:

> The fast breeder gets its name . . . because the chain reaction is so much faster than in conventional . . . reactors.

Again, this is a readable simplification of a complex idea. It's also an incorrect simplification. The *fast* in "fast breeder" doesn't refer to the rate of the chain reaction (which would be measured by the number of atoms splitting per second), but to the speed of neutrons—small subatomic particles that fly around inside reactors and split atoms. In ordinary nuclear power plants, atoms are split mostly by slow neutrons; in fast breeders, speedy neutrons do most of the splitting.

How can you avoid making such mistakes? You simply must research your subject thoroughly before you begin writing. Get help from experts on points you don't understand. Recheck any passage containing statements you're not absolutely sure of.

Finally, don't try to tell readers everything you know. That always takes you to fringe areas, where your knowledge gets a little shaky and errors begin to creep in. Statements perfectly consistent with what you know might be inconsistent with what you *don't* know. Besides, if you tell the readers everything *you* know, you're probably telling them a lot more than *they* want or need to know. Give readers just what they need to get the message.

For example, if you wished to continue the story of carbon monoxide in cigarette smoke, you might be tempted to write something like this:

Carbon monoxide, a molecule that consists of a carbon atom bonded to an oxygen atom, is dangerous because of its chemical affinity with hemoglobin. Hemoglobin, a complex chemical substance containing iron, serves as a transport mechanism for oxygen in the bloodstream. Because the affinity of carbon monoxide with hemoglobin is greater than the affinity of oxygen with hemoglobin, carbon monoxide impairs the ability of hemoglobin to carry oxygen.

This explanation, while essentially accurate, is too long. Unless you're writing for medical students or biochemists, just say that carbon monoxide impairs the ability of the blood to carry oxygen throughout the body. *You* should know all about hemoglobin and oxygen transport. But you don't need to tell everybody about it. The more you know about a subject, the easier it will be to simplify, and the less likely you will be to make mistakes.

There is one danger, though, in knowing a lot about a subject. When you have written on the subject for a while, you may find yourself using the jargon of the discipline. This is the fatal flaw in most writing on technical subject matter. If you want the audience to understand what you write, avoid using technical terms. Instead, follow the golden rule of simplifying the complex: Use plain English.

Use Plain English

Most people know plain English when they hear it. It is everyday language, free from the long words and technical terms that plague the prose of scientists, engineers, economists, doctors, lawyers and writers in other specialized disciplines. All professions and trades have special vocabularies that members use when they communicate among themselves. Unfortunately, some members use the same words—the jargon of the field—when they try to communicate with people *outside* the discipline. It doesn't work. To write plain English, you must avoid

© Lynn Johnston Productions, Inc. Distributed by United Feature Syndicate, Inc.

Source: Dilbert. Reprinted by permission of United Feature Syndicate, Inc.

using words with "insider meanings." It is especially wrong to use such language in a calculated effort to mislead your readers. That is unethical.

Semanticists refer to misleading language as *doublespeak.* There are at least four kinds, according to William Lutz: euphemism, jargon, gobbledygook (or bureaucratese) and inflated language.[12] In some cases, doublespeak fails to communicate simply because it is confusing or vague. In other cases, it is deliberately misleading, and therefore unethical and irresponsible. Misunderstanding may occur, but without serious consequences, with jargon and inflated language. Intentional deception is often the motive underlying gobbledygook and euphemism.

Avoid Doublespeak   Euphemisms may mislead deliberately, like the U.S. State Department's decision in 1984 to use "unlawful or arbitrary deprivation of life" instead of "killing" in its annual reports on the status of human rights around the world. Some euphemisms are just foolish, such as calling garbage collectors "sanitary engineers." Some euphemisms may be considered useful, to protect sensitivities or to respect cultural taboos.

Within any profession, jargon has its uses. A jargon term may stand for a complicated concept that would take paragraphs to describe in full. Once members of a profession agree on such a term, they can use it freely, because everyone within the discipline knows what it means. But to people not trained in the field it sounds like gobbledygook. (See Figure 5.1.)

Mind your FDDFSs and ACCs

HONGKONG — If the opening of Hongkong's new airport at Chek Lap Kok was a headache, then reading the official inquiry report is daunting.

The 702-page tome released yesterday was awash in acronyms.

The report used short forms of better-known companies, but also spewed out impossible gobbledygook like H0.KIA-ASP, AMFSRC and FDDFS.

Try this.

Referring to a passenger who had a heart attack and was not taken fast enough to hospital, the commission said steps were being taken to improve efficiency.

"AA and FSD are arranging a direct line to be installed between FSCC and ACC so that, in future, requests for ACC escort vehicle do not have to go through AMFSRC," it said.

— REUTERS

FIGURE 5.1

This warning about the use of abbreviations illustrates how readers not "in the know" can be left uninformed and confused.
From *The Straits Times*, Singapore, January 23, 1999, p. 28. Reprinted with permission from Reuters.

Writers must also recognize another type of jargon that may cause problems—common words that have special meanings to the members of a given group. Printers, for example, use words like *flat* and *signature* in an entirely different way from most people. Writers must make sure that readers understand when a common word is being used with a special meaning.

The lack of understanding of special terms can be extremely dangerous too. Low literacy in understanding medical terminology or health care instructions can be fatal. Public relations practitioners working in the various health care fields have some serious challenges. Most health materials are written at the 10th-grade level or above. Furthermore, few are translated into other languages. People often are too embarrassed to admit they don't know what they are reading or don't understand the directions or consequences.[13] Pretest all messages with the intended audiences.

Inflated language consists of fancy words used for common concepts, as when members of a given group use long or obscure words instead of short familiar ones that mean the same thing. Specialists, for example, often use technical terms to sound impressive. Consider the following sentence, written by an engineer explaining some of the drawbacks of solar-electric power plants:

All solar-thermal systems must accept diurnal transients and rapid transients from cloud passage during daily operation.

He was trying to say that it gets dark at night and that clouds sometimes block the sun. The idea isn't any more complicated than that, and there's no reason to make it sound complicated.

Bureaucratese is also called *gobbledygook*. A good bit of it originates with our largest institution—the federal government. In 1981 Malcolm Baldridge, then secretary of commerce, decided to purge at least his area. He issued a memo banning certain expressions and discouraging the creation of new ones. He warned commerce staff to steer clear of "bastardized words, nouns and adjectives used as verbs, and passive verbs." Included were these miscues: finalized ("finished" is OK); impact a situation (you're on safe ground if you "control" it or "affect" it); parameters to work within ("specific limits" are acceptable); I share your concern (Who cares? You still have to say "yes" or "no").[14] For more on doublespeak, see Figures 5.2 and 5.3.

Good writers never use doublespeak when common words will do the job as well. Sometimes, though, common words won't do the job as well. If a word that has no plain English equivalent is essential to your subject, you have no choice but to use it. But make sure you explain to your readers what this new term means.

It may be that all you need to do is supply a simple definition when you introduce the word. But usually there's more to simplifying the complex than defining technical terms; in fact, dictionary definitions are frequently as confusing as the terms themselves. And your purpose is not to build the readers' vocabularies but to convey an idea. Often you can get the idea across more clearly by *describing* the new term than by defining it.

Describe, Don't Define   Assume you're writing about the use of the chemical element lithium as an agent for treating psychological depression. It seems like a good idea to begin by defining lithium. So you turn to the dictionary and find: "lithium: a soft, silver-white element of the alkali metal group. Atomic number 3, atomic weight 6.941." This is not a very useful definition. If this is all you tell your readers, they won't really know much more than they did before.

Instead, you could write, "Lithium is a silvery-white metal that is very light; in fact, it's the lightest metal known. It's also very soft and can be cut with a knife. Its name comes from the Greek word *lithos,* meaning 'stone.'" Now your readers will have a picture of lithium in their heads. You've removed some of the mystery behind the name and can go on to discuss the uses of lithium.

For the same reason, it does little good to define *kilowatt-hour* as "the amount of energy consumed when an electrical demand of one kilowatt is maintained for one hour." You're much better off if you describe a kilowatt-hour as the amount of electricity it takes to run a hand-held hair dryer for an hour, or as the energy needed to toast three loaves of bread. These are not good scientific definitions of a kilowatt-hour, but they are good descriptions—and they're much more likely to be understood.

Whether you use definitions or descriptions, though, you shouldn't introduce too many new terms. Using technical terms is a luxury to be indulged in sparingly. Don't expect a reader to assimilate several new terms at once. Of course, some writers operate on the "define and proceed" principle. This is a favorite method of textbook writers. They introduce a new

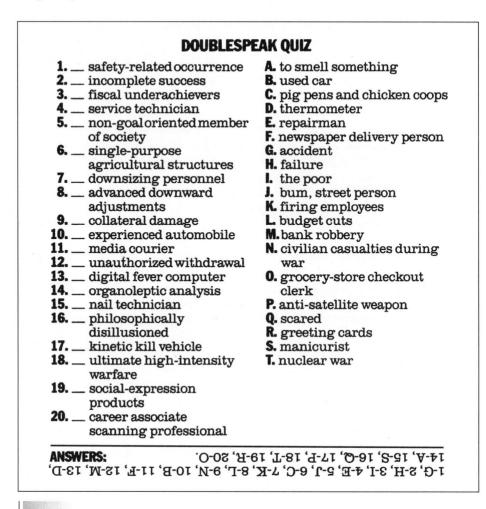

FIGURE 5.2

Doublespeak Quiz   *Test your skill at deciphering by taking this quiz. From Lloyd Shearer, "Doublespeak Quiz,"* Parade Magazine, *July 24, 1999. Reprinted by permission of the author.*

term—or five new terms or however many they need—define them and go on with the story, using the new terms freely. The unfortunate students find they must refer to the original definitions every 10 seconds or so to keep track of what they're reading.

Textbook writers don't have much choice, however, because their purpose is often to teach students the vocabulary of a new field. And this goal requires definitions. But public relations writers have a different aim: to communicate a single message. You can't do that if you introduce new terms just to educate the audience. You have to convey the main part of your message in words the audience already understands. In other words, use plain English as much as possible.

If you're writing a medical brochure about interferon, a protein substance in the body that helps to fight disease, you must use the term *interferon*. But you don't need to give your readers

If Aesop and others like him had backgrounds in drafting governmental regulations, the pithy proverbs and morals they developed might read like the ones listed below. Perhaps you are skillful enough to re-word these into their original concise forms.

1. It is undesirable for one to exhibit lachrymose tendencies when confronted by a carelessly decanted lacteal substance.

2. A lengthy verbalization concerning a given subject is less efficacious in comparison to a solitary non-verbal depiction of that subject.

3. A member of the avian family that initiates questing for helminthes prior to that same activity by others of its kind is more likely to be rewarded with success.

4. Persons with little intelligence and tendencies toward misjudgements are inclined in the direction of little-contemplated behaviors in situations in which extraterrestrial beings are hesitant to take action.

5. An antedated survey of a visual nature is recommended prior to the physical launching of one's body over a given distance or obstacle.

6. Visitations by a practitioner of the healing arts may be obviated by the expedient of diurnal ingestion of a red or yellow edible pome fruit.

7. The state of not being in attendance at a particular location gives rise to an incremental expansion of internalized emotions of affection.

8. When there exists a superfluity of preparers of viands, then the thin liquid they develop is likely to be less sapid than desired.

9. If you happen to find yourself in the capitol metropolis once inhabited by ancient Etruscans, then your activities must emulate those of indigenous personnel.

10. The one awarded the wreath of laurel in a certain athletic endeavor is not necessarily the contestant with the ability to complete the established course with the most minimal elapsement of time.

11. If the initiatory stage of one's assigned task reflects a performance of desirable quality, then the project may be considered to have a completion status of fifty percent.

12. One is more able, when employing the use of an insect-produced viscid material as contrasted with the usage of a liquid obtained by acetic fermentation of dilute alcoholic liquids, to entice and capture certain other insects.

Bureaucratic Proverbs

1. Don't cry over spilt milk.
2. One picture is worth a thousand words.
3. The early bird gets the worm.
4. Fools rush in where angels fear to tread.
5. Look before you leap.
6. An apple a day keeps the doctor away.
7. Absence makes the heart grow fonder.
8. Too many cooks spoil the broth.
9. When in Rome, do as the Romans do.
10. The race is not always to the swiftest.
11. Well begun is half done.
12. You can catch more flies with honey than with vinegar.

F I G U R E   5 . 3

Bureaucratic Proverbs

"Bureaucratic Proverbs" reprinted with permission from *Diabolical Word Puzzles* by Areff McCarty (Back Door Main Publishing, 138 South 30th Street, Camp Hill, PA 17011-4506), 2000.

Source: ETTA HULME. Reprinted with permission of *Fort Worth Star-Telegram.*

a complete lesson in biochemistry. Avoid the temptation to use words like *fibroblasts* or *lipopolysaccharides.* Even if you define these terms, using them will obscure what you're trying to say about interferon.

What if such terms are essential to the discussion? The point is, they're probably not. At least the terms themselves aren't. Fibroblasts might be important, but you can just as easily say "connective tissue cells." Describing such things without naming them will be easier for you and your readers.

Of course, you can't describe technical terms without knowing what they mean. So whenever you're writing on a specific technical subject, keep a specialized dictionary on hand. If you're writing about geology, for example, you should have a dictionary of earth science or some comparable reference work at your fingertips.

What if you replace jargon with common words where possible and do a good job of describing any necessary technical terms, and the message is still too complex for the average reader? In that case, you simply must give readers enough background so they will understand. But you have to be careful not to give too much background at once. Take one step at a time.

Take One Step at a Time

You can confuse readers by telling them too much at once. A reader can accept one new fact if you use understandable words, but don't expect to transfer several new thoughts at the same time. The reader's mind will flash "overload" and stop taking in anything. It's like blowing a fuse when you plug too many appliances into the same outlet. The brain, like an electrical circuit, can stand only so much flow.

You have to introduce one new idea at a time. And you must do so in logical order. The first idea should help explain the second, the second the third and so on.

If you start with the simplest idea and proceed one step at a time, you can eventually take the reader to a high degree of sophistication. This is Isaac Asimov's description of how he wrote a book on mathematics:

> It was about elementary arithmetic, to begin with, and it was not until the second chapter that I as much as got into Arabic numerals, and not until the fourth chapter that I got to fractions. However, by the end of the book I was talking about imaginary numbers, hyperimaginary numbers, and transfinite numbers—and that was the real purpose of the book. In going from counting to transfinites, I followed such a careful and gradual plan that it never stopped seeming easy.[15]

Using the one-step-at-a-time approach, you can eventually explain almost anything. The key is to make sure the first step is in the right place. After you've identified the main points and put them in order, look at the first point. Will your audience know what you're talking about? Naturally, that depends on the audience and their level of knowledge about the topic. Knowing where to start, though, depends on a clear definition of all steps. You must determine at the outset what the central points are. Many writers do this well enough, but somewhere between the start and the finish the central ideas get lost. Communicating the complex is bound to fail if only the writer knows what the central ideas are. Make the central points clear to the reader.

Make the Central Points Clear

Whether you're writing on a complex subject or a simple one, the objective is still the same: to convey a message. Messages must be supported with facts, figures, descriptions and explanations. You can't leave out important details. Too often, though, writers let details and descriptions obscure the message. The central point is buried in a paragraph of statistics or turns up at the end of a series of equivocal qualifying phrases. Don't lose track of your purpose. Make sure the main idea stands out.

Usually you do this by stating your main point clearly and forcefully at the outset, leaving the details for later. It is much easier for readers to follow a chain of explanations if they know the point of the story ahead of time.

If you don't make the main point clear, your audience not only won't get the message, they also won't attach much importance to what you have to say.

When you get sick, you may see a physician because you think the doctor will be familiar enough with your ailment to diagnose and treat it quickly. But if you aren't able to explain the symptoms clearly, your doctor may be stumped, at least at first. You can help your doctor if you prepare for the visit by referring to the "Family Health Manager."[16] One section of this booklet is about how to get ready for an appointment with your physician. Note in Figure 5.4 the checklist of questions you should prepare to answer for the doctor. Although these questions deal with some complex matters, they are written in plain, simple English almost anyone can understand. That is good writing because it uses familiar words to describe difficult concepts.

Preparing for a Health Care Visit

You'll get a lot more out of your visits to your primary care physician and other health care providers if you plan for them ahead of time — even if you can only manage to arrive at the doctor's office 10 or 15 minutes early, that amount of time to prepare can make a big difference. Be sure to bring your Family Health Manager; it will help you answer the doctor's questions about your own, your children's, or your family's health. And the Medical Visit Checklist will help jog your memory about things you meant to tell or ask the doctor. If you have questions or problems you would like to discuss, write them down and have the list with you during your visit. Don't forget to bring your health plan ID card, and make sure that the doctor's office staff has your correct ID number on your record.

Routine Health Care Visits

Family members usually make routine health care visits for physical examinations, immunizations, and gynecological tests such as Pap smears. Your doctor will give you advice on how often you should schedule these visits.

Nonroutine Health Care Visits

You schedule nonroutine visits when you notice a particular problem — something out of the ordinary that continues to bother you and prompts you to call your doctor. When you call your doctor with your problem, you may find yourself speaking with another health professional first. This valuable assistant to the doctor is trained to listen to your symptoms and decide whether you need to come right in to see the doctor, wait until the doctor can speak to you, or make an appointment. Try to keep the description of your problem as simple as you can, and try to explain problems in the order they occurred.

☐ What is your chief complaint? (Do you have a pain, vomiting, a fever?)

☐ When did your problem begin?

☐ What other problems do you have that relate to the chief complaint? (For example, has your sleep been disturbed or your appetite decreased?)

Use the Medical Visit Checklist as you get ready for nonroutine visits so that you will be prepared to answer the doctor's questions. He or she may need to ask for details about your life-style, including whether or not you use tobacco, alcohol, or illegal drugs. You may need to answer questions about your sexual activity. Be as honest and specific as you can because the diagnosis or treatment your doctor recommends will be affected by the information you share. Your doctor is experienced at listening sympathetically and will keep your information confidential.

FIGURE 5.4

Simplicity in Writing   *Medical terms and issues can be confusing to the average person. This checklist, however, demystifies the questions you may be asked by an attending physician.*
Source: *Your Health Care Planner*, Steven Krauss, ed. (Boston, Mass.: Madison Publishing Co., 1994). Used with permission.

Medical Visit Checklist

To prepare for a nonroutine health care visit, answer the following questions:

A. Describe the problem (chief complaint). What are the symptoms (pain, nausea, burning when you urinate)?

B. Describe the history of the problem.
1. When did the problem start?
2. What brings on the symptoms?
3. What do you think is the cause of the problem?
4. Does anything you do affect the symptoms? (For example, do antacids relieve your indigestion?)
5. Have the symptoms changed? Have they gotten worse or better?

C. If you have pain, answer these questions:
1. Where is it? Can you point to it?
2. Rate the intensity of the pain from 1 to 10.
3. Is the pain continuous or does it come and go? If it comes and goes, how long is each episode?
4. What affects the pain (motion, eating, exercise)?
5. Can you describe the pain? Is it stinging, stabbing, burning, dull, aching, or cramping?
6. Has the pain remained the same or gotten better or worse?
7. Did the pain start suddenly or come on gradually?
8. What do you think caused it?

D. Did you ever have similar pain or symptoms before?
1. When?
2. What happened?
3. Did you see a physician? When? What was the diagnosis? What tests did you have? What medications or treatment did you receive? Did they help?

E. Are you taking any prescription or over-the-counter medication for your problem? What? How much? How often?

F. Describe any medical or alternative treatment (acupuncture, massage, special diet) you are now receiving.

G. If you have seen another health care professional for your problem, be prepared to explain the tests and treatments you received.

5.4 (*continued*)

Explain the Unfamiliar with the Familiar

Readers don't easily understand complicated explanations of things they know nothing about. But if you can tie your subject to something within the reader's experience, you can skip several steps of definition and description and get right to the explanation.

Simple analogies can work wonders in getting people to understand why things are the way they are. The energy business is difficult to explain, and especially natural gas because it's usually not visible. When gas utility customers read about a British thermal unit (Btu) as a measurement for gas, it's not easy for them to visualize. The explanation in Figure 5.5 helps.

Scientific subjects especially call for explanations in familiar words. A natural science writer helped readers understand a known but seldom experienced natural phenomenon, the northern lights, in this way:

> Scientists today believe that the Aurora Borealis is caused by the "solar wind" particles interacting with the earth's geomagnetic field beyond the upper atmosphere in the area called the magneto sphere. According to Syun-Ichi Akasofu of the University of Alaska's Geophysical Institute, the solar

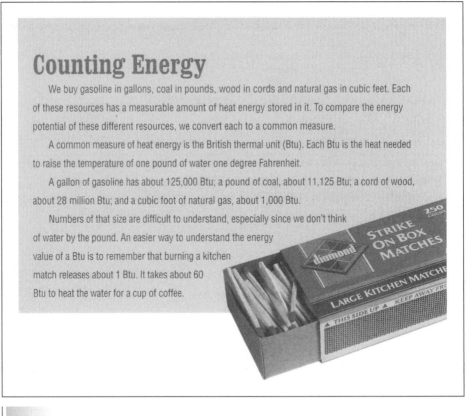

FIGURE 5.5
Explaining the Unfamiliar
"Counting Energy," reprinted with permission from *Straight Talk, ONEOK Quarterly,* publication of ONEOK, Inc., Fall 2001.

wind generates huge quantities of electricity in the magneto sphere. This energy accelerates parti-cles into the upper atmosphere where they strike atoms of various gases, producing the characteris-tic colors and staining the sky with dancing light.[17]

Analogies help audiences visualize the unfamiliar. *The Dallas Morning News'* writing coach, Paula LaRocque, cites some succinct examples.

David Stipp of *The Wall Street Journal:*

These are, to be exact, spotted salamanders. Black, six inches long and spotted with bright yellow polka dots, they resemble baby alligators in overtight clown suits.

And William Grimes, *The New York Times Magazine:*

It's a quiet site. You can hear the gentle sizzling of high-tension wires from the electrical substation serving the construction works.

 Hundreds of precast concrete tunnel segments lie baking in the sun—Snack Chips of the Gods.[18]

Helping people see something can also be aided by using concrete words instead of abstractions. Abstractions are vague and open to interpretation. The further you move away from words that are specific and concrete, the more you leave to the public's imagination.

Use the checklist in Table 5.2 when reviewing a draft of your work on a complex subject.

Make the Message Accessible

Presentation of the message also makes a difference in simplifying material. Some typefaces are easier to read, for example. Most serif type is easier to read than a sans serif because we recog-nize whole words, not characters, and we tend to scan lines, stopping at intervals. Our eyes catch the tops of the serif type and we identify the word without even seeing all of the char-acters. (See Chapter 12.)

T A B L E   5 . 2   *Checklist for Simplifying the Complex*

1. Have you researched your subject thoroughly? Do you understand its complexities and the precise meanings of the terms you use?

2. Does your writing stay within the range of your knowledge?

3. Have you told readers only as much as they need to know to understand the point?

4. Have you used plain English as much as possible and avoided unnecessary jargon? Have you substituted common words for technical terms whenever no loss of meaning results?

5. Have you fully described all technical terms you can't avoid?

6. Have you made sure all technical terms used are really necessary to communicate the message?

7. Have you taken the readers one step at a time? Have you started with a point your readers will understand?

8. Have you identified the central points you want to make? Are they made clearly and not obscured by explanation and detail?

9. Have you used familiar ideas to explain unfamiliar concepts?

10. Have you used concrete words rather than abstractions?

11. Have you made the material as accessible as possible?

In discussing ways to make materials more accessible, Kathleen Tinkel, writing for *Adobe Magazine,* distinguishes between legibility and readability. She says *legibility* refers to the ease of distinguishing one character from another. *Readability* refers to the type as it is set and can include size, spacing, column measure, leading, page layout and other such variables.[19]

Recommendations Tinkel makes include: (1) using natural letterfit and close word spacing; (2) indenting the first line of a paragraph; (3) avoiding low contrast and small sizes if you think the public may have impaired vision; (4) not using designs with fine hairlines, colored inks or colored papers if the lighting is likely to be poor.[20]

Another way to improve accessibility is by organizing and trimming materials. Among the most adaptable documents are financial pieces. The Securities and Exchange Commission, under the chairmanship of Arthur Levitt Jr., began trying a new style of prospectus for mutual fund investors. In July 1995, eight mutual funds went from a thick booklet that offered pages of tightly written copy to an 11-point prospectus that fits easily on both sides of one 8.5-by-11-inch piece of paper.[21]

Conclusions

- Remember you are writing for volunteer readers, listeners and viewers.
- Leave readers/listeners with one main thought.
- Write so people will understand what you mean.
- Know your message, your public and your medium.
- Know exactly what you want to say.
- Tailor your message to your public.
- Qualities of both the public and the medium will determine your choice of a medium. In any case, you will have to adapt the style and content of your message to the medium.
- The principles of clear writing are readability, naturalness, variety, euphony and human interest.
- Readability depends primarily on the length of words and sentences.
- A conversational style is easiest to read.
- Vary sentence structure and word choice to avoid dullness.
- Write to please the ear, but not at the expense of clarity.
- Use personal words to involve the reader.
- Eliminate clichés and bias.
- Review and edit your writing, using a checklist. Test for readability.
- Complex subjects can be simplified and made understandable, but doing so while maintaining accuracy is not easy.
- It's not enough simply to write short sentences and define technical terms. You must know your subject, as well as follow a number of important principles and rules for simplifying the complex.
- Use plain English, not doublespeak.
- Avoid euphemisms, the jargon of disciplines, gobbledygook (or bureaucratese) and inflated language.
- When you must use technical terms, don't define them and proceed. Describe them so readers will have a clear notion of what you're writing about.
- Know your subject thoroughly, and be aware of what your readers don't know.

- Start at the beginning and proceed one step at a time.
- Know what message you want to convey.
- Identify the most important point and state it clearly. Don't obscure the main idea with clouds of detail.
- If your central point is about something unfamiliar, use familiar ideas to explain it.
- If you follow these rules, along with the general principles of good writing, you should be able to explain anything important enough to deserve explaining.

Exercises

1. Find one book you enjoy reading and another you don't (both nonfiction and on the same subject). Perform a readability test by choosing the first paragraph from 10 pages of each, using a random numbers table to select the pages. (Use an alternate page provided by the table if the page begins with a quoted paragraph. You want to test the writer's work.) Is the more enjoyable book the easier one to read?
2. Analyze an article from *National Geographic* or *Scientific American.* What techniques has the writer used to make the piece both clear and interesting? Also examine devices used to simplify the complex.
3. Write directions for going through the advising and registration process at your school, for someone new to the school. Are your instructions clear? Have you overlooked a step in the process? Could someone successfully register by following your guidelines?

Use InfoTrac College Edition to access information on topics in this chapter from hundreds of periodicals and scholarly journals.

Notes

1. William Zinsser, *On Writing Well,* 2d ed. (New York: Harper & Row, 1980), pp. 56–57.
2. Robert Gunning, *The Technique of Clear Writing,* rev. ed. (New York: McGraw-Hill, 1968), p. 1.
3. David Geary, "The Readability Challenge in Public Relations," *Public Relations Quarterly* 46 (4) (Winter 2001), pp. 37–39.
4. Gunning, p. 51. Also see Cynthia Crossen's article, "If You Can Read This, You Most Likely Are a High-School Grad," in the *Wall Street Journal,* December 1, 2000, pp. A1, A11, for a quick history of readability formulas and their uses.
5. Gunning, p. 44.
6. H. W. Fowler, *Modern English Usage* (New York: Oxford University Press, 1965), p. 148.
7. Kenneth E. Andersen, *Persuasion Theory and Practice* (Boston: Allyn & Bacon, 1971), p. 126.
8. Albert Einstein, "On the Electrodynamics of Moving Bodies," *Annalen der Physik* 17 (1905): 891–929, reprinted in *The Principle of Relativity,* trans. W. Perrett and G. B. Jeffrey (New York: Dover, 1952), p. 39.
9. Rudolf Flesch, *The Art of Plain Talk* (New York: Collier Books, 1962), pp. 158, 162.
10. William Zinsser, *On Writing Well,* p. 114.

11. "Panel Issues Guidelines for Reporting Scientific Research," *pr reporter*, March 16, 1998, p. 2.

12. William D. Lutz, "Language, Appearance and Reality: Doublespeak in 1984." An excerpt from *The Legacy of Language: A Tribute to Charlton Laird*, ed. Phillip C. Boardman (Reno: University of Nevada Press, 1987), appeared with permission in *Et Cetera* 44 (4) (Winter 1987): 382–391.

13. Lauran Neergaard, "Researchers Explore Benefits of Simplifying Jargon," *The Fort Worth Star-Telegram*, November 25, 2002, p. 5D.

14. "Hacking Through the Paper Jungle," *Public Relations Journal* (August 1981): 26.

15. Isaac Asimov, *Opus 100* (Boston: Houghton Mifflin, 1969), pp. 89–90.

16. Steven Krauss, ed., *Your Health Care Planner* (Boston: Madison, 1994), p. 19.

17. Bruce Brown, "Shedding Light on the Aurora," *National Wildlife* (February–March 1985): 51. Copyright (c) 1985 by the National Wildlife Federation. Reprinted with permission.

18. Paula LaRocque, "This Analogy Clinic Fits Writers' Needs Like Cabretta Gloves," Clinic Column, *Quill* (September 1996): 32.

19. Kathleen Tinkel, "Taking It In," *Adobe Magazine* 7 (4) (April 1996): 40–44.

20. Ibid.

21. Jeffrey M. Laderman, "The Prospectus Tries Plain Speaking," *Business Week* (August 14, 1995): 72.

Selected Bibliography

Jacques Barzun and Henry F. Graff, *The Modern Researcher*, 5th ed. (New York: Harcourt Brace Jovanovich, 1992).

Rene J. Cappon, *The Word: An Associated Press Guide to News Writing* (Englewood Cliffs, N.J.: Prentice Hall, 1991).

Robert L. Chapman and Barbara Ann Kipfer, *The Dictionary of American Slang* (New York: HarperCollins, 1998).

Mary A. DeVries, *Internationally Yours: Writing and Communicating Successfully in Today's Global Marketplace* (Boston: Houghton Mifflin, 1994).

Rudolf Flesch, *The Art of Readable Writing*, rev. ed. (New York: Macmillan, 1986).

Robert Gunning, *The Technique of Clear Writing*, rev. ed. (New York: McGraw-Hill, 1968).

S. I. Hayakawa and Alan R. Hayakawa, *Language in Thought and Action*, 5th ed. (New York: Harcourt Brace Jovanovich, 1991).

Wynford Hicks, *English for Journalists* (New York: Routledge, 1998).

Robert L. Hilliard, *Writing for Television and Radio and New Media*, 7th ed. (Belmont, Calif.: Wadsworth, 1999).

Lauren Kessler and Duncan McDonald, *When Words Collide: A Media Writer's Guide to Grammar and Style*, 4th ed. (Belmont, Calif.: Wadsworth, 1996).

Paula LaRocque, *Championship Writing, 50 Ways to Improve Your Writing* (Oak Park, Ill.: Marion Street Press, Inc., 2000).

Paula LaRocque, *The Book on Writing, The Ultimate Guide to Writing Well* (Oak Park, Ill.: Marion Street Press, Inc., 2003).

Alexander Lawson, *Anatomy of a Typeface* (Boston: David R. Godine, 1990).

Michel Lipman and Russell Joyner, *How to Write Clearly: Guidelines and Exercises for Clear Writing* (Concord, Calif.: International Society for General Semantics, 1979).

Casey Miller and Kate Swift, *The Handbook of Nonsexist Writing for Writers, Editors and Speakers,* 2d ed. (New York: HarperCollins, 1988).

Mary Morain, ed., *Enriching Professional Skills through General Semantics* (San Francisco: International Society for General Semantics, 1989).

Jack A. Nelson, ed., *The Disabled, the Media and the Information Age* (Westport, Conn.: Greenwood Press, 1994).

Doug Newsom and Jim Wollert, *Media Writing: Preparing Information for the Mass Media,* 2d ed. (Belmont, Calif.: Wadsworth, 1988).

The Online Slang Dictionary: www.ocf.berkeley.edu/~wrader/slang

Kim Pedersen and Anders Kidmose, *In Black & White: An R&D Report on Typography and Legibility* (Copenhagen: Graphic College of Denmark, 1993).

Rick Poynor and Edward Booth-Clibborn, *Typography Now: The Next Wave* (Booth-Clibborn Editions, 1994).

Larry A. Samovar, Richard E. Porter and Lisa Stefani, *Communication Between Cultures,* 3d ed. (Belmont, Calif.: Wadsworth, 1998).

Frank and Francine Wattman and Paula A. Treichler, *Language, Gender and Professional Writing* (New York: Modern Language Associates, 1989).

William Zinsser, *On Writing Well: The Classic Guide to Writing Nonfiction,* 5th rev. ed. (New York: HarperPerennial, 1994).

Grammar, Spelling and Punctuation

Taking grammar, spelling and punctuation for granted can get us into a lot of trouble. One edition of this text actually got into print with the headings in the upper corner of each page in this chapter reading "Grammer." Authors don't handle headings, but the error wasn't caught in the page proofs either. Talk about loss of credibility—that is a good example. Spelling caused a credibility problem for the IRS too when their publication for tax practitioners appeared with "Practioner" on its cover. The "grammer" mistake didn't get any publicity, thank goodness, but the IRS's mistake did. A New York City tax expert called this to the attention of *The Wall Street Journal,* which put the information in its front-page "Tax Report" column, along with this question from the tax expert: "How can we rely on what is inside the manual if the outside is incorrect?"[1] The loss of credibility is more serious than the embarrassment.

Of course without the publicity, relatively few people would have observed the original IRS mistake, but what about the following case from the transit system in Dallas, Texas? DART's billboard on one of the most traveled expressways in the Dallas–Fort Worth area, Central Expressway, read: "Don't drive yourself, Crazy." Of course it was supposed to read: "Don't drive yourself crazy." The intended message was: Ride public transportation and avoid the traffic hassles. The unintended result was an insult to motorists, which in turn made DART the butt of many jokes. This story also made the front page of the "Sunday Reader" editorials section of *The Dallas Morning News.*[2]

Computers make it easy for us to check spelling and grammar, but careful reading is necessary too. Editors of a church bulletin were embarrassed when the following message was printed: "The Senior Choir invites any member of the congregation who enjoys sinning to join the Choir." Spell-check won't catch that error because *sinning* is a word and was spelled correctly.

As a public relations writer, you enter the world of professional writing. You join the ranks of skilled wordsmiths. Not only will you be expected to write expertly yourself, but you'll also be expected to edit the writing efforts of others. You'll be expected to know the rules and when to break them in order to communicate.

"Language is for communicating," writes direct-mail expert Luther Brock. "Words are simply a means of expressing one's self and, in our business, of convincing people to do business with us."[3] Writing grammatically correct prose, he points out, isn't always the best way to communicate.

"Unfortunately," writes Brock, "traditionally correct language is dishwater-dull. Why? Because it is not a reflection of the way most people talk. And talk-language just about always outsells grammar-book language."[4] As Brock indicates, the purpose of writing is to get a message across to a reader. In many respects the rules of grammar help achieve that end. But sometimes they get in the way. When they do, the experienced writer may ignore them. That doesn't mean you shouldn't bother to learn the rules or you shouldn't obey them most of the time. But you should keep the rules in perspective. "Rules," says Robert Gunning, "are substitutes for thought."[5] That's true, but they still can be useful. In many cases it's easier to follow a rule than to waste a lot of time thinking. However, when it comes to making decisions about writing readable prose, rules are no substitute for thought.

Writing expert and syndicated columnist Stephen Wilbers makes the point that writing often calls for deliberate breaking of the rules.[6] He cites at least three cases when, although your computer may advise you to use the active voice, the passive voice is better. One of these is when you intend to emphasize the receiver of the action. The example he uses is: "Millions of people have read *The Hunt for Red October*" (active voice), compared with "*The Hunt for Red October* has been read by millions" (passive voice).[7]

Another example of when the passive is the better voice, Wilbers says, is when you are trying to create coherence between sentences. The illustration he uses is: "We must decide whether to increase our prices. The possibility that we will lose some of our customers should influence our decision." Using the passive voice connects the sentences better: "We must decide whether to increase our prices. Our decision should be influenced by the possibility that we will lose some of our customers."[8]

Sometimes the passive voice is just more diplomatic, Wilbers says. A letter that says "You disregarded the terms of our contract" is likely to create more hostility and less compliance than one that says, "The terms of our contract were disregarded."[9]

Just as "always use the active voice" can be ignored at times, so can other "rules." Take the *like* versus *as* case. One of the main principles of good writing, says Gunning, is to "write like you talk." A lot of English teachers part company with Gunning here, some simply because the rules of grammar dictate that "write as you talk" is the proper way to state the principle. But Gunning responds with three good reasons for using *like* instead of *as*.[10] First, many good writers have used *like* as a conjunction (Norman Mailer for a modern example, and John Keats if you prefer the old-timers). Second, "write as you talk" breaks the rule as it states it. When speaking, people say "write like you talk"—and everybody knows what they mean. That brings us to the third point, which is that "write as you talk" has two possible meanings. It can mean "write the same way you talk" or "write while you are talking." But this is ambiguous, and unintended ambiguity is one of the worst of all possible writing sins.

Ambiguity and Grammar

The main reason grammar exists is to avoid ambiguity. Many grammar rules help us keep our meaning clear. Dangling participles, for example, are condemned by grammarians, and they should be; they can obscure the meaning of the sentence. (Sometimes a dangling participle sounds so silly that the true meaning is obvious, but even in those cases the sentence is awkward and should be rewritten.)

That Versus *Which*

The common misuse of *that* and *which* is an example of how bad grammar can tangle meaning. Using *that* and *which* correctly is important, for it involves questions of both ambiguity and naturalness. In speaking, *that* comes more naturally. "I picked up the books *that* were on the table; where are the keys *that* I left on the shelf?" In writing, for some mysterious reason, people feel compelled to use *which*. "Attached are the copies *which* I promised to send you."

Rudolf Flesch, in *The Art of Readable Writing,* explains at great length why *that* is better in such cases.[11] His discussion is worth looking up and reading. Not only is *that* the more natural word, it prevents confusion about the meaning of the sentence. In the preceding examples, the clauses beginning with *that* are restrictive; *which* should not be used to introduce a restrictive clause. When you say, "Bring me the books *that* are on the table," you want *only* the books on the table—not any of the other books nearby. The clause is restrictive. When you say, "Bring the books, *which* are on the table," you're not restricting the books, you're simply telling where they are. The comma is the clue. If the sentence reads correctly without the comma, you should use *that* instead of *which*. (In fact, try to avoid *which* clauses altogether. Clauses with commas slow readers down.)

The desire to tighten copy sometimes tempts writers to eliminate the word *that*. Often this can be done without injury to sense, but you need to watch for three problems that can occur if you strike a *that*. First, when a verb is delayed, readers might have to review the sentence to get the proper meaning. For example: "The registrar revealed the grades of the athletes being disciplined met academic standards." You need a *that* before "the grades" to make the meaning clear. Second, the time element may be rendered ambiguous. For example: "Stockbrokers said last month the decreasing bond and stock prices were a mystery." Either stockbrokers made the statement last month, or they made it recently about last month's mystery. The placement of the missing *that* will clarify which is the case. Third, smoothness may be interrupted because a clause is being used in apposition. For example: "The president's decision is one only the students will understand." A *that* between "one" and "only" makes the sentence much more readable.

Subject-Verb Agreement

Another rule that aids clarity is that the subject and verb in a sentence must agree. Subject-verb agreement helps us avoid confusion over who's doing what. There is a difference, for example, between "Growing vegetables is interesting" and "Growing vegetables are interesting."

Furthermore, merely misidentifying the subject is no excuse to break the rule. A headline in a major newspaper once said, "Workings of the SEC no longer is so mysterious." The subject is *workings,* not *SEC:* the verb should be *are* and not *is.* There is no excuse for making the mistake in less obvious cases either, as in "The general, along with his men, are marching tomorrow." The subject here is singular; the additional phrase does not make it plural. The corrected sentence reads "The general, along with his men, is marching tomorrow." If that sounds awkward, simply say "The general and his men are marching tomorrow."

Like any other rule, this one is no substitute for thought. When you write, "The *data* you need are on page 17," you are going out of your way to show that you know there is such a thing as a "datum." Most people would say "The *data* is on page 17," and there's no good reason not to. Your meaning will still be clear.

The plain fact is that in modern American usage *data* can be construed either as a singular collective noun or as a plural. The *AP Stylebook* points out that in a sentence like "The data is sound," *data* clearly refers to a collective unit, and not to the individual bits of information that collectively make up the data. If you want to emphasize the individual entities in a collection of data, of course it is correct (grammatically) to write "the data are."

The *Random House Unabridged Dictionary* recognizes the same distinctions and adds that *data* is almost always treated as a plural in scientific and academic writing. The editors also note that the singular, *datum,* meaning "a piece of information," is rarely found in any type of writing today—even in engineering, where *datum* has a special meaning and the plural used is *datums.*

Another awkward case of subject-verb agreement is the pairing *none is,* which grates on the ear and calls attention to itself. "None of the boats is going out to sea today" sounds silly. Always using a singular verb after *none*—no matter what the rest of the sentence says—is nonsense. Furthermore, any legitimate dictionary or usage manual says so. More often than not, the sense of *none* is plural. Theodore Bernstein, in *The Careful Writer,* says that the rule to follow is "Consider *none* to be plural unless there is a definite reason to regard it as a singular."[12] For example, when *none* is followed by a prepositional phrase with a singular object, the singular verb sounds better. "None of the cake have been eaten," by contrast, sounds awkward.

Myths of Grammar

Why do most people think *none* is singular and should always be followed by is or some other equally out-of-place singular verb? Even the *Oxford English Dictionary* says *none* is usually plural. Well, at some time in the ancient past, a grammar teacher decided that *none* meant "not one" and that it should be singular. That teacher passed it on to a student who became a teacher and passed it on to another student and so on. And all of these teachers were steadfastly devoted to the cause of rules as substitutes for thought. These are the teachers who, as Rudolf Flesch puts it, "tell students from grade school through college that they'd better learn not to write 'it's me' and never split an infinitive; or they'll get shunned by society in later life and never get a decent job."[13]

Some of these grammar "pitfalls" are important; others are merely grammar myths. The old *it's me* or *it's I* question, for example, isn't worth the time it takes to quibble. Almost everybody uses *it's me* these days, and most experts accept it, even though a predicate nominative is supposed to use the subject form of the pronoun. Another contraction you hear is, "aren't I." Literally it is "are not I." This is still not generally accepted.

Also, few good writers would say "between you and I." This is not only grammatically wrong but, worse, it is stilted and unnatural. In this case the correct form is also the most natural one: "between you and me." The same is true for the common misuses of *myself* when *me* is the right word. "He sent a message to John and myself" is a self-conscious and awkward way of avoiding the use of *me. Myself* should be reserved for intensive or reflexive use, as in "I hurt myself" or "I myself will do it."

Split Infinitives

As for split infinitives, every good writer knows that infinitives should sometimes be split. Let the situation be your guide. If avoiding a split infinitive makes a sentence awkward, go ahead and chop the infinitive in two and get on with writing the story. Consider E. B. White's observation in *The Elements of Style:*

> The split infinitive is another trick of rhetoric in which the ear must be quicker than the handbook. Some infinitives seem to improve on being split, just as a stick of round stovewood does. "I cannot bring myself to really like the fellow." The sentence is relaxed, the meaning is clear, the violation is harmless and scarcely perceptible. Put the other way, the sentence becomes stiff, needlessly formal. A matter of ear.[14]

Keep in mind, though, that split infinitives sometimes cause confusion, especially if the insertion of several words turns the split into a gorge. "He wanted to quickly, skillfully and perhaps even artistically complete the project" is widening the split a bit too far. Remember, clarity is the goal.

Sentence-Ending Prepositions

The split infinitive taboo originated with the fact that Latin infinitives are single words and thus can't be split. The same archaic logic led to the myth that you should never end a sentence with a preposition. Some people who remember nothing else at all from their grammar-school days remember this "rule." But in fact, this is just another example of somebody learning grammar from Latin in the Middle Ages and passing it down through the centuries until everybody says it's so but nobody knows why. In Latin it's very difficult to end a sentence with a preposition. Why allow English to do something denied in Latin?

Fortunately, some noteworthy language experts have ridiculed this rule to the point where few people still follow it. To writers, Winston Churchill's most famous line was not about blood and tears and sweat but the one in which he called the rule against sentence-ending prepositions an impertinence "up with which I will not put." Nowadays, almost all usage manuals repudiate the "rule." As a personal guide, know the "rule" before you decide to ignore it.

Usage Manuals

Once writers realize they are free from the chains imposed by grammar rules, some go off the deep end. If rules are made to be broken, why follow any of them? Well, not all rules should be broken. *Rules should be broken only when, by doing so, you can make the writing clearer, more natural, and easier to understand.* Feel free to dismiss the pedantry of critics who rank split infinitives on the same plane with arson or manslaughter. But do strive to use the language carefully and accurately.

It is no pedantry, for example, to insist that words be used in keeping with their proper meanings. *Allusion* is not the same as *illusion,* for example, and *imply* and *infer* are not interchangeable. *Parameters* are not *perimeters,* either. Countless words are misused simply because they sound like others. (See Table 6.1.)

Many writers scoff at such criticism, saying, "The reader will know what I mean. Lots of people use the word that way." If you adopt this philosophy, you put yourself in the position of confusing the members of your public who *do* know the correct meanings of words. The intelligent reader is left to wonder if the writer is using this word correctly, in which case it means something else. Using words imprecisely can lead to such ambiguity. Choose words carefully.

Even some grammar "rules" deserve a little thought before they are rejected or accepted. Any given rule can be good for some situations—possibly even most situations—though bad for others. How can you decide when to follow a rule and when not to? You must decide, of course, but it never hurts to get some advice. Check a few basic reference books. Besides a dictionary and a standard grammar handbook, you should have at least two language-usage manuals that discuss points of grammar and usage in depth. Such manuals analyze many of the tricky usage questions that writers stumble across. See this chapter's bibliography for suggestions.

When you read some of these manuals, you'll find that usage rules aren't as restrictive as you've been taught. You'll be surprised to learn what some language "purists" like Fowler and Follett have to say about split infinitives, for example. You'll also, no doubt, run across subtle but important usage matters that have escaped your attention until now. Cappon's book *The*

T A B L E   6 . 1   *Commonly Confused Words*   Here is a list of pairs of commonly confused words. If you don't understand the differences between the members of each pair, consult a usage manual, the *AP Stylebook* or *Words into Type.*

absorb, adsorb	assure, ensure	doubtful, dubious	pedal, peddle
accrue, acquire	baited, bated	dual, duel	poison, toxin
adapt, adopt	canvas, canvass	farther, further	pore, pour
adhesion, cohesion	cement, concrete	flaunt, flout	practicable, practical
affect, effect	complement, compliment	fortuitous, fortunate	principal, principle
all ready, already	compose, comprise	grisly, grizzly	rebut, refute
allusion, illusion	continual, continuous	imply, infer	reign, rein
alternately, alternatively	credible, credulous	infect, infest	stationary, stationery
apparently, obviously	deduction, induction	minister, pastor	suspect, suspicious
appraise, apprise	discreet, discrete	naval, navel	whereas, while
arbitrate, mediate	disinterested, uninterested	parameter, perimeter	

Associated Press Guide to News Writing has a chapter called "Bestiary: A Compendium for the Careful and the Crotchety."

Perhaps the most important lesson you'll learn from reading usage manuals is that there is considerable disagreement among the "experts" over what should or should not be allowed. So don't let anybody tell you there is always a right and a wrong where grammar and usage are concerned. Gather some opinions, think about each problem and then make up your own mind. Just be sure that, when you break a rule, you break it for a reason and not because you didn't know. You also need to remember your public. Materials for international use by English-speaking people need to follow more strictly traditional usage.

Verbs

Where's the action? The action of PR writing is in the verbs: They should keep things moving, capture attention and hold it.

Use active-voice verbs, and avoid using the passive voice. Recast the sentence if you have to. One simple way to put movement into your language is to limit your use of forms of the verb "to be." Consider these examples:

> An honor code is being considered by student government representatives, who want to talk with university faculty about the idea. [Passive]
>> Student government representatives considering an honor code for the university want to talk with faculty about the idea. [Active]

When writing broadcast copy, you should stay out of the past tense. The idea underlying this practice is that all broadcast news should sound as immediate as possible. A new rule on college athletes' eligibility passed yesterday by the NCAA would be written: "College athletes must make higher grades now to stay on the team." The present perfect tense is used most often by broadcasters. It implies immediacy, although the action is over. You just write "has been" instead of "was" and "have been" instead of "were." For instance, "I've been in India" sounds as though you've just returned.

Emotive and Cognitive Meaning

Cognitive meanings are information based. Emotive meanings may be positive or negative or mixed. You must be sensitive to these two different types of meaning. Emotion-charged words are often used in public relations writing, but it is imperative that you know, in advance, the emotion a word is likely to elicit from the publics it will reach. Negatively charged words are those that evoke bad images, such as prejudicial terms used for ethnic groups. Positively charged words are those that encourage "good feelings," such as *peace, love, freedom.* Some words may have mixed emotive meanings, and these can be the most dangerous to use. Words like *globalization* have different meanings to people with different value systems.[15]

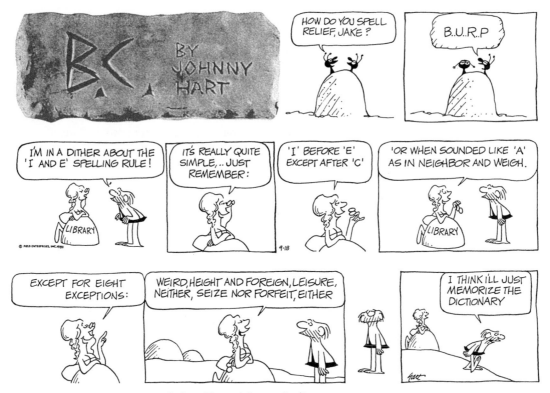

Source: B.C. Reprinted by permission of Johnny Hart and Creators Syndicate.

Spelling

You might expect that spelling would be rather clear-cut, but it isn't. For example, you can spell *benefited* with one *t* or *benefitted* with two. You must decide which one you will use for your organization; you thereby establish the style for that organization's publications. On the other hand, if you are writing for *other* publications, you have to spell words the way *their* style dictates.

With more international communications in English, you have to ask, "Whose English?" Will you use the *s* in spelling *organisations* or the *z* as in usage in the USA? Perhaps some global standardization for English is in sight, since the European Union has chosen English as the preferred language, and it is the major language of the Internet.

Who cares about spelling? Well, the people who hire PR writers for one, so if you want a job, you'll take spelling seriously. There's no excuse for *not* spelling correctly. Just keep a dictionary within arm's length whenever you're writing. If you're not *absolutely certain* that a word is spelled correctly, look it up.

Face it. If your prose is riddled with spelling errors, your readers just might conclude that your facts are also suspect. (They might also conclude that you're not too bright.) Therefore, why should they believe what you've written or even read it at all? It's little consolation to say that most readers won't catch the spelling errors. Then only the educated people will think you're wrong.

Spelling errors do crop up now and again, even in prestigious publications. Even though you make every effort to eradicate mistakes, a spelling error will someday appear in one of your finished products anyway. That's not a reason to be less diligent in your efforts. If you operate with the attitude that "just one error" isn't so bad, you'll end up with many. The old saying that "to err is human" should be applied only as consolation after the fact, not as a license ahead of time to make mistakes.

Sometimes mistakes result not from lack of diligence, but from overconfidence. Some people spell so well that they're sure they can spot any spelling mistakes. Thus they don't look up the words they should. To avoid such overconfidence, good writers and editors should occasionally test themselves on lists of commonly misspelled words. Even good spellers will find some surprises. Test yourself by counting the number of words spelled *correctly* in the list contained in Table 6.2.

Word processing systems can check spelling, but if (for example) you have used *there* instead of *their,* the system will not find the error. The system will only find words that are misspelled as nonwords, such as *thier* for *their.* It will miss homophones (words that sound alike but are spelled differently) and misspellings that produce other true words (such as *study* for *sturdy* or *sandbag* for *handbag*). (See Table 6.3.)

The same problem is likely to occur with plurals and possessives in spell-check software. Some grammar software may recognize such distinctions as "the bee's sting" (one bee) or "the bees' sting" (more than one bee). The key to possessives is the apostrophe. With the simple plural, *bees,* there is no apostrophe, but there is one when you are using a plural possessive. Another area of confusion occurs with the apostrophe when it's used in contractions—*it's,* as just used, for "it is." *Its,* a singular possessive, has no apostrophe. Sometimes *its,* the possessive, as in "The dog buried its bone," is misused for the contraction, as in "Its going to be difficult to find the bone the dog buried." Think of the apostrophe in contractions as standing for the missing letter.

T A B L E   6 . 2   *Unassisted Spell-Check*

How many of these words are correctly spelled?			
badmitton	barbiturates	procede	innoculate
sacreligious	limosine	comittee	pantomine
chaufeur	corollary	comission	inocuous
diarhea	wierd	priviledge	perogative
embarass	cemetary	knowledgable	excell
Farenheit	mispelling	sieze	
flourescent	preceed	satelite	

If you counted two correct, you're right. Only *barbiturates* and *corollary* are spelled correctly.

Source: Shoe. Reprinted with permission from Tribune Media Services.

TABLE 6.3   *Spell-Checker*

Eye halve a spelling chequer
It came with my pea sea
It plainly marques four my revue
Miss steaks eye kin knot sea.

Eye strike a key and type a word
And weight four it two say
Weather eye am wrong oar write
It shows me strait a weigh.
As soon as a mist ache is maid
It nose bee fore two long
And eye can put the error rite
Its rare lea ever wrong.

Eye have run this poem threw it
I am shore your pleased two no
Its letter perfect awl the weigh
My chequer tolled me sew.

If you answered Table 6.2 correctly without any help, you're a pretty good speller and should have no trouble with the following test. Read the passage and circle the words that are spelled *incorrectly.* Assume that the piece is part of a feature story that is to appear in a newspaper, and follow *AP Stylebook* spelling rules.

The scientists could not reach a concensus. One physicist argued that his experiments superceded earlier findings.

Beseiged by numerous complaints, the director of the labratory devised a stratagy to accomodate the researchers. He alotted each one 15 minutes to speak. One said everyone had benefitted from the experiments on liquefcation of nitrogen, but he saw no correllation between those results and the experiments on parafin.

"It would take a whole battallion of scientists to solve this dilemna," another scientist said. "We do high calibre work, but when you liquefy a miniscule amount of gas, there's no way to avoid all possible arguements about the results." Another suggested that a questionaire should be drawn up and sent out. "If we could get them all filled out, that would be quite an achievment," he said.

"That's an inovative idea," said the physicist. "I'd like to save my copy of the form as a memento of this occassion."

You should have circled 20 words. If you didn't find them all, a trip to the dictionary (or perhaps the *AP Stylebook*) is in order. By the way, although dictionaries accept *benefitted,* the AP allows *benefited* only. Some dictionaries also accept *liquify.*

Punctuation

Whereas grammar is mostly a matter of making meanings clear and spelling is basically a matter of convention, punctuation is a little of both. True, proper punctuation is usually just a matter of following the rules. But the underlying purpose of punctuation is to help make the meaning clear, and subtle changes in punctuation can change the meaning of a sentence. For example, the sentence "Woman without her man is an animal" can be punctuated "Woman—without her, man is an animal." Liz Carpenter, former press secretary to Lady Bird Johnson, likes to have people punctuate this sentence as a test for sexism.

Most reputable publications follow a fairly rigorous set of punctuation rules and apply them consistently. The virtue of consistency is simply that readers can pay attention to the message without being bothered by changes in the manner of punctuation. Sentences, for example, usually end with periods. Readers know this, and they don't have to think about it. They know that if a writer ends a sentence with some other mark, it is an intentional act to tell the reader something—as when a question mark is used to indicate a question.

Inconsistent punctuation calls attention to itself. Anything that calls attention to itself takes attention away from the message, and that hinders communication. When you're trying to communicate, there's no excuse for introducing anything that distracts the reader, however slightly.

Sometimes punctuation conventions defy logic, but these conventions are so entrenched that violators expose themselves immediately as amateurs. The prime example involves the use of periods and commas with quotation marks. Whenever a period or comma follows a quotation, it is placed *inside* the closing quotation marks. Always. Without exception (at least in the United States). It doesn't matter whether the quote is a complete sentence or a title or a single word. For example:

John's article, called "The Hands of Time," is well written.

I didn't know he wrote an article called "The Hands of Time."

The rule still applies if single quotes are used inside double quotes:

He said he "wrote an article called 'The Hands of Time.'"

Source: Peanuts. Reprinted by permission of United Feature Syndicate, Inc.

Other punctuation marks, such as question marks and exclamation points, are placed according to the sense of the sentence:

> Did he write an article called "The Hands of Time"?
>
> He asked John, "What is the title of your article?"

This may seem trivial, but many public relations writers are their own editors. If you want your material punctuated correctly, you need to know the rules. And in the case of this particular rule, there is nothing to be gained by breaking it. It is followed uniformly (in the United States), and departures from the convention call attention to themselves.

For many other punctuation rules, convention is not as binding. Often, standard "rules" should be broken to make the reading easier or to make the meaning clear. People are taught in school, for example, to place commas before direct quotations, as in

> John said, "What's going on here?"

Sometimes the comma is an intrusion, however, and can be dropped with no confusion:

> "What did he say?"
>
> He said "Let's go!"

Not all rules should be so casually violated. Some are important for keeping the meaning clear; most rules of this type involve the comma.

There are dozens of rules regarding commas, and it doesn't hurt to know them. Most help keep sentences clear and prevent readers from stumbling over tricky passages or linking clauses to wrong elements. In general, comma rules are helpful.

Some writers overdo their use of commas, though, and stick one in wherever they can. Too many commas clog up the works and make for slow reading. The best practice is to use commas only when they are necessary to avoid confusion.

The careful use of commas with nonrestrictive clauses, for example, helps avoid confusion. Restrictive clauses, which are necessary to make the meaning of a sentence clear, are not set off by commas. Consider these examples:

> Restrictive clauses, which are needed for clarity, are not set off by commas.
>
> Clauses that are needed for clarity are restrictive.

All restrictive clauses are needed for clarity. Therefore, the "which are needed" clause in the example is merely explanatory and is not essential to the meaning of the sentence. It is a *nonrestrictive* clause and is set off by commas.

Not all clauses are needed for clarity. But the "that are needed" clause is essential to the meaning of the sentence: It *restricts* the types of clauses under consideration. It is therefore a *restrictive* clause and is not set off by commas.

Restrictive and nonrestrictive clauses are also called *essential* and *nonessential* clauses. They don't always use *that* and *which*. *Who* can be restrictive or nonrestrictive, and this fact makes proper punctuation all the more important. Consider these examples from the *AP Stylebook:*

Reporters, who do not read the Stylebook, should not criticize their editors.

Reporters who do not read the Stylebook should not criticize their editors.

The first sentence says that reporters—all reporters—do not read the Stylebook. Therefore, they shouldn't criticize their editors. The second sentence says that some reporters—those who don't read the Stylebook—shouldn't criticize their editors. There's a big difference.

Another comma error that can make sentences unclear involves appositives. An appositive is a phrase that stands for a noun and bears the same relationship to the rest of the sentence that the noun does. Here is an example:

Joe Smith, the captain of the football team, signed a contract today.

The appositive following *Joe Smith* is set off by commas. The comma after *team* is essential. "Joe Smith, the captain of the football team signed a contract today" reads as though someone were telling Joe Smith (whoever he is) that the captain of the football team signed a contract.

Don't set off short titles with commas, however. "Team captain Joe Smith signed a contract" is perfectly correct. "Team captain, Joe Smith, signed a contract" is not. A similar problem sometimes comes up with restrictive appositives, when a descriptive phrase is needed for full meaning. "The American League baseball players, Garret Anderson, Nathan Haynes and Manny Ramirez, are outfielders" is not properly punctuated. This sentence makes them the only players in the American League. Omit the commas after *players* and *Ramirez,* and the sentence is correct. Avoid related mistakes too, such as the one made by a textbook author who wrote "In his novel, *The Deer Park,* Norman Mailer describes. . . ." There should be no comma after *novel;* Mailer has written more than one.

Many other punctuation rules are equally important, although it's impossible to cover all of them in a single chapter. Conscientious writers take punctuation seriously, however, and consult such books as the *AP Stylebook* for help on the fine points.

Of course, experts sometimes disagree about proper punctuation. Don't think that every rule should be followed in every instance. But make sure you know the rules. And when you break one, know why.

Global English?

All English is not the same. Not in spelling, not in word meanings, not in punctuation and not, in some instances, even grammar. The question is, which version of English do you use, the British or the American? The answer is, it depends on the medium and/or the public. You use what is accepted and familiar, not necessarily to you. Remember: public, message, medium.

Many publications using the British spellings will have *organisations,* not *organizations,* for example. In British-language publications, you'll often find *whilst,* which is considered

Source: Shoe. Reprinted with permission of Tribune Media Services.

"quaint" in the USA. British-language publications are likely to use *venue,* whereas American-language publications use *place.* Names of things are not the same, as you may know from traveling. An *elevator* is a *lift* in places using British English. British English uses different forms of punctuation too. Where American English uses double quotation marks with other punctuation inside ("."), British English uses single quotation marks with other punctuation outside (' ',).

Fortunately, you can use a computer language system to help. Most computers use American-English spelling, grammar and punctuation, but you can get a British-English system to use when needed. The question may be which system will eventually prevail. Some think it is the American-English system because of technology. Most people who buy computers get the American-English system automatically and have to get the British-English system separately. Time will tell.

To be a good public relations writer, you need to be aware of and sensitive to the differences. Fortunately, there's help available, online. At www.tardis.ed.ac.uk you'll find *The Edinburgh University Tardis Project.* Another source for help is the Association of British Language Schools (ABLS) stylebook and usage guide.

If you are attempting to communicate in another language be cautious about using the Internet for free online translations. You may not be sending the message you intended. For example, http://www.translate.ru/text.asp?lang=en offers English, French, German, Spanish, Italian and Russian. However, if you use a site like this be sure to translate the supplied translation back into English. English input: *When I go to town to shop, I enjoy taking a long walk in the park before I return home in the afternoon.* Spanish translation: *Cuando voy a la ciudad a hacer compras, disfruto tomando un paseo largo en el parque antes de que yo vuelva a(en) casa por la tarde.* English translation of the Spanish: *When I am going to the city to do buys, I enjoy taking a long walk in the park before I return to (in) house in the evening.*

If you are preparing materials in another language, hire someone fluent in both languages and someone who has recently traveled in the other country where the materials will be used. Language usage changes over time in a country. Also, as you know from experiences with American English and British English, there are significant differences in word choices, spellings and meanings between the two versions of English. This is also true of other languages.

TABLE   6 . 4   *The Quality Controlling System*

Quality Controlling	For	Some Tasks
Revising	**Ideas** • paragraphs • headings • bullets • graphics	• change • add • reorganize/reformat • eliminate
Editing	**Language** • sentences • words • symbols	• voice • tone • conciseness • parallelism • modification • diction • punctuation • mechanics
Proofreading	**Hard-copy appearance**	• headings, footers, margins, spacing • font consistency • common mistakes • typos

Source: Reprinted from *ETC: A Review of General Semantics,* Vol. 58, No. 1, Spring 2001, by permission of the author, Philip Vassallo, and the International Society for General Semantics.

Always Check

At every level of your writing check to be sure you are saying what you intend to say. With your initial product, reread, read aloud, revise or rewrite completely. When you have what you think is a final copy, then edit it severely. When you have something to send for publication and get back a proof, edit it again carefully (see Table 6.4) for suggestions at each level.

Conclusions

• Grammar, spelling and punctuation are important—not as ends in themselves, but as aids to clear communication.
• The public relations writer's chief aim is to communicate, and following the rules of grammar and usage usually facilitates that task.
• Be sensitive to the emotive meanings of words, especially for some of your publics.
• Correct grammar and punctuation help to eliminate ambiguity.

- Consistent punctuation and spelling help direct the readers' attention to the message, not to the mechanics.
- Occasionally, strict adherence to grammar rules can result in awkward or confusing writing.
- In those cases, public relations writers should ensure clarity even at the expense of traditional grammar rules. But such a step should never be taken lightly. You should know why the rule exists and why it should be broken in a particular situation.
- Conscientious writers take all construction seriously and consult reference books to be sure their decisions are well founded.
- Electronic programs can help you polish your writing but are no substitute for your own competence.
- All English is not the same. While American English is quite commonly used globally because most computers are programmed for it, British English is more familiar to and accepted by a number of global publics. Be sensitive to language usage in your global communications.
- Check your work at every level: revise, edit, proof.

Exercises

1. Choose the correctly punctuated sentence from each multiple-choice group below. You might want to consult the *AP Stylebook* on some of these. Answers follow.

    1) a. Buy a case of Dr Pepper today.
       b. Buy a case of Dr. Pepper today.
    2) a. I wondered why he asked me, "Where have you been?".
       b. I wondered why he asked me, "Where have you been?"
    3) a. Have you ever asked "What should I do?"?
       b. Have you ever asked "What should I do?"
       c. Have you ever asked "What should I do"?
    4) a. She asked, "Who played the lead role in *Hello, Dolly!?*".
       b. She asked, "Who played the lead role in *Hello, Dolly!?*"
       c. She asked, "Who played the lead role in *Hello, Dolly!*"
    5) a. She asked, "Who wrote the words to 'The Star-Spangled Banner'?"
       b. She asked, "Who wrote the words to 'The Star-Spangled Banner'"?
    6) a. Have you ever exclaimed "My God!"?
       b. Have you ever exclaimed "My, God!"
       c. Have you ever exclaimed "My God!?"
    7) a. First, call your doctor. (If you don't have a family doctor, call the local health clinic.)
       b. First, call your doctor. (If you don't have a family doctor, call the local health clinic).
    8) a. First, call your doctor (if you have one.)
       b. First, call your doctor (if you have one).
    9) a. What should I do? he asked himself.
       b. What should I do, he asked himself.
       c. What should I do, he asked himself?
    10) a. "Will you come into my office?" he asked demandingly.
        b. "Will you come into my office," he asked demandingly.
    11) a. "Did you see that catch!?," I asked.

     b. "Did you see that catch!," I asked.

     c. "Did you see that catch!" I asked.

     d. None of the above.

12) a. John Smith, author of "What's in a Name?," will arrive soon.

     b. John Smith, author of "What's in a Name?", will arrive soon.

     c. John Smith author of "What's in a Name?" will arrive soon.

13) a. John Smith, state representative from Fort Worth, resigned.

     b. John Smith, state representative from Fort Worth resigned.

14) a. State representative, John Smith, resigned from his job today.

     b. State representative John Smith, resigned from his job today.

     c. State representative John Smith resigned from his job today.

15) a. He didn't shout "Halt, thief!"; I did.

     b. He didn't shout "Halt, thief!;" I did.

16) a. Have you ever said, "Let's go for a walk."?

     b. Have you ever said, "Let's go for a walk"?

17) a. We can go to the beach, if it doesn't rain.

     b. We can go to the beach if it doesn't rain.

18) a. The spinning turbine is attached to a generator, which turns conductors in a magnetic field to generate current.

     b. The spinning turbine is attached to a generator which turns conductors in a magnetic field to generate current.

19) a. A number of activities is available.

     b. A number of activities are available.

20) a. The university has opened it's library to the public.

     b. The university has opened its library to the public.

2. Rewrite the following sentences, eliminating jargon and needless words to make the resulting sentence clear and concise. Suggested revisions follow.

   a. Johnson supported his side of the issue by saying that contemporary revenue athletics, also known as big money sports, forces athletes to cheat in school because they have no time to study.

   b. As in the case with so many of the wars over the course of time, this war was largely a result of previous wars.

   c. If methods of communication had been comparable to those of the present century, there is little doubt that this war would never have begun.

   d. The interaction of petroleum liquid in aqueous media produces a heterogeneous, layered liquid mixture.

   e. Extent of labor and its propensity to fill time is peculiarly elastic; that is, the more time available for the completion of an assigned task, the longer it takes for the assigned task to be completed.

   f. We have encountered our military adversaries and successfully engaged them, taking control of their nautical vehicles.

   g. Whatever there is that needs to be done, this machine is able to accomplish it.

   h. Financial statements indicate that the company's financial situation was negatively impacted during the preceding 12 months.

    i. After the commission's last meeting, regulations were changed so that the company no longer has to file an application a year in advance.

    j. If we use vehicles powered by compressed natural gas, it is expected that we can help reduce air pollution from cars and trucks to standards well below those required by the Environmental Protection Agency.

Answers

1. 1) The correct answer is (a). This is a trick question: Dr Pepper is a registered trademark and has no period after the Dr.

    2) (b) is correct. The period is not needed; furthermore, periods should never fall outside quotation marks.

    3) No easy answer. Logic would seem to dictate the punctuation as in example (a), but in practice three punctuation marks in a row are seldom seen. Experts say you should choose the question you most want to emphasize. In this case (b) is probably the best choice.

    4) (b) is correct. This is one of those rare cases where three punctuation marks do follow one another. The exclamation point is part of the title and should not be dropped.

    5) (a) is correct. The quotation is the question, so the question mark falls inside the quotation marks.

    6) Another tricky one. (c) is wrong; (a) seems logical, but (b) is probably the correct choice to avoid awkward appearance. The exclamation is more important than the interrogative.

    7) (a) is correct. When a complete sentence is enclosed in parentheses, so is the period.

    8) (b) is correct. When only part of a sentence is enclosed in parentheses, the period falls outside.

    9) (a) is correct.

   10) (b) is correct. Although the sentence is phrased as an interrogative, there is no question. It is more a command than a request.

   11) (c) is probably the best way to punctuate this. (a) and (b) are clearly wrong; the comma is not needed. Some might use an exclamation point and a question mark together, but most would pick one.

   12) (c) is correct. Commas are not needed in this construction.

   13) (a) is correct.

   14) (c) is correct.

   15) (a) is correct. Semicolons always go outside quotation marks.

   16) (b) is correct.

   17) (b) is correct. The *if* clause is essential to the meaning of the main clause. It is therefore a restrictive *if* clause and should not be set off by a comma.

   18) (a) is correct. The *which* clause is descriptive, not defining. It merely gives more information about a generator. It does not make a distinction between generators in general and the generator under discussion.

   19) Although number is a collective noun, when preceded by *a*, the verb is plural. When *the* is used, the verb form is generally singular. (b) is correct.

   20) *Its* is a possessive, not a contraction. (b) is correct.

2. These revisions are only suggestions. Many other revisions are possible.

    a. Johnson said big money sports forces athletes to cheat in school because they have no time to study.
    b. Like so many wars, this war was largely a result of previous wars.
    c. If today's communication methods had been available, the war would never have started.
    d. Oil and water don't mix.
    e. Work takes up however much time is available.
    f. We have met the enemy, and they are ours.
    g. This machine can do whatever needs doing.
    h. The company lost money last year.
    i. The company does not have to apply a year ahead anymore.
    j. CNG reduces vehicle air pollution to below EPA standards. (Or you can spell out CNG and EPA and still have a shorter, clearer sentence.)

Use InfoTrac College Edition to access information on topics in this chapter from hundreds of periodicals and scholarly journals.

Notes

1. Tom Herman, "Tax Report," *The Wall Street Journal,* June 26, 1996, p. 1.
2. Linda Vaughan, "Weathervane," *The Dallas Morning News,* April 16, 1996, p. J1.
3. Luther Brock, "In Direct Mail, Ignore Friends—Pay Attention to What Pays," *Southwest Advertising and Marketing* (December 1975): 20.
4. Luther Brock, "Two Professionals Disagree on the Need for Purity in Language," *Southwest Advertising and Marketing* (March 1977): 11.
5. Robert Gunning, *The Technique of Clear Writing,* rev. ed. (New York: McGraw-Hill, 1968), p. 265.
6. Stephen Wilbers, "Tarrant Business," *Fort Worth Star-Telegram,* July 13, 1998, p. 13.
7. Ibid.
8. Ibid.
9. Ibid.
10. Gunning, p. 121.
11. Rudolf Flesch, *The Art of Readable Writing,* 25th anniv. ed. (New York: Harper & Row, 1974), p. 163.
12. Theodore Bernstein, *The Careful Writer* (New York: Atheneum, 1965), p. 288.
13. Flesch, *Art of Readable Writing,* pp. 9–10.
14. William Strunk and E. B. White, *The Elements of Style,* 3d ed. (New York: Macmillan, 1979), p. 78.
15. Howard Kahane and Nancy Cavender, *Logic and Contemporary Rhetoric, The Use of Reason in Everyday Life,* 8th ed. (Belmont, Calif.: Wadsworth, 1998). See Chapter 2, "Background Beliefs and World Views."

Selected Bibliography

Grammar Guides

R. E. Allen and H. W. Fowler, eds., *Pocket Fowler's Modern English Usage* (University of Oxford, Oxford England, UK: Oxford Press, 2002).

Wilson Follett with Erik Wensburg (Compiler), *Modern American Usage* (New York: Hill and Wang, 1998).

Jeanette Harris with Donald H. Cunningham (Contributor), *Simon & Schuster Guide to Writing* (New York: Simon & Schuster, 1997).

Lauren Kessler and Duncan McDonald, *When Words Collide: A Media Writer's Guide to Grammar and Style,* 5th ed. (Belmont, Calif.: Wadsworth, 1999).

Adam Robinson and Julian Fleischer, *The Princeton Review: Word Smart and Grammar Smart Abridged* (Princeton, N.J.: Living Language, 2001).

Irene Schoenberg, *Focus on Grammar: A Basic Course for Reference and Practice* (New York: Longman, 1999).

Harry Shaw, *Punctuate It Right!* 2d ed. (New York: HarperCollins, 1994).

Dictionaries

The American Heritage Dictionary of the English Language, 4th ed. (Boston: Houghton Mifflin, 2000).

The New American Roget's College Thesaurus in Dictionary Form, 3d rev. ed. (New York: Signet, Division of Penguin).

The New Oxford American Dictionary (New York: Oxford University Press, 2001).

Shorter Oxford English Dictionary, 5th ed. (New York: Oxford University Press, 2002).

Webster's Third New International Dictionary Unabridged (Chicago: Merriam-Webster, 2002).

Word Choice and Style Guides

The Associated Press Broadcast News Handbook, Incorporating the AP Libel Manual, 2d ed., eds. Brad Kalbfeld and James R. Hood (New York: Associated Press, 1998).

The Associated Press Stylebook and Briefing on Media Law, ed. Norm Goldstein (Cambridge, Mass.: Perseus, 2002).

The Associated Press Stylebook and Libel Manual, ed. Norm Goldstein (New York: Associated Press, 1999).

Rene J. Cappon, *The Associated Press Guide to News Writing (Study Aids/On the Job Reference),* 3d ed. (New York: Arco Publisher, 2000).

Rene J. Cappon, *The Word: An Associated Press Guide to News Writing* (Englewood Cliffs, N.J.: Prentice Hall, 1991).

Rudolf Flesch, *The Art of Readable Writing,* rev. ed. (New York: Macmillan, 1986).

Robert L. Hilliard, *Writing for Television and Radio,* 6th ed. (Belmont, Calif.: Wadsworth, 1997).

John Grossman, Preface, *Chicago Manual of Style,* 14th ed. (Chicago: University of Chicago, 1993).

Karen Judd, *Copyediting: A Practical Guide* (London, UK: Robert Hale, Ltd., 2002).

Milan D. Meeske, *Copywriting for the Electronic Media: A Practical Guide,* 3d ed. (Belmont, Calif.: Wadsworth, 1997).

Allan M. Siegal and William G. Connolly, eds., *New York Times Manual of Style and Usage, Revised and Expanded Edition* (New York: Three Rivers Press, Division of Crown Publishing/Random House, 1999).

Elsie M. Stainton, *The Fine Art of Copyediting* (New York: Columbia University Press, 1992).

William Strunk Jr. and E. B. White, *The Elements of Style,* 3d ed. (Boston: Allyn & Bacon, 1995).

United Press International (UPI) Stylebook, 3d ed. (Lincolnwood, Ind.: NTC, 1994).

Barbara Wallraff, *Word Count: Wherein Verbal Virtue Is Rewarded, Crimes Against the Language Are Punished and Poetic Justice Is Done* (New York: Harcourt, Inc., 2002).

"Write On: Spotlight on PR Writing," *Public Relations Tactics* (February 2003) New York: Public Relations Society of America.

Writing for Select Publics

*P*eople who belong to an organization, as either employees or volunteers, or those who closely identify with an organization because of special relationships, whether business or personal, are select publics. The organization controls what, when and how messages are delivered to these groups.

CHAPTER SEVEN

Email, Memos, Letters, Reports and Proposals

A primary role of email, memos, letters, reports and proposals is to maintain a good, relevant and timely flow of information within an organization and with its external publics. These are the front-line pieces in public relations that help build and sustain professional relationships. It is exciting, of course, to write copy for a showpiece brochure that is a major part of a campaign. It is a professional fact of life, however, that seasoned writers probably will be assigned tasks like that. New writers are assigned what some consider more mundane tasks, such as writing memos and letters.

About two weeks into an internship a student complained about "all that clerical work" she was being given. She was writing mostly memos and letters, and an occasional email. When asked who signed off on them, she said "the PR director." And who would write them if she wasn't there? she asked. Then she answered her own question with a glimmer of understanding: "My supervisor." By the time she finished the internship, her understanding evolved into confirmed recognition that much public relations writing is business writing. It is the information that lubricates and builds productive working relationships. In that sense, it is the most critical of all public relations writing.

Public relations professionals write lots of emails, memos, letters, reports and proposals in their everyday routine office work. They also write many such pieces for key officers in the organization, because these forms of writing frequently function to persuade in some way. The purpose of this chapter is to give you some basic guidelines to follow when you must write in any of these forms.

Email

When airlines began providing services to allow passengers to send and receive email messages while flying, electronic mail clearly had become a preferred method of communication. Created just three decades ago, email has become so popular that most business cards and letterheads carry email addresses. It does have its problems, though, chief among which is that people don't necessarily access their email on a regular basis. The frequency usually depends on how important the messages are likely to be to them.

When email is part of an operation, the first thing people do each workday is to call up on their computers any mail meant for them. The design of many email systems allows a person to send the same memo or letter to all workstations on the network or to selected stations on it.

People seem to pay more attention to email messages and respond to them more quickly than to paper messages. It's easy to figure out why: It's easier and quicker.

Interoffice or external postal systems can suffer from delays in delivery. But email is instantaneous. This can be an enormous advantage when a major development—especially one that was not anticipated—begins to unfold. Speed counts, and email meets that need.

Time management can be enhanced by email. If you're working and have a question for someone, you can send the query immediately (before you forget it) and that person can respond when convenient. Your question is logged in your mailbox or electronic notebook for reference. You can also leave messages for people when they are away from their desks—at meetings or on business trips or vacations. Then they can respond and you'll get the message even if this time you're the one who's not available.

Email is interactive—that is, two-way communication can occur. So a message may be superseded immediately by an exchange of information between senders and receivers. When they use interactive systems, people tend to feel they are listened to more carefully by their supervisors. And they can "talk back" without the risk of a face-to-face confrontation.

Portable or laptop computers also have increased the use of email. Suppose you're on deadline with a major writing task and you work at home until 3 a.m. to finish it. You write a short memo to the vice president for corporate communication explaining that, because you finished the project at 3 a.m., you won't be in the office at your regular time. You send the memo and your copy to the office and go to bed. When you awaken at 9 a.m., you find an email message from the VP saying that the copy looks great and that you should sleep tight.

And email systems make it possible for you to be an integral part of your organization even though you may be working at home or in an airport lounge on the other side of the world.

With email you can attach digital images as well as text documents and database files. The world's largest provider of email and Internet services is America Online (AOL), a division of Time Warner. Founded in 1985, AOL purchased CompuServe in 1998 and now serves more than 35 million members around the world.[1]

Companies in crisis situations have found email particularly useful because it allows for a timely interchange of information across not only geographic boundaries, but also those that separate customers and investors from management and even employees from management and each other.

T A B L E   7 . 1   *Emoticons—Spin-offs of the Smiley Face :-)*

;-)	Winky smiley	:-)~	User drools	:0	Yelling	3:]	Pet smiley
:-(	Frowning smiley	:~)	User has a cold	:*)	User is intoxicated	[]:*	Hugs and kisses
(-:	User is left-handed	:'-(	User is crying	:-Q	User smokes	:-D	User is laughing
[:]	User is a robot		The invisible smiley	-)	User wears a turban	(:-)}	User is bald and bearded
8-)	User is wearing sunglasses	:^)	User has a broken nose	:-e	User is disappointed	(:-{~	User has a beard
8:-)	User is a little girl	:-#	User wears braces	*:o)	User is a clown	|-( )	User is yawning
:-{)	User has a mustache	-:-)	User is a punk rocker	:->	User is being sarcastic	oo—-oo-Bo	User is a truck driver
:-{}	User wears lipstick	:-X	User's lips are sealed	%-)	User has been staring at the screen for 15 hours	. . . And hundreds more are on the Internet!	
{:-)	User wears a toupee	:-o	Uh oh!	:-:	Mutant smiley		
:-[	User is a vampire	<:-|	User is a dunce	:-C	User is really bummed		
:-*	User just ate something sour	+:-)	Smiley priest				
		:-&	User is tongue-tied				

Formats and Content

One version of email, instant messaging (IM), allows a person to interact instantly via an email format with people on a "buddy" or "contact" list, as long as all of the people involved are online. IM allows a person to create a private chat room with another individual or group, if all are online.

A newer development in email is short-text messaging services (SMS) that allow a cell phone user to send and receive email. *The New York Times* reported, "The thumb-typing trend, Telephia says, is especially strong among American wireless subscribers between the ages of 18 to 24—45 percent of whom used text messaging this year, compared with 22 percent last year."[2]

Responding to an email is simple; all you need to do to respond to one is click the reply button, type in your response and then click "send." The problem is what you say and how you say it. The ease of this technology often works against clarity and accuracy. People tend to write "stream of consciousness" messages and send them unedited. The consequences can be mystifying to the recipients, who try to figure out what you meant from what you sent. Other consequences, such as lawsuits, are more serious. Email files are regularly subpoenaed in both investigations and lawsuits.

The spontaneity of the process often encourages intemperate remarks that can result in legal action. The system itself is regarded as a cross between a telephone message and a letter or interoffice memo, so it encourages people to put messages on the screen that they would never put on paper. The result has been some unpleasant legal battles over discrimination or sexual harassment, for example.

The ease of sending copies simultaneously to many people also can create difficulties. This method, used sparingly, is an efficient way to expedite communication. For PR people, email is especially useful in working with media representatives. Text and image files can be attached to email messages, and copies of emails are saved automatically.

Philip Vassallo says that email simply may be too easy.[3] That inspires some people to fire off messages on a whim without considering that they are using company property. This tends to saturate computers with so many messages that the management of information is more difficult and costly. It also forces readers to wade through a lot of items trying to find out what needs their attention.

Like messages in other media, you need to know exactly what you want the receiver to think, know or do. That strategic approach sharpens the focus of your message. You also need to know how much the reader knows about the subject. If it is a lot, your message can be terse. If it is little or none, your message must be longer because you must provide enough background from which the reader can make a decision.

The process of emailing is so easy that some people tend to forget that it is also writing. That can be disastrous because writing demands a lot more precision than speaking. That fact alone should warn us away from being too casual in the way we write emails.

Writing cannot duplicate speech. When talking with someone face-to-face, we can rely on facial expressions and body language to supplement what we say. But emails are made only of words on screens or printouts. For example, a word may have a common meaning, but voice inflection can give it an entirely different connotation. The point is that it is a mistake to approach emails as you do speech.

Style

Remember that although the message is electronic, the recipient is human and you need to imagine how that person is likely to respond to your message. Begin with an appropriate greeting, one that you might use in face-to-face conversation or on the phone with that person.

You need to be conversational in tone because this is a more spontaneous type of communication, but avoid words that might be acceptable if spoken but sound too harsh or inflammatory in print. They will be in print, on the screen, even if a hard copy isn't made.

Let the person know right away what the message is about so they can begin to follow your thought processes. In the subject line, use short but relevant information that will lead the reader into the messge. Make it easy to read by using simple words, short sentences and very brief paragraphs.

Let the recipient know what you expect from them. Use something like, "Please let me know about *xyz.*" Or "I'll expect to hear from you this afternoon [or a time and date] about the following: 1. *x;* 2. *y;* 3. *z.*" This allows them to respond perhaps immediately by saying something like, "Thanks for your message this morning. I can tell you now about *x* and *y.* Before I answer you about *z,* I need to make some phone calls. I'll get back to you by [date and time]. Good to hear from you."

Used the right way, email can be a very satisfying means of communication. Excessive, inconsiderate or inappropriate use can elevate your blood pressure considerably. See Table 7.2 for some email do's and don'ts.

Memos

The word *memo* is the short form of *memorandum,* meaning an informal reminder of something important that has occurred or will occur. Memos are generally used to communicate

T A B L E   7 . 2   *Do's and Don'ts of Email*   Most people think of email as quick, casual, responsive and fun. It is so easy to use, it may be abused. These do's and don'ts may help you to better use business email.

1. Always make hard copies of all important documents sent or received.

2. Make sure the email address is correct. If incorrect, it may not return to you for hours. The solution is to keep your online address book current.

3. Always write a subject line. This gives addressees an idea of the content in just a few words.

4. Verify each day that the internal clock on your computer is correct. This helps you and receivers to sort through messages chronologically.

5. Keep the caps lock key in the off position. All caps in emails is the equivalent of shouting.

6. Avoid abbreviations. However, they're acceptable in personal emails.

7. You can express yourself informally in email. But remember that email demands good writing, a level of preciseness that speaking sometimes does not require. Your writing can't duplicate speech.

8. Formal greetings or closings don't work well in email. Be more personal, as in "Hi, Diana." Don't use "Sincerely" or "Respectfully" in closing. Use something like "Cheers" or "All the best."

9. Keep sentences short, averaging no more than about 12 to 15 words. Avoid run-on sentences and conditional clauses. These can be confusing.

10. Remember that email is instant. You don't get a second chance after clicking on the send button. Make sure the message is accurate in fact and correct in grammar, spelling and punctuation.

11. Attach only documents to your email that you know can be downloaded by the receiver.

12. Be sensitive to what you say and how it may be interpreted.

13. Email is not private. Don't say anything in email that you don't want your boss to see or that you would not want to see on the front page of a newspaper. Send it another way if your message is private or confidential.

14. Read your incoming email regularly, perhaps at set intervals during the workday.

15. When an email requires action by the receiver and you don't get a timely response, follow up. Don't delay.

16. When sending to a group, ask three questions of yourself: Does each group member need the message? Does each have sufficient background to understand the message? Does each member of the group have operating responsibilities that relate to the message? If no, modify the content or exclude them.

17. Don't use business email systems to send jokes and other nonbusiness matter.

within the organization. They should seldom be used to communicate with people outside the organization, with the exception of those sent to members of boards, committees and task forces. Messages sent by email and fax are often written in memo format.

Memo Formats

A good memo disseminates information simply. It should begin with a guide to its contents, as in the following example:

To: John Gill, controller
From: Susan McConnell, investor relations
Date: September 7, 200x
Subject: Planning conference for 200x annual report, September 14, 2 p.m., in the conference room

If the writer and receiver know each other, the memo style may be even less formal, containing neither last names nor titles. This is especially common when the memo is to someone in the same office or immediate area of operations.

When people have the same mailing address, it is unnecessary to use anything more than a departmental designation. Include addresses below the names if the addresses are different, such as different internal post office box numbers. Of course, if you are using digital or printed letterhead, there's no need to include your address below your name. If you don't use letterhead or if you have stationery that does not include phone numbers and addresses, include your address. The memo would then look like this:

To: John Gill, controller, POB 311
From: Susan McConnell, investor relations, POB 286
Date: September 7, 200x
Subject: Planning conference for 200x annual report, September 14, 2 p.m., in the conference room

A variant of this format calls attention to the direction of the correspondence by using all caps for the "TO" and "FROM," and some use "RE" for "Regarding" instead of the word "Subject."

An element that may appear on memos when mailed or sent by fax is who is receiving copies of the communication, other than the person addressed. The old designation of "cc" stood for "carbon copy." No one uses carbons now, so just use one "c," either lowercase or a capital. This can go below the topic of the memo or at the end of the body of the memo. If it's only one name, you may find it easier to put the "C: Jane Penney, CFO" (chief financial officer) below the topic. If a number of people are getting the message, but only for their information, put the names at the end of the body of the memo.

When you are sending the memo to a number of people, all of whom are supposed to act on it, you need to list them all in the "TO," skipping spaces between each, but including their addresses and/or their phone and fax numbers. There's a practical reason for using the fax number last. Some fax operators only look at the last number when they get ready to transmit the message. The phone number of the recipient is included because some offices share a fax machine; the person responsible for collecting and distributing the faxes can contact the recipient when the fax arrives. In a large corporation, a department post office box or room number may be necessary to ensure delivery of the fax. Your memo or fax now looks like this:

TO: John Gill, controller, POB 311, Phone: 741-3186, ext. 322, Fax: 741-3111
           Larry Miller, public relations, POB 287, Phone: 741-2654, ext. 343, Fax: 741-2655
FROM: Susan McConnell, investor relations, POB 286, Phone: 741-2651, ext. 434, Fax: 741-5322
DATE: September 7, 200x
RE: Planning conference for 200x annual report, September 14, 2 p.m., in the conference room
C: Jane Penney, CFO

Many word processing programs include attractive preformatted memo and fax formats that include blanks for the essential information. Your organization may have templates of its own design. If so, use them.

Body   The body of a memo differs from the body of a letter by being shorter and by providing more visual cues, such as lists of numbered items.

Memos are designed to communicate salient information quickly and efficiently. Their tone ranges from formal to informal. Memos directed up the chain of command tend to be more formal, whereas those directed down the chain tend to be less formal. The least formal of all are memos that move between people at the same level in the organization. Exceptions to these guidelines turn on personal relationships. For example, an account executive in a public relations company would probably write a fairly formal memo to the president of the agency, unless the president happened to be a fishing partner.

Memos ordinarily have a limited public. They usually are addressed to just one person or to a small group. At times, however, they may be directed to a large public. For example, the president of the company may distribute a memo to all 600 employees simultaneously, stating that the company has just recorded its highest annual profits ever. This information, of course, would also be appropriate in the company newsletter and in releases to the media, but the memo is often used to share important information quickly with all employees. A common practice is to use email to reach all employees who have email addresses within the organization and to send paper copies to those without email at their work location.

Visual Cues   In addition to having an explanatory salutation, the memo usually contains a number of visual cues that help communicate important information quickly.

The most important stylistic characteristic is the use of common words, short sentences and brief paragraphs. The last is especially important, because a memo is typed single space with double spaces between paragraphs. Each paragraph represents a new but related thought. In effect, each paragraph is a subsequent "take" in the thought processes that organize information related to the content and purpose of the memo.

Other visual cues, often not found in letters, are indented paragraphs (for emphasis), numbered items (to accent important matter), fragmented sentences (for emphasis, but be cautious about using these often) and lists of items (often in vertical format rather than serially in a paragraph).

Context   Memo writers tend to assume that, because the person addressed in the memo is a member of the team, he or she knows all the pertinent background information related to the topic at hand. This is often a mistake. If you want to be understood, provide clarifying information that makes what you say comprehensible and leaves little room for misinterpretation. Do not, of course, provide superfluous information.

Establishing a context for your message is especially important if the memo is directed to people with whom you do not work regularly. When in doubt, always provide appropriate background materials. These may not be needed, but it is better to be safe than sorry. (See Table 7.3 for what *not* to do.)

When you do provide background materials, you need to say so. The way you do that is to put at the bottom of the memo the word "Attachments:" or "Enclosures:" followed by a list of everything you are including. List the items vertically and use bullets so it's easier to check them all. Sometimes not all of the enclosures make it into the envelope. The intended recipient needs to know what to expect.

T A B L E 7 . 3   *How to Make Sure No One Reads Your Memo*

1. Hide the Message in a Block of Print

You want your reader to pick up your document, and put it down again. You can get this block effect in several ways.

- Make the document as long as possible. You see how forbidding the one-page memo is. Imagine seeing two pages of it. Imagine them printed on both sides of one sheet.
- Make your paragraphs long. Think of three inches as a minimum length. Write everything single-space.
- Don't leave a blank space between paragraphs. Announce a new paragraph by indenting the first line ¼ of an inch. Add as many modifiers as you need to make sure the last line in a paragraph extends to the right margin.
- Justify the right margin.

Do this and you'll produce a formidable document. It's one most readers will glance at and immediately set aside.

2. Make the Message Appear Difficult and Irrelevant

Your goal is to lose the reader's interest.

- Send the message "To: File" or "To: Distribution." This is a strong barrier. It tells readers that the document has no relevance to them personally. The longer the distribution list at the end, the clearer the message.
- Use the "Subject" announcement to turn off the reader. It should make your topic seem dull or complex. (The word "theory" is especially useful here.)

  There must be no hint that the topic has any immediate importance.
- People who read beyond the subject-heading are a threat. You have to stop them with the first sentence of the text. This sentence *must* contain 30–50 words. It will help if a dozen of these words separate the subject and the verb.

  The first sentence should discuss a single detail of the report. There must be no suggestion of a summary or a conclusion.
- Use the second sentence as a fail-safe device. Hopefully, no one will do more than glance at it. But that glance must show it says nothing about the purpose of the document. It's a good idea if the second sentence starts with a long dependent clause. Let it begin with "If" or "Although."

Readers who go beyond the second sentence are intrepid and will be hard to stop. But they can be slowed down. You must take steps to frustrate them.

3. Make Individual Sentences Difficult to Read

Again, you should follow the example of the Fort Knox memo. It illustrates all the important techniques. Try them.

- Use a typeface that is hard to read.

  Write with a sans serif font. This is more difficult for many people to read. (A good word-processing program will let you choose from a dozen or more fonts, some of them pretty bizarre.)

  WRITE IN ALL CAPS. THIS SLOWS DOWN READING BY 10 PERCENT OR MORE.

  Use 8-point type. The tiny print puts so many words on a crowded page that your reader, on finishing one line, will have difficulty seeing where the next line begins.
- Write crowded sentences.

  Use long, compound-complex sentences. Begin with a participial phrase 15 words long, and end with a "which" clause that is 20 words long. Insert one or two parenthetical sentences in every paragraph. Keep your subject some distance from your verb. Stay with the passive voice.

continued

7 . 3   *(continued)*

- Use vague jargon that turns off the reader. Rely on abstractions, words ending in "ness," "ity," "tion," "ence," "ship," and "ment." Avoid anything specific, like proper names or sums of money.

  Devise difficult words, like "consortial," and challenging phrases, like "quantum signification." Introduce obscure acronyms, like "B.O.A. optimization."

  Sprinkle the message with high-sounding cliches, like "pursuant," "in lieu of," "per," "parameter," "closure," and "prioritize." These have deadened reading for years.

- Confuse readers with an unusual division of words. This is a subtle tactic, but quietly effective.

  It bothers most people to see merged forms like "problemsolver" and "costeffective." They are thrown off by words unexpectedly separated, like "fore men" and "counter indicated." They will be frustrated by unusual hyphens, as in "bi-nomial" and "di-agnostic." And you can unsettle them with slashed creations, like "enhance/monitor."

  Always justify your right margin. This leaves disturbing gaps between words throughout the text.

- Provide a dim copy. Make your readers work to recognize the words on the page.

By now you have the message. If you want your memo to remain unread, you can do wonders. You can offer a block of print, or introduce it with a deadly subject-head, or write awkward sentences full of strange acronyms. You won't need to do this often.

But you will see these forms every day. You'll see reports crowded with pages, and pages crowded with words, and paragraphs crowded with tiny print. You'll see messages written in all-caps or in italics or in the Mos Eisley font. You'll see dot-matrix print too faint to read and dittographed memos which have faded into obscurity. You'll throw away some important announcement because the subject-head read "Patterns of Supernumerary Clarification."

And all these documents come from people who genuinely want to be read. Somehow they never learned that effective writing takes more than facts, vocabulary, and prose style. It takes readability.

Source: The above is excerpted from Daniel McDonald's "Achieving the Unreadable Memo" in *Et cetera* (Fall 1992): 280–284. Reprinted with permission of the International Society for General Semantics.

The procedure is a bit different when you are sending a fax. You may need to use a cover page for the fax, which looks like the heading of the fax, but also tells the addressee how many pages to expect.

TO:	Alan Cooper	Phone: (313) 457-6733	Fax: (313) 457-6734
FROM:	Susan Foster	Phone: (623) 535-6354	Fax: (623) 535-7453
DATE:	October 1, 200x		
RE:	Artwork for St. Louis Hospital Brochure		
PAGES:	6 plus cover		

Classifications of Memos

The tone and tempo of a memo depend on its purpose, style and public. There are six general categories of memos: bulletin, essay, informative, action, summary and file.

Bulletin Memo   The bulletin memo usually has a sense of urgency. It is generally brief and may be terse in style. It is the telegram of the memo world. The bulletin memo gets its name from the bulletins that appear on the wire services notifying editors that something important has happened or is about to happen. Given the nature of its content, such a memo may wind up being posted on a bulletin board, even if it is addressed to just one person.

Essay Memo   An essay memo is usually much more descriptive than a bulletin memo. It is used for "let's talk it over" material or situations. Its content may range from management philosophy to questions of how to get employees to clean up the coffee room after using it. The style is often conversational.

Informative Memo   The informative memo is usually a detailed descriptive piece of writing. An example might be a memo from the account executive to the account group and client. This memo might document actions taken and their results. Or it might recommend programs and describe projected outcomes. The style and tone of these memos are usually fairly formal.

Action Memo   The action memo describes action taken or planned. Such memos, especially those dealing with future actions, often contain places for responses by recipients. For example, there might be a space for the receiver's initials on a section to indicate that he or she accepts responsibility for the initialed action. Or in the case of a supervisor, the initials might indicate approval or disapproval of the planned action.

Action memos sometimes include an element of coercion. This may be the case, for instance, when the author of the memo does not assign or suggest responsibility but seeks volunteers to assume responsibility. Coercion is at work when the implication of the memo is, "If you don't select an area of responsibility, one will be assigned to you." If you're alert to this message, you'll quickly "volunteer" for the area of action that you will do best and enjoy most.

Summary Memo   A summary memo is basically a detailed descriptive memo in essay or outline form. Discussions and actions are collected under appropriate topical headings to facilitate progress during a meeting. The summary memo is frequently used, too, in evaluating the progress of a program. In this case, it reflects an accumulation of information over time and often explains actions taken or planned.

File Memo   As its name implies, a file memo is addressed to the file—not to another person. It simply records information and is stored for reference. Memos of this type are used extensively when the program being planned is complex, when many people are involved in some ongoing action or program or when sharp divisions in points of view arise as to how or whether something should be done. In style and tone, it may be terse, almost cryptic. The purpose, remember, is merely to record information for internal use.

In a sense, a file memo is like a diary. It records names, dates, places and points of information. If serious debate arises over how or whether something should be done, the file memo should identify individuals with their respective points of view, even including verbatim accounts as necessary.

Factors Affecting the Use of Memos

Memos should be personalized. Involve the recipient with your memo by emphasizing "you." This is not only a pleasant way to write, it is also effective.

The way your memo is distributed may affect the attention it receives. Email distribution is the most common way .

Routing one paper copy to each of the people who should read it is another way. A routing slip is attached and the memo is passed from one person to the next. Each person initials the slip to indicate it has been read and then passes the memo on to the person whose name appears next on the list. Although routing is a common practice, it can be a problem if the content of the memo is timely. People tend to assign a lower priority to a message attached to a routing form than to a message addressed to them personally. Therefore, even if you save some paper and copying costs by routing memos, you may wind up paying a high price in lost opportunities.

Posting memos on a bulletin board is a common practice, but this can be even less effective than routing them. The company bulletin board is often filled with messages that remain unread by many people in the organization. If you intend your memo for posting, design it like a poster. Add graphics to gain attention, and treat the content like a bulletin to encourage easy, quick reading.

If your memo is to be distributed to a large number of people in the organization, you have several options. The best approach, of course, is to email the memo to each person. An alternative is to provide supervisors with stacks of copies and rely on them to pass a copy along to each employee. Many supervisors will be careful to distribute the information, but others will not, and communication breakdowns may result.

Some memos are best suited for special methods of distribution. For example, an announcement about changes in employee insurance coverage might best be inserted into payroll envelopes. You can count on employees opening their pay envelopes and seeing your memo, except for those who have opted for direct deposit to their bank accounts. (The payroll department will be able to tell you what percentage of employees have selected this option.) On the other hand, a memo about the company picnic might better be mailed to employees' homes, as you'll want other members of the employee's household to know about the event too.

The setting in which the memo is received may also influence its effectiveness. Obviously, the company picnic is a social event that involves the employee and the employee's family. Therefore, it is appropriate to send the memo announcing it to employees' home addresses. However, a memo calling a meeting of department heads should be emailed or sent to the recipients' respective offices, not to their homes. In general, if the memo is social, send it to the employee's home; if it is business, send it to the employee's work address.

Letters

Even though the use of email has greatly increased, letters still play a significant role in business relationships. The problem is that some letter writers think that because they are going to the trouble to write a letter it must be long. One solicitation letter from a university president to alumni was four full pages. Too long. As a rule, try to keep your letters to one page in a readable size of type. To give one-page letter writers more space, many letterhead designers put all addresses, including email, phone and fax information, in a single line along the bottom of the stationery. This also helps response rates.

Business Letter Format

The typical business letter has six parts: heading, salutation, body, close, signature and reference matter.

Heading   The heading has two parts. The first is the identity of the sender. This material is usually printed on the letterhead. The second part is the date, plus the name, title and address of the recipient. The heading should always contain these elements, even when you know the person you are writing to quite well. Always document the sender and receiver completely and accurately.

Salutation   In the salutation you address the person to whom you are writing. This might appear to be a simple proposition, but it can cause some problems if you are insensitive to your receiver.

Suppose you are writing a letter from your CEO to Doug Newsom, one of the co-authors of this text, seeking names of people who might be used as public relations consultants. You might address Doug variously as "Dear Mr. Newsom," "Dear Professor Newsom," "Dear Dr. Newsom" or "Dear Doug." The first salutation would be incorrect because Doug's name is Douglas *Ann* Newsom, but she goes by Doug. The second form would be acceptable, because she is a professor. The third form would be correct too, because she does have an earned doctorate. The last form would be correct only if your CEO knows her personally. Two points are illustrated here: Avoid using a gender-specific title if you don't know the person's gender, and do not use a title if you don't know that it is correct.

If you are writing a promotional letter to send to hundreds of clients and it will not be personalized by name, use a salutation like "Dear Customer," "Dear Client" or "Dear Colleague." Even though these salutations are impersonal, they are better than ones that might be genuinely offensive.

Body   The level of formality in the tone depends on the relationship between the writer and the recipient of the letter. If a personal relationship exists, the letter may have a casual salutation and a conversational tone. In general, the tone of the body will be more formal if the letter is addressed to a person whose status is higher than that of the writer; it will be more informal if the writer's status is higher than the recipient's.

Close   The close of a business letter contains two elements. One is a call to action (if that is the purpose of the letter) or an offer of further help. The other is a complimentary statement that appears above the signature. Most business letters close with a simple "Sincerely" above the signature block. Business letters to and from friends outside the company sometimes close with "Best regards," "Cordially yours" or simply "Cordially." Letters between strangers are more likely to have a more formal close, such as "Respectfully yours" or "Respectfully." Whatever the form used, only the first letter of the close is capitalized.

Signature   The name of the writer should always be typed; the handwritten signature will appear just above it. The signer's title should also be typed immediately below the name if the title is not printed on the letterhead.

When the recipient is a friend, the signer might inscribe only his or her first name. If little or no personal relationship exists between the writer and the receiver, however, the full signature is required.

Reference Matter   All business letters prepared by a person other than the sender should contain symbols below the signature block that look like this:

BC:rlb

The capitalized letters are the initials of the writer and the small letters are the initials of the person who keyboarded the letter. If the writer keyboarded the letter, do not include any initials.

The next element in the reference material is a notation about enclosures, if any, that go with the letter. The notation reads like this:

Enc.: [name of enclosure(s)]

This note serves both as a form of documentation by the sender of the message and a flag to the receiver that material is enclosed.

The third element in the reference material designates other people (if any) who are to receive a copy of the letter. The designation reads like this:

C: [name of people who also receive copies]

You may use "bc," which stands for "blind copy." Use this when you want to share information with another without letting those who received official copies know about it. (The "bc," of course, appears on your copy only.)

Types of Letters

Public relations writers generally find themselves writing six types of letters: information, solicitation, promotion, transmittal, cover and response.

Information   Naturally, these letters inform. They let people know about an event coming up, a decision made or an action taken. A letter of recommendation for a person would also be of this type. They are straightforward and try to anticipate and respond to any questions the reader might have. Although these letters might require an acknowledgment, they seldom require a response.

Solicitation   Letters making any kind of request can be considered a solicitation. Nonprofit organizations often write letters asking for contributions or pledges of support of one kind or another. Politicians ask for your support and your vote. These letters should be careful to suggest some sort of reward, usually intrinsic, for that support. Letters from an environmental group may ask you to "Save the Rain Forest." The question is "Why?" The letter will probably tell you that many of the new medicines that could save your life are being discovered in the rain forest.

Promotion   Causes or events are promoted in letters that encourage your acceptance and participation. There should be an emotional appeal in the letter but also a specific call to action. By using subheads, italics, boldface, underlining and indents, you can help the reader to spot these two important elements in your message.

Transmittal   Use letters of transmittal when you are sending a number of materials to someone, like a client. The letter reminds the receiver of what is being sent and why. Sometimes it is appropriate to tell the person to call after receiving the materials, especially if there are any questions or concerns. This letter should have a paragraph that lists the contents, separating items with indented bullets, and with at least the titles in boldface. You want to make it easy for the person to look at the letter, see what should be included in the package and quickly determine if everything listed is indeed included.

Cover   Some people confuse cover letters with letters of transmittal. The cover letter is a very brief note in letter format that simply tells the recipient what is being sent, why and what the recipient might be interested in doing with it.

Response   The most important form of response letter is the "Thank You." You should thank people for doing or saying something to support you or your organization. It's amazing how many people think to ask but forget to thank. You can build strong relationships by being gracious and thoughtful.

Responses can be intended for private or public use. Response letters are usually written to react to something that has occurred, which may be something said or written. The *private response* letters are written to *individuals* with the anticipation that the letter will not be made public. However, it's always possible that the recipient will make the letter public. Therefore, it's better to write all letters with the anticipation that the contents may be made public.

Some letters are written for public use, and often these are sent to news media to be published or broadcast. Some are written to correct or to put something in perspective. Others are observations or comments. You can find these in newspaper and magazine "letters to the editor" columns and hear them on radio and on television, where a brief version of the contents often is scrolled for the viewer. The important point to remember about public letters is to be direct and concise. The editor of the medium is not going to give you much time or space. Think in terms of sound bites even when you're writing for print.

Choose your words carefully, because the tone of the expression conveys both mood and character. Be persuasive in your choice, because you want to have an impact. You may be writing to change an opinion that a previous presentation in the media has created, or you may be attempting to correct an error that has been made by a medium. Be clear. These letters get a quick scan. You need to be sure your point is not missed.

Some broadcast media allow verbal responses called in to be taped. If you plan to make such a call, write the response first. Read it into a tape recorder and play it back. You should say what you have to say in 15 seconds or maybe 20. No more. It won't be used if it isn't succinct. Try out your response on some others who are hearing it for the first time without seeing the written piece. Test for tone and clarity. Many public relations writers will have to get response letters cleared by multiple levels of management. You will have to be very persistent to prevent distortion of the message. Be cautious about using humor or sarcasm. These can be easily misunderstood or taken for arrogance.

Reports and Proposals

They may look alike, which can be confusing, but reports and proposals are very different. Their differences become apparent in their purposes. A report summarizes information on some topic. A proposal details a plan of action to be considered.

You might say that a report is a summary of the status of something. Suppose you're on the management team of a food processing company and marketer. The company has endured a slight decline in market share and profitability the last two years because it has not adopted some new technologies that competitors are using to produce products at lower costs. The chief financial officer was asked three months ago to prepare a report that evaluates the economics of these new technologies. That report, contained in a 48-page booklet, is before the team now, having been distributed to members a week earlier so they could study it in detail.

After lengthy discussion, the team asked the director of manufacturing to prepare a proposal that describes in detail what the company must do to acquire these technologies, its costs and a time line that projects when the new technologies could become operational. It should be clear that when the report is presented it will deal with a planned, recommended course of action. It is then that the management team must make a go or no-go decision to take the proposal to its board of directors for ratification and implementation.

The requirements for organizing and writing reports and proposals are similar enough for both to be considered together. As used here, the terms *report* and *proposal* refer to extensive documents that are researched, written and presented much like a traditional scholarly research paper or the manuscript for a monograph or book.

In fact, if you must write a report or proposal of this type, the first thing you should do is get a copy of a style manual such as Turabian, Grossman and Bennett's *A Manual for Writers of Term Papers, Theses and Dissertations.* A style manual will save you innumerable hours of research time by showing you, as you begin to research the project, what information you need to gather and how to credit it.

Organization of Reports and Proposals

After your research on the topic is completed, you are ready to begin to organize and write your report or proposal. This requires special skills and attention to details, because a finished project often has as many as seven major sections: letter, front matter, executive summary, body, references, bibliography and appendixes.

Letter   A letter of documentation should always accompany a report or a proposal. Sometimes a letter of transmittal should also be included if there are many enclosures.

A letter of documentation, sometimes called a *cover letter,* addresses the person or people who will consider the report or proposal. It usually describes both the content of the report and the people who did the research, planning, writing and illustrating. The letter may close with a brief summary of findings or recommendations, and it may call attention to any conditions affecting adoption or rejection. Finally, it should indicate where to locate the person who signed the letter. A letter of documentation is sometimes made a part of the report, in which case it should be inserted immediately following the front matter.

A letter of transmittal is needed when a person or group has been authorized to write a report or proposal. It should seek to establish the credibility of the report or proposal. The letter should note who gave the authorization and when, as well as summarize results or recommendations. It may include a list of acknowledgments of special help or meritorious work by individuals who contributed to the project. Such a letter allows you to include information that may not belong in the body of the document but nonetheless provides additional insights into what is there.

Skillfully written letters of documentation and transmittal prepare readers of the document for what follows.

Front Matter   The front matter in a report or proposal is organized in the same general way as the front matter of this book. It consists of a cover page, a table of contents and a list of tables, figures and illustrations. These pages are numbered serially with small Roman numerals (i, ii, iii, iv, v and so on). Although the cover page is counted in this series of numbers, no number appears on the cover page.

Executive Summary   When an executive summary or synopsis is used, it appears at the end of the front matter and before the body of the report or proposal. Usually only a page or two in length, it is a concisely written digest of the content of the document. Its purpose is to give the reader a clear picture of what is in the document. (See Figure 7.1.) In the business world, *executive summary* is the term most often used, and you'll be expected to use it when your employer asks you to write a report or proposal.

Body   The body of the report or proposal follows the executive summary. It consists of three basic parts: introduction, body and conclusions.

The introduction should review the background of the problem being studied, the scope of the study and the methods used in the study. It should also explain why the study is important, what special problems (if any) were encountered in the course of research and how these were resolved. The last point is especially important because it prepares the reader for any limitations of the study. In a proposal, the introduction might review the activities that have preceded the submission of the proposal—meetings, the request for the proposal and, sometimes, the proposing organization's capabilities and competencies related to the work to be accomplished.

The body of a report should be built around a single, simple statement. Called a *thesis statement* or *hypothesis,* it unifies the entire report and helps you address the issue point by logical point. Develop each point and support it with pertinent facts. Use headings and subheads to guide the reader through the body of the report.

The body of a proposal often focuses on the objective and goals to be met if the proposal is accepted, along with the activities to be undertaken. A timeline for the activities, along with a budget and information on the people who will be undertaking the activities, also is common.

Conclusions should follow naturally from any summary findings in the report or proposal. Sometimes recommendations will stem from your conclusions. Conclusions and recommendations should be stated clearly. This may take courage, because you may conclude or recommend something that your readers would prefer to ignore. Clarity is necessary because a report or proposal that invites many interpretations is not very useful to anyone.

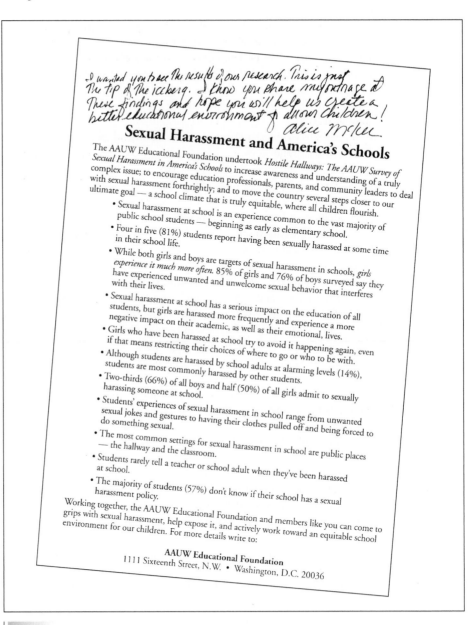

I wanted you to see the results of our research. This is just the tip of the iceberg. I know you share my outrage at these findings and hope you will help us create a better educational environment for all our children!

Alice McKee

Sexual Harassment and America's Schools

The AAUW Educational Foundation undertook *Hostile Hallways: The AAUW Survey of Sexual Harassment in America's Schools* to increase awareness and understanding of a truly complex issue; to encourage education professionals, parents, and community leaders to deal with sexual harassment forthrightly; and to move the country several steps closer to our ultimate goal — a school climate that is truly equitable, where all children flourish.

- Sexual harassment at school is an experience common to the vast majority of public school students — beginning as early as elementary school.
- Four in five (81%) students report having been sexually harassed at some time in their school life.
- While both girls and boys are targets of sexual harassment in schools, *girls experience it much more often.* 85% of girls and 76% of boys surveyed say they have experienced unwanted and unwelcome sexual behavior that interferes with their lives.
- Sexual harassment at school has a serious impact on the education of all students, but girls are harassed more frequently and experience a more negative impact on their academic, as well as their emotional, lives.
- Girls who have been harassed at school try to avoid it happening again, even if that means restricting their choices of where to go or who to be with.
- Although students are harassed by school adults at alarming levels (14%), students are most commonly harassed by other students.
- Two-thirds (66%) of all boys and half (50%) of all girls admit to sexually harassing someone at school.
- Students' experiences of sexual harassment in school range from unwanted sexual jokes and gestures to having their clothes pulled off and being forced to do something sexual.
- The most common settings for sexual harassment in school are public places — the hallway and the classroom.
- Students rarely tell a teacher or school adult when they've been harassed at school.
- The majority of students (57%) don't know if their school has a sexual harassment policy.

Working together, the AAUW Educational Foundation and members like you can come to grips with sexual harassment, help expose it, and actively work toward an equitable school environment for our children. For more details write to:

AAUW Educational Foundation
1111 Sixteenth Street, N.W. • Washington, D.C. 20036

FIGURE 7.1

Synopsis with an Appeal   *This is a synopsis of a report from research funded by the American Association of University Women. The appeal at the top is signed by the foundation's president, and the report includes a donation card and a self-addressed return envelope, along with the summary of the research. This publicizes the work of the foundation and attempts to increase donations to support other research.*

Source: Reprinted with permission of the AAUW Educational Foundation

References   In a report or proposal of this type, you must properly cite the source of every piece of information that is not common knowledge to your public. This means using footnotes or endnotes, with complete bibliographic citations, so anyone can locate and read the original materials. In this respect, proposals and reports are exactly like scholarly research papers.

Bibliography   In addition to supplying footnotes or endnotes, you must include a full bibliography. The bibliography, of course, includes all of the basic sources cited in the footnotes or endnotes, but it also includes sources you reviewed but did not specifically cite in the body of the paper. Thus the bibliography identifies the full range of works you consulted, whether or not you eventually cited them.

Appendixes   An appendix contains any charts, tables, illustrations, maps, copies of questionnaires and other exhibits that could not be woven into the body of the paper. As a general rule, the only items of this type that should appear in the body are simple tables and charts illustrating specific points. More complex material goes in the appendixes. Be certain, however, that you interpret the complex materials sufficiently to make them understandable. Each appendix should be labeled separately—Appendix A, B and so on.

Readability and Applicability

A reader of your report or proposal should be able to conclude something from what you have written. Two factors will influence this outcome: readability and applicability.

Readability   If your report or proposal is in a specialized field, your reader expects to see jargon common to that field used in your document. But this is not a license to use jargon without restraint. On the contrary, you should write in plain English with just enough jargon to establish your credibility with the reader.

Jargon invariably makes your writing more difficult to understand. Review the readability formulas in Appendix A. Try out Gunning's Fog Index on some samples of writing in your report. Then go back and do some severe editing to make it clearer and easier to understand.

Unless you are an extraordinarily gifted and lucky writer, you will not be able to write a good report or proposal in the first draft. You will probably have to write the whole report at least twice. You may have to rewrite several times. In this sense, the art of good report and proposal writing is rewriting.

If time allows, you are sure to improve the readability of your report by writing a draft and then putting it aside for a week or more. When you pick up the document and read it cold, trouble spots will jump out at you. Fix them immediately and do the reorganizing and rewriting necessary to clarify the draft.

And don't forget that headings, subheads, indented segments, underlining and other visuals can improve readability.

All these points apply to both reports and proposals, but one consideration applies to proposals alone. In a sense, proposals resemble ad copy. They are meant to persuade, to sell ideas. So showmanship with words counts more in proposals than in reports.

Applicability   When you complete a report, you will want your readers to accept the document as meaningful and significant enough to prompt a course of action. You'll want your readers to say, "This is important. We should do something." When you submit a proposal, you'll be trying to evoke this response: "This is a really good idea. Let's go with it."

You will elicit such judgments only if the reader finds what you have written to be clear, reliable and justified. Additionally, what you present should be singularly relevant to the situation. And any action you call for must appear easy to accomplish.

Conclusions

- Email is so common now that most people include an email address on their business cards and letterhead.
- When email is a major part of an organization's communication structure, it decreases response time during a crisis.
- Email also facilitates distance communication in that messages can be sent to and from anywhere in the world through cyberspace.
- One difficulty is that because email messages are so spontaneous, writers tend to be careless about content.
- The spontaneity also encourages intemperate remarks that can result in lawsuits.
- Organize email messages carefully, use simple language and tell the recipient what you expect from them by way of a response or some sort of action.
- Instant messaging (IM) allows two or more people to connect and post messages that all members of the IM group can see, identified by screen names.
- Short-text messaging services (SMS) allow a cell phone user to send and receive email.
- Memos usually are for internal communication, an exception being messages sent by email and fax, which employ the memo format.
- The form of address on the memo or fax is critical to getting a good response.
- Memos can be classified in six ways: bulletin, essay, informative, action, summary and file.
- Memos are most effective when addressed to individuals. Effectiveness decreases when they are sent en masse or are posted.
- Letters remain an important means of communication, especially for formal correspondence within the organization and for external communication.
- A letter has six principal parts: heading, salutation, body, close, signature and reference matter.
- Letters can be categorized as: information, solicitation, promotion, transmittal, cover and response.
- Reports and proposals may be done much like scholarly research papers.
- Reports and proposals can have as many as seven parts: letter, front matter, executive summary, body, references, bibliography and appendixes.
- Jargon is expected by readers in specialized fields, but it should be used with restraint.
- Style and visual elements should be used in reports and proposals to improve readability, understanding and acceptance.
- Your reader should come away with a clear sense of the problems studied and your proposed solutions.
- Your suggestions should also serve as a call to action that appears to be doable.

Exercises

1. You are a public relations writer for a hotel in a major resort community. Some extensive remodeling will begin next week on the west wing of the ninth floor. West-wing rooms will be closed, and guests in the east wing will have to put up with some noise and unsightly construction equipment. Prepare a letter for people who have reservations for next week in the east wing of the ninth floor. Explain that the inconvenience will be kept to a minimum.

2. Draft a memo that tells students in your department when the next grammar, spelling, punctuation and keyboard proficiency (typing) tests will be given. Be sure you tell them how to sign up for these tests and how to prepare for them. Let them know if these are prerequisites for taking certain skills classes. Don't forget to address the problem of transfer students who may have had tests like these before. Consult your department's policy on giving the tests.

3. Write a report on ethnic and cultural diversity as represented by your university's statistics on student enrollment over the past five-year period. Then write a cover letter to the admissions department that will accompany the copy of your report to them.

4. Write a proposal for an honors code at your university (if you don't already have one). Cite information on dishonesty at colleges and universities nationwide and information from colleges and universities that have such a code. Write a cover letter to your student government that would accompany the proposal. Remember, your letter has to get them to read the proposal.

Use InfoTrac College Edition to access information on topics in this chapter from hundreds of periodicals and scholarly journals.

Notes

1. AOL staff, "Who We Are," undated, http://corp.aol.com/whoweare/ (November 21, 2003).
2. Simon Romero, "Text Messaging Takes Off," *The New York Times* (December 23, 2002), p. C-8.
3. Philip Vassallo, "U-Mail, I-Mail—More Effective Business E-Mail," *ETC* (Summer 1998): 198.

Selected Bibliography

David Angell and Brent Heslop, *The Elements of E-Mail Style* (Reading, Mass.: Addison-Wesley, 1994).

Gary Blake and Robert W. Bly, *The Elements of Business Writing: A Guide to Writing Clear, Concise Letters, Memos, Reports, Proposals, and Other Business Documents* (Basingstoke Hampshire, England: MacMillan Publishing Company, 1992).

Ron S. Blicq, *Technically Write! Communicating in a Technical Era,* 4th ed. (Englewood Cliffs, N.J.: Prentice Hall, 1993).

Janis F. Chan, Diane Lutovich and Janis Fisher Chan, *How to Write Reports and Proposals* (San Anselmo, Calif.: Advanced Communication Designs, Inc., 1998).

Elizabeth Cohn, *Writing to Please Your Boss and Other Important People Including Yourself: Reports, Proposals, Feasibility Studies, Memoranda on Time and on Target* (Växjö, Sweden: Scandinavian PC Systems, 1990).

Richard C. Freed et al., *Writing Winning Business Proposals: Your Guide to Landing the Client, Making the Sale, Persuading the Boss* (New York: McGraw-Hill, 1995).

Rosemary Fruehing, *Write to the Point! Letters, Memos, and Reports That Get Results* (New York: McGraw-Hill, 1992).

James E. Neal Jr. and Dorothy J. Neal, *Effective Letters for Business, Professional and Personal Use,* 3d ed. (Perrysburg, Ohio: Neal Publications, 1999).

Roy W. Poe, *The McGraw-Hill Handbook of Business Letters,* 4th ed. (New York: McGraw-Hill, 1998).

Tom Sant, *Persuasive Business Proposals: Writing to Win Customers, Clients, and Contracts* (New York: AMACOM, 1992).

Barrett Soden, *Looking Good on Paper: How to Create Eye-Catching Reports, Proposals, Memos, and Other Business Documents* (New York: AMACOM, 1995).

Kate L. Turabian, John Grossman and Alice Bennett, *A Manual for Writers of Term Papers, Theses and Dissertations* (Chicago Guides to Writing, Editing and Publishing), 6th ed. (Chicago: University of Chicago Press, 1996).

Backgrounders and Position Papers

College students like to think that graduation means they can leave behind forever the chore of researching and writing term papers. But if they are going into public relations or many of its related fields, their college experience may represent only the beginning, not the end, of such activity. Beyond the reports and proposals discussed in Chapter 7, PR professionals must compose other kinds of research papers.

Outside academia, these are often called *white papers*. In public relations they are called *backgrounders* or *position* papers. There is a difference. The backgrounder is similar to a historical research paper that looks at a situation or problem in the present by considering its origins and its implications for the future. The position paper more closely resembles a research paper that takes a point of view or perspective on a situation and marshals evidence in support of the position taken.

Reports have obvious value for internal decision making and planning, but they can be critical in media relations, particularly in responding to reporters' inquiries. Reporters may ask questions like: "What's your position on [name of act] now before the Congress in Washington?" "What's your company's stand on the cause of the pollution in [name of river or area]?" "What does your company believe will be the impact of the new EPA rules?" "I'm doing a story on declining innovation in your industry. Can you give me some information?"

Your company's executives must be able to respond quickly and knowledgeably to such questions. A "No comment" response is not acceptable. And if an executive promises to call the reporter back, this must be done faithfully. If such queries are not handled with skill and dispatch, the company loses credibility in a hurry. A company's credibility is hard won and easily lost. A thoughtless response can do unlimited damage.

The role of the public relations writer in such instances is to provide either in-depth information on the topic (in the form of a backgrounder) or a clear, definitive company point of view (in the form of a position paper). As the public relations writer you are the eyes and ears of company spokespeople. You have to arm them with facts—solidly researched and documented, organized in logical fashion, clearly written and easily understandable.

Good public relations departments do not wait until a reporter calls to begin developing basic information for backgrounders and position papers. PR staffers routinely comb popular and specialized media and documents, searching for salient bits of information affecting their company or industry. These bits of information are accumulated and filed for reference. When the task of writing a backgrounder or position paper is assigned, they already have a head start on research.

Sometimes backgrounders and position papers are written and filed away for later use. The hope is that they will not be needed. But if they are, public relations personnel can respond quickly and appropriately to queries from any source.

Preparing backgrounders and position papers is often the first stage in planning a new public relations program. For example, assume that an electric utility is considering a new way of charging for the use of its electricity. The proposal calls for higher rates during the day but very low rates at night and on weekends. The PR department should prepare a backgrounder that describes the history of this time-of-day pricing structure, where such methods have been tried and with what success, the availability and cost of "time" meters and related points. Of course, the backgrounder should also compare this method to the one currently in use and to other methods.

At some point, company management will decide to stay with the present system or go with the time-of-day system. The backgrounder will help management make this decision. If the decision is to adopt the time-of-day system, the backgrounder will be used as the basis for developing and writing a company position paper on the new system. Both the backgrounder and the position paper will contain the information necessary to write news releases, ads, brochures and speeches, as well as articles for the company magazine, newsletter and Web and intranet sites.

Backgrounders tend to be heavy on facts and light on opinion. Position papers are heavy on opinion or interpretation, supported by only a few selected facts. Both can deal with broad or specific questions or issues. However, backgrounders tend to deal with general topics, whereas position papers tend to treat specific issues.

For example, a backgrounder might deal with alternate fuel vehicles (AFVs) to reduce emissions that are contributing to global warming, whereas a position paper would argue for the use of natural gas-fueled vehicles (NGVs) as a solution.

Backgrounders

Backgrounders have many purposes. They serve as an information base for company executives and employees. They provide source materials to copywriters preparing ads, news releases, brochures, speeches or articles for the company magazine, Web site and intranet. They may also be used as documents to hand out to reporters or members of the public who inquire about a certain topic. And company executives on the speakers' circuit can use them to bone up on a subject so they can field questions from the audience. Rarely does a backgrounder serve only one of these purposes; keep all of them in mind.

The hallmarks of a good backgrounder are accuracy and comprehensiveness. This means that the topic must be thoroughly researched.

Research

Doing research for a backgrounder often involves using all the research skills, techniques and sources discussed in Chapter 4. Read that chapter again and review each point as it might apply to researching a backgrounder.

You are not being professionally responsible if you leave one bit of salient information unread or ignored in your evaluation. It just might contain the germ of an idea or the fact that makes all of your other material inconsequential or misleading. This can be fatal to the company because company spokespeople have to rely on you for the information they convey to members of the media or to the public.

Research is a never-ending process. Once a backgrounder is completed, it becomes less useful with each passing day because of new information. You should establish the practice of accumulating pertinent information, filing it and updating the backgrounder at regular intervals. Backgrounders that do not include the very latest important information are worthless.

Writing

Writing a backgrounder begins first with a simple statement of the issue and why it is important. Including such a statement may appear trite, but it is necessary to focus your research and writing: It keeps you on the right track. This opening statement should be both precise and concise. Besides helping you in the writing, it tells the reader what to expect in the document.

Once your opening statement is honed to perfection, write the body of the backgrounder. Be sure to provide an adequate, clear history of the issue, a thorough discussion of the current situation and implications for the future.

Background   As the name implies, a backgrounder supplies background on a topic or issue. It should provide a fairly complete historical overview so a reader unfamiliar with the topic can understand how the current situation evolved. You have to answer the question "Why are things the way they are today?" And you can't answer this question without giving details about how things were and how and why they have changed. (See Figure 8.1.)

The typical backgrounder includes such details as significant historical events, legislative enactments, changes in government and company policy and applicable social conditions. It specifies names, books, documents, articles and reports that played an important part in the development of the issue. In sum, this section of the backgrounder should describe the evolution of the current situation.

Current Situation   Having built a foundation on the past, you should now examine the current situation, including reviewing current public and company policies. Perhaps these points could be extended to include a discussion of alternative policies now under consideration.

The purpose of a backgrounder is to assemble and convey information, not to judge it. Any discussions of policy or alternatives should be presented from an objective, neutral

Backgrounder: Tornadoes

EMERGENCY INFORMATION

1. The best protection during a tornado is in an interior room on the lowest level of a building, preferably a safe room.
2. Tornadoes strike with incredible velocity. Wind speeds may approach 300 miles per hour. These winds can uproot trees and structures and turn harmless objects into deadly missiles, all in a matter of seconds. Mobile homes are particularly vulnerable to tornadoes.
3. Injury or deaths related to tornadoes most often occur when buildings collapse, people are hit by flying objects or are caught trying to escape.
4. Tornadoes are most destructive when they touch ground. Normally a tornado will stay on the ground for no more than 20 minutes; however, one tornado can touch ground several times in different areas.

DANGER ZONES

Tornadoes can occur in any state but are more frequent in the Midwest, Southeast and Southwest. The states of Alabama, Arkansas, Florida, Georgia, Illinois, Indiana, Iowa, Kansas, Louisiana, Mississippi, Missouri, Nebraska, Oklahoma, South Dakota, and Texas are at greatest risk.

WHAT IS A TORNADO?

A tornado is a violent windstorm characterized by a twisting, funnel-shaped cloud. It is spawned by a thunderstorm (or sometimes as a result of a hurricane) and produced when cool air overrides a layer of warm air, forcing the warm air to rise rapidly. The damage from a tornado is a result of the high wind velocity and wind-blown debris. Tornado season is generally March through August, although tornadoes can occur at any time of year. They tend to occur in the afternoons and evenings: over 80 percent of all tornadoes strike between noon and midnight.

HELP YOUR COMMUNITY GET READY

The media can raise awareness about tornadoes by providing important information to the community. Here are some suggestions:

1. Publish a special section in your local newspaper with emergency information about tornadoes. Localize the information by printing the phone numbers of local emergency services offices, the American Red Cross, and hospitals.
2. Periodically inform your community of local public warning systems.
3. Sponsor a "Helping Your Neighbor" program at your local schools to encourage children to think of those persons who require special assistance such as elderly people, infants, or people with disabilities.
4. Conduct a series on how to protect yourself during a tornado in case you are at home, in a car, at the office, or outside.
5. Interview local officials about what people living in mobile home parks should do if a tornado warning is issued.

DID YOU KNOW...

- Tornadoes can be nearly invisible, marked only by swirling debris at the base of the funnel. Some are composed almost entirely of windblown dust and still others are composed of several mini-funnels.
- On average, the United States experiences 100,000 thunderstorms each year. Approximately 1,000 tornadoes develop from these storms.

FIGURE 8.1

Backgrounder: Tornadoes   *Backgrounders do just what the name indicates: they provide background information for a wide range of publics, including news media representatives. This one, from the Federal Emergency Management Agency (FEMA), is available on FEMA's Web site, http://www.fema.gov.*

- Although tornadoes do occur throughout the world, the United States experiences the most intense and devastating tornadoes.
- Tornadoes produce the most violent winds on earth. Tornado winds can approach speeds as high as 300 miles per hour, travel distances over 100 miles and reach heights over 60,000 feet above ground.
- In November 1988, 121 tornadoes struck 15 south central states, resulting in 14 lives lost and damages reaching $108 million.
- According to the National Weather Service, about 42 people are killed because of tornadoes each year.

Fujita - Pearson Tornado Scale

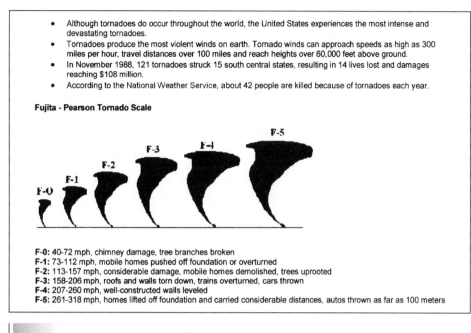

F-0: 40-72 mph, chimney damage, tree branches broken
F-1: 73-112 mph, mobile homes pushed off foundation or overturned
F-2: 113-157 mph, considerable damage, mobile homes demolished, trees uprooted
F-3: 158-206 mph, roofs and walls torn down, trains overturned, cars thrown
F-4: 207-260 mph, well-constructed walls leveled
F-5: 261-318 mph, homes lifted off foundation and carried considerable distances, autos thrown as far as 100 meters

8.1 (*c o n t i n u e d*)

position. Stick to facts. Describe policy options, discuss their good and bad points, but don't judge them.

For example, if the issue is the high cost of home heating and its effects on poor people, one policy to consider might be the use of energy stamps to help poor people pay their utility bills. This idea has its good and bad points. One writer might say:

> Using energy stamps is a poor way to solve the problem because stamps require a massive, wasteful bureaucracy and excessive government funding.

Another writer might say:

> Using energy stamps is an excellent solution to the problem because stamps could be easily administered by existing government organizations.

Both writers may be justified in their points of view, but this is a backgrounder, not a position paper. Instead of taking a position, write to inform, saying:

> Use of energy stamps is one solution to this problem. An energy stamp program would require government funding and a system for administering these funds. Such a program might be administered by existing organizations.

Implications   To this point, we have considered the historical background and the current situation. The next step in writing the backgrounder is to examine the consequences of selecting one policy over another. If the backgrounder does not address such future implications directly, it should at least highlight points that must be considered.

A backgrounder on another aspect of energy policy might deal with state and federal policies that support alternate fuel vehicles. An expectation is that such a paper would put the whole issue into historical perspective by giving first the rationale for needing such policies, second the enactment of various federal policies, primarily by the Environmental Protection Agency (EPA), and third the policy initiatives by various states. The backgrounder would also be expected to document which policies seem to be most effective, such as the EPA's clean air standards for ozone and fine particulates. The document would bring the situation up to date by explaining the current focus on market-based fuel incentives such as legislative actions that would offer tax incentives.

Identifying the implications of a certain policy includes anticipating developments. The public relations writer has to be aware of the flux of ideas about the issue and which of these may gain or lose support over time. Perhaps a public policy change is being debated now in Washington. Perhaps an extensive government study is under way, the results of which won't be released for a year. Perhaps the topic will be the focus of a convention this year. In all these cases, the issue and its implications are likely to be in the news now and in the future. As a public relations writer, you must be ahead of these developments.

Documentation

You must present full documentation of the information you use in the backgrounder. Before you try to write, as suggested in report writing, get a reliable style manual and study it carefully.

Although a backgrounder does not require the same rigorous scholarship and style required of reports and proposals, a style manual can help you properly cite the material you use in the backgrounder. Use a footnote or endnote system of citation, and include a complete bibliography at the end.

It is important to cite your sources carefully, because people using the backgrounder, whether inside or outside your company, may want to pursue a specific point more fully. Or if they find a discrepancy between the facts in the backgrounder and those in some other source, they may want to evaluate the sources you have cited. This is especially important when a backgrounder provides the foundation for a position paper.

Position Papers

As the name signifies, a position paper is designed to state an organization's position on an issue. (See Figure 8.2.) The issue may be local, regional, national or international in scope. For example, suppose your company opposes a national health insurance plan under consideration in Congress. The position paper should tell why. Your company may also take a positive position regarding a substitute proposal authored by a representative from the local district. The position paper should explain why it supports the substitute plan.

Like the backgrounder, the position paper requires extensive research. Much of the information you need will be found in the backgrounder, so new research should be minimal. At this stage, however, you will need to solicit the input of management, which must scrutinize salient information, sort out the pros and cons of alternative positions and then make a policy decision. Research on a problem may produce a backgrounder that results in a management decision to offer or support a solution. Then you may be asked to write a position paper.

Once that decision has been made, you can write a thorough position paper representing the company's point of view. If PR professionals in the company are held in high esteem, management may ask that a proposed position be written and used as a basis for discussion. A draft position paper is written with the expectation that it will be approved in principle, modified or rejected. After modifications are completed and approved, a final version is prepared for distribution to management and other publics.

Whenever a new issue surfaces, the public relations department should alert management to the need for a position paper. Recognizing an issue constitutes the first step in writing a position paper.

Stating the Issue

No position paper will have much value if it fails to state the issue clearly. Your job as writer demands that you describe the issue fairly and honestly. *Don't* distort the issue to suit your purposes or to make it easier to form—or defend—an opinion. The purpose of a position paper is to address an issue squarely, not evade it.

If you are in the natural gas industry, your position statement will support the use of natural gas-fueled vehicles (NGVs) and would argue that these provide the most desirable solution to reducing emissions. However, a good position paper would acknowledge that success of NGVs depends on recognition in the marketplace and in state and local governments that society benefits from clean, domestic fuels to the extent that there is continued financial support for private sector initiatives. Furthermore, the NGV position paper would have to recognize current limitations for NGVs, especially such critical ones as fueling and servicing.

Don't dance around an issue; meet it squarely near the beginning of the position paper. One of the most obvious ways of doing this is by providing relevant background information. (See Figure 8.2.)

Background

If you want your position paper to be comprehensible, you must provide pertinent background information. But remember that a position paper is not a historical analysis; leave that to the backgrounder. Give just enough background to provide a context for your position and to help your readers understand why the subject under discussion has become an issue. The nature of the issue often obviates the need for extensive background information, but be sure to give enough to make the basis for your position intelligible.

Position

Don't keep your readers in suspense. Come to the point immediately. Don't try to build suspense by including elaborate recitations of facts and flashy figures, and don't culminate the paper with an eloquent conclusion.

Begin by stating your position, so readers know where you stand. Then support it with facts and figures, logically organized and clearly written. Use examples or metaphors that

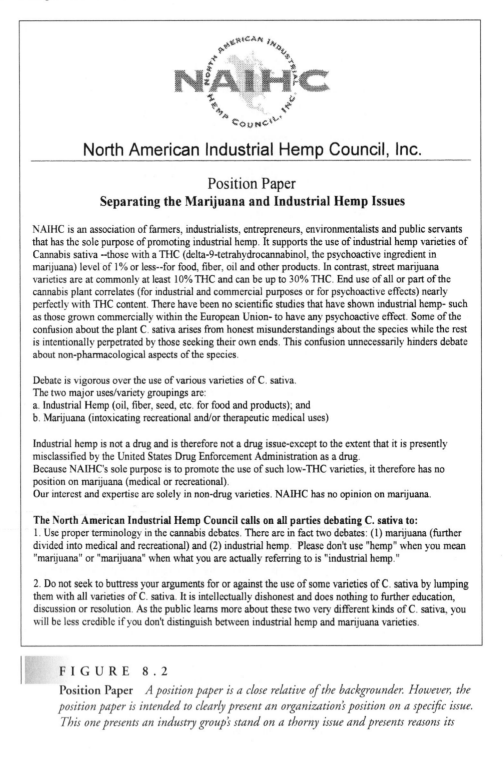

North American Industrial Hemp Council, Inc.

Position Paper
Separating the Marijuana and Industrial Hemp Issues

NAIHC is an association of farmers, industrialists, entrepreneurs, environmentalists and public servants that has the sole purpose of promoting industrial hemp. It supports the use of industrial hemp varieties of Cannabis sativa --those with a THC (delta-9-tetrahydrocannabinol, the psychoactive ingredient in marijuana) level of 1% or less--for food, fiber, oil and other products. In contrast, street marijuana varieties are at commonly at least 10% THC and can be up to 30% THC. End use of all or part of the cannabis plant correlates (for industrial and commercial purposes or for psychoactive effects) nearly perfectly with THC content. There have been no scientific studies that have shown industrial hemp- such as those grown commercially within the European Union- to have any psychoactive effect. Some of the confusion about the plant C. sativa arises from honest misunderstandings about the species while the rest is intentionally perpetrated by those seeking their own ends. This confusion unnecessarily hinders debate about non-pharmacological aspects of the species.

Debate is vigorous over the use of various varieties of C. sativa.
The two major uses/variety groupings are:
a. Industrial Hemp (oil, fiber, seed, etc. for food and products); and
b. Marijuana (intoxicating recreational and/or therapeutic medical uses)

Industrial hemp is not a drug and is therefore not a drug issue-except to the extent that it is presently misclassified by the United States Drug Enforcement Administration as a drug.
Because NAIHC's sole purpose is to promote the use of such low-THC varieties, it therefore has no position on marijuana (medical or recreational).
Our interest and expertise are solely in non-drug varieties. NAIHC has no opinion on marijuana.

The North American Industrial Hemp Council calls on all parties debating C. sativa to:
1. Use proper terminology in the cannabis debates. There are in fact two debates: (1) marijuana (further divided into medical and recreational) and (2) industrial hemp. Please don't use "hemp" when you mean "marijuana" or "marijuana" when what you are actually referring to is "industrial hemp."

2. Do not seek to buttress your arguments for or against the use of some varieties of C. sativa by lumping them with all varieties of C. sativa. It is intellectually dishonest and does nothing to further education, discussion or resolution. As the public learns more about these two very different kinds of C. sativa, you will be less credible if you don't distinguish between industrial hemp and marijuana varieties.

FIGURE 8.2

Position Paper   *A position paper is a close relative of the backgrounder. However, the position paper is intended to clearly present an organization's position on a specific issue. This one presents an industry group's stand on a thorny issue and presents reasons its*

NAIHC ADVISES
Industrial hemp advocates:
* Limit your arguments to industrial hemp.
* Whether you are for or against, keep your views on marijuana to yourself.
* Since industrial hemp is not a drug, don't allow the debate on industrial hemp to devolve to drugs.
Manufacturers, marketers and sellers of industrial hemp products:
* Don't market industrial hemp products by associating them with marijuana by the use of graphics, slang, turns of phrases, etc. (it has been overdone anyway and is too cute by half).
* Realize that industrial hemp will truly compete in the market because of quality and/or price, not the transient cachet of a product made from taxonomically related (but not intoxicating) varieties of cannabis.

Pro-marijuana (recreational and/or medical) advocates:
* Limit your arguments to marijuana and the benefits you see from its use.
* Don't conflate marijuana with industrial hemp or use "hemp" when you mean "marijuana."
* Conflating the drug and non-drug varieties together in policy debate hinders the effort to recommercialize industrial hemp in the United States.
* If you also favor the use of industrial hemp, don't advocate it in forums where you are advocating marijuana.
* Resist temptation to score debating points by discrediting anti-marijuana advocates for their failure to distinguish industrial hemp and marijuana.
* Not distinguishing between the drug and non-drug varieties leads to the same credibility problems that anti-marijuana advocates have who do the same thing (and you play into the hands of anti-marijuana advocates).
* Don't bank on the domino theory that if industrial hemp is (re)legalized, then marijuana will follow (several other nations have allowed for hemp production without changing their stance on marijuana).
Anti-marijuana advocates:
* Limit your arguments to marijuana and the dangers you see from its abuse.
* Acknowledge industrial hemp is, in fact, not a drug (you lose credibility saying that it is-and you play into the hands of pro-marijuana advocates).
* If you continue to insist that industrial hemp is no different than marijuana, you'll be increasingly fighting two opponents (NAIHC won't ally with pro-marijuana advocates, but will oppose anti-marijuana advocates who fail to distinguish industrial hemp from marijuana).
* Don't fear the domino theory that if industrial hemp is legalized, then marijuana will follow (several other nations have allowed for hemp production without changing their stance on marijuana).

CONCLUSION
The United States of America is an island of denial in a sea of acceptance. Industrial hemp is easily distinguished visually from marijuana. Industrial hemp cannot be abused as a drug. (If users confuse it with marijuana all they will get is a big headache; if traffickers sell it, they will be diluting the marijuana supply.) Industrial hemp is now grown commercially in Canada, France, the United Kingdom and elsewhere. Canadian mounties, English bobbies, or French gendarmes can tell the difference between industrial hemp and marijuana and are not concerned. Are American cops less capable? Industrial hemp can be environmentally friendly and a cost-competitive substitute for unsustainable and environmentally harmful supplies of petroleum, cotton, wood and other raw materials. There is money to be made, rural economies to be revitalized, agricultural and industrial processes to be greened. It's time to again grow and use industrial hemp as part of the move from the hydrocarbon economy of today toward the carbohydrate economy of tomorrow.

8.2 *(continued)*

members believe the industrial hemp industry should be allowed to import hemp and produce nondrug products. It is clear, simple and straightforward—hallmarks of a good position paper.
Reprinted by permission of the North American Industrial Hemp Council, Inc.

readers can understand. Use statistics sparingly but include enough of them to support and reinforce your points.

Long lists of numbers might be appropriate in a backgrounder, but in a position paper they will only clutter up your argument and cloud its sense. Make your point in clear, plain language; then select just the right statistic to support it. If you feel that a lot of statistics should be included as support material, put them in an appendix so they don't overpower the paper. Always provide the sources of your statistics. Readers who spend time with such information place a lot of weight on the authority behind the numbers.

Consider Both Sides   Although a position paper should come down strongly on your side of an issue, don't ignore opposing sides. You are expected to amass as much information as you can in support of your point of view, but don't stack the cards.

"Card-stacking" is a propaganda device whereby all the supporting arguments are given but no opposing points are mentioned. This gives the impression that the favorable evidence is more compelling than it really is. Such a position paper may seem impressive at first glance, but when readers discover other points of view, they will distrust not only this message but others you send them later.

It is far better to state opposing points of view and try to refute them than to ignore them. This is especially important when the opposition has some good points. Acknowledge the cons, but show why you think these points are outweighed by objective evidence. With this tactic, you will gain respect, even among your foes.

Consider the Public   Although most position papers are written for internal use by management, some are written for distribution to other publics. Even when writing a position paper you believe will only be used internally, you must keep in mind other potential publics.

For example, a position paper may be written for presentation to the board of directors by management in an attempt to explain company policies to stockholders. But Wall Street analysts may ask to see the company's position too. And what about the media's business editors? They may ask for and should be given copies.

This can pose a serious problem for you as a writer, because information that makes sense to your management may not make sense to the external publics or to stockholders. It would be ideal, of course, to write one version of the position paper for use by all possible publics, but the nature of the issue may make this impractical. You may have to write more than one version of the same paper. You should not tell a different story in each version; rather, you should tell the same story differently and appropriately. Remember too that different publics may be more concerned with some questions than with others. Alter the emphasis of each version of your position paper accordingly.

Recommendations

It is generally perceived as bad form to be against something without offering an alternative solution. Taking a position means being both against one thing and for something else. If you omit your alternative proposals from your position paper, you will inevitably be asked what you recommend as a suitable substitute for something you oppose.

For example, on the NGV situation, currently there are stringent regulations on the conversion of vehicles from gasoline to alternate fuels. If a bill to reduce these regulations is being proposed and you want to support it, how do you address concerns about safety? Supporting the proposal carries an implicit obligation to help arrive at a resolution of issues posed by opponents.

Sometimes position papers suggest new policy on an issue or support a recommended but not yet implemented policy. Position papers also can support existing policy in the face of proposed change.

Format

When the writing is completed, determine its format and method of distribution. A backgrounder or position paper intended for internal use is usually printed on plain or letterhead paper, copied, assembled, stapled and then delivered or distributed as an email attachment. Those distributed outside the company may be produced the same way, or they may be published as a printed booklet or monograph, embellished with art, color, design and typography and printed on expensive paper or published on the organization's Web site.

Some companies prepare backgrounders for public consumption on special forms. These forms contain a company heading with the word *backgrounder* prominent. Other companies, particularly those in heavily regulated industries that require a large number of backgrounders or position papers annually, produce punched versions suitable for inclusion in a loose-leaf notebook or—less expensive—put them on their Web sites and/or intranet sites.

Many backgrounders and some position papers include charts and illustrations to help explain topics. For formal reports, preparing graphics for either printing or Web use is often done by a graphic artist. However, you should be fully aware of their content, how they look and where they will appear in the finished report. Locating these visuals close to appropriate text segments makes the information easier to understand.

Special Uses

Although position papers have many uses, especially as frames of reference when questions come from journalists and to orient spokespeople and management personnel, they also have some special uses. An organization that wants to exploit all the avenues for advocating its point of view can use a position paper as the basis for an essay or a commentary to be submitted to the op-ed page in the local newspaper. The position paper should have enough documentation in it to stand alone as the basis of an op-ed piece. If it doesn't, go back to the backgrounder on which the position paper was based. That should give you more than enough information with which to work. Other kinds of documents can also be used as you prepare the op-ed piece, but if a position paper is executed well, there should not be much need to seek and use other information.

Another special area is the use of position papers as the locus for image ads and public service announcements (PSAs) for an organization. Position papers can be of enormous help in positioning or repositioning an organization as it tries to shape and project a consistent image.

Plans for action, as in lobbying for or against something, can spring directly from position papers. If, for example, there's a proposal to cut all government support for alternate fuel vehicles and place the determination totally in the marketplace, the position statement against that policy represents your first line of offense in furthering the cause. Backgrounders may also be of use, but it is the position paper that sets the direction and highlights the major points of contention.

Conclusions

- Every organization can count on receiving inquiries about background information and positions on issues. It should prepare for these by producing backgrounders and position papers in advance.
- Backgrounders serve as sources of information for company executives, public relations writers, media personnel, financial analysts, the external publics and a variety of other publics.
- Backgrounders should always provide a historical context, a description of the current situation and a discussion of the implications of the matter under study. This information should be free of opinion.
- Position papers state a position on a topic. They are basically opinions supported by a few facts. They should treat opposing points of view as well as supporting arguments.
- When the company takes a position against something, it should also suggest alternative solutions.
- Backgrounders and position papers—especially backgrounders—should fully acknowledge sources of information used in their preparation.
- Clear writing is a must.
- Position papers can be especially useful as the inspiration and support for essays and commentaries for the op-ed pages of local newspapers.
- Position papers may be used as the locus for image-building ads and PSAs.
- Position papers can set the agenda for action, such as lobbying for or against an issue, task or process.

Exercises

1. Choose a topic that concerns your school, such as the increasing use of drugs, getting term papers off the Internet, other forms of cheating or lack of diversity in the student or faculty population. Do your research and write a backgrounder on the topic.
2. Imagine that you are the public relations director for a city's transportation system, which includes, along with an electric subway system, fleets of gasoline-powered vehicles such as buses as well as special vans for the disabled. The city frequently has air quality alerts that keep people at risk inside. Also, exhaust fumes are killing trees and other vegetation along the freeways. To help reduce emissions, the company has decided to use natural gas-fueled fleet vehicles. Prepare the opening paragraphs of a position paper to support that opinion, and, in outline form, indicate what you would include in the rest of the document.
3. The position paper in Figure 8.2 will be subjected to criticism from various publics. List these publics and suggest which areas are open to dispute and/or skepticism.

Use InfoTrac College Edition to access information on topics in this chapter from hundreds of periodicals and scholarly journals.

Selected Bibliography

Heil Sheehan, Hendrick Smith, E. W. Kenworthy and Fox Butterfield, *The Pentagon Papers* (Chicago: Quadrangle Books, 1971). Besides being of historical interest, this book is amply illustrated with backgrounders and position papers.

Kate L. Turabian, John Grossman and Alice Bennett, *A Manual for Writers of Term Papers, Theses and Dissertations* (Chicago Guides to Writing, Editing and Publishing), 6th ed. (Chicago: University of Chicago Press, 1996).

Dennis L. Wilcox and Patrick Jackson, *Public Relations Writing and Media Techniques,* 4th ed. (Boston: Longman, 2000).

Mark Wright, "Writing Media Backgrounders: Help Reporters Find You . . . Before They Need You," http://www.markwright.com/backgrounder.htm (Washington, D.C.: Wright Communications, 2003).

PART 4

Writing for Mass Media Publics

As a relatively new medium, the Internet has made the flow of news and advertising through cyberspace a factor to be considered in the overall delivery of messages. Although the role of different media and that of media gatekeepers is changing, there is no change in the need to understand both the public and the strengths and weaknesses of each medium.

News Releases for Print Media

Want to see what a news release looks like? Go to your computer and locate your favorite corporation on the Internet. On that site, you should see a list of the company's most current news releases, with headlines presented by the dates they were distributed. There may be many or few, depending on the kind of organization you're checking.

Who Gets News Releases and How?

Getting the news your organization or client wants to send to the news sources likely to be interested is a strategic task, not a mass distribution (confetti) operation. The way you offer the news and which news channels you target are decisions made on the basis of message, medium and public. The news gatekeepers here are your intermediate public.

Some newspeople sign up for email-delivered news releases because that saves them time searching various Web sites. There are a number of distribution services that will send your releases online, and, of course, they also maintain a list of those who would rather get news releases this way.

In a local or regional situation where you are doing the distributing, it's a good idea to simply find out how each medium you intend to target prefers to receive releases. Even within media, this may differ with individuals. You need to know that too.

When you get a query from a news source, it's a good idea to get specifics about how the information is to be sent. If it's by email, you should send an email message about the story, tailored specifically to the recipient's interest in the story, with the release itself as an attachment. You want to be sure the recipient can open the attachment and read it, so compatibility is a factor here too. If it's by disk, be sure you send it in a compatible format. To keep the file size small, put art and graphics in a separate attachment from the story so this won't slow the downloading. Again, be sure this can be opened by the recipient. If you are sending a photo as an email attachment, check to see whether color or black-and-white is needed, and be sure you are sending the quality photo needed, because paper magazines need much higher quality graphics than newspapers.

Occasionally, a story is long enough that you'll want to compress it for sending. Again, be sure it can be opened successfully. Remember, the story has to be accessible. The release and supporting materials may be printed out or may be transferred electronically for use by the medium. This mechanical transition has to be smooth, or the story won't be used.

When you are sending news releases remember that regardless of what your employer might think, not everyone wants your story. If you are sending a story by email and not using a distribution service, you might be tempted to send it to a large number of recipients. This is "spamming" and not regarded charitably by most newspeople. In this case, include the news release in the body of the email, in ASCII format. In the virus-infected world of cyberspace attachments are regarded with suspicion because they may contain a virus. In fact, even unsolicited email runs the same risks. Some recipients of email won't open email from people whose email address they don't recognize because they are afraid of hitting a virus-infected communication.

The parallel of "spamming" is sending news releases by "broadcast" fax. There are a number of problems with this approach. The media receiving the "broadcast" on their fax machine see their machine tied up and their fax paper and ink used for something they didn't ask for and probably don't need or want. Furthermore, if they are going to use the information, they have to pay a news clerk to put the information into their electronic system. Clerks get paid. So the PR person is costing the news medium money.

Not only does the Internet make getting the release to the media easier and faster, but there's even more of an opportunity for media exposure because many media have online sites that are treated and edited differently than their related, traditional sites. Nevertheless, although the news release is probably the most frequently used tool for getting publicity, it also is misused. The result is that many news releases are not used at all by media people.

Why are news releases rejected? Studies generally cite the following reasons as most significant: poor writing, incompleteness, inaccuracy, poor timing and little local or no reader interest. No medium can use all the releases it receives. But basically, it gets down to this: Most releases don't get used because the PR people preparing them don't know what they're doing. Many think they do. Most news releases are rejected because they contain no news.

The first responsibility of a public relations person preparing news releases is to know what news is. If a release doesn't contain news, it won't get used. On the other hand, if it contains valuable news, editors are quite likely to overlook poor writing, typographical errors and other blunders just to get the story. It's essential to know the difference between news and non-news.

What Is News?

Different people have different definitions for news. Textbooks on beginning reporting and articles about the mass media in society construct elaborate definitions of what news is or should be. But for public relations people, no esoteric or philosophical definition is necessary. A practical one will do: News is what newspapers and magazines publish and what radio and TV stations broadcast on their news shows. News is *not* what *you* think it is or what the company president thinks it is. Realizing this will take you a long way toward writing effective news releases.

In the words of well-known public relations consultant the late Philip Lesly,

> The medium decides absolutely, in most cases, what it will use, when, and in what form. The editorial judgment or attitudes of the editors, however they may differ from those of the publicist and his organization, are the only determinants.[1]

This is not a new idea. The best public relations people have said the same thing for decades. Ivy Lee, one of the pioneers of public relations, once described how corporation executives would call on him to get their ideas printed in the newspaper. "They say you can get anything on the front page of the newspapers," an executive would tell Lee. He would reply: "I cannot do anything of the kind. If you want a subject to get on the first page of the newspapers, you must have the news in your statement sufficient to warrant it getting the first page."[2]

Furthermore, Lee would point out, what good would it do if the paper *did* print something just because you wanted it to? If a piece has no news value, people probably won't read it. And if people are likely to read it, it *does* have news value. If readers will be interested, an editor will be happy to use it without coercion or tricks.

The reason you want mass media gatekeepers to pay attention to your release is twofold. First of all, appearance in a publication that is important to your priority publics gives the information additional credibility. Second, if a news release is picked up by a newspaper that has an online service or by a news service like the Associated Press or a media-owned service like the Dow Jones Wire or *The New York Times,* then people may encounter the information from your news release in more than one place. If the news story is also used by the broadcast media then there is additional exposure. Repetition helps.

Finding News

You can encourage both mass and specialized media gatekeepers to use your materials by paying attention to what sort of material they are currently using and by building a reputation as a good source of timely and reliable information. To accomplish this, you must do two things. First, become familiar with the newspaper (or magazine, TV or radio station or other medium) you'll be sending releases to. In other words, if you want to know what news is, you have to read the papers. You have to watch TV newscasts. You should listen to radio news shows. You'll have to explore news sites on the Web. You'll soon develop a sense for what is accepted as news and what isn't.

The second step is to become familiar with your own company or institution so that you'll be able to find the news within it. Presumably, you will work for an organization that does something worthwhile or that does things the public might find some value in knowing about. If you look around, you'll find things going on in the company that are similar to what the newspapers report about other companies. You'll find people who know things the public would like to know. You'll find research on topics that affect people's lives. You'll find unusual things that are simply interesting in themselves.

Of course, a public relations writer's job is to get things into the media that will benefit the organization. Just looking for things editors consider news, therefore, may not achieve your goals. But there is a broad area where public benefit and private benefit overlap. Generating a greater public understanding of your company and its activities is almost always beneficial, and if in the process the public is entertained and informed, then everyone benefits.

Getting News to the Mass Media

Once you find the news within your organization, your next step is to get it to the public through some medium—online news sites, newspapers, magazines, TV or radio. The news release is the tool most often used to do this.

pr reporter reminds us to distinguish between reportorial media and access media.[3] News media committed to providing traditional news, defined as information that helps citizens make decisions, are *reportorial* media. They are represented by traditional newspapers and newsmagazines and the serious news operations in radio and television as well as online news sites. Newsworthiness remains the primary criterion for deciding what to use. And these media are typically the ones in which you want your releases to appear. *Access* media among newspapers, magazines, radio and television operations are more interested in sensationalizing and entertaining. Examples of access media include such forums as television talk shows, call-in shows, radio talk shows and public affairs panels and online chat rooms or "forums." Newsworthiness has low priority with access media. Provocativeness seems to be of more concern. If something can wring an emotional response from readers, viewers or listeners, it can get distribution.

News releases are placed on the Internet either through news suppliers who provide that service to organizations or through organizations who present the information on their own Web sites. These news channels offer opportunities for exposure beyond the mass media. Trade and industry editors surf the Web to look for news. Competitors frequently scan sites to see what "the others" are doing. Special-interest groups also monitor news release sites.

Distinctions between reportorial and access media are not always clear in cyberspace, where news, entertainment and advertising can appear in an indiscriminate jumble. In addition to recognized news sites, cyberspace has all sorts of "newsgroups" and chat rooms that carry information that may or may not have any foundation in fact. Furthermore, there rarely are gatekeepers, which means that anyone can write anything and stand a good chance of having it accepted as fact.

For this reason, you'll need to monitor what others may be saying about your organization or about issues your organization is concerned with. You might need to respond to false information. There's a risk to ignoring it on the premise that to respond is to give the false information credibility. You had better correct something before it takes on a life of its own as it easily can in the access media.

Actually, misinformation about your organization or an issue your organization is concerned about can provide a news peg to get you space in the reportorial media. A news peg, or something timely to hang your story on, is essential to successfully place a story.

One way you can respond to false information is by sending appropriate news media a *tip sheet* that alerts them to the story. Tip sheets usually have their own letterhead that uses "Tip Sheet" as a heading and then identifies your organization with appropriate addresses and phone numbers. These tip sheets can be sent electronically, although many news editors say they are drowning in email and faxed messages. You can also put the news tip on a news release service on the Internet. Depending on how important you feel it is to get your story out, you can wait for a reporter to follow up on your tip sheet or you can simply file a story on your own. Be sure you put the story on the news release service, but also respond in the newsgroup or chat room where the original misinformation appeared.

The widespread blurring of boundaries in cyberspace disturbs some news purists. They might see a problem with your putting a news release on your Web site, although most public relations people discount this point of view. An organization's Web site is clearly a promotional place, one that may even carry advertising. Some editors complain about the increasing fuzziness between news and advertising. Others don't seem to mind.

Those who don't mind say that newspapers and magazines already are blurring the lines with things like newspaper special sections whose editorial content is paid for by the sections' (often same-subject) advertisers, and magazine inserts and pullouts that look like news but are really advertising. In both of these cases, the material is supposed to be labeled "advertising," but often the consumer doesn't notice.

You want to be sure, though, that you know the differences between news, entertainment and advertising and that you carefully decide what you want to send to "reportorial" channels. How do you know if the release you want to send is newsworthy? There are several easy tests. Ask yourself: Is the information of general interest to readers not connected with your business? Is it about something that affects the lives of the media's audience in some way (especially economically)? Is the substance of your release something unusual, out of the ordinary or even bizarre? If you can answer yes to any of these questions, your release probably contains legitimate news, even if it also serves your own purposes.

Writing News Releases

How do you write legitimate news? The answer is simple: Prepare the material as you would if you were a reporter working for a newspaper. A news release should be written in the same form and style, following the same punctuation and spelling rules, that the publication you want it to appear in uses.

If you've ever been a reporter, writing a news release should be as easy as writing a straight news story. If you haven't, you need to know something about the methods of writing news.

Approach

Every reporter has a personal method for approaching a story. But all methods should have the same first step: Identify the most important thing about the story. In writing a news release, the first step is identical. You must answer the question: What's the most important thing I have to say? Your answer will determine what you should say in the lead.

Lead   The lead—the first paragraph or perhaps the first two—is the most important part of the release. You can't write a good release without a good lead, and you can't write a good lead until you've answered the question about what's important.

Deciding what's important sometimes takes a little judgment. *Important* must be construed broadly. What you really want to isolate is the most significant and most interesting aspect of your subject. And you have to keep in mind that news is what is happening now.

For example, if the release is about the opening of a new plant, the most important thing is the fact that the plant is *opening*. The action is the news. But is there something especially interesting about the plant itself? Is it the largest plant of its kind? The first? Will it provide a lot of jobs for the local economy? Once you've decided what's important and also what's interesting, you can write a lead.

The most important thing—in this case the action—should form the main part of the lead: "The plant is opening." The interesting thing about the story provides an "angle" for the lead: "The first plant of its kind is opening," according to *X* authority.

Sometimes you don't have to look for the most important aspect of the story. For example, it may be the appearance of someone noteworthy. That is your lead. Of course, that might explain why public relations people planning special events always try to get celebrities to attend. The appearance of a well-known person becomes the focus for the news release.

Using the most interesting angle in the first sentence may cause you some problems in constructing the traditional newspaper lead, in which the who-what-when-where-why-how all appear in the first paragraph. Traditional leads are still the rule for most wire-service stories, because the first paragraph is all some newspapers will use. However, that first sentence can get very long if you try to jam in all the essential elements. The rule is often relaxed, so that only two or three of the traditional elements appear in the first sentence, with the others following in the next sentence or two.

If you're writing a release for a wire service, try to get all of the elements in the first paragraph or, at most, the first two. When writing for dailies in your area, study the papers' styles. Are all the basic questions usually answered in the first paragraph? Or do a paper's staff writers tend more toward the attention-grabbing lead, with the details of time and place following in the next few paragraphs? The style of the papers you write for should determine the style for your releases. You may find it worthwhile to have several versions of a release to accommodate different media.

Naturally, if your lead sentence contains the most important and most interesting elements of your story, it probably already gives the who and the what. You can sneak in the when, where and why later—but not too much later. The how usually comes last.

Once you've written a lead, read it over to make sure that it states clearly what the release is about and that it grabs the reader's interest. In other words, the lead must give a quick indication of what the story is about and why it is important. And it must be interesting—both to catch the eye of the editor and to get the attention of the newspaper reader.

Angling the Lead   One lead will not suit all of your needs. The news business is not a situation where "one size fits all," not if you expect your copy to be used. Think about the medium and how the news is going to be used. If you are going to an online site, then immediacy and significance are the emphasis. Think about the time delay for the daily newspaper. The story may have been online and perhaps in the broadcast news before it can be printed. You need a fresh emphasis for the lead for the daily newspaper that picks up the story. If you are giving the story to a weekly publication, then there's even more to consider about the emphasis. What will still be "fresh" when the story is published? You must consider that. Think too about the audience. *The Wall Street Journal*'s audience is not the same as that for *USA Today.* What would each publication's audience be most interested in about your story? That's what the editor is thinking about, and so should you.

A local angle is essential in capturing the local newspaper editor's attention. Most newspapers rely on the wire services for nonlocal news, and a release without a local angle is usually dumped. In fact, some editors cite the lack of a local angle as the single most important reason releases aren't used. Be sure to identify the local angle. Make it clear and get it high in the story, preferably in the lead. If you have no local angle to interest a given newspaper, don't bother sending the release.

Timing is critical if your news is going to a newsletter or to a magazine. You must think not only of the audience and that particular audience's interest in your story, but also when the audience is going to be exposed to the story and what that audience may have learned about the news by then. The way you write the story depends on the editor's perception of its newsworthiness. You have to make it timely and interesting even if, in the case of some publications, there is a long delay, a month or more.

Amplifying the Lead   Once you have a lead that meets all these tests, writing the rest of the release should be easy. Simply amplify each of the elements introduced in the lead, giving all the details. Anticipate the questions that an interested individual might ask about your subject, and answer them in the body of the release.

Write in the style of the newswriter. Use short, concise sentences; short paragraphs; and common, concrete words. Avoid the jargon of your profession. If you must use a technical term, make sure to explain it fully. Above all, avoid editorial comment. Don't try to "sell" something in a news release. A release is not an ad. If a comment is necessary, be sure to enclose it in quotation marks and attribute it to a company executive.

Quotations   In using direct quotations, news release writers have a great advantage over reporters: They can *create* quotes. A reporter using quotation marks must report exactly what was said. You, however, can take what you've written to the executive you're supposed to be quoting and ask for approval of the words you've attributed to him or her. (See Table 9.1.) Write for time-sensitive use. (See Table 9.2.)

Sometimes you won't know what to create for the quote and will have to go directly to the person to see what he or she wants to say. Often the person will scrawl something quickly on a memo pad or ask you to take something from an official statement already prepared on the subject. Such quotes are almost always awkward and lifeless. You will need to recast the words to make them sound like someone said them in conversation. For example, in writing a release about your company's reaction to a new government report, do not write something like this:

> Company President J. T. Person said, "We have not had time to adequately review the contents of the document in its entirety, nor have we ascertained the ultimate position we are likely to take on it, though at this point in time, it seems not unlikely that we will find the conclusions, and the evidence supporting them, acceptable."

That doesn't sound a bit like spoken English. Instead, write something like this:

> "We haven't read the whole report yet," President J. T. Person said, "so we can't take a position now. But from what we've read so far, we think we'll like it."

As you write the release, keep in mind that you know much more about the subject than the editor or reader will. You can't assume any previous knowledge on the reader's part—even things you are "sure" that "everybody knows." A good rule of thumb, to quote James Marlow, is "Always write for the fellow who *hasn't read yesterday's paper.*"[4]

TABLE 9.1   *News Release with Quotations*   Integrating quotes into news stories humanizes them and gives an opportunity for releases with different emphases, as Table 9.2 illustrates. This release was created by the authors as an illustration. The company, Web site and email address, as far as we know, do not exist.

News Release   (corporate logo)
ABC Global Communications, Inc.
One Continental Plaza
Anycity, State 97989 USA
Contact: Irena Hernandez
        (123) 542-4455 Office / (123) 312-6565 Home
        (123) 542-4444 Fax / iher@ABCGlobal.worldnet.net

Communications executive says international internship experiences a must for communication students in announcing new national competition.

Anycity, State (January 16, 200X)—International working experiences are a must in today's world, according to Jamie Wallace, president and CEO of ABC Global Communications, Inc. (ABC Global).

The public relations and advertising company just announced a national internship competition for college students that would place them in ABC Global offices around the world.

"In a global communication environment, the only way to learn is to be there. That's the reason we have decided to open all 14 of our offices abroad to interns from the USA," Wallace said.

To choose the best candidates for the internships, ABC Global has posted an entry application on its Web site (www.abcglobalcom.net).

ABC Global executive Tom Fields said, "We opened the competition to students in USA colleges and universities only, at least for the time being, because we feel the size of the country limits students' experience with other cultures." Fields will be administrator of the internships.

"Reactions from offices in the UK have been very positive," Fields said, "and we just got a fax from our Mexico office. Here's what Felix Gustamante, director of ABC Global Mexico, said: 'Empathy is important, but it's experience that counts.'"

Wallace noted that living and working in other cultures create a depth of understanding that enables communicators to work easier across borders, essential in today's world.

"We want to choose 50 of the best students from their online applications, fly them in to our corporate headquarters and give them some performance challenges here before we choose those we'll send to our offices abroad," said program administrator Fields.

Fields also added that in designing the internships he had been working closely with a national center in Washington, D.C., that has some experience in administering internships.

The National Internship Academy's Deputy Director, Charlene Adams, said the major challenge for an internship is placing the right person in the right position. She added that "bringing the students together and getting to know them personally will help ABC Global place people in successful working relationships."

ABC Global provides public relations and advertising services through its offices in England, Scotland, Wales, Australia, New Zealand, Singapore, India, Belgium, Mexico, Argentina, Brazil, Venezuela, Spain and the Philippines.

-30-

ABC Global Communications, Inc., One Continental Plaza, Anycity, State 97989 USA
Contact: Irena Hernandez (123) 542-4455 Office / (123) 312-6565 Home / (123) 542-4444 Fax / iher@ABCGlobal.worldnet.net

T A B L E 9 . 2   *Adapted Leads for News Release in Table 9.1*   What follows are only a few of the different sorts of angles this story offers. Can you think of more? What would they be? Of course in each case the story has to be adjusted to fit the rearrangement of facts.

Lead for Online Release

ABC Global Communications, Inc. has an entry application on its Web site (www.globalcom.com) to choose the best candidates for advertising and public relations internships in 14 ABC Global offices outside of the USA.

International working experiences are a must in today's world, according to ABC Global President Jamie Wallace. (continuation of story here)

Lead for Release to Local Daily Newspaper

International working experiences are a must in today's world, according to Jamie Wallace, president and chief executive officer of locally based ABC Global Communications, Inc. (ABC Global).

The public relations and advertising company announced Sunday (January 16) a national internship competition for college students that would place them in ABC Global offices around the world. (continuation of story here)

What would your AP lead look like?

Lead for Area Weekly (deadline on Monday for distribution on Thursday)

International working experiences are a must in today's world, according to Jamie Wallace, president of Anycity-based ABC Global Communications, Inc. (ABC Global).

Students have an opportunity to work in advertising and public relations internships in any of the company's 14 offices outside the USA.

Administrator of the ABC Global internships is Tom Fields, a resident of Anycity.

(Follow with quote from Fields, then work in some of the rest of the story such as competitive selection, the Web site and the countries. Keep it short because weeklies typically have small news holes.)

Lead for Monthly Magazine (deadline for stories three months in advance; for news items, four weeks in advance)

College and university students visiting the Web site of ABC Global Communications, Inc. (ABC Global) find evidence of the company president's belief in international experience as essential in today's world.

The company, which has 14 offices outside the USA offering advertising and public relations services, is putting its beliefs on the line by going online with a national internship offer.

ABC Global President Jamie Wallace noted that living and working in other cultures create a depth of understanding that enables communicators to work easier across borders, essential in today's world.

(continue with the development of the story)

If the publication happened to be something like the *Chronicle of Higher Education,* what would your lead be?

That doesn't mean you write "down" to the reader. Assume that your readers are intelligent and capable of understanding something if it is explained in common English. But don't assume that they know anything about your subject at the outset.

Length   Knowing how to write a release is important. But knowing when to end the release is equally important. If a release is too long, an editor may decide there isn't time to read it, and into the trash (electronic or physical) it will go.

The essential points can usually be covered in one page. Sometimes an important event will call for two or three pages, however, so if you need that much space to cover the subject, use it. But even then, write the release so an editor can chop a few paragraphs off the bottom without damaging the story. (That's especially important for releases going to wire services.)

Long releases with pages of generally irrelevant material are annoying. A common example is the release on an executive's promotion, a subject worth only two or three paragraphs. Frequently, however, such releases give pages of company history and information on the company's chief executive, who did nothing more than announce the promotion.

Keep the release brief, at least in most cases. If you really think more information might be needed—statistics or background, for example—attach a fact sheet to the release. A fact sheet lists the basic elements of the institution and the event. (See Chapter 4.)

Ending   It's common practice to use a paragraph summarizing the organization and its operations. For example, here's the paragraph used by Blockbuster:

> Blockbuster Inc. (NYSE: BBI) is a publicly traded subsidiary of Viacom Inc. (NYSE: VIA, VIA.B) and a leading global provider of in-home movies and game entertainment, with more than 8,200 stores throughout the Americas, Europe, Asia and Australia. The company may be accessed worldwide at blockbuster.com. Viacom is a leading global media company, with preeminent positions in broadcast and cable television, radio, outdoor advertising and online.[5]

Note that the statement provides:

- the company's name,
- its New York Stock Exchange (NYSE) stock symbol,
- the name and stock symbol of its parent company, Viacom,
- the company's purpose,
- the number and location of Blockbuster stores and
- the URL of its Web site.

Form and Style

Your most important concern in writing a news release is not length, of course, but getting your message across. To be understood, you must write clearly.

Unfortunately, the writing in most releases is more complex than that in the news stories of a typical daily newspaper. You must learn to write for the editors if you write news releases. *Don't* write for your boss. Write your releases as a journalist.

That doesn't mean you should present the facts in such a way that your story makes your company look bad (as a media reporter might do). But it does mean that you leave out *no* pertinent facts, however embarrassing they might be.

When you write a story, it's not enough to conform to newspaper style in level of complexity and in basic story structure. You must follow newspaper style to the finest detail, making sure that every comma and period is in the proper place.

For newspapers, this generally means adhering to the *AP Stylebook*. Most newspapers follow AP style, but many have special style rules that you should know. It's a good practice to ask editors for copies of their stylebooks. You can get a copy of the *AP Stylebook* at a college bookstore, at Amazon.com or by going to the AP online bookstore, http://www.apbook store.com/.

The stylebook will guide you on such matters as when to capitalize, how to abbreviate and what titles to use for specific people. It also describes certain punctuation rules that may differ from common usage. In AP style, for example, there is no comma between a name and Jr. or Sr., as in "Joe Zilch Jr."

AP has adopted *Webster's New World College Dictionary* as the standard guide for spelling. Use the first spelling listed, or the spelling given with a complete definition if a word has more than one entry (like *T-shirt* and *tee shirt*). The *AP Stylebook* lists some exceptions to the dictionary spelling. If a word isn't in *Webster's New World,* check in *Webster's Third New International Dictionary* (and think again about whether you should use the word).

Because any written material you give to a newspaper will be copyedited anyway, you might wonder why it's necessary to pay strict attention to the details of newspaper style. In fact, it's *not* absolutely necessary but it's still a good idea. Even if your release is rewritten completely, the rewriter will notice if the original was in correct style—and will take particular note if it was in incorrect style. It's a matter of making a good impression. If your style is correct, an editor will know that the release was prepared carefully by someone who knew what he or she was doing. Correct spelling is even more important in this regard. If you don't bother to spell words correctly, an editor is likely to assume that you aren't very careful with the facts either. And if an editor can't trust your information, the release is worthless.

What about grammar? Some writers worry about grammar above all else, combing every line for a possible split infinitive or a *who* that should be a *whom.* Certainly good grammar is important, and awkward, obvious errors like subject-verb disagreements should not be tolerated. But don't worry more about grammar than about communication. Your first concern must be the clarity of the message. If your sentences are clear and understandable, the grammar will take care of itself. (See Chapter 6.)

One more word about style. If you plan to send releases to newspapers other than local dailies—releases about financial news, for example, might go to *The Wall Street Journal*—you should know that these newspapers sometimes have completely different style rules. Some public relations people send the same release to all newspapers, using the style applicable to the majority. You can get away with this, but it never hurts to tailor releases to individual publications. When sending releases electronically as attachments, you might mention in the message that the release adheres to the medium's style.

Electronic Transmission of Releases

Having the correct style is particularly important now that many public relations practitioners are sending releases directly from their computers to the news medium's computer via email. Other releases are sent by facsimile. One practitioner predicts that the delivery of news releases by any other means ("snail" mail, messenger or in-person delivery) soon will be obsolete. The advantage of computer transmission is that, once the release is in the medium's computer system, it can be called up for editing (or, of course, "killing").

QuickSilver Interactive Group, Inc. offers eNewsroom, an Internet-based service for an organization's use in distributing news releases automatically. Steve Lee, QuickSilver's CEO, said, "You enter an upcoming release, announcement, or information alert into the eNewsroom system and then, at the time you specify, the news item will automatically appear on your corporate Web site and an email alert is instantly broadcast. Your news items are fully searchable and printable and, of course, available 24/7."

Digital distribution systems aren't without problems, however. When Consumers Union turned over a news release to a company for distribution to about 1,000 editors, it learned later that some editors received two, three, or even eight copies of the release. That's more than a little irritating to editors, who raised a storm of complaints. More than 300 letters of apology

Source: Shoe. Reprinted with permission from Tribune Media Services.

went to these editors—at the expense of the distribution company, of course—but the damage was done.[6]

However the release is delivered, format is important. (See Table 9.3.)

Types of Releases

Once you know how to write a release, the next question is: Why and when should you write one? The reason for writing releases depends on the type of company or institution you write for and what its goals are. Frequently the release is just one of many tools a company uses to get publicity. Sometimes releases are an important communications tool for explaining the company's position on major public issues. But remember that PR people also, as Boston University PR professor Otto Lerbinger puts it, "have an obligation to satisfy people's right to know about the operation of government units and the activities of corporations and non-profit organizations that affect the public interest."[7] News releases are often necessary to meet that obligation to the public.

Another reason for issuing releases is simply to keep the record straight. Tight-lipped corporations that maintain low profiles and seldom issue releases are frequently headed by executives who complain privately about the "unfair" treatment they get in the media, or about the media's many mistakes in covering their companies. But they have little right to complain when a newspaper gets the facts wrong if they haven't provided that newspaper with the correct information. News releases are one way of helping media get the facts right when they report about your business. Most news releases do require internal clearance.

News releases are not only a matter of information. Besides getting publicity for your company, a good news release program helps build good media relations. Reporters get paid to find news and write stories, and if you help them find news—real news—the reporters will be grateful. One way to help reporters find news is to send out tip sheets.

If you've spotted a news story, you may want to alert an editor through a tip sheet. Sent to the appropriate editor by name and department, the tip usually opens with a provocative sentence or paragraph that sets the stage for the story idea. Details then follow, perhaps with suggested treatment.

If it is a good tip, the editor may call and ask you to do the story as suggested or with some other slant. You can be sure the editor's interest is high or the request would not be

T A B L E   9 . 3   *Model News Release*   Whether distributed by mail, in person or electronically, a news release should follow a basic format as shown here. Look at each of the elements and study the content. Used with permission of Doug Newsom.

Model News Release
Kevo Corporation, One Professional Plaza, Anytown, USA 65959

Contact:	Your name and title	Phone:	123 456-7890 (office)
Address:	Corporate Communication		123 789-8787 (home)
	Kevo Corporation	Fax:	123 456-8901 (office)
	9595 Constitution Avenue	Email:	xxxxxx@kevo.com
	Anytown, USA 65959		

Date release was distributed

For immediate release

(or embargo date and time)

Identifying head: Proper form for news release

Begin the body of your release about halfway from the top of the page. Use double spacing. Take advantage of spelling and grammar checkers in your computer.

Be sure the contact information is complete, including your home phone number and the date the release was distributed.

If it is a timed release, delete the "for immediate release" line and insert the proper embargo information, such as "12 noon, Friday, September 7, 20xx." Be explicit.

An identifying headline should summarize the gist of the story. Its function is to tell editors in capsule form what is in the release.

-more-

(Some organizations number releases and put the number at the bottom of each page. It makes for easier reference and retrieval.)

---

made. If the story is both newsworthy and complex, the editor may call to say that a reporter has been assigned to the story and will need your help getting background and details. The odds are good that the story, if done, will appear in print. Your task, then, will be mostly to provide liaison and assistance with gathering information. While doing that you'll have many opportunities to offer ideas about how the story might be approached and written.

Sometimes you'll find it advisable, and productive, to send along a *selling memo* with a news release. Such a memo is especially useful if you've written a story exclusively for one newspaper or one that goes to several newspapers but with different treatments. Selling memos seem to have little value for the same release that goes to all media in exactly the same way. Such releases are looked upon almost as boilerplate by editors. Many editors simply won't touch them for that reason.

A specially tooled story, one that may be a little weak on news value but reasonably strong in human interest, can be "sold" with the right mixture of persuasiveness and substance. Like tip sheets, selling memos often open with a provocative sentence or paragraph to gain attention and then follow with the selling message. The essential point to remember about writing

9 . 3   *(continued)*

Proper form for news release, 2 –

Use at least one-inch margins at the right, left, top and bottom. Indent paragraphs at least 10 spaces.

The first paragraph is the lead or summary of the most important fact(s) in the story. Paragraphs should be short, preferably no more than four lines, punctuated correctly, easy to read and understand. Sentences should average no more than about 15 or 16 words.

Use broadcast style in broadcast releases. Remember to use active verbs, spell out numbers and give phonetic pronunciation (in parentheses) for names or technical terms.

One-page releases are more likely to be printed or broadcast, but you can use additional pages as necessary. If you do, remember to insert "-more-" at the bottom of all but the last page.

At the top of the second page and following pages, flush left the identifying "slug" line from the suggested head and the page number. Never split a word, sentence or paragraph between pages.

Although the symbol "-30-" often is used to show the end of a release, some people prefer "end" or the symbol "###."

For releases sent electronically, put contact information at the bottom of the file to eliminate the need for editors to scroll back to the front. When you send or take a disk, always enclose a hard copy. Mark the disk with the slug line, software used and your name, phone and fax numbers and email address.

-30-

---

a selling memo is that editors buy for their reasons, not yours. That means that you must know the readers, listeners or viewers of the medium in order to make an argument the editor will heed. If you don't tailor your sell to a particular editor and the medium's audience, you'll end up with no sale.

When do you write releases? The rule is simple: When you have news, release it. Certain things call for news releases. Generally these fall into one of several basic categories: announcements, created news, spot news, response situations, features, bad news and special matters.

Announcement Releases   These releases can announce the marketing of a new product, the opening of a new plant, the company's latest financial results or a new company policy. Such routine items don't require long releases. Just be sure the news is legitimate. In most cases a new line of a familiar product is material for an ad, not a news release. The product has to be of a completely new kind—something unique—to deserve a news story. A good test for the value of the information is "Who cares?" If the answer is "Only a few," it's not news for the mass media, although it may be trade press or association news.

"Created News" Releases   Often, a mere announcement isn't enough to attract much media attention. A company may therefore try to "dress up" the announcement release by making sure something newsworthy is going on. The company might bring a well-known speaker to a company function, for example, or stage a formal ceremony or other event such as a concert or rally. This gives the news release writer something more interesting or newsworthy to say and an opportunity to draw positive attention to the company.

Remember one thing, though: There should never be any confusion about what's really going on and who is responsible. If the company is behind an event, make that fact clear. Deception of any kind is reprehensible, but it's doubly reprehensible in a news release.

Spot News Releases   Announcement releases can usually be planned. But sometimes things happen without warning. An electric utility's main power plant can be damaged by a storm, for example, raising the prospect of power shortages or higher costs for replacement power. An explosion can occur in a munitions factory; an airplane can be hijacked. Such occurrences are spot news, and when they happen, a news release is in order. You must fill in the facts as they become available, issue news bulletins and follow with a release incorporating as much information as you can provide.

In these cases the public relations person must function like a reporter working on deadline, gathering the information quickly and writing the news bulletins for release without delay. If media people aren't provided with information immediately, they will write their stories from whatever scraps of information they can find. And frequently in such a case the reporting is inaccurate.

A spot news release often has to be followed up the next day with a second release, explaining how the initial events were resolved.

Response Releases   Often news about a company reaches the media from sources other than the public relations department. A consumer group may issue a report critical of the company, for instance. The government may announce an investigation into company pricing practices. A research group may publish a major study on your company's industry.

When these things happen, reporters call for a response. Companies with good public relations organizations anticipate these calls and have response releases ready. Responses may be brief statements or full-fledged news releases with the company's position set down in detail.

In emergency situations, news releases may not be enough. If this is the case, public relations people must use the telephone, email and fax to transmit the latest developments to the media. Chapter 20 discusses crisis communication.

Under normal circumstances, even if you are not asked for a response, you may want to offer one anyway as a way of communicating your organization's views. For example, when animal rights groups protested against the use of animals in research laboratories, organizations including the American Heart Association (which funds research) volunteered responses, as did universities that had accepted grants for such research. Other respondents were drug companies, cosmetics manufacturers and medical professionals.

Feature Releases   Not every story in a newspaper involves events that happened yesterday or today. Feature stories about topics of special interest occupy an increasing amount of newspaper space these days. All public relations people can find feature material somewhere in their organizations—something going on in research and development, for example, like a new production process that improves efficiency or helps reduce pollution. Such feature stories can be prepared for newspapers as ordinary news releases.

Feature releases create a problem. Newspapers don't expect special treatment when it comes to regular news; they know you give ordinary news releases to all news media. But features are different. An editor is not likely to use a feature if he or she knows that some other newspaper might be running the same story. It's best to offer different features to different newspapers, or at least to develop a different angle on the story for each newspaper in the area. Magazines are even more sensitive. For feature writing, see Chapter 11.

Bad-News Releases   Sometimes events occur that a company would like to keep quiet. The natural tendency in such cases is to issue no news releases at all and hope that the problem will go unnoticed. But more often than not, attempts to keep bad news out of the media backfire. Such stories often involve a company's regulatory agency. Because regulatory agencies are supposed to act in the public's interest, you can be sure the agency will release a report. You've seen such stories: A restaurant gets a poor sanitation report from the city's health department; an industry is accused of contaminating a water supply; a nuclear plant gets a poor safety rating from a routine inspection; a manufacturing plant is accused of exposing its workers to health hazards without warning or protecting them. And what do you commonly see as the response of the accused? "No comment."

If your organization has been attacked and you have made your own announcement release on the situation, the story will still be in the newspaper—and it may be prominently displayed—but it will be treated in a less sensational manner than if you issued no comment. If you hand over the facts to a reporter, the result will usually be a straight report. When a reporter has to dig the story out, however, he or she will make the article more dramatic, and the story will be more likely to linger on the front pages, with the reporter unveiling additional bits of information as they are uncovered. This is the classic treatment of a cover-up. In recent years, organizations have begun to realize that covering up a problem can become a worse problem than the original problem itself. (See Table 9.4 for a news release checklist.)

Column Notes, Letters, Guest Columns and Photos   Sometimes the information you'd like to see in the newspaper doesn't fit the form of an ordinary news story. That doesn't mean you should forget about it. Most newspapers have special columns or sections that print unusual items, and these are often among the best-read parts of the publication. Individual columnists might make use of readers' information. Or readers might want to write a "guest column." (You might want to write one under the byline of your company's chief executive.)

Such items don't always follow the form of an ordinary news release, but they can accomplish much the same thing. Study the newspapers your organization deals with so you'll know what outlets are available.

Photos are among the most effective publicity tools. Photos must tell a story to be worth using. They can accompany a release as an illustration, or they can stand alone. In either case, they must interest the audience. Sometimes single photos and their captions even qualify as what editors call "wild art"—photos that add reader interest to the page. Captions for photos

T A B L E   9 . 4   *News Release Checklist*

1. Is the lead direct and to the point? Does it contain the most important and most interesting aspects of the story?

2. Has the local angle been emphasized?

3. Have who, what, when, where, why and how been answered in the first few paragraphs?

4. Are sentences short, concise? Paragraphs short? Words common and concrete?

5. Has editorial comment been placed in quotation marks and attributed to the appropriate person?

6. Are quotations natural? That is, do they sound as though they could have been spoken?

7. Has newspaper style (AP or other) been followed faithfully throughout the release?

8. Are spelling and punctuation correct?

9. Have all statements of fact been double-checked for accuracy?

10. Has the release been properly prepared in the correct format?

11. Is the release dated? Is the release time indicated?

12. Are names, phone numbers, fax numbers and email addresses for further information included?

13. Has the release been cleared internally?

---

that illustrate a story carry information that relieves the story of some detail. A caption for "wild art" only tells readers what they are looking at and points out the picture's significance, if any.

The AP's rules for captions are worth remembering:

The caption's job is to describe and explain the picture to the reader.
The challenge is to do it interestingly, accurately, always in good taste.
A further challenge is to write the caption, whenever appropriate, in a sprightly, lively vein.
An Associated Press Managing Editors (APME) Continuing Study Committee put together Ten Tests of a Good Caption. They are:

1. Is it complete?
2. Does it identify, fully and clearly?
3. Does it tell when?
4. Does it tell where?
5. Does it tell what's in the picture?
6. Does it have the names spelled correctly, with the proper name on the right person?
7. Is it specific?
8. Is it easy to read?
9. Have as many adjectives as possible been removed?
10. Does it suggest another picture?

And rule No. 11, the cardinal rule, never, never to be violated:
NEVER WRITE A CAPTION WITHOUT SEEING THE PICTURE.[8]

The biggest boon to PR photo distribution is the Associated Press' PhotoExpress, which delivers PR photos for a fee to member newspapers in the USA.

For media that don't get PhotoExpress, two other major delivery wires for photos are PR Newswire (PRN) and Business Wire (BW). The media make the decision about whether to accept photos from either of these services. International distribution channels move the photos via satellite.

Some organizations use digitalized photo databases for images that they may want to use for internal or external distribution. This makes images—photos and graphics—available to print and broadcast media.

Dealing with News Media

Remembering Chapter 1, you must have some idea of where you are going to send a release before you even write it. What is the news (message)? Who should get this news, by what medium? Having gone through this process before drafting your release, you already have the basic release written, as well as adaptations for the various media based on timing and their audiences. Another part of prewriting planning is distribution. How are you going to get your news releases to the media?

If you use a distribution supplier, the process is simple. You let them know which release version goes where, and it's done. You make the transfer electronically. They confirm and come back with any questions. If translations are required, the organization distributing them takes care of this. When you are sending releases directly to international news media with bases in the USA, they take care of translation and distribution.

Usually these international media are wire services, and it is important to remember the wire services. In some cases you may be preparing a release for your local newspaper and a separate one for the Associated Press. The newspaper is interested in the local angle, which you will have emphasized in the lead, while the AP wants to see the broader implications, the impact of the story on regional, national or international audiences. Your daily newspaper may be one of a chain that has its own distribution service available to its newspapers free and a service for sale to others. If so, your release will be available to those newspapers.

Some weekly newspapers also are group owned. This can be both an asset and a liability. Distribution of a release is easier, but tailoring it to the local area that the weekly serves is more difficult. One solution is to write paragraphs involving names in each region as an "add-on" at the bottom of the release. Editors can then insert that copy after the lead, which they may modify to read something like: "Three City Falls citizens are being honored by State University at services in the capitol next week." The purpose for the special event will follow and then copy listing the names. Weeklies are often more effective for reaching community audiences than dailies, which are not interested in some of the personalization of stories, unless the personalities are well known.

Most releases should also be sent to the electronic media. But remember, broadcast style differs from print style. A release prepared for a newspaper must be completely rewritten for TV or radio. (See Chapter 10 on broadcast writing.) Because the electronic version will normally be much shorter than the print version, you should attach the print version to the release you send to radio and TV stations. This makes the details available to the electronic journalists if they need them.

It's helpful to know the right person to send a release to. Most TV and radio stations have a news director, and all releases should go to that individual. Newspapers are more complicated, however. Various section editors may be interested in the news you have to offer, but sometimes their responsibilities overlap and it's hard to choose the right recipient. Most large cities have media directories, updated monthly. You can refer to these in determining your contacts. Magazines are easier because staff writers are listed and don't change as frequently.

Otherwise, a few simple guidelines may be helpful. Newspaper releases specifically aimed at a single topic (such as food or sports) should go to the section editor. If the news is of general local interest, the city or metropolitan editor is usually the right person to receive the release. If one reporter covers your company or organization all the time, send the release directly to him or her.

Sometimes it's appropriate to send a release to more than one person at the same newspaper—a reporter and an editor, for example. Some companies regularly send copies of releases to editorial writers, especially if the release addresses a controversial topic. If you send more than one copy of the release to a given newspaper, though, make sure that you indicate that you have done so on the release. To avoid duplicated story assignments, you must let the editor know that a reporter already has your release.

When should you send the release? On breaking news stories, as soon as possible. Post on your Web site. Call and see how you can help. For announcements of upcoming events, posting the story three or four days in advance is usually sufficient. For a major story that should be released at a specific time, have the release available the day before the desired date for media use.

Keep in mind that weekly papers have different deadline schedules from dailies. A weekly published on Thursdays might have a deadline as early as Monday. You must know the deadlines in order to deliver your release on time.

Calendar-of-events editors often have early deadlines and should receive notification in a short form that matches their style.

As for getting the newspapers to use your release, there is no substitute for a well-written release with genuine news value. All other considerations are secondary. But assuming that the release is properly prepared, you can do some things to enhance the chances that it will get printed. One is to choose the proper release date. Setting the release time for Sunday helps your chances, as Sunday papers are large and have more space to fill. Monday is also good, because news staffs are small on the weekend and news tends to be slow. Including a good picture or graphics with the release is also helpful, because editors are always interested in good art for page-design purposes. Perhaps the best way to get a release used, however, is to get it moved on the wire services. Newspapers use wire stories in preference to releases to save time in editing and formatting.

This chapter has covered primarily news releases to newspapers, but in practice you will be sending releases to a number of specialized news media, including trade papers and internal publications. These publications are discussed in Chapter 19. Writing news releases is just one of many activities you will be involved in.

Government Regulations

You need to be aware that the release of information—especially from a corporation whose stock is publicly traded—falls under federal regulations as well as the rules of the stock exchange where the company's stock is traded. The Securities and Exchange Commission (SEC) regulates what kind of information about a corporation and its financial affairs can—or *must*—be released and under what conditions.

In an effort to "level the playing field" for investors, the SEC issued its Regulation FD (Fair Disclosure) on October 23, 2000. In its summary of the rule, the SEC said, "The rules are designed to promote the full and fair disclosure of information by issuers, and to clarify and enhance existing prohibitions against insider trading." This regulation makes selective disclosure of information illegal, saying, "Issuer selective disclosure bears a close resemblance in this regard to ordinary 'tipping' and insider trading. In both cases, a privileged few gain an informational edge—and the ability to use that edge to profit—from their superior access to corporate insiders, rather than from their skill, acumen, or diligence."[9]

To conform to this and other regulations, the rule of thumb is to "tell no one until you tell everyone." Once information on a significant transaction or event is disclosed to anyone, regulations require full disclosure, usually in the form of a news release that is widely distributed.

Conclusions

- Many people other than media gatekeepers have access to news releases placed on the Internet.
- News releases can be a valuable communication tool, but only if they are really *news*.
- In general, news media personnel do not consider news releases to be as well written and as timely as public relations practitioners think they are.
- Internet access to news releases poses both advantages and disadvantages.
- News media personnel evaluate releases on the basis of writing quality, accuracy, completeness and timeliness.
- To understand what news is most acceptable to the media you are trying to serve, you must study the media.
- You must understand your own institution to find the news within it.
- Use news and advertising information appropriately, recognizing that lines between the two are blurring.
- The lead is the most important part of your news release.
- A local angle is important in getting a news editor's attention.
- In amplifying the lead, use short, concise sentences and be sure to cover the who, what, when, where, why and how of the story in the first two paragraphs.
- PR writers can develop quotes for stories and get them approved by the person to whom they are attributed—a luxury newswriters don't have.
- News releases should be written in a simple, clear, direct style. Format is important.
- The *AP Stylebook* dictates generally accepted news style, though some media have their own styles.
- News tips are sent to media to stimulate editors' interest in covering a story.
- News releases are written to communicate announcements, information on special events, spot news, responses to events, features and reactions to bad news.
- Some information should be placed in forms other than straight news releases—for example, column notes, letters, guest columns and photos.
- All news releases used by traditional news media will be edited, and some will not appear at all.
- Before you approach the media with releases or news tips, be sure you know the difference between reportorial and access media.
- Use tip sheets to enlist the consideration of editors for a story.

- You may need to write a "selling memo" to accompany your news release if it is a little weak on news value but has good human interest.
- Photos or graphics and their captions may be sent with a story as illustrations or alone as "wild art." In either case, they are good public relations tools.
- Digital graphics and photos can be sent electronically around the world.
- The decision of where and when to send releases is critical.
- Releases should be prepared in a style and format appropriate to the medium.
- Before distributing a news release, public relations writers should review all 13 items in the news release checklist.
- To help communicate public relations messages and to build good media relations, news releases must contain genuine news, must be written in the proper form and style and must be truthful, complete and accurate.
- Release of significant news of corporations whose stock is publicly traded is regulated by the Securities and Exchange Commission (SEC).

Exercises

1. Prepare a news release for newspapers from the position paper in Chapter 8.
2. Write a news release for a specialized publication from the same position paper. Name the publication and state its purpose.
3. Write cover letters for both, telling each editor why the story has value for that publication's audience.

Use InfoTrac College Edition to access information on topics in this chapter from hundreds of periodicals and scholarly journals.

Notes

1. Philip Lesly, "Relations with Publicity Media," in *Lesly's Public Relations Handbook* (Englewood Cliffs, N.J.: Prentice Hall, 1971), p. 348.
2. Ivy Lee, *Publicity: Some Things It Is and Is Not* (New York: Industries Publishing, 1925).
3. "New Media Strategy . . . ," *pr reporter* (June 22, 1992): 1–2.
4. As quoted by Rudolf Flesch, *The Art of Readable Writing,* 25th anniv. ed. (New York: Harper & Row, 1974), p. 25.
5. Randy Hargrove, "Alameda County Superior Court of California Rules for Blockbuster in Extended Viewing Fee Lawsuit," http://www.blockbuster.com/bb/article/details/0,7413,ART-1039%5ENT-ABT,00.html? (Dallas, Texas: March 6, 2003).
6. "Just the Fax," *The Wall Street Journal* (May 13, 1993): 1.
7. Otto Lerbinger, *Designs for Persuasive Communication* (Englewood Cliffs, N.J.: Prentice Hall, 1972), p. 69.
8. Norm Goldstein, ed., *The Associated Press Stylebook and Libel Manual* (Reading, Mass.: Addison-Wesley, 1994), p. 293. Used with permission.
9. "Final Rule: Selective Disclosure and Insider Trading, Securities and Exchange Commission, 17 CFR Parts 240, 243, and 249, Release Nos. 33-7881, 34-43154, IC-

24599, File No. S7-31-99, RIN 3235-AH82, Selective Disclosure and Insider Trading," http://www.sec.gov/rules/final/33-7881.htm (Washington, D.C.: October 23, 2002).

Selected Bibliography

Merry Aronson and Don Spetner, *The Public Relations Writer's Handbook* (Hoboken, N.J.: Jossey-Bass, 1998).

Kevin Barnhurst, *Seeing the Newspaper* (New York: St. Martin's Press, 1994).

Kay Borden, *Bulletproof News Releases: Help at Last for the Publicity Deficient,* 2d ed. (Marietta, Ga.: Franklin Sarrett Publishers, 1995).

Norm Goldstein, ed., *The Associated Press Stylebook and Briefing on Media Law,* revised and updated edition (Cambridge, Mass.: Perseus Publishing, 2002).

Carole M. Howard and Wilma K. Mathews, *On Deadline: Managing Media Relations,* 3d ed. (Prospect Heights, Ill.: Waveland Press, 2000).

Robert H. Loeffler, *A Guide to Preparing Cost-Effective Press Releases* (New York: Haworth Press, 1996).

Doug Newsom, Judy VanSlyke Turk and Dean Kruckeberg, *This Is PR: The Realities of Public Relations,* 8th ed. (Belmont, Calif.: Wadsworth, 2004).

Chris Petrakos, *Fresh Ink: Behind the Scenes at a Major Metropolitan Newspaper* (Austin: University of Texas Press, 1995).

David R. Yale, *Publicity & Media Relations Checklists* (New York: McGraw-Hill, 1995).

CHAPTER TEN

News for Broadcasting

There's something to the adage, "Seeing is believing." Seeing and hearing are influential experiences, even when the information they convey clashes with earlier experiences. As a result, credibility is always at risk in a broadcast world, especially if not much is known about an organization or an individual in the news.

Therefore, the technical aspects of providing information to news media dominate writing for broadcast. You must think of the information in a different way. What portion of the story can you get a person with authority and credibility to say so you can capture it on audiotape? What quote from the story makes a good "sound bite"? Radio stations are interested in the sounds of an event: the voice of the mayor reading a proclamation, the president of the electric company explaining a power outage, the hospital director telling about medical care for tornado victims.

On the other hand, if it wiggles, it's TV news, or so the saying goes. And the remark is only half facetious. What in your story "wiggles" or offers movement and color? How can you capture that on videotape?

Audiotape (on a roll or cassette) and videotape (with or without sound on the tape) are far more likely to be used on radio and TV than is a news release telling what happened and what was said. CDs *can* be used but aren't favored. If a station refers viewers to its Web site for additional information, the CD's digital format makes the information you send more accessible. One of the problems is compatibility. Some software is not compatible across platforms, so you need to call to check.

Consider your competition. Broadcast stations subscribe to news services that provide written broadcast-style stories and ready-to-air, satellite-fed audio and video for the stories. Additionally, there are packages of whole segments that come ready to air. What chance do you have with your news release unless you take into consideration the elements—audio and video—that constitute broadcast news?

Facts, Sights and Sounds

Facts are the vital elements of any news story, whether for print media or broadcast media. Sometimes a formal news release isn't really necessary; the public relations writer can provide the media with a fact sheet, and the reporters can write the story. But with the electronic media, facts alone are not enough. Whether you're planning a special event, holding a news conference or dealing with a crisis situation, you must also be aware of sights and sounds. These sights and sounds recorded at a news event are called *actualities*.

Announcements and Special Events

For TV, you'll have to stage some activity to film or tape for an advance announcement of your special event. Thus, after holding the first of what is to be an annual event, you'll need visuals for the next year shot during this year's event—videotape, and digital still photos for the news media to see and for your Web site. One word of caution: When you use last year's pictures as an advance story, be sure you label the pictures carefully. Sometimes editors get too busy to realize that you are sending a picture of something that already happened—and will inadvertently label last year's pictures as this year's. Protect yourself by labeling the pictures clearly and appropriately.

In preparing for an advance story, you should document the event on videotape with sound with an audiocassette for radio backup, and in case the sound needs to be on a separate cassette for easier editing. It is also a good idea to have some charts and graphs on Microsoft® PowerPoint® that show attendance figures and such from the previous year. You might also make a slide showing dates for the upcoming event. Dates for the next event of course will be on your Web page, and you may have some digitized images from the previous year's event there too. Remember that the quality of these is not suitable for television, but TV news directors seeing the pictures on your Web page may want that same image, or one close to it, for their own stories. The moral to this is to shoot events with the idea of capturing close to the same images in multiple formats. Expensive, but usually worth it.

When you stage an activity to photograph, don't *simulate* the event. You wouldn't want to perpetrate a hoax. Nor would you want to be wrongly accused of doing so. But feel free to shoot preparations for the event; they qualify as legitimate news. For audio you can use the people involved—dignitaries, if possible—to make the announcements. Have these announcements recorded by technically qualified people so they will be of broadcast quality. As the event gets closer, use interviews with some of the participants. Supply radio and television stations with your audiotapes and videotapes.

So much for the advance. For actual coverage of your special event by the news media, find out at least three to six weeks in advance what mechanical equipment you will need to supply. You'll have to check out lighting and sound systems and prepare a list of what activities (of news value) will be available for coverage. When the news media arrive, you should be able to offer (again) all the materials prepared in advance, plus an update of what is happening that day and the next. Mention any changes in or corrections of materials sent previously.

Supply these in writing when possible. Table 10.1 illustrates a special-event broadcast news release. Give reporters a copy of a brief story in broadcast style. Attach this release to a copy of the longer story prepared for the print media. In reworking the story or in writing their own to fit the coverage, broadcasters will find the longer release helpful.

T A B L E   1 0 . 1   *Format for Broadcast Release for a Special Event*

SPECIAL EVENT LETTERHEAD

Address for Event Sponsor
Phone Number for Event Sponsor
Fax Number for Event Sponsor

Your name, title, phone, fax and email address

Date (and number of release if many are being sent)*

Slug Line (for story identification instead of print release's suggested head)   Time: (in seconds, i.e., :00)

Set story for 60-space line 12-point font (Times or Times Roman) so copy can be counted and time estimated. That setting will give about four seconds a line. Use triple space on printout so copy can be easily marked and read, although few releases will be read "as is." Keep release to a single page, triple-spaced. When sending a release electronically, use double space because the receiver can convert it to triple space.

Give announcers a "lead-in" to your release before the lead. Tell people what the special event is. Get them ready for the news.

Keep your lead to between 16 and 20 words so it will be easy to read. Make the next sentence short to vary the pattern. Think of the listeners trying to follow the story they are only hearing. Think of the announcer and show how to pronounce unusual words or names. Indicate the ending of the story by ###, 30, or End. To be sure about timing, read copy and time reading with a stopwatch.

*Most large organizations number their releases, indicating purposes. For a special event you need to develop a special series with some reference alphas that tells what the event is or was, like A for Anniversary Celebration; something that incorporates the date, such as 04 for year; and something that separates the media formats, such as B for Broadcast. The number might look like A-1B04. The last release in the series might be A-10B04.

Because broadcasters will be rewriting news scripts frequently during the day, include a print release on the event too so other versions can be created by the station's newswriters. That release would carry a number like A-1P01, with the P for Print. Of course, a cover letter to the news director will explain why the longer release is being sent.

If the release is going to a television station, be sure that you include information about visuals that are available, such as videotape with or without sound.

It's important at special events to have someone at a central location to answer the telephone and respond intelligently to queries from the news media. You also need to be sure you have adequate computer facilities for that person to receive and send email and to check your organization's Web site and get updates about the event promptly. That person also needs a complete set of materials on the event and a copy of your itinerary. You should consider a pager or a cell phone too. In any case, you need to check in every hour or so regardless.

Remember that you will get only a few seconds, maybe a minute, of coverage. Use that time to direct competing media to different facets of the event. That way they will get better stories and you will get better coverage. Be absolutely sure of all your facts, because there will be no time for correction. The news media are not very forgiving of a public relations source that causes them to broadcast an inaccuracy.

News Conferences

News conferences are called by public relations directors where some interaction with the news media needs to take place. The situation may be when a major announcement needs to be made by management, or an explanation for an event given, or when a person's time in the area is limited, such as a visiting dignitary or celebrity. The whole point of a news conference is to allow as many questions to be asked as possible. The opportunity to ask questions is especially important if there is a controversy.

There are many ways to hold a news conference. The most obvious one is a live news conference where the news media come to a specific site chosen for convenience or for significance, such as the dedication of a building or memorial of national significance. Often news conferences are held by satellite. This involves considerable planning and expense, but is worth it because of increased participation from media as it doesn't require travel and does allow instant transmission. This is especially important in situations of global significance. A more low-key news conference is one by telephone, something often done by investor relations people to hook up the CEO with a number of securities analysts and economics journalists all at the same time while simultaneously offering listener access to nonparticipants such as shareholders.

However the conference is held, considerable advance planning is necessary. Ordinarily you'll prepare an announcement, giving the reason for the conference, identifying the person (giving background if he or she is a celebrity) and detailing the time, date and place and who to contact (by name, physical address, phone and fax numbers and email address) if there are any questions. Most of these announcements are sent to the broadcast media by wire. You may use a public relations wire service or you may have a news conference about financial matters carried by the Dow Jones wire. Occasionally your news conference is significant enough that information about it will be carried on the Associated Press broadcast wires (radio and/or TV). (See Table 10.2.)

If you are calling the conference to give information on a problem or to make an unexpected announcement, be sure you have prepared background materials to give to the media people who attend. A package should contain a printed copy of the announcement, biographical material on the person (if appropriate) and background materials addressing the most significant questions. You should also have prepared a "shooting schedule" for pictures. Be sure to have a still photographer, an audio recorder and camerapersons to shoot both digital photos and videotape. You will need these records for your own reference and might also need to

T A B L E   1 0 . 2   *Broadcast Wire Planning Summary*

AP v6042 rv Otx-k TX-Daybook   05-07 8:09a

For Wednesday, May 7, 2003

Eds: NOT FOR BROADCAST OR PUBLICATION

(ARLINGTON)

Event: Texas Rangers Latino players will attend luncheon saluting Hispanic businesses from North Texas. The purpose of luncheon is to build stronger relationship between the Rangers and this business community.

Time/loc: Noon-1:30 p.m. at The Ballpark, Diamond Club

Contact: Casey Gonzalez, Arlington Hispanic Chamber, 817-312-7909; Sal Morales 682-465-2185

(AUSTIN)

Event: Texas Crime Victim Clearinghouse 16th annual conference, about services offered to victims of crime.

Time/loc: Through Friday at Omni Austin Southpark.

NOTE: As part of events, Texas Atty. Gen. Greg Abbott will speak Wednesday to crime victims and advocates (5 p.m., at Capitol, south steps)

Contact: Cherri McEnelly, 800-848-4284, cherri.mcenelly(at)tdcj.state.tx.us. Abbott's contact is Jane Shepperd, 512-463-2050

Event: UIL state high school golf tournament, through Friday.

(DALLAS)

Event: Greater Dallas Chamber hosts economic forum.

Time/loc: 8 a.m. at City Place.

Contact: Brandon Rice, 214-746-6750, brice(at)dallaschamber.org

Event: Janina Bitz, first grant recipient of Mark Cuban Foundation's Fallen Patriot Fund, receives check. Her husband, Marine Sgt. Michael E. Bitz, was killed in Iraq in March.

Time/loc: 1 p.m. in Jacksonville, N.C., call for address.

Contact: Dawn Holgate w. Mavericks, 214-878-2867, Gillian Breidenbach, Bank of America, 214-673-3122

(HOUSTON)

Event: Rev. Jesse Jackson honors minority and women-owned business in the energy industry as part of annual Rainbow/PUSH Coalition energy summit.

Time/loc: Panel discussions 9 a.m. Hyatt Regency.

Reception/dinner/awards ceremony 6:30 p.m. Hobby Center.

Contact: William Thomas 713-571-0881 or Phyllis Bailey 281-438-0985.

(STATEWIDE)

Event: First drawing of Lotto Texas game with newly revised rules (including introduction of a bonus ball).

(Copyright 2003 by The Associated Press. Reprinted by permission. All Rights Reserved.)

supply them to a medium that had mechanical problems. Remember compatibility difficulties with opening art.

Remember too that news conferences are not parties for the media. You might want to have coffee or soft drinks on hand, but save the rest for a festive occasion that's not a working situation. Table 10.3 illustrates a representative set of reference materials. Table 10.4 lists logistical considerations for coverage.

Crises

A crisis, such as a plant fire or hostage situation, is a disorganized combination of a special event and a news conference. The media will need information that even you as an insider will have difficulty getting. Nevertheless, getting and supplying that information is the most important service you can perform. (See Chapter 20.)

Talk Shows

At the national level, public relations people may work directly through the radio or television show's producers, or they may use a national placement agency. These agencies have the contacts, and the reputation with the television producers, for "delivering." What producers don't want is a "no-show," or someone who appears in the studio but really is not prepared to give an interview that pulls audience response, either in ratings or in phone calls and emails, if it is a call-in show.

If the show is local, occasionally the public relations person is the talk-show guest, but this really is not greeted with much enthusiasm by the broadcasters. Try to find someone who will capture attention, from not only the broadcaster but also the audience. Shows of this

---

T A B L E   1 0 . 3   *Reference Materials for Broadcast Media*

- **News release giving basic messages or statements of conference as anticipated.**
  Generally announcements are made at news conferences, but there are responses to questions that of course can't be anticipated.

- **Biographies of all principals involved in news conference.**
  Usually only one or two people are involved in the newsmaking part of the news conference. For example, it may be a major appointment by a government official like the president, governor or mayor, or a university announcement of a new athletic coach.

- **Background information on the situation or the event.**
  For example, the news conference may be to announce an agreement that resolves a conflict. Be sure that the presentation materials are balanced and fair. This might even be a joint news conference, so materials must be shared and coordinated.

- **Who to call for additional information if it is needed when the story is prepared in the newsroom.**
  Be sure email addresses are available, as well as the Web site address.

- **Fact sheet on the event or situation.**
  For events, the details of the event can be given; for appointments, the names and dates of previous holders of the office can be useful to a reporter.

TABLE 10.4   *Logistical Needs of News Media at News Conferences and Speeches*

Broadcasters come with their own equipment bag, but what they need on site are the following:

A good microphone for the speakers and a reliable sound system in a room with good acoustics and lighting.

A mult box with enough sound system connections for the reporters to plug into to capture the audio.

Additional mult extension cords so reporters can connect their recorders and keep them with them instead of having to leave them near the podium.

Industrial extension cords for extra lights and sufficient electrical outlets.

A public address mike on a podium that is large enough to accommodate reporters' mikes.

Telephones with jacks for reporters to file from the scene. (The reporter can feed audio from an audio recorder directly into the phone circuits.)

Internet connections would help those using digital/computer gear.

Plenty of duct tape to tape down all of the wires to keep people from tripping over them. Tape your own wires before the event, but have tape and scissors available for reporters who need to tape their own connections in a hurry.

Pens, pencils and pads of paper are always useful.

Be sure the doors to the room open wide enough for larger pieces of equipment to be brought in easily, and have technical staff of your own available to help with blown fuses, fuzzy sound systems, contrary mikes and such.

Crews need a place to park, especially if they are bringing a live truck and will broadcast or transmit from the scene.

Easily accessible water fountains and restrooms are always appreciated.

nature are not as fluid as they appear. Generally, they are structured by the host in a brief period before the show is aired.

You'll need to prepare certain materials for such an event. The show's host needs to have a backgrounder or fact sheet on the institution that the individual represents, the event or occasion for the attention and biographical information on the person being interviewed. All of this information must be very brief and in a form the show's host can take on the air—use triple spacing on sheets of paper heavy enough not to rattle.

The guest should have in mind all the information he or she is going to present. To prepare mentally and to keep facts and figures fresh, the guest usually requires briefing sessions the day before and again just before airtime. The guest needs to alert the host to information that should be presented for the benefit of the listening audience. If the talk show is on television, take along materials that can be shown. Remember the wiggle.

News on Call

Some organizations offer broadcast-quality information and actualities (visual or audio) on call either through a special number or a toll-free line.

The information is changed frequently during the day so that broadcast news stories can be updated with fresh actualities.

Although Web sites continue to be an excellent source of information updates and certainly a good place for gathering background information, the audio, when there is any, like the pictures, is not of broadcast quality yet. However, in designing your Web pages, don't forget that broadcast media will be using them, so give phone contact numbers on your news pages and on your home page. The assumption of many Web site designers is that the contact will be made by computer. With broadcast media, that is less likely if what is needed is an actuality, not just information.

News Releases

Like those for print media, news releases for broadcast media are either advance stories about something soon to occur or stories explaining what has occurred or what is going on. Although no news media personnel will get excited about doing your promotion for you, many will use well-prepared advance stories if the event has enough news value. News releases on upcoming events should be extremely brief for the broadcast media—no more than two or three short paragraphs. However, you should send along your longer print-media version, a fact sheet and (when appropriate) a brochure or printed program. If the event is likely to have regional interest, send a courtesy copy of the news release to the broadcast wire services, just to alert them to an event their reporters might be interested in. Be sure to identify the courtesy copy as such when you deliver or send the release.

If you are sending your materials by email, remember to send a message with the releases, fact sheets and graphics each as separate attachments because the receiver may encounter problems opening the files or downloading the graphics.

Electronic transmission of messages, images and sound is changing the delivery of information to broadcast media. Direct feeds from satellites are common. Stations can take broadcast-quality interviews over the phone. However, the broadcast medium, be it a network or a station, has to want to receive your information. The way you accomplish that is by building a history of credibility and reliability for providing timely and accurate material of broadcast quality. (Services like QuickSilver's eNewsroom are also available, as mentioned in Chapter 9.)

For stations in your immediate area, it's a good idea to build your reputation through direct in-person contact. You want to develop working professional relationships with broadcast people so they know who you are when you call. That's very important now that broadcast stations, especially in metropolitan areas, are security conscious and not open to "drop-in" visits from strangers. Otherwise you literally can't get past the front door.

If you meet resistance, you can still leave materials with a receptionist. It's just that when you do, the opportunity to answer questions about the materials is not available unless someone calls you back. Nevertheless, it's still a good idea locally to hand-deliver advance stories to the broadcast news media whenever possible. If this is not possible, telephone the medium to alert them that a release has been sent to them and how—via email, fax or courier. Most advance stories are given short shrift. Therefore, if you have any visuals from a previous event that will add interest, offer to make them available. Media advisories help build relationships and pique media interest. (See Table 10.5.)

Timeliness is a problem for stories about events that have already happened. Nevertheless, the broadcast media will cover most events of any significance—even past events. If you are supplying audio and visual materials, be sure you prepare them to meet media deadlines and mechanical requirements. Then call the news directors to let them know that the material is coming, and hand-deliver the package. If the event was a speech, attach a complete copy to

T A B L E   1 0 . 5   *Model Broadcast News Tip Sheet*

A Compelling Headline

What: Don't just tell what is happening; give some descriptions of irresistible visual and/or audio possibilities.

When: Broadcasters live by the clock. Tell precisely when something is occurring, the date, day of the week, time of day for openings/closings and best time to catch the action.

Where: Be very specific about location and access. Give tested directions so no one is confused or lost. Also give your cell phone contact number just in case someone does get lost en route.

Who: Who is sponsoring this event and why and how significant this is to the broadcast audience because that's who matters, not you and your organization.

Contact Information: Your name, email address, organization's physical address and phone numbers including your office, cell and home numbers.

the brief release. You can file a courtesy copy with the wire service if the speech has regional interest—though, again, the wire services often provide their own coverage.

For television, you can offer graphs and charts to help explain the event; for radio, offer broadcasters a telephone interview to flesh out their story and give it a sense of immediacy. In the latter instance, be sure you have all the facts and figures within easy reach for the phone interview. Be aware that your interview will be edited. Still, if you are prepared, editors won't have to cut out dead air—gaps of silence—while you hunt down a fact.

VNRs

Video news releases are increasingly accepted by news directors, especially in the areas of science stories and health and medical news. This may be the only way the broadcast media can get access to the story because of proprietary information in the case of drug companies, the complexity of the material in science research presentations or the need to protect patients' rights in some medical stories.

Writing a video news release means writing a script, just as a news team might write it if the news team had access to the information in advance of the event. Of course, what usually happens is that broadcast news teams cover an event with reporters, photographers and technical crews. Then they go back to the station, look at and listen to what they were able to capture and write a script describing what is usable from the audio and video that they got.

In writing a video news release, the public relations writer has control of the situation. The script is written with the information in place and the visuals and sound indicated. Then the video is photographed and recorded. It is edited to a usable news segment, usually 30 seconds, but it may be longer. The outtakes are kept, and additional footage or a "B" roll usually is shot, as well as some additional actualities as long as the production studio is leased for the VNR.

Remember that your VNRs are likely to be 30 seconds, maybe a minute. A long piece is 3 minutes. If the VNR is a news feature it could run between 5 and 20 minutes. Although you will be using professional producers, some things you need to watch for in viewing the final piece are suggested by videotape editor Eric Alkire (alkire@worldnet.att.net). Look for useless cutaways and sound breaks, because these interrupt the flow of the story. The story should flow and any break, audio or video, should contribute to, not distract from, the story. Watch for flash frames or muddy audio cuts. Most importantly, Alkire advises, watch objectively and ask if the story gets told and the video is watchable.[1]

Additional suggestions come from Canadian public relations professional David Eisenstadt, who warns about being sure that the VNR is really news and not a commercial, that the production is simple, not glitzy, so that it fits most station's formats and that you use sound. Additionally, you need to know whether to send VHS or BETA. Although stations have both, one is usually preferred, usually BETA.[2]

Most broadcasters indicate that they prefer to get the VNR by satellite and want to be notified that it is coming by fax rather than wire service or telephone.[3] Although some news directors still worry about lack of flexibility in adjusting the story to their format, time frame and audience, most have figured out a way to let audiences know that the information comes from a public relations source by a simple credit line. Some VNR productions help by superimposing the words "footage supplied by XXX" over footage of a new product or over a simulation of a scientific breakthrough.

The acknowledgment of the source for VNRs has posed an ethical problem. (See Chapter 2.) However, many VNR producers, other producers and distributors now subscribe to a Video News Release Code of Practice developed in 1992 by the Public Relations Service Council.[4]

Broadcast Writing Style

The basic difference between writing for broadcast media and writing for print media is that copy for the former must appeal to the ear. (In television and video, of course, the visuals must capture the eye.) Copy must capture attention through sound and word symbolism. The words must be clear enough to be understandable the first time through. The listener will not have a chance to review what is said. In radio, the listener can't reread a sentence to understand what it meant and can't go back to the one preceding it to figure out the sequence of ideas. Each offering is a one-time-only presentation. To compensate for the lack of review opportunity, broadcast writers first tell listeners (and viewers) what they are going to tell them, alerting them to the content by calling up frames of reference. Then they present the content. Finally, in the summary, they again tell the listener what the message was. It takes a skillful writer to prepare material in this way without sounding redundant. As the writer follows this sequence, keep the time element in mind. Clarity and brevity are both important.

Because broadcast media are intimate, their style is conversational. Each listener or viewer experiences the broadcast media as an individual and responds personally. The relaxed style means that the leads, or first paragraphs, in broadcast stories, including news stories, are "soft." That is, the listener is introduced to the story before hearing it.

One type of soft lead is called a "throwaway": "Vacationers driving around the country this summer are likely to find lots of detours. The American Automobile Association says road repairs and construction are going on all over the nation." Another soft lead is the "angle" lead that hooks your attention: "Planning to drive your car on your vacation this year? Get ready for lots of detours. The American Automobile Association says road repairs and construction are going on all over the nation." If one news story is related to another, a soft lead may be used to introduce both of them: "Vacationers planning to drive their cars this summer are likely to have some unexpected problems. Road repairs and construction have put detour signs up all over the nation. The longer routes may cause motorists to run out of gas because many small service stations in outlying areas have closed during the last year. New highways bypassing towns have closed stations, and storms are the cause of the road repairs." (The story goes on to say that the American Automobile Association will help car travelers plan trips to find out about detours in advance, and that the major oil companies are offering credit card holders lists of service stations open along interstate, state and rural roads.)

We can make some other generalizations about broadcast writing. Because the tone is conversational, for instance, sentences are sometimes incomplete. We talk that way, so in broadcast journalism it's acceptable to write that way. Sentence length and structure are also governed by special rules. In broadcast writing, sentences are kept short in deference to both the announcer (who has a limited amount of breath) and the listener (whose attention span shouldn't be taxed). For the same reason, subjects and verbs are kept close together. Normally, sentences should not begin with prepositional phrases; the basic information should be conveyed first. "According to a report from the Mason County Sheriff's office today, vacationers driving through are likely to find fewer service stations than last year." By the time listeners decide that fewer service stations might be important to them, the "Mason County" is lost to all but the most attentive among them.

Broadcast writers should avoid two peculiarities of newspaper style—sometimes called "journalese"—in preparing broadcast copy. One is inverted sentence structure, where the statement precedes the attribution: "'Victims of the Mississippi tornado are all back in permanent housing,' said Scott Smith, director of emergency disaster relief." This sentence illustrates what not to do in writing broadcast copy. Because broadcast audiences may not be attending to the first part of the sentence, information should be presented as it would probably be spoken in conversation: "The director of emergency disaster relief said that all victims of the Mississippi tornado are now back in permanent housing." The name of the director is not important to the story, so his title alone is used. If the story were a long one in which Smith was quoted, his name would be used, but he would be identified in a separate sentence: "Scott Smith is the director of emergency disaster relief."

The second newspaper-style characteristic to avoid in broadcast writing is the identification of subjects by age, job title and such. In newspapers this information usually follows the name and is set off by commas. But what is efficient in newspaper copy becomes cumbersome when read on the air. Again, the name of an individual is often unimportant; title identification is enough.

Here is a typical print story:

Vacationers traveling by car may be encountering an unusual number of detours this summer, according to James R. Ragland, manager of the Dixon American Automobile Association office.

Storm damage all over the nation has resulted in more than the usual amount of road repair, and the severe winter also put a number of highway projects behind schedule, Ragland said. The result is detours in almost every state.

AAA offices are trying to help motorists plan trips to at least be able to predict delays, Ragland said.

The service is free to AAA members, and there's a nominal charge for nonmembers, according to Ragland. The Dixon AAA office is in the Chamber of Commerce Building at Fifth and Ledbetter.

Here is a broadcast version (30 seconds long) of the same story:

> That severe winter the nation had is going to make summer vacations by car more difficult than usual, the American Automobile Association says. Triple A is offering travelers plans marked with all of the detours for road repairs and construction. Triple A's Dixon manager says the plans are free to members, but available to nonmembers for a nominal fee.

An admonition to keep it short but clear comes from broadcaster and academician Dr. Suzanne Huffman: "most radio newsstories on commercial stations are *very* short. As a writer, think in terms of 30 seconds for each story; that's about five sentences long. A story that runs 35 seconds will raise an eyebrow at the editor's desk. . . . Write the bare minimum you need. You have to be clear, but you have to be concise and short."[5]

Physical Preparation

Unlike copy for print media, all broadcast copy is triple-spaced and written on one side of the page. Some broadcast news departments prefer that copy be in all caps (capital letters); others prefer the standard combination of upper- and lowercase letters. Most public relations people supplying information to the broadcast news media use caps and lowercase. For radio, select font size and margins to produce a 60-space line, to give an average of 10 words per line. Most announcers read at a rate of about 15 of these lines per minute. So in radio news, one typed line takes about four seconds to read. A 30-second story is seven to eight lines long. (See the AAA story.)

The audio copy for a TV script goes on the right side of the page, opposite the video instructions. When you are writing for television and using only half the page (the audio side), set your margins to yield about six words to the line, or about 21 lines per minute at an average reading speed—the equivalent of about two seconds per line. Thus, a 30-second TV story is about 15 of these lines.

Much of the format for a broadcast release is similar to that of print copy. Appearing in the upper-left corner of the first page of each story is a slug line—the words identifying the story—the date, the name of the organization submitting the information, your name and phone numbers where you can be reached day or night. On the following pages, all you need are the page number, slug line (story identification) and your last name. The story's end is marked by the traditional "30," and "more" goes at the bottom of each page in the story except the last. Never break a paragraph at the bottom of a page.

To facilitate reading by announcers, don't break words at the end of lines either and don't split sentences between pages. If a word or name is difficult to pronounce, give the proper pronunciation in parentheses beside it *each* time it appears. The announcer should not have to go back and look for your previous instructions. Do not use diacritical markings you find in dictionaries to indicate the proper pronunciation. Use popular phonetics like those the newsmagazines employ—(SHEE-fur) for Schieffer, for example. (See Table 10.6.)

Remember, the audience can't see punctuation marks. These exist only to help the announcer interpret the copy. Don't use them unless they serve this purpose. And don't use colons, semicolons, percentage signs, dollar signs, fractions, ampersands and other exotica.

T A B L E   1 0 . 6   *Pronunciation Guide for Announcers*

VOWELS	
A Use AY for long A as in mate.	Use AW for broad O as in fought.
Use A for short A as in cat.	Use OO for O as in fool.
Use AI for nasal A as in air.	Use U for O as in foot.
Use AH for short A as in father.	Use OW for O as in how.
Use AW for broad A as in talk.	U Use EW for long U as in mule.
E Use EE for long E as in meet.	Use OO for long U as in rule.
Use EH for short E as in get.	Use U for middle U as in put.
Use UH for hollow E as in the or the French article le.	Use UH for short U as in shut.
Use AY for the French long E with accent as in Pathé.	**CONSONANTS**
Use IH for E as in pretty.	Use K for hard C as in cat.
Use EW for EW as in few.	Use S for soft C as in cease.
I Use EYE for long I as in time.	Use SH for soft CH as in machine.
Use EE for French long I as in machine.	Use CH or TCH for hard CH as in catch.
Use IH for short I as in pity.	Use Z for hard S as in disease.
O Use OH for long O as in note.	Use S for soft S as in sun.
Use AH for short O as in hot.	Use G for hard G as in gang.
	Use J for soft G as in general.

In *A Broadcast News Manual of Style,* these symbols are used. Although getting all sounds on paper is difficult (the TH sounds in *Smith* and *then* differ, for example), this phonetic guide will aid you in understanding the usage guide and help you create useful pronouncers. It is based on the guide used by United Press International (UPI).

Ron H. MacDonald, *A Broadcast News Manual of Style,* 2d ed. Copyright © 1994 by Longman Publishers USA. Reprinted with permission of Longman Publishers USA. (Paperback by Pearson Education, 2002.)

Just use commas, periods, question marks, dots, dashes and quotation marks. Use quotation marks only when repeating the exact words is essential. It is better to rephrase a quote into indirect statements. If you feel that a quote is necessary, precede it with something like, "In his words," or "What she asked for was" or "The statement read."

Use hyphens only when you want the letters to be spelled out individually, as in Y-W-C-A, as opposed to being read as a word, as in *NASA.* Don't use abbreviations unless you want them read on the air as abbreviations. Exceptions are such titles as Dr. and parts of names like *St.* Louis. If you don't know whether to write a word out or abbreviate it, write it out.

Numbers are difficult to follow when they're heard but not seen, so avoid using them as much as possible. Throughout this book, we preach the importance of using AP style. Here is where we'll vary somewhat. If the reporter is used to getting copy from you, then use the *AP Broadcast Manual*'s instructions for numerals. It's a bit different from the AP print style in that the rule of spelling out numbers one through nine is now one through eleven. AP broadcast style calls for using Arabic numerals for 12 through 999. Above that AP broadcast style calls for using what is more conversational, such as two-thousand dollars but 12-hundred dollars. However, if you are sending copy to broadcasters unfamiliar with you as a news source, use the AP broadcast style, but in parentheses spell out the numbers. Announcers don't read anything in parentheses, and it can be marked through in the copy during the editing process or deleted if the copy is going electronically. You must be absolutely sure there is no error in delivering numbers to the news media. It's seldom a risk in print but can be a real hazard in broadcast copy. Also, to prevent errors, don't use a.m. or p.m. with times of the day; announcers wouldn't read the letters anyway. Write, for example, "this morning" or "tomorrow night." However, because your copy is going to the news media for handling, put dates in parentheses beside the weekday designation—Monday (May 1). When the copy is processed for reading on the air, that information will be omitted. But writing it in will prevent errors. Another expression to avoid when reading numbers is *per,* as in "miles per hour." Instead, use "miles an hour."

In reporting names and titles, use the title before the name, and avoid beginning a sentence with a name, especially if it is unfamiliar. If the title is long and cumbersome, break it up or shorten it. You generally do not use a person's middle initial in speech, so avoid using middle initials in broadcast copy unless they are important for clarification and identification or unless they are commonly used with the names in question. On second reference use the surname only, except when you are referring to the president of the United States or a member of the clergy. Clergy retain their titles on second reference—Rabbi Brown, for instance.

> *Print version:* Madison A. Clark, bishop coadjutor for the Episcopal Diocese of Dixon, today announced that $50,000 had been raised for the World Famine Relief project. The funds will be sent to agencies designated to purchase and distribute food in Africa, Bishop Clark said. There are three such agencies: the American Red Cross, the National Council of Churches and CARE.

***

> *Rewritten:* Dixon's Episcopal Diocese has raised $50-thousand (fifty thousand dollars) for the World Famine Relief project. The announcement came today from Bishop Madison Clark. Bishop Clark said the money will be sent to three agencies designated to purchase and distribute food in Africa.

Watch for and clarify obscurities. Be very careful about using pronouns. Listeners have trouble following the references. If you are dealing with specialized jargon, translate it. Use words and terms the audience will understand and relate to. If you are writing about little-known groups, explain who they are and what they do. Don't assume the audience will know or understand. And do use contractions, like *don't,* just as you do in speech. Use the active voice. It gives life and movement to your writing. Keep your verbs in the present tense when possible because broadcast media expect to offer timely information. When your audience's language is not English, provide a translated version of your information.

Structural Considerations

Broadcast story leads differ from print leads, in which the who, what, when, where, why and how are often all crammed into the first paragraph. This burst of information can be confusing for the listener and difficult for the announcer to read. When you are preparing your broadcast story, first alert listeners to what you are going to discuss, getting their attention with something that is important to them. Using a summary statement is a good way to get into the story. Then you can give the essentials. Make your sentences simple; don't use long clauses at the beginning or end or between the subject and verb. As you develop the story, look for ways to connect paragraphs with transitions that allow the story to emerge and flow logically. Keep the listener and the announcer in mind, and think about how each will be able to handle the words you write.

Broadcast wire stories undergo much more reworking than newspaper wire stories, because the broadcast wire serves stations that use news directly from the wire on an hourly basis. One story, repeated hour after hour, can get dull if the audience remains the same—as in offices that have piped-in radio. Research can flesh out a breaking story both to give it depth and to keep the sparse facts from getting monotonous. Broadcast leads vary dramatically from print leads. The lead-in sentence is designed to capture attention. The listener needs to know what the story is about because if it is something that is important to them, they may want to pay more careful attention. Broadcast stories more often follow a narrative format because that's the way we are accustomed to talking and sharing information. Use of the active voice conveys immediacy and importance to the story. Personalizing the story helps too, and more and more newspapers are using this format. Find a person as an example of the issue or effect and start with their perspective. Follow with expert information and understandable statistics. Then close with a summary that goes back to the individual used as an illustration, showing the consequences or choices for that person. Remember this when you furnish tape for actualities.

Supplying Tape (Audio and Video)

When you supply cassettes—audio, video or video with sound—you also need to furnish a script. Attach the script firmly to the cassette or the box of reel tape. Identify the script with exactly the same title that appears on the tape, and add your name, your institution's name and the address and phone numbers where you can be reached day and night. Also give an email address. (See Tables 10.7 and 10.8.) Broadcasters don't have time to play tapes to see what is on them. Of course, if they decide the story might be used, they will preview the tape, and they'll edit it if they schedule it to run. The station will also write a lead-in to the tape, so it's a good idea to supply additional information—for example, a copy of the news release covering the occasion for making the tape. Lead-ins identify speakers and action without detailing the content of the tape.

For example, information on the global disease called SARS (Severe Acute Respiratory Syndrome) originates from a number of sources such as pharmaceutical companies, the USA's Centers for Disease Control and Prevention, the USA's Health and Human Services Department and the World Health Organization (WHO). Because the USA's Health and Human Services Department called some 20 pharmaceutical companies to Washington, D.C., days before the WHO positively identified SARS in April 2003, many companies are working on a vaccine.

The pneumonia-like illness is created by a coronavirus that jumped from animals to humans. The virus mutates easily and can live on surfaces such as door handles and table tops for long periods of time, resisting disinfectants applied to those surfaces. Suppose that the WHO held a news conference to release the latest information on progress toward developing a vaccine from governments and pharmaceutical companies all over the world. WHO presented a scientist, Dr. E. A. Imagine, to discuss the issues.

T A B L E   1 0 . 7   *Typical Radio Script Format*

SLUG				TAPE TIMING
NAME				
DATE				
10	20	25	50	80

((THIS GIVES 3 SECONDS A
LINE—10 LINES = 30 SECONDS))

AUDIO CUES GO	ALL COPY GOES IN
IN THIS COLUMN	THIS COLUMN

ALL BROADCAST COPY IS *TRIPLE-
SPACED. NEVER* WRITE TO THE
END OF A PAGE—LEAVE AT LEAST
A ONE-INCH MARGIN—GO TO
NEXT PAGE WITH ((MORE)). *NEVER*
BREAK A SENTENCE AT THE END
OF A PAGE. *ALWAYS* USE SOME
SORT OF END MARK: -0-, -30-, XXXX,
-END-.

-END-

Source: Ron H. MacDonald, *A Broadcast News Manual of Style,* 2d ed. Copyright © 1994 by Longman Publishers USA. Reprinted with permission.

T A B L E   1 0 . 8   *Typical Television Script Format*

SLUG				VIDEO TYPE AND TIME
NAME				
DATE				
10	40	45	60	80

THIS GIVES 2 SECONDS A
LINE—10 LINES = 20
SECONDS

ALL VIDEO AND	ALL NARRATION
AUDIO	GOES IN THIS
DIRECTIONS GO IN	COLUMN
THIS COLUMN	

Source: Ron H. MacDonald, *A Broadcast News Manual of Style,* 2d ed. Copyright © 1994 by Longman Publishers USA. Reprinted with permission.

A lead-in for either videotape or audio might read like this:

A vaccine for SARS is years away despite its early identification. The bad news came today from the World Health Organization. A scientist coordinating information on a possible vaccine said global immunization is years away. Dr. E. A. Imagine is an immunologist for the World Health Organization. Dr. Imagine says: (tape) "Any potential vaccine must be tested on animals first. After those safety tests we would want to test it on health care workers, SARS victims and those in epidemic areas before giving a vaccine to the world population."

At the end cue of ". . . before giving a vaccine to the world population," you would have this closing copy for the announcer:

Despite the delay of a vaccine for SARS, the encouraging aspect is the cooperation of nonprofit and for-profit organizations to save the world from this highly infectious global epidemic.

The story, with the 38-word sound bite, totals 116 words and is about 30 seconds long. Because the sound bite copy is there, the story can be quickly cut to the following.

A vaccine for SARS is years away. That bad news came today from the World Health Organization. Any potential vaccine must be tested on animals first then health care workers, SARS victims and those in epidemic areas before immunizing the world's population. The good news is that nonprofit and for-profit organizations are working together to save the world from this highly infectious global epidemic.

That version is almost half of the first. Although not as complete a story, it would get the WHO story out.

As evidence mounts that most people depend primarily on the broadcast media for news, organizations must focus their attention on getting their information into the broadcast media. In responding to questions from PRSA's *Tactics,* Fox Television reporter Jeff Crilley said that writers should write conversationally and approach the story the way a broadcast reporter would think. The first paragraph, Crilley said, should be written so that an anchorperson could read it right on the air. Crilley also said that PR people don't use the phone enough to contact broadcast reporters with their stories.[6] If one reporter picks up on a story that's broadcast, the chances of its being used by other broadcast media are good.

Digital Delivery and Use

Video content is generally delivered to newsrooms digitally. This includes VNRs and other public relations materials such as Satellite Media Tours (SMTs). All of the materials can be sent digitally, including scripts, videos, graphics and supplemental story content as well as advisories. The delivery is not over the Internet because the results may or may not be of broadcast quality. But other digital news delivery systems do work. Reporters can take the digitally delivered material directly from the station's server to an edit system or videotape recorder.

Advantages of digital delivery are the speed of the system and the ability of the reporters to edit in supplementary material such as "B" roll and additional information to update a story and make it unique to the station's newscast. With SMT delivery, much more in-depth material is available to the reporters to flesh out stories they are working on or to develop a feature from the material sent.

Conclusions

- The sights and sounds of events are important to broadcast news.
- Electronic transmission of messages, images and sound is changing the delivery of information to broadcast media, but they still have to want it. To be recognized as a good source, you need to build a reputation for providing timely, accurate, newsworthy material of broadcast quality.
- Digital pictures shown on Web sites are not of broadcast quality but can indicate to broadcast media what types of visuals are available.
- CDs can be used, and if a station refers viewers to its Web site for additional information, the digital format makes the information you send more accessible. One of the problems is compatibility. Some software is not compatible across platforms, so you need to call to check.
- Special events are the public relations activities (other than crises) most likely to generate coverage by broadcast media, especially television.
- You'll need to prepare a fact sheet and a history of the event for the media's use, and then you must videotape some activity.
- Broadcasters need material written in broadcast style, but because that means the copy will be brief, you should attach the longer print-media release "FYI" ("for your information").
- Be sure to set up the facilities broadcasters will need to cover your special events.
- Always post someone at a central location to respond to questions, and provide that person with all the facts you have given to the media plus all new, updated information.
- News conferences are called when someone needs to interact with the news media. In arranging news conferences, be sure to provide the news media with background materials.
- You should "cover" news conferences too: make audio- and videotapes for the record.
- A crisis is a disorganized combination of a special event and a news conference.
- Whereas local talk-show appearances are usually arranged directly with the hosts or their producers by PR people, national appearances are generally arranged through placement firms although some large public relations firms do work directly with national talk-show producers.
- PR people must provide both interviewer and interviewee with appropriate information. The interviewee needs to be rehearsed, and the interviewer should be provided with biographical information and background materials well in advance.
- News "on call"—audio actualities or broadcast releases on the Web site—requires frequent updating for broadcast media to keep stories fresh.
- News releases are either advance stories of something about to occur or stories telling what has just occurred or what is going on.
- For radio, you need actualities to give authenticity and to enliven your news.
- For TV, you need audio and video—provided promptly so your story is timely and attention-getting.
- Video news releases, or VNRs, are prepared materials ready to air. Most stations prefer to receive VNRs by satellite but will accept videocassettes. Cassettes offer you the option of sending two versions of the story: one fully edited and ready to air and a second, longer version with all of the elements of the story so the broadcaster can re-edit using additional "B" roll that has the natural sound only (no announcer) and additional story material.

- Some VNR producers subscribe to a good-practices code to make their materials more acceptable to news directors.
- Broadcast writing style is conversational, and broadcast copywriters must remember that the listener has no opportunity to review or rehear a sentence or word once it has been spoken.
- When you write for broadcast, you have two audiences to consider: the person who will read the copy (the announcer) and the listener or viewer.
- The physical layout and appearance of broadcast copy are designed to help the announcer.
- The structure of broadcast stories is designed to help the listener.
- Broadcast leads differ from print leads in that they don't contain all of the news elements in the story.
- Broadcast news stories are rewritten regularly during the day to keep the material fresh, even when there are no new facts.
- When you supply news as audio- or videotape, be sure to attach a script, with the same title as the tape. Attaching an explanatory news release too will help the scriptwriter fit the tape into a context.
- PR people must know how to provide information to the broadcast media that is appropriate for the media and interesting to their audiences.

Exercises

1. Find an event from your campus calendar that you think would make an interesting news story. Get information about the event from the planners. Write a media advisory for the event. Write a news release for the student newspaper and then a broadcast version for the student radio station. If you have a television station or stream news on the student publications Web site, prepare for that editor a revised media advisory that suggest videos for their coverage along with your advance news release on the event.

2. Most universities have visiting celebrities as guest speakers to the campus or to a particular department. Find out information about the appearance of a celebrity at your school and write a news conference announcement. Prepare all materials you would need to have on hand for the conference. Where would you plan to have the conference so the sound and light would be good for the media, the guest would be comfortable and the school would look good in the clips?

3. Universities generate a great deal of research. Look at your university's publication of ongoing research and choose a topic that would make a good video news release. Decide how you would make it timely. Do the necessary additional fact-finding for a video news release and write the script.

Use InfoTrac College Edition to access information on topics in this chapter from hundreds of periodicals and scholarly journals.

Notes

1. Eric Alkire, "ABC's of Long-Form Video Edits," *News Photographer,* January 1997, p. 15.

2. David Eisenstadt, "How to Make Video News Releases Work," *Public Relations Quarterly* 47 (4) (Winter 2002): 24–25.
3. Tom Moore, "TV News Directors Report High VNR, SMT Usage; Cite Favorite Topics," *PR NEWS* 48 (45) (November 16, 1992): 8.
4. Tom Moore, "VNR Producers, Distributors Subscribing to Code of Good Practice," *PR NEWS* 49 (13) (March 29, 1993): 7.
5. Suzanne Huffman, "Writing Radio News," Chapter 6, in *Broadcast News Handbook,* C. A. Tuggle, Forrest Carr and Suzanne Huffman (New York: McGraw-Hill, 2001), p. 74.
6. Alison Stateman, "A Fox Reporter Tells All: 'Our Job As Journalists Is Always to Be Skeptical'," *Public Relations Tactics,* May 2003, p. 15.

Selected Bibliography

Marvin Block, *Writing Broadcast News: Shorter, Sharper, Stronger,* rev., expanded ed. (Chicago: Bonus Books, 1997).

Lillian Bridwell-Bowles and Paul Prior, eds., *Writing Style Differences in Newspaper, Radio* and *Television News* (Minneapolis, Minn.: University of Minnesota Center for Interdisciplinary Studio of Writing, 1991).

Charles Coates, *Professional TV News Handbook* (Chicago: Bonus Books, 2000).

Robert L. Hilliard, *Writing for Television and Radio,* 6th ed. (Belmont, Calif.: Wadsworth, 1999).

Brad Kalbfeld, *The Associated Press Broadcast News Handbook,* 1st ed. (New York: McGraw-Hill/Contemporary Books, 2000).

John Morley, *Scriptwriting for High-Impact Videos: Imaginative Approaches to Delivering Factual Information* (Belmont, Calif.: Wadsworth, 1992).

Peter B. Orlik, *Broadcast/Cable Copywriting,* 5th ed. (Boston: Allyn & Bacon, 1994).

Al Tompkins, *Aim for the Heart, Write for the Ear, Shoot for the Eyes: A Guide for TV Producers and Reporters* (New York: Bonus Books, 2002).

C. A. Tuggle, Forrest Carr and Suzanne Huffman, *Broadcast News Handbook* (New York: McGraw-Hill, 2001).

K. Tim Wulfemeyer, *Beginning Broadcast Newswriting: A Self-Instructional Learning Experience,* 3d ed. (Ames, Iowa: Iowa State University Press, 2003).

Herbert Zettl, *Television Production Handbook,* 6th ed. (Belmont, Calif.: Wadsworth, 2002).

Pronunciation Guide

Robert Burchfield, *The Spoken Word: A BBC Guide* (New York: Oxford University Press, 1992).

CHAPTER ELEVEN

Features for Print and Broadcasting

Doing most of the research and legwork for a major feature story that someone else is going to write and get credit for goes against the ideals of some professional writers who find themselves involved in public relations practice. It happens all the time. Worse than that: It's expected of you, not only by the media but also by your management. They also expect you to take responsibility for the accuracy and the tone of the story even though you will actually have little or no editorial control. The fact is that most features originated by public relations people that appear in the mass media are actually written by either media staff or freelancers.

Features that public relations people write themselves usually appear in professional organizations' publications, trade or industry publications or client or employee publications. (See Chapter 19.)

The broadcast features that public relations people write and produce are often for videocassettes used with internal or closely related external audiences. Some organizations do have their public relations people create broadcast features to be used by mass media. Often these organizations have proprietary information that prevents mass media staff from having enough access to do a feature, or the credibility of the feature depends on its being produced by the organization, such as a medical or scientific research institution.

This chapter will discuss first the process for discovering features and then the "selling" of a feature idea to a mass medium. The public relations person uses much the same process that a freelancer uses in writing query letters to media to generate interest in a feature idea. The difference is that the freelancer then develops the idea under editorial direction, whereas the public relations person generally assists representatives from the news media—writers and photographers—in developing the story idea that the editor has found interesting.

Generating and Selling Ideas

There's a chicken-and-egg problem with discovering public relations feature material. You have to know the organization thoroughly to recognize potential stories. But if you don't also know the types of media, the types of stories they use and the special interests of the writers who work there, you still won't "see" a potential feature even if you are aware of the information.

Discovering Feature Material

Remembering that what distinguishes features from news is their human interest quality, you are generally looking for stories that emphasize the unusual, the dramatic, the surprising, changes, trends and issues. Stories about people—profiles—are possibilities as are impact stories, the heavily researched story that discusses the impact of a development, a product, a disease—actually anything—on the way we live and work.

In addition to these qualities, you will find that certain types of features are used by the mass media. Although there are many ways of classifying features, the typology is not as important as the suggestions these types make to you in the discovery process. Look in the news media for features that have a "news peg"—that is, are tied to a news story—for example, the process of discovery that brought a new drug to market. Look at features that are personality profiles or sketches, like one of the discoverers of the new drug. Historical features often are used by organizations celebrating a significant anniversary year.

Personal-experience stories abound in all organizations, but not all are that related to the organization. Often these find better use in employee publications, but don't overlook them. Descriptive features and narratives often work for features about cities or restaurants, theme parks or other special sites that have tourist attractions. Some organizations permit guests to see how products are made, and the government grants access to places of interest like the White House, the U.S. Mint and such.

Some features can be developed by organizations along "how-to" lines, such as how to use a product or service successfully or in an unusual way. For example, a newspaper gave a reporter a week at home so she could use a computer lent to her by a computer company to prove that everything can be done online without once leaving the house.

Finding a Market for the Features

No, you don't research and write the feature first and then find a market. You decide where you think the feature would most likely find a receptive audience. You do that by examining stories the medium ran in the past that are like the one you've just discovered; you need to be sure it's not in the "recent" past, but at least a year or more ago. You also look at writers for that medium, magazine staff writers, newspaper columnists and feature writers, broadcast reporters and special-interest reporters who cover your area—like science, for example. See what types of stories these writers favor. They have many opportunities to generate stories, and sometimes stories are assigned to them, but often they write about what they are interested in. Look also at the audience for that medium and see what it is that they might like to know that they don't know already. Do you have access to some information that the audience could use?

If you are trying to get the name of an airline into editorial space, what about a packing story? It's good for both men's and women's magazines. One idea, two stories. And maybe a third— what about packing for a trip with children? Three different publications would use your airline's name, and maybe readers would clip articles, keep them or even pass them on to friends.

First find a single market for your idea, and then think of similar, related markets. That's how to make the most of your research time. A freelancer has to think like this to make the most money from an investment in the research. You have to think like this because you will have to sell management after you have sold the medium, and it means that whoever does the story, you or someone from the news media, will interrupt the work of others to get the story and probably cause some inconvenience. Management will want to be sure to get the most from it.

The other consideration in looking at a medium for your story idea is the public relations value of a story about your organization appearing in that medium. There are some media you don't want to be in, like the supermarket "newspapers." There may be others that you don't want to be seen in because their political, economic or social bias is contrary to that of your organization.

This is less likely to be true of broadcast media, but it may be. You also need to know that some features are generated locally and then go to national distribution, and some networks and syndicates can be approached directly if your story has broad audience appeal.

Writing the Query Letter and Following Up

Sometimes with local media a query is no more than an expanded news tip sheet. (See Chapter 9.) What you must remember is that the query letter, which draws its name from "inquiry," is really more like a sales pitch, and a "cold call" at that, if you don't know the person you are writing to.

The query letter, like all good letters, should be one page. Remember that the recipient will be judging not only the idea but you by the letter—your reliability and credibility and you as a knowledgeable source for what would be a good story for that medium. You must sell yourself, your organization, your story idea and the value as well as appropriateness of that idea to that medium's audience. Watch style and substance and determine what persuasive strategy you should use to be successful.

Following up on query letters can be risky. You don't want to irritate an editor who might have decided the story had some merit but put it aside because of other demands. On the other hand, you need to know if that publication might be interested before you approach another. Features are stories you sell one at a time. The media expect to have exclusive rights to the idea if they accept it. You don't blanket the news media with the same story idea—or even spin-offs of that story idea—unless the publications are in such entirely different markets that the audiences could never overlap.

One exception is when you are dealing with commercial and nonprofit publications, and even then the editors need to know exactly what you are preparing for them and what is being offered to the other publication. An example might be an exhibit that is appearing at the Smithsonian Institution that has a feature in the *Smithsonian* magazine and a feature about the exhibit also in *Arts and Antiques,* a commercial publication. The audiences for these publications probably have some overlap. The editors know this, and the editors have final say over the material that appears. If you are handling public relations for the Smithsonian exhibit, you need to offer different pictures and a story with an entirely different emphasis to the two publications. Neither would mind the story appearing in the same time frame because their audiences probably would want to see the exhibit. Not only is it unethical to "sell" more than one publication on a feature at a time, but also you can jeopardize your credibility as a public relations person by doing this. Word gets around, and all you really have to sell is credibility and reliability. If you lose trust, your job is next.

Suppose you do get a friendly response by letter, phone or fax—then what? You will need to flesh out the story idea. At this point, you begin to do some more research to get enough details to have a fairly good idea of all of the elements of the story, to know what is "doable." You'll have to know who will cooperate and in what time frame. You may be asking a department to help you with a story when they are facing a critical deadline. Or you may be asking someone to be a subject of a personality profile when that person is having a personal problem. You may not be able to get the cooperation or resources you might want to do the best job, so you need to discover those limitations now before you "oversell" the story to the news media and lose credibility.

Working with the Medium

When you get media representatives interested in doing the story, you still will have to give them a great deal of help. You have access to information in the organization that they would have difficulty getting, and you need to make it available to them. You also will need to find out who they want to interview and be sure those people are available when the media people need to talk with them. Be sure you have accommodations for technical crews who might accompany the writer, such as photographers. If the story is for radio or television, you need to find a place where the sound can be captured to give a "natural" background and the person or people being interviewed can still be heard.

Remember, you are going to be held responsible—by the medium and by the organization—for the outcome of the story just as if you were doing it.

There are some uncontrollable risks. First, in handling the subject, you may have "pitched" one story only to find that the media are turning that into another story. The only thing you can hope for is that it is still a positive story. This means that in the planning stages, you need to consider how the story could be turned around to be a negative one about the organization. If you detect this in the follow-up, you can try to change it, or you can try to cancel the story.

You can't control the "slant" or direction the story takes, and the emphasis is not always what you want it to be. What you and management may see as the significance of the story may seem less significant than another aspect to the media person doing the story. Gentle persuasion sometimes works, but not always.

You also can't control the subjects of the story, who may or may not say what you want them to say. What you can do in the research period before the media person arrives to do the story is to walk potential interviewees through some of the questions likely to be asked, to see what their responses are. This gives you some way of knowing which sources the reporter should be directed to. But you can't steer the reporter away from people who are the obvious sources of information in the story as you or as the newsperson has cast it. You just have to manage the situation the best way you can.

Also, once the writer prepares a story, it is going to be edited at the medium, perhaps to the distress of both of you. You have to know at the outset that doing a feature is a gamble. Why, then, are public relations people willing to take it? The value of the story if it turns out well is additional credibility. You have an outsider coming in and saying what you've been trying to tell people all along. You can get permission from the medium to make copies of the publication or broadcast segment and send those to some of your publics who might have missed it, not only extending the life of the feature but also expanding the audience greatly.

Evaluating Topics

Finding enough ideas for articles is not that difficult. The hard part is recognizing which ones are good and which are bad. Once you get an idea for an article, you must evaluate it by considering three criteria: reader interest, reader consequence and the best angle.

Reader Interest

The first question to ask about a topic is: Will the audience be interested in it? To answer that question, you have to know your audience—their interests, predispositions, likes and dislikes.

Are you writing for business leaders who are intensely interested in the state of the economy? Are you writing for workers with less than a high-school education? Are your readers professional people who are interested in job performance and growth? Is your magazine aimed at consumer advocates, government regulators, university professors? Unless you know your audience, you might as well evaluate your articles by consulting fortune cookies. And if you publish articles that do not address the interests of your audience, you're wasting a lot of time, money and energy.

Reader Consequence

The value of an article idea is also gauged by its consequence to the reader. That is, the article must be important to the reader as well as interesting. Even when good intuition helps you evaluate interest correctly, you may still trip over consequence. The reason is that some ideas that don't bubble with interest still have consequence. They are important to readers. Good writers or editors will tell you that they try to make their magazines mixtures of articles they think people want to read and articles readers ought to read.

The real problem comes when readers' lack of interest gets in the way of their reading something important to them. As a writer, this is a terrific challenge. You will have to work doubly hard to make the story so good that readers can't pass it up. Even if you can't make the story interesting, you should make it clear why the story is important. This may inspire more people to read it.

Angle

Making the importance of a story clear is not always easy. Readers may not recognize immediately, for example, that an article has consequence for them. You have to grab the readers' attention and draw them into the story by informing them at the outset that there is some point to the article. That is, you must tell the story with a specific approach, called an *angle* or *slant*. The angle must hook readers, get them interested and lead them naturally into the main topic or point of the article.

An angle does not always leap to the fore, either. For example, a writer was preparing an article for a university magazine about research in the biology department. At the time, several professors in the department were collaborating on a research project on Asian clams. That's hardly a fascinating topic in itself, although doing an article on clams was a better and more specific idea than doing one on research in the biology department. But the angle was still missing. Further interviews uncovered the information that this species of clams reproduced at a rapid rate and was becoming so populous that the clams threatened to block some waterways, such as irrigation canals and industrial water supply lines. Here was the angle—at last. Small clams the size of a half dollar were threatening to disrupt the water supply of giant industries. Again, notice that the writer did not come up with the angle immediately. First came the general topic. The specific angle was the result of alert research. In researching the subject, look for the angle with a "So what?" test. What are the consequences, intended or unintended? What is the relationship of the story to the audience of that medium? You have to find the hook for the reader/listener-viewer.

Research

Once you choose a general topic for an article, you have to research it. Research is a major component in feature writing at several stages.

You have to do some general research on the background of the article idea so you'll know where to begin. At this stage, you may have a general idea of what you want to say or even the kind of conclusion subsequent research may support. If a conclusion comes early in your research, be wary of it, because it may limit your perspective on subsequent information by encouraging selective perception. That is, it may blind you to other points of view, making your article less effective and accurate than it otherwise might be.

This is not to say that your article should not make a point, or that it shouldn't come down on one side of an issue. In fact, most public relations magazine articles do and should take a position on a particular issue. But you still want your research on the topic to be objective so that the true weight of the evidence supports the side you take. If you reach a conclusion too early in your thinking, you might ignore information that renders your conclusion invalid. An article as full of holes as Swiss cheese is usually neither credible nor persuasive.

Research techniques for writing feature articles are similar to the general techniques of public relations research discussed in Chapter 4. But it is helpful to follow a few basic steps in all article research.

Background Research

First, you should do general background research on the topic. You may already know a great deal about your topic. But if you don't, find out how your topic fits into the overall scheme of things. An article about inflation, for example, requires some general knowledge of economics.

Next, become more specific. Narrow your research down to the topic of your article. You should check the *Readers' Guide to Periodical Literature* or other appropriate bibliographies in print or online to find out what has been written and who has spoken on the topic recently.

Reviewing these articles and speeches will give you helpful background on the topic and will tell you what your audience has been reading—assuming that you know (and you should) which magazines your audience reads. For example, if your audience includes university science professors, you know they probably read *Science.* Ministers probably read *Christianity Today.* You need to know what your audience reads so you can avoid duplicating what is now old news. Offer them something they haven't read before, or at least a new perspective on a familiar idea.

After reviewing what your readers are likely to have read, go to what they probably haven't read—technical and trade journals, limited-circulation newsletters, and government documents, for example. Compile from these sources the facts and figures you will need to build your article.

Pay special attention to figures. The right statistics here and there can help make an article measurably better, and if you don't write them down when you come across them you'll have trouble finding them later. It's hard to know ahead of time which statistics you'll need, so note all the facts and figures you can find that could be relevant.

At this stage you are probably ready to develop some possible approaches to the article. Try to find angles that haven't been explored in publications to date. Once you have arrived at some tentative angles and have focused your research on specific material that will help you decide on the best angle, you're ready for step two of the research process: interviewing.

Interviewing

Some of the best material for your article will come from personal interviews with experts on the topic. Interviews not only provide additional information and insight, they can also give you the direct quotations and anecdotes you need to bring a dull article to life.

In most settings, an ample number of experts exist within your organization that you can call on for help and information. However, you may occasionally need to call on an outside expert, like a university professor. Or if you're writing about federal regulations, you might want to call one of the regulators.

You should follow a few basic interviewing protocols whether you talk with people inside or outside your organization.

Let the person to be interviewed know ahead of time what it is you want to talk about. Give him or her a chance to prepare, especially if you will be asking specific questions that may require some research before your interview. Remember that this is not a news situation in the usual sense of the term. And let the interviewee know ahead of time that you want him or her to read the story before it is published, to verify its accuracy.

Prepare a list of questions in advance. Design the questions in such a way that they will encourage the person you are interviewing to open up and extend the discussion into relevant areas you had not anticipated.

Don't ask leading questions at the outset. Be as neutral as you can with your questions early in the interview. As the session progresses, it may be appropriate to ask specific leading questions to clarify particular points.

Use a tape recorder, but first ask the interviewee for permission to turn it on. Then make the recorder as inconspicuous as possible. For example, turn it on and leave it on. Then it usually is ignored. Even though you may be using a recorder, always take notes. Do this for three reasons: (1) Writing down salient information will help you get into the flow of the conversation and understand points more clearly. Remember that writing demands thought. (2) The person being interviewed is generally pleased to see you making notes of what he or she has said. Note-taking confers importance on what is being said. (3) Machines don't always work.

Writing

Once you've researched the subject and determined the angle, you're ready to write. And the best place to start is at the beginning—with the lead. (See Table 11.1 for a checklist.)

The Lead

William Zinsser says, "The most important sentence in any article is the first one."[1] It is axiomatic that, if readers don't finish the first sentence, they aren't likely to go to the second. And they'll never read the third sentence or anything else you have to say.

So the lead must do two things. It must grab the readers' attention, and it must tell the readers what the article is about.

A bland, dull lead that says nothing a reader does not already know isn't likely to induce anyone to read on. To attract attention, leads should be concrete and visual. They should offer something that readers can relate to and understand. If the lead is about unfamiliar things, the reader is likely to think the article won't be interesting. You must link unfamiliar material in the lead to something that is familiar.

The lead must state the central point of the piece. Let the reader know at the outset what the article is about and what the point is. You can't expect a reader to read through several sentences or paragraphs to find out what the topic is.

The lead can be the first sentence, the first few sentences or, in some cases, the first few paragraphs. It can be a simple, direct statement or a quotation or even an anecdote that illustrates the main point of the article. Any device can be used, as long as it gets the readers' attention and informs them of the point of the article.

For example, here is a lead that hooks the reader into reading about the preservation of a wild garden in South Africa:

> High in the craggy mountains of South Africa's Cape at the southern tip of the continent, a helicopter disgorges a uniformed task force deployed to repel an alien invasion.

The teasing lead plays on the assumptions of the reader, using "helicopter . . . uniformed task force . . . deployed to repel an alien invasion." The next sentences keep the suspense elicited by the assumption:

> Men and women duck the chopper's rotors, dash for cover and hunker down to await reinforcements. Within an hour, 20 members of the Alien Hit Squad have assembled at their high-altitude rendezvous.

The reader is now into the story, which begins to counter assumptions:

TABLE 11.1   *Checklist for Feature Writing*

1. Is the lead interesting and specific? Does it approach the story from a slant or angle designed to catch the reader's interest?

2. Is the idea in the lead developed and supported by the rest of the article?

3. Are statements verified or properly attributed? Are general statements supported with specific examples?

4. Are anecdotes used throughout the article, both as illustrations and as devices to increase reader interest?

5. Has sufficient use been made of direct quotations?

6. Is the writing dramatic? Has the story been told in human terms?

7. Is description adequate to give the reader an accurate picture of the subject?

> Soon, a deafening whine pierces the alpine silence—a tip-off that the combatants in this elite squad are on no ordinary search-and-destroy mission. Their weapons are chain saws. Their enemy: American pines and other alien trees that threaten to engulf the indigenous vegetation, known as fynbos.

This beginning flows directly into the body of the story, which continues to develop the scene for the reader:

> Their battlefield is a floral wonderland, one of the world's hottest hotspots of biodiversity. Within the rugged boundaries of the fynbos region, more than 7,000 species of plants—twice the number found in all of Canada—grow crammed into an area barely larger than the Netherlands. This rich scrubland has survived in a harsh, fire-swept environment of poor soils and dry summers for millions of years. But until recently, it was unclear whether the fynbos could endure the onslaught of man.[2]

Development

The purpose of the body of the article is to support and develop the point made in the lead. The point must be amplified and extended to clarify its implications and importance. The story must flow smoothly and logically, with each paragraph leading naturally to the next and each paragraph adding something to the story.

As the article develops, you should answer the questions that will naturally come into your readers' minds. Make sure these answers are linked closely with what comes before and what follows, so that readers will be able to see how each bit of information fits into the picture. This requires close attention to the transitions between sentences and between paragraphs.

Besides amplifying the point made in the lead, the body of the article must also verify and illustrate it. It is one thing to make a bold statement in an interesting way to grab readers' attention. It is something else to convince them that your point of view has merit.

Verification and Illustration

You can't communicate effectively by assuming that readers will accept and absorb your statements as given to them. Generalizations must be supported with specific examples. Statements

PEANUTS reprinted by permission of United Feature Syndicate, Inc.

of fact that are not general knowledge should be attributed to an appropriate source. Contentions should be backed up with solid evidence.

Frequently you can support your position simply by stating the relevant facts. Just remember that "facts" are not opinions. They are indisputable, observable or recorded pieces of information that can be readily verified.

Some facts can be used without any specific attribution or further verification because they are so well known—"George Washington was the first President of the United States," for example. Feel free to use similar facts that can be found in any standard reference work, like "Columbus is the capital of Ohio" or "Alaska is the largest state in the USA."

Other facts—statistics and survey results, for example—are also useful, but in most instances these should be attributed to their source. If you use the results of a public opinion poll, include important information such as who took the poll and when it was taken. Furthermore, when using survey results or statistics, take care that the figures you cite are really applicable to the situation at hand.

For less well-known facts you should also give a source, whether a document or an expert in the field. A quote from an authority can be used to verify statements of opinion as well. But be sure the person you quote has the expertise necessary for forming an intelligent opinion on the topic.

Sometimes straight facts won't make your case, especially if they are unfamiliar to readers. So you must illustrate your point with specific examples. If you are writing about marine geology and want to make the point that vast mountain ranges are found beneath the ocean surface, it might not be enough to say just that. Give an example—the Mid-Atlantic Ridge, say, which winds down the center of the Atlantic and even pierces the surface at Iceland.

Another device that might help you illustrate your case is the analogy—an example of a parallel relationship between your subject and an unrelated but easier-to-grasp idea. For example, if you are trying to explain how utility rates are set, you might draw an analogy with the charges for renting a car, something that most people will more readily understand. Remember, though, that analogies don't prove anything. They merely illustrate and clarify points of information.

A good lead, logical development and adequate verification are the skeleton of an article. Good articles must then be fleshed out; the story must be brought to life. Readers must be given pictures to help them visualize what you are telling them.

Good writers use devices that involve the readers in the article. Among these devices are anecdotes, direct quotations, humanization, dramatization and description.

Anecdotes

One of the best devices for involving the reader in a piece of writing is the anecdote. As the late Stanford Professor Bill Rivers said, "No other element of an article is more important."[3] Anecdotes break monotony, illustrate points and give readers something to visualize. If they deal with familiar things, anecdotes can help people relate to the subject of the article. Anecdotes "show" readers something rather than merely telling about it.

Quotations

Another way to break monotony and make writing more natural is to use direct quotations. Quotations help make writing more personal, more like conversation and therefore more readable.

Be careful not to use too many quotations, however. They can add to interest, but often a direct quote doesn't make the point in the clearest possible way. It is best to make a point in your own words and then use a quotation to amplify or illustrate it.

As for style, the writing is usually more effective when the quote begins the sentence and the source is identified in the middle (if it's a long quote) or at the end.

Humanization

Whenever you write, you are writing for people. And people are more interested in people than in other things. As a general rule, people are interested first in themselves and then in others. Always look for the aspects of a subject that touch the lives of people. Use personal words and phrases where you can, and address the reader directly if it fits the situation.

One of the best places to find examples of humanizing is *The Wall Street Journal*. The *Journal's* front-page feature stories invariably begin not with economic facts and figures, but with an example of a specific person in a specific city. That person's problems (or business or economic situation) introduce a subject more general in scope. The facts and figures follow to verify and illustrate the point of the article. But the story is introduced and told in human terms.

The *Journal* published a piece about Sweden's welfare gone awry—where an effort to get people off government aid has actually cost the government money because citizens were quick to find a loophole in the new system and take advantage of it. But the consequences of the new policy muddle were made clear by this lead:

> UPPSALA, Sweden—It is 10:15 Thursday morning, a time when Gunilla Frodin used to be working, part time, as a teacher's assistant.
>
> But she quit for something better: full-time unemployment compensation. Oddly this came about thanks to a government attempt to cut social-welfare costs.[4]

Dramatization

The humanization of writing is best accomplished by placing the topic in a dramatic context. A discussion of a new medicine, for example, could be limited to a dry description of the chemical composition of the medicine and its biochemical action inside the body. Or the story could be told in the context of a doctor treating patients. Often such dramatization can maintain the interest of a reader who would otherwise not read the whole article.

Description

Good description can be hard to write, but it can also be an important factor in conveying a complete picture to your readers. Readers will understand and retain more information if you can place a picture in their heads. That's what description is all about: painting pictures in the mind.

One way to illustrate or describe something unfamiliar is to compare it with familiar things. It's not very helpful to say that a new machine is "big." But if you say it is "as big as a typical house," the words create a visual image in the mind's eye. The reader can visualize an average house, and although he or she may never see the machine, an idea of its size is communicated clearly. Skillful use of simile and metaphor can make your message clearer, livelier and more interesting to read.

All these devices for involving readers apply to feature articles for just about any audience. But for certain specific audiences, there is more to consider. For example, employees make up an audience of special concern to most organizations. (See Chapter 19.)

In features, your writing style is on display. You can't neglect the basics that should be reflected in all of your writing: be specific, be clear, move the story along with active verbs and involve the reader. Look at the analysis of a newspaper staff-written feature on an accident involving a Coke syrup spill in Figure 11.1.

Writing Features for Ezines

Features for online magazines must be brief because reading from a screen is tiring. More creativity is demanded too because the page needs to be lively and interesting to the viewer or it won't be read at all. Art is essential, and it's even better if it moves. Sound is another component that can be incorporated.

An online feature requires creative copy, compelling design and engaging sound. (See Chapters 14 and 19.)

Broadcast Features as a Series

Often a significant issue like the one in Table 11.2 gets a series treatment. The series treatment is used because long news features of 30 minutes or more do not hold audiences. Features on serious issues can range from investigative pieces about unsanitary conditions in local restaurants to national issues such as stolen identities or health issues such as obesity. The outline for the series is the same for broadcast or print but for television, a suggested outline for the video usually accompanies the content outline.

A public relations person can get involved in planning and writing a broadcast series in many ways. One is to work for a nonprofit organization at the national level, although some local affiliates also can and do prepare series. These organizations exist because they are concerned with serious issues such as mental health, cardiovascular disease, cancer and such. Another way to get involved is to address a commercial or local issue. An insurance company

Coke syrup spill puts drivers in a jam

Drivers heading downtown from Spur 280 onto Sixth Street enter clouds of cat litter, used to absorb syrup that leaked from a Coca-Cola tanker truck.

Star-Telegram/DALE BLACKWELL

BY DEANNA BOYD
Star-Telegram Staff Writer

FORT WORTH — Call it a Classic bottleneck.

The Friday morning commute turned slick and sticky when a Coca-Cola tanker truck sprung a leak, dumping a trail of syrup into downtown Fort Worth.

Confused emergency crews followed the trail to the company's nearby drop-off site and found out "Coke Is It."

"It led right up to that location," Lt. Billy Cordell said. "It didn't take a rocket scientist."

The syrupy trickle from Spur 280 onto Sixth Street grew to two lanes wide as it made a left on Calhoun Street and then a left on Eighth Street.

The Real Thing became the Squeal Thing as motorists hydroplaned over the glistening streets.

"Thank God for anti-lock brakes," motorist Dave Newman said.

The affected streets were closed until 9:30 a.m. while city crews spread sand on the spill, after the Fire Department spread some cat litter.

News lead tells what, when and where with words that give an amusing visual.

The "It didn't take a rocket scientist" quote from the police lieutenant contributes to the amusing aspects of the story.

The next paragraph uses another Coke slogan for a pun about the consequences with more vivid description of the consequences of the accident to motorists.

The story ends with another true, but humorous touch: the use of kitty litter to soak up the spill.

The first sentence is more like a broadcast lead-in. It teases the reader into the news lead that follows.

Development tells how emergency road crews discovered the source, and the writer uses the Coca-Cola slogan effectively for humor.

Description of the scene keeps the pace and the fun while giving the reader more about the where.

A succinct quote from a motorist illustrates the hazards of the accident.

Each brief paragraph hangs off of the other so well that it's unlikely that any reader either just looked at the photo and caption or read only part of the story. A bonus is the headline pun.

FIGURE 11.1
News Feature Analysis
Story and photo used with permission of the *Fort Worth Star-Telegram*.

T A B L E   1 1 . 2   *Outline for Broadcast Feature Series*

In developing a feature series for radio or television, the writer needs to state the problem clearly and concisely and then break it down into components. The writer must make sure to cover all questions about the problem.

Program One: Alcoholism is one of the nation's major health problems. It is an illness affecting the entire family. Help needs to be extended not only to the alcoholic, but to the members of the family as well.

Program Two: How do you know when someone is an alcoholic? Identifying an alcoholic can be as simple as answering 20 questions. (Responses to 20 questions about drinking and behavior.)

Program Three: Roles in the pattern of alcoholic behaviors: the alcoholic, the enabler, the victim, the provoker or adjuster.

Program Four: Alcoholism is a physical, emotional and spiritual disease. Patterns are the same, regardless of age or sex.

Program Five: Agencies and avenues of help for the alcoholic and the lives he or she affects.

Such an outline would be fleshed out by pulling out the research data that appear in the proposal and placing appropriate parts in each program's content. The beginning of each series needs a separate introduction to identify it as a part of a whole. The conclusion should promote (promo) the next portion of the series. The introduction and the conclusion for each segment should be about 15 seconds each, for a total of 30 seconds per segment.

did a series on estate planning. A local landscape company did one on using native plants in gardens and yards. Although these sound self-serving, and they are to some extent, they still have substantive content. Sometimes the only credit they get is a single script credit line.

Selling the idea to a station is the most difficult part because the station wants to be sure there is no slant to the story that would get the station accused of bias. However, if the content is of value to audiences, the station is often interested. The series must be prepared for the station as it would be if staff-generated. Your approach to the station should be as a resource person and writer. You do the research on the issue in considerable depth, write a proposal and contact the station most likely to be interested. You can judge that from its regular programming.

Some series prepared by national groups or government agencies are used nationally by networks. In either case, station or network, they provide the technical assistance and talent. At the local level, stations are usually stretched for resources but are interested in quality public service projects. When they control the project, in the form of editorial discretion, they are likely to go along with what you propose.

Documentaries and Broadcast Features

In most cases, you are not likely to be preparing a documentary yourself. Writers accustomed to writing documentaries generally are hired for these special assignments. However, you may be involved in preparing scripts for use by the news media on features your organization is offering because of its particular expertise or resources. For that reason, you need to know what these scripts should look like. (See Tables 11.3, 11.4, 11.5 and 11.6 for some basic formats.) Always use the *AP Broadcast News Handbook* in preparing your scripts.

Some version of the features may be used on the station or network's Web site. You need to think in those terms so you can adapt your script for that use. Suggest the idea to the station after the feature is done, but have a proposal for adaptation ready when you do. This extends the life of the story, and hence your organization's exposure.

T A B L E   1 1 . 3   *Skeleton Script Format for Television Feature*

This is the basic script page design for a television feature. There are two ways of offering features to the news media: (1) You can work out the feature and invest in it, then offer it to the news media. Again, like VNRs, this is something you probably will be working on with a production house. However, production is their business. What you want to show and tell is your business. You include all of the audio and video directions on the left-hand side of the page because you will be working with a producer and a director. You need to come up with the concepts because it is your feature. However, you also need to know that both sides of the script undergo changes in the production process. (2) If you are offering the feature to a television station for the station to shoot, you have much less control. It is not likely you would be asked for a script. However, if you are, this provides you with the format to use. In this case the audio would include any special sound effects as well as video opportunities, pictures and/or action available. If there are no special sounds available, just use VIDEO. Whether you are writing it for a production house or for a television station, remember the rules for writing for broadcast and don't hyphenate words for the sake of margins or split sentences between pages.

AUDIO/VIDEO   SCRIPT SIDE

CONTINUED PAGE TWO

T A B L E   1 1 . 4   *Radio Feature Script with Actuality (Audio on Tape)*

This is the sort of feature that can be prepared when the exhibit is being planned. The audio would have to be of broadcast quality. When the audio is given to stations, you need to also give them a copy of the script—what Donna Smyth said. If she is not actually using a script, you'll have to transcribe what she says and attach that to the cassette.

MUSEUM PEARL DISPLAY 1/16   TAPE :30

ANNOUNCER:

   If you are downtown this week, there is a forty-million dollar collection of pearls on display at the Town Hall Museum. The exhibit is open free to the public. Included are pearls set as crown jewels for kingdoms all over the world.

   Bringing the collection to her hometown answers a longtime dream of local jeweler Donna Smyth (SMITH).

SMYTH TAPE HERE.............RUN :30................ "PEARLS FROM AROUND . . ."

ANNOUNCER:

   The pearl exhibit at the Town Hall Museum closes this Sunday. Smyth (SMITH) Jewelers will have two of the necklaces from the Crown Jewels Collection on display at their downtown store until the end of the month.

-30-

T A B L E   1 1 . 5 *Script for Television Feature with Silent Tape*

If you are working with television stations and offering a feature with silent tape, you need to understand that your "script" is suggested copy only. Attached to the videotape should be not only the length of time but also a description of the scenes. If you don't do this, the station has to take time to look at it and may not unless the description of the scenes looks like something that would be good to show. Include a cover letter or memo to let the station know what else you can offer should they want to do the whole feature. The terms used to explain what the video is showing are OC (on camera) and V/O (voice-over). SIL means "silent."

PEARL COLLECTION 1/4	VIDEOTAPE-SIL :40
OC . . .	How many pearls are in a forty-million dollar collection?
	When you are talking about value, the number of pearls is less important than their quality and the setting. Some pearls are ground up for medicine and others decorate royalty. You'll see the difference in the free exhibit opening soon at the Town Hall Museum.
TAPE ON HERE V/O :40	These pearls being poured from a scoop into a pestle are then ground by the mortar you see in the hands of this Chinese drugmaker. Pearls have been used for centuries . . . (Your script would continue to describe the video before returning to an OC ending.)

T A B L E   1 1 . 6 *Sample Television Script with Sound-on-Tape and SUPER*

You may be supplying a videotape with sound (SOT) and have produced it with some clarifying titles superimposed on the video (SUPER). If so, your script would look something like this.

PEARL COLLECTION 1/4	VIDEOTAPE-SOT :40
OC . . .	How many pearls are in a forty-million dollar collection?
	When you are talking about value, the number of pearls is less important than their quality and the setting. Some pearls are ground up for medicine and others decorate royalty. You'll see the difference in the free exhibit opening soon at the Town Hall Museum.
TAPE ON HERE V/O :15	These pearls being poured from a scoop into a pestle are then ground by the mortar you see in the hands of this Chinese drugmaker.
SOUND UP HERE RUNS :45 ((SUPER: BEIJING APOTHECARY))	Pearls have been used . . . (Your script would continue to describe the video before returning to an OC ending.)

Conclusions

- Features offer vast public relations opportunities to writers in print and broadcast.
- Finding topics for features is not terribly difficult but evaluating them may be.
- Public relations writers must function in many ways like freelance writers to "sell" media on nonstaff-written material.
- The story idea has to be suitable to the medium and its audience.
- Query letters help to "sell" a feature idea to media gatekeepers, the editors.
- Often the medium will decide to do the feature with its own staff, so the public relations person must provide background information and facilitate the efforts of the staff by setting up pictures, getting access to restricted areas and arranging interviews.
- Some of the risks are a lack of control of the story's "slant" or emphasis and no control of the subjects being interviewed.
- Even after the story is done by the writers and photographers, it may suffer changes in the hands of editors.
- Nevertheless, medium-written pieces can be copied, with permission, and circulated to expand the audience and generate third-party credibility for public relations messages.
- When you are writing the story, remember that one of the keys to effective feature writing is to identify and use a clear angle or slant. A good angle is sometimes hidden and can't be discovered without extensive research.
- Backgrounding the article is critical, and the use of interviews is common.
- The actual writing should first give priority to constructing a lead that attracts readers and holds their interest. The body of the piece has to develop, verify and illustrate the central point of the article.
- Anecdotes, quotations, human interest, dramatization and description are techniques that involve readers with your writing. Use them.
- Broadcast series for radio or television are short, related features that usually are written first as a unit and then broken up for programming.
- Some public relations people produce and distribute complete series. Others may only assist newspeople with research and perhaps writing. That usually is the case with documentaries or long broadcast features.
- Both print and broadcast features offer public relations people special access to media that can result in high visibility.

Exercises

1. Select a feature story from *The Wall Street Journal,* and write an analysis of its writing style. Analyze the lead and the body. Identify the elements of human interest, anecdotes, quotations, dramatization and description, and then explain how these helped make the story interesting.
2. Compare the feature-writing styles in your local newspaper with those you see in a consumer magazine of your choice.
3. Outline a radio series based on a position paper.

Use InfoTrac College Edition to access information on topics in this chapter from hundreds of periodicals and scholarly journals.

Notes

1. William Zinsser, *On Writing Well* (New York: Harper & Row, 1980), p. 59.
2. Don Boroughs, "Battle for a Wild Garden," *International Wildlife* (May/June 1999), p. 12. Used with permission of the National Wildlife Federation, publishers of *International Wildlife,* Vienna, Virginia, USA.
3. William L. Rivers, *Free-Lancer and Staff Writer,* 4th ed. (Belmont, Calif.: Wadsworth, 1986), p. 306.
4. Lawrence Ingrassia, "For Jobless Benefits in Sweden, You Don't Have to Be Jobless," *The Wall Street Journal,* September 25, 1996, pp. 1, A12.

Selected Bibliography

William E. Blundell, *The Art and Craft of Feature Writing* (New York: Plume, 1998).

Sheree Bykofsky, Jennifer Bayse Sander and Lynne Rominger, *Complete Idiot's Guide to Publishing Magazine Articles* (Ft. Smith, Ark.: Alpha Books, 2000).

Jean Fredette, *The Writer's Digest Handbook of Magazine Article Writing* (Cincinnati, Ohio: Writer's Digest Books, 1990).

Edward J. Friedlander and John Lee, *Feature Writing for Newspapers and Magazines,* 4th ed. (New York: Longman, 2000).

Norm Goldstein, ed. *The Associated Press Stylebook and Libel Manual* (New York: Associated Press, 1999).

Barry Hampe, *Making Documentary Films and Reality Videos: A Practical Guide to Planning, Filming and Editing Documentaries of Real Events* (New York: Owlet, 1997).

Peter Jacobi, *The Magazine Article: How to Think It, Plan It, Write It* (Bloomington, Ind.: The University of Indiana Press, 1997).

Brad Kalbfeld and James R. Hood, eds., *The Associated Press Broadcast News Handbook, Incorporating the AP Libel Manual,* 2d ed. (New York: Associated Press, 1998).

Paula LaRocque, *Championship Writing: 50 Ways to Improve Your Writing* (Oak Park, Ill.: Marion Street Press, 2000).

William L. Rivers, *Free-Lancer and Staff Writer,* 5th ed. (Belmont, Calif.: Wadsworth, 1992).

Alan Rosenthal, *Writing, Directing and Producing Documentaries* (Carbondale, Ill.: Southern Illinois University Press, 1996).

Eva Shaw, *The Successful Guide to Publishing Magazine Articles* (Loveland, Colo.: Loveland Press, 1998).

C. A. Tuggle, Forrest Carr and Suzanne Huffman, *Broadcast News Handbook* (New York: McGraw-Hill, 2001).

Patricia Westfall, *Beyond Intuition: A Guide to Writing and Editing Magazine Nonfiction* (New York: Addison-Wesley, 1993).

CHAPTER TWELVE

Message Design Concepts

When you see a three-pointed star in a circle, the name Mercedes probably pops into your head. The slogan "A diamond is forever" may call to mind thoughts of De Beers. And a "swoosh" sign reminds you immediately of Nike. It isn't accidental that you make these associations. These organizations and many others have mastered the concepts of message design. They know how to shape messages and repeat them often enough that relevant publics take notice and remember.

Message design concepts involve the careful integration of words, images, motion and sounds into a message that easily and clearly conveys an idea to relevant publics. The best of these messages usually are striking in their simplicity. Publics don't need to ponder what they mean. The message comes through even if exposure to it is only momentary. That seems simple enough, but a casual review of messages in the media, including the Internet, suggests that many people don't understand this very well.

The purpose of this chapter is to share with you some broad concepts you can use as you write and design messages for different media. Study and relate them to subsequent chapters in this text. Let's look first at the creative process.

The Creative Process

Some people think of creativity as the time when an individual has a "eureka experience." That does happen sometimes, but if you wait for the lightbulb in your head to flash brightly, you may miss a deadline for your client. As a public relations writer, you're expected to produce on demand and present creative ideas to a client's publics. You simply can't wait for the muse to move you. Creativity can be a very personal process, of course, but when you're serving a client the process is likely to be a group activity that comes only after several steps are taken in concert with others in your organization.

The first step in developing a viable creative concept is to assemble as much relevant information as possible. Review Chapter 4 to refresh yourself about research. You may be expected to gather this information, but it is more likely that other people in your organization will do that.

Who gathers the information is not as important as how well the information is documented. And in the case of contradictory information, which sources of verification seem to be most reliable? These people also may provide interpretations of the information. We recommend that you review Chapter 2 because you, as a writer, are ultimately responsible legally and ethically for what you say. You can't simply say, "They gave me the information and said it was correct."

It is expected and common that you'll have much more information than you actually need. Among other things, this information should clearly describe target publics and their characteristics. The information also should lead to a concise statement of the purpose for messages in a campaign.

You're the writer. You are the person who has to convert this material into messages. So, the second step is to analyze the information in light of the needs of the client. You'll probably do this as a member of a creative team that may involve a creative director, an art director and an account services person. Several brainstorming sessions may be needed about how the information can be used. It is at this stage that no idea, even ones considered to be off the wall, should be left unexamined. After these ideas have been weighed, a few—such as three—are selected for further development.

The third step is to evaluate these ideas from the point of view of how well they communicate the client's purpose as interpreted by target publics. Does one idea convey the purpose of the campaign better than others? Are target publics more likely to respond to another idea? If so, the viability of these ideas may need to be tested for possible results. Even if there is no problem like that, message testing still may be needed when the ideas seem equally compelling. Your role as writer, then, is to write rough draft copy that can be tested.

You know what the purpose is and who the target publics are. You're now ready for the fourth step—deciding exactly what you want to say. This involves decisions about how you will finally write the message, what format is best to convey it and the overall image you want to project. If no copy tests were done, you begin with a blank sheet of paper or a blank screen. If testing was done, you have draft copy to begin with and the task is to rewrite and polish it in light of what these tests revealed.

How you write a message may be influenced also by the media used to deliver it. A magazine ad does not work well in television, for example. The concept should be the same, of course, but the message has to be crafted to fit each medium. Is the overall image friendly, open, selective, confident or what? The combination of words, visuals, sounds, layout, type, color and so on all combine to project an image. The goal is to select, shape and limit message elements to collectively project a clear image for the client. Four guidelines may help you reach that goal:

1. The verbal part of the message is the most important ingredient. It should control the selection and use of all other elements in the message.
2. Seek a consistent look from one message to the next, from one medium to the next.

3. Simplify everything. Delete all elements that are not related to the central point of the message. These are excesses that clutter the message and could confuse publics.

4. Use as few elements as possible and use only those that contribute directly to the understanding of the message.

Following these guidelines is easier to say than to do. One reason for this is that you must use symbols as substitutes for ideas.

Symbols

In your toolchest of symbols are words, type, color, sound and images of all sorts, including animation, pictures, art, logos, trademarks and graphs of various types. Even when these symbols are used well, many messages may still go awry because receivers of these messages attach their own meanings to them. Those meanings may be unlike what you intended. You must recognize up front that you do not control receivers' meanings. You control only the symbols you use to shape a message. You must select them carefully and craft them with sensitivity to how they may be interpreted.

Words are the basic building blocks of all messages. They are not ideas themselves but are representations of ideas. Words are usually thought of as being concrete or abstract.

Concrete Words   Concrete words are more likely than abstract ones to be interpreted as intended by target publics. The word *table* signifies an object, but modifiers often are needed to give it texture and form. You've seen many tables, so you have an image of what a table generally looks like. The problem is that your image of a table may be unlike the image held by receivers of your message. If you write "The solid walnut, oval table has a soft patina that glows with age, and its four gracefully curved legs are carved intricately," you've painted a picture of a particular table that target publics can "see." Now the table arouses a more precise image. A good writer chooses words carefully to make understanding easier and more complete.

Abstract Words   Abstract words are not as easy to use with the same precision as concrete words. The word *love,* for example, represents an idea, not an object like a table. It represents an abstract idea that can be interpreted in countless ways. Does love mean attraction, genuine affection, sexual relations or something else? Love, like other abstract words, needs descriptors and context to give it clearer meaning. For example, "I love being your spouse because you're also my best friend" defines what love means to the person uttering the statement. And it is likely to be understood and appreciated more fully by the person to whom it is directed.

Good writers make ideas clear. They can put words together so ideas seem to come alive. Their dynamism is arresting and stimulating. That happens only when writers remember to describe, using analogies or metaphors and similar devices that give dimension and substance to the message. Yet, the words they use must be ones that have common meanings to their target publics. Otherwise, misunderstanding and misinformation are unintended outcomes. Except when spoken, words find their primary expression in type.

Type

Type is a series of letter forms that makes a message visible. In this sense, type is one kind of visual communication. The letter forms in a font of type include all of the characters of the alphabet, punctuation marks, numbers and other objects such as quotation marks, ampersands and so forth. Figure 12.1 shows some of the major characteristics of letter forms. There also are several variations to a regular type font, such as italics, boldface and others. When used sparingly, each of these variations can be used to emphasize part of a message. What many people fail to understand is that the correct use of type depends on two key points: legibility and appropriateness.

Legibility   Computers now make many type fonts available by simply clicking a mouse. That means millions of people who select type fonts every day may be unskilled in the proper use of type. They often select fonts that are not very readable. This detracts from a message and may drive away readers of printed pieces or visitors to Web sites. Some people say that computers have done a lot of harm to the quality of contemporary message design. That may or may not be true. What is true, however, is that the first consideration in selecting type fonts is whether they are legible. If you are unsure about the legibility of a type font, consult an expert in typography.

Legibility is of special concern when you write lengthy text. Copy length presumably is driven by the need to include vital information, but long blocks of text tire readers quickly. If you use type that is even slightly harder to read, you unnecessarily build problems into your message. Be careful. If the type you like most is legible, you then should look at its appropriateness.

Appropriateness   The concept of appropriateness is more slippery than that of legibility. In its simplest sense, appropriateness is concerned with the connotative qualities of a type font.

FIGURE 12.1

Anatomy of a Letter   *Type is measured in points from the top of the highest ascender to the bottom of the lowest descender. The x-height is the height of the body of lowercase letters. Roman type has serifs—extensions at the extremities of characters that make it easy to read. Type without serifs is called sans serif.*

T A B L E   1 2 . 1   *Four Type Families*   These four fonts of type represent four type families. Each has certain characteristics that identify it with a particular family. Look at these examples and consider potential uses for each of these four type groups. Roman and sans serif fonts are what you'll use most often. Cursive and decorative fonts are used only in special situations.

Roman or Serif
This is 30-point Times New Roman.

Sans Serif or Gothic
This is 30-point Avant Garde.

Cursive or Script
This is 30-point Medici Script.

Decoratibe
This is 30-point Linotext.

Table 12.1 illustrates four type families. How do you react personally to each of the four fonts? Do they project connotative aspects that may suggest certain kinds of uses? If so, that's the idea of appropriateness.

If you're writing and designing a proclamation for an official to present during Labor Day ceremonies, you might use a decorative font in the headline or in other ways, such as in initial letters. That would seem appropriate. On the other hand, you may use a cursive or script font if you're writing and designing a formal invitation to a charity ball. That's appropriate, isn't it? And you probably wouldn't use a heavy railroad Gothic for that invitation.

A good, clean sans serif font might be very good in short headlines, but not in long texts because it is more tiring to read. And if you're designing a 24-page booklet with lots of copy you'll go with one of the most readable roman or serif fonts.

The point is that type evokes certain feelings in us. It has personality. The clothing you wear says something about you and what image you want to project to others. If you're going to a job interview, you'll not likely to dress as if you're going jogging. Like clothing, the type you select can enhance and help clarify your message or it can confuse it. When you write, we assume that you select words very carefully. Use the same care when you select type for its appropriateness.

Type as Art   Although the design of type has always been seen as an art form, the advent of computers has introduced the idea of type as art. With the right software, you can shape a word or several into spirals, waves and other shapes as you wish. In effect, you should treat this digitally altered type like a piece of art. It becomes a visual just like photographs or hand-drawn art. But be cautious about overuse.

You can get carried away with this technique and create a visual that is difficult to comprehend. That defeats your purpose.

Logos

A logo is a symbol of an organization, group or person. It is something like your face. Friends know what you look like and can relate your face to your name, much like a logo. A good logo has several purposes. First, it should make a positive impression on us. Second, it should be recognizable. Third, it should have uniqueness that separates it from all other logos, especially competitors', so people can relate the logo to the correct organization, product, cause or issue. Fourth, it should age well. Fifth, it should translate faithfully across media. Taken individually, each criterion seems fairly simple. Taken as a group, however, these criteria are difficult to meet.

Simplicity   The watchword regarding logos is simplicity. Now that many organizations are diversified and some operate across many cultures and political boundaries, logos are even more important. And simplicity is at an even higher premium. The golden arches should mean basically the same thing to publics in Singapore, Caracas, Oslo, Johannesburg, Beijing and New Delhi. If a logo is ambiguous, it fails.

Format   The format of a logo can vary. It might be an abstract symbol or a pictograph. Either should evoke an emotional response. On the other hand, it might be a logotype in which the name of the organization, group or individual is set in type, usually in an uncommon font that is legible and appropriate, such as Sony's logo. Another format is the trademark or descriptive symbol. A trademark can be a name, a symbol or a combination used to identify the product of a business. It always should be accompanied by the trademark (™) sign.

Design   If your client is a new company, you begin with a clean slate. If not, you need to know the history of the logo in current use and why a change is contemplated. Organizations that change logos or names, for whatever reason, face an expensive task. And publics don't like changes to things they're accustomed to. Expense and discontent by publics may set the stage for failure, even if the new design is good.

There are five stages of logo design, each built around questions. The first one is research. If it is a new organization, what image does the leadership want to project? If the client has a history, what was the old logo and what did it come to signify to target publics? How closely do relevant publics identify with it? Is it possible that a drastic change might confuse important publics? Why does management want to change the logo? Other questions may arise as you go about researching these questions.

Second, there must be a clear definition of target publics. Who are the people? What are they like? What do they believe? How do they relate to the client? Answers to questions like these often are critical to developing a "feel" for what a good logo might look like. If the logo will be used across cultures or political boundaries, you must be sensitive to potential problems. That makes it difficult to come up with a single logo that works everywhere and under all conditions.

Third, use in different formats may be an issue. Presumably, your original logo design may fit on a letter-size sheet of paper. Will it retain its design integrity if used as a 10-foot-high symbol on the face of the home office or on buildings at global plant sites? Can it be used as a lapel pin and still maintain its design integrity? Will it translate well in all print media, television, film and Web sites?

Fourth, does the client have enough money and a commitment to use the logo every time as it was designed? That's a critical question that is sometimes overlooked. It is a good idea, even for clients with deep pockets, to design a logo to be executed in a single color. Why? Use of a second or third color in the design may make the logo unrecognizable if it ever appears only in one color. Of course, it may appear in just one color very often, such as in retail ads in newspapers. Also, the annual cost of using a second color in a logo can be staggering. Design the logo in a single color and add color only on special occasions.

Fifth, a logo should never be designed with the intent of replacing it a year or so from now. The best logos today generally are ones that have been around a long time. Always design with the future in mind. And when you think you have a final design, ask this question: "Will it last?"

Color

Color is an important part of our lives. We encounter color everywhere. It may depress us or make us feel happy. It may suggest springtime freshness or, like odors, drive us away from something. For example, cosmetics packaged in brown often remain on the shelf. And sugar remains there also if it does not have a good bit of blue on the wrapper. Research also suggests that green is a no-no on sugar packages. Why? No one knows exactly, but color does seem to send messages to people. How people interpret color is, of course, entirely subjective. Our memories, experiences and environment apparently influence the associations we make. But there are some broad psychological implications you need to know.

Psychology of Color   No one knows exactly why, but colors seem to stimulate or calm our nervous systems. People tend to associate "warm" colors, like reds, yellows and blends of them, with heat, fire and sun. But "cool" colors, like the blues and greens, are most often related to such things as sky, sea and wilderness.

Our color preferences are complex. They seem to be influenced by emotional behavior, lifestyle, gender, age and our sense of style and fashion. You know, of course, that color in fashion changes frequently, especially as related to the clothing we wear. And it is often the case that color trends in other areas are also seen in the materials organizations prepare for their publics. You need to be aware of these trends and to know the most common emotional reactions people have to colors.

Red is a dramatic color that excites not only the bull in the ring but people as well. Red colors stimulate us and are often associated with aggressive behavior, passion, success and impulse. It is fairly common, also, to see some political candidates for major offices wearing their red "power" ties or, in the case of female candidates, blouses. The color orange is a blend of red and yellow. We tend to think of it as a bright, happy and festive color that is not as dramatic as red.

Dark blue colors seem to have calming, relaxing effects. The dark blue of night signifies the end of the day and winding down from a frenetic pace. Blues are also associated with tradition, orderliness and stability. That may explain why so many financial institutions use blues somewhat extensively. Light blues are also associated with cleanliness. On the other hand, purple is thought of as daring and it is sometimes seen as being royal, elegant and expensive. The violet colors are associated frequently with feelings of intimacy.

But bright yellow seems to raise our blood pressure, although it is often associated with health and well-being. That may explain why you see so much yellow on food packages. Yellow also is thought of as the color of optimism, presumably related to the brightness of a new day.

We tend to associate cool green colors with nature, regeneration and self-preservation. Green is used a lot by organizations and products related to the environment and cleanliness. On the other hand, white is a symbol of purity and innocence, as in bridal dress in Western countries. But in some Eastern societies it is worn at funerals. Black is especially interesting because we tend to think of it as a symbol of mourning. It also can have a sinister connotation, but if it is used in lingerie it is seen as sexy. It also may be thought of as elegant, as in a "black-tie" occasion.

These color associations are all bound by culture. Look again at how we described white and black. Because we now communicate across cultures routinely, even when we don't intend to, you must be sensitive to the ways colors are perceived in other cultures. That means you need to spend a good bit of time researching the subject because it is too extensive for this chapter.

Qualities of Color   Colors have three qualities. One is *hue.* Hue is synonymous with the word *color.* It is one of the primary colors—yellow, red or blue—or a blend of them. *Value* refers to the level of lightness or darkness in a color. Light blue has a higher color value, for example, than dark blue. *Saturation* refers to the intensity or vividness of color. A full color is saturated. Adding a complement of a color, or gray, lessens the intensity or vividness. Colors of lower intensities are said to be toned down.

Paper Color   Paper comes in many colors. Paper stock can enhance or detract from a message in a printed piece. The same holds true of background color on Web sites. When reproducing color pictures of people, skin tones are the guiding light of good reproduction. That means that you generally must confine your paper selection to whites and eggshell colors. Other colors can make people look unnatural. For example, a picture of people printed on light green paper makes them look sick. On yellows, they appear jaundiced. Test background colors on Web sites to see how they work, but remember that what you see on the monitor may not be entirely reliable. Be on guard.

Pantone® Color   Reproduction of color in printing was for decades an inexact science at best. You had to select from color swatches, much as you do when you go to a paint store when painting your room. Printers had to mix inks with a little dab of this, a little dab of that, and so on. Many of them were remarkably gifted at giving people what they wanted.

The process is more precise now because of the use of the Pantone Color Matching System. This is an international color language that lets you specify colors by numbered ink colors. Printers follow these specifications to give you exactly what you ask for. A companion system in use on computers is the Pantone by Letraset Color Markers, color guides available at most art supply stores. These guides are coordinated with Pantone color inks so you can design on a screen and specify colors that match in the printing process. Again, remember that what you see on the monitor may not be exactly what you get.

Photographs and Art

Photographs and art should be selected first because they are appropriate to the message. A well-known brand of watches once ran a large ad that said its watches are for people with inner strength. A photograph of a man filled the top half of the space. The picture was of a professional athlete but looked as if it had been taken during a police booking. All that was needed was a set of numbers across his chest. The athlete's appearance is immaterial. What is important is that no attempt was made to interpret the idea of inner strength or how the athlete reflected it. It remains a puzzle how the picture relates specifically to inner strength.

Deciding that photographs and art are or are not appropriate is a judgment call. But the process is made easier if you have a very clear idea about what the message is supposed to say. The watch ad may have turned out the way it did because its creators were unsure of what they meant by inner strength.

A primary function of visuals is to get the attention of readers or viewers. The picture in the watch ad certainly did that. But the attention was probably negative, at least momentarily. Negative attention can sometimes be useful, but mostly when the purpose of the message is to warn readers or viewers away from something or to encourage them to take protective or evasive action.

Another major function of photographs and art is to impart information. Suppose your client is a jeweler who specializes in diamond wedding rings. You might use a visual that shows a man holding out a diamond to a woman whose face is alive with excitement. The headline says, "The answer is yes." The picture distills the essence of the message because of its appropriateness.

Photographs and art also should never be used merely to dress a presentation. Each should contribute specifically to the purpose of the message. Neither should they be selected simply because they are beautiful nor because you are fond of them.

Infographics

The term *infographics* signifies the use of visual devices intended to communicate complex information quickly and clearly. These devices include charts, diagrams, graphs, tables, maps and lists. You may have endured a lengthy discourse that used a lot of economic data. Even if it was entirely accurate and written simply, it still may have been confusing. Perhaps you got lost in some of the details and had to go back to previous points to iron out uncertainties. In that case, you may have wished the writer had used infographics to explain the text. Several techniques are available and their use depends on what you're trying to say.

Devices   Among the most common are *bar* (horizontal) and *column* (vertical) charts that can visually summarize lots of statistical information. *Pie charts* are usually seen as circles or ovals in which slices or wedges of the pie show data as parts of the whole.

Diagrams can be used to show how a system works, such as the internal combustion engine that powers your car. In the case of an engine, the diagram will be what is known as a *cutaway* that shows internal parts. In other cases, the diagram may be an *organizational chart* that shows lines of authority, or a *systems flowchart* that shows sequential movement.

Illustrated graphics use images—rather than bars, lines or pies—to relate data. The Snapshots features used every day by *USA Today* are consistently good examples of this technique.

Tables are commonly used. And they are easier to design than graphs. Just because tables may contain lots of numbers isn't a reason to view them as anything less than infographics.

With the advent of computers, the availability of all sorts of *maps* on disks has increased the use of maps as informational graphics. If your organization has a plant in Borneo and you want to feature it in the annual report, for example, you can quickly give readers a geographic context in which to understand the message more clearly.

Bulleted or *numbered lists* are also infographic devices. Bullets are appropriate when you need to show related items that are not sequential. Numbered lists should be used when the items have an order.

Guidelines for Good Usage   Check and double-check all facts. Nothing is more distressing to people than to discover an error in fact or in rendering infographics. Make sure you have all the information you need before you begin designing. The design of the graphic should never overwhelm the content, but rather amplify it.

Everything should be labeled clearly. Be as precise as possible. You've probably seen tables of data in which you got lost, temporarily at least, and had difficulty understanding exactly what you were seeing. Remember that your first concern is to communicate the whole message as clearly and easily as possible. Each infographic must help. If it does not, it should be redesigned or not be used.

Sound and Motion

Radio, television, videos, film and the Internet present opportunities to use techniques and symbols uncommon to other media. When used well, these techniques can add measurably to a message. To use them well, however, you must observe certain cautions. Let's look first at sound for radio and audio for computers or television.

Radio and Other Audio

Broadcast news and features were dealt with in Chapters 10 and 11. So this section on radio and audio applies only to commercial messages and public service announcements. A message for delivery on radio requires that you resolve several questions. You know, presumably, who your target publics are and the strategy and creative tactics you want to use. You'll begin with a script sheet. (See Chapter 11 for an example.) The verbal part of the message is confined to the right of the script sheet. The left side has all of the production information.

The key thing to remember is to write the message first. Refine it until you're sure it is exactly what you want to say. Then write production cues on the left. Once these are done, break the message into chunks so what is said corresponds to the production cues. These production cues can vary a lot. For example, you may specify that a station announcer will read the script live without sound effects or music. You may produce the message in a studio in which an announcer reads the script in concert with music and sound effects. When final production is done, the message is duplicated on audiotape cartridges and sent to separate stations to be played as scheduled.

Sound effects can be copied from sound libraries. Music can be used from music libraries. Some of it may be in the public domain so you can use it without charge. Much of it, however,

"See! Right there, in between all that scrolling data and those
splashy graphics, right next to that little station ID thingy ...
I think I can actually see the news anchor!"

Cartoon from *Quill* magazine. Used by permission of Alan Vitello.

is copyrighted and you'll need to pay a fee to use it. You'll need to rely on the station or recording studio that does your production to advise you of the music's copyright status. In some cases, you may need to commission professionals to compose original lyrics and scores to get the particular effect you want. If so, be sure to work out in advance who owns the copyrights to this new material.

You may want to do location sound recording to get the "feel" that you want for your message. That involves a sound crew, a truck, travel, lodging, meals and so on. Expect to pay a lot more than if it is done in a station or recording studio.

Much audio is now produced digitally. Digital sound is much cleaner and represents cutting-edge technology. You may want to transfer your message to digital disks for this higher level of quality, but you'll pay more than if you use traditional audiotape cartridges.

Television, Video, Film and the Internet

Each of these media uses moving images as well as sound. Designing a message for television begins with the development of a storyboard if it is for an ad or a public service announcement. See Chapter 13 for a sample storyboard. A storyboard shows sequential rough sketches of major scenes. The script appears below or adjacent to each frame of the board so it is easy to connect verbal content to the visual. Production of the message can be on film or on video, and can use traditional or digital animation.

If your message is longer than a traditional spot or PSA, you may construct the message in production script form. Ask your instructor for a copy of a production script in the instructor's manual that goes with this text. This example is a segment of a time-coded film script. Time coding measures the length of each scene, many lasting no more than seconds. Action cues, music and other production information appear down the left side and the narration is on the right, just like a radio script.

Try to maximize a major asset—the ability to show movement. Generally, avoid talking heads because they don't exploit this quality. Movement attracts attention and it can hold it if the verbal content and sound effects blend well with it. Don't use action for the sake of action. Use it for a purpose. Make it fit what is being said.

Production of these messages usually is assigned to television stations or to film or video production studios. They ordinarily are selected through a bidding process based on the lowest and best bid. The latter point is critical because some production people are better than others at doing some kinds of production. You want to be sure that your message is produced as intended.

Even if your message is short, the costs of production can be high. And the way you build your message may drive the costs even higher. For example, the nature of your message may demand that production be in the field. On-site production is generally a lot more expensive than in studios, if for no other reason than travel, meals, rooms, the production crew, equipment and other expenses. So be sensitive to costs as you develop the message. Your client will appreciate that.

If your production is to be distributed through a Web site on the Internet, it is a good idea to search sites that have canned video segments you can use. Some segments are free. Others require fees. Look closely at what is available, but don't be surprised if you can't find something that fits your needs perfectly. You may have to produce project-specific video for use on the site. Web sites are expensive to build and to maintain. Adding the price of project-specific video production can drive up the costs dramatically.

Music and film or video images usually are copyrighted. Check carefully on the copyright status of everything. Be prepared to pay fees. These usually cover a limited number of plays so if your message will be used repeatedly over long periods, residual fees may be an issue. In the case of talent, such as models and performers, residuals are routine. Be sure to evaluate the long-term costs.

Qualities of Good Message Design

There's no mystery to good message design. Certain qualities should be kept in mind as you work.

Clear Creative Concept

We've already noted that you must have a clear strategy that focuses on the key point you want to communicate to publics. But a clear message concept is not the same thing. It is the creative way you decide to interpret the strategy. It is the tactical way you finally shape the message. It affects all elements in the message.

Suppose your client is a candidate for governor in your state. The candidate's strategy is to make family values an essential part of every campaign message. The question is: How do you interpret family values so that it is meaningful to target publics?

One message in a series might be built around the candidate's personal view of the importance of education. For example, the copy might say "(Name) believes a good education helps people realize their potential." This can be expanded in the body of the copy and illustrated, perhaps, with the candidate addressing students at a university commencement.

Another message might say something like "(Name) believes that people must take personal responsibility for their own behavior." Of course, the copy should develop that idea and it might be illustrated with a picture of a felon in prison, representing someone paying the price for not taking personal responsibility.

The point is that a good creative concept is one that focuses all elements of the message on a specific idea. Not two or three ideas. Just one. Creative interpretations of strategy for a client are limited only by your imagination.

Getting and Holding Attention

A good creative concept gets and holds attention. Getting attention may be fairly easy, but holding attention can be difficult. That's because publics are inundated with information and they're busy. A well-executed concept encourages readers and viewers to pay attention to the whole message, not just a small part of it. This calls for the careful integration of words, visuals and design. Weakness in any of these areas can drive people away.

Understanding Publics

One of the most critical problems in developing a good creative concept is the degree to which you really understand the publics for which a message is intended. Refer to the gubernatorial candidate again. Family values may, and often do, mean various things to different publics.

For example, are there differences in perceptions of family values among Asian Americans, Hispanics, blacks, American Indians and Caucasians? Yes. Are there significant differences within these groups? Yes, in some; maybe no, in some. If so, what are they? You'd better find out if you don't know. This is where the research information mentioned earlier can be of special use. Will the same message work for all of these groups or must you tailor the message to each group? It depends. You'll be lucky if a single message will work for all.

Publics often discount quickly messages they perceive as not reflecting their beliefs. Unless they are predisposed to the point of the message, they're likely to discount it. The claim that you should know publics goes well beyond semantics. It signifies the degree to which you are limited by your knowledge of their beliefs and behavior. Developing a message without this kind of knowledge guarantees that it will be less successful than expected.

Good Organization

Your message should be organized so that it seems to flow naturally from point to point. When readers or viewers encounter a message that challenges their ability to decipher content, they are likely to move on to another and forget you. You have to give them a reason to volunteer their time to understand what you are saying.

The way you write the message helps with its organization. And the way it is laid out in printed form or presented on a computer screen also gives a sense of organization. Layout—the physical arrangement of elements showing how they are related—that seems haphazard is recognized quickly by publics as disorganized, even if they are unskilled in such matters. They wonder if they should volunteer their time to pay attention to what you say. Many decide not to.

Visual Principles

You should keep in mind a few visual principles as you put together a message. These principles should be applied after you've written the verbal part of a message. They should be applied when you do a layout for a printed piece or a storyboard for television, video or a Web site. Layout deals with the physical arrangement of elements and how they are related. A storyboard is a series of layouts that shows the sequential development of an animated message.

These visual principles are important for several reasons. The human eye tends to perceive a message by grouping information by similarity, proximity and continuity. Elements that don't fit arouse dissonance, which may prompt questions about the message itself as well as the source of the message. That tends to drive publics away.

People also sometimes "see" messages that are not overt, but only implied. This can be especially devastating if an implication is unintended, because it invites unwanted speculation. It is best not to rely on inference. It is difficult enough to communicate overtly. Why create potential problems by using inference? Some people are more visually acute than others. They "see" much more in a message than do other people. This explains, at least in part, why the meanings they attach to a message may be quite different from interpretations by less visually acute people.

When people look at your message, they filter it through their past experiences. They apply their own values and belief systems to interpret the meaning of a message. Remember, also, that in Western cultures people are taught to view messages from left to right, top to bottom and front to back. People in some other cultures learn to consume messages from right to left, bottom to top and back to front. Those points need to be kept in mind if your message is going across cultures.

With those points as background, let's look now at eight visual principles.

Balance

Some people say that balance is the most essential of the visual principles. Perhaps the easiest way to envision this concept is to draw an imaginary vertical line down the center of a sheet of paper. Keep this sheet in mind as we look at two kinds of balance.

Formal When all of the message elements are equal in visual weight on both sides of that imaginary line, the balance is *formal* or *symmetrical.* Formal balance connotes stability, security, authority, leadership and thoughtfulness. It also may be seen as unexciting, unimaginative and lacking tension or movement. Its primary value is that readers or viewers don't have to work hard to see relationships between message elements.

Informal   Placing elements of unequal visual weights on either side of that imaginary line produces *informal* or *asymmetrical* balance. It offers less stability but it generally is seen as being more interesting and exciting. It seems to require more effort by readers and viewers to perceive the whole message. It can be a little unsettling to some people. A message using informal balance is seen as dynamic, fresh, inviting, casual, creative and friendly.

Visual Weight

Applying the principles of balance depends also on your ability to understand the concept of *visual weight,* which transcends size. For example, a small, dark visual may have as much or more visual weight than one much larger in lighter tones. Black is heavier than white. Intense colors are heavier than those that have been toned down. The point is that you have to think in terms of visual weight and size as well as the distribution of elements on either side of that imaginary line.

Horizontal and Vertical Lines

Horizontal and vertical lines tend to stabilize our visual perception of a message. But diagonal lines seem to create visual or dynamic tension. This contrasts sharply with our normal view of up to down and side to side. A single diagonally shaped visual can alter entirely our perception of a message on a page or on a screen. Does that mean that you should never use diagonals? Of course not. You simply need to remember that diagonals tend to jar readers and viewers. Used with restraint, they can be very effective.

Contrast

There is a saying that opposites attract. Keep that in mind because contrast is a primary way to indicate differences as opposed to similarities. Contrast builds interest and stimulates our attention. Without contrast, a message quickly gets boring. That turns away readers and viewers. You can think of it in another way, too. A photograph without at least a small area of pure black and white keeps us from seeing the full range of grays or colors in it. Contrast helps anchor the eye so it can see a visual more clearly.

Use contrast to exaggerate, emphasize, accent, dramatize, excite and attract attention. One of the easiest ways to call attention to a large visual is to put a small one next to it. You can build contrast into a message by contrasts in size, type, colors or images.

Large, dark type in a headline contrasts with smaller, light type in the text. If a darker image is contrasted with a lighter one, each seems to enhance the other. Remember, too, that dark images will seem closer than ones of equal size but lighter. If you put a dark image in a light space, it appears to be even darker and heavier. You can also build in contrast by content. For example, if you're trying to show the size of a 5-carat diamond, put it next to a familiar object, such as a golf ball or a small pager. Search for ways to build contrast into your message. A message without contrast is boring.

Movement

Return now to that sheet of paper with the imaginary vertical line down the center. Now draw an imaginary line horizontally through the center. That divides the paper into four equal parts. Where the lines intersect is the symmetrical center. Move up the horizontal line about one-fifth of the way from the symmetrical center to the top of the sheet. Put an imaginary X on the vertical line. The area of the X is called the optical center.

The point of this exercise is to illustrate the idea of natural eye movement. When you pick up a blank sheet of paper your eye first looks at the area of the optical center. If there's nothing there to move it in another direction it will move up through the upper left quadrant, then over to the upper right quadrant, then back through the symmetrical center into the lower left quadrant and then into the lower right, where it will then exit from the space. That pattern produces something like a stylized reversed "S."

If this is the way the eye behaves naturally, then it is a good idea to place a key element in the general area of the optical center. That does not guarantee that people will read your message, but it does help get them into the message. Once into the message, arrangement of elements can lead the eye through other patterns. Arrangement of elements creates the illusion of movement and keeps the message from being seen as static and uninteresting.

Several techniques can be used to enhance the sense of movement and rhythm that leads people through a message. People tend to look in the same direction as figures in photographs and art. A guideline to remember about this is to always place these visuals so people always look into a page or screen. If you don't, that's an open invitation for readers or viewers to go elsewhere. Visual elements, including blocks of text placed in certain relationships, can lead people naturally through a message. Contrived devices can also be used, including pointing fingers, arrows, sequential numbers and letters of the alphabet, to lead people from one element to the next.

Harmony

This is a slippery concept. To understand it better, think of a jigsaw puzzle with all of its pieces in place. The message of the puzzle is harmonious because each piece is where it is supposed to be. Good layouts and storyboards have harmony. All of the pieces fit together in what appears to be a natural, cohesive way. They collectively convey a clear message that is enhanced by the type, visuals, color and paper or screen. They "speak" with a single voice.

Unity

This principle is related to harmony, obviously, but it goes beyond that to deal with how all of a message's elements tie together visually. A message with good unity is one where all of its elements are complementary. They enjoy a relationship that is more than spatial. Some of the most common techniques to unify a message include, but are not limited to, the use of borders, screens, background colors and overlapping elements. Overlapping some elements also can help the natural eye movement through a message. Another important technique is to group related small visuals into a single block. Grouping gives them the impact of a larger visual without taking away from the content of each. If they aren't grouped, the message may have a checkerboard look that is generally uninviting.

Proportion

If you stand on the sidewalk in front of the Empire State Building and look straight at the building, you see only a small part of it. If you cross the street and look again, you can see more of it. You may have to go several blocks before you can see the whole building.

The point is that messages in printed, electronic and film forms are read, viewed and scanned up close. People have difficulty seeing the whole of extreme shapes. Visuals with a proportion of height to width approximately three to five or five to three are easier for the eye to see. Must every element fit that exact ratio? No. But it is a good idea not to vary too much from it. Avoid extreme vertical and horizontal shapes.

Another way to look at proportion is to think of the relativity of all the elements. When we see a message, we see several elements, each in relationship to all the others on the printed page or screen. We react automatically to their size, shape, weight, color and so on. Varying the proportions of elements also can add to the contrast in the page or screen and can help to gain attention.

Conclusions

- Skillful message design involves the careful integration of words, images, motion and sounds to convey a message to target publics.
- For public relations writers, creative work is expected to be produced on demand and it is usually the end result of group activity that involves several steps.
- Writers use symbols to represent and convey ideas.
- Words are the building blocks of all messages. They transcend all other elements in a message.
- Type is the most basic way of expressing ideas. It must be legible and appropriate.
- Computer software can be used to massage type in ways that convert it into art.
- A logo is a symbol of an organization, group or person.
- A good logo is simple, can be used in all sorts of media, is easy to recognize, maintains its design integrity and is durable.
- Color tends to send subtle messages to people, although its perceptual meaning varies from one individual to another and is influenced by culture.
- Different colors have psychological implications.
- Color has three qualities: hue, value and saturation.
- The Pantone Color Matching System is an international color language that allows specification of color by numbers.
- *Infographics* is a term that signifies the use of visual devices used to convey complex information.
- The most commonly used infographics are bar, column and pie charts, diagrams, graphs, tables, maps and lists.

- Sounds are recorded in studios, taken from sound-effect or music libraries or recorded at on-site locations.
- If prerecorded sound or music does not fit, original lyrics and scores can be composed to fit the message.
- Use movement in video and film messages.
- Generally avoid talking heads when producing messages for television, video, film or the Internet.
- Prerecorded video segments may be downloaded from several Internet sites for free use, but these often don't precisely fit a message.
- Some recorded audio or video segments may be used without paying fees, but most are copyrighted and do require fees, usually for a limited number of plays. More plays mean residual fees.
- A clear creative concept is requisite of good message design, which must get and hold attention.
- A good writer creates messages that publics interpret as being meant for them, not some generalized other.
- Good message design reflects keen organization so that the message emerges naturally and without effort by target publics.
- Visual principles of good message design include balance, visual weight, horizontal and vertical lines, contrast, movement, harmony, unity and proportion.

Exercises

1. Find a printed message that leads your eye easily through the whole message. Find another that your eye has difficulty following through all the elements. Write an analysis in which you compare the two pieces, including recommendations for improving the second example. Attach copies of the pieces to your report, which should not exceed two double-spaced pages.

2. Find a logo that you think is especially good and another that you believe is not very good. Write an analysis in which you compare the two. Be sure to explain what are the good and bad features in both logos. Attach copies of the logos to your report, which should not exceed two double-spaced pages.

3. Several visuals are discussed in this chapter. Find a printed piece that illustrates most or all of these principles. Analyze the piece critically and focus on principles that are not exploited as well as they could have been. Attach a copy of the piece to your report, which should be no more than two double-spaced pages.

Use InfoTrac College Edition to access information on topics in this chapter from hundreds of periodicals and scholarly journals.

Selected Bibliography

Erich Gamma, Richard Helm, Ralph Johnson and John Vlissides, *Design Patterns* (Boston, Mass.: Addison-Wesley, 1995).

Robin Landa, *Graphic Design Solutions,* 2d ed. (Clifton Park, N.Y.: OnWord Press, 2000).

Marcelle Lapow Toor, *Graphic Design on the Desktop: A Guide for the Non-Designer,* 2d ed. (Hoboken, N.J.: John Wiley & Sons, 1998).

Douglas K. van Duyne, James A. Landay and Jason I. Hong, *The Design of Sites: Patterns, Principles, and Processes for Crafting a Customer-Centered Web Experience* (Boston, Mass.: Addison-Wesley, 2002).

Robin Williams, *The Mac Is Not a Typewriter,* 2d ed. (Berkeley, Calif.: Peachpit Press, 2003).

Robin Williams, *The Non-Designer's Design Book: Design and Typographic Principles for the Visual Novice* (Berkeley, Calif.: Peachpit Press, 1994).

CHAPTER THIRTEEN

Writing Advertising Copy

Advertising is ubiquitous. You go to the home page of Microsoft Internet Explorer or Netscape Communicator and ads pop up everywhere. You drive down streets lined with signs and billboards. Your radio station is likely to have commercials unless it is a public station and then you hear about sponsors. Television content is sometimes difficult to isolate from commercials, and in some cases the content is all commercial.

So, everyone knows what an ad looks like, you might think. Wrong. Sometimes you have to look carefully. Product advertising used to be fairly easy to identify. That's not the case now. Ads and promotional pieces often blend into a confusing composite.

Generally advertising agencies prepare the direct sales ads for products and services. Promotional pieces may be done by ad agencies or by PR companies. But as a PR writer, you are in the business of selling ideas. The result may look like editorials or features, or exactly like advertising.

Ads that promote ideas run the gamut in terms of content. Some, like the ad in Figure 13.1, address public policy issues. Sometimes ads like this are called *advertorials*. If they are presented in the broadcast or film media, they are often called *infomercials*. Other ads, as in Figures 13.2 and 13.3, simply present organizations as good corporate citizens. Such ads are often called *institutional, identity* or *corporate-image ads*.

Ads mistaken for features look just like their editorial counterpart. They have a story and art, often both pictures and graphics, like Figure 13.4. The difference is that the ads are paid for, and although they are clearly designated as advertising, readers often don't notice that they are not editorial copy.

If you are in charge of a special event you may have a whole section inserted in a newspaper or magazine. These inserts also look like editorial material except for their dedication to a single topic. Often a nonprofit organization will find a commercial sponsor for an event and its advertising.

Two other types of ads you'll be doing are public service ads and house ads. No money is exchanged in the placement of these pieces, but the two qualify in every other way as advertising.

Public service ads are ads that are carried at no charge in the print and broadcast media. When they appear on radio and television, public service ads are called public service announcements (PSAs). United Way, Girl Scouts, the American Heart Association and a wide variety of similar organizations and causes benefit from such ads. (See Figure 13.5.) PSAs also appear on the Internet. Global crises such as earthquakes, floods and droughts generate online appeals for help.

House ads are advertising messages that appear in a company's own publications. They may, for instance, urge employees to buy savings bonds or give blood or not to litter. Regardless of the sources or special purposes, ads always try to persuade.

F I G U R E   1 3 . 1

Public Policy Ad   *Ads attempting to influence public policy may originate with either nonprofit or profit making organizations. Shell often uses ads that resemble and read like editorials in publications like* Time *magazine. This ad, used with permission, is from the American Civil Liberties Union. The four-color ad appeared in* Vanity Fair *magazine. The copy below Take A Stand reads: "At the heart of freedom lie our basic civil rights. And we hold these rights to be sacred. It takes more than a display of pride to protect those rights. It takes action. LOG ON: ACLU.ORG."*

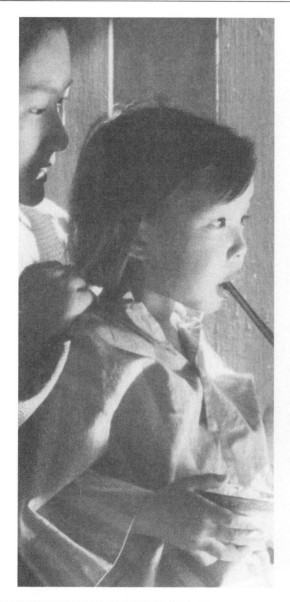

Biotechnology
researchers call it
"golden" rice.

For the color.
For the opportunity.

"When mothers and their children eat an adequate amount of vitamin A in a daily meal, it could help alleviate more suffering and illness than any single medicine has done."

The excitement expressed by plant biologist Charles Arntzen reflects the golden opportunity that many see in a new strain of rice being developed with biotechnology. "Golden" rice contains increased amounts of beta-carotene, a source of vitamin A. Because rice is a crop eaten by almost half the world, golden rice could help relieve a global vitamin A deficiency that now causes blindness and infection in millions of the world's children.

Discoveries in biotechnology, from medicine to agriculture, are helping doctors treat our sick, farmers protect our crops – and could help mothers nourish our children, and keep them healthier. To learn more about biotechnology and agriculture, visit our Web site or call us.

COUNCIL FOR
BIOTECHNOLOGY
INFORMATION

good ideas are growing

1-800-980-8660
www.whybiotech.com

FIGURE 13.2

Global Positioning for Biotech Crops   *Helping the world grow more nourishing rice is the Council for Biotechnology Information's positive positioning for biotech crops that do not have universal acceptance.*
Used by permission of the Council for Biotechnology Information.

FIGURE 13.3

Image Ad   *This ad from XTO Energy for a concert program booklet plays on words for the headline and the copy. The ad is also a good example of creativity with words only and no art, except the logo.*
Source: Used with permission of XTO Energy.

AN ADVERTISING SUPPLEMENT TO THE WASHINGTON POST NATIONAL WEEKLY

KOREA

Roh-Bush summit to cement strong ties

PRESIDENT ROH MOO-HYUN, who was sworn into his country's highest office in February this year, plans to use his summit with President George W. Bush today as an opportunity to reassure Washington of Seoul's unwavering commitment to their long-standing alliance.

His visit comes amid concerns over heightened tensions on the Korean peninsula caused by a bellicose Pyongyang which in recent months restarted its nuclear weapons program and in late April told an American official that it already posses a nuclear bomb.

President Roh took office with a commitment to pursue the engagement policy with the north of his predecessor, Kim Dae Jung, while sounding a note of caution over too rapid integration, in the light of expected heavy costs for the south.

He has also endorsed US policy towards the North, with one exception. He would like Washington to rule out a military option, something the American government has been unwilling to do, reserving the right to attack the North to destroy its nuclear capability.

President Roh told The Washington Post in an April 11 interview that, "Strategically, it's natural for the United States to take this approach, and I fully understand its position. But the reason I cannot say I agree with it in public is because it would become an unstable factor for the Korean economy."

In an April 29 speech to the 700 military engineers Korea has contributed to the reconstruction effort in Iraq, Roh said, "I've been persuading the countries involved under the conviction that war should not occur. I've maintained the coherent principle of resolving the North Korean nuclear issue peacefully."

His decision to send army units to Iraq, and to contribute $10 million to humanitarian relief efforts there, came against a backdrop of virulent opposition to the war by most Koreans. They are gestures intended to underline his personal

President Roh Moo-hyun

commitment to maintaining strong ties with Washington.

However, Korean companies, which have long experience in building major infrastructure projects in the Middle East, including Iraq, are interested in securing reconstruction contracts there now, in the aftermath of the war.

President Roh has said that he doubts North Korean assertions that it already possesses nuclear weapons, and he be-

Roh sees Korea as a worthy democratic partner for America

lieves that a policy of dialogue will bring about the results both sides say they seek: peaceful reunification.

He is fully aware of the impact the war on Iraq has had on Kim Jong Il, who heads the Stalinist regime in the North. "I'm sure they are very much terrified... petrified by the Iraqi war," he said in the same Post interview.

In his first official meeting with President Bush, President Roh will also seek to reassure Washington that Korea is a safe place to invest for American companies, despite the troubles with the North.

A centerpiece of his government's program is to make Korea the financial and trading hub of Northeast Asia, serving as a bridge between Japan, on one side, and northern China and eastern Russia, on the other.

Korea has long wanted to reverse its historical position as a battleground for rival Chinese and Japanese empires rising instead to become the central meeting point of commerce between the two.

With its physical infrastructure now highly developed, especially in transport and telecommunications, it is tackling obstacles to foreign investment and movement of capital of its financial market growing into a credible rival to Hong Kong and Singapore.

President Roh is a strong advocate of democracy and has made a name for himself as a leading campaigner against the endemic corruption that bedevils the Korean political system.

His vision is of Korea as a worthy democratic partner for America, a friendly beacon of peace and prosperity across the Pacific.

Roh wants Korea to be Northeast Asia hub

PRESIDENT ROH MOO-HYUN wants Korea to end its existence as a nation on the periphery of world affairs and to take its place as the hub of the rapidly-developing Northeast Asia region.

In his February 23 inauguration address this year, he mentioned the importance of the region over a dozen times, referring to a view held by some scholars that the 21st Century will be the Age of Northeast Asia.

He put Korea's opportunity this way: "For a long period of time, we have lived on the periphery. At times, we were forced to go through a history of dependence, unable to determine our own destiny. But, today we are at the threshold of a new turning point. The opportunity has come for us to take off as the hub of Northeast Asia. We should seize this opportunity."

seek solutions to problems "through dialogue and compromise, not through confrontation and conflict."

He applies this approach both to domestic politics, where inter-party rivalry is traditionally fierce, and to his approach to the regime in Pyongyang, which has for decades made bullying and brinkmanship the hallmarks of its public policy towards the south.

He believes part of the solution to perennial political troubles in the south is to decentralize power to the provinces and to move the administrative center of the national government from Seoul to a central area of Korea.

This would free Seoul to develop as a financial and commercial hub for the wider Northeast Asia region, a key ambition of his government.

Seoul has an opportunity to develop as a regional financial

The gleaming new Inchon International Airport serves the Seoul region.

Korea goes to the head of the class

IN LITTLE MORE than a generation, Korea has developed from an agrarian society into a world leader in cutting-edge technologies, and today it is the world's 12th largest exporter.

Perhaps the best indicator of this rapid development, which has taken Korea through the industrial age and into the information age in a rush of progress, can be seen in the fact that wireless telecommunications now rival semicon-

FIGURE 13.5

Public Service Ad   *Public service messages like this one from CARE are run free by the media. When they are in print media, they are called public service ads, but they are called public service announcements (PSAs) when aired on radio and television. The media run these messages on a space- or time-available basis.*
Source: Created for CARE by McCann-Erickson Atlanta. Used with permission.

Advertising as a Persuasive Force

Many people believe that advertising has the power to make people buy things they neither need nor want. If this were true, it would follow that advertising could be used by public relations professionals to make publics accept ideas they might otherwise reject. But advertisers will quickly tell you that advertising does not work that way.

Advertisers know that the power of advertising is limited to persuasion. It cannot coerce. Used skillfully, advertising may stimulate in an audience a predisposition to buy a product, use a service or accept an idea. Advertising has proved itself to be economically efficient at persuasion, because it works on the principle that you attract more bees with honey than with vinegar.

Appeal

The key element in a successful ad is the relevance of the appeal it has for the receiver of the message. This appeal should be as direct as possible. In writing ads, don't leave the appeal to inference. Spell it out. An appeal can be emotional, rational or a combination of the two.

Emotional appeals tug at the heart. They suggest that the receiver can become happier, healthier, prettier, sexier, more successful, more patriotic or richer in any number of other qualities if he or she behaves in a specific way. The number of emotional appeals open to the ad writer seems to be infinite. Note the emotional impact of the copy in Figure 13.6. Rational appeals, on the other hand, appeal to the receiver's reason. Such appeals are likely to be based on economy, durability, profit, efficiency and performance, among others, as seen in Figure 13.7.

Combination appeals use emotion first to get people to pay attention and then use rational appeals once the receivers are interested in the copy. The copy will usually close by returning to an appeal to the heart.

Positioning

A particular appeal works in concert with the marketing idea of "positioning the product." The writer expresses the appeal creatively in an attempt to carve out a special niche for the advertiser in the minds of the public. For example, Hertz has been the dominant rental car company for decades, with Avis in a distant second position. At some point, Avis decided to capitalize on its No. 2 position and appeal to the public's inclination to root for the underdog. In this way, the "We Try Harder" idea was born.

Viewed rationally, a Lexus is a Lexus, whether it has the Hertz logo or the Avis logo on it. If there is no significant difference in the rental fees and services offered by the two companies, why should you rent a Lexus from Avis rather than from Hertz? There is no rational reason. Avis makes an emotional appeal to the prospective customer by positioning itself in the public's mind as No. 2. Everybody knows that No. 2 has to try harder to be No. 1. Therefore, the suggestion is, you should rent the Lexus from Avis, because Avis tries harder. When employees bought the company, the slogan was modified to say "Owners Try Harder."

This principle of positioning was aptly applied when a major city wanted to pass an enormous bond program to rebuild and improve an extensive portion of one of its oldest freeways.

FIGURE 13.6

Emotional Appeal   *Extraordinary customer service is a form of "bonding" for a company to its customers. You expect "wake-up" calls from a hotel, but your mail-order house? Used with permission of Lands' End.*

FIGURE 13.7

Rational Appeal   *A rational appeal generally is used with high-value products, and certainly the company handling your investments is one from which you want some assurance of the company's own values and standards. American Century's ad accomplishes that and reinforces its conservative image.*

Used with permission of American Century and Michele Clement Photography.

Each time they were asked, voters denied the bonds. On its last try, the city launched a "safety bond" program to finance the project. Positioning it as a safety project focused attention on its benefit rather than on its cost. The issue passed by a comfortable margin.

Behavior

Understanding what people think and do in different parts of society is critical to developing credible advertising. Good advertising writers understand that there may be a little bit (and perhaps a lot) of snob in all of us, because we like to relate to others and have others relate to us. Behaviorists spend a lot of time trying to understand our reference groups—organizations to which we belong or want to belong. We all want the comfort of belonging, of being accepted. For this reason, friends and family are important to us, and we seek their approval. We are also influenced by opinion leaders. Different segments of society have different opinion leaders, and each of us reacts to those leaders differently based on our own personality. For example, authoritarian types are more vulnerable to leaders who have status and authority.

If you are getting the idea that people don't respond rationally to a lot of advertising copy, you are right. Most of the decisions we make are based on emotion, not reason. That is why good advertising copy is a complex blend of information (facts) and appeal (emotion).

Basic Guidelines for Writing Advertising Copy

Advertising copywriters are often believed to have a great deal more creative freedom than most other writers because they work under few artificial restraints. For example, you might view writing a news release as less creative than writing copy for an ad, because in the former case you must conform to newswriting style. But there are rules and restraints on ad copywriting too.

Purpose

To begin with, you must have a clear understanding of what you want to accomplish with the ad. Do you want your public to support the bond issue? Do you want shareholders to vote for the recapitalization of the company? You must know the single (never multiple) specific purpose for the ad. And everything you put in the ad should contribute to that purpose. In editing the ad, delete as excess baggage any word, phrase, sentence, paragraph or visual that does not specifically further the purpose. The receiver should not have to wrestle with excess baggage in discerning the message you are trying to communicate.

Objective Facts

You'll be able to select a specific purpose for the ad only after carefully and thoroughly reviewing all the pertinent facts about the issue. You should review these facts not only from your side's point of view but also from that of your opposition. In fact, the latter review is just as important as the former. And both reviews have to be done with objectivity. Only then can you make an informed judgment about the strengths and weaknesses of your position and those of your competition. And only then should you attempt to derive a purpose calculated to capitalize on one of your strengths or to attack one of the opposition's weaknesses.

The Publics

You should review the facts and select a purpose for the ad with a full awareness of the uniqueness of your public. You need to know their wants, needs and values. This is where demographic and psychographic information assumes great importance. If the members of your public are blue collar, average less than a median income, have a ninth-grade education and suffer from a high rate of unemployment, you may have difficulty in persuading them to support a large bond program to build a junior college in the community. This doesn't mean you won't be successful in gaining their support, but it does mean that you will have to write credible messages that clearly demonstrate the rewards such support will bring.

Media

Before you write the copy, you must know which medium or media you are writing for. One of your first concerns, of course, is to meet the technical requirements of the medium. An ad prepared for a newspaper may not meet the requirements of a magazine, and it certainly won't meet those of radio or television or the Internet. If you are writing ads for a medium with which you are unfamiliar, first check the technical requirements in the most recent issue of *Standard Rate and Data Service (SRDS)*. *SRDS* will also provide you with deadline information, a list of key personnel and other data. *SRDS* is one of the bibles of the advertising business.

Beyond technical issues, you need to know a lot about the medium you will use. How credible is it? How evocative is it? How do people react to it? What audience does it reach? What audience does it seek? What is its editorial slant? What have other advertisers experienced who have used it in similar situations? These are important questions, and you must know—not guess at—the answers. In some cases you may have to rely on word-of-mouth, but in other cases you will be able to gather a lot of information from the medium itself simply by writing or calling.

The Creative Approach

Never try to develop a creative approach or write a line of copy until after you have made the decisions specified above. These decision areas are parts of what advertising professionals call a *copy platform*. A copy platform is a succinct document that spells out pertinent information about the public and contains a simple statement of creative strategy. For example, a creative-strategy statement for a little-known candidate running for senator against an incumbent might read like this:

> To convince voters that Mr. X will represent the views of eastern Kentuckians better than Mr. Y.

This statement clearly expresses your purpose (strategy). The question then becomes: How will I do it? That's where creativity comes in.

Let's suppose that Mr. Y is noted for being absent from the Senate floor when important bills that may affect eastern Kentuckians are up for a vote. You could construct a series of ads in which Mr. X pledges to be in the Senate chamber during every important vote. The voters would probably want to hear this message, though they might consider the claim to be mere political rhetoric.

You could take the offensive and attack Mr. Y by showing his empty chair during a roll call. You could then support the point with a table, showing not only the bills on which Mr. Y did not cast votes but also the number and dates of his absences. In other words, you could provide a lot of solid, verifiable, convincing information that Mr. Y is not doing his job properly. Still another approach might be to show Mr. X, dressed in hunting garb and following some coonhounds on the scent. Mr. X would look up and explain that he and his "dawgs" were looking for Mr. Y. An obvious close would be a superimposed message like this:

Where *is* Mr. Y? Vote for Mr. X. You will always find him in the Senate.

Of these three approaches, the first is mundane. It is low on persuasiveness because there is nothing unique about its claim. The ad neither excites the emotions nor challenges the reason. The second ad is more creative, and it contains lots of convincing and damning information about Mr. Y. It is more likely to be persuasive. But the third approach, which is obviously best executed for television, is not only more creative but it is also dramatically persuasive. How could a voter see that ad and remain free of resentment toward Mr. Y? And as resentment builds, voters will be more easily persuaded to vote for Mr. X. Emotion is the essence of good creativity in advertising.

Visualization

As you read the discussion on creative approaches, it may have occurred to you that creative strategy in advertising involves visual as well as verbal thinking. If so, you caught on to an essential difference between writing news copy and writing advertising copy. A good advertising copywriter always thinks in visual as well as verbal terms. The reason the hunting example just described is so dramatic is that the visual element graphically characterizes the verbal message. In the best advertising copy, verbal and visual content harmonize perfectly so that each complements and extends the message of the other. See how visuals take the reader through the message in Figure 13.8.

Language

It is axiomatic that, if you want to communicate with someone, you must use language that the other person will understand. Language has certain rules, and if they are not generally observed, communication may be impossible or the result unwanted. Thus the common rules of grammar and syntax are the standard in advertising, as they are in other forms of writing. You can break a grammar rule for a purpose—for example, to achieve a specific effect not possible with traditional rules—but doing so should be the exception, not the rule.

Always choose the simple over the complex word. Your public might be able to read and comprehend at the college-graduate level, but people generally prefer to read copy that is two to four grade levels below their ability. And if you have any doubt about the educational level of your audience, you should gear your writing to about three grade levels lower than you believe it to be. Obviously, if you are writing an idea ad for your company that will appear in a highly specialized professional journal, you should use language appropriate to that public.

FIGURE 13.8

Art and Copy   *In this Menlo ad the old map captures the reader's curiosity and a provocative headline draws the reader into the copy for the worldwide shipping and distribution company.*
Source: Used with permission of Menlo Worldwide.

This may mean using some professional jargon. If your ad is to appear in a general mass medium, however, simplify the language and avoid jargon.

Not only should you use simple words, you should also use short phrases, sentences and paragraphs. Sentences should average no longer than 12 to 15 words. Paragraphs should average about three to five sentences. Following these guidelines will improve your writing's readability.

Repetition

Do you recall the outcome of Pavlov's experiment with his dogs? As the number of repetitions mounted, the dogs began to associate the meat powder with the sound of the tuning fork. When the repetitions were plotted on a graph, a learning curve took shape. Finally, the curve leveled; that is, after a while additional repetitions did not cause the learning curve to go higher. Thus repetition is an essential principle of learning. You can apply this principle to your message in two basic ways.

The repetition principle applies first to the actual writing of copy. The general rule is that you should repeat the essential point of your message at least three times in your ad. This does not mean that you have to repeat it verbatim, but only that you must repeat the idea. This is absolutely crucial in broadcast messages, because they are so fleeting.

The principle of repetition also applies to how frequently you repeat the message to your public and in what time frame. Generally, if you are introducing a new program or idea, you will have to present your message fairly frequently during the early stages of your program. As your audience becomes familiar with what you are promoting, you can reduce the number of presentations and space them out, while still maintaining a reasonable level of awareness.

When your campaign ends, the public will begin to forget at approximately the same rate at which it learned. Still, the public's awareness about what you said will not drop back to zero. Hence, it will take less effort in a subsequent campaign to raise public awareness to former levels. This is a good argument for sustained programming, of course, because it suggests that sustaining awareness is more efficient than building it.

These general guidelines apply across all media and in all copywriting situations. Now let's review some guidelines for specific media.

Copywriting for Broadcast and Film Media

Brevity, clear style and sharp technique are the hallmarks of good broadcast and film copywriting. Specific time frames vary among stations, but you will usually write for periods lasting 10 seconds (25 words), 20 seconds (45 words), 30 seconds (65 words) or 60 seconds (125 words). Word count is approximate. Count it! The actual word limits may vary a little from radio to television to film, but in any case you have to tell a complete story in just a few well-chosen words. This is seldom easy.

Because an audience's attention is easily distracted, your copy must be simple, direct and provocative. Avoid clichés and slang. Be careful to make smooth transitions from one point to the next. Personalize the message by emphasizing "you" at every opportunity. People are more likely to respond personally to a message if they think it is directed to them. So try to write your copy as if it were a personal conversation between you and a friend.

Avoid exaggerated claims; don't make any claims that you wouldn't make to your closest friend. Your persuasive appeal must be distinctive so that your audience will remember it when they see or hear it again.

You must capture the attention of your audience in the first few seconds or you will lose it completely. Be sure to register the name of the company or organization, and let the audience know what you want it to do. A sense of urgency may help move the audience to action.

Radio, television and film have different technical capabilities, of course, but some styles of message presentation are common to all three media. One is the "slice of life," which is a mini-drama that presents a situation anyone might experience. It provides the context for the message.

Another is the jingle approach, in which music and words are combined to make the message memorable, identifiable and entertaining. A humorous approach is appropriate in any of these media. This may include anything from a cartoon (television or film) to a joke (usually radio only) to a mini-sitcom (situation comedy). The difficulty with humor is in finding universal themes that will not go stale quickly. And remember, never make your audience the butt of the humor.

Another technique is the interview. Here an announcer talks with representative members of your public. Still another approach is the testimonial. If you use a testimonial approach, however, be sure to establish the credibility of the people testifying. Otherwise, the audience will tune out your message.

You can use sound effects with any or all of these approaches. And you can combine the techniques themselves in some fashion.

Television and film have the additional benefit of permitting visual demonstration. This may be done through live action, animation or a combination of the two. In writing for television or film, consider the visual aspect carefully.

Your choice of a copy approach will depend above all on your resources—that is, money and facilities. Be prepared for the frustration that comes when you have to reject a creative idea because you can't afford to realize it. As you consider various techniques, you may want to review what others have done in similar situations. You won't want to copy from them, but you should not hesitate to adapt ideas that have worked for others.

Public Service Announcements

If you write much advertising for broadcast media, it is likely to consist mostly of public service announcements (PSAs). To do PSAs well, you must decide first whether your primary purpose is to *inform* or to *persuade.* If it is mostly to inform, you'll need to amass lots of information, sift it wisely and use it selectively. You must be able to say a lot in a little time. If the purpose is to persuade, you'll still need information, but you'll put more emphasis on its interpretation. And you'll arrange it so it has the maximum persuasive impact.

A variation on these two purposes is a "positioning" PSA. Think of the safety bond program described earlier. That was essentially an exercise in positioning or focusing people's attention on safety rather than cost. A positioning PSA seeks to position an idea in some unique way against all other related ideas. Effective positioning can have a significant impact on what people understand, accept, reject or feel about something. It also may influence what they recall and how they associate it with other relevant information.

Whatever your purpose, PSAs for nonprofit organizations can be created on elaborately produced videotapes, film with sound, some types of pictures with audiocassette, audiocassette only or computer-generated pieces on a CD-ROM. Many organizations' national headquarters provide their own PSAs in these forms, and they usually leave room for a tagline to be added at the local level. More often, however, PSAs are produced locally for local agencies. Because the agency is begging for the broadcast time—and occasionally for the production time too—most PSA scriptwriters try to keep things simple. (See Figure 13.9.)

For television PSAs, local agencies may provide film or video footage to be edited as the visual for the PSA. A station announcer or a local personality may volunteer services to do the audio. If the volunteer is a local personality, you should write the script to match as closely as possible that personality's style of speaking.

The visual part of the PSA could be a set of slides supplied to the station, with a script to be read by a station announcer. If the script has too many words to permit good delivery, it is likely to be thrown away. You should realize how little control you really have over whether your message will be broadcast. Your best assurance is to write an infallible script.

PSAs are more likely to be read live on radio than on television. Scripts, without a cassette, are sent to the local station. If the script is no good, local announcers will often improvise, but if improvisation does not work, the script will be thrown out. To guard against this, listen to the announcers who might read your PSA, study their styles and write for their rate of delivery. If you are in doubt, *under*-write—that is, use fewer words.

Copywriting for Television and Film

When writing copy for television or film, imagine how your ad will look as well as how it will sound. This will help make the message stronger and more persuasive. Remember that you have to think visually and verbally.

Divide your paper down the middle so that you have two equal columns. Label the left column "description" and the right column "script." In the right column, begin to write the words you want your public to hear. Concentrate on the single, basic idea of the message, and remember to promise your public some reward—a benefit that is both explained and supported.

Now go back and polish what you have written. Pare away unneeded words, phrases and sentences. Get the verbal message into what you consider finished form. Then have someone read the script aloud to you. Make sure the reader doesn't study the message beforehand, but reads it "cold." Listening to your copy being read aloud by someone else will help you to spot parts that need to be corrected, eliminated or rearranged.

Now repeat the process, this time working down the left side and describing the visuals that are to accompany the verbal message. Make certain that the visual images match and interpret their verbal counterparts. In some cases, you may be working from a prepared television script sheet, like the one in Figure 13.10.

Remember that television and film are visual media and that one of their strengths is action. Avoid static scenes. If the image does not move, the audience will shift its attention to

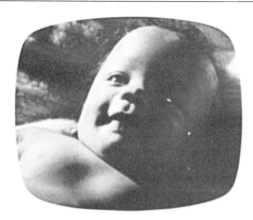

MALE V/O: Oh, she has her daddy's smile . . .

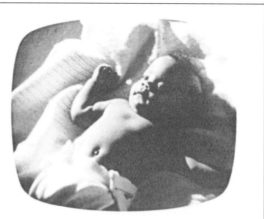

FEMALE V/O: and her grandmama's eyes . . .

V/O: and her mother's AIDS.

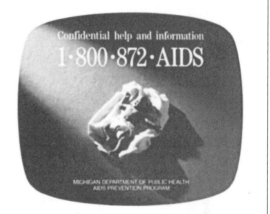

Don't share a bed with someone who shares a needle.

FIGURE 13.9

Public Service Announcement for Television   *This 10-second PSA, done by Brogan and Partners of Southfield, Michigan, for the Michigan Department of Health, AIDS Prevention Program, delivers a message like a karate punch—swift and hard. It uses finished art—hence, it is called a presentation storyboard—to show the sequential development of nonverbal and verbal content. (V/O means voice-over.)*
Source: Reprinted by permission of Brogan and Partners.

something more interesting. You must pay attention to the visual, but don't become so carried away with it that you forget the message you want to convey.

In television, it is common to carry the aforementioned process a step further and create a storyboard. Figures 13.9 and 13.11 illustrate this idea. The storyboard depicts graphically what you have described down the left side of your script sheet. Although an artist is often

CLIENT: TIME:
                                 DATE:
TITLE: WRITER:

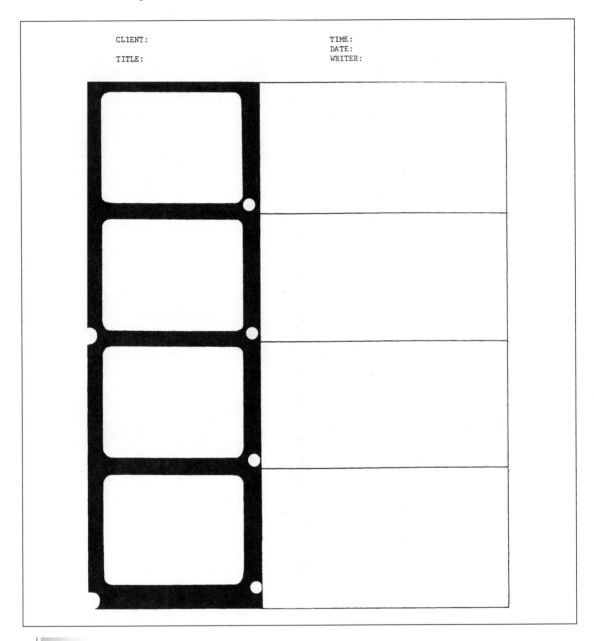

FIGURE 13.10

Blank Television Script Sheet   *This blank television script sheet may be helpful to writers as they try to conceptualize how words and visuals fit together to form a cohesive, effective message. Review the message in Figure 13.9 to see how well it fits this model.*

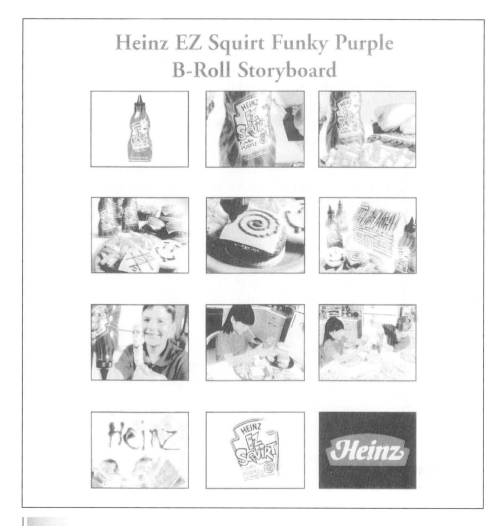

(Heinz EZ Squirt Funky Purple B-Roll Storyboard — Used with permission of Heinz.)

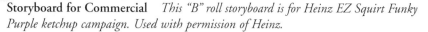

FIGURE 13.11

Storyboard for Commercial   *This "B" roll storyboard is for Heinz EZ Squirt Funky Purple ketchup campaign. Used with permission of Heinz.*

assigned the job of making a storyboard, many copywriters find it is helpful to make their own, using stick figures to properly sequence the visuals. They often write their copy under each frame so they can better judge its unity. Internet ads must be carefully planned also, as these involve color, movement and sound.

Copywriting for Radio

Approach copywriting for radio as you would that for television and film—by dividing your paper and labeling the columns to make a script sheet. That is simple enough, but writing really good radio copy is more difficult than writing for television or film. In television and film, you have visual images to help you convey your message. In radio you have only the visual theater of the mind. Although this is a vast territory, it is one in which many copywriters get lost.

Begin your copy in the right-hand column. You'll have to search especially hard for just the right words to evoke the images you want to paint in the public's collective mind. That is, you'll have to imagine exactly what you want the public to see. Language can be your best ally or your worst enemy. It will be the latter if you use uncommon words, especially those that have regional or local usages. Be wary of these. Also be cautious about using dialects.

Once you have written the message in the right-hand column, have someone read it "cold" so you can listen for semantic traps. Verify that the mental images you evoke unfold in a logical, easy-to-follow sequence, or you'll lose your listeners. You'll need to build excitement and drama, but be sure to drive home the message by repeating it at least three times in the script.

With the verbal content completed, work in the left-hand column providing complete cues regarding music, volume changes, announcers, sound effects and similar production concerns. Check your descriptions against the verbal messages in the right-hand column to make sure they match. (See Figure 13.12.)

Although most commercials are prerecorded, some are read live. If you distribute your ad to stations in script form to be read live, make sure the words are simple to pronounce and flow smoothly, so the announcers will not foul up the announcement by mispronouncing them. Placing the wrong inflection on a word or phrase can distort the message by giving copy elements the wrong emphasis. The safest step is to prerecord your spots. This applies to television and film as well.

Broadcast Production Relationships

Your role as writer may not end with the completion of a script. You may find yourself involved in a working relationship with production professionals. If you're in an agency, someone in account services will likely assume the role of being the liaison with production specialists. If not, or if you're not in an agency, you may be called on to coordinate production of your script with these people. You need not be a production expert to do this.

Key Players   There are certain specialists who are critical to the successful production of your video or audio script. You must clearly understand their functions and establish good working relationships with them. Good relationships are built on mutual professionalism, respect and attention to detail. Who are these people, and what do they do?

Executive Producer   This person is in charge of one or more projects or programs. The executive producer coordinates with clients, station or corporate management, advertising and public relations agencies, investors, talent (and their agents, if they have them) and approves and manages the production budget. This person's word is final. Get to know him or her well. If problems arise, the executive producer can be your best ally or worst enemy.

Producer   The producer is the person who will directly supervise the production of your script. He or she has direct supervision of all the production personnel working on your script and coordinates all of the technical and nontechnical elements. In larger operations, there may

---

"FREIGHT TRAIN" :30 SECONDS

MUSIC: *Ominous and Foreboding Music*

SFX: *Distant Train Horn*

MALE V/O: *"It's coming again."*
                  "In seconds it will be here."
                  "Your heart pounds."
                  "You can't breathe."
                  "You're terrified."

SFX: *Train Horn Getting Louder and Swiftly Closing In*

MALE V/O: *"You're sure you're about to die."*

SFX: *Pounding Heartbeat*

FEMALE ANNCR:

For people with Panic Disorder, this is how it feels to have a panic attack. Find out how you can get help. Call 1-800-64-PANIC. 1-800-64-PANIC. Panic Disorder. It's real. It's treatable. A public service message from this station and the National Institute of Mental Health.

FADE OUT

FIGURE 13.12

Public Service Announcement for Radio   *The National Institute of Mental Health Panic Disorder Education Program produced its "Freight Train" PSA in 30- and 60-second versions. The two are identical up to the segment in which a female announcer reads the copy. SFX refers to sound effect.*
Source: NIMH Panic Disorder Education Program, Radio Public Service Announcements, Spring/Summer 1994. Used with permission.

be *associate producers* (APs) who share some of the producer's responsibilities. In small production houses or stations, the producer may also double as a writer and/or director.

Studio and Field Producers   In large operations, producers may have different assignments. Studio producers supervise only studio productions. Field producers are assigned to on-location, out-of-studio field productions.

Director   This is the key person to direct all talent in the production and technical operations. The director is also the key to transforming your script into effective video and/or audio messages. In smaller production houses or stations, the director may also serve as the producer.

Bidding   When your script is approved by the client, it will probably be put out for bids. Invitations to bid can vary extensively in their complexity. Depending on the nature and

---

"FREIGHT TRAIN" :60 SECONDS

MUSIC: *Ominous and Foreboding Music*

SFX: *Distant Train Horn*

MALE V/O: *"It's coming again."*
                    "In seconds it will be here."
                    "Your heart pounds."
                    "You can't breathe."
                    "You're terrified."

SFX: *Train Horn Getting Louder and Swiftly Closing In*

MALE V/O: *"You're sure you're about to die."*

SFX: *Pounding Heartbeat*

FEMALE ANNCR:

This is how it feels to have a panic attack. And for millions of Americans with Panic Disorder, attacks happen over and over again. They come out of the blue. They don't last long. But they can change your life. Trips to the emergency room and medical tests may show nothing's wrong. But you know there is.

If you think you have Panic Disorder, find out how you can get help. Call 1-800-64-PANIC. 1-800-64-PANIC. Panic Disorder. It's real. It's treatable.

A public service message from this station and the National Institute of Mental Health.

FADE OUT

▌ **1 3 . 1 2   (c o n t i n u e d)**

length of your script, bids may be sought from video production houses, audio production houses, film production houses, television station studios or radio station studios.

If you're lucky the winning bidder will be close by, so that eye contact with a minimum of telephone discussions and travel is possible and desirable. But the winning bid may come from a distant source, making substantial travel more likely. In that context, it is more difficult to build and sustain good working relationships with production specialists. But getting what you want is the point, not the difficulty of getting it. Simply remember that professionalism, respect and attention to details are critical.

Copywriting for Print Media

Some general guidelines apply to ad copywriting for the print media. These guidelines turn on the concepts of attention, interest, desire, credibility and action, sometimes referred to as AIDCA. Let's look at each of these concepts separately.

Attention

It is axiomatic that, to communicate a message to a public, you must first command attention. Two elements of a print ad perform the attention-getting function: the headline and the visual design. Although some argue the point, most great copywriters believe that the headline is the single most important element in an ad, period. The headline is the element most often responsible for stopping readers and luring them into the ad. A terrific visual may do this too, but it is the headline that makes the greatest and most lasting impact. Of course, the visual elements should be harmonious with the headline and its content. A good headline offers a promise to the reader. More often than not, it spells out a benefit to the reader as well. And it does this provocatively so that the reader will pay attention.

The visual, in addition to gaining attention, helps to amplify the content of the headline. Thus the headline and the visual express the same message in different ways. Remember the principle of repetition mentioned earlier in this chapter? Showing the message is a way of repeating what the headline says. Whether verbally or visually, however, the message must convey—powerfully but simply—some benefit to the reader. Ads with the greatest attention-getting value are those that speak to the reader's self-interest.

The use of color can help gain attention. When you buy advertising space, however, remember that the use of color costs extra. This may affect your budget, so check the costs before you commit yourself to using color. Though color generally increases attention, it does not necessarily increase readership or retention of your message.

Interest

Remember that, by offering a benefit, the headline stops the reader. Thus the next phase is to heighten the reader's interest. You can do this by making sure that the first sentence or paragraph of the copy flows naturally from the headline and expands on the headline's promise. For example, suppose your company is launching a recapitalization program. The success of this program will depend on whether a majority of stockholders support the program. Many stockholders, if not most, don't really understand recapitalization, so they are not necessarily apt to return a ballot. Your task is to make the program appealing enough so that they will want to find out more about the benefits to them of supporting the issue. An attention-getting headline in this case might be:

HOW TO INCREASE YOUR INVESTMENT IN [NAME OF COMPANY] BY 36%

That headline would attract the attention of any investor. The task now is to get the reader to understand the how-to. That becomes the function of your copy, especially the first sentence or first paragraph. This must tie in directly to the headline itself. Thus the first paragraph of your copy might read:

> Each of your shares in [name of company] will increase from $50 to $68 if you support the recapitalization program recommended by the board of directors.

If you owned stock in this company and you received this message, you would pay attention to it, because you would recognize how much money you could make by merely marking a "yes" on your ballot. The headline and first paragraph would speak your language. It would clearly be in your self-interest to pay attention to what the company was saying to you. That is the essence of "interest" in good advertising copy.

Desire

Once you have developed self-interest, the next step is to talk about why the idea is desirable. You can do this by filling in details of the plan in subsequent paragraphs: Describe what the plan is, why it is needed, how it will benefit the company and its shareholders and when it will go into effect, and supply other supporting bits of information. This part of the copy promotes the idea that the suggested action is a desirable thing to do.

Credibility

Even if your message is provocative, your public may not believe it. The cardinal rule in this regard is to be as specific as you can. Note the specifics in the preceding headline. The line did not say "about 36%"; it said "36%" specifically. And the first paragraph of the copy did not equivocate on the dollar increase per share. It was very specific: "from $50 to $68." There is no room in this instance for misunderstanding the message. Never leave to inference what you want the reader to know. All your copy should reflect that same degree of specificity. If you hedge your claim, the reader will spot it immediately and begin to discount what you say. So be specific, concrete and direct. You will more likely be believed, even if the reader decides against your point of view.

It also pays to remember that truth is sometimes stranger than fiction and more difficult to believe. This can be a major problem when you are asking readers to accept something that defies common experience—even if it is entirely truthful.

Action

Action is the "bottom line" in advertising. You are paying for the space in which to present your message. Therefore, it makes sense for you to ask the reader to do something. Action is not as important in some idea ads (especially ones that simply want to convey a positive image of the company) as it is for product ads. But in some idea ads, such as the preceding example, you want your readers to take an action—in this case, to support the recapitalization program. It would be at least a partial waste of the company's money if you did not ask the reader to do something specific. For example, you might close the ad by saying that a ballot will be in the mail tomorrow and asking the reader to mark it and return it immediately in the postage-paid envelope. That kind of close to the ad would leave no doubt as to what course of action you want the reader to take.

Now that we have reviewed these points about copywriting for print media, let's look at each print medium separately.

Copywriting for Newspapers

Newspaper advertising falls into two categories: display and classified. Display advertising is the advertising that does not appear in the classified portion of the newspaper.

For display advertising, words and visuals must provide a unified message, as audio and video do in television commercials. Newspapers are read hurriedly and have a fairly brief life. So it's a waste to use words and visuals just because they look or sound good. If they don't have a purpose in the ad, they should be deleted. Readers won't read "fat" ads, because they don't have the time. Although newspapers are known as a mass rather than a class (or selective) medium, they can saturate a specific geographic market more thoroughly than magazines, radio or television. And even though a newspaper is mass in appeal, some segmentation of audiences typically occurs through features and special sections, such as the sports or business section.

Display   Display advertising is especially good at promoting an immediate demand for products or services or achieving the acceptance of ideas. It works if you have a unified concept to convey designed along the lines of the earlier AIDCA discussion. The size of the space you buy will determine the proportions and sizes of the headline, copy, visuals, logos and other elements of the ad.

How much space to buy is a critical decision, for it determines how much competition for readers' attention there will be on the page where your ad appears. If you buy a full page, there will be no competing message on the page. If you buy a half page, there are likely to be two or three other competing messages—in addition to the editorial matter—all clamoring for the reader's attention. The smaller the space you buy, the greater the competition for attention on the page.

Most newspaper ads are for local companies and are addressed to local readers. A good copywriter takes advantage of the research information about both the medium and its market and tries to tailor a message that will "fit" the market. Of course, national advertisers who use newspapers ordinarily can't tailor their ads to this degree. They might run the same ad simultaneously in newspapers all across the country. Remember, though: If you have the opportunity, write your ad with the local market in mind.

Classified   Most classified advertising sections contain excellent examples of creativity in the use of a limited number of words. Classifieds are also big business on the Internet. Ads in these sections are not for garage sales alone. Classified ads are used extensively by real estate agencies and transportation- and recreation-related companies. A professional copywriter for an agency is likely to prepare hundreds of classified ads for clients. The technique employed here is simply to determine how many words you can get into a specific space. Deduct from this count the number of words that you *must* include—such as the company's name, address and telephone number—and compose your message with the number of words left. Read the classified columns before you begin writing, to help you appreciate the ingenuity of others and to learn the accepted abbreviations in that market. In the process, you'll also find out what your competitors are doing.

Copywriting for Magazines

Magazine audiences are highly specialized. Specific magazines appeal to particular types of people, regardless of where they live. Magazine advertising copy should exploit this specificity in magazine audiences. Both demographic and psychographic information are relevant here.

Although magazine readers do not necessarily devote immense amounts of time to reading magazines at a single sitting, they usually put them aside for rereading as their time and interests dictate. When writing ad copy for a particular magazine, you may want to get in touch with the sales-promotion department for specialized information on the readership.

In writing your magazine ad, you should know its size and placement before you actually begin. Magazine space is ordinarily sold by the page or by a fraction or multiple of a page. It is possible to buy a special position for your ad, but you'll have to pay a premium for it, and that can run up the cost in a hurry. Be aware that most magazines allow, and even expect, a higher level of reproduction quality than newspapers exhibit, especially in the use of color and highly creative visual materials.

Look at several issues of the specific magazine your ad will appear in before you begin writing, so you can get a feel for its character and the tone of its advertising content. Then check the editorial bent of the magazine. These inspections may cue you to use or avoid a particular approach.

Like those in newspaper ads, the verbal and visual elements in magazine ads should be complementary, not disjointed.

Public Service Ads   Both newspapers and magazines run public service ads for nonprofit organizations and causes. (See Figure 13.5.) If you are preparing one of these ads for use by these media, observe all the rules that apply to ads you would buy. Remember, you are asking these media to give your message a free ride. If you want your ad run, play by the rules. Be as helpful as you can. You're not buying. You're asking—and hoping.

House Ads   Newspapers and magazines run house ads on a space-available basis. Although no money changes hands, the promotion department of the medium is often given a budget for this purpose. It is then the department's responsibility to prepare various house ads and to have them available to run on demand. Some house ads, however, are scheduled as if they were paid ads. These usually promote the magazine or newspaper as a good medium in which companies can reach a market or an audience. Or they may promote subscriptions (particularly in newspapers) or the use of the classified ad section. Even though these are house ads, they are written and prepared just as other ads are.

Copywriting for Web Pages

News and advertising professionals in traditional media have a history of separating news, entertainment and advertising. That does not hold true for the Internet. Commercial messages, known as banner ads, pop up in some of the most unexpected places. In other cases they are integrated into the news or entertainment program content so that it is seamless. Separation generally does not exist on the Internet. As one example among many, the travel page on CNNfn's financial news blends travel articles with reservation services and promotions from a sponsoring travel agency. And such sites as Amazon.com present promotional pieces thinly disguised as book reviews. In addition, many of the Internet search services now put all sorts of links to advertisers above and to the side of actual search results.

Most ads on the Internet don't resemble what we see in other media. They are stripped-down, quick bursts of information with a simple message and a visual. And because of the blending of content, in many cases it is difficult to know what is an ad and what is not. Writing advertising for some Web uses is somewhat like writing for an outdoor poster. It is short—often fewer than 10 words. But if the message is integrated into program content, then it may be somewhat lengthy. It also must fit the style and thrust of program content. Hence, building an ad to be integrated limits the creative latitude copywriters ordinarily have. And space for the display of ad messages on computer screens is always limited. Therefore, good copy for Web sites should avoid overuse of adjectives, adverbs and conditional clauses. We recommend that you review Web page reading habits in Chapter 14 before you attempt to construct an ad for the Internet.

Copywriting for Direct Response and Direct Advertising

The severest test of your ability as a copywriter is whether you can write effective direct-response or direct-advertising copy.

Copy that is designed to promote direct action by the audience is called *direct-response copy*. It is the type of message that urges people to take immediate action such as mailing in a coupon, calling an 800 number, entering a sweepstakes or figuratively raising their hands and saying, "Hey, we're interested."

Direct-response copy can appear in most any medium. The key is not the type of medium in which the message appears, but the type of message conveyed. If it urges the audience to do something now, it is direct-response copy. For example, a commercial on television from Publishers Clearing House touts its subscriptions and provides an incentive by offering fabulous sweepstakes prizes. All you have to do is to call a toll-free number, but you have to call *now*.

Direct-advertising copy appears in written, printed or processed form and is sent via a controlled method of circulation to individuals. There are three types of direct advertising: direct mail, mail order and unmailed direct advertising.

Direct Mail   This covers all forms of mailed direct advertising, except mail order. It includes letters, postcards, booklets, broadsides, brochures, circulars, catalogs and stuffers, among others.

Mail Order   Mail-order copy is responsible for the entire "selling" job. It may appear in a variety of forms, from catalogs such as L. L. Bean to a letter urging the recipient to give to the Disabled American Veterans.

Unmailed Direct Advertising   Unmailed direct-advertising copy differs from direct mail and mail order only in its method of distribution. It includes promotional pieces that may be delivered to a person's home or may be picked up in a store, showroom, fair or exhibit or at any other site allowing promotional efforts.

All forms of direct-advertising copy are especially difficult to write effectively because you have to create the medium as well as the message. You don't have the support of a preselected audience from the standard media.

Each message has to stand alone and produce results. In fact, success is carefully measured by the number of responses generated. These can be in any number of forms—for example, coupons, orders or queries—and the response rate measures precisely how much action you have generated with your writing. Once you have designed and written a successful ad that has proved itself, you are not likely to change it very much in the future.

Obviously, the overall design of coupons, order forms and related material has to be very good, so that people can respond easily.

Copywriting for Out-of-Home Media

The term *out-of-home media* refers to a variety of media—outdoor, transit, skywriting and the like. The key feature they share is that readers go to them rather than the other way around. This characteristic imposes severe constraints on what you can say and how you can say it. Each out-of-home medium is unique, but the general guidelines for outdoor media apply to all.

There are two basic kinds of outdoor billboards: the poster panel and the painted bulletin. Poster panels, which are printed on large printing presses, are a standard size: 12 feet 3 inches by 24 feet 6 inches. Three sizes of messages can fit onto these panels. A 24-sheet poster measures 8 feet 8 inches by 19 feet 6 inches; a 30-sheet poster measures 9 feet 7 inches by 21 feet 7 inches; and a 30-sheet bleed panel measures 10 feet 5 inches by 22 feet 8 inches. The 24-sheet poster panel has been the standard in the medium for decades, but currently the 30-sheet panel is replacing it.

The "sheet" unit of measurement has its roots in the time when it took 24 or 30 sheets of paper to cover a panel. Printing presses are larger today, so most panels can be covered with from 10 to 15 sheets.

Many advertisers use poster panels routinely, changing their messages monthly or several times a year and advertising in many markets simultaneously. Once the cost of designing and producing the panel is absorbed, the costs become incrementally smaller as additional sites or markets are used.

The painted bulletin, as the name indicates, is painted by hand. It goes on a board measuring 14 feet by 48 feet. An advertiser will use "paints" only when cultivating one or a very few markets and when the message will not be changed within a year. Usually an advertiser will not use more than two or three painted bulletins, or "paints," in a specific market, depending on the size of the market.

Outdoor advertising—called *outdoor* for short—is remarkably cost-effective when you need to saturate a market with an idea. The price of an outdoor campaign is based on what are called *showings*. A 100-show is a campaign in which enough panels, including some illuminated for night viewing, are set up to provide 100 percent coverage of the mobile market for a 30-day period. Studies show that it is not unusual for a 100-show to produce a high level of message repetitions—an average of 25 or more per month. A 50-show thus would involve half the coverage and repetition of a 100-show.

Copywriting is especially difficult for outdoor. Because your message may be seen for only a second or two, it has to be especially simple and compelling to register with the viewer. As a general rule, you can't use more than about eight words, including the company's name, and expect the message to punch through. No more than three verbal and visual elements should appear in the message. Hence, you must restrain yourself in both your verbal and visual thinking if you expect to write a good outdoor message.

Simplicity is the hallmark of good outdoor. If your message is complex, don't use outdoor. But if you can reduce your message to just a few words, and if you can employ bold, even garish, visuals, you will be able to do a lot with a little.

Although ads for subways, taxis and similar media have different size specifications, the same guidelines apply to them as to outdoor.

Copywriting for Sales Promotion

Point-of-purchase advertising, samples, contests, advertising specialties and cooperative advertising are sales-promotion pieces, as are coupons, booklets, brochures and mailers. (See Chapter 18 for brochures.)

Point-of-purchase advertising is advertising displayed with a product, service or idea and specifically designed to inspire the customer to buy on impulse. Most point-of-purchase advertising is strong on emotional impact, particularly symbolism, and ties in with other existing promotional materials to create additional recognition. Another promotional device is the sample, a free product sent out along with descriptive literature. The copy accompanying a sample often tries to inspire a sense of obligation in prospective customers by urging them to accept the "gift."

Contests are designed to offer customers something extra and to maintain their awareness of the idea through participation and anticipation. Advertising specialties can be anything with the corporate logo on it, but generally they are useful objects, like ice scrapers for windshields, or things with high visibility that will be remembered.

In cooperative advertising, the retail outlet appeals for direct sales while receiving support from the manufacturer. When the manufacturer's logo appears alongside the retailer's in a local company's advertising for a product or service, this is usually a tip-off that the ad is a cooperative one, with the retailer and manufacturer sharing in the cost of space, time or position.

Conclusions

- Most advertising copy that PR people write involves promoting ideas.
- These idea ads are in print and electronic media and take many forms, some looking like traditional ads or commercials and some looking like editorial matter.
- Advertising uses persuasion. It cannot coerce.
- Successful persuasion is based on the right appeal, proper positioning and an understanding of how people will respond to the appeal.
- Basic requirements for advertising copywriting include an understanding of the ad's purpose, a careful review of the objective facts to be conveyed, an awareness of the public to be addressed, and a thoughtful decision as to the media to be used. Internal requirements are a creative approach, visualization, precise language, blending of art and copy, and repetition.
- Television and film media are dynamic, so movement must be integrated into messages for these media, and the verbal and visual elements of the ad must be complementary.
- Internet advertising also involves color, movement and sound.
- Copy for radio is written for the ear, not the eye. Words and sounds must be especially well chosen for radio ads so that the public can "see" the message.
- Although newspapers and magazines are static media, messages placed there must be dynamic and move people to act. Stages of audience response that must be addressed in developing these ads include attention, interest, desire, credibility and action. The headline is the most important element.
- Direct-mail messages are difficult to execute effectively because the message must also be the medium.
- The audience goes to out-of-home media, rather than vice versa, so time is short and simplicity in both words and visuals is crucial. The total message is limited to eight words and three elements.
- Writing copy for sales promotions often involves writing for a variety of media and methods. It is a good idea to review the descriptions and illustrations in this chapter before writing any sales-promotion materials.

Exercises

1. Write five different headlines for ads addressed to shareholders, explaining the recapitalization program discussed in this chapter.
2. Select one of the five headlines you have just written, and write three alternative lead sentences or paragraphs for it.
3. Write a double truck ad (two facing pages) for *Business Week* for the following situation: Your client is an industrial park. It has a lot of undeveloped land, plenty of water and power and the resources to build high-tech facilities for companies relocating to your area. In fact, state and local taxes will be waived in perpetuity for any company locating in the state. This is, of course, a big incentive for companies to move to the area. You are free to expand on this information using a local situation.
4. Write a television commercial for the circumstances described in Exercise 3.

 Use InfoTrac College Edition to access information on topics in this chapter from hundreds of periodicals and scholarly journals.

Selected Bibliography

David Angell and Brent Heslop, *The Internet Business Companion: Growing Your Business in the Electronic Age* (New York: Addison-Wesley, 1995).

Frank Biocca and Mark R. Levy, eds., *Communication in the Age of Virtual Reality* (Hillsdale, N.J.: Lawrence Erlbaum Associates, 1995).

Robert L. Hilliard, *Writing for Television, Radio and New Media,* 8th ed. (Belmont, Calif.: Wadsworth, 2003).

Institute of Outdoor Advertising, *The First Medium* (New York: Institute of Outdoor Advertising, undated).

Daniel S. Janal, *Online Marketing Handbook* (New York: John Wiley & Sons, 1999).

Jerome Jewler, *Creative Strategy in Advertising,* 7th ed. (Belmont, Calif.: Wadsworth, 2001).

Barbara K. Kaye, *Just A Click Away: Advertising on the Internet* (Boston: Allyn & Bacon, 2001).

Milan D. Meeske, *Copywriting for the Electronic Media: A Practical Guide,* 4th ed. (Belmont, Calif.: Wadsworth, 2003).

Roy Paul Nelson, *The Design of Advertising,* 7th ed. (New York: McGraw-Hill, 1996).

CHAPTER FOURTEEN

Writing for Web Sites

The Internet has become an integral part of our lives. Organizations of every type, as well as individuals, have active sites, and the Internet has made possible ubiquitous email and instant messaging. Nearly 47 million sites on the World Wide Web had been registered by February 2004.[1] More than half a billion people (580 million) worldwide now have Internet access, according to a Nielsen/NetRatings study released in February 2003. Forecasts indicate 709 million will be online by year-end 2004.[2]

And the Internet is a public relations professional's dream-come-true—the ultimate PR tool. It combines the benefits of sight and sound, print and video as well as interactive communication capabilities. Organizations of all types and sizes are taking advantage of the Internet. An inventory of corporate Web sites found more than 65 kinds of public relations content—from *About Us* to *Webcasting*.

A Web site begins with a *home page,* which is the opening page of a site and serves as the site's introduction, starting point, and guide. From there visitors are directed to information about the organization, product, service or individual. The best sites offer a kaleidoscope of information. Many offer products or services as well. USA online consumer sales for 2002 were about $74 billion, according to comScore Media Metrix.[3]

As a public relations writer, you may be involved in creating the concept for a site, organizing the site and writing some or all of its content. You also may serve as liaison with other professionals who build and maintain Web sites, but you're not likely to be expected to build a site. That's why this chapter offers only an overview of activities in which you may be involved. It focuses on basic concepts, issues, questions and techniques with which you should be generally familiar. The intent is to make it easier for you to adapt your writing style to this medium. The chapter should also help you to talk more knowledgeably with professional Web site supervisors. Let's begin by reviewing the basic nature of the Internet.

Nature of the Internet

A careful look at the Internet suggests that it is really about *people,* although most people think of it in terms of computers and information technology. They think of it as existing somewhere in cyberspace, a space that seems infinite. It is true that computers and software link countless computers worldwide into a network of astounding dimensions. But it isn't infinite. It is limited by the hardware that is used and the software that controls it. These elements are both finite and inanimate. They are meaningless without the people who direct their usage and those who use their outputs. Therefore, a view of the Internet primarily as a people phenomenon is valid, although somewhat uncommon.

Accessing the Internet

In the simplest terms, the Internet is nothing more than a delivery mechanism through which digitized information travels. Sites on the World Wide Web and email both depend on the Internet. Email is pervasive, of course (see Chapter 7), but the focus in this chapter is on Web sites. You get to a Web site by keying in a URL (Uniform Resource Locator). That typically brings up the home page of a site. Then you navigate through the site to get the information you want from other pages.

Inside a site, a user navigates by clicking on a button or a text link or pulling down and selecting from a menu. This will take you to another page or window in which related, but different, information appears. More buttons or menus lead you to deeper information from the same or other sources. Available information seems endless at times. In that sense, the Web provides a service to users by helping them quickly access information stored in many different computers connected to the Internet. You might envision the Web as a constantly expanding spiderweb that is alive with activity.

Although it began as a text-only medium, the Web now displays text with graphics in full color on the same screen. It also can combine sound and video, making it a *multimedia* vehicle.

Cross-Platform

Visitors to a site get there by using a *browser*—a software tool that helps you locate and retrieve information. The two most popular browsers are Microsoft Internet Explorer ("IE") and Netscape Communicator.

Each browser is a software application. The application directs your queries to Web sites. For example, when you type in a domain name (a critical part of the cyber address) such as http://www.qsigroup.com, the computer contacts a Domain Name System (DNS) server. The server translates the domain name into a digitized address, with a format such as 123.456.78, which is the identifying number of the Web server that hosts the site. When your request for qsigroup.com arrives at the server for the QuickSilver site, the server automatically serves up the digital address assigned to qsigroup.com, the site's home page, which appears on your screen. Search engines like *Google, Yahoo!* and *MSN Search* can be accessed by browsers and are heavily used to locate sites through key words.

A server is simply a high-capacity computer that feeds information to browsers that ask for it. Think of the server on which your Web site is stored as your publishing house, just like Wadsworth is the publisher of this book. The key point is that popular browsers can work successfully in cross-platform environments, serving up text, graphics, audio and video for both PCs and Macs.

Importance of URLs

A *Uniform Resource Locator* (URL) is an address that directs a browser to a page of information on the Web. URLs are universal and are used to link to additional information. So URLs are critically important to how visitors navigate the Web and find your site.

Two Types of Web Pages

Web sites have two types of pages—the home page and the destination page. The *home page* is the main page that is the entry point for visitors to your Web site. It is what visitors see first when they connect with your site. It's promotional in nature and should lead the reader into more detailed information. It usually has a high-level form of table of contents, typically the navigation buttons, and summarizes for visitors, often in bullet form, what they can expect to find on the site. (See Figure 14.1.) The second type of page is the *destination page,* typically the secondary and tertiary pages. It's informational in nature, and it's where people go to get the information they want.

Organizing the Site

Before a Web site is designed and built, some basic questions must be answered that will be helpful in organizing the site:

- What's the site's main purpose? To sell products? To provide information to members? To attract investments or contributions? To encourage volunteers? To recruit personnel?
- What are its secondary purposes? Some corporate sites sell products but also provide information for investors, financial analysts, brokers, students and other groups.
- What kind of content is important for each purpose?
- Who are the publics or constituencies to whom the site must appeal? What are those people's main interests? Ages? Income levels? Education levels?

Site Map   With this type of information, you can begin organizing the site. The best way to proceed is to prepare a *Web site map*—a graphic representation of the site's structure and contents.

Figure 14.2 shows the site map for QuickSilver Interactive Group's Web pages. The home page features buttons that link to four main sections—*About Us, Clients, Services* and *Stories.* These four sections compose the main navigation for the site, and links to those sections appear on each of the landing pages for those sections. The firm's logo is used on all pages as a link to the home page. On each of the main section pages (secondary pages) are links to additional pages with information about each of the four main categories.

FIGURE 14.1

Home Page   *A Web site's home page, or main page, gives the user an important first impression of the organization represented by the site. From the home page, links allow users to navigate to specific pages that are available. Many Web sites, like this one for the White House, offer information in more than one language.*

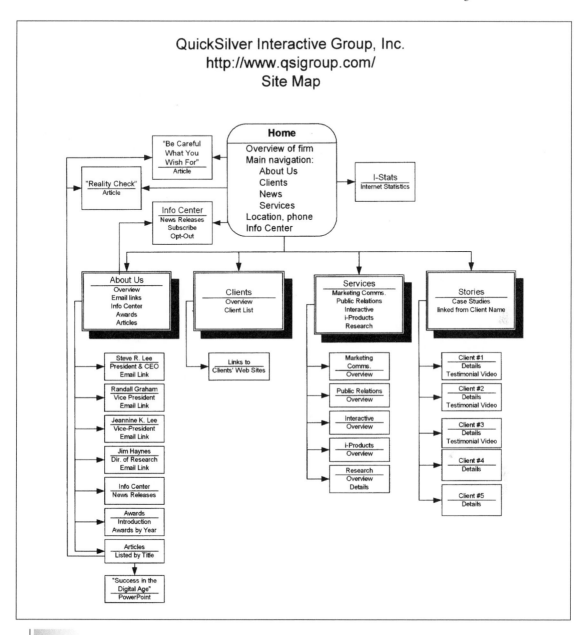

FIGURE 14.2

Site Map   *This is the site map for QuickSilver Interactive Group, Inc.'s Web site, http://www.qsigroup.com. Many site maps have active links to the site's content.*

- On the *About Us* landing page is an overview and a list of senior management, with an email link to each person. The page also has links to *Info Center, Awards* and *Articles* written by QuickSilver personnel. On the *Info Center* page, there are headlines from news releases, with each headline linking to the full text of the release.
- The *Clients* landing page presents a list of clients, with links to the clients' Web sites.
- The *Services* landing page has a heading for each type of service provided, with links to more detailed information about that particular service.
- On the *Stories* landing page are short summaries of programs that QuickSilver has completed for selected clients. Links provide access to *Details* of the program and video *Testimonials* by clients.

Once a site map has been prepared, the next step is to prepare a *content matrix*. The content matrix outlines and explains all the content elements recommended for the site. It becomes an effective reference document as you build the site. This document typically is sectioned based on the site map's categories arranged in columns. The name of the page is in the first column. The second column has the names of the content on the page. The next column shows the deadline for the content. Other columns indicate the person(s) responsible for the content, the method to be used in updating the content and the frequency of updates (hourly, daily, weekly, monthly and so on).

Web Site Writing

The Web is a relatively new medium. The Internet has taught people that they can access information quickly, so visitors coming to your Web site want the information "now." We are in a world that communicates in sound bites. Make them wait more than 20 to 30 seconds and they'll bail out. Make them work to find the information they need and they won't return. It is unlike any of the traditional media we're taught to write for. Web sites can be updated instantaneously, making updates (or those tricky typos) easy to change. Audience expectations are higher too. A Web site requires frequent updates to its main content pages. How frequently they are revised depends on the type of parent organization and the kinds and uses of information provided. Updating can be done manually, from a database or by an automated system. With the right authorization and software, Web site changes can be made remotely from anywhere in the world.

A Web site is its own delivery system. Once a site goes online, it can be accessed by millions of people around the world. In that sense, you can't predict clearly or control who might visit your site. However, software can count the number of visitors and assemble other information about them. This information, in time, can give you a fairly clear picture of who visits and why. It is also invaluable information as you seek to improve your Web site so it is more appealing and useful to the publics you want to reach.

There are some technical issues over which you have no control but that impact how you write and what you publish on your site. You don't know what kind of browser or computer system visitors may be using. Nor do you know the limitations of their printers. Visitors probably have color monitors with their systems, but many use black-and-white printers. Some will have audio and video capabilities. Others won't. This should cause you to wonder how your site will look on their systems. It is important to do a test on various browsers before publishing a new site and even a new page to the "live" site. The best approach is to design for the common denominator. And that includes restrained use of audio and video.

Visitor Reading Behavior

You need to know how visitors behave when they visit your site. Web readers *scan information* rather than *read.* That's the conclusion of a Sun Microsystems study reported by Lawrence Ragan Communications, Inc. Sun found that 79 percent of site visitors scan content.[4] Only 11 percent actually read *word for word.* Sun also found that copy on the screen is about 25 percent more difficult to read than in printed form.

When writing for a newspaper or magazine, you are expected to lead people through stories, from beginning to end. In that sense, print writing is linear. But visitors to Web sites are more nonlinear. They skip from place to place. Therefore, you must break information into small chunks. Reading on the screen also is slower than reading the same information in printed form. You must give visitors minimal directions so they can locate the information they want with the least effort.

How can you deal with that kind of reading behavior?

Writing Basics

Our purpose as communicators has not changed. Our call is to write clean, clear and concise copy with the audience in mind and to provide content with a purpose—whether it's information, education or entertainment. So know your audience, and write what they know and understand. Don't assume that they will understand abbreviations, acronyms and jargon.

Is writing for the Web really that different? Yes and no.

Yes, it's different, because information is presented in short bursts, or should be, because Web readers scan, jumping from one point to another and looking for key words or facts. This does not justify sloppy writing. In fact, this behavior demands the best, most precise and concise writing. The point is to deliver copy in smaller chunks, not necessarily to write half as much copy.

No, it's really not different. The pyramid style of writing still applies, and a good lead is critical to drawing in the audience.

According to Jeannine K. Lee, APR*, vice president of QuickSilver Interactive Group, Inc., we can categorize writing for the Web into three formats:

• Headlines
• Briefs
• Navigation buttons and links

Lee says effective writing for the Web can be summarized in the following way.

Headlines   Effective Web headlines have a subject and a verb, are written in present or future tense and are no more than 10 words. If they occupy two lines, the lines should match in length. Here's an example:

Technology moves data collection from factory to the road.

*Accredited Public Relations (APR) is a designation for practitioners accredited by PRSA.

Briefs   An effective Web brief meets the following criteria:

- It is no more than one to two sentences long.
- Each sentence should be 20 words or fewer.
- It should entice the reader to explore further.
- First and second person establishes dialogue with audience and allows you to talk to your reader.
- It uses "relevant" questions to capture the reader's curiosity. Example:

> **2003 Series Tickets**
> Buying series tickets gives you first pick of seats for the 2003 Texas Stampede. And you now have the right to retain your seats for next year too. *Sign up now* to be notified this spring when the series ticket packages are available. [Links to a form to subscribe to the email alert system. That person will now be notified by email right before the tickets go on sale.]

> **Volunteer Kickoff Planned**
> Want to get in on the action early? *Contact us* about our Volunteer Kickoff planned for April 15. [Links to RSVP form. The event organizer is provided a list of all the people who registered before the event.]

> **April 15**
> Tell us who you'd like to see on stage. [Links to an open text box where visitors vote for their favorite concert artist. This is reviewed by the marketing department and used to help make the decision of what artist(s) to bring into the event.]

Navigation Buttons and Links   These should be one to three words long (*New Products, Global Directory, Benefits*), yet clear and precise.

Destination Page Writing   On destination pages, Lee says, break your text into paragraphs composed of two to three short sentences. Keep each destination page as close to one screen as possible, and structure for facts and figures using links and bullet points. Always provide an option for the full-text version.[5]

Writing Style

Good grammar, proper punctuation and correct spelling apply to Web sites as they do to all other media. Beyond those points, writing style on the Web is a little different. Minimize the use of adjectives and adverbs, because they fatten a block of copy unnecessarily. Avoid conditional clauses also. These not only lengthen sentences, they can be confusing to some visitors. Remember how visitors behave as they search for information. You must write tight and edit even tighter.

It should be a given that you will spell-check your document. Visits to a few Web sites show that some writers don't do that. Spelling errors are far too frequent. They are especially easy to overlook in large headline type. In fact, read headlines and subheads letter-for-letter, even when you use a spell-checker. Such simple errors cast doubt on the reliability of information in the whole site.

Emphasis

You've probably seen lots of Web sites. And it was difficult in some cases to figure out what was important about them. That's because everything seemed to be emphasized. A simple idea worth remembering is that *total emphasis results in no emphasis.* When you see a block of copy in which half of the sentences seem to be underlined, boldfaced, italicized or in all caps, it is understandable that a reader may struggle to figure out what is important and worth remembering.

Use restraint if you want to emphasize a point. Think of a young woman who has bangles from her wrists halfway to her elbows. Your attention is drawn to the excess of jewelry, not to *her.* Italicizing, boldfacing, underlining and all caps are devices similar to those bangles. They should be used to complement the message, not compete with it. Overuse of these devices also impedes readability and reading. We suggest you use underlining rarely because visitors will assume it's an inactive link.

With this background on writing for Web sites, now turn your attention to some design issues, even if you don't do the actual design. Some of these also may impact what and how you write.

Design Issues

No amount of good writing can hold up to a poor design. Designing a Web site involves a lot more than designing a page in a book, brochure or other printed matter, although some principles are the same. Designing Web sites is sometimes viewed by nondesigners as a complex, baffling process. But it can be simplified if you follow a few basic guidelines.

If you have produced creative work in other media, you can expect to use some of the same principles. However, you'll find that design options are more limited. Yet, there's enough flexibility to create an inviting Web site.

Getting Started

You've probably noticed that some Web sites are quick to come up on the screen, are inviting to look at, are a pleasure to read and allow a user to find information easily. Other sites are slow to display on the screen and many of them are cluttered with graphics or text. Clutter is confusing and hard to read—another reason to bail out. Sites that require excessive scrolling also can be an irritant to the visitor.

Why are these pages so bad? One reason may be that their creators didn't have a clear idea of what they wanted to do, what content to include or how to present it well, and they lacked an idea of how visitors might use their sites. Another reason may be that some Web site designers are "techies"—people skilled in digital nuances but who may know little or nothing about communication processes. According to Lee, "Techies tend to build pages with many bells, whistles and doodads simply because they can. They are engineers, not communicators, and they understand little about information flow, intuitiveness and business objectives."[6] All of which are critical to a Web site's success.

Basic Guidelines

Books could be written on guidelines that should be followed when designing a Web site. In fact, many have been. But we're going to mention only a few selected guidelines here.

Simplify   We earlier urged you to simplify everything. That applies equally to the design of Web sites. Limit the number of elements. Elements in this context include everything visible on the screen without scrolling. That includes background, headlines, subheads, text blocks, boxes, rules, buttons, visuals and so on. An average of *five elements per screen* is our arbitrary recommendation. Using an average makes it possible for you to have more on some screens and fewer on others. If you can come close to that goal, you'll quickly see that simplification helps the look of your site.

Limit Visuals   Watching a large, full-color visual come to life on the screen can be exciting to a designer. But it can be painful to visitors because it takes so long for the image to come up. If it takes more than 20 seconds, it tries the patience of visitors so much that they may simply move on to another site. Even if they stay with your site until the image is fully up, they may have formed a negative attitude that could make them wary of information they find there.

Hold the content of a screen to no more than 85K. That guideline will generally let visitors download in about 10 seconds or less. If a large visual must be used, consider using a thumbnail sketch (2 × 2 inches) and provide a link for visitors to click on a larger version. That cuts down the time to bring up a screen and it does not increase the time for printing unless visitors make that choice. That's a win-win proposition.

Headlines and Subheads   The traditional use of a headline is to summarize the key point in a block of text. The size of type in the headline also grades the importance of the text block for visitors. Subheads are mini-headlines dealing with portions of a long text block, breaking it up to make the text more visually appealing. Subheads also help readers go quickly to certain sections in the text. Note how the headlines and subheads in this book help you see quickly what the page content is about. You may want to consider the use of small icons or rules as substitutes for subheads. That can be a good design technique, but its use must be restrained or the screen quickly gets cluttered.

Consistent Look   Strive for a consistent look for each screen. That's comforting to visitors because after seeing three or four screens, they know what to expect. They don't like to be jarred into wondering if they've somehow stumbled onto another site. Again, look at the page design of this book. Page numbers are always in the same place. Tables are presented in the same basic style. Heads and subheads never vary, except in size. These and other elements illustrate the concept of a consistent look. The basic layout of your site should remain the same, just like the pages in this book. Although each screen is similar to the next, the content, just like the pages in this book, makes them different.

Family Look   If your organization requires a standard look but will allow various departments or subsidiaries to add their own personalization within designated areas, that's a family look.

Links

You may have heard a lot about the importance of links. And you may have benefited from the use of them when searching for information. You have probably discovered, also, that some links are useless because the information in a link may not really be salient or the link is to a *dead site* (one that is no longer active). Your experience may suggest several things about links.

Purpose   Each link should serve a specific purpose. Never link just because you can. The casual mention of a term like *integrated communication* should not be linked. However, link it if the mention contains significant facts or points of view or describes techniques that may be useful to others.

Relevance   You can't know in advance why a specific visitor may bring up your Web site. It may be only curiosity. But most visitors have specific reasons to tune in. So add to purpose the idea of relevance. You may think that a crystal ball is needed for this but you only have to think about the publics you're trying to reach. Who are they and what do they want? If you can answer those questions clearly, you'll know what is relevant.

Utility   Although the text you've written should all be relevant to the purpose of your Web site, that does not mean that all of it will be useful to all visitors. So, all of your text should not be linked. Link only points that seem to offer real usefulness to visitors.

Easy, Quick Access   Each link should help visitors zero in on additional information they want. The ease and speed with which visitors can navigate your site and extract what they want are huge considerations. Useful links can make a difference in whether a visitor will return or not. Poor links are a liability. In some ways, links are as important as the content and the look and feel of your site. Navigating should be quick and easy and require no more than three clicks before visitors find what they want. More than three clicks often tries the patience of visitors. They sometimes move on to other sites.

Home Link   It is also a good idea to include a Home button or link on every page so visitors can return directly to the home page. It's common practice to use the organization's logo as a link to the home page or to include a Home button. This practice gives visitors a quick way to escape from the depths of links when they've concluded that they've gone too far, that they're lost or that they've gotten the information they want. A Home link avoids navigating back through a link hierarchy visitors may not fully remember.

Graphics

The term *graphics* is used here to include type, color, background and visuals. Making good choices about graphics helps build a consistent look, one that has eye appeal and that helps guide visitors to important information. If you seek advice from graphic design specialists, you're likely to get as many different recommendations as the number of people you consult with. What follows is a set of guidelines to help you sort out what is best for your Web site. We'll begin with one of the most important areas—type.

Selecting and Using Type   Set a goal of selecting no more than two typefaces that you'll use exclusively. Some people say this is too restrictive. Remember this is the Internet and you're limited to four or five type styles. Maybe it is, but it also works well if you select wisely. Select one typeface for text blocks and, perhaps, another typeface for displaying headlines and subheads. The faces you select must meet one absolute criterion—*readability.* It is important to select faces that are widely available, because they must be installed on each computer used to view your site. Otherwise, type will appear as the default browser type that will blow out any formatting or design you've incorporated into the site.

Type Font   Understand that each computer's browser views fonts differently. This is important to remember. Experienced users can set their browser preferences to view fonts larger or smaller. You can't control this. Your position is to, once again, design for the common denominators. The only fonts you can be sure are installed on PCs running Windows are:

- *Times New Roman*
- *Arial*
- *Verdana*
- *Courier* (default)

You can be sure that a Mac has the following installed:

- *Times* (default)
- *Arial*
- *Verdana*
- *Courier*

That's *it!* The font you select should, in addition to its regular typeface, allow you to bold and italicize. That's usually more than enough to meet your needs. Run several tests with combinations of text, headlines, subheads, italics, extended type and bold to determine compatibility. If you desire something with more flare or design for your headers, you will need the designer to create them as graphic elements.

Font Size   The newspapers and magazines you read probably use 10- or 11-point type for text. People with near-normal eyesight have no difficulty reading type in those sizes. Reading from a computer screen, however, is more difficult and slower than reading from a printed page. That's because the type you read on a screen is made up of *pixels* (electronic dots) that move along the screen at the speed of light. Even if the image appears stable, it is in constant motion. Hence, smaller type is more difficult and tiring to read on the screen than on paper, especially if it is a long block of copy.

On Web pages, font type sizes are, for all practical purposes, meaningless. PCs display type about a third larger than Macs, and browsers allow each user to set the size in which HTML type will be displayed. We suggest that you use the default setting of "12"—equal to 12-point type—for text. Resist the temptation to use type smaller than default 12-point equivalent. If your copy won't fit the space, edit until it does. We recommend a 24-point type equivalent for headlines. For subheads, 18-point equivalent works well if you're using the equivalent of 14-point text but 14-point is good for subheads if you're using "12" text. Be aware that the settings on the browsers used by visitors actually control the size of type displayed by the browsers. And remember to test your pages on *both* a PC and a Mac, as well as Microsoft

Internet Explorer, Netscape Communicator and AOL. If you have a document that you want displayed a particular way, your options are to create an image file (depending on its size) or a PDF.

Line Lengths   Lines too long for the size of type being used reduce the ease and speed of reading. If it is a long block of copy, readers tire quickly and tune out. You can overcome this by using a line length of 400 pixels—between 40 and 70 characters, depending upon type size, or about 60 characters in "12" size type.

Screen Resolution   You may work with a large monitor, such as 21 inches (diagonal measure), but the monitors many people use are no larger than 17 or 14 inches. Some laptops are even smaller. And the printers they use may not print anything wider than eight inches. You must construct your site so that it will fit comfortably within these limits. Standard screen resolution is set at 800 × 600 pixels, although many are transitioning to 1,024 × 768 pixels. Typically a page design is set for a width of 720 pixels. Height will vary based on the content displayed.

Avoid Typographic Chaos   Because the computer makes it easy to change fonts, sizes and line lengths, be on guard against creating typographic chaos. Be careful about the following points and apply them consistently.

Use caps (capital letters) and lowercase (small letters) throughout your document. Avoid all caps because they are harder to read, especially in headlines. You can use it minimally in subheads. Larger type is more difficult to read, especially if it is in all caps, and spelling errors are not as easy to spot.

People are conditioned to begin reading at the upper left of a block of copy and to read from left to right until they get to the end. Type placed vertically is much harder to read. By doing that you're inviting visitors to lie on their sides so that your message appears normal to them. Also, type tilted dramatically is harder to read. If you must tilt type, limit it to no more than about 15 degrees.

Wrapping type around visuals is acceptable, but only if the reader isn't expected to jump across a visual to read the rest of a line of text. Visuals inserted in text probably should be placed on the left or right side of a copy block, not in the middle. The shape of visuals also may affect wrapping. If visuals have square corners, a wrap may work with a graphic on the left or right. If they have irregular shapes, don't even think about placing them on the left of a copy block because that produces a ragged left margin. The only place they may work is on the right side so that the wrapped type has a ragged right margin.

Using Color   Many computers are capable of creating and displaying millions of colors. This is possible because computers can mix—in an incredible array—the primary colors yellow, red, blue and black (although pure black technically is not a color because it does not reflect light). Only people with the most acute color-sensitive vision can see more than a tiny fraction of this spectrum. It makes little sense to select and use electronic colors many visitors can't actually see and printers can't duplicate.

This problem can be solved easily. It's important to know that Pantone Color Matching System colors do not match Web colors easily. There are only 216 Web-safe colors that can be used in matching the multitude of Pantone Color Matching System colors. Work with your design team to get as close to matching that color as possible. It will differ slightly. Also remember that each person's color printer prints colors differently as well, so don't expect that "brochure" you put on the Web site to look just like the real thing—it won't. Your options are to redesign it for the Web or accept its limitations.

Background Color   Your best choice for readability and printing is a white background. It's clean and crisp, and you can still design a knockout Web site without losing pizzazz. That said, the purpose of a background color is to provide a visual framework that unifies all of the elements on the page. It should not intrude on content. It is simply background.

Also note that background color, if not selected carefully, can interfere with color visuals. For example, a graphic with a lot of red may appear to bleed into a pink background. That's another reason why a white or light gray background may be the most useful.

Background tiles are used on some sites. Tiles often trigger to the visitor the impression that the site is "homegrown" or has been designed by an amateur. These usually have colorful patterns or discernible content that, alone, may be very attractive. But they can be visually annoying as background for screens and can interfere dramatically with reading. Generally avoid tiles, although they can be used now and then to enhance a screen or a portion of it. Just don't overdo it.

Visuals   The first thing to know about visuals is to think small. Second, select and use only visuals that have direct, obvious relevance to the idea of your Web site. Third, limit the number of visuals per screen to no more than two, preferably one. We've already suggested that colors be kept to 216. We also suggest that visuals be reduced to no more than 72 dots per square inch. Reducing the dots makes downloading and printing faster. We also recommend that 85K be the limit of everything on a screen. If you observe that guideline carefully, you'll have a more attractive Web site.

Visual Sources   You can get visuals from several sources: photographs, original hand-drawn art, digital photographic images, clip art and video. Photographic prints and hand-drawn art must be scanned (digitized) for use. Clip art comes in two forms. One is art clipped from printed sources, which must be scanned to produce a digital file. The other is clip art from a digitized library. Images from digital cameras can be transferred directly to your computer. Video segments can be downloaded from many sites on the Web. They certainly help to grab attention but they eat up enormous hard drive space and slow downloading. Remember also that printers can't reproduce animation, so generally avoid video. If you must use video, exercise restraint.

Copyright   If you are using content from another source, check its copyright status. If it is copyrighted, don't use it unless you get permission from the copyright holder. You may have to pay a use fee. If you quote an excerpt of 100 or more words from some text source, check the copyright status and get permission, if needed. Otherwise, paraphrasing the information, but with proper attribution, is usually enough to forestall legal action claiming infringement of copyright. Be careful. If you are purchasing a graphic, be sure you select a graphic that is "royalty-free." This will enable you to use it more than once in your Web site and any supporting marketing materials you might design to go with the launch or promotion of your site.

Making a Web Site More Useful

Of course, you want to make your Web site as useful to visitors as possible. To do this, you must first get their attention. You can do several things to help achieve that.

Branding

Think of the design and construction of your Web site as an exercise in branding. Everything on a site should conform and contribute to the image people already have of your client or organization. If it is a startup, however, you may use the site as a primary focus for establishing a brand image. But that image for existing or new organizations must be consistent with what is projected by other media and means of communication. That's one of the primary principles of good public relations. Use your client's logo for this purpose. Don't tinker with it. It should remain identical to the logo when it is used in other media. Remember that consistency of look and feel is mandatory if you expect to realize cumulative impact. If your Web site is personal, you must design a logo for yourself. That can be a challenge. Keep it simple, yet distinctive.

Site Search Software

Some Web sites are huge, and finding information on them can be a challenge. A *site map*—an outline or graphic overview of the entire site with links to each portion of the site—can be helpful but often doesn't pinpoint what a user wants. A better solution is to use a site search capability—a search engine that is housed on the same server as the Web site. Site search engines work in the same way Internet search engines like Yahoo! and Google do but search only within a particular site. A wide range of such software is available, ranging from simple, free packages to sophisticated products. Once such software is in place and the site has been indexed in the search software, the search engine will quickly find and display links to locations on the site for key words. Most will present those locations in order of relevance.

Visitor Response

Give visitors to your Web site an easy way to respond to you. They may want to comment on your site, make suggestions for improvements, place an order, ask for specific information or seek clarification of some point. Include response forms that collect this information. These forms are usually built with boxes to be checked, buttons to be clicked, menus to be pulled down, one-line text boxes or scrollable text boxes on which visitors can write to you. Include *submit* and *reset* buttons so visitors can send you their feedback. Create a file to store this information and review it regularly so you can make changes to your Web site, fill orders or respond to visitor queries.

Many companies fail to acknowledge receipt of customer email inquiries or if they do, fail to respond in a timely manner. More than 90 percent of the companies surveyed by Jupiter Research said that they provide an email channel for customer inquiries. But nearly one-third of them took three days or longer to get back to customers through email or failed to respond at all, falling short of customers' expectations.[7]

Refreshing Your Site

Depending on the intended use, the site should be refreshed regularly. The frequency is a judgment call, but it should be updated at least monthly. Some sites are updated daily simply because of their purposes and the number of visitors who access them. When visitors learn that you update the site frequently, they are more likely to return for new information. Many corporations update their sites every few minutes.

Tracking Usage

If you want to know who visits, which specific screens of information they view and how they use the information they get, you must monitor and analyze the traffic on your Web site. This information is especially critical if you expect to advertise or to sell goods or services. You can get a lot of information from the forms that you've built in, but you also need to know such things as: What are the busiest days of the week for traffic? What are the busiest hours of the day for traffic? What is the daily average number of visitors? Which are the most visited pages on the site? Experience may prompt you to add several other questions, depending on your purpose and the way visitors use your site. Software programs like WebSTAR Log can automate the gathering and charting of usage statistics.

You can use this information to improve the site and to evaluate your niche in cyberspace. You'll want to register your site in all the right places so it will show up when search engines are employed by visitors cruising the Internet. Don't overlook Web directories, business search engines and Yellow Pages. These are ideal places to register your site, especially if you advertise or sell products or services on your site. You also should consider registering your site with category-specific or industry-specific directories.

A Dozen Tips to Remember[8]

1. Build a site that can be easily maintained.
   - Don't build a site that only one person knows how to maintain; train several.

2. Be sure your pages can be printed.
   - People still like to print pages they want to read.
   - Test print for frames, colors, background images or colors.

3. Just because you know how to do something doesn't mean you should!
   - Flash, video, etc. It's all in fun, right? But use sparingly, if at all. After seeing/hearing them once, they're distracting.

4. Tables can be a real asset when designing.
   - Use cells and tables to organize and compartmentalize your pages.

5. Be considerate of how your viewer is accessing your page.
   - How quickly does your page load? Less than 20–30 seconds is a good aim.
   - Are they inside or outside your firewall?
   - Don't make them "dig down" very far.

6. Color is a great accent.
   • Use color to draw attention to an area.

7. Keep your navigation intuitive and helpful.
   • Don't make your reader guess where to click.
   • Always give them a way back to the home page and/or section they're in.
   • The Back button is not a navigation button.

8. Use graphics sparingly.
   • Make it load quickly or people will go away.
   • Icons and graphics that act as buttons and links can confuse the reader and slow down the page load time.
   • If using graphics, also provide a text link for those few who prefer to view text only in their browsers.

9. Web readers are scanners.
   • Be sure your copy has "context."
   • Provide strong summary paragraphs with links.

10. Size your pages to fit the need.
    • Your 8 × 10 page format will not always fit in a 600 × 800 screen resolution.
    • Minimal scrolling.

11. Use links effectively.

12. Don't try to do everything on your front page.
    • Make it *look* simple, even if it's complicated.
    • Make it easy for the user.

Conclusions

• Strategic thinking must precede the act of writing.
• The Web is an extension of your more traditional communications tools.
• The best Web sites offer a kaleidoscope of information about organizations and/or individuals.
• Good grammar, proper punctuation and correct spelling are as essential to Web sites as they are to other media.
• Good writing for Web sites minimizes adjectives, adverbs and conditional clauses because these unnecessarily fatten sentences and lengthen blocks of copy.
• Successful writing for Web sites is more nonlinear than writing for other media because visitors tend to scan, rather than read, for key words or facts—that is, they jump around a lot.
• Keep information as brief as possible.
• Too much emphasis results in no emphasis. Use restraint.
• Simplify both the writing and the design of Web sites.
• Limit the number of visuals per screen and keep them small.
• A good Web site has a consistent look from one screen to the next.
• Select only two type fonts. Use one for text and one for heads and subheads.

- Use the default setting of "12"—equal to 12-point type—for text, a 24-point type equivalent for headlines and an 18-point equivalent for subheads.
- Be aware that the settings on browsers actually control the size of type displayed by the browsers and that PCs display type about a third larger than Macs.
- If you have a document that you want displayed a particular way, create an image file or a PDF.
- Limit your line lengths to 400 pixels—between 40 and 70 characters, depending upon type size, or about 60 characters in "12" size type.
- Keep the width of a Web page to 720 pixels and the length to 600 pixels (when possible).
- Use caps and lowercase consistently. Avoid using all caps.
- Be consistent in the use of justified or ragged right margins. Do not use ragged left margins. Don't mix margin styles.
- Don't wrap type around an irregularly shaped visual on the left because that makes reading more difficult.
- Limit screen content to no more than 85K.
- Background color can provide unity to the site, but avoid intense colors. Select white, light gray or a soft pastel.
- Content can come from many sources. Some must be digitized before being used. Get approval for all copyrighted content before using. Purchase royalty-free graphics.
- Use a logo to create an identity for your site. It must match exactly the logo as it appears in other media.
- Think of creating a Web site as an exercise in branding.
- Build in response forms so visitors can get in touch with you.
- If video is included, use it with restraint.
- Devise a plan to refresh your site on a regular basis.
- Track the usage of your site so you have statistical information that may be used to improve the site and to promote the site.

Exercises

1. Select a Web site designed to market a product and one designed to promote a service or an idea. Critique the two sites and compare them according to similarities and differences. Evaluate whether the differences can be explained by their purposes.
2. Find a Web site that is not just poor, but awful. Write a report in which you analyze what makes the site so bad and what can be improved.
3. Use your search engine to explore the Web to build an annotated bibliography of sites that offer guidance on how to write for the Web. Restrict your report to no more than two double-spaced pages.
4. Evaluate the content of your university's Web site. You've been here awhile, so you have points of view about the place. How well does the information on the Web site match your experience? What information is included that you have found especially useful to you? What information has been included that you have found to be useless, incomplete or misleading? What information is missing that you wish you had known before you got to the campus? Write an analysis of your findings, not to exceed two double-spaced pages.

5. The following headlines break one or more of the guidelines we discussed. Rewrite them so they are improved (*Make up details where necessary*):

   - DWDM: Beyond Multiplicity
   - New Benefits Handbook
   - Company Stock Price Soars to Record High
   - Sales Increased from Last Month's Report Due to Strong Marketing Program Launch

 Use InfoTrac College Edition to access information on topics in this chapter from hundreds of periodicals and scholarly journals.

Notes

1. Netcraft Ltd., "February 2004 Web Server Survey," http://news.netcraft.com/archives/web_server_survey.html.
2. Robyn Greenspan and CyberAtlas Staff, "More Than Half-Billion Online Globally," February 2003, http://cyberatlas.internet.com/big_picture/geographics/article/0,1323,5911_1593591,00.html.
3. Gail Chiasson, "2002 U.S. Online Sales Forecast Up 39%," PubZone.com (Montreal, Quebec, Canada: Rice Wine Communications, Inc., 2003).
4. Shel Holtz, *How Should I Put This? Interactive Public Relations* (Chicago, Ill.: Lawrence Ragan Communications, Inc., undated), p. 4.
5. Jeannine Kadane Lee, APR, "Precision Writing for the Web" (Dallas, Texas: QuickSilver Interactive Group, Inc., 2003).
6. Ibid.
7. Kimberly Hill, Report: "E-Mail Fails to Deliver Customer Service," September 2002, http://www.crmdaily.com/perl/story/19261.html.
8. Lee, "Precision Writing for the Web."

Selected Bibliography

D. Keith Denton, *Empowering Intranets to Implement Strategy, Build Teamwork, and Manage Change* (Westport, Conn.: Praeger Publishers, 2002).

Jane Dorner, *Writing for the Internet (One Step Ahead Series)* (New York: Oxford University Press USA, 2002).

Irene Hammerich and Claire Harrison, *Developing Online Content: The Principles of Writing and Editing for the Web* (Hoboken, N.J.: John Wiley & Sons, 2001).

Shel Holtz, *Public Relations on the Net: Winning Strategies to Inform and Influence the Media, the Investment Community, the Government, the Public, and More!* (Watertown, Mass.: AMACOM, 1999).

Shel Holtz, *The Intranet Advantage: Your Guide to Understanding the Total Intranet and the Communicator's Role* (San Francisco: International Association of Business Communicators, 2003).

Shel Holtz, *Writing for the Wired World: The Communicator's Guide to Online Contact* (San Francisco: International Association of Business Communicators, 1999).

Crawford Kilian, *Writing for the Web,* writers' ed. (Bellingham, Wash.: Self Counsel Press, 2000).

Laura Lemay, *Teach Yourself Web Publishing with HTML in a Week,* 4th ed. (Indianapolis, Ind.: Sams Publishing, 1998).

Keiko Pitter et al., *Every Student's Guide to the Internet* (New York: McGraw-Hill/Irwin, 1996).

Karen A. Schriver, *Dynamics in Document Design: Creating Text for Readers* (Hoboken, N.J.: John Wiley & Sons, 1996).

David W. Schumann and Esther Thorson, eds., *Advertising and the World Wide Web* (Mahwah, N.J.: Lawrence Erlbaum Associates, 1999).

Diane F. Witmer, *Spinning the Web: A Handbook for Public Relations on the Internet* (Boston, Mass.: Allyn & Bacon, 2000).

PART 5

Writing for a Media Mix

The combination of media and audiences discussed in these chapters emphasizes the need for integrated communication planning and writing.

CHAPTER FIFTEEN

Media Kits and Media Pitches

Media Kits

Working with the mass media requires the development of a *media kit*. Media kits used to be easy to describe: a pocket folder containing information for print and/or broadcast media. Media kit folders have ranged from basic pocket folders from the office supply shelf with a letterhead sticker on the cover to elaborate four-color packages with pockets for videos. Now a media kit more likely is digital—on an organization's Web site or in a colorful envelope with a CD-ROM that contains the media kit.

Yes, these are "media" kits, not "press" kits. The difference is that public relations practitioners prepare packages of information for all media to use, not just the newspapers or "press."

Traditionally the contents of the kits have varied based on their use, but the contents are always prepared with the medium in mind. For example, black-and-white glossy photographs that might be useful to print media are not included in broadcast media kits. Sound on CD-ROMs that might be in radio news kits are not included in television news kits, which might have videotape cartridges.

On the other hand, media might prefer that the entire textual contents of the media kit be available to them on a Web site or CD-ROM. The problem with CD-ROMs is knowing which computer system format to use. When media lists are compiled, it helps to discover this detail. But, if you don't know, having disks that are PC-compatible and Macintosh-compatible available to insert in kits will help. A better option is to put both formats on a CD-ROM.

If you are considering producing not just a text disk, but a CD-ROM with both text and graphics, you should first assess how many of the media you are serving are likely to use this technology for a media kit. You will also need to answer the same question as with a text disk of which system to choose or whether to produce a "cross-platform" CD-ROM that will run on either system.

To develop a good CD-ROM you may need a team of skilled people because it's unlikely at this stage of development for the technology that you can find all of the necessary talents in one or even two people. According to Tony Harrison, who has won some awards for this interactive technology, you need the skills of copywriters, graphic designers, illustrators, multimedia developers, computer programmers, videographers, photographers, audio engineers and voice talent.[1] You also may need some good musicians because most of the better packages have original music.

A CD-ROM can hold as much as 700 megabytes, and if you include a good access menu for your CD-ROM-based media kit, it will be easy to use. Harrison says his company includes helpful features on the CD-ROMs it creates, such as a search function that identifies stories by 36 key words and an inventory of almost 50 stock photos and illustrations. The text documents adhere to AP style and can be printed or saved to disk as editable text files. Also included are outside contacts, which can be used as additional sources.[2]

The advantage of using an organization's Web site for a media kit is that it can offer news media not only much more material but also much more flexibility. When information becomes outdated, changing the information on the Web site is fast and quite inexpensive, compared to trashing a supply of printed materials and reprinting.

In a study of corporate Web sites, QuickSilver Interactive Group, Inc. found that various companies offer as many as 65 features on their Web sites. Some of the more popular contents for both Web-based and printed media kits include:

- *About Us*—summary or overview of the organization
- *Annual Report(s)*—most recent year(s)
- *Biographical Information*—principals of the organization: officers, founders and others with pictures (head shots), downloadable or reproducible ones for print media, small ones for identification for broadcast media, high-quality ones for magazine use
- *Board of Directors*—names, affiliations and addresses
- *Calendar of Events*—information on coming teleconferences, webcasts and executives' speeches
- *Community Service Programs*—information on charitable and civic activities and policies on contributions
- *Contact Information*—information on who to contact for media inquiries, customer service and investor relations
- *Downloadable Logos and Photos*—various sizes and forms of organization's logo and photos of typical operations
- *Fact Sheet*—gives information about the organization: officers, offices with addresses and phone numbers, a description of what the organization is or makes or does
- *FAQs*—Frequently asked questions and answers
- *Financial Information*—earnings releases, financial highlights, stock charts, dividends history
- *Historical Facts*—background on the organization and historical milestones in its development—that is, when founded and where, when new activities began and so on
- *Position Papers*—selected copies of any position papers the organization has prepared on current issues

- *Profile or Backgrounder*—tells about the character of the organization and the nature of what it does, including Board committee charters and corporate code of ethics
- *SEC Filings*—information on filings with the Securities and Exchange Commission
- Hard-copy media kits often contain selected copies of the organization's serial publications such as magazines or newsletters.

Media representatives are going online in increasing numbers. A 1998 *Editor & Publisher* study of nearly 6,000 newspaper and magazine editors and broadcast news editors found that nearly half of respondents said "they or a colleague go online daily in search of news." That's up from the 33 percent who said they went online on a daily basis the year before.[3]

If you are using hard-copy media kits, then you need to think about how much material you are going to send and how to make it appealing. The most conservative choice is to use a *shell.* The shell for media kits is usually a basic folder that has the name and logo of the organization, and you can have these made up in bulk so they are available when you need them. The only time you would want to have a different shell printed would be for a special event. Then you want the theme of the special event to dominate, although not at the expense of losing the identification of the organization.

Media Kit Use

Media kits are used by organizations for basic information about the organization, special events (preliminary and on site), news conferences and crises. In all cases, the kit has a letter to the medium's user identifying the contents of the kit and the people to contact for more information. When kits are mailed, the kit letter is replaced by a cover letter explaining why the kit is being sent, its contents and any other particulars that would be important such as important dates or people who may be contacted.

The key to developing useful and used media kits is to think of who is going to be using them and what that newsperson is likely to need. (See Table 15.1.)

Media kits are not created to be sent to new members of the board of directors, for example. They are not packages of information for general use by someone who wants to know something about the organization. They are for hands-on use by working members of the news media: reporters, editors, news directors and producers. Remember that before you begin stuffing one with copies of ads or sales materials.

Media Kits for Special Events

The use of the kit is particularly important when you are preparing one for a special event. Special-event kits are somewhat different in their contents, which are as follows:

- A *basic fact sheet about the newsmaking event* should detail the event and explain its significance in strictly factual terms. This should be a "stand-alone" sheet that gives a contact's phone and address, because it may become separated from the rest of the material. You need to include all important dates, times, participants and their relationship to the organization and to each other, such as those who work for wholly owned subsidiaries.
- A *historical fact sheet about the event* that tells when it was first held, where, who attended and how many if that is significant. You need to give milestones in the event's history, being sure to make clear why each is significant.

T A B L E   1 5 . 1   *Preparing a Media Kit*

1. Define the purpose for the media kit.
2. Identify the publics you need to reach.
3. Identify the media reaching those publics.
4. Determine which media will receive the kits.
5. Consider how each item in the media kit relates to the purpose for the kit.
6. Consider how the news media recipients will use each item in the kit.
7. For every item included in the kit ask these questions:
   a. How do you expect the audience of each news medium to use the information?
   b. How does what you are providing the news medium convey that expectation to the medium's audience?
   c. What do you expect audiences of these media to do as a result of receiving this information? How will you measure that? (This question is significantly different from asking if the news media used the media kit or how much of it was used and when. That is easily measured. It's their audience's response that you need to know in order to determine if the kit's contents were effective.)

- A *program of events or schedule of activities* should have detailed time data, as that is especially significant to broadcasters. Provide a script if you have one. This is especially useful for the broadcast media but can be important for print photographers too.
- A *complete list of all participants* should explain their relationship to the organization and why they are a part of the event.
- *Biographical information on the principals as well as head shots* of them should be included. The black-and-white prints for newspapers and magazines should be of reproduction quality, and you should indicate when color pictures are available.
- A *straight news story* should give the basic information about the event in an announcement news approach. This should be about a page and a half, double-spaced on a 60-space line for print media and one or two short paragraphs triple-spaced for broadcast media. Be sure to give broadcast media both print and broadcast stories so they have the benefit of the additional information in the longer story. The print media need only the print version.
- A *longer general news story* that ties in the background information may be as long as three double-spaced pages for print media and one full page for broadcast media.
- A *feature story* or two should be included to offer some insight into the more interesting aspects of the special event. There need be no broadcast version of these, but these features should be included in the broadcast kits for information.
- A *page of isolated facts* about the special event and others in the past, if this is an annual event, should be included. These facts are often picked up by broadcasters to use if they cover the event, and sometimes they are incorporated in print copy written by reporters covering the event.
- *Visual materials* should be included, and this can be a problem if the event is a first-time affair. You'll have to develop photos about parts of the event in progress. If the event is an annual affair, you can include pictures from the past, but be sure these are properly labeled so they are not misleading. *Do not include any pictures that have been used in advertising.* Also

don't include any pictures of participants if they can be identified unless you have a written release. Attach information to the pictures so it can be removed without marring the photo.

- *Information on cooperating organizations* is important for their recognition and support as well as for the news medium. However, you don't just stuff the kit with what cooperating organizations give you. You get the information about the organizations, then prepare information sheets explaining their contribution to the event and their relationship to your organization. For example, an organization may be supplying picnic lunches for volunteers who are taking children on an outing. You need to tell how much food and something about the supplier as well as why that organization is participating in your special event. Use quotes from people in the cooperating organization. If the contribution is significant enough, you may want to do a special news release on one or more of the cooperating organizations. This is especially important for them if your organization is a nonprofit one and you have called on profit-making organizations for help in making the event a success. It is easier for you to get media attention than it is for them, and if you see that they get credit for their support, they will be more willing to participate in the future. Be sure that you clear the information you have prepared with them to be sure it is factually accurate. You don't want your credibility undermined by some participant saying that what you have said about them is inaccurate.

Cover letters for special-event kits should tell the news media why you think the event deserves the attention of each medium, in terms of the interest of that medium's audience in the event. You want to be sure you make coverage easy for them too. Let them know what arrangements are being made, such as the facilities of the media room, and how to schedule an interview with celebrities or other participants.

You'll need to include information about how they gain access to the event, such as how to apply for badges and vehicle passes. You might even want to include information about transportation or eating facilities in the area of the event if this is important. You could save the information about the immediate area in which the event is held—such as food facilities and so on—for the cover letter that goes with on-site media kits.

On-site cover letters are different. You will need to let the news media know who to contact at all hours of the day and night in case they have problems or questions, and you'll need to let them know how to get others from their news medium in (such as technical crew) and what to do about personal and vehicle passes.

On-site media kits are different too. You need a sheet of changes in the front, and you must replace every piece of paper where a change has created an error. Keeping dates on your news releases and all other information elsewhere, such as on fact sheets, makes this easier for you to do. Things get so hectic in a special event though that some people use different-colored paper for different days so there's not a mistake. But this can be a problem with materials like news releases.

Your on-site kits should have materials arranged in order of importance and have a story for each day of the event or each feature of the event if it is a one-day affair. An example of the latter would be a story on a speaker, a feature on the food for the luncheon or the chef, and perhaps a feature on the planning for the event if there are unusual aspects to that. You can include in on-site kits any promotional brochures about the event that have been used. These often have dates and times that can be a quick reference for the person covering the event. *Do not include these if facts have changed since they were produced.*

Media Kits for News Conferences   When you are preparing a media kit for a news conference, it makes a difference what the occasion for the conference is. News conferences should be called for only two reasons: (1) to provide media access to a celebrity or expert whose time is limited; (2) to offer face-to-face access to a spokesperson for the organization when there is a controversy. The latter will be covered later in this chapter in the section on crisis kits. So if you are preparing a media kit for a news conference in which you are providing access to a celebrity, you need the following materials:

• A *biographical sketch of the celebrity* that is up to date and a recent photo. If there are any restrictions on the use of the photo, you should not include it, because you probably won't be able to control its use.

• *Information about the relationship of the celebrity to your organization,* such as providing entertainment or being a spokesperson in promotions, on issues or on new developments. You need to think of "celebrity" in very broad terms here. The "celebrity" may be a researcher who has done breakthrough research that your organization is able to take advantage of through serving clients in a medical facility or through providing medication or medical procedures. You can provide this information either in a fact sheet or as a backgrounder.

• A *general news story* that is the kind of story someone covering the news conference would write. To do that, of course, you will need to have interviewed the person and asked the kind of questions the news media attending are likely to ask and incorporated the responses in the story.

• A *basic fact sheet about the organization.*

Promotional Media Kits   Promotional media kits are made up differently. (See Figure 15.1 for an example.) These kits often include advertising used in the promotion, quotes from critics or reviewers when appropriate or even reprints of entire newspaper stories (reprinted with permission). It may be that the promotion is part of a larger event such as a national touring performance or exhibit. In that case, many of the materials will be provided by those planning and sponsoring the event, but you will need to add your organization's information to the materials and tailor news and advertising for the media you'll be using.

One example of coordination was the General Motors sponsorship of "A Slave Ship Speaks: The Wreck of the Henrietta Marie," an exhibit of the only identifiable slave shipwreck in the Western Hemisphere. The exhibit of artifacts and objects recovered from the ship, which sank in the summer of 1700 in waters 35 miles off of Key West after unloading the cargo of slaves, went to 20 cities over a three-year period.

General Motors had the basic media kit materials prepared by the Chisholm-Mingo Group in New York. To these, each exhibit venue added its own information. Accompanying the exhibit was a 63-page softcover book that included articles about the exhibit's materials from the National Association of Black Scuba Divers, whose members worked with the Mel Fisher Maritime Heritage Society, a brief history of the slave trade, a piece on the African diaspora and an article on the archaeology of the *Henrietta Marie.* Also, with the exhibit, was a hardcover book available for purchase at the exhibit. The hardcover book was entitled *Spirits of the Passage: The Transatlantic Slave Trade in the Seventeenth Century* by Madeleine Burnside and Rosemarie Robotham, published by Simon & Schuster. Many special publics needed consideration in promoting this exhibit, and the expectation of the sponsors was important to the exhibitors at each venue.

FIGURE 15.1

Media Kit   *A good way to get news media representatives' attention is to produce an unusual media kit. This three-dimensional kit from the Heinz EQ Squirt Funky Purple Launch—winner of a top national award from the Public Relations Society of America—was distributed to introduce a new ketchup from Heinz. Called EZ Squirt, it's purple, as the name suggests, and joins other EZ Squirt ketchups in Tomato Red and Blastin' Green. The lead for one of the accompanying news releases began, "Grab your buns, and brace yourself."*

Reprinted with permission of Heinz North America.

HEINZ 57 CENTER
357 6TH AVENUE
PITTSBURGH, PA 15222

CONTACT: Michael Mullen
Heinz North America
412-237-3562
michael.mullen@hjheinz.com

Kristin Sofran
Jack Horner Communications Inc.
412-473-3407
kristins@jackhorner.com

FOR IMMEDIATE RELEASE

HEINZ KETCHUP GETS FUNKY WITH NEW PURPLE EZ SQUIRT

Pittsburgh—July 31, 2001—Purple reigns. Purple reigns. Heinz Ketchup announced today that Heinz EZ Squirt Funky Purple® will join Heinz EZ Squirt Tomato Red and Blastin' Green in its growing complement of colored condiments. Consumers will start seeing the color purple on grocers' shelves in early September.

"The tremendous success of Heinz EZ Squirt Blastin' Green showed us that kids love decorating their food with colors that are bright, wild, even a little … funky," said Casey Keller, Managing Director for Ketchup, Condiments and Sauces at Heinz North America. "Literally thousands of people called, wrote or e-mailed us demanding a new Heinz EZ Squirt color, and the vast majority of kids asked for purple."

The Heinz EZ Squirt color team turned to the experts for help – kids. After all, children are the No. 1 consumers of ketchup, devouring more than half of all ketchup in the United States – roughly 5 billion ounces annually. Kids and the Heinz EZ Squirt color team developed new prototypes that would give kids a bold new color they can use to personalize everything from hot dogs and french fries to macaroni and cheese.

"Boys and girls alike love the cool purple color," said Brian Hansberry, Vice President of Marketing for Ketchup, Condiments and Sauces at Heinz North America. "Just look at kids' entertainment, and you'll find everything from purple computers to Harry Potter purple lightning bolts. Purple is a bold, fun color that brings a hint of mystery and magic to kids' condiment creations."

Funky Purple Makes Meals More Fun

"Purple is one of the hottest colors for kids right now. In an era when kids can't get enough monsters and wizards, the bold, powerful color purple has reached new heights of popularity. It's consistently a kid favorite," said Jay de Sibour, President of the Color Marketing Group, a not-for-profit international association of 1,700 color designers involved in the use of colors as they apply to marketing of goods and services. "Purple is a color with attitude that appeals to kids of all ages and is equally liked by both boys and girls."

-more-

WWW.HEINZ.COM

1 5 . 1 *(c o n t i n u e d)*

Kids like psychedelic purple flowers on hamburger buns and purple racing stripes on hot dogs. The curvy soft plastic of the Heinz EZ Squirt bottle is designed for smaller hands and the typical, two-fisted grip favored by kids. The nozzle is notably narrow to create a thin stream, enabling young condiment artists to use more precision when decorating their dinners. Moms and dads are sure to like the added Vitamin C that Heinz EZ Squirt Funky Purple offers.

Nearly a year ago, Heinz EZ Squirt Blastin' Green captured the imagination of consumers – kids and grownups alike. More than 10 million bottles were sold in the first seven months, with Heinz factories working 24 hours a day, seven days a week to keep up with demand. Desperate consumers eager to get their hands on Heinz EZ Squirt Blastin' Green tried everything from impersonating Heinz executives' relatives to bidding for bottles posted on eBay. The product launch made headlines around the world, even though its distribution is only now expanding outside the U.S.

Kids can learn more about the new Funky Purple EZ Squirt product by logging onto www.heinz.com.

About Heinz

With sales over US$9 billion, H.J. Heinz Company is one of the world's leading marketers of branded foods to consumers everywhere, whether in supermarkets, restaurants or on the go. Its 50 companies operate in some 200 countries, with more than 20 power brands, including the Heinz® brand with nearly US$3 billion in annual sales. In addition to the Heinz brand, other famous brands within the company include: StarKist®, Ore-Ida®, 9-Lives®, Wattie's®, Plasmon®, Farley's®, Smart Ones®, Bagel Bites®, John West®, Petit Navire®, Kibbles 'n Bits®, Pounce®, Pup-Peroni®, Orlando®, ABC®, Olivine®, Juran® and Pudliszki®. Heinz also uses the famous brands Weight Watchers®, Boston Market® and Linda McCartney Frozen Meals® under license. Information on Heinz is available at www.heinz.com.

# # #

B-Roll Satellite Coordinates for Tuesday, July 31, 2001

10:30-10:45AM/ET C-Band Telstar 5/Transponder 16/Audio 6.2 & 6.8
2:00-2:15PM/ET   C-Band Galaxy 3/Transponder 3/Audio 6.2 & 6.8

Note to Media: Photos are available at www.businesswire.com.

1 5 . 1   (*c o n t i n u e d*)

Media kits that are offered on a CD-ROM—other than simple text that can be produced quickly and easily—should be for something special due to their production cost and the time it takes to make them. Depending on the organization, it's possible that you could have a basic one made for the organization. However, such material is easily dated so you need to be sure to provide for periodic updates. It's more likely that you'd create a media kit for a special event or a special observation like a 50-year anniversary.

15.1 (*c o n t i n u e d*)

Some of the materials needed are the same:

- Basic fact sheet
- Historical fact sheet
- Backgrounder
- Biographies of all principals (company officers, speakers, celebrities and others)
- Isolated facts about the situation that can be used as column items, fillers or a story idea

15.1 (*continued*)

- Visuals that include photos of the principals, pictures of the company or the event or whatever is appropriate to illustrate the purpose of the kit, but carefully chosen and edited with accompanying identification
- News stories
- Features
- Information on any cooperating organizations or perhaps on the site if the event is being held in an unusual place
- A source information directory so reporters or editors can locate names of people to call or to send faxes or email messages. Be sure to include a technology "help" number in case the disc is unreadable.

These suggestions for creating an effective CD-ROM are offered by Tony Harrison:[4]

- Make the CD-ROM as interactive as possible with a wealth of information.

Heinz EZ Squirt Funky Purple Media Highlights

Funky Purple was taste-tested on CNBC

Heinz EZ Squirt Funky Purple press kit, on the desk of *CNBC Squawk Box*

Heinz CEO Bill Johnson promoted Funky Purple on CNBC

On *Today*, Anne Curry shared the Funky Purple news with Katie and Matt

Bryant Gumble tried Heinz EZ Squirt Funky Purple on *The Early Show*

Regis and Kelly demonstrated a live Funky Purple taste test

CNN Today featured images of www.ezsquirt.com

15.1 (*continued*)

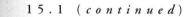

- Make the CD-ROM easy to use by creating easy interfaces with big buttons, large type and readable fonts providing easy navigation from point to point so the users don't get lost offering mini-indexes for different locations so users know what's there without having to go into the location.
- Arrange your images in an easy-to-use order by

  - Scanning photos (or copying digital images) onto CD-ROMs if you have a lot of still photography
  - Organizing the images well, so using and choosing the images is easy
  - Creating an image-placement database so that, if a photo or illustration is needed in several places in the CD-ROM or needs to be replaced, the change can easily be made
  - Saving (archiving) each step in the process of graphic images so that you can make changes without having to start the process over (for example, an image created in Illustrator, touched up in Photoshop and saved as a PICT file has a typo)

- Get rid of all of the bugs in the system so the CD-ROM will perform at the bottom of the system as well as at the top of the line.
- Update periodically to keep contents current.

Media Kit for a Crisis   You may find that you are using your crisis media kit at a news conference because the confusion caused by crises generally means that at least one news conference is necessary. In the event of a severe, ongoing crisis such as effects of a natural disaster like an earthquake or hurricane, you may be giving daily briefings as well.

With information changing so quickly in a crisis, you will need to keep updating your Web page. This keeps down the number of direct media contacts you have to handle. It does mean, though, that in addition to your computer at the media center for the crisis communications, you must have a printer and a copier available.

Because crises are largely unpredictable, you need to have a supply of basic materials set aside for quick assembly. There won't be time to locate and print these items. You will have the media kit shell, which is a basic folder for the organization. You also should have on hand:

- Basic fact sheet about the organization, with names and titles; addresses of the home office and all branches or subsidiaries (if any); phone numbers, including the numbers of security people and night numbers that override the main control and put the caller through to the person on duty
- Backgrounder on the organization itself—what it is and what it does
- Biographical information on the principals of the organization—officers and board, including long in-depth pieces on the principals, often called "current biographical summaries," which are used for speeches and introductions but in this case may become "standing obits" (material ready for use in case of death)
- Detailed description of all facilities, giving layouts and square footage in each area as well as the number of people who work there at what times, as some of these may be involved in the crisis
- Information on all the activities of the organization, including products, services, research funded or ongoing, and equipment
- Visual material, including pictures of facilities and principals
- Historical fact sheet on the institution, giving important milestones in its development

- Statistics on the facilities and the institution, including number of people employed; annual financial statements; major contracts with unions or suppliers; details of lawsuits pending against the institution; information on regulatory or accrediting agencies with some sort of oversight authority over the institution, its products and its services (for instance, the Food and Drug Administration or a hospital's accreditation bureau)

Keeping these materials updated for hasty assembly may be demanding for some organizations, but most have this material available on a fairly current basis from their annual report. *Material to be added* includes:

- A statement from the crisis spokesperson about the crisis (provided in audio for the broadcast media)
- Information about who to contact for information about the crisis as it continues or moves toward resolution

(Also see Chapter 20 for information on planning for crisis communication.)

Materials for Media Rooms—Crises and Special Events

The media room in any crisis or special event is an information hub. You need to be sure it is that and not a hubbub. So that staff and reporters are not frustrated, you need to have racks of information available that include all of the materials listed for the kits. In summary, you need:

- Fact sheets, informational and historical
- Backgrounders on the organization and situation
- Annual reports and informational brochures
- Biographical data and photos of organizational principals
- Special facts, such as information on the site if it's a crisis, or on the event
- Statistics on the organization and/or event
- News releases, dated and numbered
- Quotes from principals, dated and numbered, and any actualities you have of these
- Visuals, with information and identifications attached

What you will be adding to these are *news briefs* on breaking or developing news. You should have a daily summary of new information, something that might be given at a crisis news conference or news briefing and something usually put out each day of a special event to let reporters know what's going on and what has happened that day. Like news releases, these should be dated and numbered so you have a reference later. Unfortunately, the reference isn't always for quick retrieval later. Sometimes in crisis situations, news releases and news briefs are part of the documentation in a court case. If you have a crisis, you will be sued in all probability. Keep that in mind as you prepare materials. Stick to the facts. Think in advance about what reporters will want to know.

In case of crises, here are some facts reporters are going to want to know (and will find out from other sources if you don't provide the information):

- Numbers of dead and/or injured
- What was damaged and how (descriptive, not dollar amounts)

- Time of crisis events
- Location of all crisis events
- Names of dead and injured (released only after the next of kin are notified)
- Relationship of the casualties to the organization
- Number of people within your organization who were involved and who they are
- Who the spokesperson is and how to get in touch with that person
- What the effects of the crisis are on the organization

This last item is the troublesome question. Don't speculate. Don't sound too upbeat, because you'll appear to be insensitive. Don't be too negative, because your words will affect the morale of employees and the responses of other publics, such as investors and regulators, to the crisis. Keep a written account of everything released, to whom and on what date.

Special-event news briefs are generally on more positive news than a crisis, but you need to be sure you have good stories every day for print and broadcast media. Think in advance and plan in advance for good print stories and broadcast coverage. You will need to move around the event interviewing people and getting story material to provide to various media representatives as tip sheets or story ideas. This is your job, not theirs. If you want the event covered, you will have to do the fact-finding and initial story preparation. Again, keep copies and dates and names of the people you've given a story idea to. Remember, feature ideas are given to only one medium at a time. If a medium seems interested but doesn't use the story in a reasonable period of time, you are free to give the same information to another medium after confirming that the first medium is not likely to use it.

At news conferences for crises and special events, you need to be sure you cover the news conference and capture what occurs on video- and audiotape so you can write a follow-up release afterward. That story will incorporate what actually occurred at the news conference. You send the news conference media kit with this story as a substitute for the earlier news story to news media who were unable to attend the conference. You have to be careful about doing this because in writing the coverage story you don't want to take advantage of good questions asked by media people who were energetic enough to cover the news conference. Nevertheless, you want to get as much mileage as you can out of the news conference.

Media Pitches

A *media pitch* is just what it sounds like—a proposal to a media outlet. It's intended to "sell" a story idea on a specific topic. The media pitch can be in the form of an email, a phone call, a fax or a letter, depending in large measure on how well you know the person for whom the pitch is intended. (See Figure 15.2 for an example.)

The pitch can be for a new product or service, a new use for an existing product, an event or a movie—in other words, just about anything. The media pitch is the accepted way to make media representatives aware of a story idea in a clear and concise format. Each pitch should be targeted to a specific medium and should contain specific, unusual story angles.

Perhaps the most important part of a pitch is to present enough information to demonstrate that the story idea is of interest to their readers, listeners or viewers.

Sample Email Media Pitch

1600 Saratoga Ave., Ste. 403, #191
San Jose, CA 95129
www.prtrainingco.com

Hi, John:

I'd like to talk to you about the <u>world's first live, full-length sporting</u> <u>event to be webcast Feb. 15 at 2 p.m. EST.</u>

This is the first of more than 150 European pro soccer events that will be webcast by XYZ Company and 123Sports.com over the next two years.

Are you available Monday between 1 and 3 p.m. or Tuesday afternoon between 2 and 4 p.m. for a phone interview with our CEO John Hancock?

Please let me know which date and time work for you. You can contact me at 408-559-6090 or email me at joeblow@pragency.com

Look forward to hearing from you.

FIGURE 15.2

Media Pitch   *One way to let media representatives know about an event or other newsworthy activity is to use a "media pitch." This is an example of an email pitch; telephone contact also can be effective in "pitching"—making media people aware of what you have to offer.*
Source: Reprinted with permission of The Public Relations Training Company, San Jose, California, www.prttrainingco.com.

Be Prepared and Be Persistent

Before you send your pitch letter or email, be sure you know the publication or station. Check *Bacon's* or another media directory, and check with PRSA members or others in the market where it's located.

Todd Brabender, president of Spread The News PR, says that one media pitch isn't enough and that your opportunity for placements "increases with meticulous, media follow-ups and re-pitches." "Based on my professional experience as a PR/Publicity specialist," he said, "I would estimate that media placements occur in the following manner:

25% occur after the 1st–2nd pitch,
50% occur after the 3rd–5th pitch,
25% occur after the 6th–8th pitch."[5]

The California Association for Health Services at Home (CAHSAH) encourages its home care provider members to use a series of media "hits" in selling a story idea. They recommend that "Media Hit #1" be made by fax, mail or email if specifically requested. ". . . Craft your pitch letter to stand out from the crowd." They advise opening with an interesting statement "that motivates the reader to read on. Next, explain why the media should be interested in the pitch. Finally, address your proposal to a particular person, not just 'editor,' in the form of a standard, one-page professional letter."[6]

CAHSAH says the second contact should be by telephone and should focus on how the story will appeal to the reporter's audience. The third contact, they say, should be by mail and should include your organization's media kit. Finally, they recommend following up by telephone to be sure the media contact has all of the information needed to develop the story.[7]

Check the editorial calendars of magazines—especially trade and professional publications. The editorial calendar is a tentative list of topics that the publication intends to cover during the next 12 months. By examining a publication's editorial calendar, you should be able to develop story "angles" that will give each magazine or newsletter editor reasons to include your organization in one or more issues. If you have questions about whether your story will "fit" into an issue, call the editor, briefly explain your idea, and ask if it sounds as if it will work. A phone call may save both the editor and you considerable time developing a pitch that doesn't have a chance of success. Editorial calendars include submission deadlines, so you need to pitch your article concepts well in advance of those deadlines to allow time for developing the article before the deadline. (See Table 15.2 for more tips on media pitches.)

Conclusions

- Media kits, a part of campaign writing, may appear in many forms, including digital versions on Web sites and on CD-ROMs.
- Media kits are prepared especially for the use of particular media. It's not a situation in which one kit will do the job. The way the kit is delivered to the medium usually depends on the situation. It may be mailed if it's something the reporters need in advance. It may be hand-delivered to local media if it's a local event. It may be distributed at a news conference or available in the media room set up for a special event or a crisis.
- When you are using a CD-ROM for your media kit, you need to make a decision about what system to use or whether you need a "cross-platform" CD-ROM so it will run on either a PC or a Macintosh.
- Prepare for a sizable budget to produce a CD-ROM and assemble a good team of compatible people who bring to the job the skills of copywriters, graphic designers, illustrators, multimedia developers, computer programmers, videographers, photographers, audio engineers, vocal talent and musicians.

T A B L E   1 5 . 2   *10 Commandments of Successful Media Relations*

"Pitching," or proposing stories to news media people, requires skills that can be acquired by public relations practitioners. Here are 10 rules that one media relations practitioner uses in her successful business.

1. **Stop Doing Stupid Things!**
   - Stop promoting every press release
   - Stop getting on the phone before you're ready
   - Stop pitching without all the facts
   - Stop calldowns and smiles and dials
   - Stop sounding like a PR person

2. **Start with the Goal in Mind**
   - Creating a relationship is your primary goal
   - Know what you want the reporter to do *before* you pitch
   - Avoid competing messages
   - Keep It Simple

3. **Think Like a Reporter**
   - Is this a good story?
   - How does this relate to the publication and the reporter's interest?
   - Is it worth the time?
   - Do I have all the information I need to sell this story?
   - Does the story have legs, or is it just a fluff piece?

4. **Find the Story Before You Sell**
   - Media relations is 98 percent preparation and 2 percent execution
   - Research the reporter
   - Research the publication
   - Read what the reporter writes
   - Know your client and product and how they differ from the competition
   - Know why this story is right for the media outlet

5. **Prepare Your Pitch Bag**
   - Prepare and use "pitch points"—a one page cheat sheet with client facts, background and important features—and keep it in front of you during the pitch
   - Have two or three different story ideas in mind if the first one doesn't work
   - Be able to switch tracks mid-conversation
   - Know extra things about your client—human interest, etc.
   - Be willing to get additional information for the reporter

6. **Get in and Get out**
   - Be yourself
   - Speak and think in bullets
   - Don't ramble—have your pitch points in front of you
   - Don't dress the pitch up—stick to the facts
   - Be conversational and casual

7. **Give a Clear Call to Action**
   - Say WHAT you want, then WHY they should do it *"There's a new hockey team in town. I thought it would make a great feature for the sports section."*
   - Not IF, but WHEN—*Are you available Wednesday or Thursday between 10 and noon?*

8. **It's Never "A Good Time"**
   - Don't always ask, "Is this a good time?" Do you have time for telemarketers?
   - Don't apologize for pitching—it's your job and they know it (just do it well)
   - Give a brief qualifier: *"I wanted to talk to you about a new time management device that's saving companies $5 billion a year . . ."*
   - By the time you qualify and apologize, you could have sold the story

9. **They Won't Buy if You Don't Believe**
   - Don't pitch until you "get it"
   - Get excited about what you're pitching
   - Enthusiasm sells
   - Be committed to the idea and why it's right for this pub
   - Ride the wave—when you feel it, go for it
   - Trust your intuition

10. **Become a Valued Resource**
    - Be willing to not sell your story the first time you call
    - Give quality information when they need it
    - Anticipate their needs and take care of them
    - Take time to get to know reporters as people
    - Give a story away to get more later

Source: From the forthcoming book, *Secrets of Successful Pitching: How to Talk So Editors Will Listen* by Margo M. Mateas, Copyright 2004. Public Relations Training Company, www.prtrainingco.com. Reprinted with permission.

- The advantage of a digital media kit on a Web site or a CD-ROM is that it offers more material and more flexibility.
- The CD-ROM's envelope needs to provide easy identification and visual appeal to get people in the media to consider using it.
- Although the shell for a traditional media kit is something you usually have made up in quantities, you probably will have a special media kit made up for an event, one that promotes the theme of the event. Each media kit has a letter to go with it. The letter is for the person who will be using the kit. If the kit is mailed, it's a cover letter. If the kit is given to a reporter, the letter is inside and generally tells the reporter basic facts and what is in the kit.
- Media kits are used by organizations to convey basic information about the organization, to tell media about special events, to hand out at news conferences and to make available in times of crises.
- Media kit contents vary according to not only the technology of the medium but also the situation for its use. Nevertheless, media kits do have some basic contents: organizational fact sheets, historical fact sheets, biographical material on the organization's principals, a backgrounder and perhaps position papers, serial publications and the annual report if there is one, plus a page of isolated facts about the organization. The kit may or may not have a news release, but ordinarily it does have at least one straight news story related to the occasion for the media kit's use. It may or may not have visuals.
- The key to developing useful and used media kits is to think of who is going to be using them and what that newsperson is likely to need.
- Media kits for special events in addition to being thematic are likely to have visuals and more news releases, especially features on certain aspects of the event. You want to be sure that you include information on organizations cooperating with you in the event, information that you should clear with them before including it.
- Media kits given out at news conferences are designed especially for that occasion and should provide substantial background information for the reporter, whose time at the news conference is going to be limited.
- Media kits offered on CD-ROMs require some of the elements of basic kits, but you need to make the material easily accessible and be sure the CD will work in different systems.
- Some media kits given at news conferences deal with crises, but generally the crisis media kit has to be prepared quickly from available materials with a brief summary of the situation and quotes from the principals added. The core of these is regularly updated, reliable basic information on the organization itself as well as how to get more information.
- The materials in media kits should also be available in media rooms set up to accommodate reporters covering special events and crises. All materials should be dated and numbered or otherwise coded so you can identify the specific piece later. You need to keep a record of what was given to whom with what medium and when, not only for internal tracking but also for later reference. Media kits project an image of the organization, and it's important that you remember that the media kit is speaking for the organization when no one else is there. Be sure it's a good representative of the organization.
- Keep your Web page updated during a crisis. That helps handle media demands for fresh information. You'll need at the crisis communication center in addition to your computer a printer and a copier to provide hard copies of the updates.

- A *media pitch* is just what it sounds like—a proposal to a media outlet. It's intended to "sell" a story idea on a specific topic.
- The media pitch can be in the form of an email, a phone call, a fax or a letter, depending on how well you know the person for whom the pitch is intended.
- The pitch can be for a new product or service, a new use for an existing product, an event or a movie—in other words, just about anything.
- The media pitch is the accepted way to make media representatives aware of a story idea in a clear and concise format.
- Each pitch should be targeted to a specific medium and should contain specific, unusual story angles.
- By examining a publication's editorial calendar, you should be able to develop story "angles" that will give each magazine or newsletter editor reasons to include your organization in one or more issues.

Exercises

1. Plan a basic media kit for your university to use. If you were an intern in your university's news service and were asked to assemble a media kit for "general use," what would you look for to put in it? Write the letter that you think should go with it.

2. Write a media pitch letter for a local nonprofit organization, Computers For U, that puts computers into libraries for public use. The organization has received a $500,000 grant from a local entrepreneur who wants to remain anonymous. Due to the grant, Computers For U can double the number of computers in each library and is having a "ribbon cutting" event at the main library, where the first computers purchased with grant monies will be installed. Focus on how the computers will help job seekers and low-income citizens using the computers and Internet connections without charge. Insert blanks where numbers and/or names will be inserted.

 Use InfoTrac College Edition to access information on topics in this chapter from hundreds of periodicals and scholarly journals.

Notes

1. Tony Harrison, "The ABCs of CD-ROMs," *Public Relations Tactics,* September 1996, p. 14.
2. Ibid.
3. "Traditional Journalism Is Changed Irrevocably," *Editor & Publisher,* February 17, 1998, http://www.nua.com/surveys/index.cgi?f=VS&art_id=887722978&rel=true (accessed March 24, 2003).
4. Harrison, "The ABCs of CD-ROMs."
5. Todd Brabender, "Turning Your Media Pitch into a Media Hit: Increase Your Coverage by Increasing Your Pitches," March 18, 2001, http://www.saleslobby.com/Mag/0401/FETB.asp (accessed December 12, 2003).

6. California Association for Health Services at Home (CAHSAH) "Media Relations," undated, http://www.cahsah.org/HCMonth/HCmonthmediatips.htm (accessed March 24, 2003).

7. Ibid.

Selected Bibliography

Jim Avery, *Advertising Campaign Planning: Developing an Advertising-Based Marketing Plan,* 2d ed. (Chicago: Copy Workshop, 1997).

Mary Anne Morfitt, *Campaign Strategies and Message Design: A Practitioner's Guide from Start to Finish* (Westport, Conn.: Praeger Publishers, 1999).

Sandra Moriarty with John Burnett (contributor), *Introduction to Marketing Communication: An Integrated Approach* (Englewood Cliffs, N.J.: Prentice Hall, 1997).

Doug Newsom, Judy VanSlyke Turk and Dean Kruckeberg, *This Is PR: The Realities of Public Relations,* 8th ed. (Belmont, Calif.: Wadsworth, 2004).

Ronald E. Rice and Charles K. Atkin, eds., *Public Communication Campaigns,* 3d ed. (Thousand Oaks, Calif.: Sage Publications, 2000).

Charles T. Salmon, ed., *Information Campaigns: Balancing Social Values and Social Change* (Thousand Oaks, Calif.: Sage Publications, 1989).

Donald E. Schultz and Beth E. Barnes, *Strategic Advertising Campaigns,* 4th ed. (Lincolnwood, Ill.: NTC Business Books, 1998).

Gary W. Selnow, *High Tech Campaigns: Computer Technology in Political Campaigns* (Westport, Conn.: Praeger, 1994).

V. A. Shiva, *The Internet Publicity Guide: How to Maximize Your Marketing and Promotion in Cyberspace* (New York: Allworth Press, 1997).

Speeches and Other Presentations

Speeches are presentations, but the presenter is one person who may or may not use any visuals. Other presentations are more elaborate, always with visuals and/or handouts for the audience and sometimes complex productions with music and costumed performers. Presentations may involve a single presenter, but often involve more than one.

What speeches and presentations have in common for public relations writers is the consideration of two critical elements: the impression the audience will take away from the experience and the information that audience will retain. In some situations, a persuasive element is crucial because of what the audience is expected to do or to think as a result of the experience.

Speeches and presentations are strategic tools. Organizational, business and functional strategies collectively influence and shape message strategy, as you'll see in Chapter 20. Each poses some questions that must be answered by the public relations writer before launching the project.

Regarding organizational strategies, what is the reality within the organization's mission, its goals and objectives, its resources? What strategic function does a speech or presentation serve in fulfilling a goal? How will that speech or presentation be accepted internally? How will the speech or presentation affect the organization's primary publics, those most closely identified with the organization?

In terms of business strategies, what does the organization expect as a result of the speech or presentation? Is direct action a needed consequence? Is delayed response not only anticipated but desired? What has to happen from the organization's investment in the time and trouble to give the speech or make the presentation?

The functional strategy is how the speech or presentation fits into the overall communication tactics. Is publicity a crucial factor? Or is a subtle, low-key persuasive approach needed?

What effects are anticipated from the various publics who will have direct exposure to the speech or presentation? What about side effects from those who read or hear about the speech or presentation? How will these be measured?

All of these considerations are critical ingredients in preliminary planning. A significant consideration also is how close the audience is to the information being presented. If the speech or presentation is for internal audiences such as employees or related trade or professional groups, some allowances can be made for assumptions about familiarity with the topic. If the audiences are primarily external, nothing can be taken for granted, and some special care needs to be taken to eliminate misunderstandings or misinterpretations. Some speeches or presentations can have negative public relations consequences, often just because of one word or phrase.

Speeches

Delivering a speech is a hazardous undertaking. A speech takes place in real time—once. Without audience attention, no communication can occur. A speaker can only send messages, verbally and nonverbally, to an audience. It's the audience that gives those messages meaning.

For this reason, writing speeches and scripts demands more attention and care from the public relations writer than almost any other writing task. You can't simply write down your thoughts on a subject and expect them to be delivered successfully by any speaker. Audiences react emotionally to the speaker's authority, trustworthiness, tolerance and friendliness, so the speechwriter must consider these factors when writing. In essence, this means the speech must be personalized. The words must go with the person. A speaker must sound natural and not as though he or she were reading cue cards. A person who feels comfortable with the words being spoken will be a more credible speaker. Direct interaction with an audience in either a speech or a visuals/words presentation brings out the best in most of us. The person preparing the material must remember that, although the audience is the ultimate receiver of the information, the person presenting it is most important. The speaker is both medium and message.

Sometimes public relations writers deliver speeches themselves, and in these cases it should be easy to write a natural-sounding speech. But there's more to consider than just the speaker. Whether writing for another person or for yourself, you must have an idea of what the audience will be like. What experiences do audience members bring with them? What do they expect from the speaker? What stereotypes do they hold? That is, what are the "pictures in their heads"? If you don't know these things, you won't be able to write an effective speech.

You need to know the language patterns of the audience as well as of the speaker, because certain words used in particular ways can send thoughts down familiar paths. Remember that the connotations of words are as important as the denotations. And keep in mind that meanings change with time and that the same words may mean different things in different contexts or in different parts of the country. This means you can't write like you talk (or like the speaker talks) without considering how the audience talks.

Words, important as they are, aren't the only thing to be considered. Nonverbal cues can help emphasize points or obscure them. Audiences are sensitive to body movements, gestures, facial expressions, physical appearance and displays of personality and emotion. Effective speakers use these nonverbal expressions to hold attention and to help get the message across. Most speakers videotape rehearsals to perfect the blend of words and nonverbal expressions.

Many speechwriters get stalled at the beginning because they don't ask some important questions: Why was the speaker invited to address this particular group? What do the group members expect to hear? What does the speaker want to accomplish by giving a speech to this particular group? What particular topic will meet the speaker's needs and the group's expectations? You have to answer these questions before you start writing.

The next two questions have to be considered together: How long should the speech be, and what is the physical setting? A luncheon group won't tolerate as long an address as a dinner group, for example. People attending luncheons usually have other obligations; people who go to dinner are making an evening of it. Are there other speakers? Who are they and what are their topics? (These last questions are especially important if the speech is part of a seminar.)

Types of Speeches

Public relations people usually deal with four basic types of speeches: informative, persuasive, entertaining and technical. A fifth, less formal type of speech is termed brief remarks.

Informative   The informative speech generally—but not always—makes use of visuals. The subject matter is information that can readily be understood by audiences with little or no background in the subject matter. It thus is an educational opportunity for the organization. Such a speech may consist of telling a civic organization what the speaker's organization does, or it may involve telling an advisory body or an internal public what the organization is planning to do or has done. The speech given by the head of an organization at the annual meeting falls in this category.

Persuasive   The persuasive speech attempts to sell an audience on an idea, a person or a course of action. It could also be used to promote a specific product—anything from T-shirts to season tickets to the opera. More likely, though, the subject is something more abstract and therefore more difficult to sell. The speech might be aimed at convincing employees to take an early retirement opportunity or to contribute to a political action committee. It could be intended to convince a union of the desirability of accepting management's proposal or to favorably impress investor rating agencies like Moody's with the state of the organization. Presentations like these may also make use of graphs and even booklets of charts and supporting documentation.

Entertaining   The presentation may be designed primarily to entertain, such as an after-dinner talk or a luncheon speech. In some cases, a keynote address may be classified as chiefly entertaining, although these are generally more purposeful. Even when emphasis is placed on giving the audience an enjoyable experience, information about the organization is presented and the speaker tries to leave the audience with a favorable impression not only of herself or himself, but also of the organization.

Technical   The technical presentation almost always involves visuals, usually Microsoft PowerPoint slides, or a videotape, and printed handouts. A problem with technical presentations is that the technology often fails. PowerPoint presentations are particularly vulnerable to incompatible components or unfavorable lighting. Videotapes sometimes don't work as well as planned either, for a variety of reasons. Tapes from broadcast stations, for example, need to be transferred to another format to be used in VCRs, the equipment most likely available to speakers. Technical presentations are usually for peers at trade or professional meetings, or an official presentation to a regulatory body or a board of directors. The audience is likely to be less forgiving because it wants and needs the information. Be sure to have a backup plan for a verbal-only presentation with handouts.

Brief Remarks   Other speeches fall into the category of brief remarks, which are given on special occasions as expressions of thanks, welcome or acceptance. Although certainly important, these need not be entirely scripted unless the person speaking is uncomfortable without a script. What works best for these occasions is to develop the gist or content of the remarks and have the speaker put them in his or her own words. If it is a highly official function, it may be better to use a script and rehearse the speaker a number of times until she or he is comfortable with the brief remarks.

Planning

After you know the length and the setting of your speech, make a list of proposed topics and begin your research. One of the best places to begin is the *Readers' Guide to Periodical Literature,* especially if the audience is a general one. You can look up the articles listed and find out what the audience might have been exposed to recently. If the audience is a specialized group, consult the publications that group members receive and find out what is being written. You'll learn their current concerns and get an idea of what the group is like.

Most speeches written for public relations purposes are informative speeches. After you have determined what the audience has already been exposed to, you will need to do research on the topic chosen. Although you may feel you already know the material well enough to write a speech in your sleep, do some library research. Some can be done from your computer using various search engines. Most libraries have access to collections if you are not a subscriber to information services. All your knowledge of the topic is likely to be from an insider's point of view. You probably have seen some materials that come from competitors and critics, but you should look at what has appeared in the mass media as well. *The New York Times Index* is a good source. Most public libraries in metropolitan areas and in cities with a university have electronic research capabilities. Select your topic and have the literature searched for sources. Remember that, in writing an informative speech, you are charged with offering members of the audience new and valuable information and then helping them understand and retain it. When you are writing a speech for someone else to deliver, you need to meet with the speaker after this initial research to get an idea of what he or she thinks is most important and to determine the slant or approach for the presentation.

Paring and Timing

If you have done your research well, you will have many more ideas than you can or should introduce in a single speech. Begin paring. Cut away until you have no more than three items you want to communicate.

Select the three most important ideas you want people in the audience to carry away with them, and then present the ideas as something fresh and meaningful. (It helps if the ideas are startling in themselves, but don't fake it.) Give the listeners some way to associate these ideas with others they hold. You'll have to repeat the ideas often to make sure they are retained, but don't be redundant. You don't want the audience thinking, "You just said that a few minutes ago." You also have to introduce the ideas in a logical sequence, using relationships that aid retention. It helps if you can break the pace of the presentation, adding some visuals when appropriate. Injecting humor helps people retain information, but problems can arise with this if the speechwriter and the speaker are not the same person. Humor is very personal. It's difficult to write humor for someone else unless both people are real professionals at their jobs. To be safe, use anecdotes—narratives that don't depend heavily on the style of delivery.

At each rehearsal do more trimming. Sometimes you'll find whole chunks of copy to delete. Do that, but add transitions so the speech won't become choppy. You need to physically time the speech with a stopwatch. If you are writing the speech for someone else, attend rehearsals and time the delivery. When visuals are used, you'll have less copy because visuals take more time than the actual showing. There's lost time in the movement from voice to video or slides. You'll lose less time if you have someone else handling the visuals so the speaker can concentrate on delivery and be more attentive to audience reactions. Time the whole presentation at each rehearsal. It should get shorter, up to a point. That's fine. Good presenters always leave the audience wanting more, rather than getting eager for the end.

Persuading

As you convey your three main ideas, keep in mind what you want to accomplish with this message. Do you want to move the audience to take some action? If so, you'd better let the listeners know what you want them to do, how they can do it and what their rewards will be. Perhaps you want to change their belief about something. Remember, a belief is acceptance of a truth—an acceptance based on experience, evidence and opinions. If you are going to try to persuade people to change a belief, you'll have to offer both logical proof and some emotional appeal.

Alternatively, you may only want to reinforce a belief. Many public relations speeches are of this nature. Give the audience reasons for retaining their belief, and inform them of reference groups who also hold the belief. This will reassure your listeners that they are right in believing what they do.

The Mechanics of Organization

A speech has three parts: an introduction, a body and a conclusion. Contrary to what you've probably done all your life, don't write the introduction first. Just as you wouldn't write an introduction for a speaker until you knew who the speaker was, you shouldn't write an introduction for a speech until you know what will be in it.

Start with a title. The title should keep the main point of the speech in the forefront of your thinking. After you have a title, write down your purpose: to entertain, explain, convince or motivate. Then list the three ideas you want the audience to retain. Next, state precisely what you want the audience to do as a result of hearing the speech. You should then be able to write a conclusion.

Go back now to the three main ideas you want to convey, and devise a theme to tie them together. You ought to be able to tie this theme in with the purpose of the speech. At this point, you should be ready to prepare an outline.

Begin the outline by listing the three main points on separate sheets of paper. Under each point, list the pertinent information you have gathered from your research, along with what you already knew. Keep this list on the left side of the page. On the right side write a key word for an anecdote or illustration to go with each point. Now arrange all of the information under each point in a logical sequence, and you are ready to write.

Formal speeches have a format that you need to consider: response to introduction; greetings to audience and effort to build rapport with them; overview of topic; summary of three points to be covered; discussion of each point with verbal and/or visual illustrations; reiteration of three points in light of purpose of speech; desired response from the audience—what to remember and why; conclusion and thanks for the audience's time and attention.

Style

To be effective in stimulating images in the audience's mind, you need to employ vivid words and expressive language. Be clear. Choose your words with precision. Be specific. Keep a thesaurus and a dictionary on hand to find precisely the words you need. For emphasis and retention, use repetition, but use it effectively. Use transitions not just to connect thoughts but to underscore a point by reiterating it. Confirm that all your words are appropriate to the purpose of the speech, to the audience and to the speaker. Involve the audience by using personal pronouns and asking questions that listeners must answer for themselves. Find some way to establish rapport—by citing common experiences or using familiar situations and imagery, for example. Use quotations if they are not long and if they can be integrated with your ideas to give authority. Be direct. If you are ambiguous, an audience may leave wondering what you meant and may come up with the wrong answer.

When you deliver the speech, support your points with various timely, meaningful exhibits—audiovisual aids, statistics (not too many), detailed illustrations and hypothetical or real situations. Comparison and contrast are effective too.

After you've completed the body of the speech, go back and write an introduction. The introduction is an integral part of the speech. It should lead smoothly, logically and directly into the body. It shouldn't appear to have been pasted on as an afterthought. The introduction must create attention and build rapport. It should give the audience some sign of the direction the rest of the speech will take.

You can use various devices to create an effective introduction. For example, start with an anecdote or illustration to capture the audience's interest. Use a quotation or a bright one-liner that makes a startling assertion or asks a provocative question. You might even use a suspense gimmick, which you can then refer to throughout the speech and finally tie in to the conclusion. Some speakers begin with a compliment to help establish rapport, but there is some risk in this. You could come off as patronizing. You never want to apologize for yourself or the speech. You shouldn't have to!

When writing for someone else, keep in mind that person's favorite words, expressions and normal speaking pattern—long sentences or short, snappy ones. One speechwriter records the speech-planning session and plays it during this part of the work. The basic speech is then personalized for the speaker. After the speech, be prepared for responses from the audience, either formal or informal. Think of questions the audience might ask and have your answers ready, in writing if necessary. Jot down some examples of your three points that you can develop extemporaneously—provided, of course, that you are the one delivering the speech!

Source: Wizard of Id. Reprinted with permission of John L. Hart FLP and Creators Syndicate, Inc.

For another speaker, develop some examples and write them down for review. If possible, take a real example from the speaker's own background, or use that background to create a story or metaphor that the speaker might have thought of to illustrate the point. Summarize the three points so the speaker can reiterate them.

If you are delivering the speech, find out all you can about the physical location so you can think of appropriate gestures. If someone else is delivering the speech, you need to inform the speaker of the physical arrangements so appropriate delivery can be rehearsed and non-verbal expressions developed to reinforce the message. The physical situation is extremely important. For example, subtle gestures are lost in a large auditorium, whereas the slightest movement is magnified by television cameras.

Be sure you are comfortable with any visual aids or demonstrations. If you are not the one giving the speech, go over these carefully with the person who is. Mechanical failures can undermine a speaker's authority and poise. Eye contact is important. Audiences don't like to be talked *at*. Find individual people to look at and direct your message to them. Be sure they are scattered about the room so that attention doesn't seem to be focused in one spot. If you're facing a television camera, the audience is the red light.

Setting the Stage and Writing the Finale

In addition to writing the speech, the public relations writer must provide a written introduction of the speaker. How the person with the message is presented is important to audience acceptance. Content has to be controlled. For example, it's common for the person inviting the speaker to ask for a résumé. The problem is that the résumé is often *read*. Such an introduction is lethal. In public relations practice, you should offer to write the introduction for the person who will be presenting the speaker. There are problems in writing for a speaker you don't know. So keep it short and simple and easy to read. Think about what this particular audience wants and needs to know about the speaker. What will best set the tone and context for the speech? The slant will change for each audience even if the speech is basically the same.

Another part of the presentation that you'll need to write for the speaker is what she or he says immediately following the introduction. The speaker needs to acknowledge the introduction and say something nice about the person who invited him or her to speak, or about the person in charge of the gathering or the members of the audience. It's not only good manners, it's good public relations. You'll need to do some research to write something meaningful, such as finding out who issued the invitation and why. The reason to prepare this is because some speakers have destroyed the positive atmosphere for their speech before they begin by some extemporaneous, inappropriate remark. The acknowledgment comment does need to sound sincere, but planning and rehearsing it should accomplish that.

The other major writing job is to prepare a news release about the speech. Because the audience for the speech may be limited, a news release gives the message broader circulation. For a major address, an institution usually includes publication of the speech in the promotion budget. The format is similar to a brochure, with the introduction of the speaker included, along with a description of the occasion on which the speech was presented. Copies are then mailed to lists of important publics for the message who were unlikely to have been present, usually with a cover memo (rarely a letter) or simply a business card. Specifications for reprint are also usually included. Reprinting the speech is usually permitted, although in some cases the speech is copyrighted. When the latter is the case, it should be made clear so that those who want to use the speech or large portions of it will know that permission for use is required.

Presentation Scripts

Speeches, as discussed here, are presentations that a person delivers before a live or electronic audience. Scripts are formats for integrating visuals from a computer projection, slides, film or videotape into a presentation by one or more people.

Differences and Similarities

Another major difference between preparing a script and a speech is the audience consideration. A script is not tailored as specifically for a single audience or single event as a speech. Many audiences may be seeing it *individually* (as in the case of employee videotapes on benefits) or *collectively* (as when salespeople all over the world see it in their own company group). Ordinarily, these pieces are expected to have a longer "shelf life" than a speech, even one given frequently. Furthermore, the audiovisual presentation may be an educational tool from which the listener/viewer expects to gain a skill or information to progress in the workplace.

Approach script planning by first determining what you want to accomplish. Then think about the various publics who might be exposed to the presentation. After you have identified these publics, make a list of what each needs to know about the subject.

Types of Presentations

Basically there are two types of presentations that involve public relations writers: the primarily informational and the primarily persuasive.

Informational presentations are generally to employees and/or organizational advisory groups, external advisory groups such as government regulatory or supervisory bodies or nongovernmental organizations (NGOs) who are a special public because of their interest in issues related to the organization, educational organizations or associations or trade and professional groups. Some informational presentations are instructional, and these are usually more repetitive in content than strictly informational scripts. For example, safety instructions or how to use new equipment presentations are in this category.

Persuasive presentations may be directed to any of these groups too, but usually persuasive presentations are a call to action or a particular point of view. These presentations are often given by lobbyists to governmental staff or elected officials themselves or to special-interest groups that the organization is trying to enlist in a joint effort to affect policy. Persuasive presentations may be given to employees too, especially those given in connection with a campaign to get them involved in and supportive of the effort before going to other publics. One type of persuasive presentation that public relations people in agencies or firms are always involved in is new business solicitations in which it is the organization itself that is being promoted with the idea of persuading the prospective client to hire them.

Planning

List the principal ideas you want to convey in the presentation. Arrange these logically so development is easy to follow. Use a narrative approach if you can. Make a master chart of the ideas, listing under each, as you would for a speech, the points you want to make. Beside each, describe in detail how you might present the point visually. Be sure each point has these elements: something to set the scene for the idea, something to carry the action of the line of thought forward and something to relate to a common experience that audiences can identify with.

Because scripts are more like a play than a speech, there must be an element of drama that builds. You can't put your punch lines first. You need to build to climaxes, give comic relief, offer suspense and/or surprise. You are more of a dramatist than a speechwriter—but it's not all that different from writing a television commercial or a PSA.

Development

At the point of developing audiovisuals, there is no single path forward. Often because the speech is composed on the computer, the writer will prepare the major points as a visual or series of visuals. If graphs or charts are important, these are added. Of course, you can incorporate other art from the computer or use art that you scan into the computer. The presentation is projected to a large screen directly from the computer. The speaker can then go from one point to another easily and back up if there's a need to revisit a point. Having visuals on the computer also makes it easy to copy the visuals onto transparencies for overhead projection if the location does not allow for computer projection.

The scriptwriter has to work closely with the person preparing the graphics and other visuals, because these tell the story. The words are just there to help. There are two ways to go about this double-track operation: Select your visuals and write a script that fits them, or prepare the script and then "illustrate." When the visuals come from outside the organization, it is logical for the script to come first.

If you are getting help with visuals, plan for a series of conferences. The first adds details not in the proposal. The writer can explain the outline of points and suggest how these might be told with visuals. If pictures are needed, a photographer then develops a shooting schedule, interpreting the intent of the script in terms of shots that need to be taken to tell the story. Additional visuals may have to be sought or created elsewhere.

After the first visuals are ready, another conference should be held to ensure that the visuals match your conception of the message. And when all are completed, another conference is needed to see what is missing or needs replacement. At this point the stronger art should be selected. The most compelling illustrations must be arranged in the best way to tell the story. In addition, the script may have to be revised at this stage. The importance of flexibility can't be overstated—although it is sometimes difficult to be objective about finding the best way to tell the story.

After the art is chosen and the sequences are planned, the script is ready for polishing, if it has been written. If it has not been written, you are ready to start.

Matching Words and Sights

Visuals have the power to set a mood, inject drama and explain in powerful ways. The words of the script should help the visuals do this. Too many words interfere with the listener's ability to absorb the visuals. Allow time for the pictures to have an impact.

The question always arises as to whether the script should carry the same information that is being seen, perhaps on charts or graphs. Usually the audience is given the charts and graphs as a handout. These need to be in a suitable format for keeping as a reference. It's best to handle charts as they are handled in the print media. First the textual material prepares readers for the illustration by discussing it. Below the illustration there usually is a caption explaining the graph or chart. Readers then expect to see the relationship between the illustration and the point being made explained further in the textual matter.

Writers with television-writing skills adjust easily to presentation scripts. Their experience with the medium transfers easily to writing film or videotape scripts too. Sometimes, though, they have difficulty with the time period. Television writers are accustomed to working with fragments of time. In a visual presentation, the time is usually about 30 minutes, but it can be twice that. In a long presentation, both unity and pace make the job quite different from that of writing an ordinary television script. For elaborate presentations consider the use of sound. It can add emphasis and recall. Think of music and sound effects to accompany the words.

Pace can be varied in both the script and visuals. And to keep audience interest it is essential to employ some of the techniques of the dramatist—suspense, dramatic foreshadowing and comic relief among others. In a way, the script constitutes half of a dialogue and the visuals form the other half; together both tell the story.

Just as in the case of speeches, promotion is involved in calling attention to the ideas presented in the script. Like speeches some presentations may be prepared as publications. A news release may be written if the presentation is for important or large groups or is a "traveling" presentation. If the production is a long presentation going to a number of audiences, a promotional brochure should be developed.

Computer Advantages/Disadvantages

Advantages seem fairly clear—retention and flexibility. Facts and visuals for the speech or script and various versions can all be stored on disks for reconsideration. Editing is simplified and printed copies of various versions can easily be produced. Computer graphics programs can produce excellent illustrations transferable to slides or overhead projections. Illustration can be changed easily on the computer. Some points can be highlighted, colors added, backgrounds changed and designs reconfigured. Photos can be scanned into the computer and stored. Digital cameras can capture images for downloading and viewing, printing as photos, emailing or for use in videotapes. Photographic images from 35 mm slides also can be used to make a videotape.[1]

Computer-mediated presentations can be developed using a program like Adobe Persuasion or Microsoft PowerPoint presentation software. Computer-mediated presentations use a computer, a color LCD panel and a high-intensity overhead projector, or the computer can be connected directly to a large-screen monitor.

When the presentation version is completed, it's best to copy that and a runtime version to a disk. The runtime permits the presentation to be run on another computer without the software application, but it doesn't allow for revisions.[2]

Because one major advantage of computer presentations is flexibility, you always want to maintain that and keep open the opportunity for revisions, up to the last minute if necessary. Another advantage of computer-generated presentations is the opportunity to use the projected visuals as prompts for an experienced, knowledgeable speaker for whom the projection is the script. Preparing scripts for experts often means preparing just the points the speaker wants to make along with associated charts, graphs or other visuals. The speaker will use these to keep the presentation on track but will speak extemporaneously. This makes for a very persuasive presentation as long as the speaker's delivery is effective. You'll probably go through a number of designs for this sort of presentation until the speaker is comfortable with all of the computer screens that will be used. This must flow easily and nothing can be overlooked. Here the ability of the speaker to return to previous screens in a question-and-answer session following the presentation makes it necessary to have a script there for reference so the screen can be found promptly.

Disadvantages of computer presentations are not as obvious as the advantages. One disadvantage is having equipment problems. First make sure the equipment needed for the presentation is on site and working. If the presentation is to a large group, you may be using projection to large screens or even to a remote site. In these cases you need top-notch technical support. The equipment may check out fine in rehearsals and then break down while the presentation is going on. You want to be sure you have backup equipment, and someone there who knows the mechanics of the setup. That is a delivery problem, though. A not-so-obvious problem for the PR writer is inexperience in using PowerPoint or another presentation software effectively. (See Table 16.1.)

Presentation software offers endless possibilities, and some scriptwriters find it tempting to use all or most of them. The effects can be dazzling and dizzying. Shapes and forms that seem to melt into each other or surprisingly emerge, wonderful color for background and type often are more of a detriment than an asset to the presentation. Before attempting a computer presentation script, reread Chapter 12 on message design concepts and Chapter 14 on writing for Web sites. Much of the information there pertains to presentation scripts on the computer.

Other Types of Presentation Aids

Overhead Projectors   Often PowerPoint slides are printed as transparencies for use on overhead projectors. Information on the individual transparencies needs to be spare for easy reading and the slide should not be cluttered with artwork. If color is used, be sure it will show up well on the transparencies. Also the type should be large enough to be read easily in the back

TABLE 16.1   *Computerized Graphics*

When should you use computer graphics?
- When you want to have a screen show at the touch of a key
- When the equipment is available and the technology would enhance your communication with the audience
- When your competitors are using it or a similar presentation mode

Creating graphics

Graphics can be either static (still) or dynamic (animated).

Examples

Still: Charts—Bar/line, organization, text, pie, area, high/low, etc.
Should be used for communicating information such as budget disbursement.

Animated: Product rotated on the screen, internal view of how something works, simulated growth history of sales in animated form, flow of information in a communication network, etc.
Should be used for communicating information such as product capability.

Hints for effective use

- Use graphic techniques and maintain audience focus and attention.
  Transitions include zooms, fades, overlaps, dissolves, and others.
- Use a different color in graphics to emphasize major points.
- Present only pertinent information. *Avoid* excessive *Details.*
  Use as a guideline: No less that 28-point type
  Maximum of 33 characters per line
  No more than 6 lines of text per screen
  No more than 3 or 4 screens per minute
- Use upper and lower case (rather than all caps) for text. Headers can be upper case, if desired.
  - For readability from across a room, use a very dark background and large, very light-colored type.

Contingency plan

- *Before your presentation, check whether equipment is functioning properly.*
- Have transparencies, an overhead projector, and a screen ready in case equipment failure prevents your computer screen show.

Know your material well enough that you can still give an organized presentation during a power outage (even if it means giving your presentation in the dark).

Reprinted courtesy of Dr. Gay Wakefield, Director of the Center for Professional Communication in the M. J. Neeley School of Business, Texas Christian University.

of the room. Normally what you would want to put on the transparencies are graphs, charts and statistics that are difficult to follow verbally.

Flip Charts   If you are giving a presentation that depends on audience participation, use a flip chart. Pages can be torn off and taped around the room. You'll need a good supply of multicolored markers and masking tape.

Sound   Your presentation may call for sound from audiotape or CDs. You should get someone to help with the sound systems, including the microphones. Nothing is worse than not being able to hear or for the sound to be overpowering. When you use prerecorded sound, you'll need to be sure the recording is cued so that it will blend into the presentation and not detract from it.

Always rehearse, rehearse, rehearse. And time the presentation with the aids. Although aids may add significantly to the presentation, they also will add to the time you'll use.

Other Speech/Presentation Occasions

Some speaking opportunities are under less controlled circumstances than the speeches and presentations discussed so far. Two common situations are television interviews and news conferences.

Television Interviews

Normally in setting up the interview, you will have covered with the interviewer what you will be discussing. If it is a friendly interviewing situation, the interviewer will meet with you prior to the show, although sometimes just before airtime or the taping. The interviewer wants a good show, and you want to make certain points, never more than three, and maybe fewer depending on the length of the interview. Make the most important point in the first 15 to 20 seconds.

You need to organize your thoughts mentally because you will be speaking extemporaneously. Think of good sound bites, but use them appropriately. Listen carefully to the questions as they are asked, and respond specifically to each question.

Keep a friendly, open demeanor, even if the questioning gets tough. You need to keep calm and relaxed, but be strong in your voice. You want to engage the audience so they'll remember your points. Be sure you know all of the information you are likely to be asked. Your preparation should seem effortless, though, and come out in a natural conversation.

If you are participating from another location, you will be wearing an earpiece. Be sure that it fits properly before the show or the taping starts. You don't want the distraction of fumbling to adjust the piece to your ear to get the right volume. Usually you'll be wearing a lapel microphone, but the sound staff probably will get this adjusted properly for you and test the pickup of your voice before the interview begins.

News Conferences

Because you will have called the news conference, you have more control than you do in a television interview. It is your choice of site, your setting, your equipment and your staff. However, you want to be sure you have anticipated all of the questions. If you are responsible for having an executive interviewed, go through the types of questions likely to be asked and her/his general response. You should be working with a media-trained executive so they have some on-camera experience.

Occasionally news conferences call for demonstrations or injections of visuals, usually from videotape. Be sure these work as expected and add significantly to the point of the news conference. Have microphones set up for news media to use them so their questions can be picked up by everyone, and also on your videotape of the news conference that your staff is making. If the news conference is being carried in real time on your Web site, be sure the set is designed for easy viewing on a computer. The setting will have to be tighter than just for television.

In most news conferences, the executive or you will be speaking from a prepared script, although it should be brief. Afterward, you'll be responding to questions. Don't try to dodge them or be evasive in your response. Also, don't get defensive; it shows.

Because you are controlling the presentation, remember the broadcast rule: Tell them what you are going to tell them, tell them, and then tell them what you told them. It's OK to be repetitive, just not redundant.

Some good advice comes from media trainer T. J. Walker, who says to watch your performance within 24 hours of the airing or taping to evaluate and improve it.[3]

Evaluations

Public relations writers, as well as presenters and certainly management, want to know if the speech or presentation was effective. What often is used on site is a simple evaluation form. It may be handed to attendees at the presentation and either collected at the door or left behind on tables. Sometimes if the presentation is at a conference, the evaluation is sent later to those who attended and includes all of the speeches and presentations for respondents to evaluate.

Remember, these forms are generally distributed and collected by the organization where the speech or presentation was given, and when that organization is different from your own, you may or may not know the results. To assess the evaluation, you need a copy of the questionnaire used, the method for soliciting responses and the number of completed responses used in the assessment. Why? Because your job may be on the line. A presentation can get "bad reviews" that you get blamed for when your part of the job was fine. Or it may be that the opinion "survey" is not a good indicator.

When a presentation is an informative one, the best assessment is an evaluation some time after the presentation to test recall of information as well as what was best appreciated or liked about the presentation. This helps you design better presentations.

If the presentation is a persuasive one, the measures are more complex. You can't always judge long-term effects by short-term reports. However, you certainly can tell something about the presentation by the verbal and written responses the organization gets. You can document these and draw some conclusions from them, as long as you remember that those you don't hear from may be significantly different from those who make the effort to express themselves. Be alert to any pointed criticism about bias or insensitivity that a presentation may have aroused. Even one critic's message can be important here.

Conclusions

- Writing speeches and scripts for presentations is a demanding task because of the combination of words and images and the performance element.
- Direct interaction with an audience in either a speech or a visuals/words presentation brings out the best in most of us.

- Preparing material especially for specific audiences is the key to pleasing them.
- The person preparing the material must remember that, although the audience is the ultimate receiver of the information, the person presenting it is most important. The speaker is both medium and message.
- Speech subjects need to be thoroughly researched, but the main points must be pared to three.
- The effect you want the speech to have on the audience should be the governing factor in how it is constructed.
- You need to be sure you are using words and symbols that are meaningful to the audience and appropriate for the speaker.
- Most public relations people are in the business of preparing materials for others to use, so they must be skilled in this task.
- Preparing material for presentation by others is a hazardous task, but a highly creative one.
- Scriptwriters must be able to visualize the combination of pictures and words that will occur when messages are presented.
- Speeches and scripts must have a sense of pace—a rhythm appropriate for both the material and the speaker.
- The script is a dialogue with visuals. Scripts are more like plays than speeches and are closely akin to television commercials and PSAs.
- Presentation of any kind of audiovisual or speech is a public relations function that demands rehearsal.
- Part of the public relations function is to prepare the introduction for a presentation, releases about the presentation, and brochures (which in the case of a speech may be a reprint of the speech or important graphics from the presentation with captions, to be sent with a cover memo).
- Overhead projectors, flip charts and sound are other useful aids, but will add to the length of the presentation. Time and rehearse.
- Television interviews, live or taped, are another type of opportunity to speak. Organize your points mentally. Carry on a conversation with the interviewer and keep a pleasant demeanor even if the questions get tough.
- A news conference offers more control, but needs to be carefully planned to keep it that way. Be concise and think of sound bites in advance. Don't evade questions in the Q&A that follows.
- Evaluations of speeches and presentations are important because your job may be on the line. When other organizations do the evaluating, you may or may not get the results, so you need to build in mechanisms for your organization to evaluate the value of speeches and presentations.
- Informative speeches and presentations are easier to assess than persuasive ones because the long-term effects of persuasion are more difficult to measure.
- Be alert to any pointed criticism of bias or insensitivity in speeches or presentations, even if it's from only one critic. Sometimes only one word can cause public relations problems.

Exercises

1. You are the vice president of communication at O. Joyitz Funn Manufacturing Systems. OJF is a major producer of children's toys made of plastics. The management team recently got a confidential staff medical report confirming that OJF employees have a much higher incidence of respiratory illnesses than is normal in the surrounding community and region. The report cites as the probable cause a key ingredient used in the manufacture of several OJF products, although more study is necessary to confirm this chemical as the offending agent. Management immediately ordered more study for definitive answers. But it also decided to keep the information confidential until the results of these studies are known. Your task now is to come up with a persuasive rationale that will give support to running a story about the staff medical report in the company magazine now. What arguments will you use? Consult Chapter 3 on persuasion for some clues.

   How would you treat this subject in writing a speech for the CEO to present to:

   a. employees?
   b. a local civic group?
   c. an activist group for clean air in your city?

2. Develop a presentation script to recruit students to your school.

Use InfoTrac College Edition to access information on topics in this chapter from hundreds of periodicals and scholarly journals.

Notes

1. Barbara A. Ross, Sarah V. Beckman and Linda V. Meyer, "Learning to Produce and Integrate Presentations, Videos and Stills," *T.H.E. Journal* (September 1995): 78–81.
2. Ibid.
3. *tips and tactics* 41 (10) (May 5, 2003), pp. 1–2.

Selected Bibliography

Steven Ascher and Edward Pincus, *The Filmmaker's Handbook: A Comprehensive Guide for the Digital Age* (New York: Plume, 1999).

Susan Avallone, comp. and ed., *Film Writers Guide,* 7th ed. (Los Angeles, Calif.: Lone Eagle, 1998).

Jeanne Tessier Barone with Jo Young Switer (contributor), *Interviewing Art and Skill* (Boston: Allyn & Bacon, 1995).

Douglas Biber, *Variation Across Speech and Writing* (Cambridge, U.K.: Cambridge University Press, 1992).

Lillian Brown and Edwin Newman, *Your Public Best: The Complete Guide to Making Successful Public Appearances in the Meeting Room, on the Platform and on TV* (New York: Newmarket Press, 1992).

Thomas D. Burrows, Lynne S. Gross and Donald N. Wood, *TV Production: Discipline and Techniques,* 7th ed. (Dubuque, Iowa: WCB/McGraw, 1997).

Michel Chion and Claudia Gorbman, ed. and trans., *Audio-Vision: Sound on Screen* (New York: Columbia University Press, 1994).

Mary Ellen Guffey, *Business Communication: Process and Product,* 2d ed. (Belmont, Calif.: Wadsworth, 2000).

Peter Hager, *Designing and Delivering Scientific, Technical and Managerial Presentations* (New York: Jossey Bass–John Wiley & Sons, 1997).

Thomas K. Karam and James Gaut Ragsdale, *Can We Talk?: A Handbook for Public Speakers* (Lanham, Md.: University Press of America, 1994).

Milan D. Meeske, *Copywriting for the Electronic Media: A Practical Guide,* 4th ed. (Belmont, Calif.: Wadsworth, 1997).

Sandra Moriarty with Tom Duncan (contributor), *Creating and Delivering Winning Advertising and Marketing Presentations,* 2d ed. (Lincolnwood, Ill.: NTC Publishing Group, Business Books, 1996).

John Morley, *Scriptwriting for High-Impact Videos: Imaginative Approaches to Delivering Factual Information* (Belmont, Calif.: Wadsworth, 1992).

Thomas A. Ohanian, *Digital Nonlinear Editing: Editing Film and Video on the Desktop,* 2d ed. (Boston: Focal Press, 1998).

Jo Robbins, *High Impact Presentations* (New York: John Wiley & Sons, 1997).

Linda Seger, *Making a Good Script Great,* 2d ed. (Hollywood, Calif.: Samuel French, 1994).

Elizabeth Urech, *Speaking Globally: Effective Presentations Across International and Cultural Boundaries* (Dover, N.H.: Kogan Page Ltd., 1998).

Kathleen S. Verderber and Rudolph Verderber, *Inter-Act: Using Interpersonal Communication Skills,* 9th ed. (Belmont, Calif.: Wadsworth, 2000).

Rudolph F. Verderber, *The Challenge of Effective Speaking,* 10th ed. (Belmont, Calif.: Wadsworth, 1999).

John Watkinson, *The Art of Digital Video,* 3d ed. (Boston: Focal Press, 2000).

Newsletters

Newsletters often are rated as the single most important benefit of membership in organizations. Subscriber newsletters operated as businesses carry valued information to people willing to pay substantially for it, and these newsletters often are monitored by the business press for trends and other news. How has the Internet affected the value attributes of these print media? The answer seems to be *enhancement*.

The Internet has a proliferation of newsletters and ezines—short for "electronic magazines." The difference is that newsletters usually are distributed by email or an email attachment, while ezines reside on Web sites. When a new edition of an ezine is available, a link to it may be distributed by email.

Some ezine and newsletter subscriptions are free; it's just a matter of signing on to be included in the "distribution." Why would an organization do this? Obviously, whether it is commercial or nonprofit, the access to extended audiences is seen as an opportunity. An email newsletter written by the prime minister of Japan is believed to have broken subscription records for a publication of its kind, attracting 1.82 million subscribers during its first two weeks.[1]

Ezines are especially popular among marketing professionals. Around 65 percent of marketers say they plan to increase their use of email newsletters, according to a survey by Intermarket Group, a San Diego, California-based business information publisher. They said, "Fifty-nine percent of B2C (business-to-consumer) marketers identified direct sales as an important objective for their email marketing efforts, while 56 percent mentioned customer relations. Among B2B (business-to-business) marketers, 65 percent said that generating sales leads was the most important objective, while 63 percent said they use email marketing to educate sales prospects."[2]

Web Content Report offers these tips for creating effective enewsletters:

- *"Grab 'em in the subject line.* Keep your subject lines less than 60 characters; otherwise, it may get cut off. (Hotmail allows 80 characters and spaces; AOL, 52; Outlook Express, 64; Outlook, as wide as the screen allows.) . . . Include some content in the subject line. Users typically decide whether they open e-mail based on the subject line." . . . Nielsen Norman Group said to avoid words like *free* and *debt* in email subject lines to distinguish newsletters from spam.
- *"Offer both HTML and text formats*—and tell AOL users which one to choose. . . . AOL has a different way of processing mail. . . .
- *"Don't send your e-newsletter if there's nothing new to say.* Sending e-newsletters with similar information too frequently may prevent users from paying attention to what you're providing. . . ." Of course, the same could be said of printed newsletters.
- *"Newsletters must be designed for easy scanning.* In the Nielsen [Nielsen Norman Group] study, only 23 percent of the newsletters were read thoroughly; the remaining were skimmed or partially read. And 27 percent were not even opened."[3]

You can even get evaluations of newsletters and ezines on the Internet. One site, "Best Ezines," rates the electronic magazines on original content, as opposed to rehashes of print-published material, and what it calls "responsible advertising." An ezines database provides a list of more than 3,000 ezines, electronic newsletters and other electronic publications in addition to listing newspapers and magazines, more than 900 offering subscription discounts. Ratings of newsletters are more likely to be by category—that is, the best site for investor newsletters or newsletters for managers and such. Just click on search, type in "newsletters" and the latest information is at your fingertips.

What does this have to do with writing? It provides a new challenge. Now newsletters are being delivered both by the U.S. Postal Service and by the Internet. Writing for the two is not the same, as you discovered in Chapter 14 on Web page writing. Nor can designs move entirely comfortably between the two, as you found out in Chapter 12 on message design concepts.

Most newsletters now carry their Web site address on the printed version. (And if the newsletter is membership-based or subscriber-based, the Web site likely has a home page with an opportunity for the member/subscriber to enter a password to get into the information.)

As organizations began to downsize in the 1990s, many public relations people took advantage of their job loss to go into business for themselves. Early on, those were the people most comfortable with the journalistic tactics of public relations and the ones who had mastered desktop publishing. Now the emphasis is on people who are comfortable working in cyberspace and preparing newsletters and ezines that are unlikely to appear in a printed form.

The significance of this to public relations writers is that many college graduates find their first jobs in the newsletter industry. The opportunity usually comes because they understand how to gather information, write in a compelling and interesting way and know desktop publishing.

For organizations, the increasing number of professional newsletters requires that they be aware of those that follow their activities because the coverage is often more objective and critical than they may be comfortable with.

As for this chapter, the emphasis will be on printed newsletters because your best guide to electronic newsletters and ezines is your computer. Search for both newsletters and ezines, separately, although both searches will yield some information on each. Get familiar with what is on the Web so you'll know how to make your printed materials compatible with an electronic version. Surf enough to know what your competition is and where opportunities lie for you to connect with people interested in your information.

Criteria for Successful Newsletters

Several criteria affect the success of any newsletter:

- It must fill an unmet need.
- It must be able to do things for its audience other media can't and it must convey information in some unique way so people will pay attention to it.
- It must be distributed in a way that is efficient and regularly reaches its intended audience.
- There must be a person or a staff of people interested in it, skilled enough to produce it and with time committed solely to its production.
- It must be a serial publication (Vol. #, No. #) issued with enough frequency that its contents remain timely in the eyes of its readers.

Filling Unmet Needs

Memos, letters and bulletin boards are commonly used to communicate inside an organization. But as an organization grows, these media sometimes aren't sufficient to carry all the interesting and important information that should be shared. A newsletter can be as large, within budgetary limits, as necessary to carry important information.

For organizations like the American Association of Retired Persons (AARP), membership is massive and widely dispersed. A newsletter can reach out and mobilize the self-interest of such vast audiences. Even if an organization has a magazine, it often emphasizes feature material, but a newsletter, as the first part of the name signifies, can focus on information that is current, thus making it more useful to its readers.

Other media, such as newspapers, magazines and television, provide data, but none of them provides the select, in-depth and sharply focused information found in newsletters.

Uniqueness

A successful newsletter is one that conveys information particularly useful and interesting to its audience. Of the two general types—organizational and subscription—the organizational goes to employees of an organization or members of an association. As an employee or as a member of an association, you have special interests related to that involvement. For example, if you fish for bass, you may become a member of a bass fishing club. That club will have a newsletter that informs you regularly about forthcoming fishing tournaments, who is the current leader in club points and related matters. No other medium provides you with such targeted information.

Subscription newsletters also address special interests, both personal and professional. Some of your interests or hobbies may lead you to subscribe to newsletters that give you "inside information." For example, if you invest in the stock market, you may subscribe to at least one market newsletter that keeps you abreast of news relating to the market. If your interest is in precious metals, you may even focus narrowly on a gold and silver market newsletter.

As an avid booster of a professional or collegiate sports team, you may get a personal view of that team through a newsletter that goes only to its contributing boosters.

Note that in all these examples and others, although information about the organizations and interests is available from other sources, none can speak to your special interest as directly as a newsletter.

Distribution

Getting a printed newsletter into the hands of its target audience is a key element of success. And it can be quite expensive. If you can't create a mailing list with names and addresses, you can't be successful. Names of people and their addresses usually are easy to get when distributing a newsletter through interoffice mail.

On the other hand, if you must create your own list from scratch, be prepared to spend much time and money building it. Maintaining its accuracy over the years also is expensive and time-consuming. So is delivery by the U.S. Postal Service, even if your newsletter qualifies for a second-class mail permit. Distribution sounds easy, but it often isn't. So be resourceful and persistent in creation and maintenance of an effective distribution system.

Knowledge and Skills

Producing a newsletter that earns the loyalty of its readers is time-consuming work. It also takes specialized knowledge and a combination of skills at writing, editing, designing and visualizing. Many who start newsletters are short on both knowledge and skills, but if they are long on commitment, they learn by doing. That's often the case in small organizations because there probably isn't someone on the staff who has the academic or professional training needed for the task. Small budgets also may preclude hiring someone with the knowledge and skills needed. Newsletters from big organizations usually aim for and achieve higher professional standards. But it is the restricted, focused coverage of news that makes readers look forward to the next issue.

Frequency

The frequency of a newsletter is governed by three primary issues—budget, timeliness and serialization. Your budget may restrict your frequency as well as the number of pages in your newsletter. There are trade-offs you can make. If you cut the number of pages, you may be able to publish more often and stay within a tight budget. If timeliness is critical, you must publish more often, even if with fewer pages. If the timeliness of newsletter content is not an issue, you may publish less often but with more pages.

Perhaps the least understood influence is serialization. For a publication to be classified as a newsletter, it must be issued on a regular basis, and each issue must contain volume and issue numbers. A publication issued on an irregular schedule, although it may have every appearance of a newsletter, isn't one unless published at regular intervals. Also, the only way the U.S. Postal Service will grant a second-class mailing permit is for you to publish it on a regular schedule. If you distribute your newsletter through interoffice mail, there can be some variability in your schedule, but you still need volume and issue numbers. If you use the U.S. mail, you must keep a rigid publishing schedule.

Format

The best format for a specific printed newsletter is a curious blend resulting from content, budget and readers' convenience. If the intent is, as in most newsletters, to write tight, edit tighter and present information in almost-bulletin form, an 8.5-by-11-inch page size may be perfectly suitable. Readers who keep backfiles of the newsletter in binders or in cabinets like the convenience of an 8.5-by-11-inch sheet size. Copies of newsletters that routinely get routed from office to office within an organization also seem to work better in an 8.5-by-11-inch page size. If your newsletter routinely runs longer pieces, especially feature material, a larger page size—such as 11-by-17 inches or tabloid—may be more appropriate. If pictures and graphs are important parts of each issue, larger sheet sizes may be needed.

Format also requires that you weigh the relative merits of vertical versus horizontal layout of content. Small sheet sizes can accommodate either vertical or horizontal displays, if they are done skillfully. Nevertheless, horizontal displays of content are usually more attractive in larger sheet sizes. That apparently is a function of the more pleasing proportions produced by the vertical length of a large sheet size, such as 11-by-17 inches.

Unless your budget is generous, money may restrict your choice of formats as well as the extent to which you can afford to use visual materials and color. Four-color printing can hit your budget hard, but is very important if your distribution is large. Of course that drives down the unit cost. It also, as noted previously, influences the frequency of your newsletter and the number of pages per issue.

Although it is important to know about the criteria that can make a newsletter successful, it is equally important to know about the types and functions of newsletters.

Types and Functions of Newsletters

The main purpose of newsletters is to communicate regularly with members of a special public. Sharing information sustains the unity of those bound together only by a special interest.

Employee and Member Newsletters

Good managers know that the success of the company or institution rests on the cooperation and support of employees as much as on their own managerial skills. As an organization grows, however, it becomes increasingly difficult to communicate policy or other information on a personal basis. A newsletter may serve this purpose.

An organization's endurance depends on maintaining its membership base and attracting new members. Frequently a newsletter is a periodic reminder of the organization and invites or structures the member's participation in the organization's activities.

In the case of both employees and members, though, the timeliness of newsletter information may suffer from the production and delivery process. There's something to the term *snail mail.* For employees email systems may be a better delivery system for messages that need immediate attention, and members of organizations often turn to Web sites for news and updates. (See Chapter 14 for a discussion of Web sites.)

Internal Communication   Newsletters nevertheless are an effective channel of internal communication. (See Figure 17.1.) Their content is carefully selected, written and presented to

FIGURE 17.1

Member Newsletter *Newsletters such as this one provide regular information to members of all kinds of organizations including professional and trade associations, schools and universities, religious organizations and health care institutions. Many organizations, including the Texas School Public Relations Association, have discontinued printing their newsletters on paper and—instead—make them available via email and/or on their Web sites.*

Source: Used with permission of Texas School Public Relations Association.

convey a common experience and a feeling of belonging, and to promote identification and unity with the group.

Personal Touch   Newsletters are often expected to help humanize what may otherwise be viewed as an impersonal relationship. Because of this, a common thread of content runs through newsletters: a focus on accomplishments.

Employee newsletters often focus on work-related accomplishments. For example, an employee may be given special recognition in the company's newsletter for having developed a new materials-handling system that saves the company thousands of dollars annually. The company is obviously better because of the employee's contribution, which is acknowledged among his or her peers in the newsletter. Such recognition also implies that others can get the same kind of treatment if they contribute beyond the normal call of duty.

Employees often are recognized, too, as people worth knowing because of their dedication, skill or accomplishments in areas not related to their jobs. For example, Rose McKenna devotes many hours of volunteer service weekly to the Big Sisters program. Rose McKenna is someone you should know, not because she is one of three quality-control supervisors at the plant but because she is who she is. Companies and institutions routinely encourage employees to take an active interest in community affairs because they create goodwill toward the company or institution.

Newsletters for organizations also call attention to the accomplishments of the organization, primarily as achieved through its members. (See Figure 17.1.) This kind of recognition encourages others. If it is a nonprofit organization that is primarily driven by volunteerism, the recognition may be critical not only to encourage other volunteers but also to convince potential donors that the organization engages in worthwhile projects.

In their efforts to humanize the company or institution, newsletter writers sometimes use humor. Humor is, of course, a good method of conveying some information. However, unless you have a special gift for writing humor, avoid it, because poor humor can come across as trite. And it can be inadvertently offensive as well. If you use humor now and then, remember that you should never poke fun at anyone other than yourself or the company or institution.

Gary F. Grates, vice president of GM North America Communications and former president of the public relations agency GCI BoxenbaumGrates, says today's employees "receive enormous volumes of unsolicited information and are unable to handle it all.

"Just when organizations have made improving relationships with employees a priority, they've encountered an interesting, sobering reality—employees aren't listening. In addition to information overload—or, most likely causing it—is the startling fact uncovered in recent surveys that a low percentage of the workforce, including managers and supervisors, understand the company's strategy, and that leadership is aghast at that fact. This knowledge deficiency among managers is a serious problem, because these are the very people who must drive the strategy." As an example, he said poor communications with workers at General Motors was the main factor in a 54-day strike that cost the company $2 billion.

Grates said that employees are watching but choosing not to listen. "They are inundated with so much information—most of which is irrelevant or conflicting—that it overwhelms and confuses them. Instead, they look for visual cues and pay attention to what's going on around them. For instance, they may hear or read in a company publication about a new initiative that realigns the way things are done. But then they see leadership or their managers operating in the same manner as they always have. What's the real message for them? Is the company embarking on a new paradigm, or not? 'Probably not,' employees say to one another. The result is widespread cynicism instead of the enthusiasm and commitment that business organizations need in order to grow and thrive. Just as some football fans watch Monday Night Football with the volume off to escape the incessant blather posing as commentary and insights, employees learn to discern company strategy by watching behavior rather than listening to the noise."

He continued, "What employees are looking for, in addition to respect for their intelligence, is information that will help them do their jobs better. They want to help the company survive and thrive so that they can keep their jobs, send their children to college, pay their mortgages and feel good about their lives. Yet conventional internal communications is out of sync with that model. Internal communications is not public relations. It is not about touting, advocating and creating noise. It is about listening, hearing and acting. Internal communication is not about being a trumpet, but about being an organization's ears. Internal communication is becoming a management priority where leaders recognize that a real competitive advantage can be gained through an engaged, motivated, knowledgeable, and respected work force.

"What does this mean for senior management and communicators who understand this paradigm? It means they should stop using tired clichés like teamwork, loyalty and empowerment. Instead of acting as though the employees' volume is still on, leadership should focus on what employees are really concerned about: job discretion, respect, privacy, recognition and reward."[4]

Special-Interest Subscriber Newsletters

The term *special interest* describes group relationships bound by a common interest other than as an employee or a member.

The purpose of these newsletters is to communicate information about the special interest that binds the group. Information is thus highly targeted and seldom presents anything not directly related to the interest of the group. (See Figure 17.2.)

Writing style is often informal and, depending on the field of interest, may involve jargon. For example, a newsletter for personal computer hackers may be filled with computerese. If you are really interested in communicating fully, though, you'll minimize the jargon and stay with simple English.

What's significant about special-interest subscriber newsletters is that the information has to be substantive enough that people feel they are getting value for their money. They are paying for information about lifestyles (traveling, health, economics); earning money or investing it; computers (new software and technology updates); hobbies (gardening, scuba diving); collecting (everything from antique glassware to baseball cards); or renovating old real estate (from houses to office buildings). Subscription newsletters offer a lifeline to important information for people concerned with these and other topics.

Technical and Content Considerations

There is no best way to prepare a newsletter. The writing style may range from informal to formal, but it is always keenly focused on the interest of the group at hand. Some newsletters are simply prepared on a computer, printed, photocopied, folded and mailed. Others are

pr reporter

The Newsletter of Behavioral Public Relations,
Public Affairs & Communication Strategies
603 / 778-0514   Fax: 603 / 778-1741
E-mail: prr@prpublishing.com
www.prpublishing.com

Vol.45 No.25
June 24, 2002

UNIVERSITY FINDS EXTREME OPENNESS WITH PRESS BEST TACK TO DEFLECT NEGATIVE ATTENTION DURING CRISIS

When suspected pipe bomber Luke Helder allegedly planted a series of 18 explosive devices in mailboxes throughout five Midwestern states, officials at University of Wisconsin (Stout) found themselves roiled in a crisis; Helder was a junior majoring in industrial design at their University. **The story unfolded rapidly**, according to John Enger, exec dir, university rels. "The story broke in Texas at 11 a.m.," he told prr. "By 11:15 it was all over the world."

The story was a tricky one for University officials because **it had threads leading directly to the school**. The initial tip off came from Helder's roommate, who told authorities about some suspicious comments Helder made prior to the bombings, and about some pipe remnants found in the pair's off-campus apartment. Furthermore, in a letter to the University's main campus in Madison, postmarked the day before the first bomb was discovered, Helder states that he is willing to die and threatens to hurt others. Finally, while Helder was still at large, there was a great deal of concern that he might be lurking around the campus. "A lot about the story centered on the University."

The FBI contacted the school and told them that a student at U Wisc was under suspicion for planting mailbox bombs. "We knew that given the state of the country after 9/11, this would be big news." The FBI requested the University keep the news under wraps, but **evasiveness had to be abandoned once the floodgates opened**. "Our first call was from MSNBC; then all of the major news outlets began calling."

INTERNAL AUDIENCES ALERTED FIRST

The **crisis management team was in place** to decide what to do and who to contact. "One of our main concerns was that we needed to alert the campus as to the status of the situation. We sent several e-mails to all students and staff. We also needed to establish contact with UW System Administration and with some other key contacts such at the Baldrige Office. (Stout is the first university recipient of the Malcolm Baldrige National Quality Award, see prr 5/27.) "This has created national attention and we needed to assure the office that the crisis would not interfere with inquiries generated by the award."

> **Previous prr crisis articles from two different schools** – where each had to deal with a single, high profile story that was lurid, scandalous, and had threads leading back to both universities – **are also good case studies**. In them, the student – an exemplary campus leader and "good deed doer" who even organized a service to escort girls to their dormitories late at night – hid in the closet of a local anchorwoman and attacked her; he was shot & killed during the attack. He was a student at Drury College and prior to that, at Southwest Missouri State U. Reports later surfaced that the student had been caught peeping into windows and had received counseling. **Both schools had to deal with resulting media and public scrutiny**. (See prr 5/22/89 and 6/19/89)

EDITOR & PUBLISHER, OTTO LERBINGER • CONTRIBUTING EDITOR, REGINA LAPIERRE
READER SERVICE MANAGER, PAMELA J. KING
A PUBLICATION OF PR PUBLISHING COMPANY, INC., DUDLEY HOUSE, P.O. BOX 600 EXETER, NH 03833-0600 • ALL RIGHTS RESERVED
FOUNDED 1958 • $250 YEARLY • SPECIAL RATE FOR MULTIPLE COPIES: CALL FOR INFORMATION • ISSN 0048-2609 • COPYRIGHT 2002

FIGURE 17.2

Subscription Newsletter *Although public relations has no formal continuing education for practitioners, most PR professionals try to keep up with changes by subscribing to a newsletter that follows recent PR research, trends and people. Once such newsletter is* pr reporter.

Source: Used with permission of *pr reporter.*

elaborately designed and printed on fine-quality paper. Budget, of course, is a key factor in determining the appearance and method of reproduction. The important point to remember is that the newsletter's content, not its appearance, counts most. If the content is perceived as important by readers, you have accomplished your purpose.

Reporting and Writing for Newsletters

Reporting and writing for newsletters are two very different tasks. Reporting deals with getting information. Writing deals with analyzing and packaging information.

Reporting

Getting useful information is the lifeblood of any newsletter. There is no reason for a newsletter if it doesn't have information other media don't have. Otherwise, potential readers may simply yawn away its existence. So reporting is a key element of a good newsletter.

Relying on standard journalistic approaches to fact gathering won't do. You must have an angle that sets your search process apart from others. For example, the *White House Bulletin* began in 1990 with the idea that other media reporting on White House activities were overlooking many important details. Written by an editorial staff of former White House and congressional officials relying on inside sources and wire-service reports, the newsletter is a daily, Internet- and fax-delivered news service for subscribers. In a few years it has become a mainstay of the Washington press corps as well as government leaders. As it sifts continually for overlooked details, the *White House Bulletin* has scooped national media several times on some major stories.

You can look for a newsletter angle by identifying a gap and trying to fill it. Examples of filling gaps show in these newsletter titles: *Cold Water Oil Spills, Underground Storage Tank Guide, Iranian Assets Litigation Reporter, Back Pain Monitor* and *Anesthesia Malpractice Protector.*

Get It Right or Get Out   Every reporter makes mistakes. But mistakes often are deadlier in newsletters than they are in the mass media, because you're dealing with an audience with specialized knowledge. Readers spot mistakes quickly and they are not forgiving. Because of your mistake, they feel that you've broken faith with their trust. Your credibility and the future of your newsletter may go down the drain. That's especially the case if you're reporting for a commercial, profit-making newsletter. Even a decimal point out of place can be disastrous for your readers. You must be right all the time. Impossible? No, it just means that you do what all reporters should do routinely, but often don't—check, double-check and check again.

No-Nonsense News   Commercial subscriber newsletters, especially, adhere to a hard-news policy. Fluff, features and humor have no place in these newsletters. However, employee and member newsletters may carry soft news, but if the news is all soft the newsletter loses its audience. Audiences read newsletters expecting to find current information that is important to them. So go light on soft stuff.

Writing Tips for Newsletters

Newsletter recipients are likely to be fairly cohesive groups. Those receiving a particular newsletter already belong to a club or are employees of a company, or are philosophically aligned with or at least inclined toward a group. Assume but also reinforce readers' areas of shared knowledge and commitment. Use acronyms and other abbreviations accordingly.

As their name implies, newsletters have much in common with newspapers. They are often read for their content and then discarded.

The standard rules of grammar, punctuation and spelling apply to newsletters as they do to all other media. However, there are some different emphases.

Crisp, Clear Style   Sentences in newsletters are mostly bare bones—subject-verb-object. Adjectives and adverbs are scarce. Compound clauses and sentences are uncommon. In short, the writing style in newsletters is simply spartan. Much of it might even remind you of what you'd see in a news bulletin. There are two secrets to this type of writing. First, you must know the subject matter very well. That comes from good reporting as described previously. Second, write in your usual fashion but then edit out about half of what you've written. If you allow yourself to get enamored with your prose, you can't be a good newsletter writer. You have to cut and trim until only a polished diamond of information remains. In that sense, editing your copy properly is more difficult in newsletters than it is in most newspapers or magazines.

Five Ws and the H   The who, what, why, when, where and how of standard newswriting also is important in newsletters. But the angle chosen for the newsletter may put the emphasis on one of these in story after story after story. Angle not only influences the focus of your reporting, it also may shape the way you write a story. If you concentrate on entertainment celebrities, the "who" is paramount in your newsletter. If you focus on back pain, "what" gets emphasized throughout your newsletter.

You also should remember to avoid summary leads. Put the key point into the lead sentence and build the body of the story on that key point only. If there are several key points, make each one a separate story. Use the KISS method—Keep It Short, Simple.

Fitting Newsletter Copy and Design

Designing newsletters to display information attractively is important in gaining attention for your message.

Some newsletters may have a great deal of room for copy, if they do not use many, if any, illustrations. The danger is in crowding the piece with too much copy. Headlines, indentations and generous paragraphing help break up the copy in a word-heavy piece. Others tend to use too many illustrations and look cluttered.

Use   The purpose of a newsletter is closely aligned with its use. When you are deciding how to communicate with an audience, you have to determine what you want to accomplish, and then you have to approach that goal in the way most likely to succeed. If you have a dive shop in the Virgin Islands, for example, you can excite the imagination and probably stimulate business better with a brochure that presents more pictures than words. On the other hand, if you want to keep in touch with all the Corvette owners in your state, you're better off with a newsletter full of copy about rallies and parts.

How you plan to distribute the newsletter also has a great deal to do with its design. If you intend the newsletter to be a self-mailer, one side will have to carry your return address, the postage and the mailing label. Furthermore, the whole piece will have to meet the specifications of the U.S. Postal Service. Always check with the postmaster in the community where the newsletter will be mailed. Postal regulations may seem to be pretty clear, but in practice they are often subject to local interpretation. It is better to check first than to be sorry later.

With so many organizations becoming international in scope, you may be dealing with postal systems that you don't know anything about. For example, you might inadvertently use U.S. postage stamps that don't have the numerical value on them for newsletters going abroad. If you read the fine print carefully, those stamps say for USA use only. If you don't read the fine print, your newsletter will come back from or not even reach the destination country, which does not accept postage that doesn't have the value on it because they don't know whether or not the amount paid is appropriate.

What the receiver is likely to do with the newsletter also has a bearing on the design. Will it wind up on a bulletin board, for example? Some newsletters are designed with that purpose in mind. A copy is sent to the president of a group, who then posts it for others to read. Others may be designed for display in a rack or countertop display unit. In both cases, the display unit has to be designed to call attention to the newsletter, and the newsletter should call attention to itself.

Writing to Fit   When you are writing the copy, you have to prepare the message to say what you think needs to be said in an appropriate way. Then you have to decide how you are going to convey the information on hand in the space available. Some professionals are experienced enough to be able to "write to fit," but most prepare the message and then spend a lot of time trimming it to fit and generally tailoring the message to the medium. A newsletter is somewhat flexible because pages can be added, but that usually costs more money. A better solution is to determine your information hole first and then write the message to fit it.

Writing for Other Cultures   The USA is very culturally diversified, and you can get yourself in trouble within its borders by not being sensitive to mores and taboos. However, the difficulties you can create in the USA are nothing compared to the problems you can cause for yourself abroad if you don't know what is culturally acceptable. Because English has become an internationally accepted language, many newsletters are produced in English and distributed internationally. It is easy to forget that some contents—photographs, for example—are not accepted in some countries, especially those governed by religious and not secular laws. If you have any questions, it's best to ask. Most embassies and consulates are helpful on such matters.

Writing and Designing Newsletters on Desktop Systems

The rules of the game regarding newsletters remain imperative, even if you write, edit, design and produce camera-ready copy on a computer system. That's a point you must understand fully; otherwise, you may wrongly assume that a computer system is the answer to all your prayers.

A desktop system can provide three major benefits to a person engaged in writing, editing, designing and producing matter for duplication or printing:

1. It can speed up the process of getting verbal and nonverbal material into condition for many purposes.
2. It allows you to experiment at little cost (except for time) with formats, graphic treatments, typefaces, type sizes and the like.
3. It enables you to exert more direct control over how things fit and look before you release your work for duplication or printing.

However, a computer can't make you a better writer or designer. Those are uniquely human qualities that no computer has yet been able to simulate. You should use your computer to its maximum advantage, but don't let it mesmerize you. It is a wonderful device that helps you do things you could only dream about without it. But it is still a dumb machine that can only move digitized information through electronic gates. Its behavior is controlled by which gates are open and closed. You open and close gates each time you enter a command. What comes out are your ideas, not your computer's. If your ideas aren't good, your computer can't make them better.

The value of the computer for writing, editing, designing and producing newsletters depends on how you use it. That's what this portion of this chapter is all about: how public relations people can use the computer productively and wisely.

Expediting Editorial Matter

The process of writing, editing and producing finished materials on typewriters was slow and tedious. Manual typewriters were much faster than writing in longhand, and electric typewriters were a little faster still. But both systems required long delays between drafts for hand editing and subsequent retyping.

When using a word processing program on a computer, you are actually using the computer much like a typewriter. A major difference is that your computer has enormous resident storage and useful tools. That's important because, if you're doing a 12-page, 8.5-by-11-inch newsletter every month, you're dealing with a lot of content. You need enough storage to keep all the information at your fingertips, without having to keep track of 50, 60 or more pieces of paper.

Clearly, your computer can speed up your work. And the time you save can be better spent on thinking. If the quality of your work improves, it may be because of this additional thinking time.

Extra time may also result in more *accuracy* in what you write—accuracy in facts, spelling, word choice and grammar. Review Chapter 6 for a more extensive discussion of these points, some of which are repeated here because they bear so directly on the successful use of desktop publishing systems.

Facts   If you're on deadline but you doubt the accuracy of a quote or piece of data, you can check it quickly and make the change instantly in your text, without disturbing other content. This remains true until just seconds before you must release your work for duplication or printing.

Spelling   If you're not gifted at spelling, your computer may save your job. Many good word processing programs include an electronic dictionary of more than 150,000 commonly used words. And these programs usually let you add thousands of other words, especially jargon particular to your needs.

Word Choice   Some programs may also include a *thesaurus*—a dictionary of *synonyms* and *antonyms*—so you can easily review your choice of words. Dictionaries and thesauri also are available on the Internet. But even with a thesaurus, you must remain sensitive to shades of meaning. Just because a synonym or antonym is listed does not mean it will work in a particular situation. You can't simply substitute one word for another, without thinking about them and the context in which they are used.

Homophones   Your computer also is blind to homophones. So when you mean *rein* but spell it *reign,* your computer's dictionary will read *reign* as correct and won't flag it as a misspelled or wrong word. Your computer may be able to flag misspellings like *regn* that are not words at all, but this feature does not relieve you of the need to read and edit your text for content, context and usage. You still must know the difference between *rein* and *reign.*

Grammar   The development of word processing software has reached fairly high levels of sophistication. But software that deals knowingly with grammar and syntax remains pretty crude. Programs can help some writers spot and correct grammatical and syntactical errors. But skilled writers can't get much help. Nevertheless, it is probably wise for every writer to use what is available as a safety net. Even the most skilled writer can't spot dumb mistakes all the time.

Designing

Although efficient word processing was fairly common by the mid-1970s, desktop publishing only began to emerge in the early 1980s. And it was not until the late 1980s that easy-to-use systems at affordable prices began to appear in substantial numbers. The term *desktop publishing* then came into vogue. Although the system certainly fits atop a desk, the operation isn't publishing in the usual sense. A personal computer is used to assemble verbal and nonverbal material into a cohesive unit; and this, if produced on a laser printer, may be used as camera-ready copy for duplication or printing.

In its comprehensive "Comparison of Desktop Publishing Software," PubCom of Takoma Park, Maryland, headed by Bevi Chagnon, said "PageMaker, InDesign and QuarkXPress can be thought of as solutions for basic page layout—they are ideal for brochures, newsletters, advertisements, pamphlets, posters and other items that require a high degree of design and control. FrameMaker and Ventura are best suited for long documents, technical documents and database publishing."[5]

Because the software that drives these systems is now easier to use, many people and organizations have been motivated to produce materials in-house that traditionally would have been done by professional designers, typesetters and printers. The results are a mixed bag. Some are superbly done; others are tawdry at best. The reasons for this rainbow of results are many, but a few are vital for you to know as you prepare for a career.

Format   A key production issue to settle about newsletters is the question of format. This simply refers to the visual frame within which verbal and nonverbal content is displayed. Is a vertical rectangle, a horizontal rectangle or a square most appropriate? Will the design elements be balanced, unbalanced, modular or free-flowing? One of the features of desktop systems is that you can quickly produce a seemingly endless variety of formats.

This cornucopia of formats can so dazzle the unwary that the next issue of a newsletter may not look at all like the present one or the one before that. Just because you *can* change the format instantly does not mean that you *should.* The best use of a desktop system is to experiment with formats until you create the one that is right for your purpose. Once you have found it, use it consistently. Don't change just for the sake of change. You can create a template of the right format, store it and use it on demand. By using the same format you create a visual identity for your newsletter, one your audience comes to recognize and to trust.

Fit   Desktop systems can show you how a story fits into the space assigned to it. This feature simplifies the task of fitting copy to type, because the computer does it for you, instantly. But this does not mean that you should let the desktop system control how much you write. (See Appendix B.) To avoid this trap, observe these steps:

1. Write for content first. Make sure you say what must be said.
2. Then try to fit the content to the space.
3. If it does not fit and you can't excise the surplus without affecting sense or add the deficit without being redundant, change the size of the type or the spacing to fit the content.
4. Never let space rule content.

Visuals   The very best systems can't improve the quality that a professional production artist or photographer can achieve. However, when these systems are used by people who have little or no visual sense or artistic skill, the results may be highly undesirable. If the finished product is to be four-color throughout, you can use a system to input information and to provide a basic design for initial approval, but you may want to turn to vendors for the finished work.

Most computer art is clip art. It is generic and general, not organization-specific, and it often is used as "wild art" to dress up a page. It contains little real information. Some software lets you modify clip art to your own needs, but unless you are remarkably deft, your efforts may well be in vain.

Scanners allow you to scan a photograph or printed visuals and create digital images. Digital cameras provide pictures directly to your computer. You also can modify this art, but often with the same results as with clip art. Also available are pencils you can use to draw on an electronic palette. If you can't draw well with pencil on paper, however, don't even try this alternative. No computer can overcome a lack of basic talent.

The mix of desktop publishing for print and for the Internet has created some serious design and content problems for both. It is possible to design a newsletter that can go on the Internet and be printed and mailed, but it requires a great deal of time and talent. Use the separate and different assets of each medium to their fullest.

Conclusions

- Newsletters combine some aspects of newspapers and letters and are issued regularly.
- Newsletters appear in print and on the Internet. Digital ezines are especially popular among marketing professionals.
- Newsletters are serial publications that must carry volume and issue numbers.
- To qualify for a second-class mailing permit, printed newsletters must be published on a regular schedule.
- Newsletters represent a growing opportunity for college graduates seeking their first jobs.
- A successful newsletter must meet an unmet need in a distinctive way, be distributed so that it gets into the hands of its intended readers, be issued frequently enough to remain timely and have a person or staff committed to its production.
- The primary purpose of newsletters is to communicate regularly with a special group.
- An employee or member newsletter is one way an organization communicates with people important to its existence.
- These newsletters also seek to humanize the organization with a personal touch.
- The content of subscriber newsletters runs a wide gamut but in all cases offers information of value—worth the cost of the publication.
- Gathering information for a newsletter is much more sharply focused than is reporting for other media.
- Mistakes are deadly in newsletters because readers have specialized knowledge.
- Writing in newsletters is likely to be bare bones—subject, verb and object. Adjectives and adverbs and compound clauses and sentences are less common in newsletters.
- The process of writing, editing and designing newsletters using a desktop system depends more on your own limitations than on the system's.
- Desktop systems can't make you a better writer or designer of newsletters.
- Word processing and design software has improved dramatically in recent years.
- Desktop systems are cost-effective and efficient for newsletters that need not be produced at the highest levels of quality.

Exercises

1. Find a newsletter for members or employees and another that goes to subscribers. Write an analysis that compares their purposes, content, writing styles and formats.
2. Select a newsletter of your choice. Review the focus of its content. Write an essay describing your perceptions of the readers of that newsletter.
3. Write a story for a newsletter of your choice assuming that the newsletter will be mailed as well as appear on the Internet. How does the dual delivery system affect your writing style, the timeliness of the copy and the number of words you use?

Use InfoTrac College Edition to access information on topics in this chapter from hundreds of periodicals and scholarly journals.

Notes

1. Olaf Jüptner, "Japanese PM's Ezine Breaks Records," June 25, 2001, http://www.e -gateway.net/infoarea/news/news.cfm?nid=1694.
2. Intermarket Group, "Marketers to Increase Use of Email Newsletters," August 23, 2002, http://www.nua.com/surveys/index.cgi?f=VS&art_id=905358300&rel=true.
3. Lawrence Ragan Communications, "Web Site Tips . . . E-newsletters: Substance or Spam?" *Web Content Report,* December 1, 2002, http://www2.ragan.com/html/main.isx ?sub=180&bum=0&maga=&reach=22730&base=story2&ma=WCR&tt=.
4. Gary F. Grates, "Working with the Volume Off: Cutting Through the Noise of 'Today's' Communications" (New York, N.Y.: GCI BoxenbaumGrates, undated).
5. PubCom, "Comparison of Desktop Publishing Software," July 11, 2003, http://www .pubcom.com/downloads/dtp_comparison_table.pdf, p. 13.

Selected Bibliography

Barbara A. Fanson, *Producing a First-Class Newsletter: A Guide to Planning, Writing, Editing, Designing, Photography, Production and Printing* (Bellingham, Wash.: Self-Counsel Press, 1994).

Chuck Green, *Design It Yourself Newsletters: A Step-by-Step Guide* (Gloucester, Mass.: Rockport Publishers, 2002).

Howard Penn Hudson, *Publishing Newsletters,* 3d ed. (Rhinebeck, N.Y.: HEM Publishers, 1997).

Peggy Nelson, *How to Create Powerful Newsletters: Easy Ways to Avoid the Pitfalls 80 Percent of All Newsletters Face* (Chicago, Ill.: Bonus Books, 1994).

Lisa Shaw, *How to Make Money Publishing from Home: Everything You Need to Know to Successfully Publish: Books, Newsletters, Greeting Cards, Zines and Software* (Rocklin, Calif.: Prima Publishing, 1997).

Roger Walton, *Typographics 2 Cybertype: Zines + Screens* (Cincinnati, Ohio: North Light Books, 1998).

CHAPTER EIGHTEEN

Brochures

Brochure is a term most people are familiar with. The problem is, it doesn't mean the same thing to everyone. This chapter will clarify usage, at least for this text. Public relations people write lots of copy for brochures. But if you ask them to tell you what a brochure is, you'll get a rainbow of explanations. That's because the term can mean booklets, fliers, circulars, leaflets, pamphlets or tracts. The difference between a brochure and these other pieces is sometimes a judgment call, so here are some quick guidelines for you to consider.

When the term *brochure* is used in its narrow sense, it signifies a printed piece of six or more pages, published only once and distributed to special publics for a single purpose. Brochures aren't serial publications like newsletters.

A *booklet* is basically a piece of at least eight pages, stitched on the spine. It often is small enough to fit into a pocket or small purse. *Fliers* and *circulars* are usually single-sheet pieces printed on one side that may be mailed, often in bulk, or distributed directly, like those you may find stuck on your car's windshield in a parking lot.

A *leaflet* is similar but it is usually folded, although not stapled or trimmed. A *pamphlet* is also folded and usually has more pages. A *tract* is a pamphlet or booklet whose content promotes a political or religious point of view.

These differences are pretty nominal. What these pieces have in common is more important, including:

- Message statements are always singular.
- Their purposes are to persuade, inform and educate.
- They are published only once, but multiple printings of some are common, with or without updates.
- They must attract and hold the attention of their own publics.

- Because they aren't parts of other media, they are their own delivery systems.
- They must have clear writing and be visually attractive.

Although the term *brochure* will be used in the remainder of this chapter, the principles will apply to all the types of pieces discussed above. The creation of a brochure is a complex process that includes six basic steps:

1. Clearly define its purpose.
2. Develop an organizing concept for it.
3. Write the content.
4. Design the presentation of information, including format and the use of type, visuals, paper, space and color.
5. Produce the brochure, including the selection of a method of reproduction.
6. Distribute the brochure.

Purpose

The first step is to define the purpose of the brochure. What is it that you really want to accomplish? That sounds simple, and it is. But it can be tricky. That's because people often begin with a general rather than a specific idea of what they want to do. If you force yourself to write a single declarative sentence that describes the purpose, then you can move ahead with relative ease. If you can't reduce the purpose to a simple sentence, you need to think about it some more. You also can define purpose by developing a basic message strategy. A message strategy simply defines the key idea that you want to convey to your publics.

Real estate agents use brochures to show property and to describe the advantages of owning it. Sometimes realtors use a brochure to "sell" the services of the company, rather than specific properties offered by the company. Those reflect very different purposes. Many professional public relations people receive at least one brochure a week describing a seminar that has been designed to help improve their skills—yet a different purpose. Public relations professional groups publish brochures offering members as speakers to interested groups. "Selling" talent is selling a service from which others can benefit. Other brochures may promote membership, affiliation or participation. These serve all different purposes.

Still other brochures sell intangibles, by describing the worth of an idea—for example, those designed to get support (usually financial) for foundations. One mental health foundation sends out brochures "selling" its publications and audiovisual materials at prices that barely cover mailing costs. The foundation "sells" ideas for sound mental health but offers the materials to educate the public about its mission.

Brochures also can be informational and educational in the strict sense. The Hogg Foundation for Mental Health publishes a list of publications and reports on mental health. Typically it offers a booklet that provides content summaries of each publication, complete with order forms in the back. A person seriously interested in the study of mental health issues would find this an invaluable resource.

Informational brochures about subjects like a suicide prevention hot line or accident or crime deterrence are often produced as a community service. A druggist may dispense, along with prescriptions, a brochure on how to prevent poisoning accidents and what to do if an accident occurs. Such informational brochures perform a service and generate goodwill for those who distribute them.

Persuade

Brochures always try to persuade. In that sense, brochures try to "sell" or publicize a product, service or idea. You may find it useful to review Chapter 13, "Writing Advertising Copy," because advertising copy is common to a majority of brochures. Brochure copy, however, is usually much longer and more descriptive.

Your purpose, of course, influences not only the way you write copy for the brochure but also the design you evolve, the visuals you include and, perhaps, the way you reproduce it. If your intent is mostly persuasive, your copy will lean heavily on adjectives, similes and metaphors intended to tug the emotional heartstrings of readers. Although factual information has its place in persuasive efforts, the copy appeal is mostly emotional.

Inform and Educate

If your purpose is primarily to inform or educate, the copy you write will contain lots of factual information, perhaps replete with tables and graphs. This kind of copy appeals to the cognitive behavior of readers. It is a good idea to review the basic persuasive strategies in Chapter 3, one of which is cognitive strategy. This does not suggest that you should use only cognitive strategy in brochures.

But writing copy that informs and educates is more fact-intensive and descriptive than is copy intended only to persuade. You should remember, however, that even the purest of information can have a persuasive impact. (See Figure 18.1.)

Concept

Once the purpose of a brochure is settled, you're ready to take the second step, which is to define a concept for it. An effective concept is one that helps you to organize words, visuals, color and space so they work well together to tell your story in a way that gets and holds the attention of your readers. How does that work? Begin by referring back to Chapter 13 on advertising copy, especially the portions dealing with creative treatments.

First you need a simple message statement. That statement becomes the basis for a creative concept. The concept has to include some symbolism for conveying the message. Then you need a headline that encapsulates the message. The visual must complement, not compete with, the message. The remaining pages explain the offer, give the reader response options that are easy to complete and urge the reader to send or to call for further information or to take another action.

A good concept takes a key idea and interprets it, shapes it and, in turn, is shaped by it, and follows through with the production of a fully coordinated message that blends all the elements into a cohesive unit so that the whole is a sum greater than its parts.

Purpose and Object

Although the purpose is to persuade, inform or educate your readers, those broad purposes usually aren't enough to give you the firm direction you need for an effective brochure. You have to combine them with an object or application. Persuasion is usually the dominant purpose of a brochure, but some educate or inform.

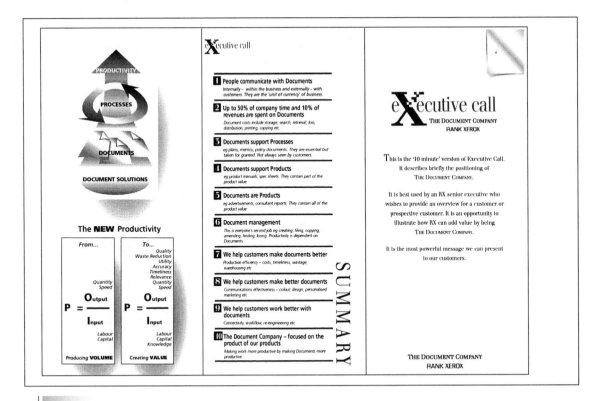

FIGURE 18.1

To Inform and Educate   *This brochure was designed to reach a very select public—senior executives at Rank Xerox. Its purpose was to provide them with information to be used in discussions or presentations. Reprinted with permission.*

The guideline is: Begin with a general purpose—persuasion, information or education—and then extend it to the specific—an object or an application.

The Farmers Insurance Group, like most insurance companies, was very concerned about the rising number of young people killed or maimed annually in automobile accidents because of driving and drinking. FIG wanted to educate young people about the risks they take when they drink and drive. The general purpose was primarily to educate. The object was to offer advice on how to break the drinking and driving cycle. So the concept evolved into "young drivers at risk." The six-page, 8-by-10-inch color brochure used a magazine design treatment to convey stories about how individuals can make a difference, comments about the rites of passage, the impact of fantasy and a first-person account of how "A Drunk Driver Changed My Life." The last page carried a signed statement from the chairman of the board and chief operating officer of the Farmers Insurance Group. Remember to proceed from the general to the specific.

Uniqueness   Not only must you have a well-refined concept for the brochure, but you also want it to stand out from all others that readers may see. You want it to be memorable. That

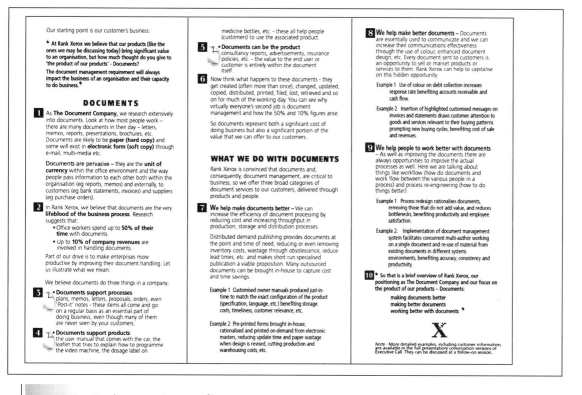

1 8 . 1 (*continued*)

means that you must be concerned with making your brochure different. The struggle to be unusual can lead you into some bad decisions, so be careful.

Cleverness   Inexperienced writers too often depend on cleverness to make a brochure stand out. Being clever is desirable, of course, but cleverness can be a slippery concept. Cleverness may turn out to be terribly trite, as in the case of a brochure for an electronics discount retailer that shouted "You've shopped the rest. Now shop the best."

Genuine cleverness takes something familiar to readers and gives it a *new and different twist*. Suppose you're creating a brochure to "sell" the idea that writing, designing and producing a brochure is really an exercise in packaging information. Talking about packaging information is fairly routine. So you might give it a different twist and call it giving shape to information. Giving shape to information also is more descriptive of what you're actually doing as you prepare a brochure.

Puffery   In their zeal to be unique, writers may stretch the truth. It is true that the Federal Trade Commission allows the use of puffery in language as an essential part of promoting goods, services and ideas. Even if puff words like *best, greatest, lowest, richest* and so on are sanctioned, they often are viewed skeptically by many readers. Readers usually recognize puffery for what it is: truth stretched to the point of unbelief. Puffery can help to create a memorable brochure, but it may be remembered for the wrong reasons.

Suppose the Rose Petal, a chain of 21 high-quality cleaners, has given you the job of developing a small brochure, claiming that the Rose Petal gives customers the cleanest clothes in town. The brochure will be clipped to the plastic bags that cover the cleaned clothing. The story can be told by describing the care Rose Petal's professional staff gives to clothing, including comments about special chemicals they use and so on, but it is best to avoid an exaggerated claim like "cleanest." In the absence of an objective measure, "cleanest" is a red flag that may inhibit credibility.

The guideline to use is: Avoid puffery.

Validity   Puffery aside, you naturally want to put your best foot forward. But your best foot must stand firmly on the accuracy of what you say. You must be careful in collecting information about the subject of the brochure. If you're writing a brochure that encourages prospective clients to lease space in a new office building, make certain, for example, that each office indeed does have its own working thermostat control before you claim that in your copy. If a company rents space and installs computer components that need special temperature control—and there is no thermostat—you can be challenged for misrepresentation in the brochure you produced.

Brochures about financial matters are especially hazardous—investments in particular. You must carefully spell out all the financial considerations and review the copy with both an accountant and an attorney before going into production. The underlying reason in cases like this is the same as with the new office building. People should be assured of getting their money's worth.

A professional organization's foundation offered a brochure detailing for potential contributors the benefits of membership in the foundation. The group's attorney was adamant that the mechanism for providing these benefits be in place before the publication went to press. Colleges and universities now do more careful reviews of their catalogs and brochures after being told by counsel of cases in which institutions were taken to court for promising more than they could deliver. The same caution extends to college and university Web sites.

Suppose you're promoting contributions to a local philanthropic group and claim that "all your dollars remain in the community." Keeping contributions at home is a powerful appeal to many potential donors, but if you're using a professional fund-raiser, the claim might be perceived as misleading because of the sometimes-inflated commissions that go to fund-raisers.

Brochures that inform and educate are much easier to write than ones intended to create or sustain an image. Image is often nebulous. Informing and educating are more concrete. Accuracy is critical. So is completeness. Now, we're ready for the third step.

Giving Shape to Information

You may not realize it at first, but the overall task in producing a brochure simply is giving shape to information. You do that by what and how you write, and how you illustrate and display it.

Notice that writing is the third basic step in creating a brochure. And you should take that step only after you're thoroughly convinced that the purpose is clear and you have a well-understood concept that helps you to organize and shape the information that goes into the brochure. Before going further, we suggest you review Chapter 12.

Rules

The rules of good grammar, punctuation and spelling apply to all brochures as they do to other media. Fractured grammar wreaks havoc with the language in a brochure as it does in a news release or a feature story. Reader reaction also may be even more virulent to mistakes in brochures. That's because of the specialized publics of brochures.

Suppose you're 21 years old and in good physical condition, but you find yourself in the office of a urologist. You're there because in the last three days you've had some severe back pain. You wonder if you have a kidney infection or if something is wrong with your back. As you try to relax in the waiting room, you pick up a brochure on kidney diseases. You begin to read it carefully and in the third paragraph you discover a subject-verb disagreement that results in confusion about the number of causes of kidney infections. The earth doesn't open and swallow you but your anxiety level does go up. You begin to wonder if you can really trust a physician who would produce such writing. Your skepticism may lead you to cancel the appointment and see another physician or, at least, to get a second opinion.

Accuracy

Accuracy is essential. Most brochures have lots of information. To be able to write good brochure copy, you must first be a good reporter. Gather, sort, evaluate and synthesize facts carefully. Check and double-check information you're unsure about. Learn as much about the topic as you can. This is necessary because it is when you are writing about something that stretches your knowledge to its limits that you make mistakes. If you aren't careful, you may not even realize you've made a mistake.

In a sense, when you produce a brochure you're making a contract with readers. They expect to be able to depend on you. Accuracy is one of the key elements of good brochure copy.

Active Voice

Use the active voice. There will be times when passive voice seems to better fit the context of what you're saying. So it is permissible to use the passive voice, but a general guideline is to avoid it when you can.

Style

Every piece of writing should conform to a specific style. Your organization may have its own. Use it. If a client has a style that is unique to that organization, you should use that style. If neither your organization nor your client has a standard style, adopt one. If you must adopt one, consult the *Associated Press Stylebook and Briefing on Media Law* for help. AP style is used widely, but often with adaptations. The particular style you use or adopt is not an issue, but being consistent is. That's what style is all about—consistency. Don't use *Mr.* or *Ms.* in one place and not in other places. Such inconsistencies in style nag subconsciously at readers. They may not overtly recognize such glitches in your writing, but they "know" something is wrong. They just can't place it. Adopt a style and use it.

Tone

Good brochure copy has a clear, distinct tone. It may be light or heavy or formal or informal in treatment. The tone should be appropriate to the brochure's purpose and subject matter. It may have a lilting quality or it could be a dirge. It really depends on what you're trying to do. It may walk slowly or run across the reader's consciousness. It might jump, crawl or turn cartwheels. For example, think about writing brochure copy for a funeral home. Death is not easy to talk about. Getting people to *plan* for their own death is a special challenge. You walk slowly, carefully. You might begin by talking about consideration for others who must handle funeral arrangements—physical and financial. Few people want to inflict inconvenience or financial obligations on those they love. Your persuasive appeal and tone have to be personal but not too emotional or sentimental.

Visuals

Thinking visually as you write brochure copy is as important as it is when writing advertising copy. The *process* is exactly the same. Because of space limitations in an ad, however, you may be able to use only one visual. Brochures usually have more space, so you can use more visuals. But it is a mistake to use visuals just because you can. The general rule for using visuals in brochures is: Use a visual to substitute for a paragraph or a section of copy. If you can say it visually, do it. If you can't, then write it.

That raises a question: Do you visualize, then write? No. Write first. Write as much as is necessary to tell the story. Then go back and examine each new idea to see if it can be conveyed visually—by photographic or drawn art. If it can be shown, use a visual. In effect, what you write governs the extent to which you use visuals. And don't forget to use charts and graphs. Done well, they can simplify complex information so it can be understood at a glance.

There are two types of visuals. One is *line art.* This is art with no gradations of tone. For example, a pen-and-ink drawing is all black and white. There are no grays. The other type is *screened* or *halftone art.* Art that must show gradations of tone must be screened. For example, a photograph must be screened before it can be printed. This is done by filtering the picture through a screen that breaks up the image into dots. Screens are designated by their relative coarseness. An 85-line screen means that the screen will break up an image into a dot pattern that has 85 rows of dots vertically and horizontally per square inch. That computes to 7,225 dots per square inch. By comparison, a 200-line screen has 40,000 dots per square inch. This is a much finer screen. Most of the art you'll use in a brochure will likely be screened at about 150 or higher, because coarser screens simply can't reproduce subtle gradations of tone.

Only your imagination and budget limit your sources of visuals. The most common is clip art. Clip art can be literally clipped from any printed source (but you can't use it without written permission). Clip art can also come from a variety of digital sources. There are many sources that provide clip art—Web sites, PC- and Macintosh-formatted disks or CD-ROMs. You are free to use this art without additional payment or permission. If you have a scanner, you may clip from a printed source, scan it to convert it to a digital format and then edit it to suit your needs (but you must get written permission to use it).

The problem with clip art is that it is rare to find exactly the art needed to convey an idea quickly, precisely and accurately. That's because it was created for some other purpose or it is generic art. The alternative is to hire photographers and production artists to execute the unique art that you want. This is, of course, the most expensive method of getting visuals, but it is usually the most satisfactory.

Writing brochure copy is, in a sense, an exercise in integrating words and visuals to their highest degree, more so than even in the best magazines. That's because magazines operate with fixed formats. The format of a brochure is controlled by you, so you have much more flexibility in creating a fully integrated message. In effect, you let the content of what you say dictate the format in which you say it. All of which brings us to the fourth step in producing brochures.

Designing Brochures

The fourth step in creating a brochure is designing. It includes several major elements: format, type, paper, space and color. Each of these elements may be worthy of a complete book. What follows are selected comments intended to give you a general sense of direction. They are not, and can't be, definitive in such limited space.

Format

First of all, a brochure format should complement the content and the method of distribution. Suppose the purpose of a new brochure you're assigned to write for a bank client is to promote the use of the bank's electronic (paperless) banking system. You learn that the brochure will be inserted with monthly statements to customers. The content of the brochure will not demand much space and the brochure must fit into statement envelopes. With those two pieces of information, you can begin to shape the message to a complementary format.

Because an 8.5-by-11-inch sheet of paper will fold to fit easily into a regular business envelope, you can begin with that size of paper. Now you must decide whether it will be done in a flier format (one wide column printed on one side) or in a folded-page format. Because the sheet must be folded to fit into the statement envelope, it makes sense to design the format as a six-page folder where each page measures 3.667-by-8.5 inches.

Consult Figure 18.2 and look at 2A and 2B. The first folding option, 2A, is called a *gatefold*. When folding back page one so you can see the second page, it is much like opening a swinging gate—thus the name. *Accordion fold* is the name applied to 2B because it folds and unfolds like the bellows of an accordion. Folder options 1A and 1B, called four-page folds, do not work well for this project because its page dimensions don't fit into the statement envelope. Folder options 3A, 3B and 3C are referred to as eight-page folds. Folder options 4A and 4B represent standard 12-page folds. Folder options 5A and 5B represent 16-page folds. Folder options 3, 4 and 5 usually are used with much larger paper stocks, like 17-by-22 inches.

A different kind of project might call for something other than a folder-type brochure. For example, if you're doing a recruiting piece for your university, you may end up with a 36-page, 8.5-by-11-inch booklet in full color. If that's the case, you'll work with an 8.5-by-11-inch format and adjust the number of pages to those needed to display the content fully. The key thing to remember about these larger formats is that the number of pages must always

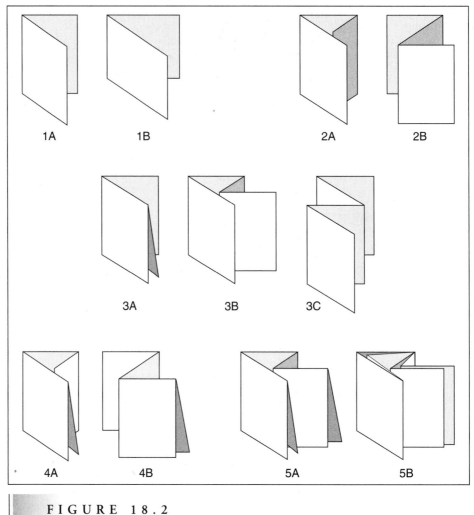

FIGURE 18.2

Brochure Folding Styles   *These are the most common folder options used when producing brochures.*

be in multiples of 4-, 8-, 12- or 16-page flats. A *flat* is the number of pages on one side of a large uncut sheet of paper stock. Which one you use will depend on the press sizes available from your printer and the number of pages in the brochure. Look at Figure 18.3 for illustrations of the most common flats. Booklets like these usually are stapled along the spine, but some are pasted.

Type

Review the sections on type in Chapters 12 and 14. In addition to the points made there, consider these ideas. Typography is an important design element in brochures. Although you need

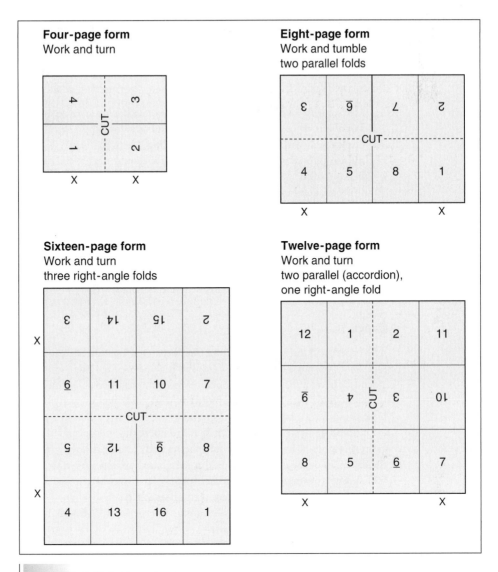

FIGURE 18.3

Most Common Page Flats for Large Paper Stock   *The actual size of a brochure is determined by its content. Selection of a printing flat is based on the number of pages in a brochure and the size of the printing press on which it will be reproduced. Flats are always done in multiples of 4, 8, 12 or 16 pages.*

to stay with traditional text faces in brochures, as you do in newsletters, you have a good bit more flexibility regarding display type.

You will find that your use of decorative or specialty type fonts is much greater in brochures than in newsletters, and even more than in some magazines. However, that isn't a suggestion that you use a myriad of display faces. Choose one and stay with it. If your software offers families of fonts, you can use these family variations to their best advantage in brochures. You also can do special things with type, like using a large initial character (called a *drop cap*) to begin each new section in the brochure. And you can use rules around blocks of type (but don't overdo this) and screens and tint blocks to give variety, yet consistency, to the overall look of the brochure. Here are some typographic guidelines to remember:

1. Use subhead lines to break up long copy blocks. This gives air to copy blocks.
2. Put about twice the space above a subhead as below it.
3. Experiment with additional space ("leading") between lines. This also gives air but don't overdo it. Spacing between lines generally should not exceed the point size of the type being spaced. The problem is that some font faces are denser and bolder than others. Only trial and error can lead you to a good, readable design.
4. Avoid using uneven left margins unless fitting copy around art.
5. Don't tilt type at odd angles. If you must tilt it, keep it to no greater than 15 degrees.
6. Don't run type vertically. It kills readability.
7. Select typefaces—text and display—that are legible and appropriate.
8. Avoid sans serif faces for text.
9. Generally, don't try to wrap text around odd shapes.

Paper

The paper stock on which your brochure is printed can add a lot to the impact of your message. If it is printed on inappropriate stock, your message loses some of its impact. Printing stock can be a baffling topic and one far too complex to explain fully here. The best advice is to work closely with a printing expert who can guide you properly. However, there are some basic things about paper that you should know before you talk to a paper authority.

Paper has a *grain*. That means that the fibers run in a specific direction. Knowing about grain is important because paper folds better and cleaner with the grain, and paper is stiffer in the direction of the grain. Paper is also designated by its *basis weight*. Seventy-pound paper is 500 sheets (a ream) of 25-by-38-inch paper. That size, by the way, is the standard for U.S. book papers, which include coated, text, offset, opaque and so on. The basis weight of typical business letterheads is 20 pounds, meaning 500 sheets of 17-by-22 inches. Cover stocks come from different sizes of basis weights.

Curl refers to the degree to which paper tends to buckle because it has excess moisture. This usually isn't a problem except when you use a cover stock that is coated on one side only. *Paper-ink affinity* refers to the speed with which ink dries on the printed stock. If the paper is very porous, as is newsprint, the ink is absorbed and dries quickly but the images are not as sharply defined as on better stock that dries more slowly. Gas and electric dryers often are used on many paper stocks to speed the drying process.

Paper color can affect color reproduction of lighter tints. Type is generally easier to read on a soft (yellowish) white stock, but four-color process reproduces more accurately on neutral white stock. *Brightness* also can be a factor. It affects contrast, brilliance, snap and sparkle of the printed content. *Opacity* refers to the show-through of printing from the other side of the paper or from a sheet under it. Papers with higher basis weights usually are more opaque than those with lower basis weights. *Smoothness* is a very important quality. If you're printing using a letterpress or gravure process, you need a smooth surface for the best results. Smoothness seems not to matter as much when printing offset.

Paper also is *graded* by its primary uses. Although there are many grades, those that follow are the ones you'll most likely use:

- *Bond* paper is typical business correspondence paper.
- *Coated* stock is what you will likely use when you must have the highest-quality reproduction.
- *Text* paper is noted for its interesting textures and colors. You'll use it mostly for announcements, fliers and brochures.
- *Book* is a grade that is common for trade books and textbooks.
- *Offset* stock is similar to coated and text papers but it is less moisture absorbent to compensate for the extra moisture present in offset printing.
- *Cover* papers have heavier basis weights and are made to complement coated and text papers.

If all of this is baffling, remember the simple rule: When in doubt, consult an expert.

White Space

The term *white space* refers to the unused portion of the total space in your brochure. Good design includes a judicious use of white space because it is, indeed, a design element, just like a piece of art.

The most important decision about the use of white space is how much margin you will use at the top and bottom of a page and on the left and right sides. There are no fixed rules to follow. A rule of thumb you may find useful is that the smaller the page size the smaller the margins can (not must) be. The reverse is also true. For example, if you are working with a page size of 8.5-by-11 inches, you might use three-quarters of an inch margins at the top and left and right sides and one inch at the bottom. Should the bottom margin be wider? Yes, to compensate for the optical center (not the symmetrical center) of the page.

The next most important decision about white space is the line length of your text. Try for an optimal length that is plus or minus one to three picas from the result of the following formula:

Text type point size × 1.5 = line length in picas

If you're using 12-point type, then the best line length for that size would be from 15 to 21 picas. If you stay within that framework, you'll generally improve the readability of your brochure.

Another decision affecting the use of space is the space between columns of type, or gutter space. A space in points 1.5 times the point size of text type is about the minimum space to consider. For example, 12-point type should have no less than 18 points between columns.

The next consideration is the amount of space you'll use to separate text from artwork. This can vary a good bit, but a general rule is to use the point size of text type as the minimum.

The final major consideration is whether you'll bleed artwork. Bleeding refers to running artwork off the edge of the page. Always stop artwork at the margin or bleed it off the page. Never stop it between the margin and the edge. Bleeding often requires a larger paper size, because the paper must be trimmed into the artwork (and discarded) to provide a sharp edge.

One major rule to remember about white space is: Never trap white space inside the page design. The reader's eye tends to fall into these "white holes" and it is hard to escape them. Always arrange your visuals, heads and copy blocks so there is white space opening to the outside of the design. This avoids the "white holes."

Color

Color enhances the attractiveness of most any publication. Even so, don't use color just to make things look better, because many messages don't need color at all. Using it in those situations is simply a waste of money. But other messages not only need but demand color. If you're creating a brochure for a new luxury hotel, you not only need color but four-color process to show the decor of the hotel. The same is true if you're trying to raise funds to send underprivileged kids to summer camp in the mountains. How can you really show the thrill of a child catching a trout in the splendor of a mountain stream if you don't use color? So color can be an important element in the success of many brochures.

There are four basic components of color that you need to think about when working with electronic images. First is *pigment*—red, yellow and blue—the primary colors that mix to produce all other colors. The second is *light*—red, green and blue—the color that you see on your computer or TV screen that comes from beaming three light sources at triads of red, green and blue phosphor pixels, which then causes the pixels to glow at different intensities. The third component is *complementary colors*—cyan, magenta and yellow—created by mixing two light sources such as in theater lighting. A fourth component is *print colors*—cyan, magenta, yellow and black—also referred to as process colors or CMYK (the K stands for black), that are mixed in printing to create all other colors.[1]

For electronic colors, the brightness of each pixel is determined by *voltage*. The range is from zero voltage or black to equal voltage or white. The range of brightness is greater than for ink on paper because the brightness of the ink we see depends on the amount of light reflected from the image to our eyes. Different surfaces and different inks affect brightness as does ambient light. Our eyes have rods that detect black and white, and cones that see color—but not well in low light.[2] You need to know how different colors will show up on the screen because this affects the balance of the design and readability.

Review the section in Chapter 12 regarding the uses of color, the psychology of color and how the Pantone Color Matching System takes the place of traditional color swatches for printing.

There are two broad types of color usage. One is called *spot color*. That's where you use a second color to supplement a basic ink color, usually black. If you use still another color, it will be called the third color. Spot color is fairly inexpensive, and with the creative use of screens and tint blocks you can get a rainbow of effects for a modest investment. Spot color also is not, in printing terms, close register—that is, it does not have to line up within thousandths of an inch.

The other kind of color is called *four-color process*. Photographic art is screened four separate times with special filters that sequentially block out all colors but yellow, red, blue and black (the primary colors). When they are printed properly one on top of the other, they produce the full range of colors visible to the human eye. Four-color process is close-register printing, meaning that the dot patterns must align precisely or the picture is fuzzy, requiring additional paper and press time for setup. That is why four-color process color is more expensive than spot color. So check your budget carefully.

Reproduction

Unless you are relying on photocopying machines or desktop publishing, you must prepare your brochure for reproduction, meaning you must choose between three types of printing: letterpress, offset or gravure. Each method has its own distinguishing quality and characteristics. Because of rapid technological improvements, differences in the final images produced by these methods are not as noticeable as they were just a few years ago. All three are capable of producing the same copy and art with satisfactory results.

Letterpress

Letterpress printing is the oldest of the three. It reproduces images from raised surfaces, working on the same principle as a rubber stamp. Letterpress is noted for its sharp, crisp printing and slight embossing (because paper is pressed into direct contact with the raised image to be printed).

Well-tooled letterpress printing plates are good for long pressruns into the hundreds of thousands. Quantities of a half million or more will likely require a second set of printing plates. Because there are so many press sizes, letterpress can be an efficient choice, even for small, short-run brochures.

Offset

Offset or offset lithography prints from a flat surface. It works on the principle that oil and water don't mix. The image to be printed is burned into a light-sensitive printing plate and developed with special chemicals. The developing process sensitizes the image so that it will accept ink. The unsensitized area rejects ink. The image is transferred to a rubber blanket that then offsets the image to paper. Thus the printing plate never comes into contact with the paper on which the image is offset or printed.

Offset printing is characterized by soft, smooth transitions of color and tones and slight differences in color balance throughout a pressrun. It is a good method for creating a mood piece, especially if soft contrast in tones is needed. Generally, offset printing is less expensive than letterpress and gravure. It is also easy to work with if you're using a desktop system to produce camera-ready pages.

Gravure

Gravure is a printing system that transfers an image from recessed images on printing plates—the opposite of the raised surface in letterpress. The image is etched into the printing plate so that ink fills the individual dots (wells). A device called a doctor blade moves across the surface and wipes away excess ink, leaving ink in the holes. When paper comes into contact with the printing plate, it lifts the ink from the wells, thus creating an image.

Gravure is known for the finest quality of color reproduction and is often used in high-fashion printed pieces, which many years ago got it mentioned in the song "Easter Parade." It is also known for high-quality printing on a variety of surfaces like transparent and flexible films, cartons and even vinyl floor covering. If you use gravure, get ready for a budget shock, because it is more expensive than letterpress and offset.

Distribution

The way you distribute a brochure may influence its overall design. If it is to be mailed in an envelope, its finished form must conform to the size of the envelope chosen. If it is to be a self-mailer, the back page or panel must be designed with a return address in the upper left corner and a place in the center lower half for the mailing address.

If you're using a postage meter or stamps, postage must be affixed in the upper right corner. If you're using some sort of mail permit, this must be printed in the area where postage normally appears. Be sure to check with the postmaster at the post office where the piece will be mailed to be sure that you know and conform to appropriate regulations. In fact, you'd be wise to create a dummy of the brochure and take it to the postmaster for inspection and guidance. It is a lot easier to prevent a mailing problem than to correct one.

Of course, if your brochure will be distributed from racks, as in waiting rooms of physicians, your concern is that the size will fit readily into such display racks and that the paper stock on which the brochure is printed is stiff enough to remain vertical when placed in racks.

Converting your brochure into digital images is an additional option. Once in digital form, the brochure can be loaded onto a Web site or distributed via email. Here you have several options:

- If your computer has Adobe® Acrobat® software installed and you use desktop publishing software to prepare your brochure, you can produce a portable document format (PDF) file by selecting the Acrobat Distiller® as your "printer."
- If the brochure was designed by a vendor, that person probably can produce a PDF file, but don't expect that service to be done without charge. As you are preparing your budget before the work is done, ask your vendor to include in the quote preparation of a PDF file.
- Another option is to use a scanner with PDF capabilities to scan the printed brochure and produce a PDF file. The result will be digital images with the same colors as the printed brochure.

If you convert your brochure to a PDF format and distribute it via your Web site or email, you should provide a link to Adobe's Web site where a free download of Acrobat Reader® is available.

Conclusions

- The term *brochure,* used in its narrow sense, means a printed piece of six or more pages, published once and distributed to special publics for a single purpose.
- The term *brochure* is often used to refer to booklets, fliers, circulars, leaflets, pamphlets or tracts.

- Common elements of brochures are: (1) message statements are singular; (2) they attempt to persuade, inform and/or educate; (3) they are published only once; (4) they must attract and hold their own publics; (5) they are their own delivery systems; and (6) they must have clear writing and be visually attractive.
- The general purpose of brochures is to persuade, inform or educate.
- An effective brochure can be developed only from a clear concept.
- An effective concept is one that links a broad purpose to an object or an application.
- A good brochure is distinctive. It seeks cleverness by giving a new or different twist to something that is familiar.
- The best brochures avoid puffery and build credibility by offering only valid information.
- Writing and designing a brochure is the art of giving shape to information.
- The rules of grammar, spelling and punctuation apply to brochures as they do to all other forms of public relations writing.
- Use the active voice. Strive for accuracy, consistent style and appropriate tone.
- Write first. Then design.
- Visuals should be used to substitute, when possible, for what is written, not just to dress up a brochure. For best reproduction of visuals, art must be line art or screened art.
- Good brochure design involves selecting the right format for the information, using type wisely, finding the right paper on which the brochure will be printed, using white space judiciously and using color creatively.
- Aside from brochures produced on all types of copying machines, brochures will be printed by way of letterpress, offset or gravure.
- The method of distribution must be considered at the time the brochure is being planned. Distribution can also affect the choice of paper stock on which it is printed.
- Your brochure can be converted to digital images for loading onto a Web site or for distribution via email.

Exercises

1. Select brochures of your choice from a bank and a hospital (or two other dissimilar organizations). Analyze the two brochures in terms of purpose, concept, writing style, clarity of information and design. Evaluate whether these brochures are attuned to their publics and explain why you believe that is the case.
2. Get a copy of the recruiting brochure from your university. Do a readability analysis of the writing (refer to Chapter 5). Is the readability level appropriate for the intended public? Select three or four consecutive paragraphs and rewrite them to a ninth-grade level.
3. Develop a concept for a brochure to promote the department or field in which you are majoring.

 Use InfoTrac College Edition to access information on topics in this chapter from hundreds of periodicals and scholarly journals.

Notes

1. Noel Ward, "Translating the Languages of Color," *Desktop Publishers Journal* (March 1995): 26–27.
2. Ibid.

Selected Bibliography

Barbara Radke Blake and Barbara L. Stein, *Creating Newsletters, Brochures, and Pamphlets: A How-to-Do-It Manual* (New York: Neal-Schuman, 1992).

Robert W. Bly, *Create the Perfect Sales Piece: How to Produce Brochures, Catalogs, Fliers, and Pamphlets* (New York: John Wiley & Sons, 1985).

Herman Holtz, *Great Promo Pieces: Create Your Own Brochures, Broadsides, Ads, Flyers and Newsletters That Get Results* (New York: John Wiley & Sons, 1988).

Gordon Woolf, *Publication Production Using PageMaker: A Guide to Using Adobe PageMaker 7 for the Production of Newspapers, Newsletters, Magazines and Other Formatted Publications* (Hastings, Vic., Australia: Worsley Press, 2002).

Magazines and Annual Reports

W hat an organization *says* is always the measure used to judge what it *does*. The responsibility and expectation of the "spokespersons" for organizations is that they will craft the significant messages for the organization: magazines and annual reports. Magazines are serial publications, but annual reports, as the name indicates, are published once yearly and report on the previous year.

The magazines may be for internal publics primarily or external publics primarily and occasionally for a mix. Organizations may publish a variety of magazines, but each should have a clear and distinct purpose that sets it apart from the others.

This chapter focuses on the demands made on the writer of these two significant tools of organizational communication.

Magazines

Even though the contents of Internet and intranet sites have replaced printed publications in many organizations, magazines still can be powerful public relations tools. They allow greater depth of treatment than most other media, permit more vivid and attractive display and enable writers to compose messages for specific target publics. Their life is longer and they have more "pass-along" readership.

Sometimes the public is internal—when a magazine is published for the employees of an organization, for example. Sometimes it is external, like that of *Frontiers,* published by BP plc, which goes to selected industry, media and community leaders. By one estimate, more than 10,000 public relations magazines are published in the United States. Many such magazines now are published only on Web sites to increase their availability and eliminate printing and distribution costs.

The success of such publications is determined in part by format, illustrations, design, editing and proper distribution. But the most important element of any magazine is the writing—its quality, its relevance and its appropriateness for the target readers. The most beautifully designed, illustrated and printed magazine in the world cannot sustain success without well-written articles, because it won't communicate much.

Topics

When you are choosing topics, it pays to look again at the mission statement for this public relations tool. What is it supposed to do? Who are its readers?

Most magazines conduct readership studies and, for budget purposes, a magazine must show a cost-effective benefit as a public relations tool. Because organizational publications compete with mass media for the time and attention of their readers, even if they are "free," you must be sure of their appeal. That means you must give priority to developing good topics for articles. Sometimes your topics will be assigned to you by your superiors, but more than likely you will be left to your own devices most of the time. Although a good writer can usually make a mundane topic interesting, success can be assured only with a consistent inventory of good article ideas.

Finding Topics   If you know your readers well, certain topics will virtually suggest themselves. Your own flashes of insight may not be sufficient, however, to fill every issue of the magazine you work on. Fortunately, they don't have to be. There are other sources for article ideas.

First, however, let's talk more about knowing your readers. As a writer, you need to move about your organization and get to know people from all areas of the operation. You can't know everyone personally, of course, but you should get to know at least a few people in every area. Personnel can be good sources of ideas, and they also can help you gauge the value of your own ideas.

A growing concern these days among employees is the lack of information about where their organizations are headed and the reasons behind these and other decisions. They also want management to listen to them, not just talk down to them. They further believe that, despite claims to the contrary, management does not actually encourage free exchange of information. If this is a correct assessment, your task is greatly simplified. Simply talk to other employees throughout the company. Listen carefully. You'll turn up a wealth of topics your readers want to know more about. If you research and write the stories well, your magazine will be greeted with eagerness rather than a yawn.

But be prepared for the politics of getting some topics approved by management. Many of the things employees want to know are exactly what some managers don't want to talk about. The latter may support you, however, if you prepare them to look at story ideas from strategic points of view.

Doing a story now may defuse a small problem before it becomes large. An organization may gain a lot more support in the long run if it sensitizes employees now to a delicate situation rather than issuing edicts about it later when it may be even more delicate. Yet another strategic consideration is that the pain caused by candor, especially in a crisis, is usually temporary. Candor clears the air quickly, so an organization can get on with its business.

It is becoming common for companies or organizations to perform what is called a *communication audit*. This is a systematic evaluation of the effectiveness of the organization's communication programs, including the magazine, if one is issued. The audit zeros in on strengths and weaknesses in the organization's communication program. Some of these findings become fodder for good magazine articles. Refer to Chapter 4 for more information about communication audits.

Managements sometimes conduct organizationwide employee surveys. Survey participants may include readers of the magazine who are customers or who have more than a passing interest in what goes on at the organization. Such surveys may be treasure troves for article ideas.

Public opinion surveys, like those done by the worldwide Gallup Organization and the Roper Center, are common sources of ideas. They regularly take the pulse of the American public. You should make it a practice to read, study and save these polls for future reference. Even if the topic of the poll report seems unrelated to your company or industry, later analysis may show otherwise.

Additionally, you must regularly consult both local and national newspapers and a variety of consumer magazines. Save items that strike your interest, even if a specific article idea does not leap out at you. Watch both network and local television news, public affairs broadcasts and special-events programs. Listen to a broad spectrum of local radio stations, and tune in some of the news and commentary programs on public radio.

It should be obvious that you must read the appropriate professional, trade, industrial and scholarly journals. And you should go to meetings of all types. These can range from local service-club meetings to national professional conventions. The point is that you must go.

Any one or all of these may be the source of an idea. And an article idea may come into focus when you least expect it. But the idea you want won't come looking for you. You have to be on the alert all the time. If you're not tuned in, you may not recognize it. The clue may be a word or phrase, even out of context, or a major event. You have to pay attention to what goes on around you.

Form Versus Substance   This chapter began by saying that magazines are good communication tools for organizations. And they are. But are they as good as they can be? No. Who can make them better? Writers. Who are the writers? You. At least, you expect to be. So it is you—not "them"—who will improve company magazines and other publications.

That's not a small challenge, because it seems that everyone interested in the organization is more concerned with the substance of your writing than with your writing skills. That's no license to lessen your attention to proper grammar, syntax and other technical matters. Rather, it is an indication of the trap that some writers fall into: They substitute form for substance. What you must strive for is both good form *and* substance.

Good substance is defined as what interests readers. There is growing uneasiness among employees about how they relate to their organizations. Many don't have the depth of personal identification with or loyalty to their organizations that was characteristic some years ago. They sense they are interchangeable pieces in a chess game being played by management. They feel frozen out of decisions about which moves to make and why. If they get jumped, they are summarily removed from the board.

As a writer, you can help. But you can do this only if you listen carefully to your readers and are sensitive to their information needs. When you identify those needs, meet them.

Just choosing the right word can make the difference in whether or not you convey your meaning and—if you do—what the emotional reaction might be. Two studies published by the Mid-America Communication Foundation, one from Opinion Research Corporation and another from Hill & Knowlton, call attention to the different vocabularies of management and employees. In the ORC report, the findings show that employee-effective words satisfy three criteria:

1. Familiarity: Employees know the word well enough to define it.
2. Understandability: In workers' dictionaries, *capitalism* may be understood differently.
3. Emotional impact: Beyond familiarity and understanding, a word might trigger a different emotional reaction from employees than from management.

A current example might be the word *downsizing,* which management might see as positive (that is, becoming more efficient), but employees probably see as negative (that is, firing a lot of people). The H&K study cited identifies 30 words and 25 phrases that show how inflated language used by management during a steel strike made matters worse. For instance, instead of the word *accrue,* simpler words like *pile up* or *collect* would have been better understood. Similarly, the phrase *exclusive function* should have been translated *sole right.* Both study results came from talking to people to find out what worked for them. Such consultation is important if the publication is to be useful.[1]

Some people think that magazines and other employee publications are perhaps expected to carry too much of the communication load for organizations. That may be true. But it is certainly true that employees place more value on information they get from personal sources than from impersonal ones.

You can't change a magazine or other publication from its impersonal form, but that's no reason for you as a writer to treat your readers impersonally. Talk to them. Listen to them. See things through their eyes. Be them. Then write to them. Focus on the substantive information they want and need. If you do these things well, maybe you can make your magazine a lot better.

Employee Publications

Most organizations have a publication of some sort for employees. Often the employee publication is a full-fledged magazine; sometimes it looks more like a newspaper or newsletter. But whatever the format, the writing in employee publications should follow most closely the style of magazine articles.

Why? Because even if an employee publication looks like a newspaper or a newsletter, it rarely functions as a medium for hard news. Unless it comes out daily (and few do), an employee publication cannot compete with other information sources available to employees. Informal communication networks among supervisors and secretaries can spread news faster in the organization than can the AP wire. And when important events occur or major decisions are made, they are generally announced at once rather than held for publication in the next month's employee magazine.

Furthermore, employee publications can be an extremely potent tool of internal public relations, and they should be used to accomplish more than telling of the shop foreman's new baby or the vice president's successful fishing trip. (This is known as the dead-fish-and-live-babies syndrome.) As experienced employee publication editor Don Fabun points out, employee publications today must appeal not only to a telephone operator, but "to an atomic physicist, a systems engineer, a market analyst, and an operations analyst. These latter are not likely to be interested in, or motivated by, bowling scores and a detailed account of the company picnic."[2]

Employee publications can help generate support among employees for corporate goals and objectives. Articles can build employee morale and enhance job satisfaction, thus boosting productivity. Publications can create a broader understanding among employees of the problems a company faces.

How can these goals be accomplished? Mainly by keeping such objectives in mind when you're writing articles for employees, and by following the principles of magazine writing outlined earlier in this chapter. Specifically, you must orient the writing to the reader. Explain the significance of events from the point of view of the employee—not from the point of view of the board of directors. In other words, don't relate verbatim a new company policy as handed down from on high. Explain the policy and tell what it means to the reader. But explain it in an interesting way: Find a good angle, write a good lead and make the article as human and dramatic as possible.

If you take this approach, your company's employee publication can be a valuable asset to the organization. Articles about a company's achievements in research can generate pride among the employees, giving them a good feeling about being part of the company. Articles about the need to save energy or improve safety records can motivate employees to improve their performance in those areas. Articles about the relationship between your company's work and the well-being of the community can give employees a sense of involvement in a socially useful occupation. Articles about the accomplishments of individuals can be an incentive to other workers.

If you write articles on such subjects skillfully, so that employees will read them, you can accomplish much more than you would with a publication written strictly to provide entertainment or to relate social fluff. This does not mean that an employee publication should be a propaganda engine for the views of management. Rather, such a publication should be mutually beneficial to the individual employees and to the organization as a whole.

Association Publications

Members feel very involved in their associations and look forward to receiving the publication that their membership fees entitle them to. Even the government of the USA has associations with membership fees and publications such as the *Smithsonian* from the Smithsonian Institution.

Other well-known associations that have magazines include the National Geographic Society, the American Automobile Association (AAA), the National Wildlife Federation, the National Trust for Historic Preservation and various social groups such as college sororities and fraternities. (See Figure 19.1.) The American Association of Retired Persons publishes *AARP The Magazine,* which has the largest circulation of all USA magazines—larger than *Reader's Digest.* Some of the publications carry advertising from external sources and others have only house ads or no advertising at all.

What's important for a public relations writer to remember about them, though, is their high credibility and in-depth reading. Although these publications compete with commercial, newsstand magazines for their audience's attention, they are likely to get it.

Q&A

Anne Saunders, vice president of interactive, Starbucks

Starbucks Brews Up Success on the Web

BY SHANE MCLAUGHLIN

Starbucks has conquered the coffee business. Throw a rock and it will land in someone's Café Americano. Now the ubiquitous chain is brewing up java of another sort, the kind that refers to the programming language of Web sites.

Starbucks.com is that rare corporate site that stays simple and sophisticated while it reaches out to several audiences. It percolates with substantive information for employees, job seekers, reporters, investors, customers and coffee-growers alike.

As a communications tool, it's proving its return on investment. According to Anne Saunders, vice president of interactive, 11 percent of all in-store sales are prepaid through the company Web site. Customers who have the "Starbucks card," which holds cash for store purchases, can charge it up online through a credit-card transaction. Java addicts everywhere may have found the eternal caffeine buzz.

Saunders's own experiences in e-commerce and marketing have shaped her technology philosophy at Starbucks. Prior to her current job (which she found through the Starbucks Web site), her career included being CEO of e-commerce company E-Society and working as one of the 10 highest-ranking women at AT&T Wireless. *The Strategist* recently spoke with Saunders about the power of technology to drive communications.

You have an extensive background in both e-commerce and marketing. Now you're in charge of technology for one of the biggest business brands ever. How have you incorporated your experience into the Web medium?

Saunders: I can't take sole credit. We have a great design team with the philosophy that a Web site should have information people need, load fast and be easy to navigate. There's a lot of content from many company functions on one site. However, we also make an effort to highlight different facets of the company at different times. It's important to keep the site fresh with new offerings to keep people coming back.

Your Web site reflects the look and feel of your stores, which are distinctive customer experiences. Was that a challenge?

Saunders: Our goal is to have our site look and feel like it's that same Starbucks you visit for coffee. We want people to connect online like they connect in our stores. We are exploring using the Web site to profile what's going on in local communities, for example, poetry readings, book-club meetings or charitable events. This information would be accessed through our store-locator function, one of the site's most popular features.

Is your site an effective employee recruiting tool?

Saunders: We have built out the functionality of our job center site considerably. We have 65,000 employees worldwide. I found my job initially through the Starbucks Web site.

How are you recruiting customers through the Web?

Saunders: We're excited about our online section for Starbucks cards. A year and a half ago we introduced a card for customers to load up with cash. We've installed a payment mechanism online so people can reload their cards without going in a store. It's billed right to their credit card.

They can register to have the card automatically reloaded when it drops below $20. This Web-based program is part of the reason that 11 percent of our store transactions are prepaid using the Starbucks card.

FIGURE 19.1

Association Publication   *One benefit of membership in the Public Relations Society of America (PRSA) is the magazine* The Public Relations Strategist, *published quarterly.*

TECHNOLOGY

Are there any concerns about privacy issues for Web-based customers?

Saunders: We have a very stringent privacy policy that appears at the bottom of every page. Unlike some companies, we never give customer information to third parties. We also encourage people to register their card, which means submitting your name, address and e-mail online. That way if the card is lost or stolen, we will replace it free of charge.

Are registered users automatically

sent e-mails from Starbucks? That could be a reason not to register.

Saunders: You choose whether or not you want to receive information about new products in an "opt-in" format. Registered cardholders are also eligible for vacations and giveaways. We've given away several trips so far.

Your philanthropy is extensive. Is that a high priority moving forward?

Saunders: A lot of our philanthropic initiatives come out of suggestions from our customers and employees. The in-

formation on our Web site aims to empower people to make a difference.

Online we also have information about fostering sustainability in the countries that produce our coffee. We pay a premium price for coffee because it's grown to high standards and the dollars are funneled back to the local farmer. The life of a coffee partner is challenging. We want to be an industry advocate for change.

Your Web site is also a source for new media, especially free music.

Saunders: Providing digital content free of charge is innovative. You can hear interviews and download tracks from a diverse group of artists like Yo-Yo Ma, Ray Charles and Sheryl Crow. Additionally, 2,200 stores currently offer wireless Internet connections to customers for a fee. We are projecting 2,600 stores will offer this service at the end of the year, or 60 percent of company-owned stores. On average, customers who bring in their laptops and log on to the Web stay about twice as long in our stores.

What does the future hold for the Starbucks technology strategy?

Saunders: We view the wireless Web as a platform for our company, a device for the achievement of business objectives. Our corporate communications and marketing leadership are important in the brainstorming process as we move forward. We have a unique and special work environment that is reflected on the Web. ■

Coffee talk: Starbucks chairman Howard Schultz (*front*), Michael Capellas, president of Hewlett-Packard (*left*) and John Stanton, chairman of T-Mobile, use a high-speed wireless connection at a Starbucks store in San Francisco.

Shane McLaughlin is a freelance writer and senior associate at Best Practices in Corporate Communications, a Washington, D.C.-based member organization. He recently authored "Champions of Change," an investigative report analyzing the change philosophies of communications in the world's most respected companies.

FIGURE 19.1 (*continued*)

This article uses an effective question-and-answer format that you may find helpful during your public relations career.
Source: Reprinted by permission of Public Relations Society of America.

Trade and Industry Publications

Most trade and industry publications are of little interest to anyone outside that particular area of business. (See Figure 19.2.) But for people in the business, these magazines are a major source of information. You can find the *Cattleman* in most cattle raisers' homes or offices and the *Grocer* in most food store owners' and managers' offices.

Although most of these trade and industry publications are the product of associations, they differ somewhat from the lifestyle or interest associations that produce such publications as *National Geographic*. If anything, though, their readers are even more dedicated and more avid. If you go to work for a trade or industry publication, you'll find that the smallest mistake will result in countless phone calls, faxes and letters to the editor. It's nice to be noticed, but it's better if the notice comes from some creative or inspired writing, rather than from a mistake.

Corporate Publications for the Public

More companies are producing magazines about their product line, offering advice and services. Health maintenance organizations (HMOs) publish magazines about their services. Manufacturers like Sony are likely to have more than one publication. Sony publishes *Sony Style* and *Sony Electronics*.

Although these are published for customer convenience and information, their purpose is to establish brand loyalty.[3] Slick and expensive, these publications do have subscriptions, but the subscriber costs are generally low, intended to cover marketing and distribution costs. Subscribers also benefit from coupons in the publications and special prices to subscribers.

Another type of corporate magazine sells image. One of the most impressive magazines of this type is *Aramco World*, published by Aramco Services Company. The oil company uses its magazine to share information about the history, art and culture of the Middle East. There is no charge for this publication, which goes to a limited audience of appreciative readers. Another, a slick four-color magazine, *food&family*, is published by Kraft Foods North America, Inc. and includes feature articles, full-page ads and recipes touting its products while building its image.

Promoting an image is, of course, a major role for many organizational magazines. But there's another type of publication that also contributes significantly to an organization's image—the annual report.

Annual Reports

First you need to know that a corporation whose stock is publicly traded is required to prepare not one but *two* annual reports. One is the SEC Form 10-K annual report to the Securities and Exchange Commission. The other is the annual report to shareholders.

The SEC Form 10-K is prepared in a format decreed by the SEC that is plain—no graphics, no photos, no color, just black type on white paper. Because it contains all of the information that a company is required to provide shareholders, some companies choose to print extra copies of the 10-K and wrap around it a cover and information that management wants to provide to shareholders and other constituents.

F I G U R E   1 9 . 2

Trade Magazine   *The front cover of this issue of* Presstime *reflects stories and features on multimedia and technology sure to appeal to NAA members. Reprinted with permission of the Newspaper Association of America.*

Because it is a legal document, the SEC Form 10-K usually is prepared by accountants and attorneys. On the other hand, the annual report to shareholders is a principal public relations responsibility. It is the latter annual report that we will discuss in this chapter.

The annual report to shareholders may look like a magazine but the similarity is mostly superficial. Annual reports are publications required of publicly held companies as a way of documenting fiscal soundness and chronicling the year's events. Many privately held companies and nonprofit organizations also produce annual reports, although they aren't required to. Whether public, private or nonprofit, many annual reports seem to have one thing in common—obscure language.

Here's one sentence from an actual report—a good example of how *not* to write: "Net Profits from the sale or disposition of a Partnership property are allocated: first, prior to giving effect to any distributions of Sale Proceeds from the transaction, to the General Partner and the Limited Partners with negative balances in their capital accounts pro rata in proportion to such respective negative balances, to the extent of the total of such negative balances; second, to the General Partner, in an amount necessary to make the balance in its capital account equal to the amount of Sale Proceeds to be distributed to the General Partner with respect to the sale or disposition of such property and third, the balance, if any, to the Limited Partners."

Some obscurity may come from meeting regulatory requirements of publicly held companies, but that does not justify it in the annual reports of private and nonprofit organizations.

Indeed, the SEC itself encourages simple writing. It publishes *A Plain English Handbook—How to Create Clear SEC Disclosure Documents.* The handbook is available free on the SEC Web site and by calling (800) SEC-0330. It contains details on the following writing tips:

- Use the active voice with strong verbs.
- Don't ban the passive voice, use it sparingly.
- Try personal pronouns.
- Omit superfluous words.
- Write in the "positive."
- Use short sentences.
- Replace jargon and legalese with short, common words.
- Keep the subject, verb and object close together.[4]

The SEC changed the reporting rules so that what the shareholders get now is a considerably leaner publication that is more of a promotion piece than a disclosure document. Many annual reports still don't read very well, however. Shareholders used to be able to count on the "devil being in the details"—that is, the footnotes. Footnotes used to be read assiduously by shareholders hoping to find out what was really going on instead of what the report suggested. Then in 1995, the SEC, which already was asking for annual reports to come to its office electronically, decided that although it still had to see all of the footnotes, it wouldn't be necessary for organizations to furnish all of these to shareholders anymore. Supposedly this saves money because the longer reports could cost from $300,000 to $500,000 to produce.[5]

Following this was the SEC decision permitting companies to produce what is in effect summary annual reports. (See Figure 19.3.) Shareholders always can request a copy of the 10-K, of course, to get all of the information the SEC has. Driving the SEC decision was an effort to provide investors with a document that was not so overwhelming.[6] The problem may still be that "concise" is not always the same as "clear."

F I G U R E   1 9 . 3

Annual Report with SEC Form 10-K   *Many companies, like ONEOK, Inc., a diversified energy company, insert the corporation's SEC Form 10-K, their annual report to the Securities and Exchange Commission, into their Annual Report to Shareholders.*
Source: Reprinted by permission of ONEOK, Inc.

The SEC requires corporations to send annual reports to security holders at least 20 days prior to the annual meeting of the company's shareholders. If directors are to be elected at the annual meeting, then the annual report must be distributed with, or prior to, the company's proxy statement. Rule 14c-4—a part of the Securities Exchange Act of 1934 and still in effect—requires that information in the report be "in roman type at least as large and as legible as 10-point modern type except that to the extent necessary for convenient presentation, financial statements and other tabular data, but not the notes thereto, may be in roman type at least as large and as legible as 8-point modern type. All such type shall be leaded at least 2 points."[7]

Ninety-five percent of corporations surveyed by the National Investor Relations Institute (NIRI) early in 2003 said they make their annual reports available on their corporate Web sites. In addition to annual reports, companies say they provide the following information on the Internet:

- Quarterly earnings releases (99%)
- Press releases other than earnings (95%)
- SEC filings such as the 10K or 10Q (92%)
- Transfer agent information (87%)
- Detailed information on products and services (77%)
- Calendar of events (76%)
- Archive audio of conference call (75%)
- Biographies of senior management (72%)
- Fact sheets or corporate profiles (68%)
- Historical stock price information (68%)[8]

Clarity Versus Accuracy

If a more readable report is more popular, why don't more organizations produce them? Evidently, readability is related to truth, truth is often equated with fact, and fact sometimes does not make a company look good. Because management has to have new capital to work with—and that means attracting new investors to the company's stock—writers of annual reports sometimes resort to obfuscation. That is, they fog up the report with writing that may be entirely truthful but is nonetheless so murky that hardly anyone understands what it says. On this point, a federal judge once said, "What has developed is a literary art form calculated to communicate as little of the essential information as possible while exuding an air of total candor."

There are other reasons, of course, why annual report writing is so bad. Some company executives demand formality in writing because they believe this makes their divisions look more important. Some company presidents, for example, wouldn't think of writing a letter that just anybody could understand. Furthermore, some presidents who know nothing about writing insist on writing their own letters without the help (or subsequent editing) of a seasoned public relations writer. To do otherwise would imply that they did not know how to write. Contrary to the way some of these letters read, apparently writing them is one of the chief executive's most time-consuming tasks, according to a study by Yankelovich Partners for Potlatch Corp.[9]

Another reason the writing in some annual reports is so bad is that it has to be cleared at many levels in the company before it is finally approved. Everybody wants to add, delete or change words. "The legal department, the accounting department, and all the others tend to put in a few more terms or qualifications, just to show, if nothing else, that they are on the job," says Robert Gunning, an expert on clear writing.[10]

Once you are in an organization and have turned out an annual report or two, you'll probably begin to anticipate such changes and start writing gobbledygook to begin with. But this won't help, because the same people who made changes before will make them again. So it's best to resist the temptation to join the crowd, and instead to write simply, directly and clearly, as usual. Remember, the annual report is a public document, intended to communicate the status of the company to the public. Says Gunning, "Many writers fool themselves into believing they are writing for the public when they are actually writing to impress the boss."[11] He says that no accountant would fake the net income figure just to make the boss feel better. Yet writers often do the equivalent in annual reports. The result is that annual reports end up containing long words, long sentences and long paragraphs, many of which are not needed at all.

Say It Right and Simply   Some executives will scream when you start shortening sentences and cutting out vague words. "You need those words to be accurate," they say. "It won't be correct if you say it any other way." You must recognize, too, that they may be right. Listen to them because they are experts in their fields, although they may not be expert writers. The point is not to say it right or to say it simply, but to *say it right and simply.*

You will quickly find that it is not always easy to say it right and simply. You may have to spend an inordinate amount of time with a sentence or paragraph to make it both right and simple. The fog that billows through some annual report writing is not produced by adherence to the dictates of strict accuracy but by the inclusion of details and qualifications that don't bear on the main point of the sentence or paragraph. If a detail or qualification alters the point, include it. If it does not, delete it and make it the primary occupant of another sentence or paragraph.

The key point here was stated clearly many years ago by U.S. Supreme Court Justice Benjamin Cardozo: "There is an accuracy that defeats itself by the overemphasis of details. . . . The sentence may be so overloaded with all its possible qualifications that it may tumble down of its own weight."[12]

Comprehension   Vague words are also known as "glittering generalities." They are usually very abstract and impressive, but they don't communicate much. As a professional writer, you must be dedicated not only to truth but also to making your copy understandable. Comprehension increases in direct proportion to your use of simple, concrete words. Remember, you are writing to communicate, not to obfuscate. Annual reports that are not clearly written breed distrust.

In the following example, a company is having trouble selling some worthless land it owns in the West. But thanks to a deal made with another company, it may be able to dump its real estate soon. How did this relatively simple fact get reported in the annual report?

> We were less successful than we had hoped last year in achieving our goal of disposing of the properties of our land division, located principally in the western part of the United States. While conditions in real estate were difficult, we did conclude an important joint venture with [name of other company], which we expect will facilitate the disposal of our real estate assets.

Is it any wonder that people find fault with the writing in annual reports? The situation is changing though as government regulators are getting serious about requiring companies not only to tell the truth in annual reports but also to tell it plainly. The problem now may be that there's often not enough information, unless you ask for the 10-K.

It is easier to point out what is wrong with the writing in annual reports than to explain how to do it right. The first step, however, is to follow the principles of good writing. But even this is not enough; for your annual report writing to be successful, you must do it with a purpose. This means that you must proceed from a carefully drawn plan. One does not write an annual report on the basis of whimsy; rather, one approaches it as an important undertaking. The annual report is costly, time-consuming, sensitive and important. It makes sense to do such an important task right.

Planning the Report

Although our main concern here is writing, in writing an annual report you should never forget that the report is a publication—much like a magazine, in fact. It takes careful planning to produce a unified product. Art, design and writing must all mesh if communication is to be effective. Before you decide on format, choose type or begin to write, you must establish the report's purpose.

Purpose   The fundamental purpose of most annual reports is to provide investors with financial data and a description of the company's operations. But annual reports can do much more than this, and good ones do. Not only can the report tell the company story to investors, it can present the company's views to many other publics—the media, community leaders, employees, prospective employees and financial analysts, for example.

Thus the first step in annual report planning is answering these questions: What should the report accomplish? Do you want to comfort investors, sell stock or paint a glowing picture of the company in order to attract new customers or employees? Is the purpose merely to maintain good employee or investor relations? Will the report be used to convey the company's point of view on key issues to community or industry leaders and to the media?

Obviously, the purpose is closely related to target publics. Whatever you want to say, you must know who will be reading the report so you can tailor your message to them. Step two of annual report planning, then, is to define your publics.

Publics   Annual reports are written primarily for stockholders, but stockholders are rarely the only public, and they may not be the most important. Some companies—for example, those owned by holding companies—don't sell stock directly to the public. Annual reports for these companies might be directed to entirely different groups—perhaps to employees or legislators. The readership of annual reports is even broader now than before because many are available online. After the SEC required electronic filing, many companies decided to make the information generally available electronically because many brokers, analysts and financial editors would also be interested. The first annual reports available online were just text, but now that many companies are recognizing the electronic versions as another information tool, most include graphics, and some also have sound and animation.

As with any piece of writing, then, it is important that you first define your readers. If there are two or more significant publics, you must also establish their relative importance. That means you must set some priorities. For example, if you are writing the annual report for a company in a heavily regulated industry, logically you will be concerned with both stockholders and regulators. But these are only two entries on what might be a fairly lengthy list:

Stockholders	Suppliers
Potential stockholders	Legislators
Stockbrokers	Regulators
Financial analysts	Reporters and business editors
Employees	Editorial writers
Potential employees	Community leaders
Customers	Consumer advocates
Potential customers	Educators

The list could be extended by several additional publics. However, you get the point that your annual report might be directed to several groups. And depending on the type of company and its industrial field, the list may include some of the preceding or a completely different list. It all depends on the purpose behind the report.

Don't start writing until you have listed all your possible publics. Then establish some priorities. The publics are not equally important. If you have difficulty establishing priorities, enlist the help of company management. Construct a short questionnaire that lists the options and a scale of importance for each. Company executives who know the relative importance of these publics can be of great help. Once you have clearly identified your major publics, you should direct your report to them.

Even if you identify and direct your report to only one public, remember that others may also read it, including competitors. If you are writing for stockholders, for example, remember that some stockholders may also be employees. If so, you will not improve employee relations by stressing how well your company is holding the line on costs by paying low wages.

Writing the Report

Once the purpose is set and publics have been identified, you can begin compiling information to use in the report. The first concern at this stage is content: What should the report say?

Determining Content   Determining content is probably the biggest problem in writing an annual report. In probably no other writing task is determining content so difficult. An individual writer composing a piece on a single topic merely gathers information, decides what to say and then says it. As an annual report writer, however, you will have to please many people before the report ever reaches its intended publics, and you are likely to run into some difficulty in trying to write material that is truthful, clear and acceptable to all.

Fortunately, there are some guidelines regarding content. For instance, government rules specify certain items that must be included. Among the essentials either required by law or generally demanded by the investment community are these:

Financial summary
Letter from the chief executive officer
Corporate description
Narrative section describing operations
Balance sheet and income statements
Statement of sources and use of funds
Notes to financial statements
Auditor's statement
Chief executive officer and chief financial officer's certification of financial statements
Ten-year statistical summary

Most of these essentials are simply tables of numbers, and they won't be of immediate concern to you as the writer, but their content may provide important clues to points you should emphasize in the narrative portion of the report. Accountants supply the numbers; writers supply the words. Providing the words usually means writing the chief executive's letter and the narrative section of the report.

CEO's Letter   When preparing the chief executive's letter to shareholders, you must first meet with that person to find out how the letter is to be written. Sometimes the executive will write a letter and turn it over to you for editing or rewriting. Sometimes it works the other way around. And sometimes the writer interviews the executive and then prepares a letter based on the executive's responses. Above all, the letter should "sound" like the chief executive. Any of these procedures is acceptable as long as a good letter is the result.

But what makes a good letter? There's no agreement on this—or even on what the letter should contain. Some simply summarize the year's financial results. Others may ignore money matters and talk about social problems facing the company and its industry. Still others may combine financial material and social commentary in a lengthy treatise designed to convince everybody that things are better than they seem. Different letters are appropriate in different circumstances. Pfizer's 2002 annual report was titled, "Toward a Healthier World." Many annual reports for 2001 and 2002 dealt with the September 11, 2001, terrorist attacks, deaths of employees from those attacks and terrorism's negative effects on the USA economy.

Annual reports that are rated highest by financial analysts usually contain letters that adhere to a few basic principles. First, the best letters don't delve deeply into financial matters. Letters crowded with statistics are difficult to read. Except in brief mentions of key financial results, the numbers are best left for the tables and charts in the body of the report. Second, an incisive, concise letter is preferable to a lengthy dissertation that attempts to cover the minute areas of operation. Third, analysts expect the executive's letter to be devoted primarily to results of the previous year and expectations for the coming year or two. In this regard, the letter should include a discussion of future problems as well as anticipated successes.

Whatever the focus of the letter, it sets the stage for the narrative of the report, where the company's operations are described in detail.

Narrative   The body of the annual report is where you tell the company's story. This section contains a general description of the company or institution; its location, purposes, products and services; and its related activities. The narrative reports the company's results of the previous year and its plans for the future, even if these are mentioned in the executive's letter. The narrative must disclose and discuss events, management decisions, sales, mergers and conditions that have had significant effects on the company's operation.

At the same time, the narrative must also achieve the communication objectives set for it during the planning process. If the report's purpose is to get people to buy stock, the narrative must give reasons why the company's stock is a good deal. You can do this best not by talking dollars and cents but by describing the company's position in the industry, its management philosophy, and its foresight and record of success.

The narrative of most annual reports also covers such topics as plans for expansion, research and development programs and the nature of the company's customers or markets. But merely presenting such basics isn't enough. Financial analysts want information on the problems facing the company and its industry, and a discussion of current economic conditions and their impact.

Analysts become specialists in certain industries and then carefully follow selected companies in those fields. You can't make your company look financially healthy if the numbers show that it isn't. What you must do is treat problems candidly but emphasize what the company plans to do to solve them. If the plans are sound, your candor may sell lots of stock.

Even if it does not, you'll certainly earn credibility for your company in the financial community.

Discuss the status of the natural resources (if any) your company depends on, including the possibility of shortages and how the company will cope with them. Describe the marketing, advertising and public relations strategies that have been designed to communicate your company's goals and objectives. Tell how the company is responding to demands for greater corporate responsibility. All these matters are just as relevant in annual reports as the bottom-line figures of the income statement.

It is inevitable, of course, that even if you are determined to include all these things, you will have to fight the space battle. Something may have to be left out. How do you determine what can be deleted? First, check with the corporate attorney to identify items that must be included by law. As examples, the company may be involved in significant legal action or in some major financial transactions. Next, identify the items that most stockholders and analysts expect to see in any annual report. These include industry trends, financing, capital expenditures, consolidations, research, marketing and energy supply.

Selecting specific events to include in these categories is more difficult, however. One approach is to ask the executives in charge of company divisions which events and actions of the past year were the most important. This personal-interview technique is quite common. In fact, some annual reports simply use verbatim interviews with division heads, in a question-and-answer format. If you do this well, the technique can provide the necessary information whether or not you use that format in the report. Just keep in mind that the purpose of most interviews is to provide raw information that you need to sift and shape for your readers.

Another way to gather information from company executives is to use a written questionnaire. A simple survey can often help you get the information you need to gauge the relative importance of different topics—and thereby help you decide what to leave out. The simplest questionnaire merely asks executives to rate the importance of a few key areas. Such a form might look like the one in Table 19.1. To meet the needs of a given situation, you could add or leave out categories. In addition, you might leave space for comments or observations about the problems or successes a respondent designates as most important. A more extensive questionnaire might be called for if you want more detailed information. A series of short-answer questions like those in Table 19.2 could bring more useful responses.

Responses to questionnaires like these will help you choose topics to include in the annual report. But you should never rely solely on such surveys. If your own research shows that something else is important and should be in the annual report, don't leave it out just because it didn't appear on the survey forms. Put it in and be prepared to explain why you included it.

Double-Checking the Narrative   Once you're in the throes of writing the narrative, the following points may prove useful. The SEC is concerned particularly with three areas: results of operations, liquidity of assets and capital resources. You must couch your discussion in the context of the three years of financial information required by the SEC. You can't simply list material items, unusual occurrences or infrequent transactions. You must discuss them in sufficient detail so that your least knowledgeable readers can understand them. The SEC provides no boilerplate solutions on how to write the narrative, but it doesn't want a line-by-line discussion of the financial statement. However, if a line item represents a significant change, that item should be discussed in detail. You are expected to find a way to characterize the

TABLE 1 9 . 1   *Simple Structured Questionnaire*

In column A, rank the areas in which the company has achieved the greatest successes during the past year (1 = greatest success). In column B, rank the areas in which the company has experienced the greatest problems in the past year (1 = greatest problem).

A		B
_____	Marketing and sales	_____
_____	New product development	_____
_____	Employee relations	_____
_____	Community relations	_____
_____	Stockholder relations	_____
_____	Government relations	_____
_____	Energy supply	_____
_____	Media relations	_____
_____	Customer service	_____
_____	Competition	_____
_____	Laws and regulations	_____
_____	Other: _____	_____

TABLE 1 9 . 2   *Annual Report Questionnaire for Executives*

1. Inside the company, what do you think was the most significant event of the past year?
2. What external event of the past year do you think had the most significant impact on the company?
3. What do you believe was the most significant accomplishment of your division of the company during the past year?
4. What do you believe is the most significant problem facing the company as a whole?
5. What was the most important event or development in your division of the company during the past year?
6. What do you believe was the most significant accomplishment of the company as a whole during the past year?
7. What do you believe is the most important problem facing your division of the company?
8. What event of the past year had the most significant impact on the company's industry?
9. What do you believe is the most important problem facing the company's industry?
10. What are the most significant things the company is doing to deal with companywide, divisional and industry problems?

Source: Adapted from a questionnaire by permission of Armstrong World Industries, Inc., Lancaster, Pa.

company's business experience of the last year. The narrative is also expected to talk about trends and uncertainties. This expectation calls for you to peer into a crystal ball, however darkly, so be cautious and choose your words carefully. Remember that you and your organization must live with those words.

Theme Once you have settled on the content, the next step is to put it together in a cohesive way. You want the company to appear to be well managed, well organized and unified. The annual report should mirror these qualities from cover to cover.

The most common way to ensure cohesiveness is to find a theme. A theme is an organizing principle that provides a creative peg on which you can hang content. It helps you position content so that it flows naturally. Although each element should be sufficiently strong to stand alone, when all elements are taken together they have superadditive qualities that yield a sum much greater than the individual parts.

For example, you might build an effective theme out of a significant event in the life of the company that occurred during the past year or that is on the horizon. Or you might find a theme in some major event or development that affects the entire industry, not just your company. A new product or service could supply a theme, especially if it signifies that the company is moving in a new direction. A good theme is one that provides a context for content. It should never overpower content, and it should never call attention to itself.

Prudence, however, shouldn't interfere with developing good, creative themes. Sara Lee built its annual report around paper dolls. That theme is much less sober than those usually seen in annual reports. Scissors, pages of paper dolls and an invitation to order paper doll books went with the annual report to investors. Paper dolls decorated the cover. They also were on inside pages to represent the company's business lines—packaged meats and bakery, coffee and grocery, personal products, and household and personal care. The response to this unusual theme was so good that Sara Lee printed more than 10,000 paper doll books. Some investors even bought stock for children and grandchildren. They equated this creative strategy with a management style that signifies a good investment.[13]

Style With purpose, content and theme defined, you can begin to write. That means dealing with the question of what style of writing to use in the report. Degree of formality is often the first question of style to be answered.

Many annual report writers and most corporate executives might object to the informal style generally advocated by readability experts like Flesch and Gunning. Such objections are often based on the belief that an annual report is a very serious document and that informality is therefore inappropriate. It is true that the style should be appropriate to the document and to its readers. However, neither the document nor the readers should be the sole determinants of style.

Style is part of what you say—content and purpose. If your company wants to portray itself as a friendly, informal, neighborhood company eager to do business with just plain folk, then a stuffy style is as inappropriate for the annual report as it would be for a commercial on television. But a company that wants to be viewed as formal and sophisticated may use a refined writing style in its annual report, with contractions and humor kept at a minimum or prohibited altogether.

A formal style is no excuse for foggy writing, however. The annual report must be readable and comprehensible, whatever the style. No company wants to be viewed as incoherent and confusing. And no company wants to give the impression that the person representing the company in print is incapable of thinking clearly enough to write understandable prose. Many astute observers note that in one way or another fuzzy writing is usually a sign of fuzzy thinking. You should keep that point in mind—and it might help if you also passed that word to the legal staff.

The fact is that the final wording of the annual report is frequently the result of a clash between writer and lawyer and sometimes the chief financial officer, usually a CPA. Attorneys should have the last word in matters of law, but too often attorneys are given the last word, period—even regarding writing style. And that can be bad news for simple writing. "If a man draws a document that only he can interpret," Gunning writes, "he has built himself a degree of security. He must be retained to interpret it."[14]

In general, neither attorneys nor accountants would lose their jobs if their writing was not understandable. Most don't intentionally confuse things, but many are not good writers. They are not trained as writers. So when it comes to issues of style, the professional writer must have the last word.

Timing   Clearly, an annual report is a major project for any company, and it is critical that the report be issued on time. That means setting and meeting deadlines over a long period. It is not unusual for the production of an annual report, from its inception at the planning stage until its delivery to its readers, to take six or seven months. One reason it takes so long to produce a good annual report is that the writer has to await the final version of the financial data following the close of the fiscal year before wrapping up the final details. Then the final report has to be approved at many levels in the organization.

There is no foolproof method of scheduling and producing an annual report. However, review the approximate schedule in Table 19.3 of a typical annual report of a company whose regulatory agencies require copies no later than March 31 of each year. This timetable will not work for every company or institution, but it will serve as a rough guideline for most situations.

Conclusions

- Magazines may be for internal or external publics.
- Magazines remain a powerful public relations tool because of their depth of treatment and "pass-along" qualities that increase exposure.
- Choosing topics for these magazines is critical to capture the "volunteer" readers because public relations publications must compete in the broader marketplace for reader time and attention.
- Substantive stories are important.
- These publications done well can contribute a lot to the success of the organization.
- Look to employees and association members for story ideas. Listen carefully to them.
- Many of the stories readers are most interested in are ones managers least want to talk about. So be prepared for the politics of getting clearance to do certain stories.

TABLE 19.3 *Annual Report Timetable*

This is a sample production timetable for the annual report of a company whose regulatory agencies require a copy of the report by March 31.

September: Begin preliminary planning.

October: Send questionnaires to company executives. Compile research from company publications and other sources on events of the year.

November: Interview executives. Decide on theme and approach. Begin development of publication design options. Collect photographs and assign additional needed photographs to the photographer. Begin production of charts, graphs and other artwork.

December: Begin writing preliminary draft of chief executive's letter and narrative. Decide on publication design. Complete photographs, graphs and artwork, except for financial charts. Determine approach for Web site version of publication.

January: Circulate draft of narrative for review by various company departments. Begin publication production art. Revise draft of chief executive's letter and narrative as required.

February: Circulate final draft of letter and narrative for approval by executives, lawyers, auditors and other company departments as appropriate. Make final corrections. Complete production art on narrative, letter and financial tables (if available). Deliver disk of production art to printer by end of the month. Begin production of online version of report.

March: Review proofs provided by printer. Make final corrections to print and Web site versions. Distribute printed copies to regulatory agencies with required forms and to stockholders and appropriate distribution lists.

Source: Adapted from a timetable by permission of Armstrong World Industries, Inc., Lancaster, Pa.

- Many magazines now are published only on Web sites to increase their availability and eliminate printing and distribution costs.
- Trade and industry publications are important and are read carefully by knowledgeable readers.
- Some annual reports are getting briefer and some companies are working to make them more clear and more creative.
- Foggy writing may be caused by a conflict between telling the truth and looking good.
- Writing in annual reports should be clear and simple.
- Preparation of good annual reports includes careful planning, definition of purpose and identification of important publics.
- Some major divisions of content of annual reports are the chief executive's letter, which sets the stage for the entire report; the narrative description of the company's operations for the last year; expectations for the future; and financial summaries.
- Writing style may range from informal to formal, but should reflect the purpose behind the report.
- Production of an annual report is usually spread over several months. This is due, at least in part, to the fact that content has to be cleared through so many levels in the organization.

Exercises

1. You are the vice president of communication at O. Joyitz Funn Manufacturing Systems. OJF is a major producer of plastic toys. The research and development department has recently created and successfully tested a new toy. Tests seem to suggest that the new toy, called "Rotzie," will be a huge seller. OJF is frantically working on a plant expansion to help accommodate the demand it expects when Rotzie is introduced. You are equally busy getting communication plans ready for a formal announcement two months from today. Although some employees are aware of Rotzie, most of them have no clue as to how its potential sales will affect them or OJF. You know that you must put together news releases for local and national media as well as trade journals, and prepare speeches, brochures, sales literature and other things. But right now, you're pondering how to approach a feature story about Rotzie for the OJF employee magazine and the leading toy trade journal. Should the approach be the same for both? Why? Why not? Explain your decision.

2. Get a copy of an annual report from a publicly held company and another from a foundation, or access such annual reports on Web sites. Do a written comparative analysis of:

   a. Purpose
   b. Publics
   c. Content
   d. Style

3. Get an annual report from a publicly held company and compare the writing in it to the writing in Figure 19.1, "Starbucks Brews Up Success on the Web." In your analysis, look especially at:

   a. Purpose
   b. Readers
   c. Content
   d. Style

   Your report should be no longer than two double-spaced pages. Attach a copy of the annual report to your analysis.

 Use InfoTrac College Edition to access information on topics in this chapter from hundreds of periodicals and scholarly journals.

Notes

1. "How Word Choice Impacts Employee Communication," *Mid-America Communication Foundation* 2 (1) (1996): 47–55.
2. Don Fabun, "Company Publications," in *Lesly's Public Relations Handbook,* ed. Philip Lesly (Englewood Cliffs, N.J.: Prentice Hall, 1971), p. 135.
3. Eleena DeLisser, "Luring Loyal Customers to Pay for Product News," in "Marketing," *The Wall Street Journal,* August 23, 1993, p. B1.

4. Nancy M. Smith, *A Plain English Handbook—How to Create Clear SEC Disclosure Documents* (Washington, D.C.: U.S. Securities and Exchange Commission, Officer of Investor Education and Assistance, 1998). Available online at http://www.sec.gov/pdf/handbook.pdf.

5. Roger Lowenstein, "Investors Will Fish for Footnotes in 'Abbreviated' Annual Reports," *The Wall Street Journal,* September 14, 1995, p. C1.

6. Ibid.

7. "Rule 14c-4—Presentation of Information in Information Statement," *General Rules and Regulations Promulgated Under the Securities Exchange Act of 1934,* 1934, http://www.law.uc.edu/CCL/34ActRIs/rule14c-4.html.

8. Louis M. Thompson Jr., "2002 Trends and Technology Survey," National Investor Relations Institute, February 11, 2003, http://www.niri.org/publications/alerts/ea20030211TrendsSurvey2002.pdf.

9. Pamela Sebastian, "A Time Bandit," in "Business Bulletin," *The Wall Street Journal,* September 19, 1996, p. 1.

10. Robert Gunning, *The Technique of Clear Writing* (New York: McGraw-Hill, 1968), p. 227.

11. Ibid.

12. Rudolf Flesch, *The Art of Readable Writing,* 25th anniv. ed. (New York: Harper & Row, 1974), p. 135.

13. "Sara Lee Finds a Way to Cut Through the Clutter," *inside PR* (November 1992): 6–7.

14. Gunning, p. 244.

Selected Bibliography

American Society of Magazine Editors, *The Best American Magazine Writing 2002* (New York: Harperperennial Library, 2002).

Jeanne Tessier Barone with Jo Young Switer (contributor), *Interview Art and Skill* (Boston: Allyn & Bacon, 1995).

Robert Bohle, *Publication Design* (Englewood Cliffs, N.J.: Prentice Hall, 1990).

Lyn M. Fraser and Aileen Ormiston, *Understanding the Corporate Annual Report: Nuts, Bolts and a Few Loose Screws* (Englewood Cliffs, N.J.: Prentice Hall, 2002).

Edward Jay Friedlander and John Lee, *Feature Writing for Newspapers and Magazines: The Pursuit of Excellence,* 4th ed. (Boston, Mass.: Allyn & Bacon, 1999).

Mary Ellen Gaffey, *Business Communication: Process and Product,* 2d ed. (Belmont, Calif.: Wadsworth, 1997).

Paul Martin Lester, *Visual Communication: Image with Messages* (Belmont, Calif.: Wadsworth, 1995).

Brian Stanky and Thomas Zeller, *Understanding Corporate Annual Reports* (Hoboken, N.J.: John Wiley & Sons, 2002).

Anne Wyle, *Planning Powerful Publications,* 2d ed. (San Francisco: International Association of Business Communicators, 2002).

CHAPTER TWENTY

Crisis Communication and the Planning Process

September 11, 2001—"9-11"—is a date that screams "CRISIS" to people throughout the USA and around the world.

- At 8:46 a.m. (EDT) that day, American Airlines Flight 11 struck the World Trade Center North Tower in Manhattan.
- Seventeen minutes later, United Airlines Flight 175 struck the South Tower.
- At 9:38 a.m., American Airlines Flight 77 crashed into the Pentagon.
- At 9:59 a.m., the South Tower collapsed, and the North Tower fell at 10:28 a.m.
- At 10:00 a.m., United Airlines Flight 93 crashed in Pennsylvania.
- The Federal Aviation Administration suspended all air traffic in the United States and diverted international flights to Canada.
- 3,062 people died: 2,829 in New York, 189 in D.C. and 44 in western Pennsylvania.[1]

Every type of organization was immediately plunged into deep crisis. New York City police, fire and other emergency organizations were immediately affected, along with government agencies at all levels. Charitable organizations responded immediately to the crisis and began collecting donations for the victims. News media represented many voices from around the globe.

Hundreds of organizations with employees and facilities in the World Trade Center and the Pentagon and in areas nearby were at "ground zero" in the heart of the crisis. The effort to account for people was a huge undertaking. Morgan Stanley, one of the world's largest diversified financial services companies, had employees in both towers of the World Trade Center. Philip J. Purcell, chairman and CEO, said, "The loss of just a single life is too many. But when you consider the incredible destruction that occurred, the loss of fewer than 40 of our people out of the 3,700 who worked there is a near miracle."[2]

Airlines were heavily hit by the 9-11 tragedy. Dozens of American Airlines and United Airlines employees lost their lives in the crashes. Financial losses by the airlines alone climbed into the billions of dollars as they cut flights and laid off thousands of employees in response to reduced passenger loads. United Airlines filed for protection under Chapter 11 of the U.S. Bankruptcy Code on December 9, 2002.[3] AMR, American Airlines' parent corporation, reported net losses of $1.4 billion for 2001 and $2 billion for 2002.[4]

Even the highly respected American Red Cross, founded in 1881 by the Civil War nurse Clara Barton and providing disaster relief to the victims of more than 67,000 disasters annually, faced a major crisis following 9-11. Ray Suarez reported on PBS television's *The NewsHour with Jim Lehrer*, "As the contributions poured in, Red Cross President Bernadine Healy took the unusual step of not putting the money in the agency's general funds, rather in a separate place, the Liberty Fund, which most people assumed would be used solely for September 11 victim relief." But less than one-third of the $543 million pledged was spent on relief efforts. The Red Cross planned to spend more than half of the contributions for other purposes. This brought heated criticism and a threatened lawsuit by New York's attorney general. On October 26, 2001, the organization's president and chairman resigned, and the American Red Cross was faced with the difficult task of rebuilding its credibility.[5]

Public relations people were confronted with crisis situations for which they were not prepared. *Tactics,* published by the Public Relations Society of America, reported, "Tim Doke, vice president of corporate communications for American Airlines, Brig. Gen. Ronald T. Rand, public affairs director of the U.S. Air Force, and Gil Schwartz, executive vice president–communications for CBS Television, all agreed that no crisis plan or contingency planning could have prepared them for the disasters of Sept. 11, 2001, and the nightmares that followed."[6]

Planning for Crisis Situations

In less horrific crises, planning can be extremely valuable. No one likes to think about calamities, but public relations people are expected to consider and plan for worst-case possibilities. If you work for a refinery, you need to assume that there will be a fire sometime, somewhere. If you work for a chemical company, there will be a "hazardous substance" case sometime, in some form, somewhere.

But you don't have to be involved in a "dangerous business" to encounter a crisis. For instance, a Dallas CEO was kidnapped and held for ransom; a truck crashed into a busy cafeteria; an angered employee went home, returned with a rifle and killed supervisors and fellow employees. Anything that *can* happen, *will.* You need to be prepared for it.

Mark Palmer, vice president for corporate communications at Enron, said, "We all thought there was no way to go but up. We were a $160 billion company, number seven on the Fortune 500 list and in the top three for innovation, quality of employees and quality of management. Then on October 16, 2001 the wheels came off." That was the day the company announced a $1 billion loss for the third quarter of 2001. A few days later, the Securities and Exchange Commission began an investigation. Rumors of document shredding circulated. The company was unable to secure the financing it needed, and Enron began the slide toward bankruptcy. "We didn't sleep well," Palmer said. "I lost 30 pounds in six weeks. We marched along that path with our CEO (Kenneth L. Lay) thinking it was just a giant PR problem.

'Enron will never go bankrupt,' he said, 'and anyone who thinks that probably shouldn't be working here.'" On December 2, 2001, Enron filed for Chapter 11 bankruptcy.[7]

The term *crisis communication* includes within its meanings *issues management,* because it is good public relations to intervene in a developing situation before it becomes a crisis. And issues management, in turn, is primarily a research function, the purpose of which is to identify and track trends and events likely to affect the institution and any of its publics. But beyond issues management, which involves all of the communication tools and planning previously discussed, there is the critical event—the serious unforeseen development. In this chapter, we will use the term *crisis* exclusively to refer to the critical event. Refer to Table 20.1 for a brief outline of what is usually included in planning for and dealing with a crisis.

Research suggests that there are only six types of crises—three in each of two categories. Review these in Table 20.2. The two categories are violent and nonviolent. Within each are crises that are caused by nature, by accidents or by deliberate acts.[8]

Corporate Information

Part of being prepared is a matter of routine. It involves maintaining current corporate fact sheets containing all necessary basic information in the files at all times. See Chapter 15 on media kits.

The most important precrisis action, though, is getting your positive messages out daily and educating your publics so they are knowledgeable and you can draw on their trust and goodwill when the crisis occurs.

When the Columbia space shuttle disintegrated on February 1, 2003, killing all seven astronauts aboard, NASA immediately put its crisis plan into action. Carl Gustin and Jennifer Sheehy of the Clarke & Company Crisis Communication Center evaluated NASA's communications this way: "One lesson already learned from the Columbia disaster is the value of preparation in dealing with a future crisis. NASA's senior management team was obviously ready to put its crisis communication plan into action, and has been getting high marks for its openness, availability, knowledge and sensitivity. . . . NASA management was prepared. It learned lessons from the [1986] Challenger and put in place, and no doubt 'drilled,' its crisis plans. Those plans clearly include communications with clear lines of authority for speaking to media and government officials. That was evident in the frequent updates that NASA started broadcasting within the hour of initial reports of a problem and the speed with which the first press conference was convened. . . . No one would accuse NASA, at least to this point, of remaining silent. NASA should be commended for its two-a-day press conferences and the apparent availability of a smart, talented press staff."[9]

There is never a good time to plan for a crisis, but sooner is better than later. And it is critical not only to have a plan but also to make sure that everyone understands it.

In a crisis, the media's first response often is to contact the creators of the institution's public relations image. But before the situation arises, it's important to develop a good plan and be sure everyone likely to be involved knows what to do. Seminars involving role playing can help those who might be responsible in a time of crisis to understand the plan. It's important for you, as the writer of the plan, to know who will play specific roles as well.

Crisis planning by organizations goes beyond communication to specific employee actions.

T A B L E   2 0 . 1   *Outline of Crisis Communication Plan*

Planning

1. Develop a series of scenarios that reflect the kinds of crises your organization may face. Pay particular attention to the worst cases. Evaluate realistically the probability of their happening. Review current policies and strategies that may be impacted.

2. Identify a crisis management team. Assign specific roles to team members. Designate one person to speak to external publics and another to keep internal publics fully informed. Rehearse the crisis management team regularly. Train and retrain the spokespersons, emphasizing the need for them to coordinate and share information so the organization is seen as speaking with one corporate voice.

3. Insofar as is possible, implement policies and strategies designed to minimize the impact of crises. If needed, lobby government and seek public support for changes in laws and/or regulations that may prevent crises or reduce their impact.

4. Review the entire plan at least annually. A quarterly review is better. Make sure that members of the crisis management team have copies of the current plan and can access them immediately.

Crisis Event

1. When a crisis occurs, activate the crisis management team immediately. Designated spokespersons should take charge of all communication functions.

2. Strive for a timely, consistent and candid flow of accurate information to both external and internal publics to allay fears and stifle rumors.

3. The organization should continue to function as normally as possible, leaving it to the crisis management team to contend with the crisis.

4. Make adjustments to policies and strategies as needed to arrest the crisis. Seek public support as needed.

Recovering from the Crisis

1. As needed, make changes in policies and strategies to speed recovery from the effects of the crisis.

2. If necessary, make changes to the structure of the organization. If these changes are needed and the organization has a history of an open management style, such changes are often slight.

3. Seek as soon as possible to re-establish the operation of the organization to the level it had before the crisis or even better.

Evaluation

1. Learn from the crisis experience. Evaluate its causes, the organization's responses to it and the outcomes.

2. Modify policies and strategies in light of this experience.

3. Update the crisis management/communication plan in light of this most recent experience.

TABLE 20.2   *Crisis Typology*

Source of Crisis	Violent: Cataclysmic—Immediate Loss of Life or Property	Nonviolent: Sudden Upheaval But Damages, If Any, Are Delayed
Act of nature	Earthquakes, forest fires	Droughts, epidemics
Intentional	Acts of terrorism, including product tampering, when these result in loss of life or destruction of property	Bomb and product-tampering threats, hostile takeovers, insider trading, malicious rumors and other malfeasance
Unintentional	Explosions, fires, leaks, other accidents	Process or product problems with delayed consequences, stock market crashes, business failures

Reprinted with permission from Doug Newsom, Judy VanSlyke Turk and Dean Kruckeberg, *This Is PR: The Realities of Public Relations*, 8th ed. (Wadsworth Publishing Company: Belmont, Calif., 2004) p. 321.

Most institutions where crises are especially likely—such as chemical plants, hospitals, prisons and banks—have employees who are crisis-trained. The way a situation is handled as it is occurring can make the public relations job easier or more difficult. For example, writing about hostage-taking, which is a fairly common experience in hospitals, clinical psychologist James Turner says that staffs need to be trained in handling the hostage-takers in the first few minutes, before police officers and negotiators arrive.[10]

Designated Spokesperson   The most important strategy in crisis communication is to have only one person communicating with the news media and other external audiences. You may sometimes use both an expert and a management representative, with the crisis determining which is the principal spokesperson. The other person is a support voice and should coordinate messages so these *never* conflict or contradict themselves. When the messages fail to match, a severe credibility problem develops. The best precaution against this is to develop a communication plan.

A Communication Plan   First, identify people likely to be the principal participants in the communication plan. Then decide what media to use in a crisis: memos, closed-circuit television, computer terminals, intranet telephones—whatever is likely to work in a given situation. You should create a system for checking message statements. Usually, an internal message for employees is developed first, and the external one is composed from that. You don't want employees and others close to the organization to hear about a crisis from outside sources unless this is absolutely unavoidable.

When time is critical and people are not where they are usually found, a telephone operation becomes particularly important. You or the person in charge of communications needs to be highly skilled in getting facts, taking questions and dispensing information accurately.

You must act like a reporter first, finding out as much as you can about the situation. Anticipate questions from the news media. Have your own photographers and interviewers out gathering the story. If you don't take these steps, you won't have enough documentation later, and you will not know what the reporters are getting or how accurate their information is.

Your first job will be to get a statement on the severity of the disaster or crisis from someone in authority. You'll need to have the statement both in printed form and on audiotape. Then you'll need to develop a fact sheet telling what is known. Review this information with the organization's attorney to assess the legal ramifications of the information you will be releasing. All information released over the telephone should be drawn only from these prepared and checked sheets. Never speculate.

Crisis Teams   The organization (corporate or nonprofit) involved will create crisis communication teams from staff members—as well as public relations and crisis communications consultants—to create the necessary level of expertise. These teams should be able to deal with the crisis so the organization can go on about its regular activities as normally as possible. Nothing contributes more to the atmosphere of uncertainty than involving all the institution's decision makers in the crisis and thus causing day-to-day business to come to a halt. When this happens observers can conclude that there is not much depth to management and that the company needs everyone it can get to handle a problem.

Handling the Crisis

When a crisis first occurs, the announcement results in some sort of consultation within the organization. Ordinarily this is a face-to-face meeting, but it could be an electronic one—for instance, a telephone conference call or a video teleconference. Of primary importance at this meeting is that a record be kept—a fairly detailed one—of the points discussed and the responsibilities assigned. In fact, it may be your specific responsibility to write and circulate a memo detailing this.

Almost immediately, and sometimes before such a meeting takes place, you will need to make a response release addressing the situation. You must characterize the crisis in language that will become a symbol of the event. In doing so, you will need to check attributed quotes with the organization's attorney if the release contains any mention of responsibility or damages.

For the broadcast media, you should have an actuality of the statement from the spokesperson. And you will need your own photographer's pictures from the crisis scene— black-and-white and color stills, and videotape or film (maybe both). Some companies maintain ENG (electronic news gathering) equipment so that they can receive pictures of the disaster immediately at corporate headquarters. Here, too, the art chosen should represent the way you want the event symbolized.

You may need to call a news conference so that news media representatives can pose questions. If you do, you should be prepared with a list of the points you want to make, and you should anticipate the reporters' needs and questions.

As news develops, you will be issuing bulletins to keep internal and external publics informed. Some of these bulletins may be put on an electronic system such as teletext or videotex. Additionally, you will be preparing letters to various related publics to keep them aware of your control of the situation. For example, a university experiencing a number of fires sent letters to parents, and a company that found a problem with a certain lot of its product sent letters to all affected consumers it could identify through warranty cards. In some cases, you may need to plan special advertising. One utility that had gotten a bad safety review of its nuclear plant and several days of bad publicity thereafter felt it necessary to buy space for its own message.

Often crises involve materials or conditions that the average person (including reporters) may not know much about. With nuclear plant accidents and chemical-related stories, scientists often are called on to help reporters explain these situations. But because of scientists' concerns about being misquoted, Sigma Xi, the Scientists' Institute for Public Information, provides a free service to journalists—a database clearinghouse with a computer file of more than 30,000 scientists, engineers, physicians and policy-makers who have agreed to answer queries from reporters.[11]

Getpress.com, a firm that specializes in crisis communications, says the basic tools needed in a crisis situation include the following:

- *"Statement* This is usually a clear and concise press release that highlights a company or organization's position in a particular situation. Within this statement, a series of messages clearly articulating that position are highlighted.
- *"Media Q&A* This includes a series of questions most likely to be asked by members of the media, customers and employees regarding the issue/crisis at hand. This document includes direct answers reflecting the company's position and key messages addressing the situation.
- *"Employee Communication* Recognizing that your employees can be your best spokespeople, clearly articulating the company's position or statement regarding the crisis at hand is instrumental to any well-managed crisis communication plan.
- *"Regulatory Communication* Depending upon the size and scope of the crisis at hand, communication with various governmental regulators such as the EPA, SEC and FCC may be required.
- *"Customer Service Phone Scripts* A complete Q&A that addresses and answers anticipated questions."[12]

The Planning Process

Whether your organization is dealing with a crisis situation, a short-term public relations campaign or an ongoing public relations program, it is impossible *not* to communicate.

As an individual, everything you wear, everything you do and everything you say communicates something about you. The same is true of organizations. The way buildings, signs and office decor look, the way telephones are answered (or not answered), the logo, the letterhead, the annual report, the Web site . . . everything communicates something about your organization.

So we can't choose whether or not we want to communicate. What we *can* do, though, is decide how to communicate and whether we choose to manage communications.

That's what public relations planning is all about. An organization without a written plan is like a runner in a race without a finish line. There's a lot of activity, but without a plan, there can be no success—no "finish line."

For you as a public relations professional, writing a plan is *defining success for yourself.* For your organization, planning is a lot like drawing a *map*—providing a direction toward a desired destination. A plan can equip the organization to speak with one voice, like a choir whose members sing from the same page of music.

A public relations campaign or program is a series of coordinated, unified activities and messages, driven by a single strategy, delivered to relevant publics by a variety of means. These activities and messages are intended to inform, educate or persuade those publics to buy, use or support something. Therefore, the public relations plan should fit properly into an overall strategic plan. A strategic plan and its public relations component focus the resources of an organization on a particular purpose. It is a way to ration and use resources—human, financial and physical—to help an organization accomplish its purpose. A plan defines first *what* is to be done, second *how* it will be done, third *who* will do it and fourth *when* and/or *how often* it will be done. Resources are deployed in what is believed to be the most effective and efficient way to accomplish an organization's purpose.

A plan's design is dictated by the organization's strategic objective. What the organization wants to achieve determines the priority publics. Once the publics are identified, the media to reach them are clear, or should be. Thus a campaign might be designed that involves no mass media at all, either for publicity or for advertising. The whole effort might be carried out through specialized media, if that's the most effective way to reach the publics.

On the other hand, the primary publics might best be reached through the mass media, and the mass media they hold credible may be needed for one or both of two public relations purposes. One is employing publicity to give third-party credibility to other messages originating from the organization. The second is advertising to give guaranteed exposure in targeted media.

If the latter is more important—the case with introducing new ideas, services or products—then the campaign is primarily an advertising campaign with publicity and special-event support. If the campaign is primarily information centered or focused on conveying complex messages, then publicity is the driver of the campaign.

When a campaign is primarily directed to specialized audiences, there may be little or no use of mass media. Some ads may be bought in trade or professional journals supported with publicity in the same media. Or the campaign may be entirely driven by presentations. (See Chapter 16.)

But in public relations, *anything* can be used as a channel for communications—doorknob hangers, mayors' or governors' proclamations, open houses, marathon races, parades and so on—the list is almost endless. The most effective programs encapsulate the individuals composing the target publics in carefully selected messages delivered through channels that are highly believable and credible to the individual public.

A public relations writer usually is directly involved only in helping to review or craft message strategies and in the implementation phase. Does that mean a public relations writer need not be too concerned about the overall thrust of a campaign? Certainly not. The public relations writer is a vital part of the total success of a campaign because it is the writer, more than anyone, who interprets the objectives, goals and strategies to relevant publics. So a writer must be fully aware of what the campaign is expected to accomplish and why. The entire campaign plan must be studied carefully and understood exactly, to ensure that the writing supports the total effort.

Often the most workable planning strategy is to develop numerous "mini" plans—one for each aspect of the public relations program. One international corporation has separate plans for employee communications, marketing publicity, community relations, media relations, urban affairs, government affairs, investor relations and customer relations.

Let's take a step-by-step look at how a public relations plan is put together. (See Figure 20-1.)

1. Review, Revise and Affirm the Mission Statement

The organization's mission statement establishes the scope, domain and fundamental purpose of the organization and provides a guiding philosophy. It should be a clear, simple statement of the overall purpose of the organization, provide a focal point for objectives, goals and activities and define success for the organization.

Southwest Airlines' mission statement meets those criteria: "The mission of Southwest Airlines is dedication to the highest quality of Customer Service delivered with a sense of warmth, friendliness, individual pride, and Company Spirit."[13]

The mission statement should never be "carved in stone." It should be regularly reviewed and updated as the organization changes. The beginning of a public relations planning process is an excellent time to do just that.

To review the mission statement, answer the following questions:

- Is it current? Does it reflect the organization as it exists today?
- It is explicit? Is there any room for misinterpreting what the organization is all about?
- Is it understandable?
- Is it brief?
- Is it memorable?
- Does it contain the key words that reflect the organization's focus?

If these questions can all be answered "yes," then the mission statement can be affirmed, and the public relations planning process can proceed. If there is a "no," the statement should be modified. If this is done, most organizations require that the revised mission statement be approved by the organization's senior management or board of directors. Such approval will represent affirmation of the revised mission statement.

2. Examine the Present Situation

Now that the mission of the organization has been reviewed, changed if necessary and affirmed, you can begin the task of gathering relevant information, analyzing it and preparing forecasts. You might want to review Chapter 4 on research before you read further.

Questions you will want to answer in this work include:

- What are our strengths?
- What are our weaknesses?
- What might restrict our success in accomplishing our objectives and goals?
- Will we have the support of our internal publics (board of directors, senior management and employees)?
- How about our main external publics (shareholders, contributors, media and others)?

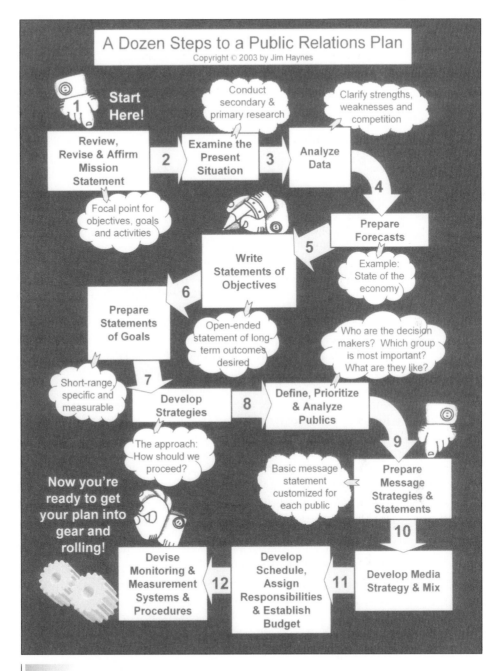

FIGURE 20.1

A Dozen Steps to a Public Relations Plan

Copyright © 2003 by Jim Haynes, APR, Fellow PRSA. Used with permission.

- What level of financial support can we expect?
- Will we be working within the boundaries of the current cultures in the areas where we operate?

Kinds of Information   The overall quality and effectiveness of a public relations program is heavily dependent upon the quality of information on which it is based. There are two broad kinds of information available. The first is secondary information. This is information available to you from existing sources. The second is primary information. This is new information generated by original research, such as surveys, interviews or meetings. (See Chapter 4.)

3. Analyze the Data

The next step is to analyze the information gathered from secondary and/or primary sources. Gathering much more information than you may use is a good idea, because it is better to have too much than too little. The first step in analysis is to sort the information into categories. This information may fall naturally into quite a range of categories, such as audience, market, geographical area, product, service, economics, politics, behavior and so on.

Each piece of information in each category then is reviewed carefully for its direct relevance. Duplicate information is discarded. The least useful information is set aside for further research, if needed. Information judged most important is extracted from the rest and put into usable form. Much of it is converted into tables and graphs, especially if the information is complex. Tables and graphs help people to "see" things they might overlook if the information is reviewed only in narrative form. All of the information is carefully documented as to its original source. This is necessary because during the analysis you may find that you must refer to an original source for additional information or to clarify a technical point. Returning to original sources may be necessary also to resolve contradictions in information between sources.

It is also common at this stage to look especially at an organization's *strengths* and *weaknesses,* as well as those of the opposition or competition. Strategic planners covet information that leads them to match one of their strengths against a weakness of an opponent or competitor.

Then efforts are made to synthesize these groups of information into a cohesive set of documentation that is linked by a terse narrative. Synthesizing is simply the art of tying diverse pieces of information together in some unique way so that it leads to clear, new insights as to what may be ahead in the near future for the organization.

4. Prepare Forecasts

If the information is well defined, it will lead management to draw better conclusions about the future. For example, if the data indicates the economy is static or in a downturn, this might be interpreted to mean that an organization may have a hard time reaching its profit or fund-raising goal. This might lead to a reduction in the goals. On the other hand, if the economy is heating up, the organization might adjust its target upward.

The point is this: Objectives, goals and strategies adopted for a program should be based on solid information, not whimsy, that supports the clearest possible view of the future.

After the information is gathered and analyzed, conclusions can help you set achievable objectives, goals and strategies.

5. Write Statements of Objectives

In some organizations, the term *goal* is used to denote long-range outcomes desired, while *objective* is used for short-term outcomes. Other organizations reverse the meaning, with objective meaning long range and goal referring to short term. Neither is incorrect, but it is important to clearly identify the meaning of each as you go into a planning activity.

Using the latter definition above, an objective should be:

- A long-term outcome desired
- An open-ended statement of purpose
- Based upon mission statement

Each objective should add value to the organization and should:

- Be feasible
- Be acceptable to those involved

Most public relations plans have only a few long-term objectives—often only one—and numerous short-term goals.

6. Prepare Statements of Goals

Whereas objectives are long-term and open-ended, goals are:

- Short range
- Specific as to time and degree
- Fully measurable
- Finite extensions of objectives

A goal should answer the question, "What one result do you want to accomplish?" Well-written goals are closed-ended statements of purpose oriented toward an *end result.* (What happens *after* the special event occurs or the newsletter is delivered?)

Each well-written goal contains the following four components:

1. What is being measured (awareness? attendance? contributions?)
2. A starting point or base against which to measure
3. Quantities or percentages to be achieved
4. A deadline or amount of time for accomplishment

Evaluation of success is only as good as the quality of the goals. By including these components, you're setting the stage for measuring your success.

Here are two examples of how a weak goal can be made stronger by including the above components:

Example 1

Weak: "Enhance our public image."

Stronger: "Improve recall of important facts about our organization—from three to five—among key media representatives by June 1 of next year."

Example 2

Weak: "Improve media relations."

Stronger: "Increase by 10 percent—from 60 percent to 70 percent—positive media coverage on 10 key issues by the end of the year."

7. Develop Strategies

Once objectives and goals are spelled out, you're ready to take the next step toward a plan—the development of a basic strategy. A strategy is an approach to solving a problem or capturing an opportunity and should answer the following questions:

- How shall we proceed?
- What approach will guide us?

For example, a nonprofit organization could adopt a strategy of public recognition of donors, calling attention to the benefits of their generosity to individuals and to the community. Good news and feature stories could be developed around success stories. If these could be tied to current programs in the community, the general awareness of both the organization's focus and the organization itself could be increased, thus making it easier to raise money.

Other strategies for both nonprofit and profit-making organizations might include training and rehearsing the staff for group and one-on-one presentations, coordinating the timing of all presentations, coordinating invitations to and dates of group presentations, providing model scripts to follow when making phone contacts and a range of other activities.

8. Define, Prioritize and Analyze Publics

The next step in the planning process is to define your publics or constituencies. Each public is a group of people with similar characteristics (demographic and/or psychographic) that can help your organization achieve the objectives you have set, hinder your organization in achieving its objectives, or hurt your organization in some way.

The basic questions to be answered are, "Who can make the decision (or take the action) that I want made? And what are those people *like?*

Identifying the characteristics of publics—whether the public is employees, shareholders or others—allows the public relations person to make communications more personal and relevant and therefore more memorable to the individuals composing the public. For example, if you work in public relations for an organization that sells pet-related products, knowing who owns pets can help you target your efforts and make your public relations program more effective. Or if you work in a corporation, you know that the company's shareholders have in common the ownership of shares of stock in the corporation.

Further segmenting each public into homogeneous segments who will respond in similar ways can help you make communications more targeted and effective. This kind of segmentation is accomplished using one or a combination of two criteria—demographics and psychographics or lifestyles.

Demographics   Demographics are the statistical characteristics of human populations and include such factors as:

- Age
- Sex
- Race
- Geographic location
- Occupation
- Marital status
- Education
- Household size
- Income or household income

Knowing any of these factors about the members of a target public can be of great help in public relations planning. For example, if you work for a grocery retailer, marketing research might indicate that the company's target audience is a married female between the ages of 26 and 34. The research might also indicate that a typical shopper is employed as a professional, has one or two children and prefers to shop at the end of her workday, stopping at a store on the right side of her homeward drive. With this information, you could develop a public relations plan for new store openings focused on events to include children and emphasizing products that offer both nutrition and ease of preparation. One large grocery chain that determined that their target public fit the above demographic profile decided to build new stores on the right-hand side of evening drive-time traffic arteries to make stopping on the route home from the office more convenient for the women shoppers.

Census bureau demographic characteristics are used extensively in demographic segmentation.

Psychographics and Lifestyles   Psychographics involve identification of personality characteristics, interests (like children, music, art, pets, travel or hobbies) and attitudes that affect a person's lifestyle and purchasing behaviors. Psychographic data points include opinions, attitudes and beliefs about various aspects relating to lifestyle and purchasing behavior.

Prioritizing Publics   Once you have identified your main publics and conducted as thorough an analysis as time and budget allow, you'll find it's helpful to list the groups in order of priority, with the most important first on your list. This small step will equip you to always consider your most important constituency first—when you allocate budgets and staff time. (See step 11 below and pages 20–29.)

9. Prepare Message Strategies and Statements

Notice that deciding what to say, how to say it and in what media messages should be conveyed are *not* decisions made at the outset of the planning process. Making those decisions before steps 1–8 have been completed would be like a physician prescribing medications before examining the patient.

Yet another step—developing message strategies—is important before messages are conceived.

Organizational, business and functional strategies collectively influence and shape message strategy. A basic message strategy focuses on what is the basic message to be conveyed to target audiences in every message. A good message strategy is simple, adaptable to any medium, applicable to all messages in the campaign and durable.

Simplicity   There is a temptation to overwrite message strategy. One way to avoid that is to look carefully at all three levels of organizational strategy in the plan. Think about your organization's purpose and the precise nature of the problems it tries to solve.

The Texas Education Agency called upon LaMancha Group, a small not-for-profit organization dedicated to working with nonprofit organizations, to assist the agency with a statewide program called "Child Find." Challenged to devise a public relations plan for implementation through the state's 20 Education Service Centers, LaMancha Group did just that.

In its planning process, the group developed the following message strategy:

> Child Find is a federally financed program designed to locate handicapped children who are not in school, assess their individual needs and provide them with the educational services they need.

That simple statement captures the essence of the program's strategy. It is neither fancy nor especially memorable. It is, simply, the basic message that was to be conveyed in every message from and about Child Find.

Adaptability   The Child Find message was unusual because it was adaptable and was used as an "umbrella" statement with a "tag" for each major public. For example, for a religious organization presentation, the statement might be:

> Child Find is a federally financed program designed to locate handicapped children who are not in school, assess their individual needs and provide them with the educational services they need. *We want to allow each child to develop to his or her fullest potential.*

For a Rotary club or other business group, the statement might be:

> Child Find is a federally financed program designed to locate handicapped children who are not in school, assess their individual needs and provide them with the educational services they need. *We want to help these handicapped children become voters and taxpayers.*

The statement cannot appear as written in every message. The medium used to carry the message may not be able to carry the message that way. For example, you could not use posters effectively if you had to carry that message statement as it appears. So the posters used in the program carried a large photo of a hearing-impaired child and the message:

How do you find the children
who stay at home all day
because their parents don't know that
free education is guaranteed to every child
by our state laws?

YOU ASK EVERY PERSON IN TEXAS TO HELP.

Maybe you know a handicapped child who needs
Help. Maybe you can help.
Call 1-800-XXX-XXXX

Applicability   Functional message strategies must apply to every message. This is one criterion, perhaps more than any other, that keeps writers from straying from the strategic fold. You may write a perfectly good news release about the record gifts coming in to a nonprofit organization. But if you fail to get across why they are coming in at record levels, then you're not being faithful to the organizational, business or functional strategies. That's when your supervisor gives the release back to you, tells you to remember what it is we're trying to do and suggests that you review the strategy and rewrite the piece. If that happens often, your supervisor soon knows that, although you may be a gifted wordsmith, you really aren't wired into what the organization is doing. That may lead to a suggestion to look for another job.

An illustration may be wonderful in all details except that its content does not communicate the central message strategy in any form. That's an illustration that should not be used. Clearly, the message strategy should be a central thrust of both the verbal and nonverbal portions of every message. If it isn't, the message should be scrapped or modified to make it applicable.

Durability   This may be the toughest part of evaluating the usefulness of a potential message strategy. Who can predict with accuracy when a message strategy reaches its wear-out stage? When does it become trite? When does it become boring to audiences? No one really knows. What *is* known is that a good message strategy will easily last a year without wearing out or becoming trite or boring. "A diamond is forever" is a message strategy that De Beers has used for decades. It is as fresh and pertinent today as it was the first time it was used.

If the organizational strategy changes, then even the most durable of message strategies must change to remain consonant. Durable message strategies are sometimes changed only because organizations, not their audiences, get tired of them. That can be a mistake, because a really durable message strategy may be difficult to replace with one of equal or better quality. Building recognition levels so there's instant awareness also takes time. This sometimes leads an organization to seek another agency to come up with better creative work. That can be elusive. And costly.

To be durable, each message must meet the following guidelines:

- Be consistent with and supportive of all other messages
- Be tailored especially to a particular public
- Be written to fit the format of the medium used to deliver it

Now that you have a basic message strategy, you can turn to another important segment of the communication plan—media strategy and mix.

10. Develop Media Strategy and Mix

Media strategy and mix represent one of the most important areas of a public relations plan. However, it sometimes does not get the careful attention it deserves. It deals with what kinds of media will be used to deliver campaign messages, which specific media will be used and how they are mixed. It also deals with the timing of the delivery of messages and the frequency of delivery.

"The key is the media choice, what specific television shows or magazines people watch or read," says Joel Steckel, a professor of marketing at New York University's Stem School of Business. "Different people read *U.S. News and World Report* than read *Tiger Beat*."

You first would make a list of all the kinds of media—mass and specialized—that you can possibly use to effectively reach the publics that have been defined. In public relations, almost everything is a communications medium—from doorknob hangers to videos. The list might include such things as all of the local mass media and such specialized media as face-to-face contact, brochures, annual reports, backgrounders, position papers, newsletters, direct mail, ads, PSAs, faxes, email, news releases and so on.

You then would apply several criteria to each of these media before you begin to make strategic decisions about them. These criteria are: attending, persuasiveness, credibility, timing and effective reach.

Attending   The first consideration is to review who the public is so you can identify which media they "attend to" most. A fund-raising nonprofit organization has two primary publics: current donors who make the largest gifts and potential donors who are capable of making large gifts. Because you know who they are, you can now judge which kinds of media they pay attention to. You might then review the media list and rank-order these media in terms of their ability to draw the attention of our target publics.

Persuasiveness   The next step is to look at the persuasiveness of these individual media. Some media inherently are more persuasive than others. For example, the most persuasive medium is face-to-face delivery. After that, a presentation to a small group is most persuasive. Then come such media as the telephone, email and fax. The latter three media tend also to impart a sense of urgency to a persuasive message. In a nonprofit's program designed to raise money, persuasiveness implicit in the media can be a critical factor. When you look at our priority list of kinds of media, you may produce a different rank-order because some kinds of media may be fairly low on attending but high on persuasiveness or vice versa.

Credibility   A message posted on the bulletin board may be believable but certainly not to the same degree as one delivered face-to-face by someone you know and trust, or even by someone who is an authority but whom you don't know personally. Most people would agree that the same message appearing in *The Wall Street Journal* is more credible than if it appears in the *National Enquirer*. Some media tend to impart more credibility to the messages they carry than do other media. If you expect to set the stage to raise money, you must consider carefully the credibility of the media used to deliver the organization's messages. That may cause you to change your rank-ordering a little.

Timing   Proper timing of the delivery of messages can affect the overall productivity of a campaign. For some aspects of a campaign, it may be important to control message delivery down to the hour. Such media as face-to-face, small group and telephone give us the greatest control. On the other hand, a news release does not. In fact, it may not ever appear. So we have to score traditional mass media as fairly low on timing. If timing is not critical, however, local mass media can provide wide exposure.

Effective Reach   It isn't enough to deliver a message to massive numbers of people. For example, we might get *Time* magazine to run a public service ad on what a nonprofit organization is doing. That would be impressive to many people and it would give us a potential reach into the millions. Suppose that our two target publics number only 3,600 people and all of them subscribe to and regularly read *Time* (which is improbable). The fact is that maybe no more than a quarter of those who read *Time* can recall seeing the message. Of those who recall seeing our message, perhaps no more than 10 percent can recall substantial parts of it and connect it with the organization. That means that we communicated effectively with only about 90 members of our target public, yet the readership of the medium is in the millions. The difference between potential reach and effective reach often is dramatic. Of course, we didn't pay for the space in *Time*, but it did cost us a good bit to prepare the message to *Time's* specifications. The idea of slippage, or waste, in this example applies equally to other mass media.

Effective reach relies on the economic efficiency of reaching the target public with messages that break through the clutter of other messages and cognitively penetrate so that information is correctly associated with its source. And it must do that with the maximum persuasive impact and at the right time. The lesson is: Don't be mesmerized by massive numbers.

Strategic Use of Media   Having evaluated the different kinds of media that could be used, you now can begin to create a basic strategy for your organization. Three communication guidelines should be kept in mind here. First, you stand a better chance of getting the message across to your target publics if you use a multimedia approach. Research shows that people learn easier and retain information better if they get the same message from different kinds of media. Second, the media chosen should engage as many as possible of the human senses. Research indicates that this improves both learning and retention. It is easy to see how sight and sound can be involved in many of the media we've discussed. But what about touch, smell and taste? Are there things that can be done to engage those senses, also? Third, some media should be used and messages designed to get the target publics intellectually involved with the message.

Repetition   Repetition is key to building memory. Of course, we remember information that is *personal* and *relevant* to us, so making information as personal and relevant as possible to members of selected publics should be a priority in planning. Once that's done, repeating the message in various formats and through a variety of channels is critical.

To achieve repetition in an acceptable way, using a strategy with three tiers is often appropriate. Let's assume our client is the APEX Foundation, whose mission is to provide community grants to nonprofit organizations and institutions to help children overcome learning disabilities caused by dyslexia. For its fund-raising campaign, we might use the following three-tier approach.

Tier One: The first and most important tier is to develop well-scripted presentations for small groups and one-on-one presentations. Everything thus far points to the fact that if these aren't done well, the fund-raising campaign may fizzle because it is here that we should make our most eloquent pleas for help. Note that these two media score very high on persuasiveness, credibility and effective reach. The highest quality of support materials must be developed for these sessions. These support materials might include such things as a videotape, tent cards, name badges, brochures, pledge cards and Web site content. The Web site should have the capability of accepting contributions online, but only if a secure server is used.

Tier Two: This tier would include the development of a series of information pieces that can be used as direct-mail items, as well as for other purposes, such as backgrounders, fact sheets, position papers and other items. We might also try to design some sort of crossword puzzle that is provocative enough to get people in the target audience directly involved in its solution while learning about dyslexia. Most or all of these should be loaded onto our organization's Web site. We should develop some specialty items that are uniquely appropriate to the campaign, such as a nice paperweight that illustrates dyslexic behavior. We might stage an event like a celebrity golf tournament where the flags are tampered with so hole 6 looks like hole 9 and hole 12 looks like hole 21. For a special event like this we also would prepare a media kit. (See Chapter 15 for media kit information.)

Tier Three: Here we could rely on a range of news releases—print and broadcast—to local media. We'd work to get spokespeople on local talk shows. And we could provide a series of coordinated PSAs to the local media. We also would provide tip sheets to editors and make sure they had a continuing supply of newsworthy art about APEX and its campaign. We would be sure that the slogan we use is part of every activity. We could even put the line on our standard news release letterhead.

11. Develop Schedule, Assign Responsibilities and Establish Budget

Having made those decisions, you would now develop a schedule or time line. You could divide the year into weeks and list them in columns across the top of a planning board or a spreadsheet software program. Down the left side you'd list the various media and activities that will be used, thus forming a grid. You'd then insert dates into appropriate blocks in the grid. When timing is critical, you may want to create specialized subschedules. For instance, you may want to create a special schedule that deals only with the days, times and locations of group presentations. Similar schedules might be made for individuals who will make the one-on-one presentations. Other subschedules can be developed as the need arises. A schedule grid—some available on specialized software—makes it easy to track activities very closely. Of course, much narrative material about each of these activities will accompany the plan.

For each activity, one person with overall responsibility should be identified. Other people probably will be involved in various parts of the activity, but they do not need to be named in this overview of the plan.

A budget for each activity also should be included. Arriving at a budget may involve obtaining estimates from outside suppliers for printing, still and video photography and so on. For annual reports and printed brochures, envelopes, mailing labels, preparation for mailing and postage can be major costs. In large projects such as annual reports, it's a good idea to add a contingency of 10–15 percent for unexpected costs.

12. Devise Monitoring and Measurement Systems and Procedures

Control   When functional plans are presented for review, management looks for, among other things, methods of controlling the campaign so that everything is done when it is supposed to be done and in the way it is supposed to be done. Under normal operating conditions, lines of responsibility and authority remain unchanged. For example, the directors of internal and external communications both report to the vice president for corporate communications, who in turn reports to the president. Copywriters and designers both report to their supervisors, who in turn are responsible to the creative director.

However, if a campaign has unique features, it may be necessary to designate unusual responsibilities to certain staff. For example, if a plan calls for a special event, but the organization has never before developed a special event, explicit assignment of responsibility for its management and implementation is necessary. This might be handled by assigning this duty to a current staff person or it might require creating a new permanent position. It also might be done by an outside vendor specialist. Some organizations don't try to produce their own media kits, for example, but give that task to people who specialize only in doing them. Decisions such as these are an organization's first line of control: assigning responsibility.

Budget is another means of control. As expenses are incurred, they must be paid. It should be clear who approves payment and who has the responsibility for making payments. Rules on bidding, working with vendors and work-for-hire employees should be spelled out clearly.

Production control is yet another major area. Everything in a plan is supposed to happen as scheduled. A figurative time line is established and particular activities are inserted at various places on that line. Elements of a campaign happen in prescribed sequences. Some elements overlap. So several or a great many activities may be unfolding simultaneously. Each is to be finished at a certain time. In fact, many organizations use a large board on which each activity is listed down the left side and blocks of time are arranged across the top. Entries are often color coded for ease of visual tracking. For example, the entire time frame for activities may be entered with a red felt-tip pen. Progress for each activity is entered with a blue felt-tip pen. That makes it easy to check the exact status of an activity and to know quickly that it is or is not on schedule. If it is the latter, questions must be raised by management to get back on schedule.

From the point of view of the communication function in an organization, perhaps the most significant control is the degree to which the communication program consistently and effectively supports organizational strategy. Really good top management teams know how important it is for communication strategies to be carried out at the highest levels of quality. In the review process, they often look at the functional communication plan with especially critical eyes because they know that problems in communication may put the organization at risk quicker than problems in some other areas. Less sensitive managements learn that lesson the hard way.

Control is also closely related to our next topic of coordination.

Coordination   Coordination relates to control, of course, but it is a much broader, richer concept. Every organization, even very small ones, is divided into functional areas. Each of those areas has its own roles to play and its own contributions according to the mission of an organization. Even if they are separate functional entities, they are also interdependent. Suppose that a new product rollout is scheduled for the first of the month. The public relations people have been busy placing news and feature stories in trade magazines and in the mass media and producing sales training aids and brochures. The marketing people have been working with distributors to negotiate shelf space, passing out product specifications, pricing sheets, and brochures. The special promotions people have a sweepstakes program ready to launch with the new product. When the magic day comes, more than half of the distributors don't have the new product on their shelves because someone failed to make sure that all truckers knew the last date on which the product was to be delivered. The buildup for the rollout was terrific. There was excitement about the new product. But the new product didn't get to all the destinations on time. Consumers came to stores but didn't find it. They got angry at the stores and decided to shop elsewhere. The stores got mad at the company for letting them down and causing them to lose sales. That illustrates what coordination is all about: making sure all the players know what they are supposed to do and when. Control is following through on the schedule.

But coordination can include even more than the preceding scenario, especially when the campaign involves working in tandem with other organizations. Suppose APEX works out a cooperative arrangement with American Airlines for six free round-trip airfares for two to Honolulu. Hertz is brought in to provide free rental cars. And the Hyatt Regency agrees to provide free luxury suites for one-week vacations. Winners of these prizes will be drawn at a victory banquet at the conclusion of a successful campaign. That is a nice way to say "thank you" to donors. The catch is that none of the promotion from APEX notes that these vacations are good only from June 15 to August 15 of next year. Winners may be elated but three of them may find that other obligations will keep them from enjoying the prize. That isn't a tragedy, because they can give the vacations to their children or friends. That's when it's discovered that clauses with Hertz and Hyatt Regency prevent transfers. These problems arose because there wasn't clear coordination on every detail of the agreement.

Coordination may be the most difficult aspect of any campaign. It might appear that because all functional areas are within the same organization that coordination would just happen because each functional area is working according to its plans. And those functional plans are supposed to be driven by a single organizational strategy. That's theory. In practice, top management must regularly check to see that things are working as they should and to take corrective actions when they aren't. It should be remembered that an organization can act only through people. People make mistakes. They sometimes forget. Knowing that, the top management must be constantly alert.

Tactical Implementation   When functional strategic plans are finished and approved, it is time to set them in motion. This is when the public relations writer begins to play a major role. Assignments are made for a range of tasks. Copy supervisors do careful reviews with the writers to make sure they know what they are supposed to do, what the basic message strategy is and how it can be interpreted in particular writing tasks.

Suppose you are assigned the task of writing a brochure that explains to donors and potential donors the background and philosophy of APEX. There are countless ways this task could be approached. Because this brochure will be used as a "selling tool," you'll probably want to avoid a chronology, preferring to concentrate on the philosophy behind the organization that created its unique history. That provides a context in which you can tie APEX's history and philosophy to the new campaign. Of course, your work must be coordinated with that of designers and production people.

A key element, regardless of the writing task, is to make sure that what you write is consistent with the strategic thrust of the campaign. That's what makes a campaign a campaign. As more and more messages are created and distributed, awareness of what APEX is doing begins to rise.

Another requirement is that each message must be written so it will fit the format of the medium used to deliver it. Of course, every message should be directed especially to the target audiences. Yes, other people will see many of these messages. But it is a good idea to regard them as incidental receivers. Don't let them divert you from the basic strategy.

While you are writing, others are designing, videotaping and doing myriad other tasks, such as negotiating with vendors about printing a brochure or producing a slide show. At the same time, people in other functional areas of the organization are doing their own things, such as arranging for financing, clearing legal requirements for the use of copyrighted materials, securing releases from models and various other tasks.

Monitoring and Evaluation   Monitoring a program is essential. Functional strategies collectively define what is expected to happen to achieve stated goals. One of the primary functions of supervisors at all levels in every area is to monitor progress. This is a routine part of their jobs, but their efforts are mostly focused inside the organization. What about monitoring things that go on outside? That's a different situation. Certainly the leadership of the communication program should routinely and regularly scan the environment for problems, issues, developments, trends, opportunities and other things that may affect the organization or the campaign in progress.

How can we tell whether the program is working? Do we go by intuition or do we set some routine procedures to take the pulse of our target publics at regular intervals? One measure we might consider is to review progressive reports on the number of inquiries. If there is an increase in inquiries, how can we be sure the increase is a result of the campaign? Another might be to count the house at special events to gauge how well people are responding to the campaign. It may be that an overflow crowd attended a concert simply because of the quality of the singer but they will soon forget the sponsor, if they ever realized who the sponsor was. If we are selling a product or service, weekly sales reports can give us some insights. But are sales or the number of orders a clear indication of how effectively we are communicating with our audience? Lots of variables affect sales and orders other than messages. If we are promoting a candidate or a political issue, telephone canvassing can tell us a lot, but can we predict with great accuracy a victory at the polling booth?

Although those indicators, as well as many others, may be prominent parts of many campaign plans, the information they yield is ambiguous about what the target public knows about us or whether there have been any shifts in attitudes toward us because of the campaign. These two issues deal exclusively with the communication function. The only way they can be evaluated objectively is to do systematic research on relevant publics at regular intervals. That means that we need incremental research on our relevant publics to get a clear picture of how the campaign is doing. Such information may help us spot problems that can be corrected during the remainder of a campaign.

The monitoring process results in an assortment of writing tasks. Prominent among them are memos and letters. Analytical reports may also be written, along with cover letters. If something is awry in the campaign and ways of righting it are found, then recommendations or proposals for specific actions will need to be written. Monitoring should be, of course, a part of every functional plan.

When a program is completed, it is necessary to evaluate its productivity. The most effective evaluations are those with known benchmarks in place at the time the campaign begins. For example, pertinent data gathered in support of the strategic plan would ordinarily contain a good bit of benchmark information. Depending on the nature of the organization, this information might be found in measures of attitudes and behavior, brand shares, market shares, sales volumes, unit sales, contributions and pledges received, aided and unaided recall scores and others.

Particular measures should be selected that are uniquely appropriate to the campaign and its parent organization. In the case of APEX, a critical measure is the dollar volume of contributions and pledges. This can be compared directly to the level from the preceding year. It is easy to see whether the organization met its goal. If it did not, efforts must be made to determine why so that those mistakes will not be made in future campaigns. If the goal was exceeded, we need to know why. Is the greater-than-expected increase due to the campaign or is it attributable to some influence beyond the scope of the campaign? Is the awareness of APEX higher now than when the campaign began? Do people have more appreciation for APEX now than before the campaign? Clearly, many of these questions, and many like them, can be answered only if we expand the systematic research program that we used during the monitoring phase. Both monitoring and campaign evaluation cost money. This needs to be provided in the campaign budget. If there is not enough money for good monitoring and effective evaluation, then we can't really do these tasks correctly. An absence of evaluation cripples strategic planning for future campaigns.

Although many memos and letters will be written as part of a campaign's final evaluation, the most daunting writing task is likely to be a thorough, lengthy report that summarizes the results of the campaign. Such reports must be highly persuasive, yet be careful not to mislead management as you try to marshal your arguments in support of conclusions. Much of the information in these reports is complex. That may make it useful to break out some pieces of information and recast them into backgrounders, position papers, letters and memos in support of forthcoming planning efforts. The reason for doing that, of course, is to make sure that the responsible managers get information that is in its most usable form without having to wade through a lengthy report.

Conclusions

- Crisis communication entails issue management, as the best public relations is preventive.
- The critical event is the crisis.
- You need to plan for crises and, when you do, always anticipate the "worst case."
- Routine corporate communication becomes critical in a crisis and must always be up to date.
- A corporate crisis plan must be developed and placed in the hands of the people who will need it.
- Crisis plans can often be "taught" by role playing.
- There should be no more than one or two designated spokespersons in a crisis.
- These spokespersons should be trained in handling media and individuals who are under stress.
- Crisis communicators must consciously supply the symbol (visual and verbal) for the crisis, incorporating the symbol in language for a response statement.
- Spokespersons handling internal and external communication must coordinate their messages to avoid discrepancies that would reduce their credibility.
- Crisis teams should take over the crisis situation and permit all others in the organization to go on about their daily work. This will inspire continued confidence in the organization's ability to cope with the problem.
- Almost all the communication tools discussed in this book can be used in a crisis.
- Effective campaigns are built around a unified message strategy. The organization must speak with one voice.

- A campaign is a series of coordinated messages and activities, driven by a single strategy, delivered to relevant publics by a variety of means.
- A campaign intends to inform, educate or persuade its relevant publics to buy, use or support something.
- The writer's primary role in a campaign is to craft messages that are consistent with campaign strategy.
- A campaign plan defines what is to be done, how it will be done, who will do it and when or how often it will be done.
- Public relations writers are involved in campaign planning mostly at the stage of crafting creative message strategies and in tactical application of those strategies.
- An effective organizational strategy is rooted in the mission of the organization.
- A mission statement must be explicit. It should be reviewed at the outset of strategic planning.
- A good mission statement leads to a clear understanding of the business mission of an organization.
- Organizational and business missions collectively give focus to the information-gathering process.
- Information in support of strategic planning is of two types: secondary and primary.
- Information must be analyzed carefully, put into usable form, synthesized and used as a basis for forecasting.
- Relevant information is reviewed before setting objectives. Objectives are long range, are unspecific as to time and degree and are not measurable.
- Goals represent incremental movement toward fulfilling objectives. Goals are short range, are specific as to time and degree and are measurable.
- Strategy is shaped directly by an organization's mission, objectives and goals.
- Organizational strategy defines what is to be done that will help to meet the goals specified.
- Coordination of activities and messages is important to build unity and credibility.
- Functional plans for each area of operations are developed in support of the organization's basic strategy.
- A communication plan takes its strategic cues from organizational strategy.
- Good message strategy is simple, adaptable, applicable and durable.
- Good media strategy considers who in the target audience pays attention to which media, how inherently persuasive the media are, how credible the media are, how easy it is to achieve precise timing of delivery of messages and whether the media provide effective reach.
- Effective management of campaigns depends on control so that what is to be done is done as it should be and when it should be.
- Coordinating communication campaign activities is a major challenge, especially if it involves working with other organizations.
- Tactical implementation is that stage at which writers and other creative people craft and distribute campaign messages.
- At the monitoring and evaluation stage, writers are most likely to be called on to write memos, letters, short or long reports, proposals and the like, most of which must be highly persuasive.

Exercises

1. Select a public relations campaign that is now under way in your area. Get as many pieces of campaign materials as you can. Work out a clear set of statements that reflect that organization's mission, objectives, goals and strategy.

2. Using your work from Exercise 1, identify the message and media strategies in use by this organization. Write a short evaluation that judges the degree to which these strategies support what appears to be the organization's mission, objectives, goals and strategies. Is that the best plan for this organization? Why? If not, why not?

 Use InfoTrac College Edition to access information on topics in this chapter from hundreds of periodicals and scholarly journals.

Notes

1. U.S. Department of State, "September 11 One Year Later: A Selected Chronology of Key Events, September 11, 2001–Present, Compiled by the Office of International Information Programs, U.S. Department of State," September 11, 2002, http://usinfo .state.gov/journals/itgic/0902/ijge/gjchron.htm (accessed March 24, 2003). The *Wall Street Journal* reported on January 26, 2004 that the death toll had been lowered to 2,749.

2. "Grief at Cantor Fitzgerald, Relief at Morgan Stanley," September 14, 2001, http://www .foxnews.com/story/0,2933,34357,00.html (accessed December 21, 2003).

3. UAL news release, "UAL Corp. Files for Chapter 11 Reorganization," December 9, 2002, http://www.united.com/press/detail/0,1442,50461-1,00.html (accessed March 24, 2003).

4. AMR news release, "AMR Reports Fourth Quarter Loss of $529 Million," January 22, 2003, http://www.amrcorp.com/newsreleases.html (accessed March 24, 2003).

5. Ray Suarez, "The Controversial Liberty Fund," December 19, 2001, http://www.pbs.org/ newshour/bb/business/july-dec01/redcross_12-19.html (accessed March 25, 2003).

6. Chris Barnett, "Crisis Communications Now: Three Views," *Public Relations Tactics,* January 2003, p. 15.

7. Enron Corporation news release, "Enron Files Voluntary Petitions for Chapter 11 Reorganization; Sues Dynegy for Breach of Contract, Seeking Damages of at Least $10 Billion," December 2, 2001, http://www.enron.com/corp/pressroom/releases/2001/ ene/PressRelease11-12-02-01letterhead.html (accessed March 24, 2003).

8. Doug Newsom, Judy VanSlyke Turk and Dean Kruckeberg, *This Is PR: The Realities of Public Relations,* 8th ed. (Belmont, Calif.: Wadsworth, 2004), p. 321.

9. Carl Gustin and Jennifer Sheehy, Clarke & Company Crisis Communication Center, "Handling a Crisis: Lessons from NASA," February 14, 2003, http://www.clarkecrisis .com/article1.htm (accessed April 16, 2003).

10. Jack C. Horn, "The Hostage Ward," Psychology Today 21(7) (July 1985):9.

11. Media Resource Service of Sigma Xi, The Scientific Research Society. http://www.media resource.org/ (accessed January 20, 2004).

12. Getpress.com, "Crisis Communications Support," undated, http://www.getpress.com/crisis_communications.htm (accessed April 16, 2003).
13. Southwest Airlines, "The Mission of Southwest Airlines," January 1988, http://www.southwestairlines.com/about_swa/mission.html (accessed April 16, 2003).

Selected Bibliography

Jim Avery, *Advertising Campaign Planning: Developing an Advertising-Based Marketing Plan,* 2d ed. (Chicago: Copy Workshop, 1997).

Robin Cohn, *The PR Crisis Bible: How to Take Charge of the Media When All Hell Breaks Loose* (New York: St. Martin's Press, 2000).

Kathleen Fearn-Banks, *Crisis Communication: A Casebook Approach,* 2d ed. (Hillsdale, N.J.: Lawrence Erlbaum Associates, 2001).

Jack A. Gottschalk, ed., *Crisis Response: Inside Stories on Managing Image Under Siege* (Detroit: Visible Ink Press, 1993).

Peter Sheldon Green, *Reputation Is Everything* (Burr Ridge, Ill.: Richard D. Irwin, 1994).

Roger Hawood, *Manage Your Reputation: How to Plan Public Relations to Build and Protect the Organization's Most Powerful Asset,* 2d ed. (London: Kogan Page Ltd., 2002).

James E. Lukaszewski, *Current Crisis Communication Issues: Getting Your Boss to Buy into Crisis Planning; Building a Crisis Response Plan That Works; When to Send Your Boss Out to Meet the Press; Managing the Lawyers; Managing the Violent Threat* (White Plains, N.Y.: Lukaszewski Group, 1996).

Dan Millar and Larry L. Smith, *Crisis Management and Communication: How to Gain and Maintain Control,* 2d ed. (San Francisco: International Association of Business Communicators, 2002).

Mary Anne Morfitt, *Campaign Strategies and Message Design: A Practitioner's Guide from Start to Finish* (Westport, Conn.: Praeger Publishers, 1999).

Sandra Moriarty with John Burnett (contributor), *Introduction to Marketing Communication: An Integrated Approach* (Englewood Cliffs, N.J.: Prentice Hall, 1997).

Doug Newsom, Judy VanSlyke Turk and Dean Krukeberg, *This Is PR: The Realities of Public Relations,* 8th ed. (Belmont, Calif.: Wadsworth, 2004).

PASE, Inc., *The Emergency Public Relations Manual,* 3d ed. (1993) (available from PASE, POB 1299, Highland Park, NJ 08904 and online at http://www.paseinc.com/public relations.html).

Lester R. Potter, *The Communication Plan: The Heart of Strategic Communication,* 2d ed. (San Francisco: International Association of Business Communicators, 2002).

Sally J. Ray, *Strategic Communication in Crisis Management* (Westport, Conn.: Quorum Books, 1999).

Ronald E. Rice and Charles K. Atkin, eds., *Public Communication Campaigns,* 3d ed. (Thousand Oaks, Calif.: Sage Publications, 2000).

Donald E. Schultz, *Strategic Advertising Campaigns,* 5th ed. (Lincolnwood, Ill.: NTC Business Books, 1998).

V. A. Shiva, *The Internet Publicity Guide: How to Maximize Your Marketing and Promotion in Cyberspace* (New York: Allworth Press, 1997).

Ronald D. Smith, *Strategic Planning for Public Relations* (Mahwah, N.J.: Lawrence Erlbaum Associates, 2002).

Patricia Westfall, *Beyond Intuition: A Guide to Writing and Editing Magazine Nonfiction* (New York: Longman, 1994).

Steve Wilson and Luke Feck, *Real People, Real Crises: An Inside Look at Corporate Crisis Communications* (Winchester, Va.: Oakhill Press, 2002).

Readability Formulas

Research in readability goes back at least to the 1920s. Early work identified various factors—like sentence length, word length, prepositional phrases—that affected the readability of prose.

In *What Makes a Book Readable,* published in 1935, William Gray and Bernice Leary discussed 64 different aspects of prose that seemed to affect reading difficulty. It would have been nearly impossible to devise a usable formula covering that many variables, so when readability formulas were developed, most emphasized two of the most important factors: sentence length and word length.

Dozens of formulas have been designed to measure readability. In 1959 George Klare identified 31 formulas and 10 variations, and he didn't cover all the different types of formulas. Many more formulas have been designed since then, although only a handful of these are in general use. The three best-known formulas are those devised by Rudolf Flesch, by Robert Gunning, and by Edgar Dale and Jeanne Chall.

Flesch's Reading Ease and Human Interest Formulas

The first formula to gain much notice was the one proposed by Flesch in the late 1940s. His formula is based on average sentence length and average number of syllables per word.

To use the Flesch formula, select 100-word samples at random from your text. Divide the number of words by the number of sentences to obtain an average sentence length (*asl*), expressed in words per sentence. Next count the number of syllables in the sample and divide this by the number of words to obtain an average word length (*awl*), expressed in syllables per word. Then insert these values into the Flesch "Reading Ease" formula:

Reading Ease = 206.835 − (84.6 × *awl*) − (1.015 × *asl*)

The resulting score should fall between 0 and 100. The higher the score, the easier the material is to read. A score in the 70–80 range is "fairly easy"; a sixth-grader could understand it. Scores below 50 are considered difficult reading. Scores below 30 are generally found only in scientific and technical journals.

When using the Flesch formula, count contractions and hyphenated words as one word. When counting sentences, count clauses separated by colons or semicolons as separate sentences.

Recognizing that there is more to easy reading than short words and sentences, Flesch devised a "Human Interest" formula that measures the degree of reader interest. It is not used as often as the Reading Ease formula. It is based on the number of personal words (*pw*) per 100 words and the number of personal sentences (*ps*) per 100 sentences. Personal words include personal pronouns and any other words that are either masculine or feminine. Personal sentences are direct quotations, exclamations, questions—sentences that address the reader directly. The formula is as follows:

Human Interest = (*pw*/100 words × 3.635) + (*ps*/100 sentences × 0.314)

A score below 10 is dull; 20 to 40 is interesting; above 40 is very interesting.

Gunning's Fog Index

Gunning's formula is much simpler to apply than Flesch's. The "Fog Index," as Gunning calls it, measures reading difficulty rather than reading ease.

Gunning also counts words and divides by the number of sentences to find an average sentence length. But rather than counting syllables, Gunning's method is to count the number of long words—those of three syllables or more. He excludes from this count all proper nouns, verbs in which the third syllable is an *-ed* or *-es,* and compound words made from two short words, like *worktable.*

To apply the formula, take the average sentence length and add to it the number of long words per 100 words. Multiply the total by 0.4.

The resulting score is roughly equivalent to the grade level of difficulty. A score of 12, for example, indicates that an average high-school senior should be able to read the material. In practice, no general-audience magazine would rate above 12 on the Gunning index. *Time* magazine rates 11, *Reader's Digest* scores about 5 and comic books score 6.

Source: http://www.helpforschools.com/ELLKBase/practitionerstips/Fog_Index_Readability.shtml

Dale-Chall Formula

The Dale-Chall formula is more difficult to apply, because it requires the use of a list of 3,000 words. Words on the list are known by 80 percent of fourth-graders. [The list is included as an appendix to Gunning's book, *The Technique of Clear Writing,* rev. ed. (New York: McGraw-Hill, 1968).]

To use the Dale-Chall formula, select 100-word samples and determine the average sentence length (as with the Gunning and Flesch tests). Then count the number of words not on the Dale-Chall list. Here is the formula:

(Average sentence length × 0.0496) +
(Words not on Dale-Chall list × 0.1579) + 3.6365

Dale-Chall scores are usually lower than Gunning scores for a given piece of writing. A Gunning index of 16, for example, indicates readability at the college-graduate level; the same piece would score about 10 on the Dale-Chall test.

Keep in mind that readability scores do not reflect a "recommended" level of reading difficulty. They only indicate the readability level that an average reader (average seventh-grader, average high-school senior or whoever) is likely to understand. To make the reading easy, the writing level should be a couple of steps below the educational level of the intended audience. Rarely do popular magazines—even those read by college graduates—score higher than the readability level of a high-school senior.

ELF Formula

The Easy Listening Formula (ELF), developed by Irving Fang, measures readability sentence by sentence, identifying a sentence as a "package of information." Look at each word in the sentence. Subtract one from the number of syllables in each word. A one-syllable word counts zero, a two-syllable word counts one, and so on. If your count passes 12, examine the sentence. It may be all right, or it may be hard to understand. What has pushed up the count? Unnecessary adjectives and adverbs? Clauses that might be better as separate sentences? Abstract words? The more abstract a word, the more difficult it is to understand.

Example:
Communication receivers have preset opinions about certain linguistic features such as pronunciations, sentence structures and words that are outside of their usual vocabulary—that is, "different" words.

Rewrite:
The way words are said and used, and how familiar they are, triggers opinions.

Other Readability Tests

A completely different type of readability test is Wilson Taylor's "Cloze" procedure. This test, first used in the early 1950s, was developed from concepts of Gestalt psychology. It tests readability by seeing how easily a reader can "fill in the blanks" when words are left out of a passage.

For example, readers might be given a passage with every fifth word deleted. From the context, the reader should be able to fill in some of the missing words. The more words the reader can fill in, the more readable the selection is.

This unique readability test has one major drawback: It can't be applied simply by making calculations. The prose must be tested on real readers, and those readers must accurately represent the intended audience. All readability formulas are approximations, because no single formula can cover all the variables that affect readability. With the increased use of computers, though, more complicated formulas may soon come into use. Computers can be programmed to calculate readability automatically when a sample of a story is typed in at a computer keyboard.

An early formula appropriate for computerized use is the Danielson-Bryan formula. It is based on the total number of characters (letters) per word and per sentence. Here is the formula:

$$(1.0364 \times \text{characters per word}) + (0.0194 \times \text{characters per sentence}) - 0.6059$$

Wayne Danielson devised an even more elaborate formula to measure the probable time period of prose. It has long been known that English sentences have, on average, become shorter over the centuries. Taking a random sample of novels published between 1740 and 1977, Danielson found several other variables that have changed with time, such as paragraph length (shorter now than in the past), presence of long words (less frequent now than in the past) and presence of "internal apostrophes" for possessives and contractions (more frequent now than in the past). Using data from his sample of novels, Danielson produced a formula that would predict the publication date for a fiction selection. These predictions work with a fair degree of accuracy on fiction, but the formula in no way predicts the publication year for nonfiction, because only novels were included in the original sample. However, any prose can be given a style year rating by applying the formula. And although the formula is not a readability measure by design, style year scores show a very high correlation to readability scores obtained by standard formulas. (See Table A.1.)

A computer program has been written to apply this formula, and tests show that a selection with a style year of 1900 or later rates "very readable" on standard readability tests. Style year scores of 1850 or before are not very readable.

T A B L E   A . 1   *Comparison of Readability Scores with Style Year*

Gunning Score (Fog Index)	Grade Level	Style Year
4	Fourth	1948
5	Fifth	1939
6	Sixth	1929
7–8	Seventh–eighth	1916
9–10	Ninth–tenth	1897
11–12	Eleventh–twelfth	1879
13–15	College	1856
16 and up	College graduate	1838

The formula, which must be applied to an integral number of paragraphs, is as follows:

Style year = 1949 $+$ (36.41 $\times$ internal apostrophes per sentence)
$-$ (2.57 $\times$ words per sentence) $-$ (2.92 $\times$ sentences per paragraph)
$-$ (16.71 $\times$ long words per sentence)

In Danielson's system, long words are defined as words with 10 or more letters.

Software Programs

Most grammar software programs provide more than one readability measure. In addition to word, sentence and paragraph statistics, Grammatik IV offers the Flesch Readability Formula, Gunning's Fog Index measuring years of education and the Flesch-Kincaid Reading Grade Level.

In addition to a qualitative assessment of the writing, *StyleWriter,* a plain-English editorial program, provides word and sentence statistics with an index that gives the percentage of passive verbs plus a count of words in such categories as jargon, legal, abstract, complex and such.

Copyfitting

You need to fit copy accurately for two reasons: (1) to determine how much space a given amount of copy will occupy when set in type, and (2) to determine how much copy to write to fill a predetermined space. Occasionally both circumstances are important. If an editor has prepared copy and a layout showing space where the copy is to go, some adjustment will usually be necessary. The copy will have to be cut (or lengthened) to fit the space, the layout will have to be redesigned to allow more (or less) space for copy or both.

In either case the principles of copyfitting are the same.

Sizing Copy

To fit copy, an editor must know the type specifications. Relevant data include:

1. The typeface, type size, and amount of leading
2. A "characters per pica" count for the typeface
3. The column width of the copy after being set in type
4. The total number of characters in the original copy

Computers allow the total number of characters (letters and spaces) in the original copy to be precisely counted.

Computer programs will give you the character count, number of words and number of sentences. If lines are uneven, you may have to determine an average line length by hand. One way to do this is to draw a straight line down the right margin so that half the lines go beyond your line and half don't reach it. Then measure the number of spaces from the left-hand margin to the line you've drawn.

Partial lines should be counted as full lines, because space will appear at the end of paragraphs.

Once you've determined the total number of characters, you must determine the specifications of the type to be used. The *typeface* is simply the name of the style of type you are using—Times Roman, for example. The *type size* is measured in *points;* it takes about 72 points to make 1 inch. The type size in most general publications ranges from 8-point to 12-point.

Leading refers to the amount of space between lines of type. Sometimes type is set solid—that is, without leading. Often, to improve legibility, the type is leaded 1 or 2 points. This simply means that 1 or 2 points of space are added between each line of type. On the computer, you can use full, expanded or condensed.

Copy space on a layout is usually measured in *picas;* there are 6 picas to the inch. One pica of copy depth is equal to 12 points. Thus one line of 12-point type occupies 1 pica of copy space.

If the type is set solid—no leading—100 lines of 12-point type take up 100 picas, about 16⅔ inches. The general formula for determining copy depth is:

$$\frac{\text{lines of type} \ \times \ (\text{point size} + \text{leading})}{12} = \text{copy depth in picas}$$

Thus if you use 10-point type with 1-point leading, 100 lines of type will occupy:

$$\frac{100 \ \times \ (10 + 1)}{12} = 91.7 = 92 \text{ picas}$$

Notice that, if 10-point type is used and is leaded 2 points, the number of lines of type is equal to the copy depth in picas.

The number of lines of type can be determined only after the width of each line is known. In other words, how many characters will each line contain?

Type books commonly give a "characters per pica" count for different typefaces and type sizes. Ten-point Helvetica, for example, has a count of 2.4 characters per pica. Thus if your copy space is 10 picas wide, the number of characters per line will be 24.

Sample Copyfitting Problems

Suppose you want to set the original copy—calculated at 3,250 characters—in 10-point Helvetica. The width of a column of type will be 14 picas. How many lines of copy will you have?

Step One: Characters per pica times line width in picas gives characters per line:

2.4 × 14 = 33.6

Step Two: Total characters divided by characters per line gives number of lines:

$$\frac{3,250}{33.6} = 96.7 = 97 \text{ lines}$$

Given 97 lines of 10-point type and 1-point leading, what will the depth of the copy be when set in type?

Step One: Point size plus leading times number of lines gives depth in points:

$$(10 + 1) \times 97 = 1,067$$

Step Two: Depth in points divided by 12 gives depth in picas:

$$\frac{1,067}{12} = 89 \text{ picas}$$

If the copy had been 10-point leaded 2 instead of 1, the copy depth would have equaled the number of lines: 97.

Suppose the layout is flexible. You have copy with 3,250 characters. The typeface is 10-point Helvetica leaded 2. You want the length of copy when set in type to be 49 lines. How wide will the column of copy have to be?

Step One: Total number of characters divided by number of lines gives characters per line:

$$\frac{3,250}{49} = 66.3$$

Step Two: Characters per line divided by characters per pica gives picas per line:

$$\frac{66.3}{2.4} = 27.6 = 28$$

The column width will have to be 28 picas.

Finally, you are given a layout with columns 21 picas wide, and you have a depth of 120 picas. Copy must be written to fill the space. If you set your margins to provide a 60-space line, how many lines will be needed to fill the space? (Assume type will be 10-point Helvetica leaded 2 points.)

Step One: Characters per pica times line width in picas gives characters per line:
$$2.4 \times 21 = 50.4$$

Step Two: Characters per line times number of lines gives total characters:

$$50.4 \times 120 = 6,048 \text{ characters}$$

(number of lines equals depth in picas because type is set 10 point leaded 2)

Step Three: The number of lines equals the total characters divided by characters per line:

$$\frac{6,048}{60} = 100.8 = 101 \text{ typed lines}$$

Broadcast Copy

Radio

Set margins for a 60-space line. That setting will give three or four seconds per line.

Use 12-point type in Times Roman or a serif type of equal measure that will give you about 10 words per line.

For 30 seconds of copy, there are about seven or eight of these lines.

For one minute, plan for about 15 lines.

If you are going to print out the copy, use triple spacing.

Television

Set margins for about a 30-space line in a column on the right side of the page.

Use 12-point type in Times Roman or a serif type of equal measure that will give you about six words per line.

For 30 seconds of copy, there are about 15 of these lines.

For one minute of copy, plan for about 21 lines read at an average speed.

Print out triple-spaced. (Video information goes in the left-hand column along with other instructions not being read.)

The best gauge for estimating time is to read the copy and time it with a stopwatch. This is more complicated with estimating TV scripts because you have to allow additional time for visuals, even when it is voice-over.

Index